MW01627055

NINA
CHANEL
ABNEY

M

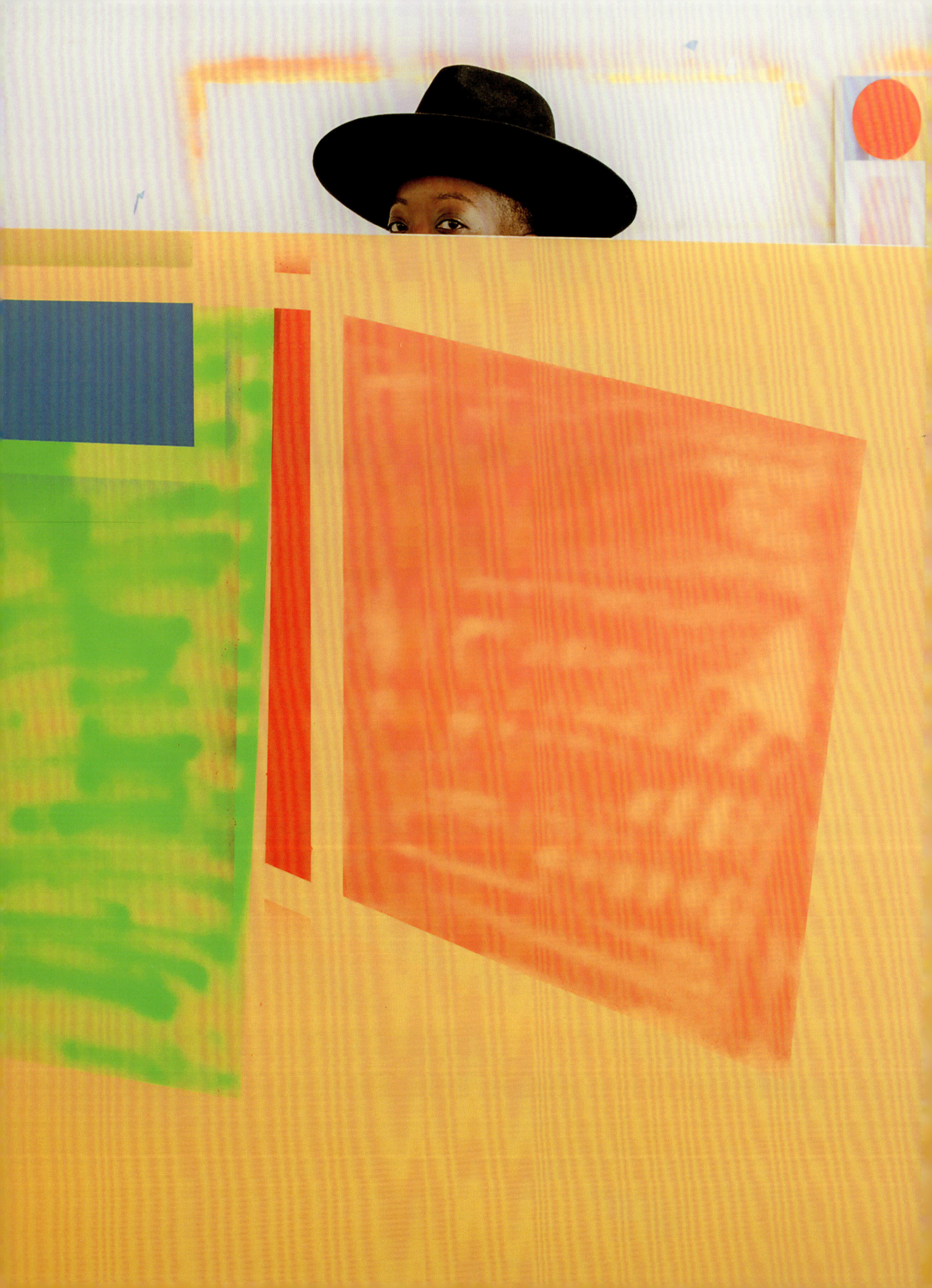

CONTENTS

FINDING THE TRUE ARTIST'S VOICE:

JEFFREY DEITCH IN CONVERSATION WITH NINA CHANEL ABNEY

Jeffrey Deitch: Nina, I've always been inspired by your expansive vision of what an artist can do. Your achievement in painting and works on paper is really outstanding—as is your NFT startup; your interest in multiples—but I'm very curious about your interest in public art murals. We did several of them together; so I'd like to ask you to start [by speaking] about this expansive vision you have about being an artist and reaching a broad public.

Nina Chanel Abney: I think it first comes out of my natural inclination to work in many different mediums. Growing up and looking at [the work of] Henri Matisse and Andy Warhol, my understanding of a masterful artist was an artist who evolved their practice through experimentation with different mediums. When I knew I wanted to be an artist, I aspired to have a career in which each body of work propels my practice forward.

Deitch: I remember a discussion we had some years ago about proposing a balloon for the Macy's Thanksgiving Day Parade. They didn't understand how great you were, but I was very impressed then—and that was some years ago—very impressed by your ambition to reach people with your art.

Abney: I have always appreciated graffiti artists and their ability to reach a broad audience. The idea that anyone could access art just by walking by it and the idea of being able to share my work with a larger public has become more interesting for me, showing people how you can discover art in the everyday—whether that's a sneaker or a billboard. I am always looking to find new ways to do that.

Deitch: Our first project together was your great mural at Coney Island. Somehow, I had the instinct that we had to position you right at the center, give you the great entrance wall, and your work was phenomenal.

Abney: Thank you very much.

Deitch: Was that one of the first public murals you did?

Abney: Yes, it was one of the first. The very first one I did was in Newark, New Jersey, off of McCarter Highway with Project for Empty Space. They did a program where they worked with about eighteen different artists through a long span of the highway, and each artist got a section of the wall. When given the opportunity, I said, "Of course I'll do it." Most everyone involved was a full-time time graffiti artist. I completely underestimated what

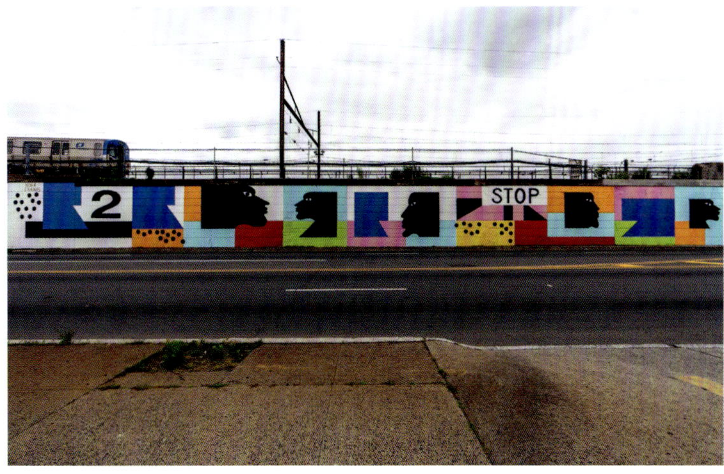

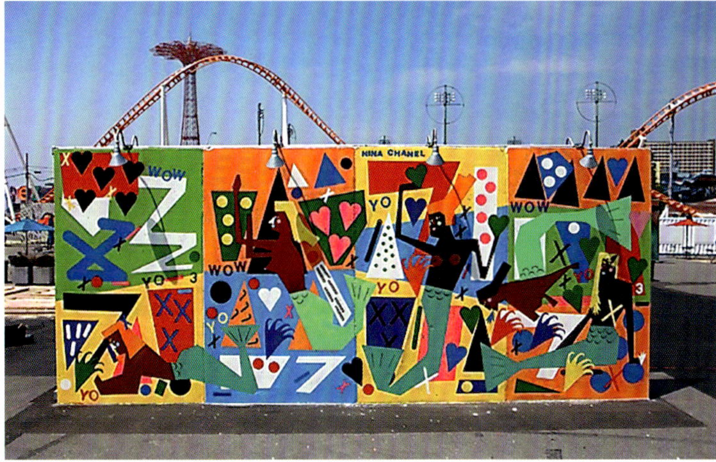

[TOP] Untitled, 2016, McCarter Highway, Newark, NJ
[BOTTOM] Untitled, 2016, Coney Island Art Wall, Brooklyn, NY

the project would entail. We were working crazy hours to avoid traffic, basically midnight to 5:00 a.m. It was about 1:00 a.m. and I went there with spray paint in hand, arrogantly thinking I could just start working directly on the wall. I realized, "Oh my God this is... an entire other way of working, a talent I don't have." I was on the verge of tears, panicking at 3:00 in the morning on the side of the highway, thinking, "I don't even know how to do this." It was a learning curve.

In that moment, I had to figure out how to translate my work into a large-scale mural. That's when I began using tape and creating stencils to adapt my imagery to a larger scale. That was the very first mural. After I conquered the first mural, I did one in Detroit with Library Street Collective and Coney Island came after. Fortunately, every opportunity led to another, allowing me to improve my technique along the way. I might still do a balloon [for the Macy's parade]. I found a loophole, I think.

Deitch: That would be very exciting. I love how you think. By the time you did your third mural at Coney Island, you had totally perfected it. It was incredible and so impressive to see you and your team. We more recently did this project in Miami with two gigantic multi-story walls and a tunnel, and that was phenomenal. It was amazing to see how you had put together this team that allows you to create massive works of public art.

Abney: At first, I was doing the murals with one studio assistant, which was labor intensive because I work intuitively. It truly felt like doing an extremely large painting in a very condensed timeline, sometimes less than a week. It didn't seem sustainable. Also, I realized that maybe I'm a little afraid of heights. That's when I came up with a different strategy.

My friend JJ, who helps me manage my mural projects, introduced me to an amazing team of women painters who are capable of working on the side of skyscrapers with no fear. They're badass and have been helping me paint murals ever since. There's great synergy.

Deitch: Oh, that's fascinating. I'd like to talk about how you approach the work. I read in a previous interview that you do not do preparatory sketches. Is that correct? It seemed with the complexity your work, one would think that there are numerous preparatory sketches.

Abney: There are not. If I sketched the piece beforehand, I'd lose interest and wouldn't want to paint it. The excitement for me comes from the unknown—the spontaneity and problem-solving in the moment to create a cohesive composition.

Deitch: That's extraordinary. It's very rare that an artist can create these large-scale complex works without numerous preparatory drawings. I've seen that with Keith Haring, who would be able to start a large painting or mural in the upper left corner and move across, but that's amazing that this is all internalized. It's almost like a jazz improvisation that you do.

Abney: Each painting becomes a puzzle for me to solve.

Deitch: Something that I admire immensely in your work is the inherent rhythm of the composition: in classic critical art terms, one talks about the color, the edge, things that you associate with painting. Rhythm does not generally come up, but that's something that's so inherent in your work. Looking at a large painting of yours, I can see it move. I can feel the rhythm. I'd like to ask you about that aspect of your work, because that's quite unique.

Abney: The work is rhythmic because I aim to create movement across the canvas so that the viewer's gaze is never stagnant. To achieve this, I have created systems and techniques that utilize color, shape, repetition, and text. I want the work to keep your attention.

Deitch: Do you have a background as an athlete or a dancer? The rhythm is so physical.

Abney: I played tennis. I still play tennis. I played soccer, basketball... I was always very athletic when I was younger, and I play the piano.

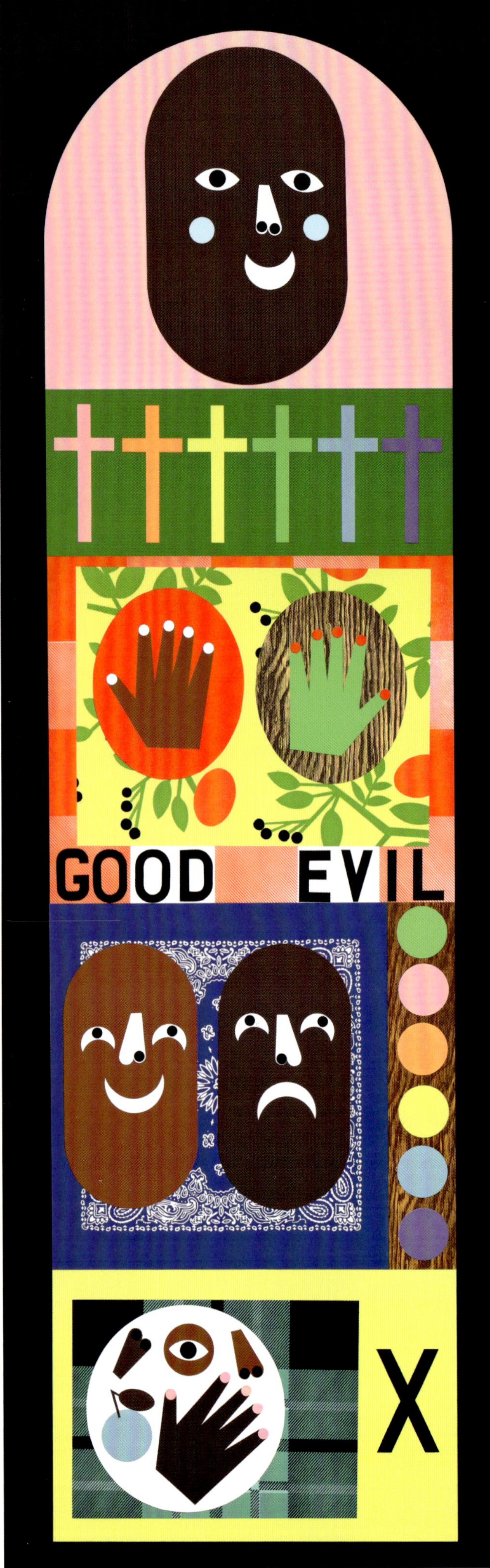

Throwing Light, Catching Shade #4, 2024

Deitch: I didn't know that. Do you have a classical training or was it more jazz piano?

Abney: Classical, but I have always wanted to learn jazz. I have several cousins who were self-taught jazz [musicians].

Deitch: Your improvisational talent goes into the painting?

Abney: Yes.

Deitch: That's so fascinating, because your paintings do have a sound, in a way.

Abney: I would love to learn jazz. I recently bought some books and a piano to try to teach myself.

Deitch: Did you get to the point where you were a performer also or was it more just your own study?

Abney: With classical, I performed in recitals as a kid with my stepsister, who was, at the time, learning opera. It's so wild when I think about it. We would do some recitals together, I would play and she would sing. Outside of that, after a certain point, I didn't really take it up. I feel like I quit after I realized I needed glasses or something. That was in the '80s, early childhood, but I kept with it. I can still play now.

Deitch: Let's talk about your trajectory. There's an unusual year where you worked in a Ford factory, one of the only contemporary artists I know who actually had that kind of experience. It seems that and other aspects of your background had given you a sympathy for the working class. Your art addresses everyday people in the city, not only the art elite.

Abney: I am everyday people, I come from everyday people. My mom worked for almost forty years at the unemployment agency, my stepfather delivered Pepsi®. I come from humble beginnings, so being catapulted into this elite art world has been interesting. I still feel like an outsider sometimes, though I am a part of this "art world."

Deitch: A lot of your work has a strong social-political message. I'd like to ask you about how you integrate messaging with the formal aspects of the work.

Abney: My whole way of working, from color, humor, and seducing the viewer into challenging topics in a way in which they want to stay, comes from my own experience with artwork. I noticed that with works that are overly didactic, people tend not to spend much time with them since they feel like they already have the work figured out. I want to create work that can be visually engaging: it can make you think, but also, provoke self-interrogation.

Deitch: It's also fascinating the way you invite entry into the work by your use of humor.

Abney: When I was younger, I wanted to be a cartoonist. I love the most sarcastic animations. I was a big fan of Hanna-Barbera. That's where I got my sense of humor. With animation, you can walk the line of inappropriateness. I'm interested in that play, too.

Deitch: Do you have some plans for an animated film?

Abney: I actually wrote a cartoon with my partner, Jet Toomer, and our friend, Zoe Lister-Jones. We wrote a cartoon based off me and my younger sister's relationship, but we threw a wrench in. We have turned the family structure that's usually depicted in animation on his head.

Deitch: It sounds brilliant. Maybe I can help you to make that happen.

Abney: Maybe. I'm even thinking maybe a short film, centered around the same concept, and would love to do it at the Sundance Film Festival because they have an animation program. The film industry, from what I've learned, is so different, even in the approach to ownership and intellectual property. I feel like I'm more independent-minded when it comes to that, where I'd rather take the time and do it myself.

Deitch: Well, that's one of the greatest things about being an artist: You do not have a boss. Nobody's telling you what you can do.

Abney: I don't want to have to compromise my vision to make things more mainstream. When you're not conforming, people might see it as risky, but there are communities that are rarely considered in film and television and that's who I would like to prioritize.

Deitch: Fascinating. I anticipate you will be able to realize this.

Abney: I hope so.

Deitch: In your approach to your art, there's a lot of references from the vernacular—you mentioned strip clubs and sororities—but you also have so many deep art historical references. I imagine you've deeply studied Pablo Picasso, Romare Bearden, Stuart Davis... I want to ask you about these art historical references that you build on, that are inside your work, that you must have studied.

Abney: Actually, funny story, Stuart Davis... I hadn't even heard of him until I was working on a show called *I DREAD TO THINK* [October 18 – November 24, 2012, at Kravets Wehby Gallery, in collaboration with Anna Kustera Gallery, New York, NY]. When I was working on that show, Lowery Stokes Sims came to my studio and brought up Stuart Davis, assuming I was aware of his work. Immediately after that, I was obsessed.

I didn't know much about contemporary art until I came to New York for graduate school at Parsons School of Design. The first show I went to was a Marina Abramović performance at the Guggenheim and my mind was blown. Parsons was an intense education because I was playing catch up to the contemporary art history while trying to become a contemporary artist, myself.

My references came from what was available to me when I was younger. I mean, *everyone* knows Picasso. I had field trips to the Art Institute of Chicago, where I learned about Chuck Close and Georges Seurat. I had some exposure to Black artists through *The Cosby Show*.

Deitch: Really? From the TV show? That's fascinating. It must be thrilling for you to see your work influencing artists who are of the younger generation.

Abney: It's surreal to know that my work is being studied in classes. I still can't believe it. Because I have become an influence to others, I feel a responsibility to keep pushing the boundaries of my own practice, exploring new mediums and delving into industries in which people who look like me aren't represented. It's crazy to think that I could be a part of art history. If you named the period of art we're in now, what would it be? I don't know...

Deitch: Well, you're one of the people defining it. Fascinating to know that you studied both computer science and art, because most artists, if you ask, "What did you study?" they'll probably say poetry and art. I think maybe part of the rigor that's in your work comes from this study of computer science. Could you elaborate a little bit about that, about the dual mind that you bring to your artwork?

Abney: I intended on being a computer programmer because I couldn't fathom having a career as an artist. I didn't know how artists made money and I needed a sustainable job, but I didn't like going to work. When I started the major, however, I quickly thought, "This isn't for me." It was hours of trying to figure out a program that may simply not work because of a missing semicolon.

Everything happens for a reason. My grades were horrible. I was barely holding onto my computer science major. And just when I thought things couldn't get worse, I was helping a friend with his homework and he accidentally turned in a copy of my homework as his. When I get my assignment back from the professor, I have a big F written in red marker. I look at my friend like, "What happened?" The professor had circled my name on his paper—he also had an F. It was a major assignment and she would not change my grade. That class was so vital, it put my major in jeopardy, so I dropped computer science and focused on art.

I also wanted to be a graphic designer. I was learning how to design websites during my summers off. I thought, "Graphic design, that's how I'll get paid as an artist," but when I got out of undergrad, I got pretty much rejected

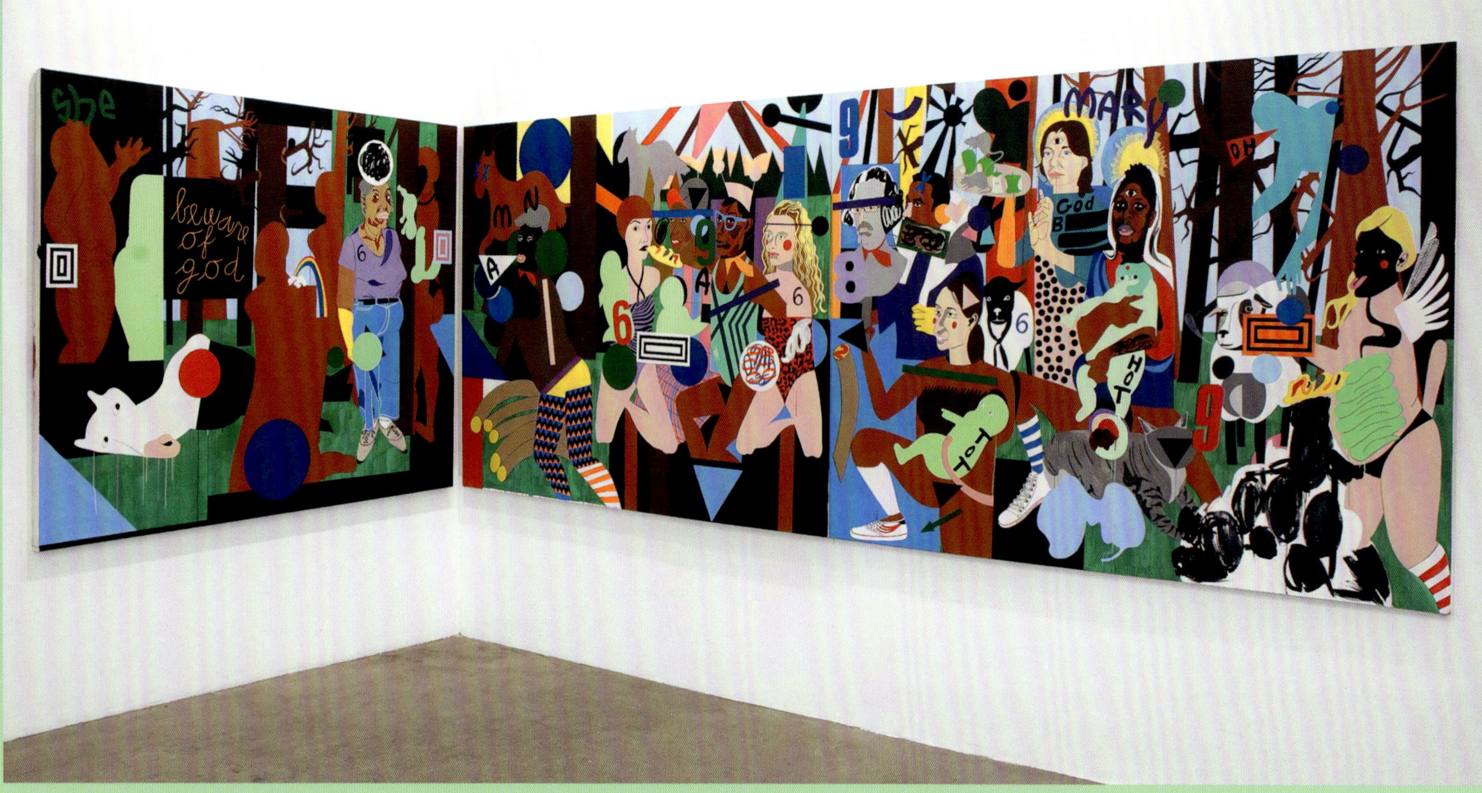

I DREAD TO THINK, 2012

from every graphic design program I applied to. I worked for a little bit and that's when I said, "Maybe I'll try painting." That's how that all came about.

I still have a definite interest in graphic design... I feel like most people don't realize that we were all teaching ourselves HTML code to create cool pages on Black Planet. We were learning HTML to play music play or feature graphics on our social media pages. I was fascinated by it.

Deitch: Prior to our talk, I was looking through the catalog of your exhibition at the Nasher Museum of Art. It's very interesting to see how your work has evolved. The figures were much looser, I'd say a little less rhythmic in the composition, and progressively become more abstracted, the rhythms more complex. I'd like to ask you about the evolution of your work over this period.

Abney: My work was always critiqued for being too flat, so I had a specific preconceived notion of what a "good" painting was, and that was one that was rendered realistically. The earlier work is a by-product of this mentality. Over the last twenty years, I have been moving away from this way of thinking and towards abstraction, which I feel is more freeing.

Deitch: You've evolved a completely unique style that's only you, that is instantly recognizable, which is quite an achievement.

Abney: Thank you. It's been a long journey to block out the noise and be in tune with my own voice.

Deitch: You have your own artistic vocabulary that's yours. It's remarkable. Very few artists can achieve that.

Abney: Thanks. I'm still trying to unlearn a few things that have been restrictive to my practice, but I feel like I'm now at 80 percent of my true artist voice. There's still work to be done.

Deitch: It's good that you still have another 20 percent to achieve. Something that fascinates me is that you've been able to put together a narrative, where some of your work tells a story with an abstract set of images. That's quite rare to be able to be narrative, bold, and abstract at the same time. I think that's quite an achievement.

Abney: When approaching my work that is representational, I aim to figure out the least amount of information needed. That's how I approach the imagery in my work now. For example, what's the least amount of information needed for one to register a figure? How do I break this down to the simplest form? I try to remove unnecessary information to create a language that becomes universal.

Deitch: Another characteristic of your work is the integration of text. You're using text almost as an abstraction, but it also becomes an essential part of the narrative.

Abney: I started using text because there are certain things I felt I just couldn't paint. Some things just need to be said plainly. I also see letters and numbers as forms and shapes. I'm also interested in the use of text in advertisements.

Deitch: I look at your work as taking Pop art into the present.

Abney: I love Pop art, so that's what I would hope to be achieving right now with my current work.

Deitch: You're expanding into other media—some ambitious sculpture is coming. I'd like to ask you about your sculpture in relationship to the painting.

Abney: I've always wanted to work in sculpture, but I was waiting until the right moment. I could not figure how I could organically translate my paintings to sculpture. I had no idea what my sculpture was going to look like. It took so much time to figure it out and now it's finally here.

I took the first step by making a vinyl toy, which allowed me to see how my work could look three-dimensionally. That was the start and things have been quickly evolving. In the past year alone, I've made over ten sculptural works. Eventually, I want to do large public sculpture that can be interactive. I'm not necessarily interested in creating monuments, but works that people can sit on, sculpture that is functional.

Deitch: I read some exciting news this week about your being selected as one of the artists commissioned for New York's new John F. Kennedy International Airport terminal. It seemed that you were thinking of doing a sculpture.

Abney: I am. I'm working with a material I've never worked with before, stained glass, inspired by New York City iconography.

Deitch: That will be brilliant. Now, we're here at Pace Prints in New York City for this conversation and you've really reinvented how to make a print, how to make collage. I'm fascinated by how you've taken this well-traveled medium of all the artists who have made prints or works on paper and you've done it in a fresh way.

Abney: I held out for years when it came to doing prints. Many printmakers or print shops would approach me and say, "You know, your work would translate so well to printmaking," and I would turn them down in hopes of working specifically with Pace Prints. Also, my understanding of prints was limited. When I thought of an edition, I only thought of an image of an existing work. So for the longest time, I was not interested in doing this.

I got a C in my printmaking class. I didn't have enough patience for the process. I did an etching, and it was the most tedious thing, so I never thought I would end up loving printmaking. Fortunately, I was introduced to [President of Pace Prints] Jacob Lewis and the printmakers of Pace Prints. I was blown away by the work that they were doing.

We started working together and it's such a collaborative process. We challenge each other to think beyond traditional printmaking and create unique works that explore collage and expand the conversation around paper as a medium.

Deitch: Well, your prints have the impact of complex paintings.

Abney: That's what we hope to achieve.

Deitch: Of all the important contemporary artists I follow, your work is sexier than almost anyone else's, but it's never vulgar. I'd like to ask you about how you insert the sexuality and the sexual power in the work in this strong way that's elegant and impactful, but never vulgar.

Abney: It comes from a sincere place of wanting to destigmatize the idea that sexuality is vulgar... and that's one of the reasons I moved to New York—it's forward-thinking energy fosters self-expression and challenges outdated norms.

I've always wanted to tell you that when I first came [to New York] to go to graduate school, your gallery was one of the first that I went to. You had a show with Kehinde Wiley with a band that performed on Wooster Street and that blew my mind. It was a very impactful experience that expanded what I thought of art as an expression and as a career.

Deitch: That was our goal, to inspire people. I really, really love hearing that it had such an impact on you.

Abney: I have always wanted to work with you because your exhibitions are ambitious, fun, smart, and not so uptight. With our February 2025 show [*Winging It*], it's a full circle moment.

Deitch: Let's close by talking about what you hope to realize in the next few years, expanding your work, both pushing the painting practice and also expanding into more popular areas.

Abney: I want to prioritize sculpture and public work in the coming years. Right now, I'm very interested in installation. I've been thinking about Yayoi Kusama's Infinity Mirror Rooms—something more experiential that can travel. Also, animation production, and I can do something new in that space that hasn't been done before. I'm also very much interested in creating more products, specifically, sneakers.

Deitch: A lot to look forward to.

This interview has been edited for length and clarity.

THE NCA☺ CODE

RICHARD J. POWELL

The art of painting was at a conceptual crossroads in the initial years of the twenty-first century. No longer the inevitable, tried-and-true art medium, painting frequently took the proverbial backseat in contemporary art practices to photography-based work, large-scale installations, body art, and digital media. For those tenacious, early twenty-first century painters like Mark Bradford, John Currin, Nicole Eisenman, Kerry James Marshall, Julie Mehretu, and Nina Chanel Abney, it was clear that the medium, as it was historically framed, could no longer maintain its esteemed former status. At a moment of radical realignment in the art world and in the midst of profound global changes, painting would need to be reimaginged not only to remain relevant but to participate in an increasingly theoretical discourse within contemporary art.[1] As curator Jamillah James reminded viewers in her 2024 Museum of Contemporary Art Chicago exhibition *The Living End: Painting and Other Technologies, 1970–2020*, painting's relationship with its so-called "successors" in these years demonstrated "an expansive understanding of image production, a wider lens on continuities of artistic practice, and as such a broader definition of painting."[2]

Abney entered this dialogical exposition with, on the one hand, the tools and expertise that one might have expected from a recent graduate of the Parsons School of Design: a broad-based art education encompassing traditional art media as well as the latest imaging technologies. On the other hand, Abney embarked on a singular path through the progressively metamorphosing medium of painting, a course differentiated by her reformulations of painting's core attributes and methodological fundamentals. Abney's compositions, colors, her pigment's dynamic traces, each work's collagelike parts, and her malleable uses of signs and symbols all shifted painting's time-honored position—from its halcyon years during the High Renaissance to its perceived provocations in the postmodern era—in a largely unexplored yet captivating direction.

Not beholden to painting's a priori status in art history, and yet not entirely renegade, Abney interjected into the medium a new pictorial program governed by her cerebrations, ideological positions, and inclinations toward digitally informed encryptions. Her designs and painting strategies collectively gestured towards a personal protocol: a code that responded to the exigencies of the twenty-first century, and that saw visuality as adept at grappling with ethical conundrums without abandoning art's allure and mythos.

Abney's collage sensibilities, in which painting's essentials subscribe to silhouettes and segments—the latter invoking parallelograms, trapezoids, circles, and other geometric shapes—have numerous modern art precedents, as

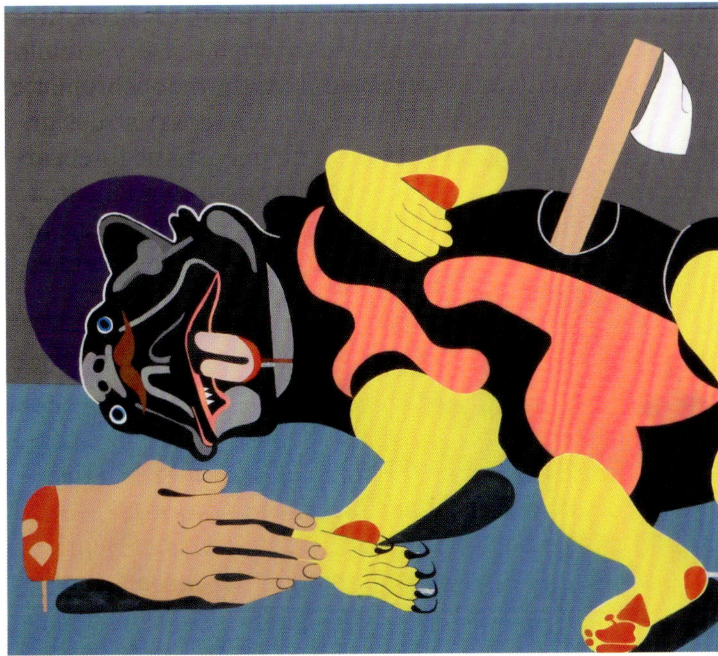

[FIG. 1] DETAIL, KING OF SORROW, 2011

seen in the works of Stuart Davis, Richard Lindner, Romare Bearden, and others. But unlike the works of her predecessors, the cartoonlike ingredients that Abney incorporates into paintings like *Law and Order* (2010), *King of Sorrow* (2011) (fig. 1), and the mural-scaled triptych *I Dread to Think* (2012) (pp. 50-55) hedged Pop art's representational reductivity with the visual supremacy of geometric abstraction, a formula that in the 2010s underscored that era's political divisions and moral ambivalences.

I Dread to Think's hallucinogenic patchwork of shapes, signs, texts, and numerals, silhouetted and minimally rendered, superficially resembles the psychedelic murals of the 1960s and 1970s, especially those of painter/illustrator Mati Klarwein. Racial difference in *I Dread to Think*—shown in a dizzying spectrum of flesh-colored torsos and dismembered body parts—was an act of cultural equivocality, where human skin tones, graphic symbols, and isolated texts, in tandem with primary and secondary palettes, produced a new abstraction, unencumbered by abstraction's repudiations of content and yet clearly foregrounding social and cultural matters.

A sprawling *Untitled* painting of 2017 distills elements from previous works, such as *I Dread to Think*, resulting in an evocative, semiabstract frieze of placard-carrying brown and near-black human prototypes set against an image-scape of wedges, emblems, and forms from nature, words in pronounced fonts, and stenciled symbols. The key characteristics in this and related paintings are tapered, collagelike bodies, with selected organs (especially noses and breasts) having racially marked complexions that contrast with their hosts. As with early twentieth century Cubist painting, Abney's diagrammatic noses are more allusive than naturalistic, and the eyes of her figures—axiomatic and open—appear as if hovering over each face. The illusionistic signboards in *Untitled* are not just allusions to protests or vague proclamations; they're extensions of their anthropomorphic exponents, as well as compositional companions, with their accompanying pictographs and characters slipping between content, decorative pattern, and surface energy. Discovering a way out of a solely narrational approach, as well as a route beyond the nonrepresentational, Abney employs showy colors and geometric configurations to create a painted sensation, and to elicit in viewers intense and deep-seated feelings not necessarily attached to well-defined subjects of introspection or self-analysis.[3]

The roller-coaster racial realities in the wake of *I Dread to Think*—from Barack Obama's reelection to a spate of widely publicized vigilante and police shootings of unarmed African Americans across the United States—precipitated a more sophisticated chromaticity and brasher graphic statements from Abney. For example, rather than advancing the painting's superficial, agitprop trappings, the five heads placed among the multihued semblances in *Untitled (FUCK T*E *OP)* (fig. 2) serve other purposes, their burnt sienna profiles (with racially White appendages) narrativizing the vividly patterned picture and putting race at the center of this work. The contrasting tones and dense placements of design units in the work level their criticisms of law enforcement through comprehensive, visual means: the sharp, angular, and well-defined shapes of Abney's painted forms implicitly expressing restlessness and anger.

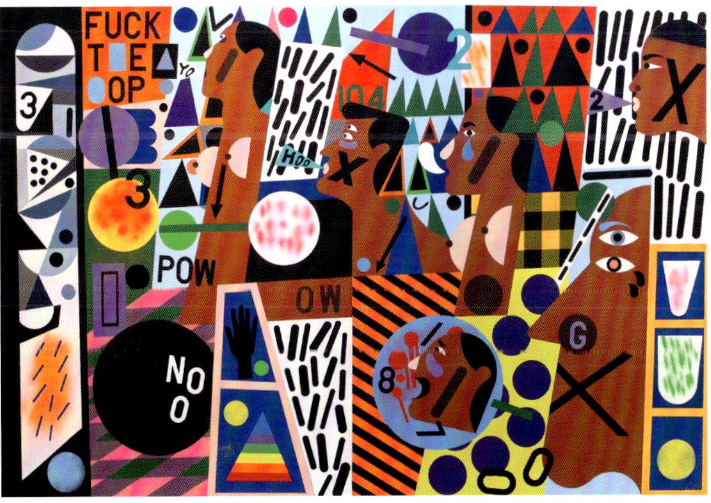

[FIG. 2] UNTITLED (FUCK T*E *OP),

If the profanity-laden subtitle of the work—and its strident text in red, black, and light blue in the painting's upper left corner—did not allow the composition to slip into an absolute fantasy, a subsequent series of canvases depicting the police arresting disorderly protesters makes no pretenses at narrative open-endedness. In addition to the pinkish hues of White people and the brown complexions of Black people, Abney's incorporation of the shades of blues associated with police uniforms brings that era's incendiary clashes between law enforcement and African Americans under scrutiny. Without actually depicting the

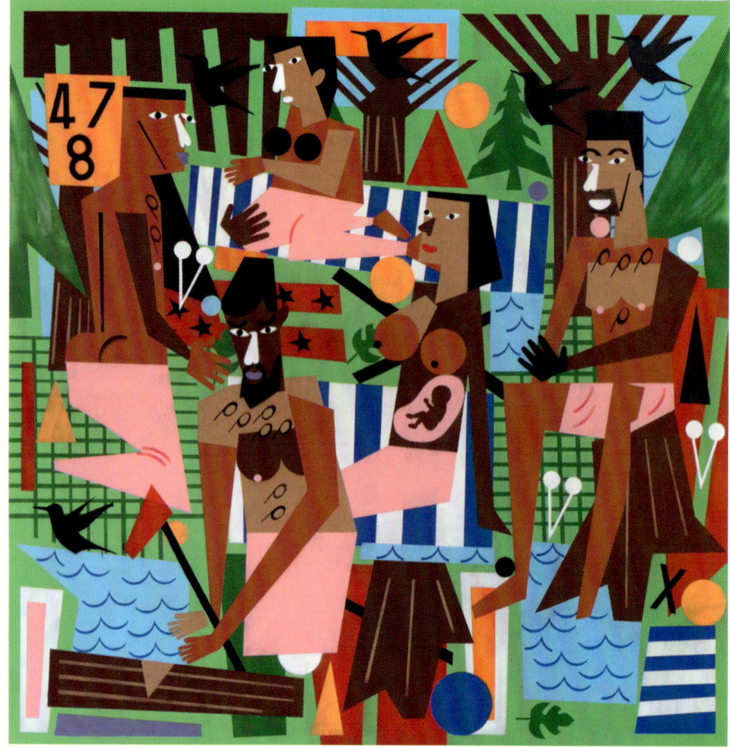

[FIG. 3] FEMME GAMES, 2020

police chokeholds and shootings of Black men such as Eric Garner and Michael Brown, Abney puts colorful motifs and heavy black lettering to work but distilled through the selected forms' universalizing capacity for reportage. Paradoxically, these combat scenes seem less accusatory than simply statements of fact: accounts in which institutional authority, community unrest, and racial difference serve the cool, disaffected objectives of the nonconcrete.

Abney's idiosyncratic approach to color—referential and yet unbound, and spectral in its psychological effects—grew exponentially in subsequent paintings such as *A Vanilla Position* (2019) (pp. 62-63) and *Femme Games* (2020) (fig. 3). The rainbow range in *A Vanilla Position* fuels the painting's transgressive tenor, disrupting racial and gendered conventions via a largely phenotypic White character flanked by multiple Black personae, and by way of an unconstrained Pop art palette. Indeed, Abney's colors metaphorically hang glide in paintings like *Femme Games*, paying homage to the Impressionist pastorale while also dismantling such art historical tropes with high-key, contrastive silhouettes and chop-block insertions. A big part of Abney's destabilizations is her use of the color brown: in one aspect, it is racial. But in other ways it is nonrepresentational, or in the theoretical framework of the French philosopher Jean-François Lyotard (in his arguments about inscrutability in the visual arts), a *figural* factor that, vaulting a conscious grasp of pictorial matters, conveys its affective powers physiologically and directly onto the corroborator's nervous system.[4] The color brown functions counterintuitively in *Femme Games* as a physical trait, a chromatic accent, and as the painting's metronomic pulse. Abney's brown effigies not only racially integrate her compositions, they infiltrate the audience's inner eye (as encoded throughout her oeuvre via ocular details), resulting in a state not unlike one's reactions to external sensory stimulation.[5] Although decades removed from the monochromatic murals by the Harlem Renaissance's premier artist/designer Aaron Douglas, Abney shares with her artistic forebearer the power of a brown-to-plum chromatic component: a prismatic dimension that when augmented by a retinue of graphic symbols and a Black cultural subtext, invigorates the picture and animates the viewer's psyche.[6]

"Nina Chanel Abney's bold, scratch-and-chop approach in her raucous paintings," stated the press release for the 2018 group exhibition *Travelogue*, "[push] to the fore her subjects and [emphasize] the frenzied pace of life in the 21st century."[7] Among Abney's works in *Travelogue*, *#5* (2018) (p.93) and *#21* (2018) (fig. 4) acknowledge Henri Matisse's Fauvism by way of unmodulated chroma and dynamic paint applications. Mixing planar treatments, stenciling, and sprayed sections, Abney's irreverent basketball shooter in *#5* exudes an unalloyed vibrancy: the painting's acrylic expanses and latex waves pushing viewers' responses to this subject towards agitation, excitement and, ultimately, an inner jouissance.[8] These graffiti-conversant constituents—aided by the effects of brown, black, and other darker shades against brighter and more chromatically saturated parts—propose color/rhythm relationships. In *#21*, the bust of a geometrical figure affixes and anchors itself to the surrounding chromatic actions, while in *Peep*

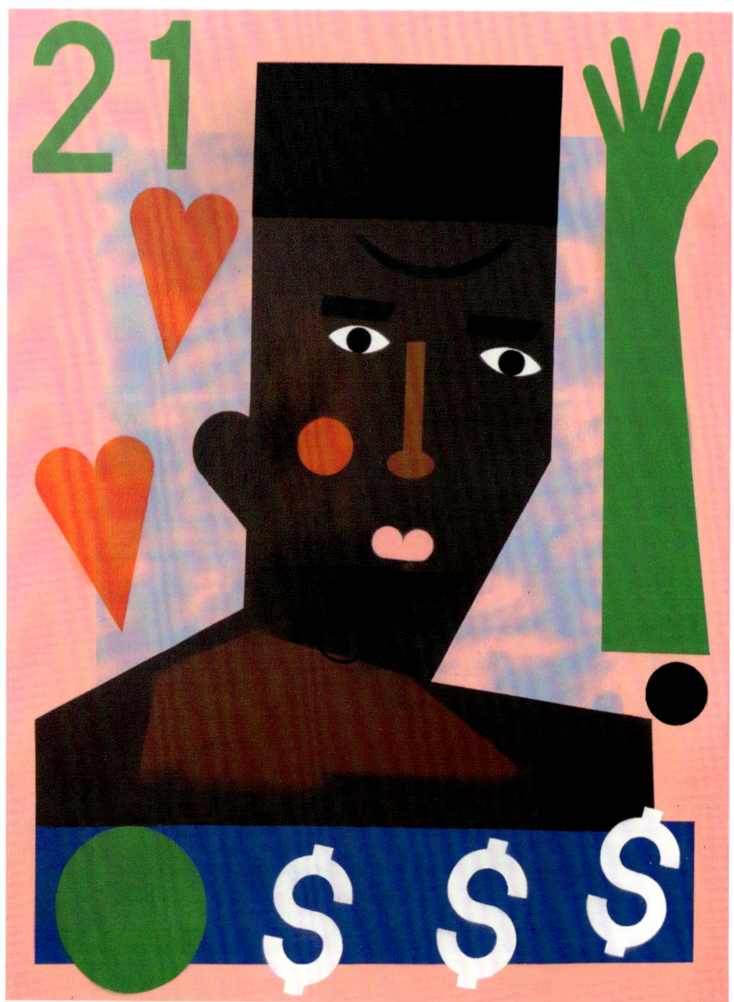

[FIG. 4] #21, 2018

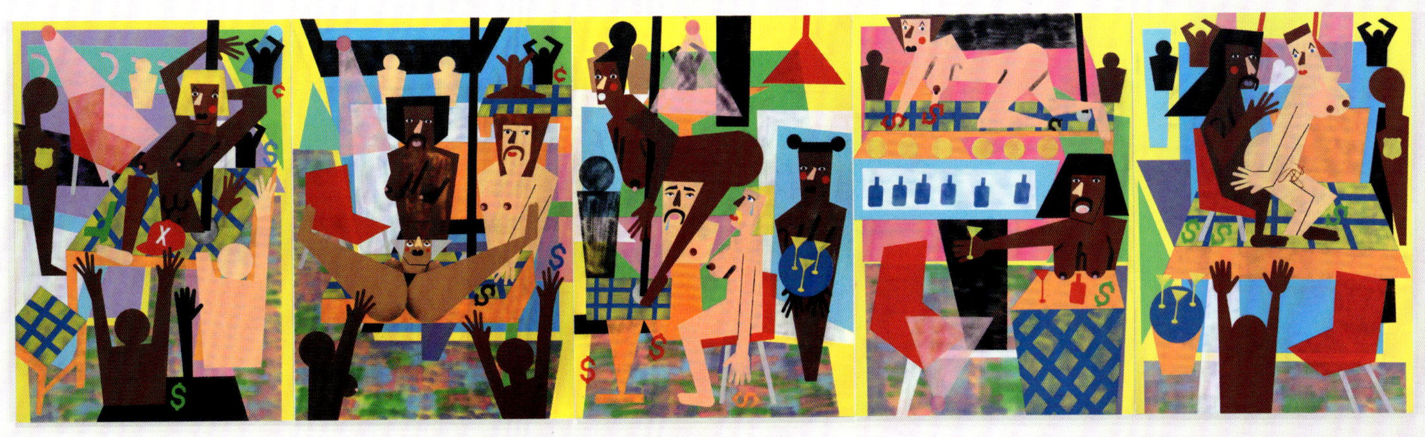

[FIG. 5] PEEP, 2019

(2019) (fig. 5), sprayed and stenciled zones turn the painting's strip-club subject into an allusive, fractious banner, as rhythmical and haptic as it is graphic and anecdotal.

This interplay between a painting's recognizable features and Abney's artistic actions—wryly alluded to in the imagery and title of her major 2017 work *Catch Me If You Can, Catch 22* (pp. 74-75)—inevitably pushes these paintings towards something as double-edged and proactive as, say, Pablo Picasso's *Women of Algiers*, after Delacroix (1955). But unlike Picasso's colonialist reverie and overtures to four-dimensional space, time dilation, and relativity, Abney's point in time of domestic and global instability and the related concerns surrounding climate, poverty, identity, privacy, and technology, all demand a detached yet subtly engaged approach, one which avails itself of iconic structures, brash gestures, and redolent colors in service to the tumultuous times in which the paintings were created. "Cubism allows me to manipulate time and space on the canvas, making the figures dynamic, as if caught in a perpetual dance between the seen and the unseen, the said and the unsaid," acknowledged Abney about that artistic movement's impact on her work.[9]

Approximately a century after Picasso created his visual disruptions, Abney embarked on her own pictorial upheavals. However, the differences between Cubism's radically modified figures and still lifes and paintings like Abney's *Catch Me If You Can, Catch 22* reside in a format that, while dispersed and motley, was aesthetically germane to its fraught moment of creation. In the midst of a cultural explosion informed by an African American urban artform such as hip hop, Abney made similar uses of Cubistic shards and chunks to connote aural blasts, exhortations, and the honed outlines of what felt like a frenetic, contemporary existence. As seen in Abney's use of stencils and aerosols to apply paints, and in her composite, racially combined renderings of human figures, works such as *Catch Me If You Can, Catch 22* and the 2015 *Why?* (pp. 104-105) gave a tangible if eclectic delineation of that era's rallying cry of "Black Lives Matter."

Under Abney's aegis, Cubism's colloquies with modern physics and its reimagining of an art object's geodesic position vis-à-vis its subject have been expanded to include a hip hop aesthetic whose planes and facets establish a nexus with contemporary African American culture. Abney's stenciled and spray-painted sections in *Catch Me If You Can, Catch 22* are like a DJ's record-scratching on a turntable: a device that incorporates textures, hard edges, and heightened tensions into a work of art. Or consider the orthogonal figures in Abney's *Big Butch Synergy* (pp. 128-31) series: six life-size, oval-shaped canvases of seated individuals, whose undermining of the cisgendered binary in figurative art exemplifies Abney's characteristic, jagged interfacing—not unlike a rapper's distinctive flow on top of a song's improvised beat.[10] Abney's applications of pigments and serrated references to human bodies rise above their assumed social categories in these paintings and, instead, draw audiences into a speculative experience, something akin to contemporary hip hop's immersive capacities.

Flipping the allegory of a racially integrated utopia on its head, Abney's paintings of Black and White policemen, street combatants, and, as seen in her 2016 *Hothouse* (fig. 6), women in suggestive "pin-up girl" poses give augmented meaning to the notion of spectacle, where race is both the object and the subject of an intense, disciplinary gaze. "It's a terrifically energetic, feminist update of Picasso's brothel painting *Les Demoiselles d'Avignon*," wrote an art critic upon *Hothouse*'s appearance in a 2016 exhibition at the Whitney Museum of American Art.[11]

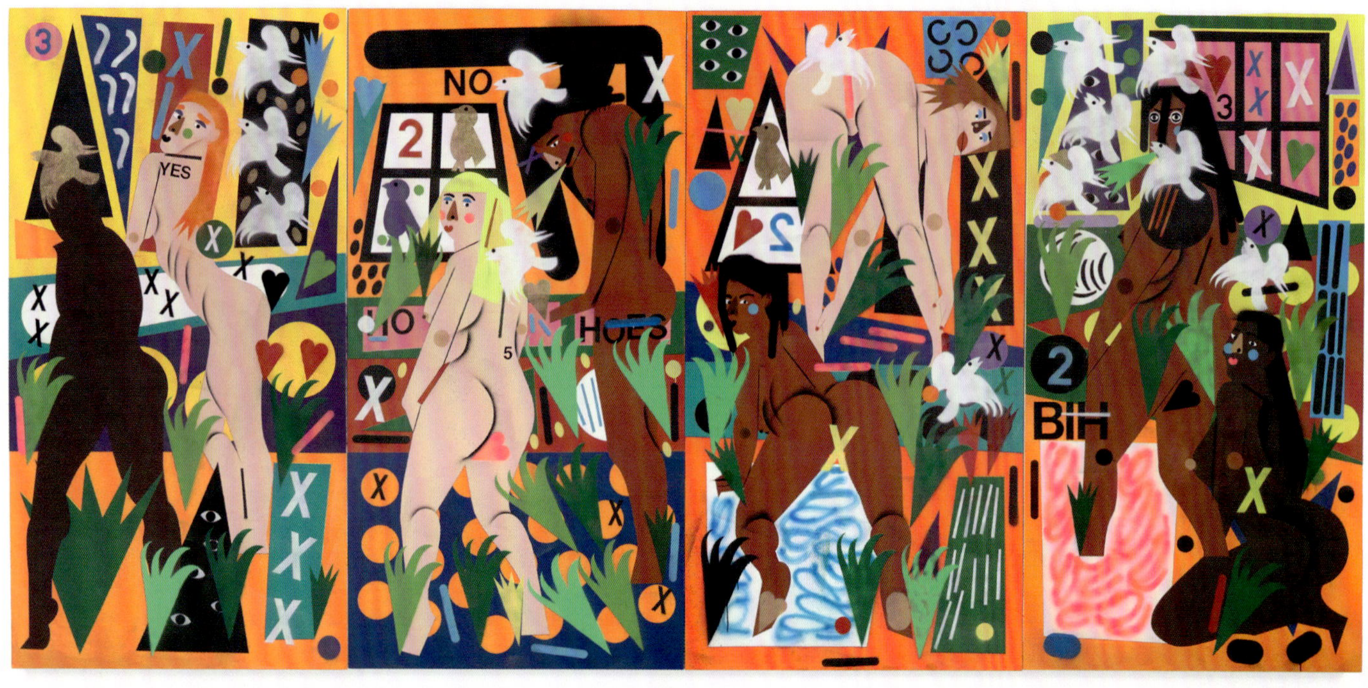

[FIG. 6] HOTHOUSE, 2016

Along with references in these paintings to obstruse and conflicting signage, the exemplifications of racial Blackness and Whiteness, while front and center, ultimately distracts and deludes spectators (as indicated by each figure's racially mismatched noses), and contributes to Abney's musings on information systems—aural, textual, and pictorial—and their inherent limitations for accurate and clear communications, especially at this moment of an assumed, limitless access by way of the internet. "Abney's two-dimensional canvases pack gossip, race, sex, politics, jokes and sleaze," observed a *Huffington Post* reporter, "mixing and matching symbols until the aforementioned categories become jumbled into one. . . Gazing into her works feels like falling asleep in front of your laptop and TV, leaving the open windows and random commercials to wedge their way into your dreams."[12]

"Symbols are as ubiquitous as language," Abney told an interviewer about her use of dollar signs, eyes, *X*s, and other insignialike motifs in paintings, "and with the advent of mobile technology and rapid-fire communication, they are shaping up to be a benchmark of communication for our time. . . I have been especially influenced by emojis and their layered meanings," she continued, expanding upon the semiotician Henry Dreyfuss and the futurist R. Buckminster Fuller's shared notion of "a visible language."[13]

Riding the waves of the emoji's popularity—beginning around 2015, when an expanded selection of the pioneering telecommunications designer Shigetaka Kurita's "picture-words" were made available in Unicode 8, the international encoding standard for electronic communication—Abney wholeheartedly embraced this new pictorial/logographic writing system, seeing in it a vehicle for her adjunctive, semiotic approach to abstract painting.[14] "Someone once said to me that my work is indicative of the digital era that we are embarking upon—and I'd like to think that the disassociated use of letters, numbers, and shapes is akin to a time capsule."[15]

In Abney's 2019 diptych *Junk Mail Scribble #2* (fig. 7), one sees how fantastic figures with standardized eyes and other physical features help contextualize an otherwise inchoate, symbol-filled field. However, the painting's amalgamated human facsimiles with racially distinctive complexions nonetheless added to the work's oblique gestures toward recognized phenomena, encouraging viewers/readers to take into account the punctuation, numbers, interjections, and emblems in the context of an ontologically comprehensive composition. Abney's titular acknowledgement of the painting's information-overload theme underscores her career-long preoccupation with the fault lines that the internet era has wrought: rifts that are often exacerbated by misrecognitions along racial, gender, and sexual gradients. Abney's punctuation signs vault their linguistic functions, and like their geometric counterparts, create status-quo-breaking interruptions and flashing signals. Hearts and dollar signs pose ethical quandaries in these pictures and, along with the silhouettes of both natural phenomena and cultural icons, they prod us to choose between reverie and reality. When words, letters, and numbers do materialize, they quarry the subconscious, where sounds, quantifications, and profound concepts propel themselves through a borderless and depthless frontier.

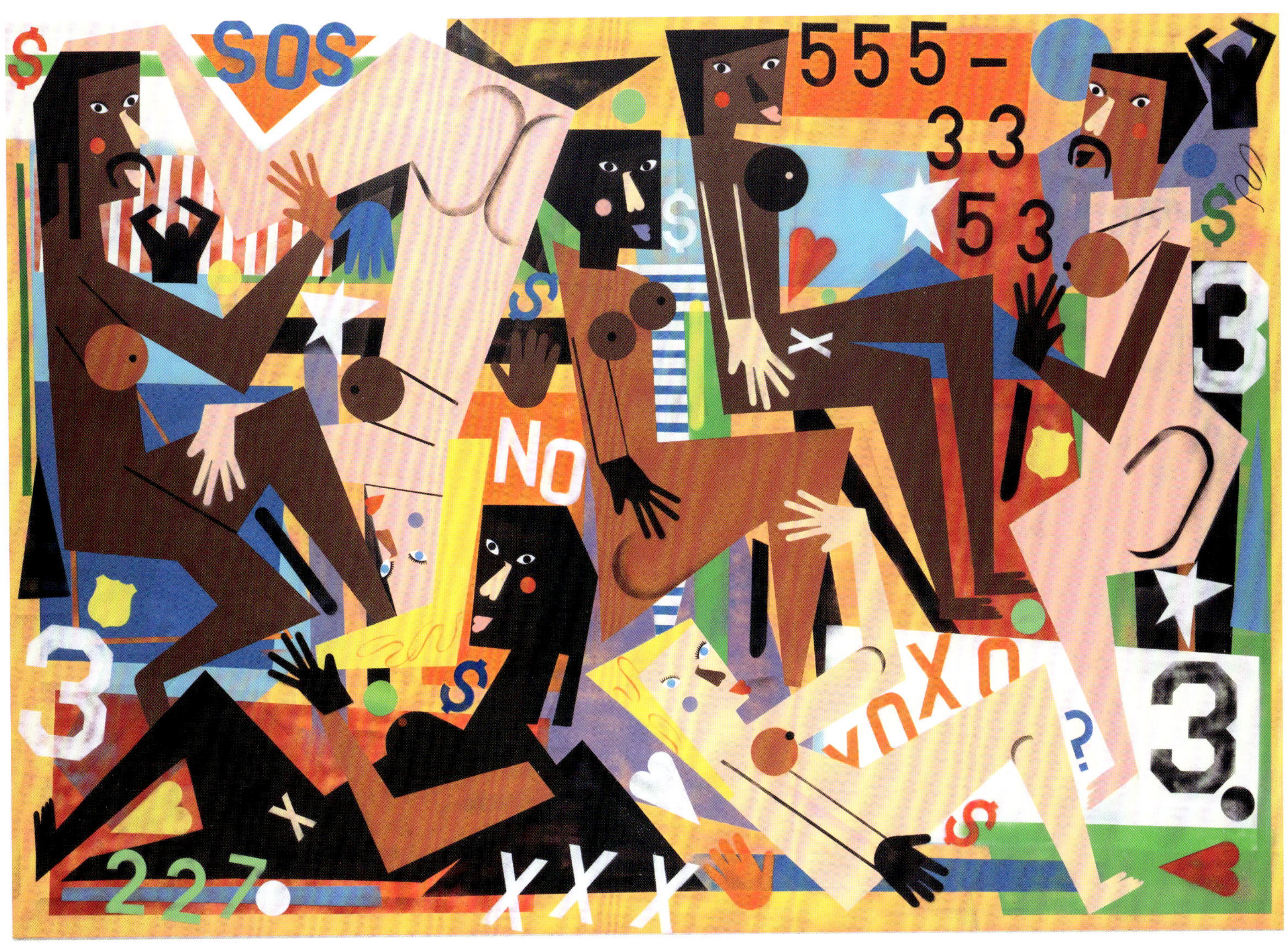

[FIG. 7] JUNK MAIL SCRIBBLE, 2019

In a major artistic statement that would marry Abney's commentaries on symbols with providing the public a much-needed history lesson, the artist created *San Juan Heal* (Public Works insert pp. 80–81), a mammoth latex, ink, and vinyl graphic attached to the fourteen windows along the north side of the Lincoln Center for the Performing Arts' David Geffen Hall in New York City. Under any circumstance, putting a work of art on public display in Manhattan is challenging, but in spotlighting Lincoln Center while also acknowledging its role in the destruction of San Juan Hill, an established Upper West Side working class neighborhood, Abney faced additional pressures. Her answer was a thirty-five-panel compendium: not a linear narrative about San Juan Hill but a patchwork of illuminations—pictorial, textual, and grammatical—that collectively recounted the neighborhood's history in a crosslinguistic, semiotic therapeutic.[16] Neither exhaustive nor insubstantial, *San Juan Heal*'s individual anecdotes aligned with the terse phraseology and vibrant-hued, hemmed abstractions that characterize Abney's work, but to spectacular effect against Geffen Hall's precast concrete, marble, and glass facade. Among *San Juan Heal*'s various sections are several featuring the letter *X*, a multipurpose proxy for that which requires witnessing, as well as a powerful insignia for Black lineages lost yet honored (to paraphrase the 1960s Black activist Malcolm X).[17]

Along with the *X*'s, another repeated motif in *San Juan Heal* is human hands, either disembodied or the gesturing extremities of musicians, saints, and neighborhood heroes. As seen throughout Abney's work, hands and limbs are as much in the realm of signs as is the letter *X*, alerting viewers to not just a potential human interest story but to corporeality writ large as symptomatic, such as in signage for recreation, warnings, or indicators for seating the elderly or the physically challenged on public transportation. Abney's imagery doesn't so much tap into sentimentality as turn potential human dramas into two-dimensional glyphs that require deciphering, interpretation, and a measure of irony-attuned humor.

This balancing act between the body politic and a tongue-in-cheek corporeal facticity are on full display in *Marabou* (fig. 8), a diptych that, spoofing the 1980s artist Keith Haring's faceless, gesticulating bodies, situates those cyphers in a maternity ward where the ambience is more a factory's assembly line than a hospital. The intersections of gender and race in *Marabou* are additionally entangled with the idea of childbirth; here infantlike circle-and-trapezoid entities tumbling from splayed bodies and into eager arms.[18] A commentary on the rise in surrogacy, especially its employment of women of color as gestational carriers?

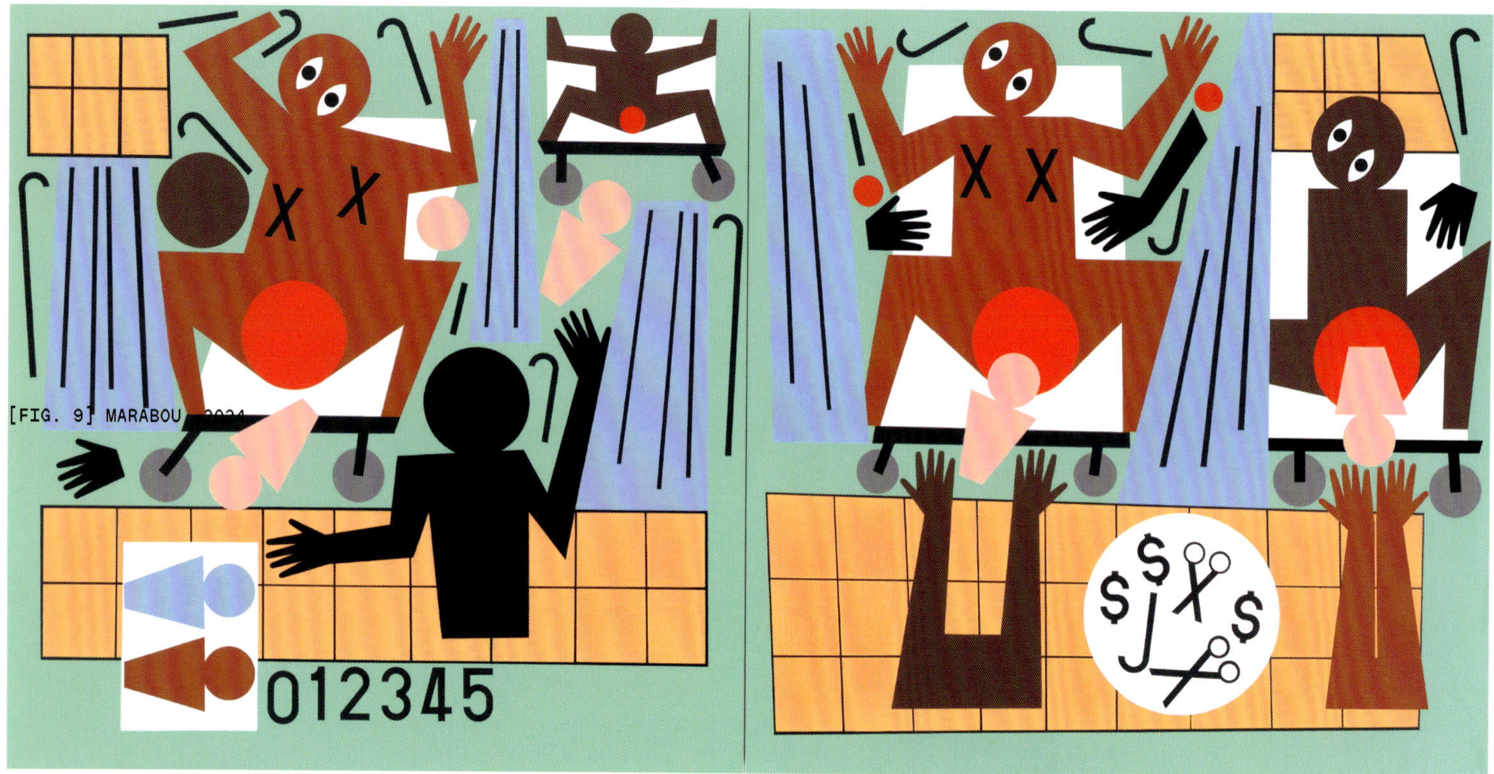

[FIG. 8] MARABOU, 2024

A riposte about the reproductive value placed on Whiteness? Perhaps. What is clear is that in lieu of the proverbial baby-dropping stork (or marabou), this delivery room is equipped with curious shapes, institutional tinges, numerals, dollar signs, and the letters *X* and *J*, the former morphing into scissors or forceps and the latter mutating into walking canes or weapons.

Across Abney's output, metamorphosis is not just something signs and symbols execute; the physical sign itself—a cardboard sheet, a digital animation, a piece of clothing, and a canvas, vinyl, or metal panel—can rotate (or appear to oscillate), thus augmenting a viewer's initial impressions with added perspectives and interpretations. Serialization and repetition implicitly suggest motion, and the barbed forms in her work cognate with a perceived dynamism and action even if the objects themselves are static.

Exploring the possibilities of the manifold meanings of a given sign or symbol and sense of dimensionality and material presence, Abney increasingly turned to sculpture to investigate the contours and corollaries within these markers. The almost ten-foot-high *TOK* (fig. 9) comprises a standing figure holding aloft a placard/truncated head in one hand and a figural bust on a platter in the other. And yet the figure's schematized breasts and racial mashups both indicate and problematize its identity, which is also undone by the figure's combined declaratory/conferring gestures.

A pathway to Abney's sculptural simultaneity was surely forged by Picasso, especially in his late-career sculptures. In numerous examples one can see how Picasso's Cubist representationalism was finessed by his manipulations of rolled steel sheets, where the cutout, sharp-cornered, and welded components—similar to Abney's *TOK*—revealed multiple characters, states of being, and even different species.[19] The reverse side of *TOK* enacts comparable machinations, downplaying the White arm behind a brown torso and limbs, and replacing the aforesaid heads on the placard and platter with two allegorical standees on their reverse: a ghostly, black-and-white effigy and a brown face enveloped by an American-flaglike do-rag. Titled with half of the name of the highly popular social media app, *TOK* soars above the average person in both height and easy explanations, and yet circumnavigating the sculpture and discerning its different aspects mirror TikTok's invitation to its content creators and consumers to perform while pondering life's contradictions.

Through her career-long gauging of the culture's social media pulse, Nina Chanel Abney's work stands apart from an art practice that simply comments on contemporary issues or society at large. What distinguishes her work is an inordinate preoccupation with the tools and mechanisms of signification in the information age, or what Roland Barthes in 1964 presciently described as "the Kitchen of Meaning."[20] However, this semiotic concern is always conceived with a mind's eye on *affect:* exegeses in painting, sculpture, and other art genres that all possess a transcendent essence and a conspicuous visual imprimatur.[21]

In the wake of Cubism's artistic bequests—and also in response to digital/post-analog theories of computer imaging and semiotics—Abney's twenty-first-century entrées into a reconceived abstraction and a mass-media-conversant symbolism is certainly noteworthy, and was

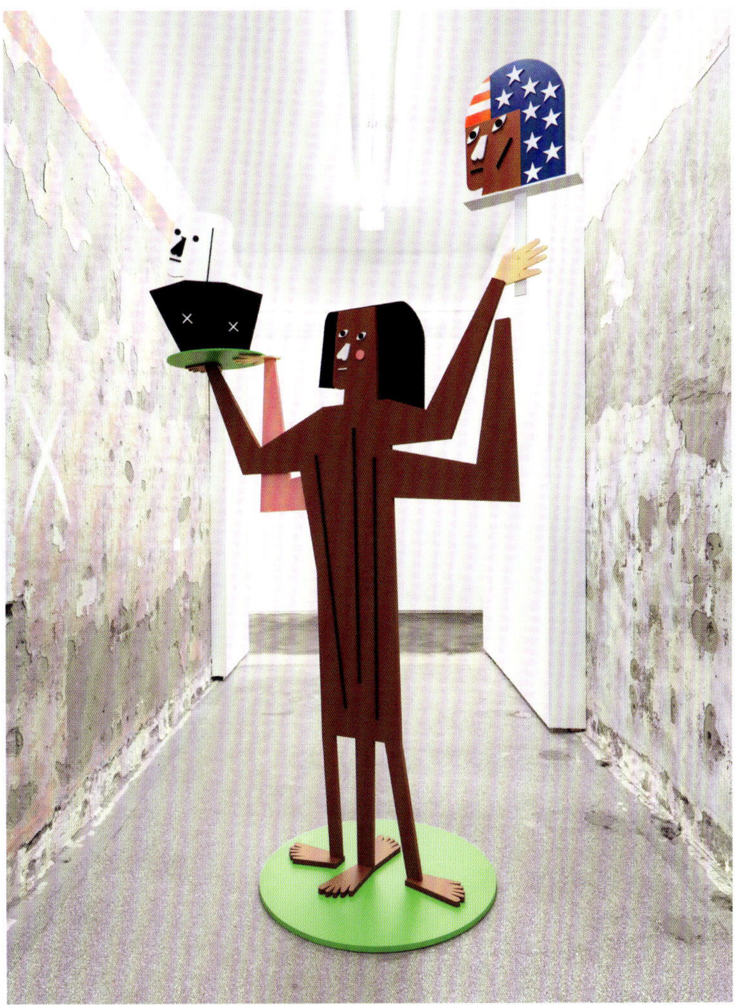

[FIG. 9] TOK, 2024

also quite prophetic. When the Harlem Renaissance's Aaron Douglas called in 1925 for doing "the impossible" in art, and creating "something transcendentally material, mystically objective" and "dynamic," who could have imagined that a hundred years later someone would take up his audacious invitation?[22] Who could have guessed that through a reimaging of the medium of painting, the language of signs and symbols, and the emoji's tripartite tenets of representation, interpretability, and contextualization, an artist would reformulate the vexing questions of identity, as well as use her work's miscellaneous modes to reconcile the perceived gulfs between imagined worlds and material truths?[23] As Abney's multifaceted career has demonstrated, of paramount importance in the "NCA ☺ Code" is the interfacing of the virtual with the real, while also addressing the pressing topics of the day with an understanding of how art can engage contemporary issues by way of a sophisticated yet precise and lucid outlook.

Endnotes

1 Griselda Pollock, "Painting in a 'Hybrid' Moment," in Jonathan P. Harris, ed., *Critical Perspectives on Contemporary Painting* (Liverpool: Liverpool University Press, 2003), 38.

2 Jamillah James, "... And It's Still Living," in *The Living End: Painting and Other Technologies, 1970–2020* (Chicago: Museum of Contemporary Art, 2024), 12.

3 Daniel W. Smith, "Deleuze's Theory of Sensation: Overcoming the Kantian Duality," in Paul Patton, ed., *Deleuze: A Critical Reader* (Oxford: Oxford University Press, 1996), 44.

4 Jean-François Lyotard, *Discourse, Figure*, trans. Antony Hudek and Mary Lydon (1971; Minneapolis: University of Minnesota Press, 2011), 268.

5 Ibid.

6 On the "purplish" Harlem Renaissance palette, see Nicholas Gaskill, *Chromographia: American Literature and the Modernization of Color* (Minneapolis: University of Minnesota Press, 2018), 215, 220.

7 Press release, *Travelogue* (Kinderhook, NY: The School/Jack Shainman Gallery), May 20–October 6, 2018.

8 Jane Gallop, "Beyond the *Jouissance* Principle," *Representations* 7 (Summer 1984): 110–15.

9 Ella Martin-Gachot, "Artist Nina Chanel Abney Cements Her Place in the Contemporary Canon With a Colossal Upstate Show This Summer," *Cultured*, May 16, 2024. https://www.culturedmag.com/article/2024/05/16/nina-chanel-abney-jack-shainman-upstate-show.

10 "These works are reflective," Abney told an interviewer, "but also are reimaginations and subversions of exclusionary social rituals that are widely circulated in visual media." Eliza Jordan, "Nina Chanel Abney Reconstructs Representation at ICA Miami with Big Butch Energy," *Whitewall Magazine*, November 30, 2022. https://whitewall.art/art/nina-chanel-abney-reconstructs-representation-at-ica-miami-with-big-butch-energy

11 Ken Johnson, "'Flatlands,' Where the Familiar Becomes Hypnotically Strange," *New York Times*, January 28, 2016.

12 Priscilla Frank, "Nina Chanel Abney on How Art Basel Is the Art World's Spring Break," *Huffpost*, December 7, 2013. https://www.huffpost.com/entry/nina-chanel-abney_n_4401255.

13 Syma Mohammed, "In Conversation with Nina Chanel Abney: Using Bright Colors to Tell Dark Realities," C&, January 11, 2018, https://contemporaryand.com/magazines/using-bright-colors-to-tell-dark-realities/

14 "Full Emoji List, v15.1," Unicode – The World Standard for Text and Emoji. https://unicode.org/emoji/charts/full-emoji-list.html.

15 Ibid.

16 Will Heinrich, "Geffen Hall Commissions New Art That Honors Black and Latino History," *New York Times*, October 8, 2022.

17 Malcolm X, *The Autobiography of Malcolm X, as told to Alex Haley* (New York: Ballantine Books, 1965), 199. For an extended meditation on the *X* symbol, see Carl G. Liungman, *Dictionary of Symbols* (Santa Barbara, CA: ABC-CLIO, 1991), 139–40.

18 Conversation with the artist, August 14, 2024.

19 Werner Spies, "Sculpture in a Plane," in *Sculpture by Picasso, with a catalogue of the works* (New York: Harry N. Abrams, Inc., 1971), 226, 260–61.

20 Roland Barthes, "The Kitchen of Meaning," originally published as "La cuisine du sens (sur la sémiologie)," in *Nouvel-Observateur*, December 3–10, 1964, English version: *The Semiotic Challenge*, trans. Richard Howard (New York: Hill and Wang, 1988),157–59.

21 I discuss the role of *affect* in Nina Chanel Abney's work in a forthcoming book chapter: Richard J. Powell, "The Bronze Thrill" (unpublished manuscript, April 3, 2024), typescript.

22 Aaron Douglas to Langston Hughes, circa December 1925. Langston Hughes Papers. James Weldon Johnson Collection in the Yale Collection of American Literature, Beinecke Rare Book and Manuscript Library, Yale University. I compared Nina Chanel Abney's contemporary figural abstractions with Aaron Douglas's Jazz Age "Afro-Deco" imagery in a public lecture at the Metropolitan Museum of Art: Richard J. Powell, "The Leonard A. Lauder Distinguished Scholar Lecture—Blackbeats: Cubism Reimagined," YouTube Video, 1:06:55, April 1, 2024. https://www.youtube.com/watch?v=b2npnMbDyiY.

23 Marcel Danesi, *The Semiotics of Emoji: The Rise of Visual Language in the Age of the Internet* (London: Bloomsbury, 2017), 40–42.

FUTURES YET TO BE IMAGINED:

THELMA GOLDEN IN CONVERSATION WITH NINA CHANEL ABNEY

Thelma Golden: Nina, I'm thrilled to get to do this. I saw your work in 2008, in a group show called *30 Americans* which was presented at what was then the Rubell Family Collection (now the Rubell Museum) in Miami. It was shortly after, at your solo exhibitions at Kravets Wehby Gallery, that I really had the chance to immerse myself in your practice. When I saw these works, I knew them—they were already there for me in my visual imagination. That's because then, as now, your visual language is so distinct. And it's distinct not only in its form but in the ways in which it occupies its surface. Whether we see it in a print, a painting, an interior wall mural, a public work, or as a reproduction in person, it speaks through the visual language you've created in such a broad and bold way.

The first person I probably spoke with about your work, Nina, was one of your early collectors and one of my most significant mentors and friends, and that was Peggy Cooper Cafritz. Peggy lived deeply in her enthusiasms; when she was excited about an artist, she would say that artist's whole name over and over and over again in ways that opened up space. We are very proud at the Studio Museum [in Harlem] to have received a bequest from Peggy, who, long before her untimely, too-early passing said, "I'm leaving my collection to the Studio Museum in Harlem." So she collected with the idea that some of your works would come to the Studio Museum. Often our conversations about artists were about the way in which Peggy was collecting, and this idea of her stewardship of artworks into the future for the public and in the public realm. I think that's very resonant with what I've always felt has been an important mission of your work, Nina: to have work that is accessible and in the public realm, there for now, but also for futures yet to be imagined.

Nina Chanel Abney: Peggy was amazing. I have so many funny stories about her. When I [first] sold her a painting, I was so nervous. It was my first direct sale to a collector, so I created a makeshift agreement. Peggy rewrote it on the spot, casually reminding me that she had her law degree. Peggy was so deeply supportive.

Golden: Nina, I am very interested in you talking about some of the artistic influences you've had, because when I first saw your work—and I continue in these years to watch it evolve and develop—I noticed a potential lineage to some of the artists that are important to the art history that I'm so privileged to steward. For example, I went to the Harlem Renaissance exhibition last spring at the Metropolitan Museum [of Art], I had the rare occasion to see, in person and up close, those amazing Aaron Douglas murals. And I think about the way in which Douglas worked, creating art for the ages but also doing it in places that folks would get to see it, such as magazines and newspapers. I know you've talked in lots of publications, but for this, I'd love for you to think about the things that you look at and have looked at that have inspired who you are as an artist.

Abney: My influences have shifted, but in many ways, my current approach returns to how I worked as an undergrad. Grad school and New York initially pushed me toward a more painterly style, but I eventually found my way back to my true voice. Growing up in the Midwest, my first exposure to art was through Annie Lee and Romare Bearden prints in Black households. Later, at the Art Institute [of Chicago], I studied Picasso and Matisse, but my real awakening to contemporary art happened in New York. A key moment was making my first collage for *The Bearden Project* at the Studio Museum. The process of flat layering became foundational to my painting practice. Lowery Stokes Sims introduced me to Stuart Davis, whose work changed my perception around form and text, further shaping my visual language. Now I look at artists like Kenny Scharf, who fluidly move between fine art and commercial work, which resonates with how I want to position my practice—blurring boundaries while staying accessible.

Golden: Well, that's why when I brought this up I was thinking about artists, of course, like Douglas. And I was also thinking about Charles W. White, who made works to be shown in museums but also works that were illustrated in *Ebony* magazine, so that they were quite literally in people's homes through the '50s and '60s. You bring up those prints, and I add to that greeting cards and that era when the big greeting card companies commissioned Black artists to make works. Everybody had these similar images, and people would keep them.

All of it speaks to an idea that I think pushes away from when people talk about art being accessible in a negative way. It's actually about what the power is for art that can live in these different worlds and speak in those ways. Those Bearden prints, of course, are not the same as a Bearden that you see in a museum, but they profoundly spoke to the ideas and the ways of working that Bearden believed in. You encapsulate that as well.

It's so interesting, you say that you've not done collage. When we thought about how to celebrate Bearden—this enormously significant artist not only in the many ways that he worked throughout his long career, but the role he played in creating space for artists, places like the Studio Museum, the Spiral Group, and his involvement and investment in being a real leader in the arts community—it was also because he was such a master of collage. And when we were thinking about that project we invited lots of artists whose work perhaps didn't feel like it was aligned with Bearden. But in your case, it really did feel like our ask was because you were already working in parts of Bearden's tradition, so it's interesting to hear you say that that was a first moment where you returned to flat work and collage work.

What I have long appreciated about your work and the way in which I see where it lives in the beautifully diverse community of contemporary artists of African descent working in this city, country, and world right now, is your commitment to a deeply complex formal exercise. And that's this visual language which we've come to begin to understand. We can see it in the way you use perspective and the way signs and symbols live within your work. That's why I say that when I finally saw your work, I was like, *Wow*, but in a way, I also already knew it because I had seen it and it impacted me so deeply.

What's also interesting are the ways in which, across your career, the narratives in your work have addressed so many ideas. And those ideas are often in conversation with the work of many artists of your generation—even if there's no visual connection—who are thinking about how we understand history, how we engage identity, how we place ideas around race, gender, and sexuality, and how we explore representation and what that means. You are pushing in interesting ways at a sometimes overwhelming desire for certain kinds of figurative art, and you're giving us a way to see a different version of the figurative that can live within this conversation.

Actually, there's a word that I often think of when I see your work, and that is *syncopation*. I didn't really think about that a lot until we were beginning to think about potential artists for the Lincoln Center [for the Performing Arts] public art project [for the facade of David Geffen Hall]. I instantly began to have the conversation about you, and that word syncopation came back. And obviously in talking in that moment, it felt attached to some of the ideas there. But more broadly I feel that there's a very specific kind of rhythmic, visual way of working that you have, which I find super engaging.

Abney: I work intuitively, guided by rhythm. Colors act as notes, symbols move in syncopation. I don't preplan compositions; I feel them out in real time. This approach can be frustrating under deadline, but it keeps my work dynamic.

Golden: It feels like the kind of code that makes sense of your compositions. That's it.

What music do you listen to in the studio? What music inspires you generally? What music did you grow up with? What would you say is your musical era? For me, it's '94: Biggie, Tupac, all of that.

Abney: Nineties R&B—D'Angelo, Mary J. Blige. Jazz is a constant, and I'm currently teaching myself jazz piano and learning how to DJ. I rotate between music, podcasts,

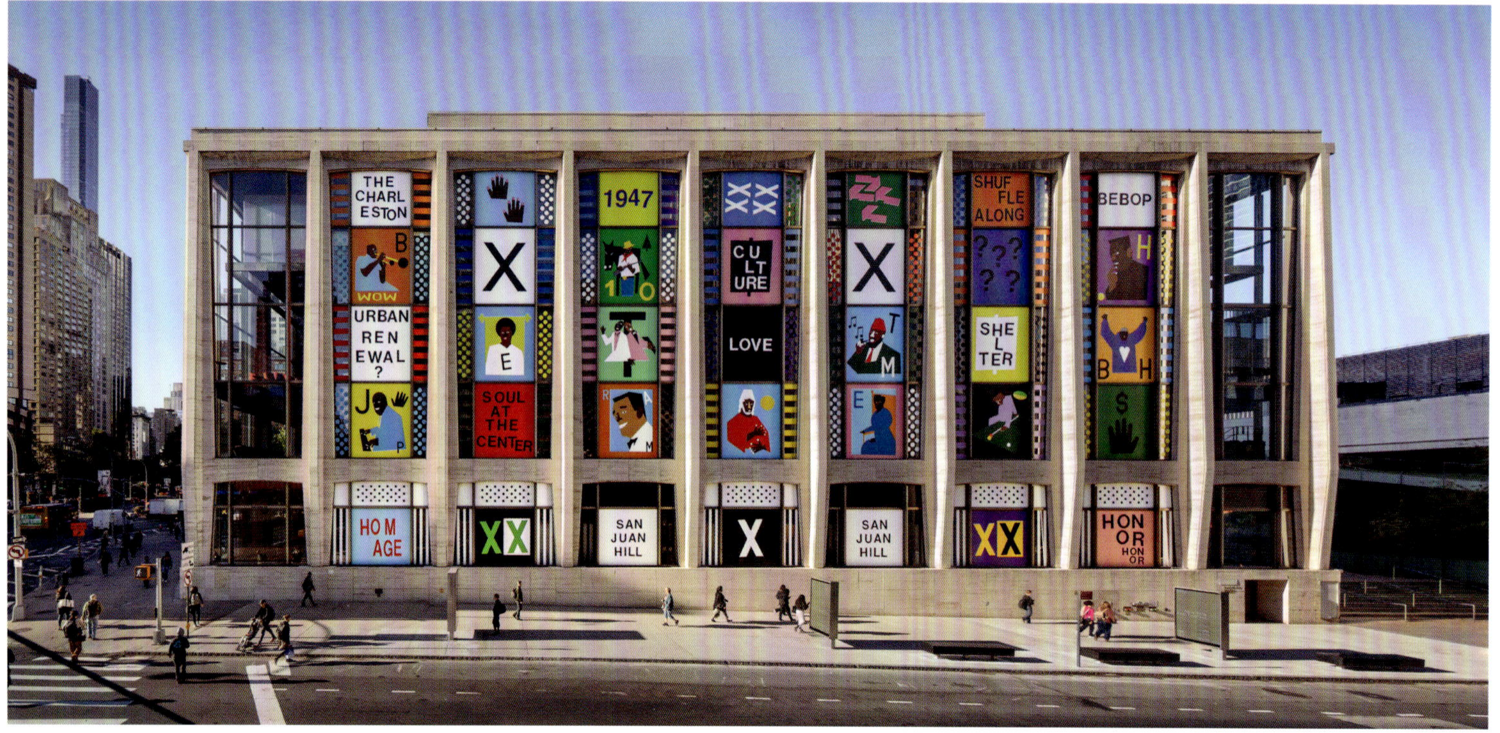

SAN JUAN HEAL, 2022

and even phone conversations while working. Oddly, background noise helps me focus, especially when executing precise details.

Golden: How do you make a painting? But first, let me say something. I say this to all artists: Don't tell any secrets.

Abney: I'm definitely not going to give out any secrets! I start with a solid background color, then build layers of shapes and colors. As I work, I research references, sometimes cutting paper to pre-visualize forms. Each painting evolves through layering and intuition until it tells me it's done. My process makes it difficult to delegate, therefore I rarely work with studio assistants, but when I do, they can help with base layers. After that, it's all instinct.

Golden: Yes, yes, yes. Can I ask about your use of text?

Abney: Stuart Davis's use of letters as formal elements inspired me. Certain numbers and letters appeal to me visually, so I use them for compositional balance. In larger works, text also directs the viewer's eye and can be used as a tool to evoke various emotions.

Golden: Let's turn back to Lincoln Center for the Performing Arts, and our work together on David Geffen Hall. In 2018, when we closed the Studio Museum so that we could build a new building on the site of our old building, it necessitated us thinking about how we would still be in the world, how we would still work, how we would still present, how we would still serve, and most significantly how we could still be of service, in very real ways, to artists.

We envisioned a couple different kinds of projects. We had a show featuring our collection travel around the country. We had a partnership with the Museum of Modern Art. We began doing lectures and talks at the Schomburg Center for Research in Black Culture, our neighbors in Harlem, and all kinds of programs outside of the city. I made it known that we were deeply open to this and that we were no longer a physical space that you could visit on 125th Street, but we were down to be in the world.

I got a call from the then chair of the board of Lincoln Center, the amazing Katherine Farley, who said, "I want to talk to you about what we're thinking about at Geffen Hall in terms of art." Now, of course, on the Lincoln Center campus, there's a long tradition of commissioning or acquiring major works of art that are resonant with the performing arts experience, so that you have the opportunity to engage with amazing works from the lobby, up the stairs, at the second balcony, and all across Lincoln Center. This became an idea in that tradition.

It also, in the renovation and restoration of the space, was an opportunity to think about the building in its historic architectural form. The Studio Museum was asked if we would partner to commission two artworks, one for inside the Geffen Hall lobby and one for the 65th Street facade. In my mind I was like, *How are we going to do this? We don't know how make public art*, but out loud, I was like, "Yes."

I called my amazing, dear colleague Nicholas Baume, artistic and executive director at Public Art Fund, and I said, "Okay, we have this opportunity. We don't know how to make public art. Can we partner?" So we made this partnership, we went through a jury process, and we came to a group of artists which we narrowed down. And I have to say Nina, you felt to me, from moment one, like an artist who could tackle this. I don't even remember how high the project space is. I know Nina does because it's like two stories.

Abney: Yeah. I remember it was like thirty-five windows. A lot of windows.

Golden: Right. On 65th Street. Now, public work does require a different kind of sensibility, because artists have to figure out not just what the work will be, but how to make it, and how to make it work for the space. When we called you, Nina, and made a proposal, you brought a layer that was significant because of its interest in engaging very directly in the history of San Juan Hill and how the Lincoln Center of today came to be. And how it came to be was by erasing, displacing, and ending a Black and brown neighborhood—a working-class neighborhood, and a neighborhood that was defined by not just the lives of people, but culture, music, jazz, and so many other things. Nina's piece speaks to that history by situating *San Juan Heal* (2022) on the corner of 65th and Broadway as a way to mark where we are and picture, symbolically, the people, so that passersby could encounter the work on the bus going down Broadway, walking across the street, and going into Geffen Hall.

I love walking down Broadway and seeing people arrange themselves to be photographed in front of the work, which prompts them to want to know more about some of the people or images or ideas. There are also a number of Nina Chanel Abney superfans who make pilgrimages to go see it, but we also hope that they get up on that plaza and realize that, just as your work is about so many things, there are so many amazing things that you can experience and encounter at the Lincoln Center itself.

It was an amazing way to create a great work of art and imagine its life in the public space. And for us at the Studio Museum, we've done public work—we do a lot of work in the parks in Harlem, commissioning artists to make work—but we had never done something like this. It was such an honor and such a pleasure, and it gave us a lot of pride as well, because of course, you were enthusiastically willing to do it. I know you can talk about how technically complex that piece was. It was the Public Art Fund and my colleagues there that were able to wrestle with that to make this happen.

Abney: *San Juan Heal* is my most successful public work to date. When doing public art, I feel responsible for understanding the site's history. Learning about San Juan Hill—how Lincoln Center displaced a Black and brown neighborhood—made it clear I had to acknowledge that erasure. Public work is a balancing act: it should engage visually while provoking thought and, in this case, educate about unspoken histories.

Golden: I can't speak for you, but certainly my understanding of this piece was this was not intended to heal all the issues that need to be dealt with in regard to San Juan Hill, but it was a way to say, this is the present reality that now should be addressed, meaning more people should know about this neighborhood. Books should be written; documentaries should be made. As you surfaced this, it also became clear that our colleagues at Lincoln Center were already thinking about doing this work in a significant way. The work therefore serves as a portal to reimagine our understanding of that history.

I also want to add that, if people know that building, it's a building that alternates the stonework and windows. There's a lot of unmovable, unchangeable, architectural detail. You worked so hard to create a work that allowed all that detail to be there and worked around it and looked at it, I think, not as a constraint but as an incredible opportunity.

Abney: Thelma, I actually have a question for you. As I continue making work, I've been thinking about how, as a Black artist, there's this unavoidable dynamic where our work, regardless of its subject, is often politicized or immediately framed through the lens of race. It's not necessarily a burden of representation, but even when we don't engage explicitly with those themes, the absence itself can become a statement. What I appreciate about the Studio Museum is that it offers a space where our full complexity as Black artists and individuals can be seen and celebrated. But outside of that context, our work is often flattened into a singular reading. Thelma, how do you see that shifting in the future?

Golden: Well, first I will say thank you for the question, really. Thank you, thank you, thank you for the question. The gift that I received from being able to have had the path of my career, touch the lives of curators, artists, collectors who were a full generation older than me, is that I understand that change is incremental, and that quite often, with the work of change in the present, one can't see its results in the future. As you say, how do we change that?

Well, one way that that got changed in the '60s is we began to create more of our own institutions, which in turn allowed us to create our own worlds and our own realities. One of the things that would often make me laugh is that we had all kinds of exhibitions at the Studio Museum, and sometimes we'd have an exhibition, for example, of an abstract artist. And I remember a collector who was not of African descent had come to the museum, and we had a beautiful show of an abstract painter and sculptor. This collector said to me, "Oh, it doesn't look Black." And that has become a way in which I think about the craziness of those

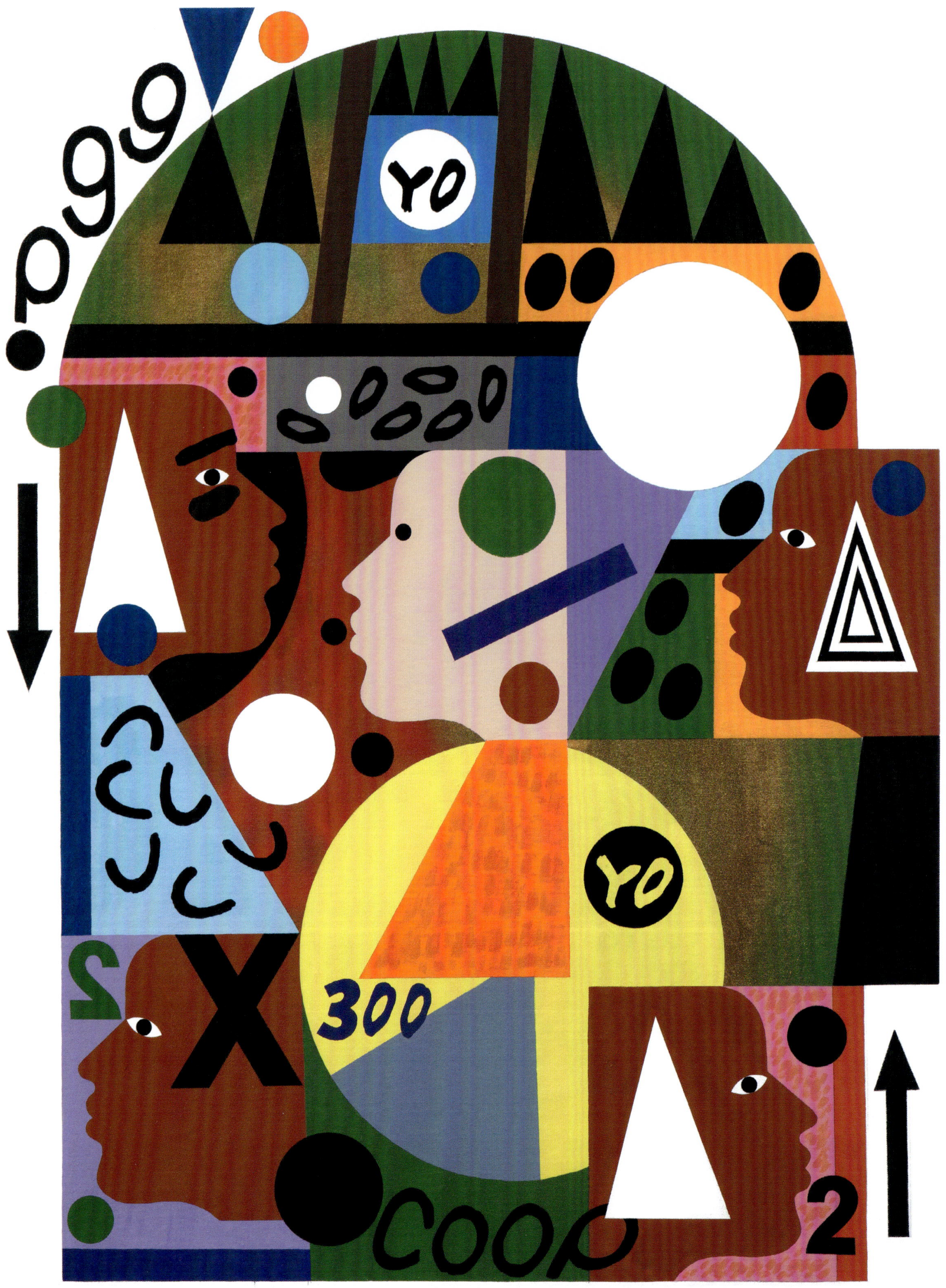

UNTITLED, 2012

ideas, that there is a thing that Black artists have to make. And some of that, Nina, is about what the market says. So the first takeaway from that story is that I don't see the market as making meaning. Meaning is made through the deep and profound intellectual exchange that we can have through exhibitions, through the writing that can be done about artists, through the critical apparatus, through the ways in which work can live in the world. I also don't acknowledge the narrowness of possibility for us because it's the only way that I can imagine into real spaces of possibility for Black artists in all forms. So as the young folks say, I practice a little bit of controlled delulu.

Abney: Yeah, for sure.

Golden: You have to, because I know the strength, the breadth, the genius inherent in the work made by artists of African descent. Now, I'm not saying there's not genius everywhere, but when we see the narrowness that can come in the face of what we know is in the work, I have to keep going and keep imagining what it means to have all artists be understood through their humanity, which is defined by many things.

It goes the other way, too. I often find, every once in a while, I get in these conversations where someone will say to me, "Why do all these Black artists have to make art about being Black?"

Abney: We're Black.

Golden: Right? Again, I don't answer. This is my delulu. Are they all making work about being Black or are they making work about who they might be? I was taught in art history that things that we know, are. They just made those universal, and we had to argue everything against it. I want us to have a broader and deeper sense of how we can name and create big spaces of ideas for Black artists. I also think one of the things we can do when we create a certain space of our own definition is also push back. It's something you said as we began. The way these lines are made between an artist who works in an art space and an artist who is quote-unquote commercial. I think through and around how that has been damaging for certain practices that are not seen and understood in their totality because of these lines. And I feel now, my own trajectory has been to support the idea of what it means to create more power around how we can name who we are and what we are without it being so narrowed and cyclical. Nina, what are some of the things you are thinking about in work that you are making and imagining right now?

Abney: In the studio, I'm thinking about what's next politically and socially. Art should respond to its time. Lately, I've been considering how the American flag—once a national symbol—now feels co-opted. What does it mean to be a Black American today? I'm also thinking about the role of Black churches and why younger generations are disengaging. I am currently pulling from these observations, and I'm interested in how people navigate faith and meaning outside traditional institutions.

I'm also expanding my sculptural practice and rethinking my relationship to commercial work. I see product as an extension of my art, and I'm considering how a web store can function as a space for experimentation. After nearly twenty years in galleries, I'm asking: Who is the next generation of collectors? What are they drawn to? Art collecting is changing—it's not just about high-value paintings but also cultural touchstones, like the Annie Lee prints that were in every Black household. I want to engage with that audience in a way that feels authentic.

Golden: Fantastic. I think that really, in a way, what you're saying is that you are reimagining the space that you are creating for yourself to operate in—not reacting to those that are there, but really creating your own. By doing that, you are also continuing to expand on how we engage with your artistic vision and voice, and how it can manifest in all of these forms. Nina, is there anything else you want to say or you want said? This is big. This is about your work.

Abney: I intentionally blur the line between fine art and commercial projects. Historically, artists like Keith Haring, Kenny Scharf, and [Jean-Michel] Basquiat challenged these hierarchies. I'm aware that the art world often views commercial work as lesser, but I reject that distinction. My goal is to redefine what prestige means on my own terms.

Golden: Nina, I think you sit in this tradition of these iconoclastic artists who see an art world in its traditions and reimagine it. What we know though is that sometimes the way that's understood shifts and changes over time. I think that in and of itself, when you say to me, "Where do you fit?" What I say often is, "Artists create their places through the work. The work is what's out there speaking." And I think that idea is evident in your work, and, as your practice grows, you are going to continue to set the terms for how your artwork is defined. And that, I think is very much in the form or the example of an art world, a culture world that is shifting to embrace more and different and new.

Abney: I agree. I feel like we're all working in the future.

This interview has been edited for length and clarity.

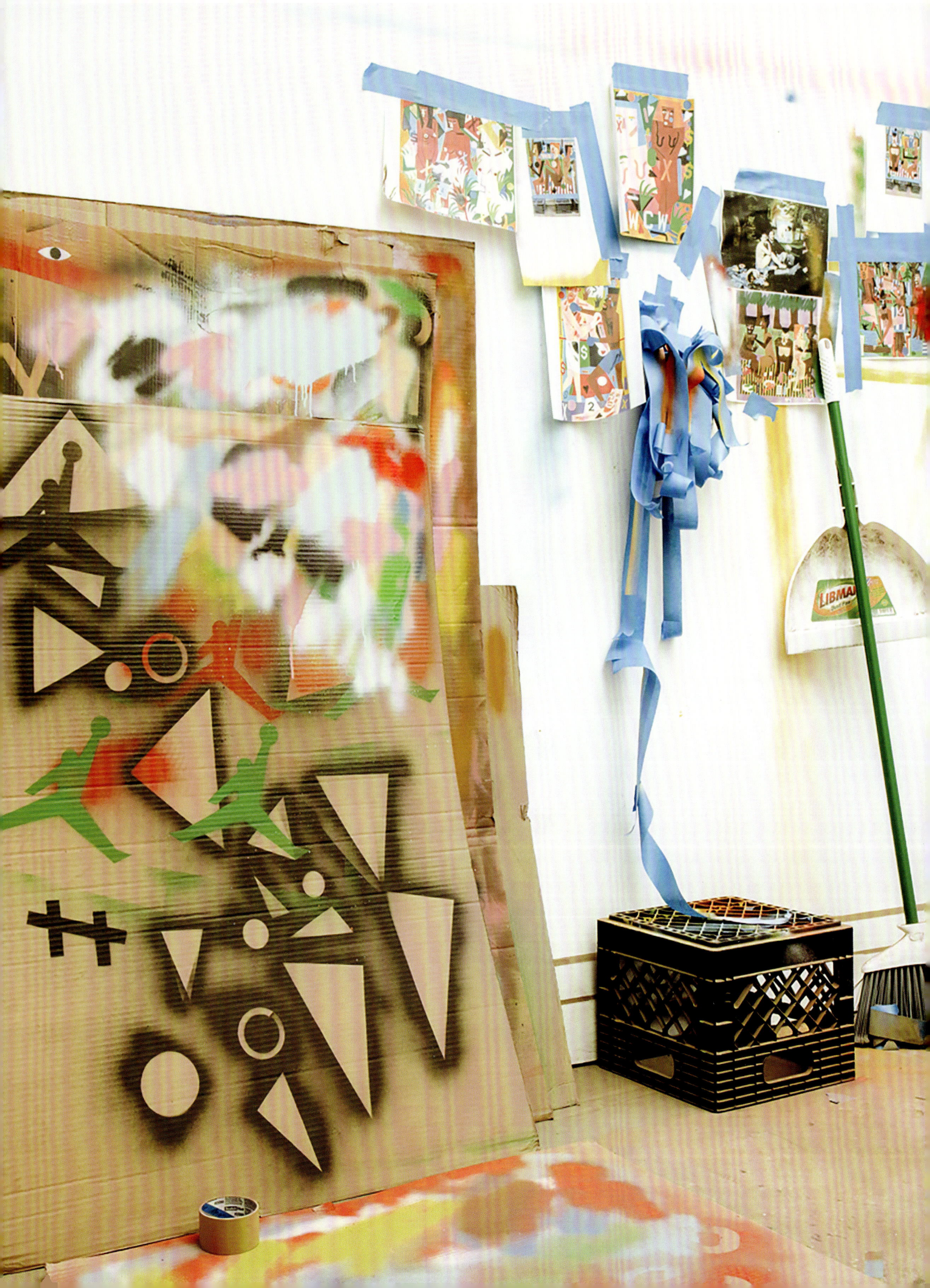

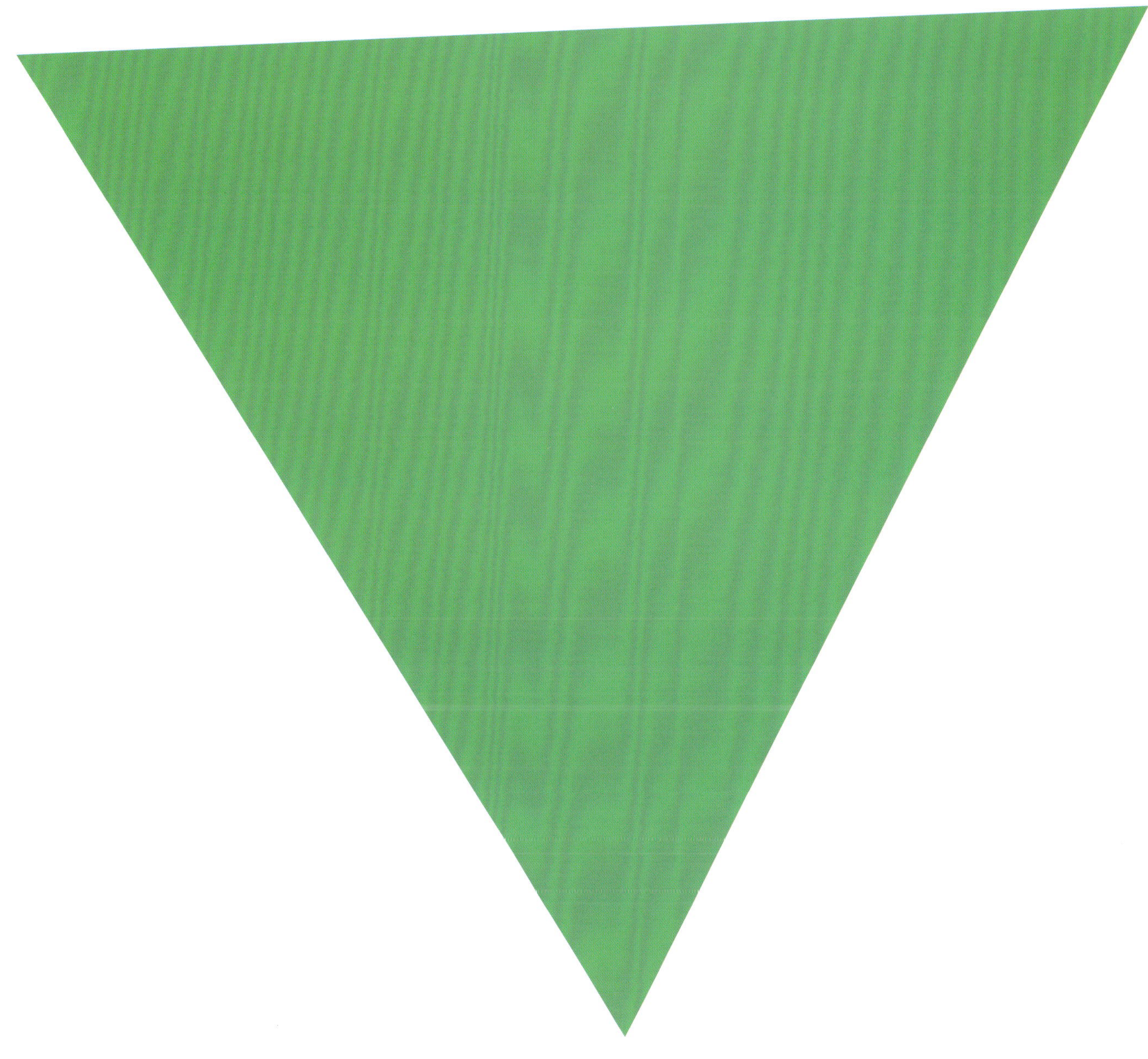

PAINTINGS

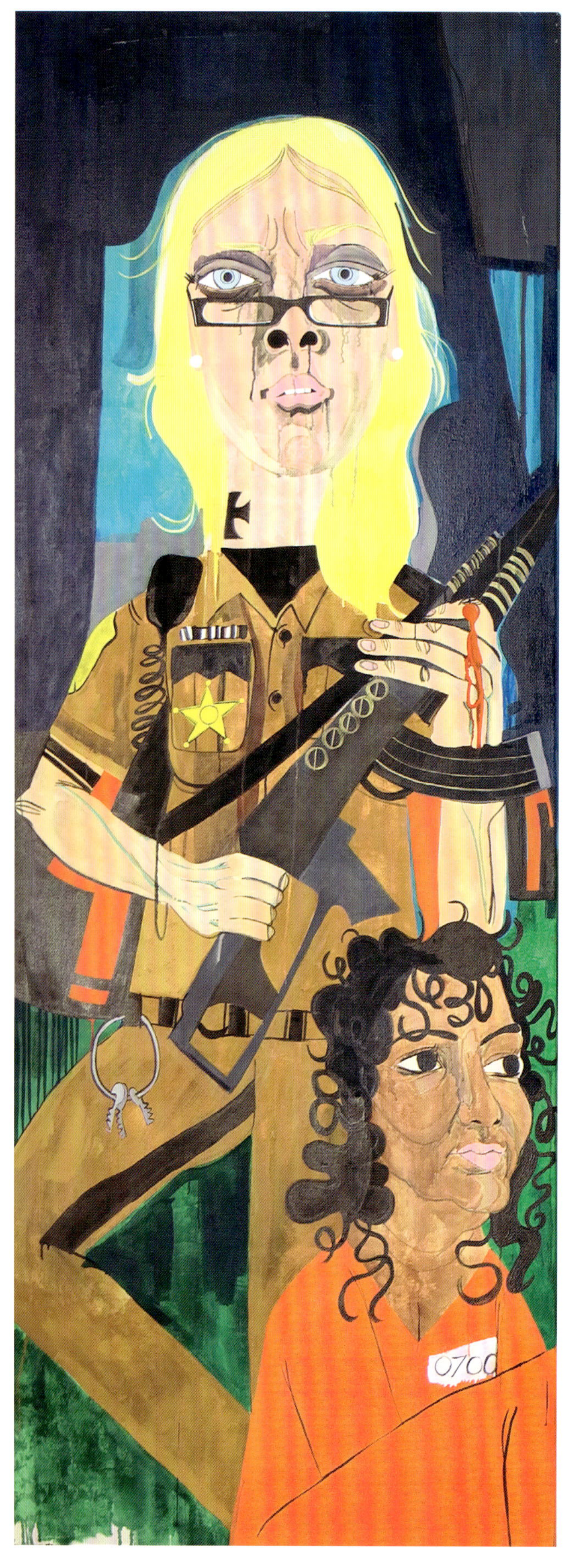

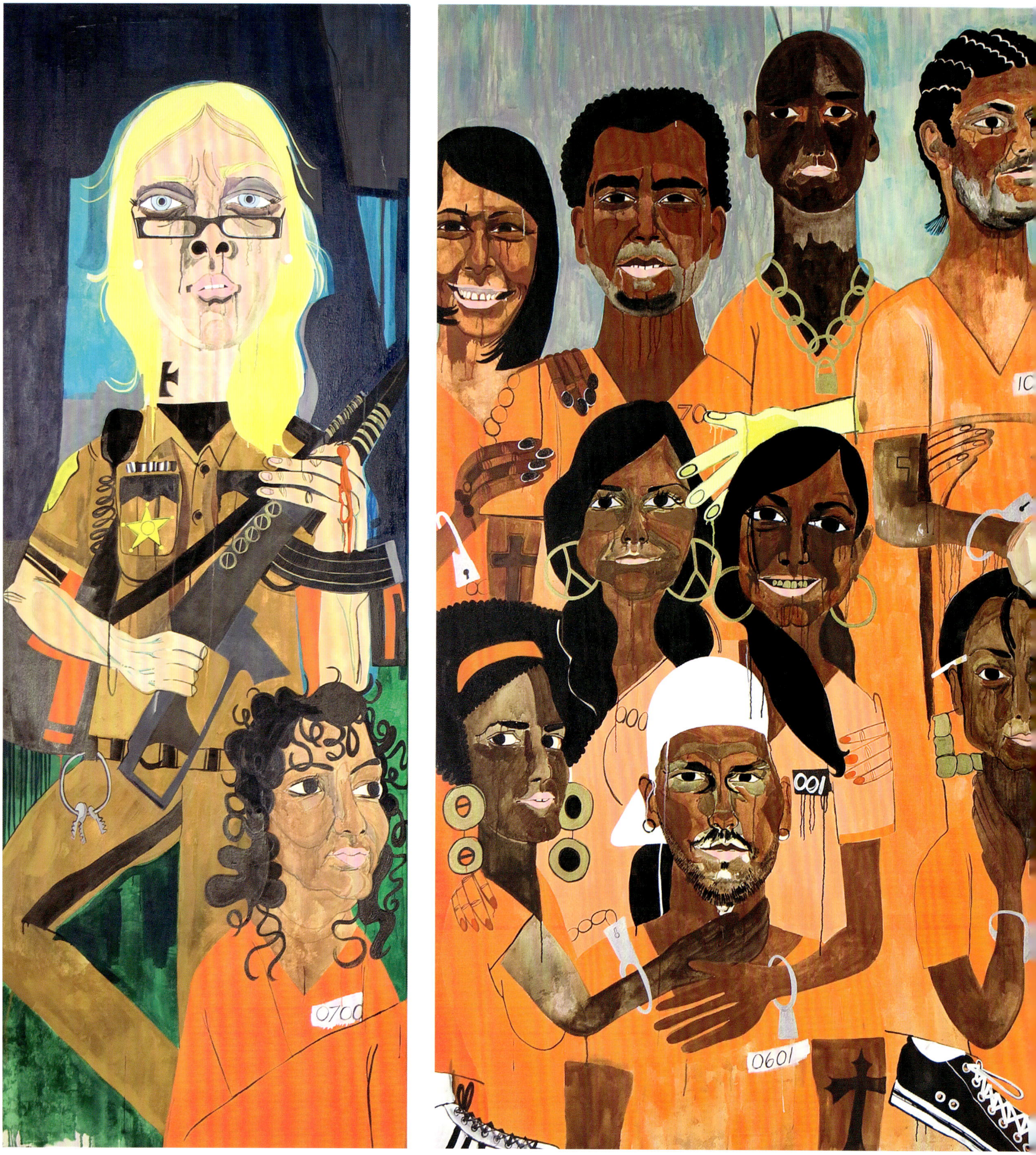

Class of 2007, 2007

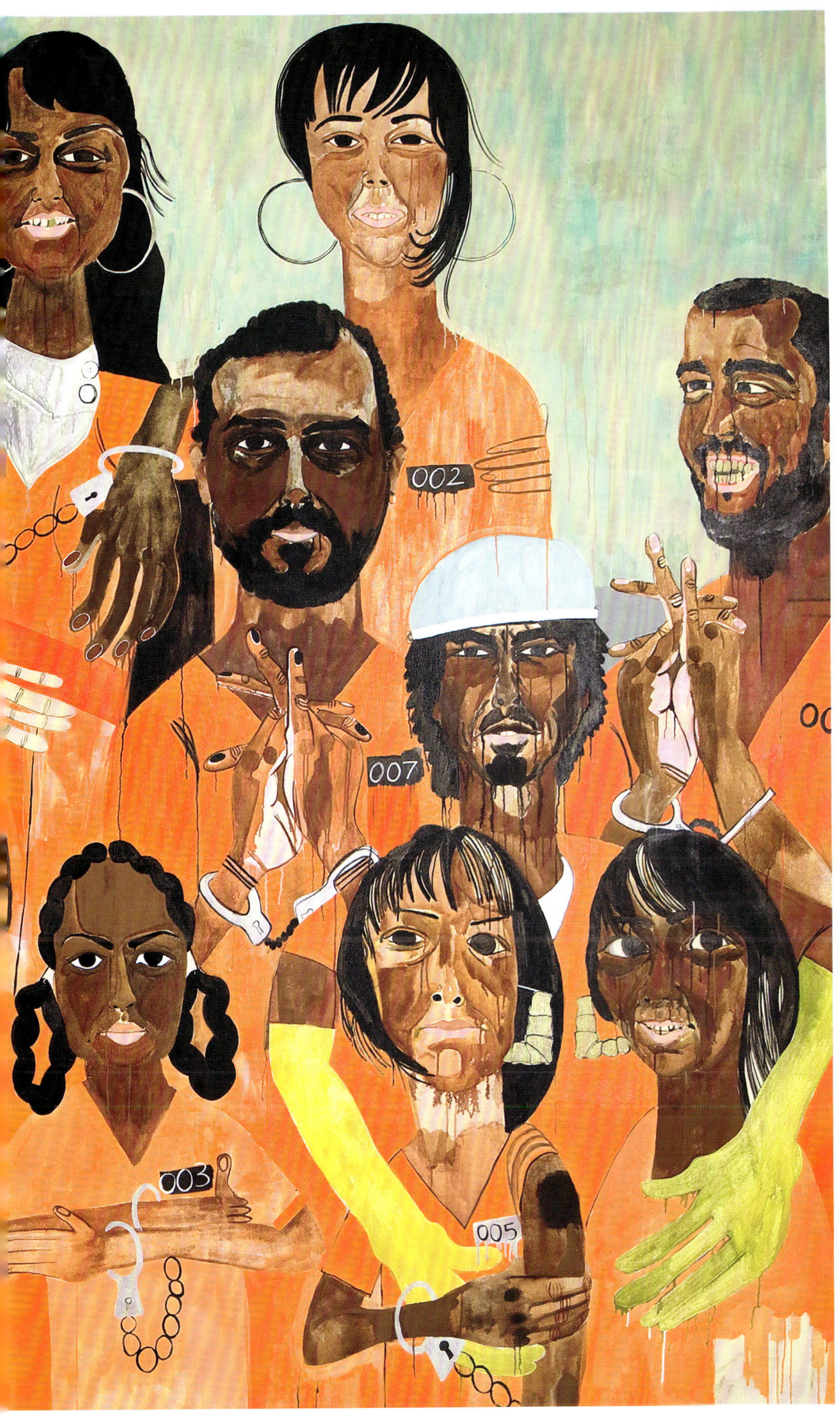
002
007
003
005

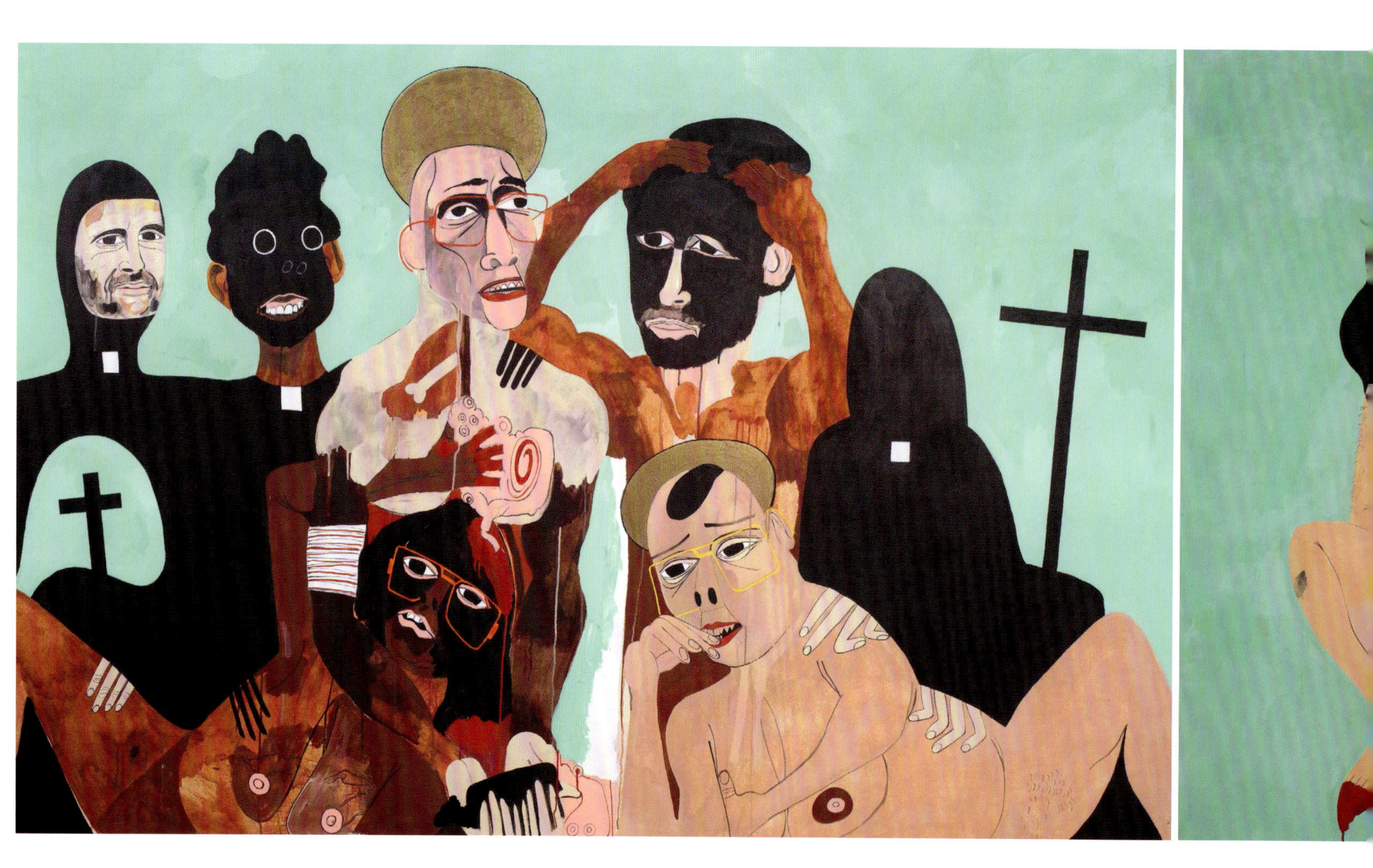

Untitled (Black Soap), 2007

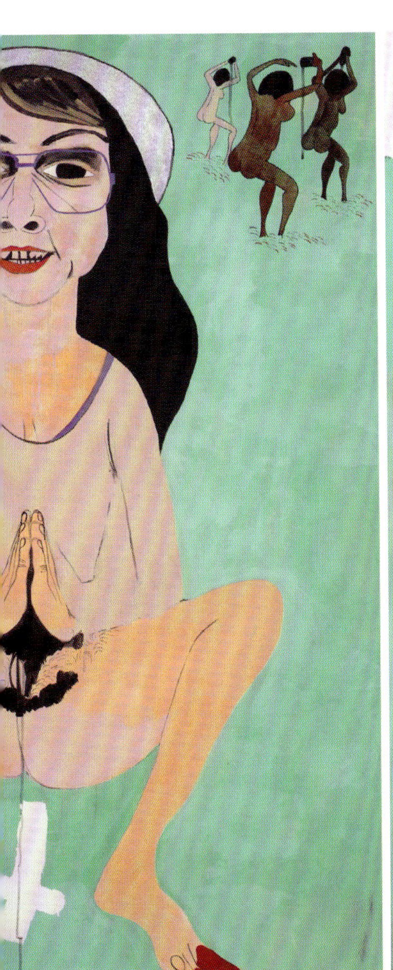

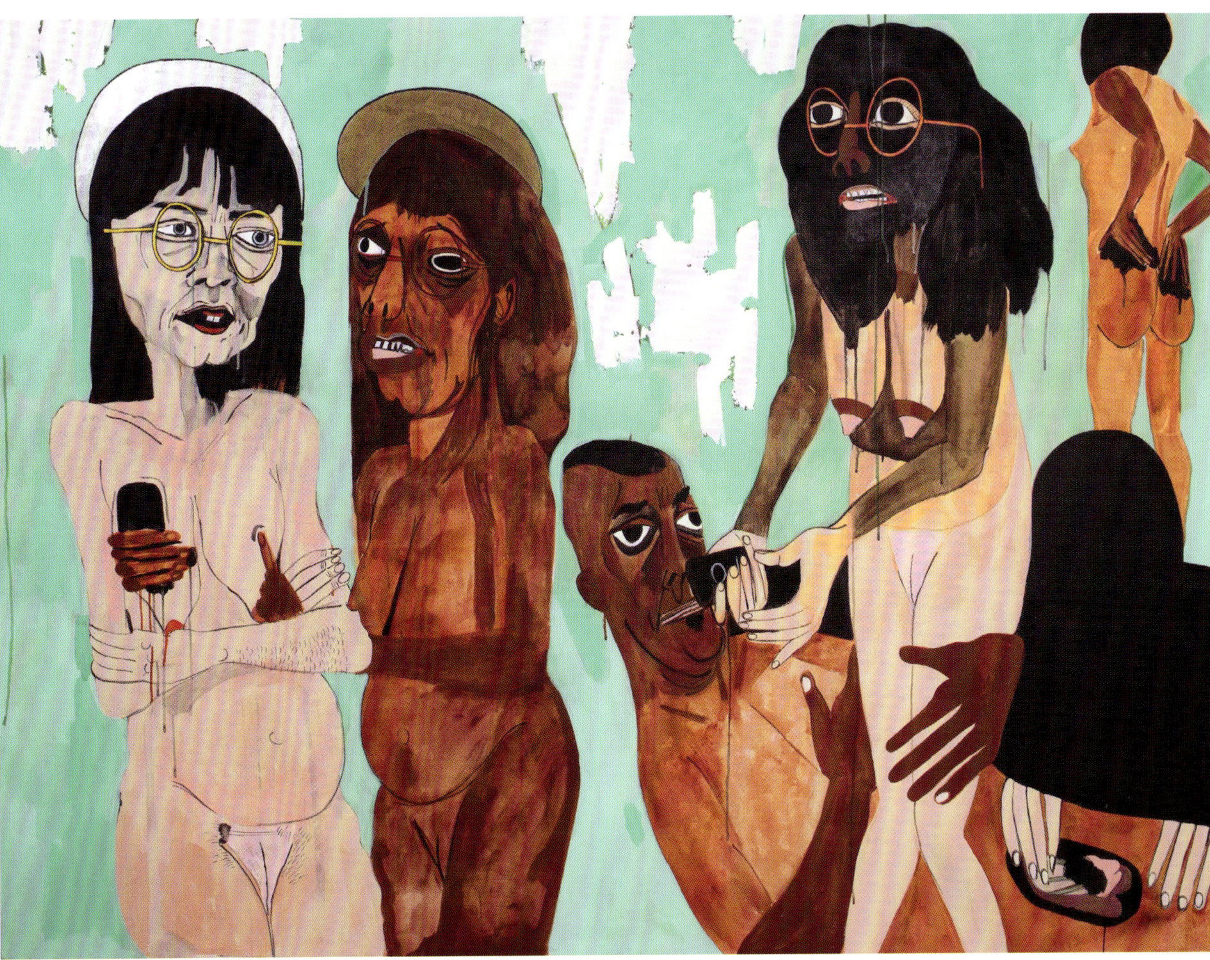

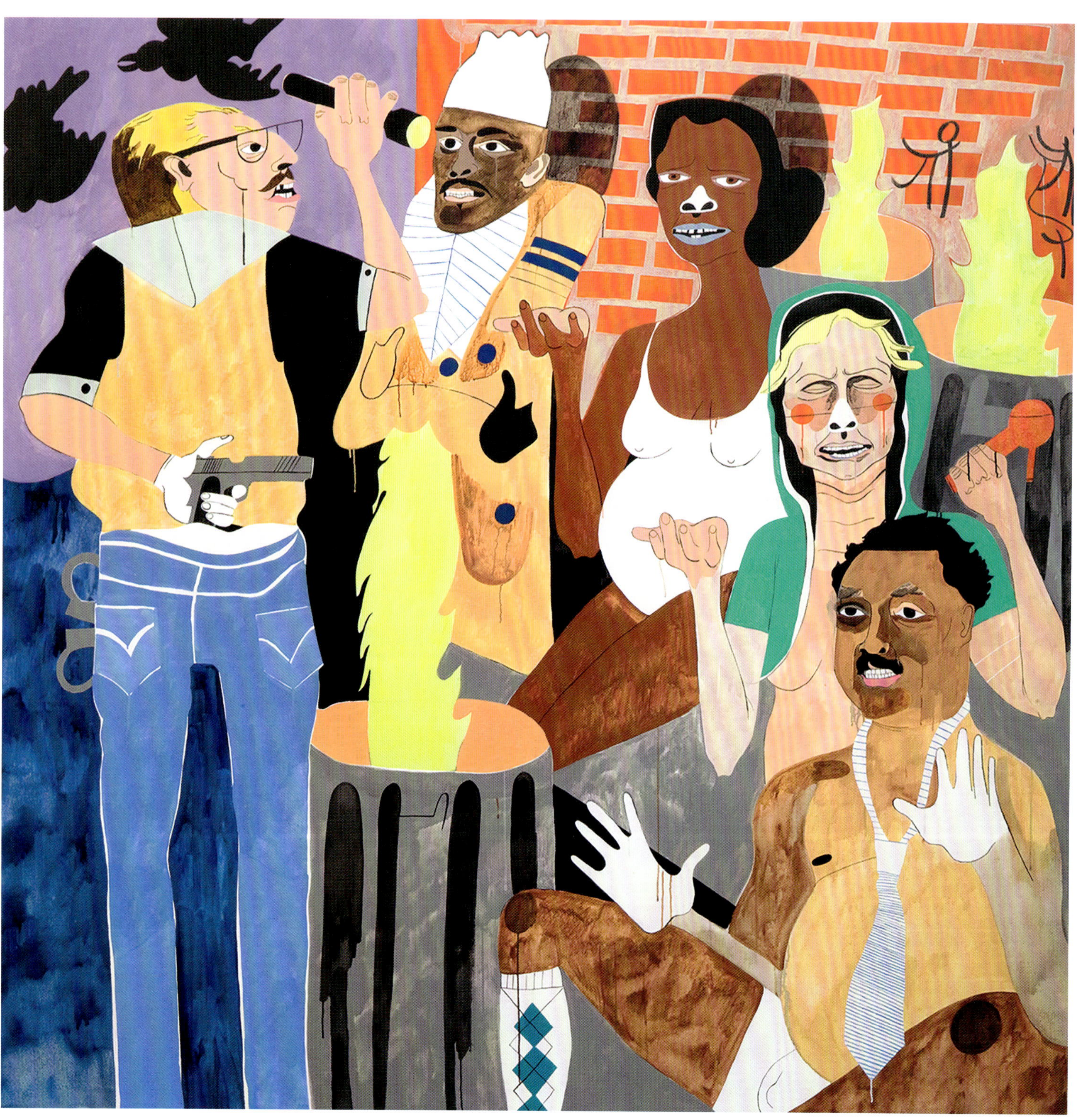

Rainblow, 2008

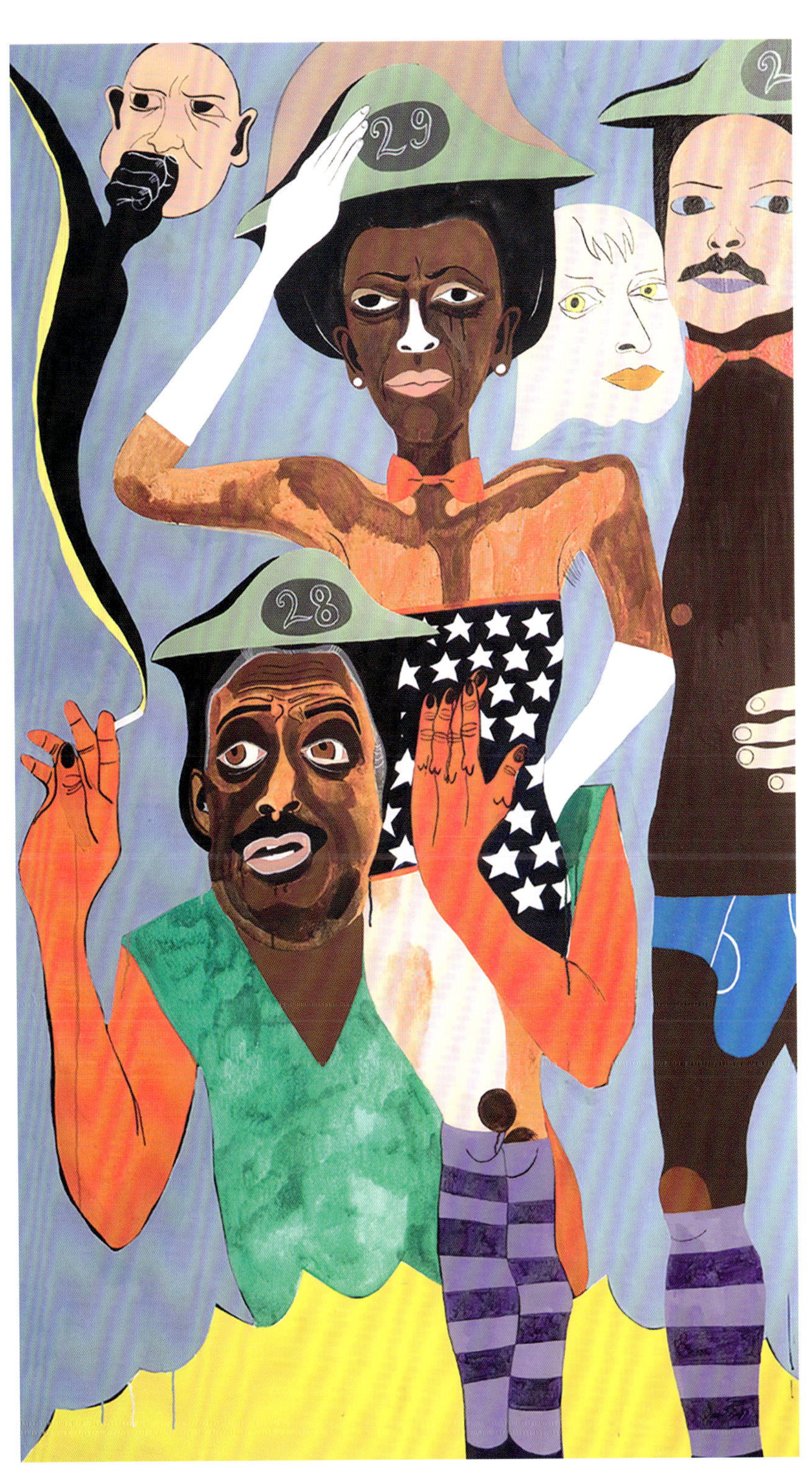

The Ugly, 2008

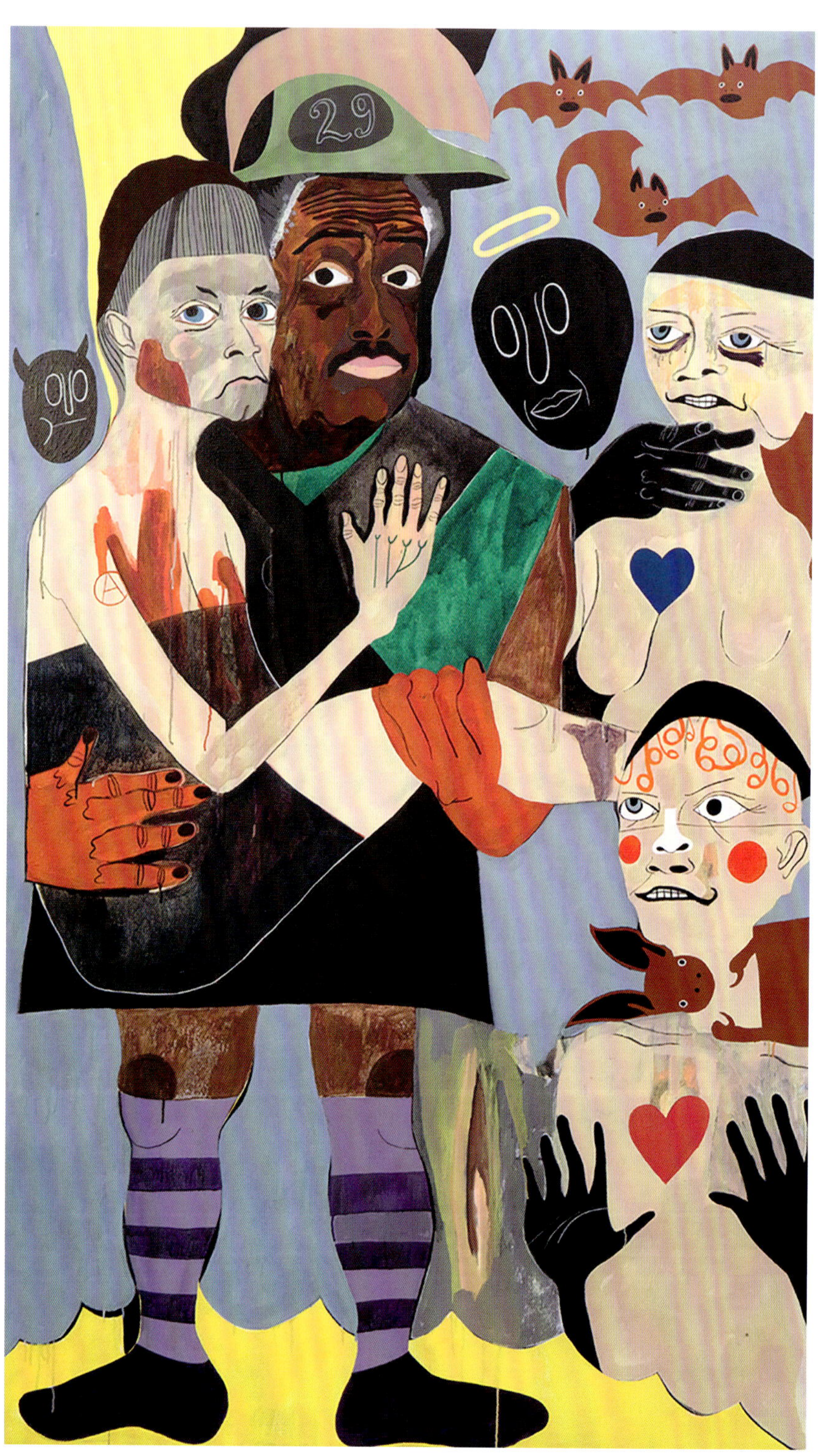

The Good, The Bad, 2008

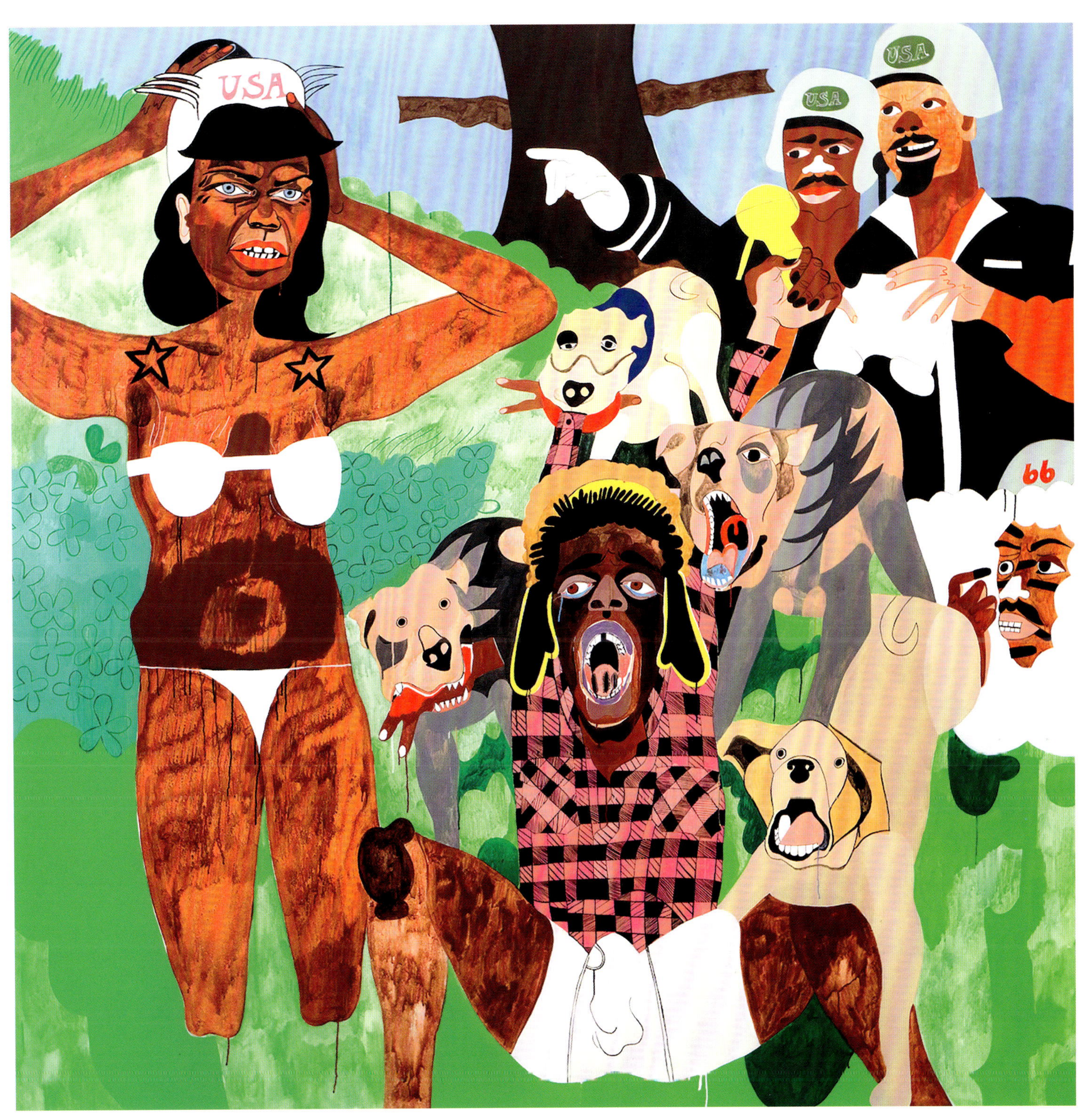

Randaleeza, 2008

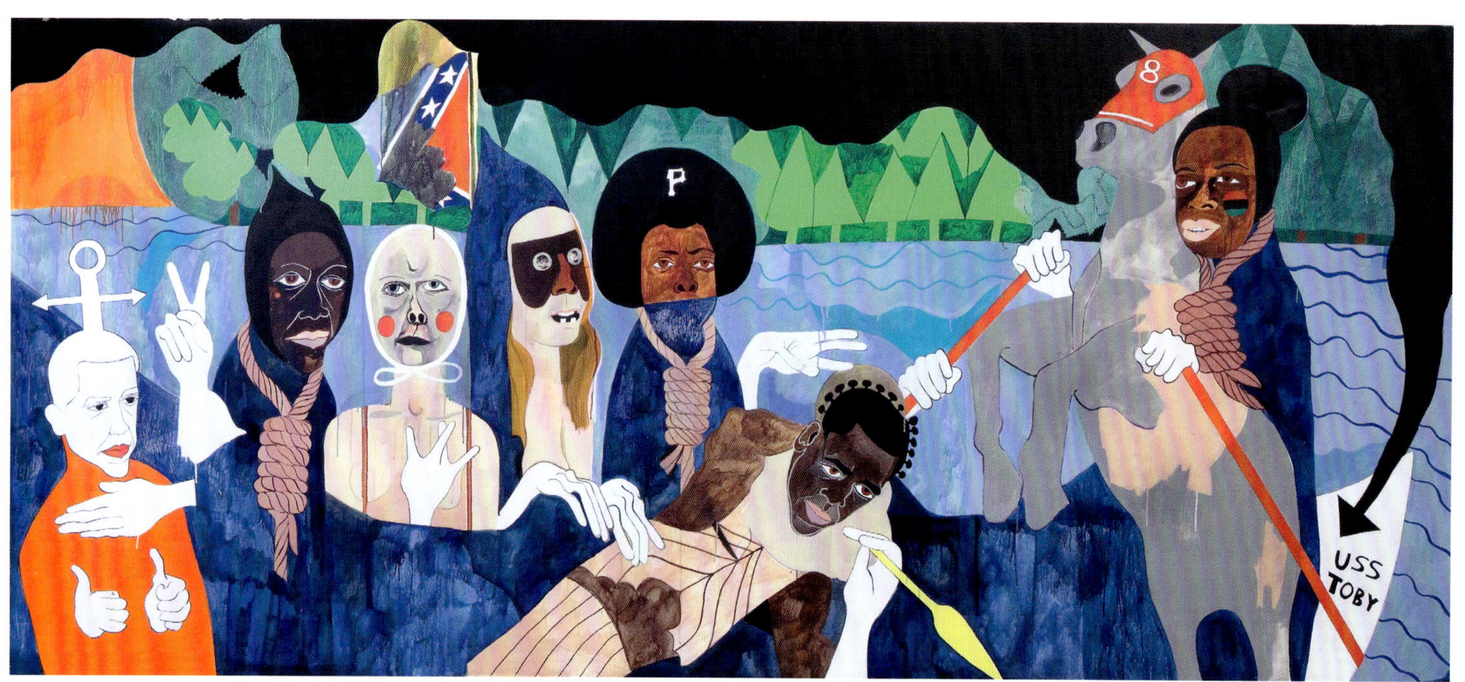

The Takeover, 2008

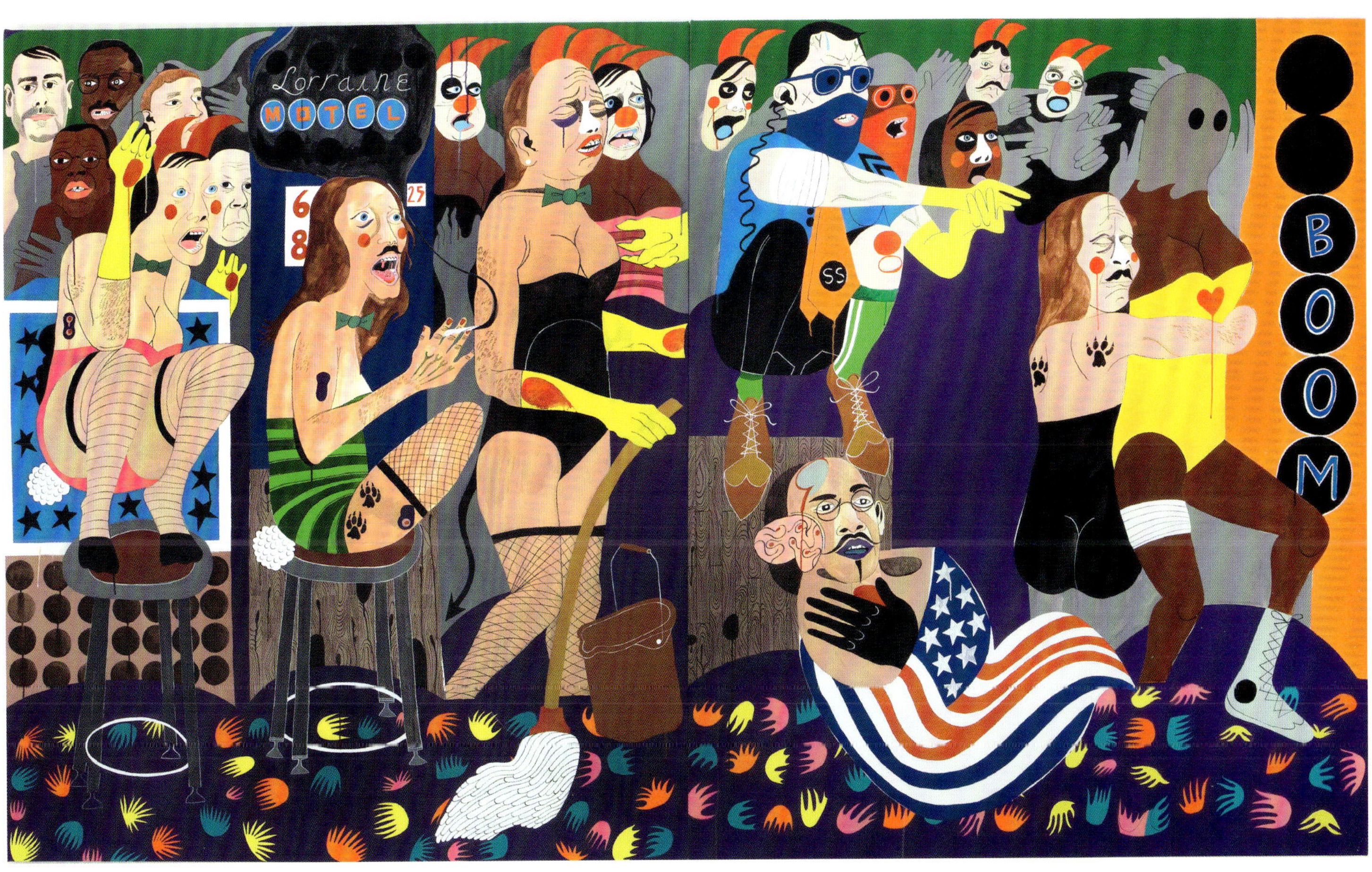

Close, But No Cigar, 2008

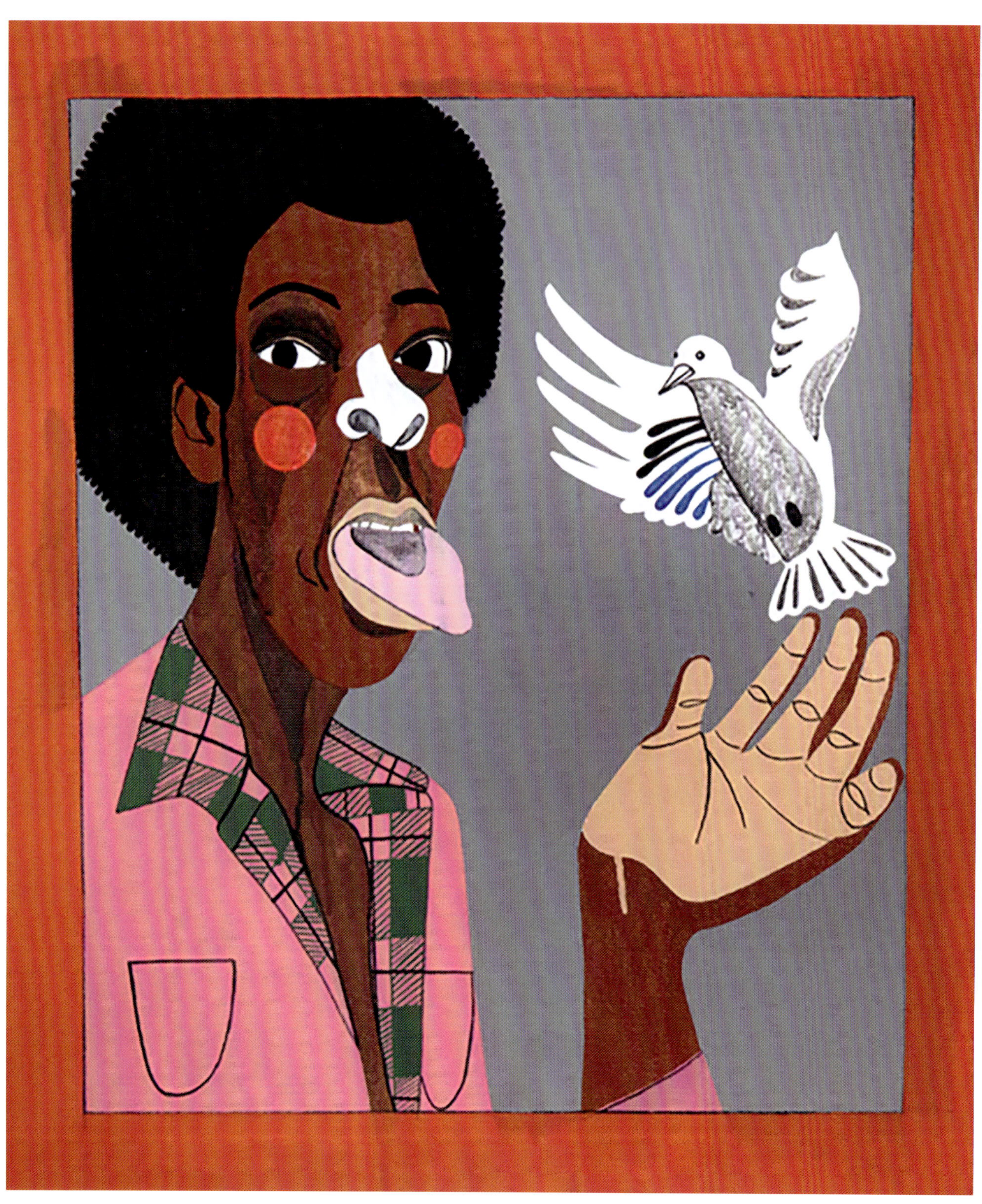

The Paris Portrait, 2008

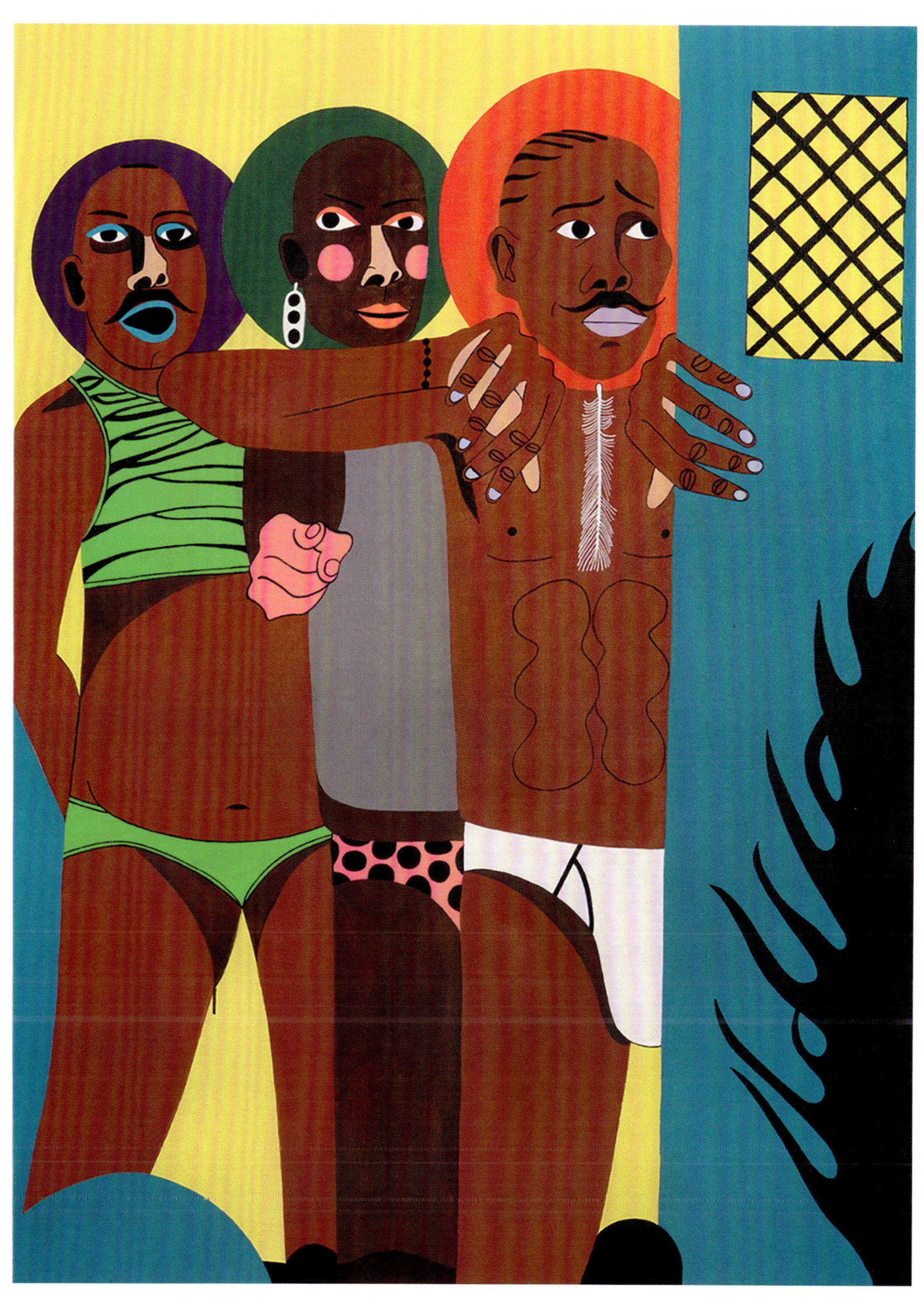

Another Midnight Run, 2009

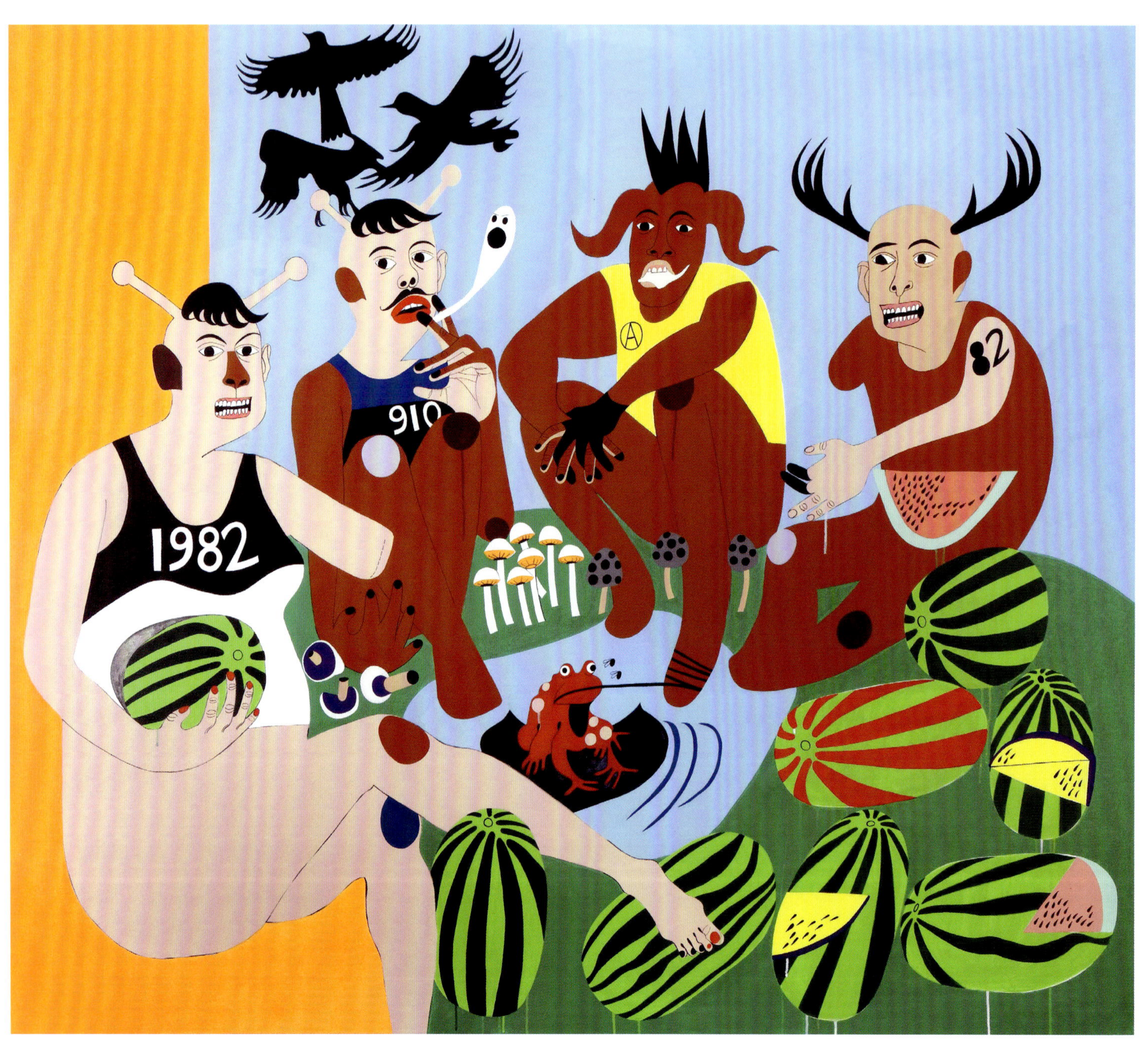

Forbidden Fruit, 2009

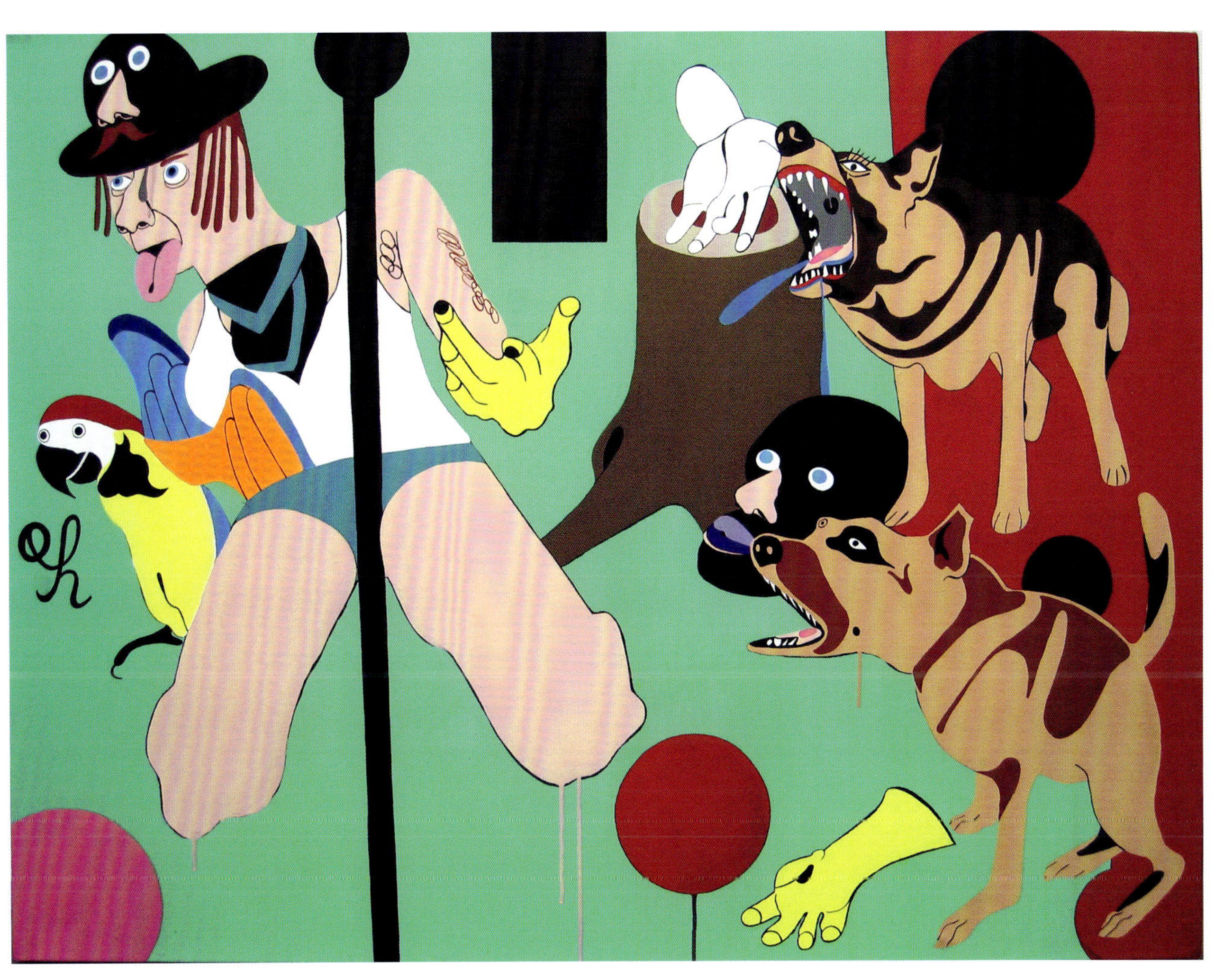

Make it Reign, 2009

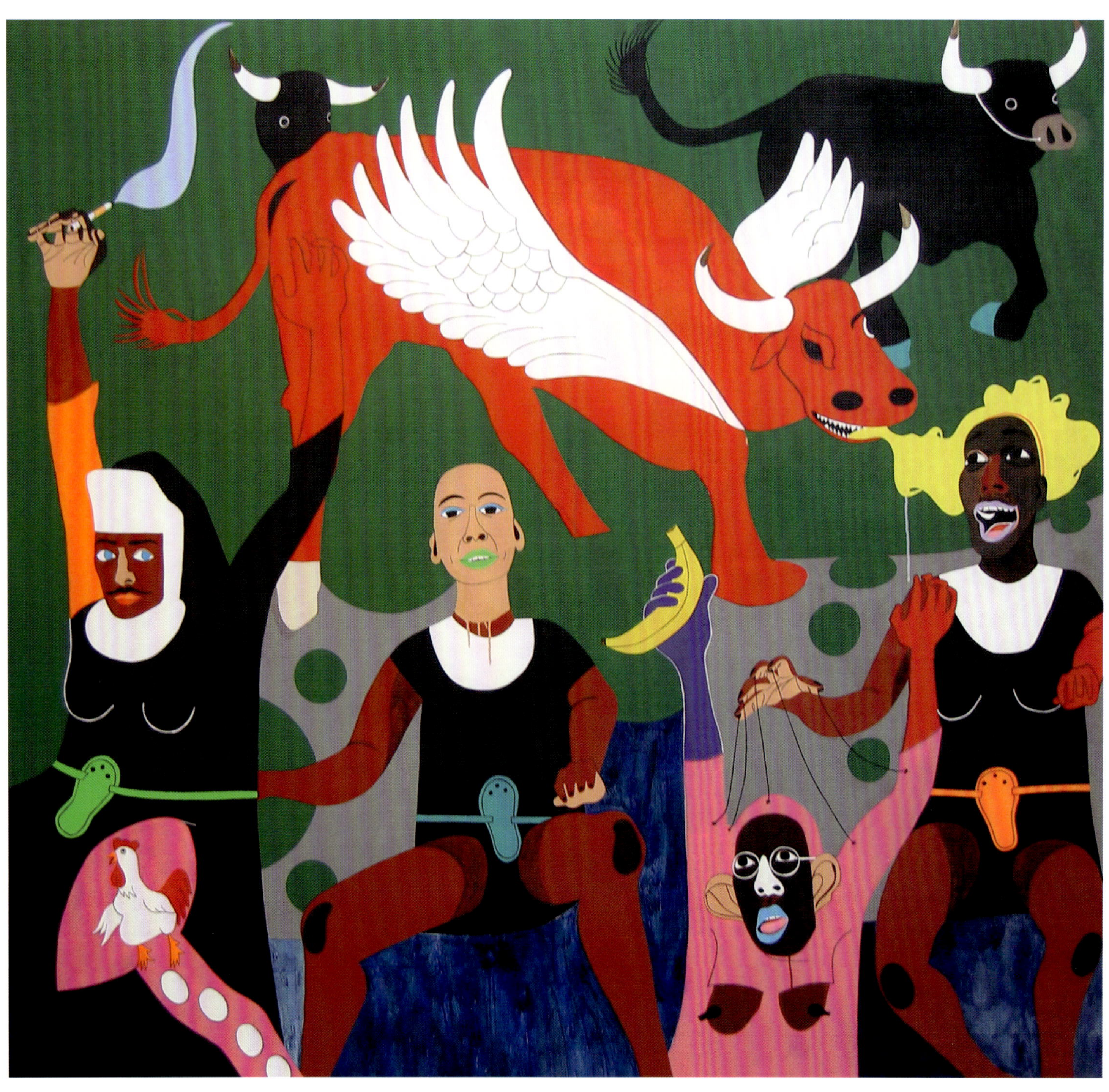

Who, What, When, 2009

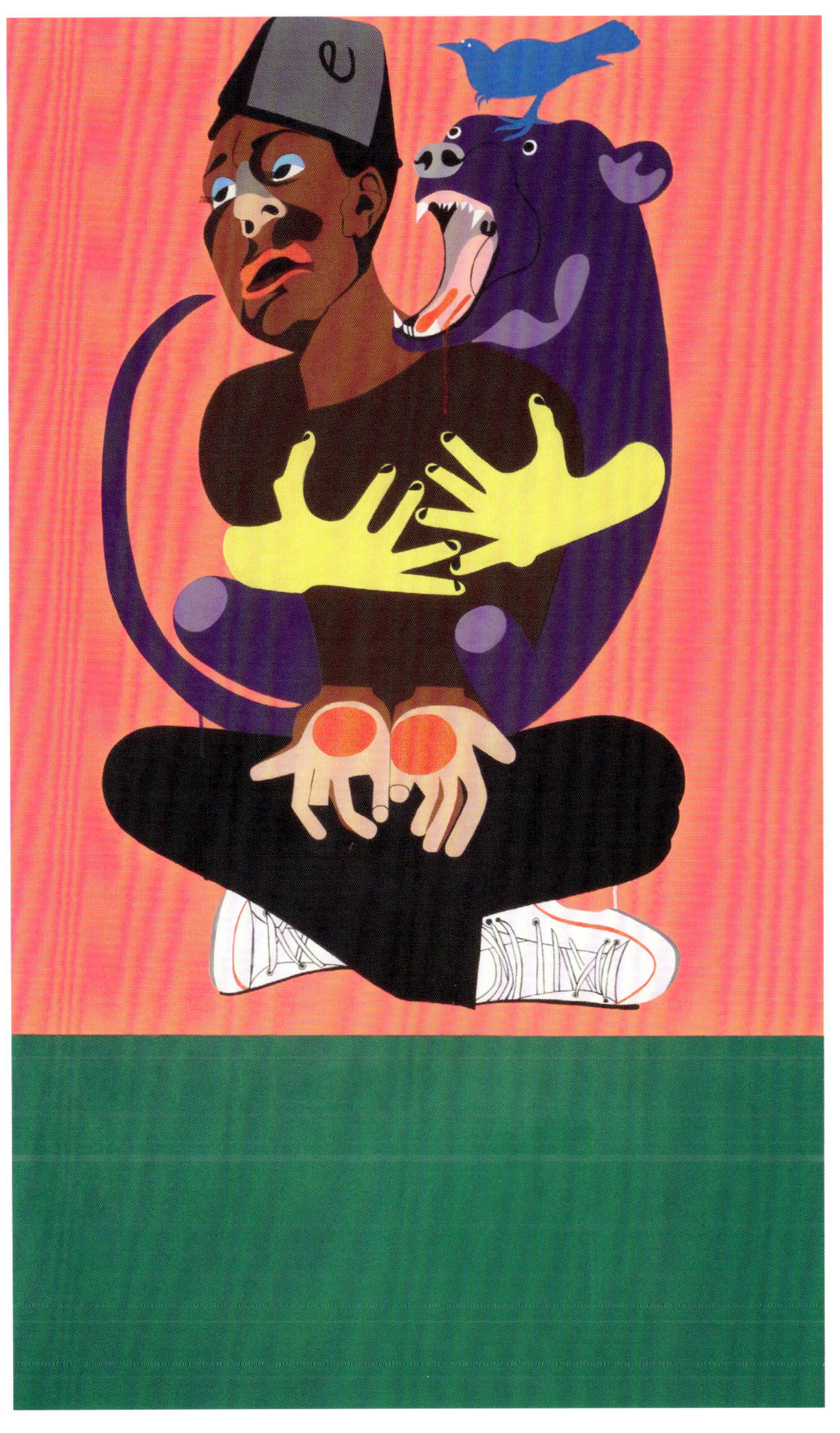

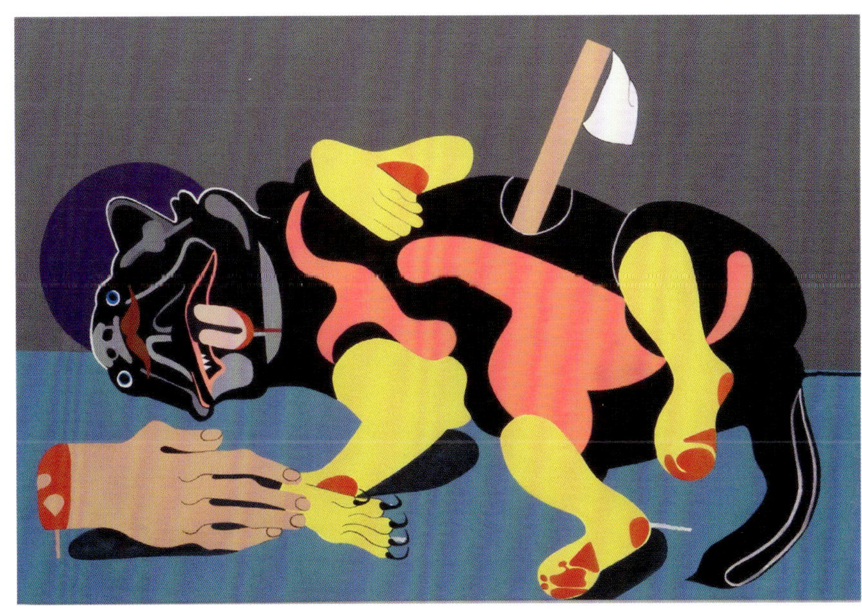

King of Sorrow, 2011

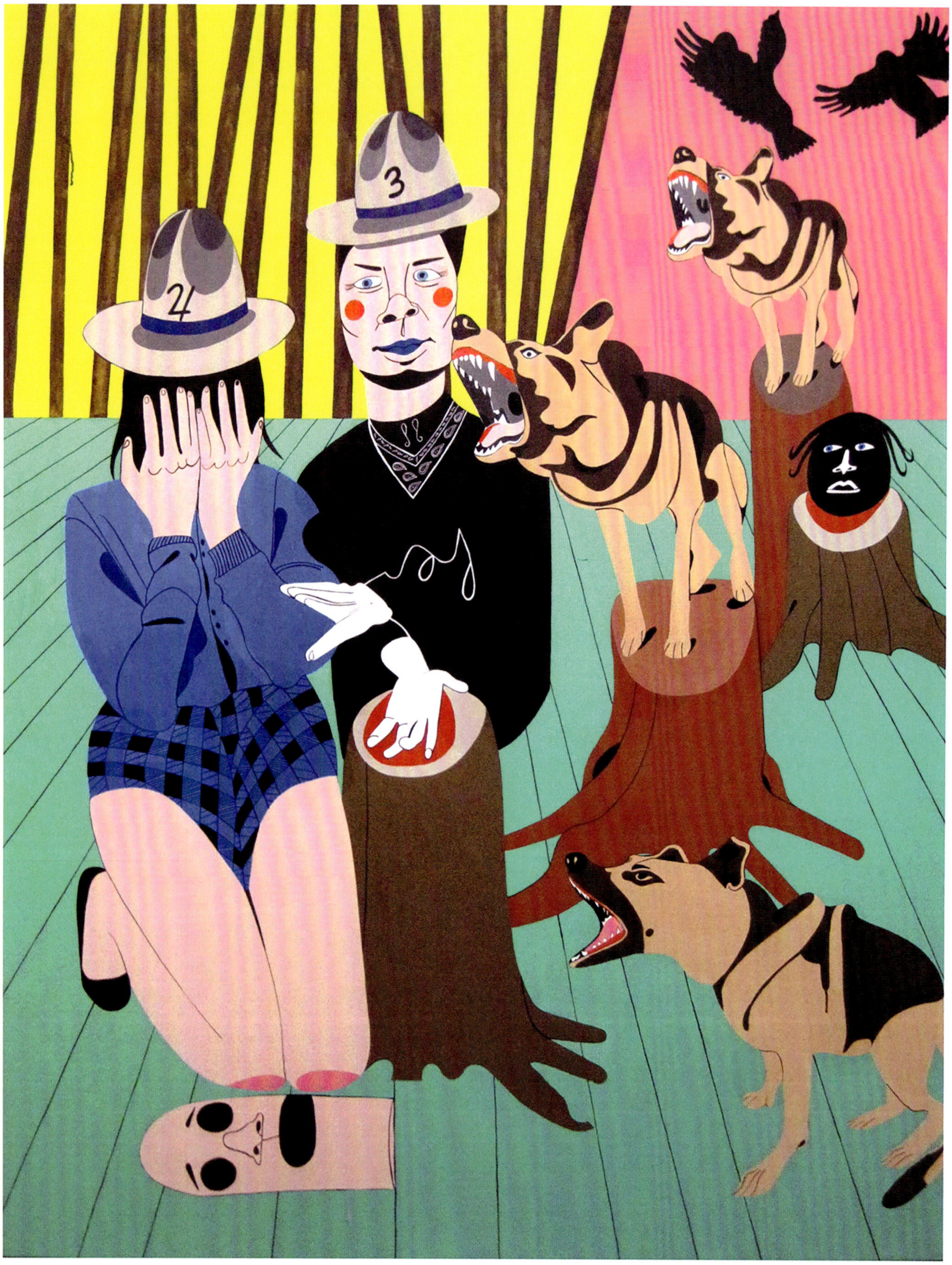

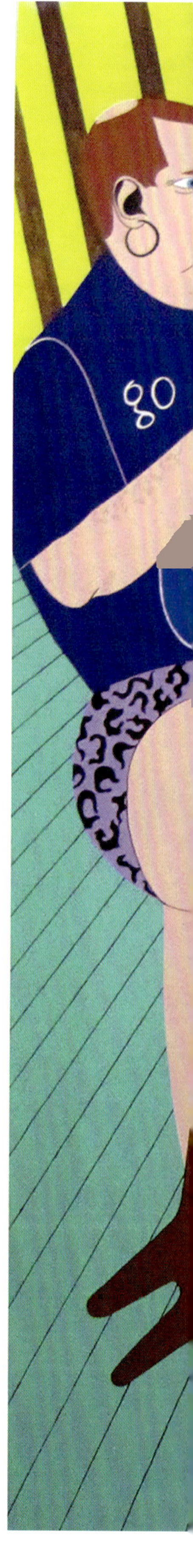

Your Gig Is Up, 2009

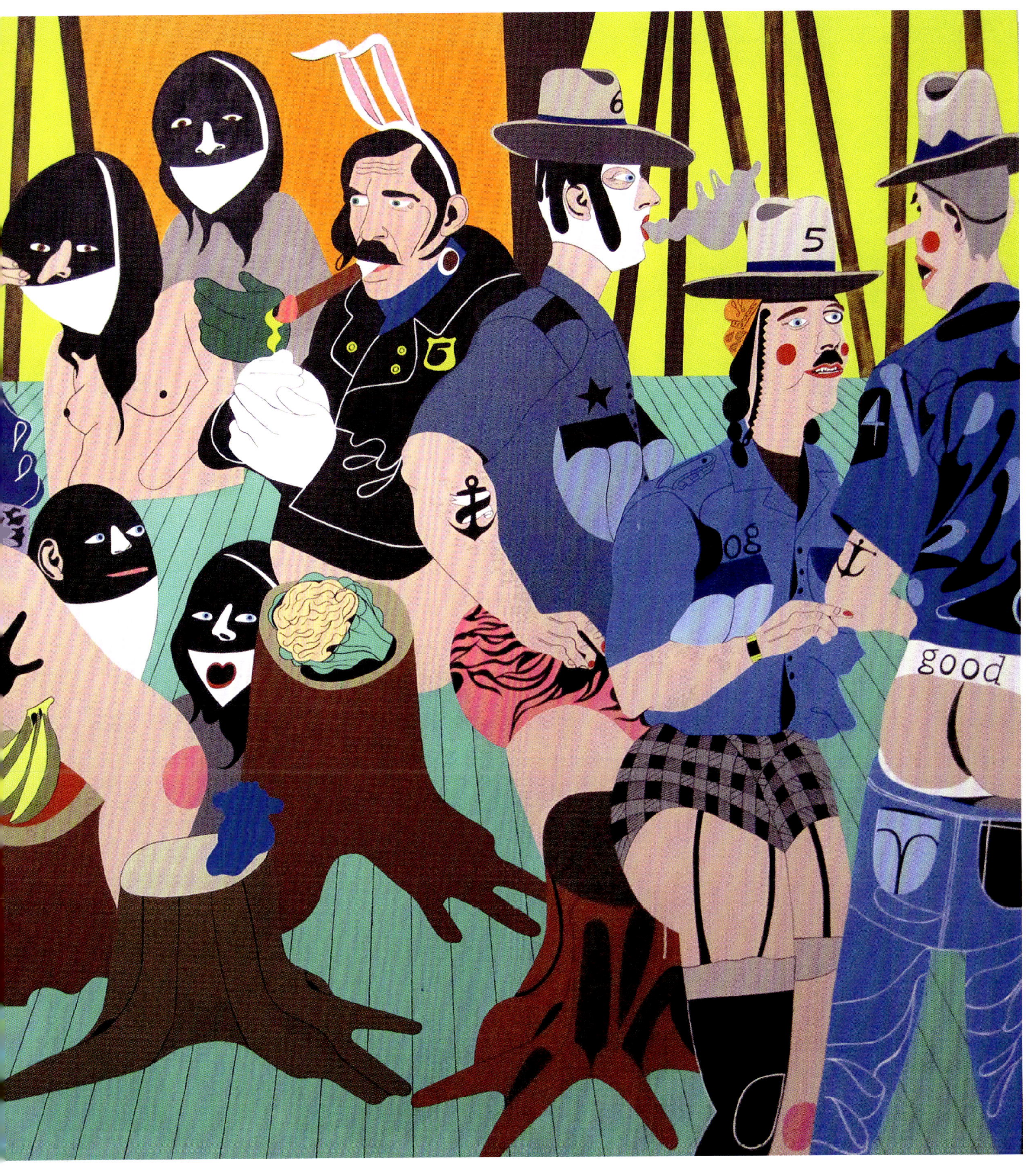
6
5
4
good

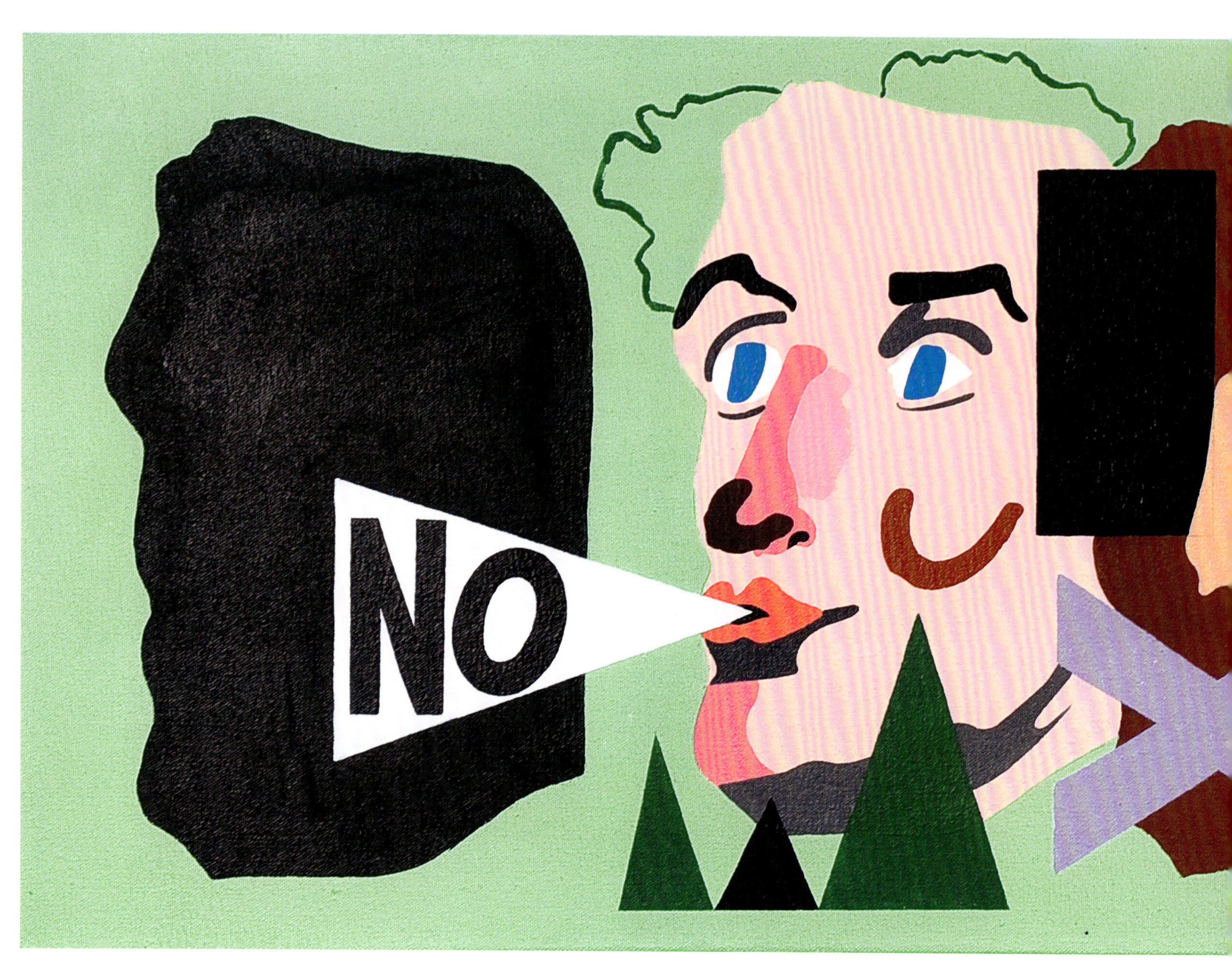

Superstar Ken, 2012

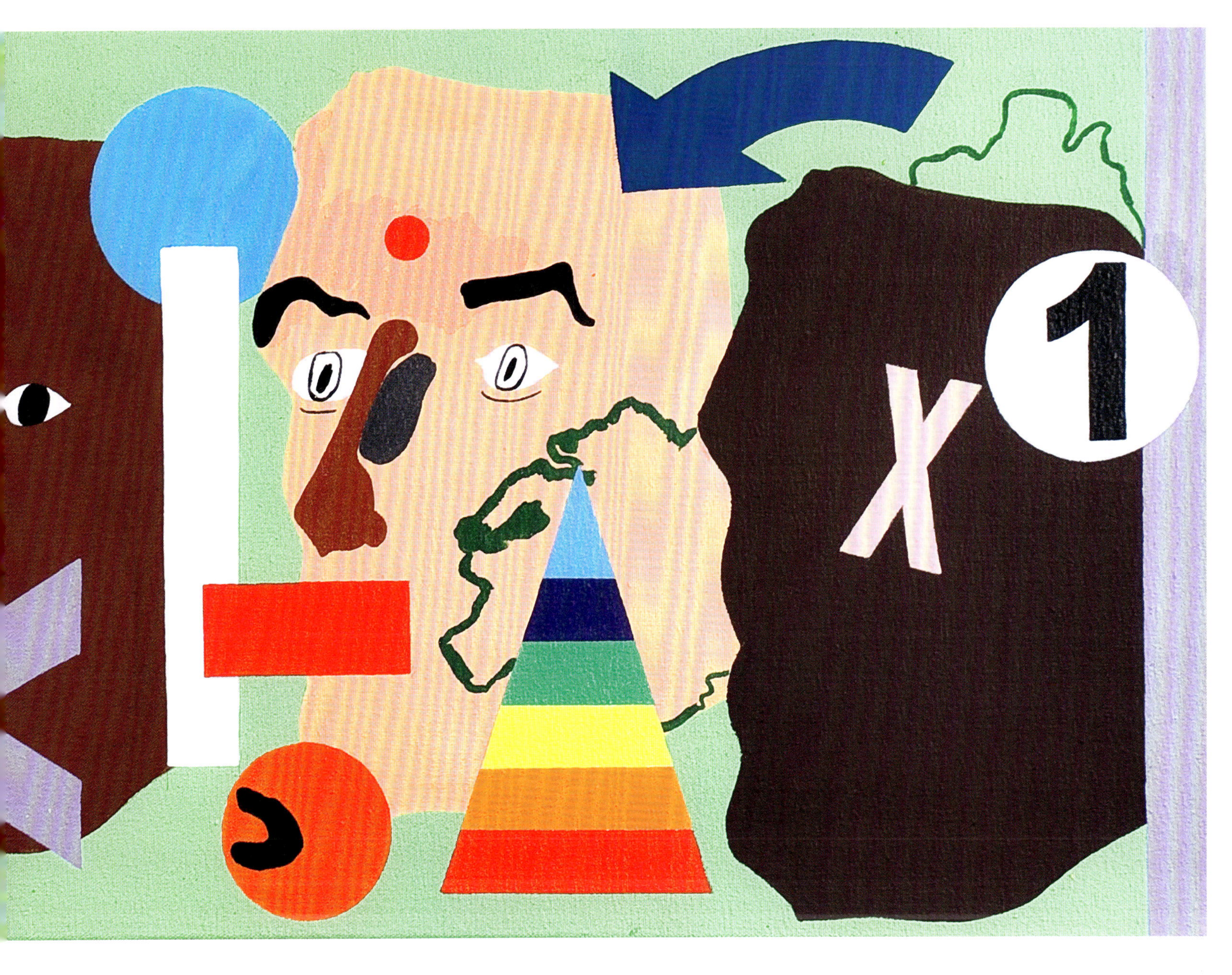

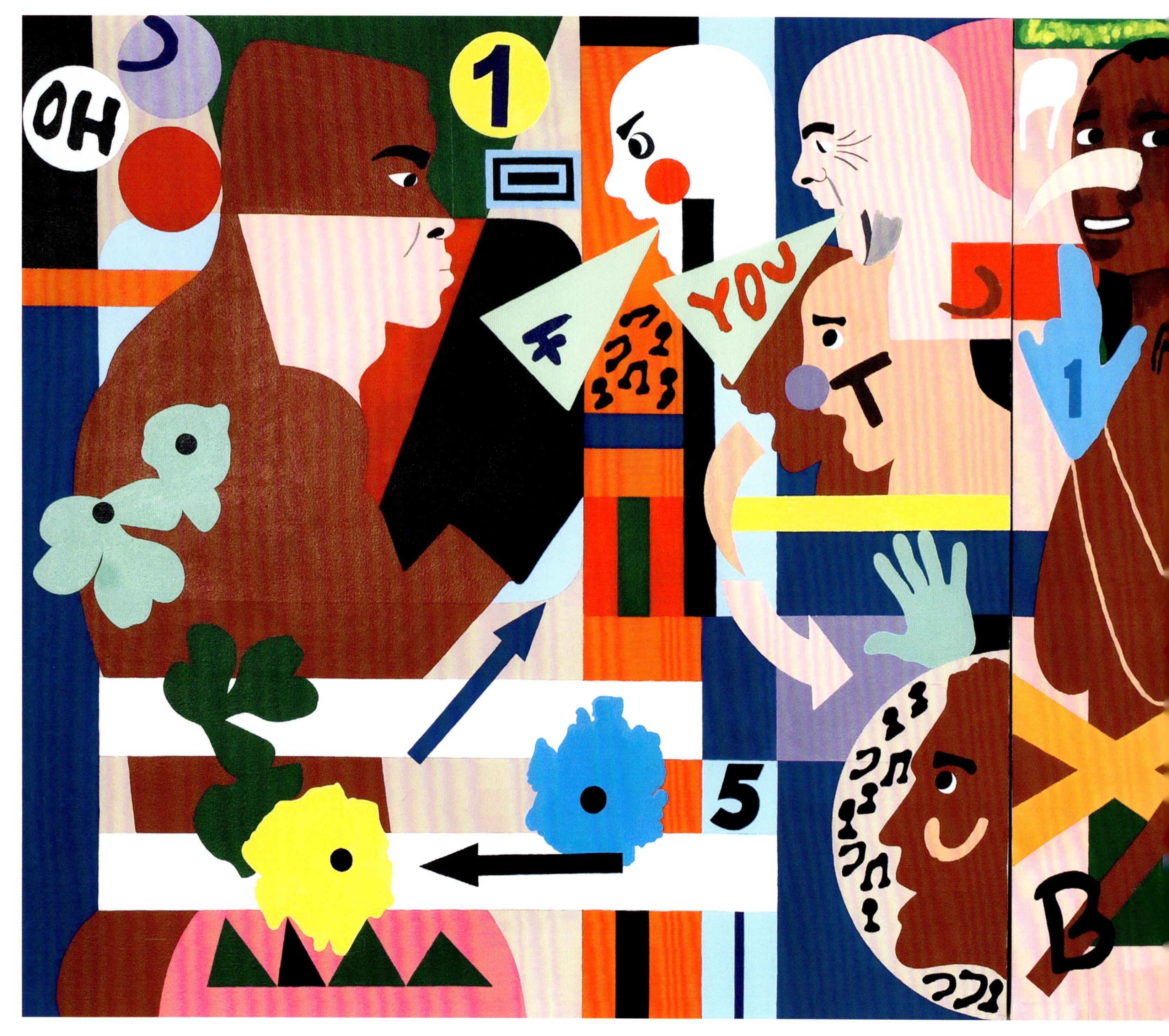

Untitled, 2012

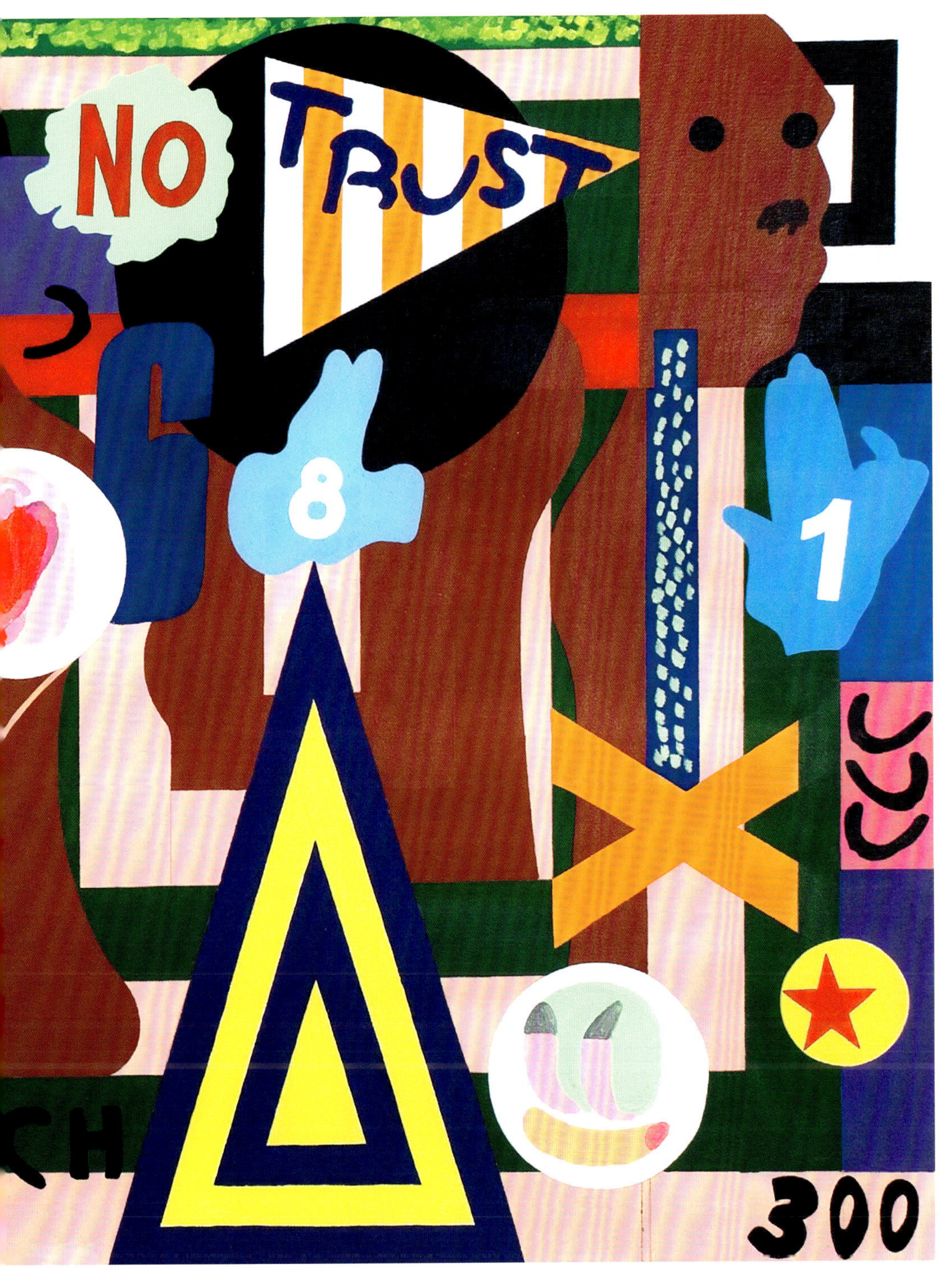
NO
TRUST
8
1
300

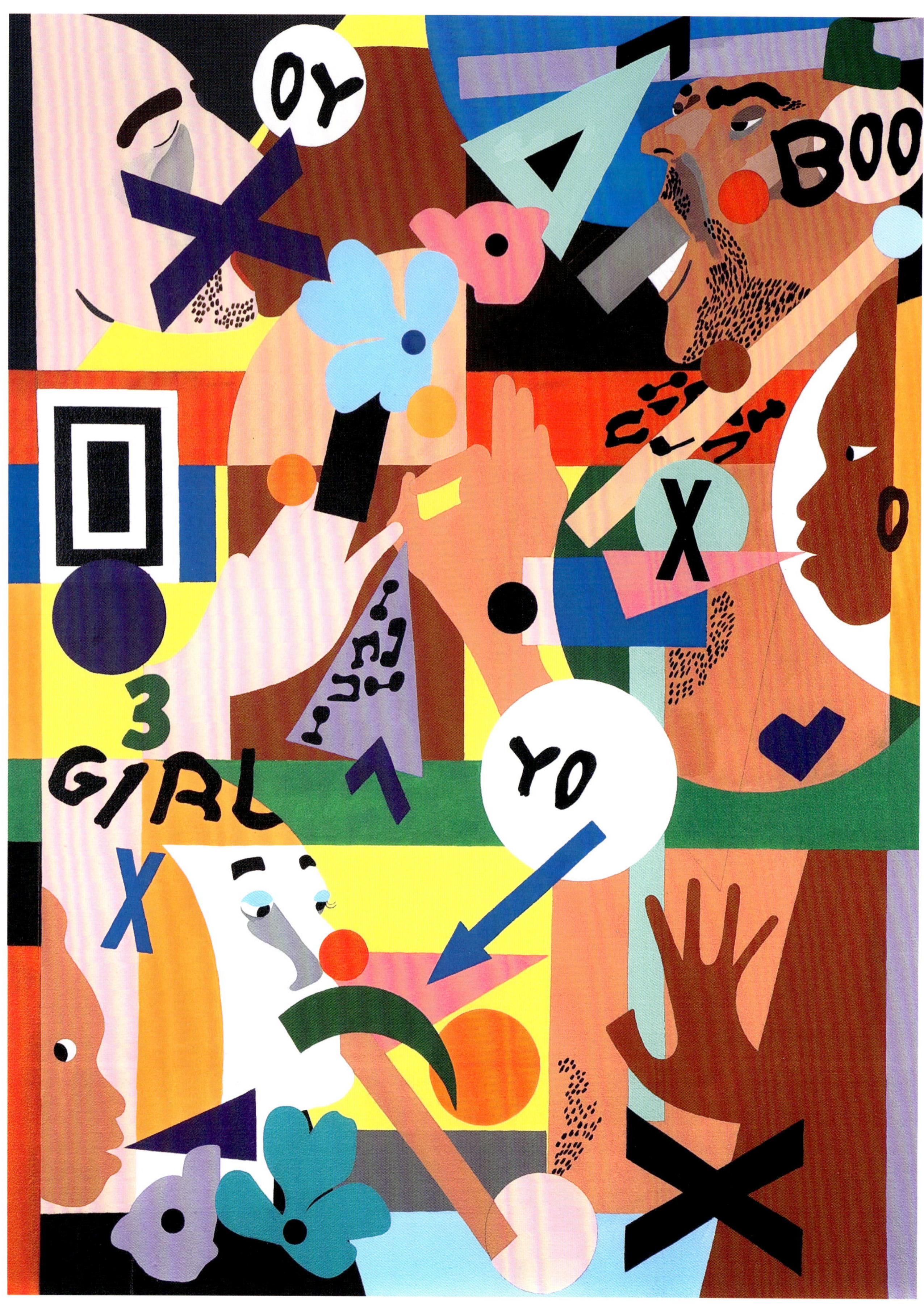

Mad 51st, 2012

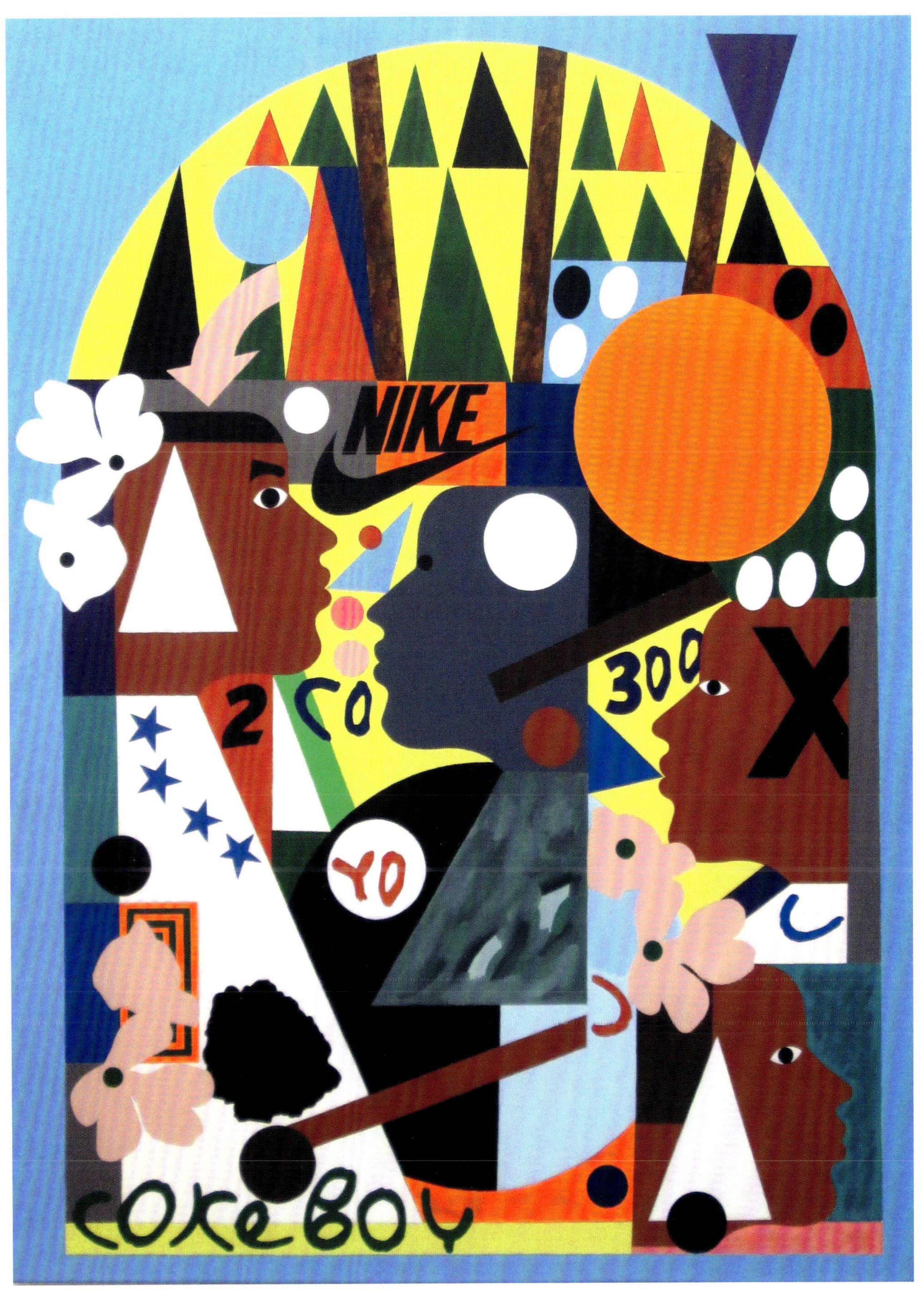

Let's Go Hoop, 2013

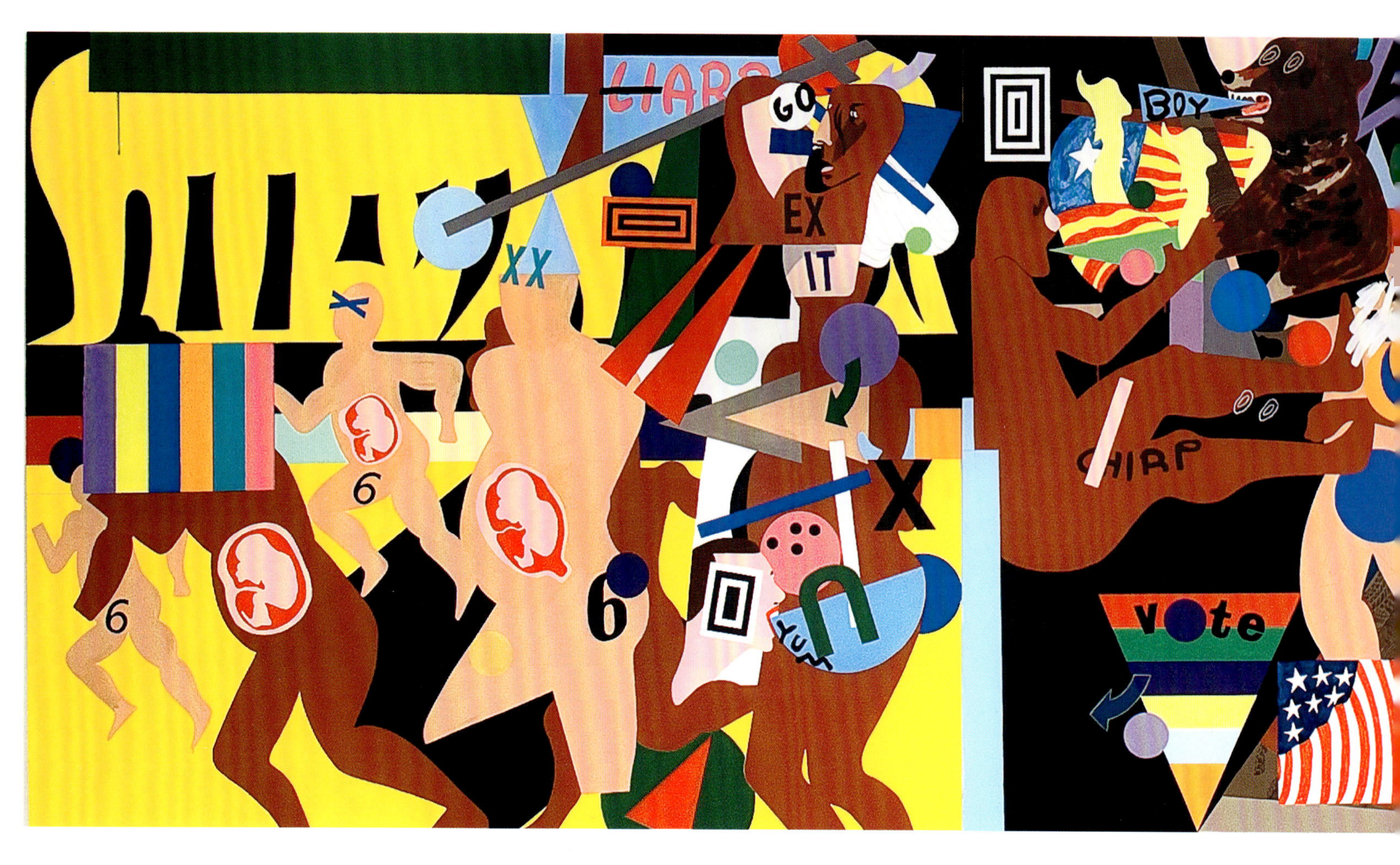

I Dread to Think (1 of 3 panels), 2012

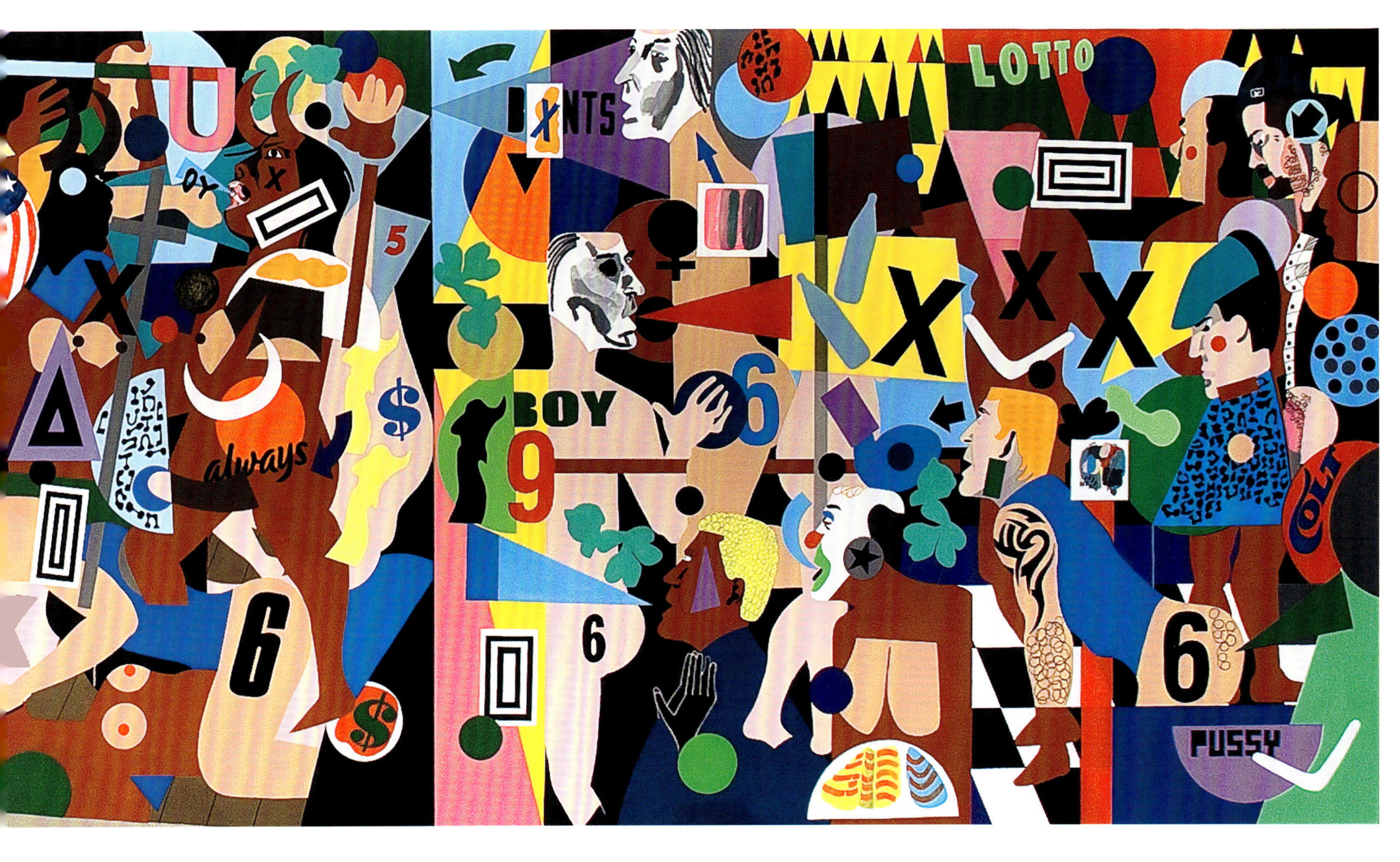
LOTTO
BOY
always
COLT
PUSSY

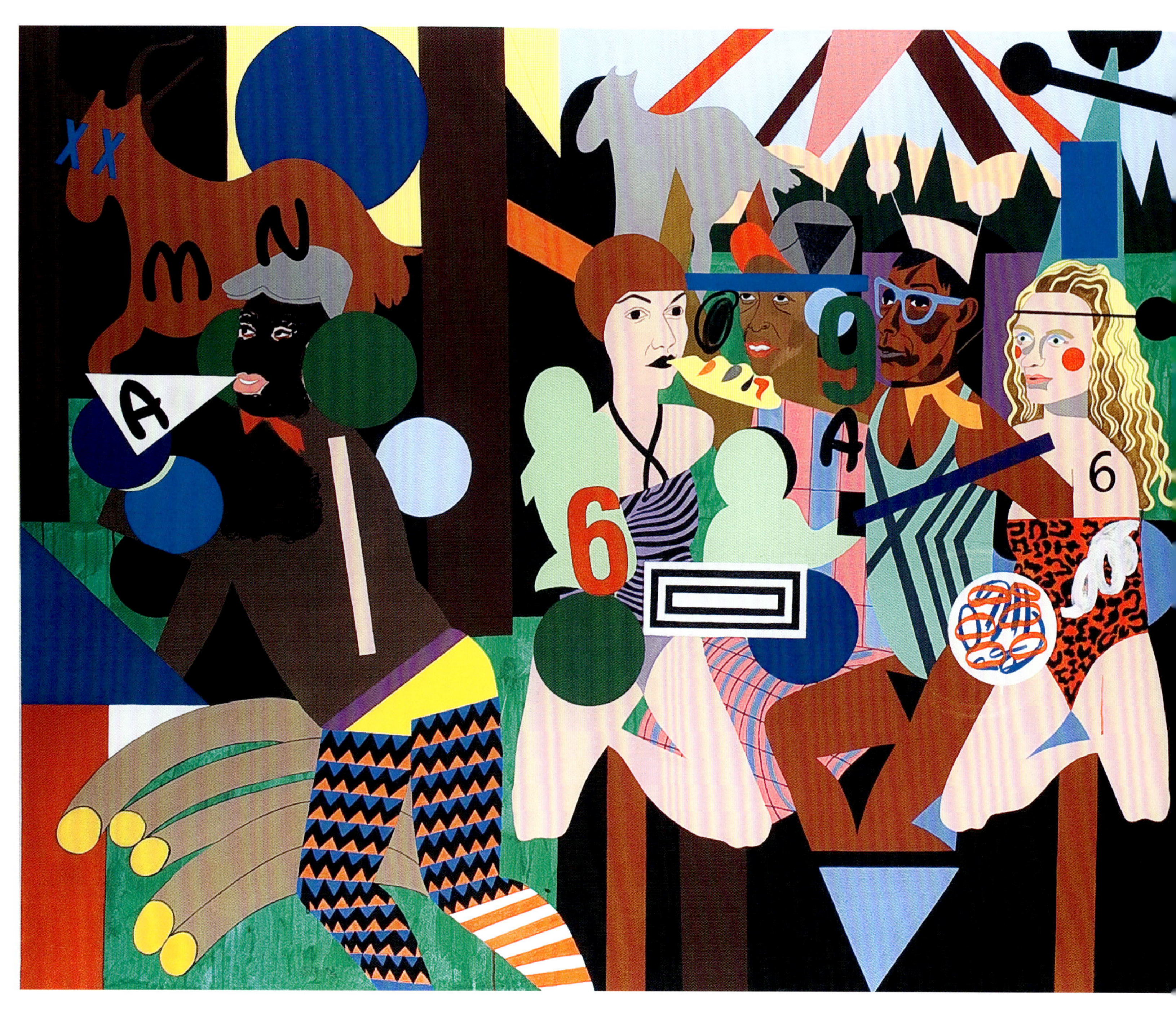

I Dread to Think (2 of 3 panels), 2012

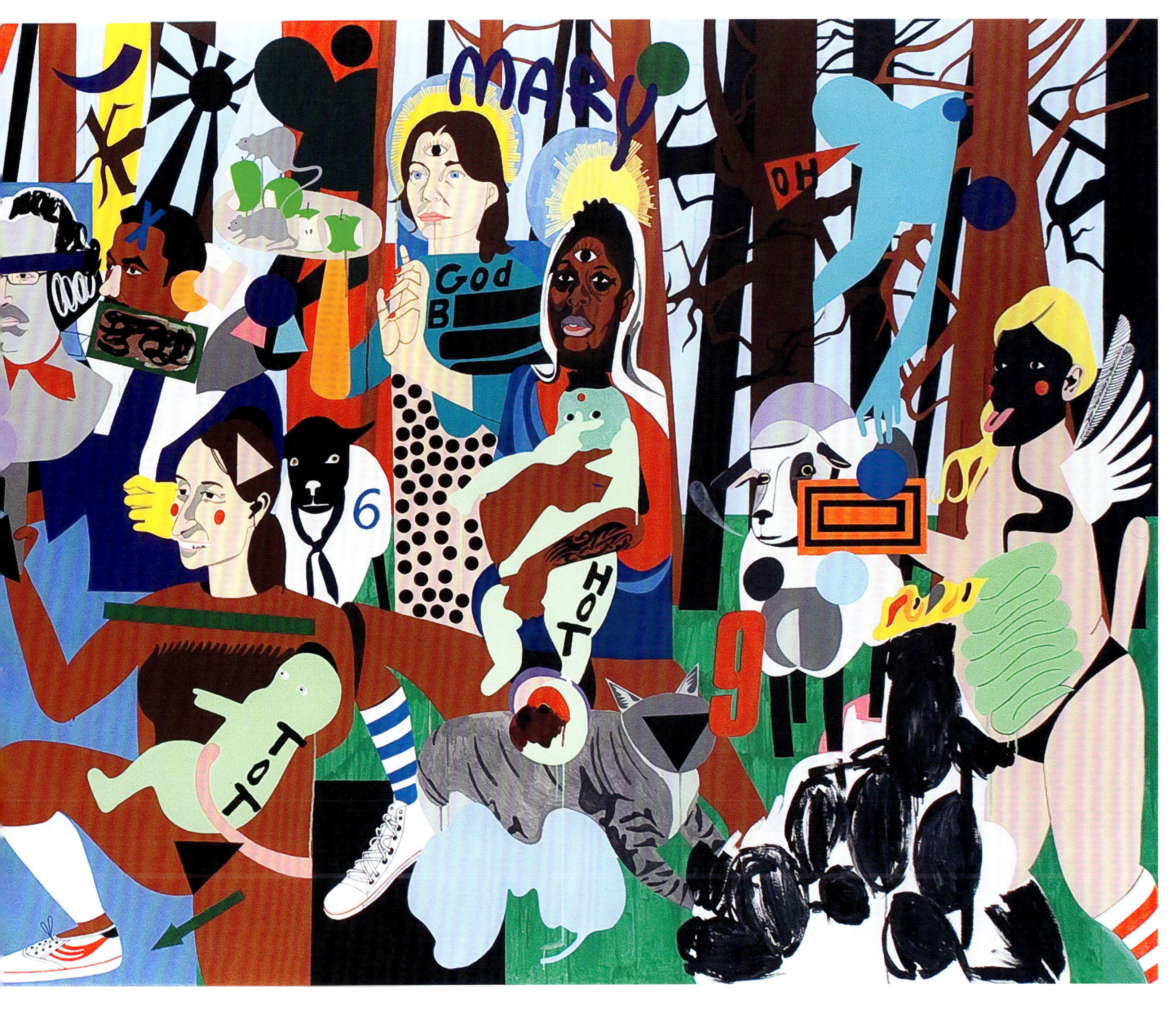

MARY
God
B
OH
6
HOT
TOT
9

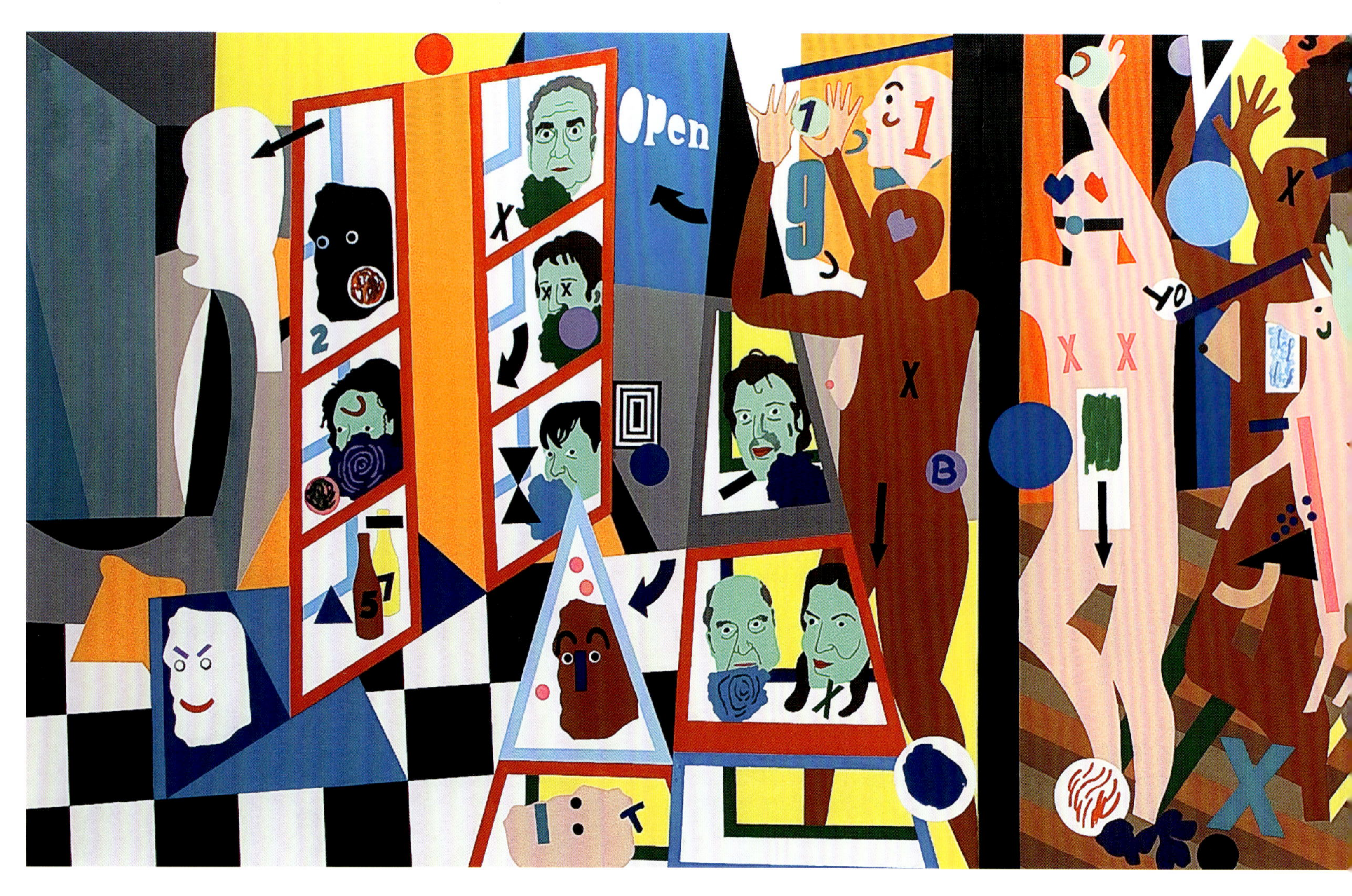

I Dread to Think (3 of 3 panels), 2012

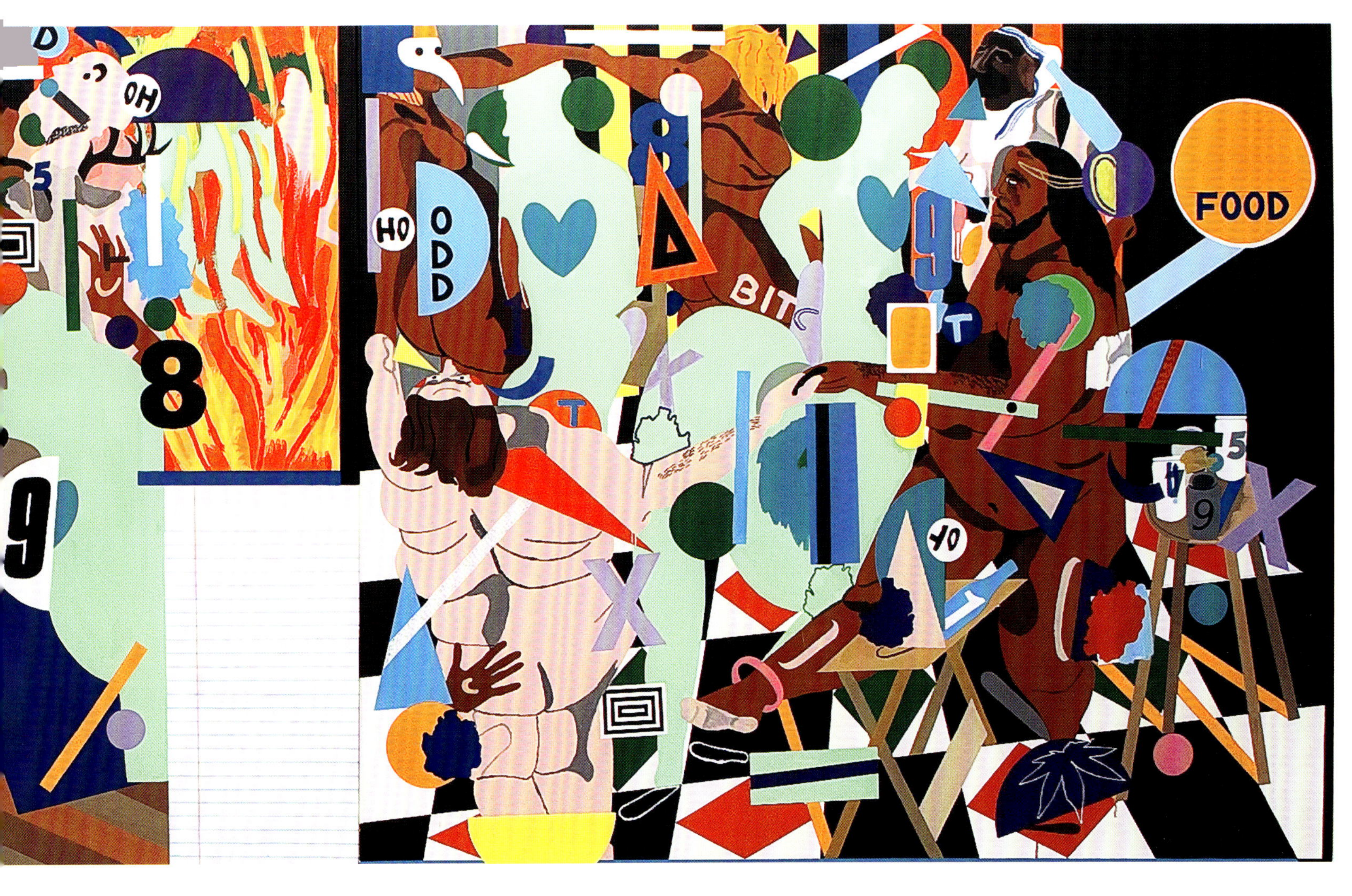

OH
HO
ODD
BITC
FOOD

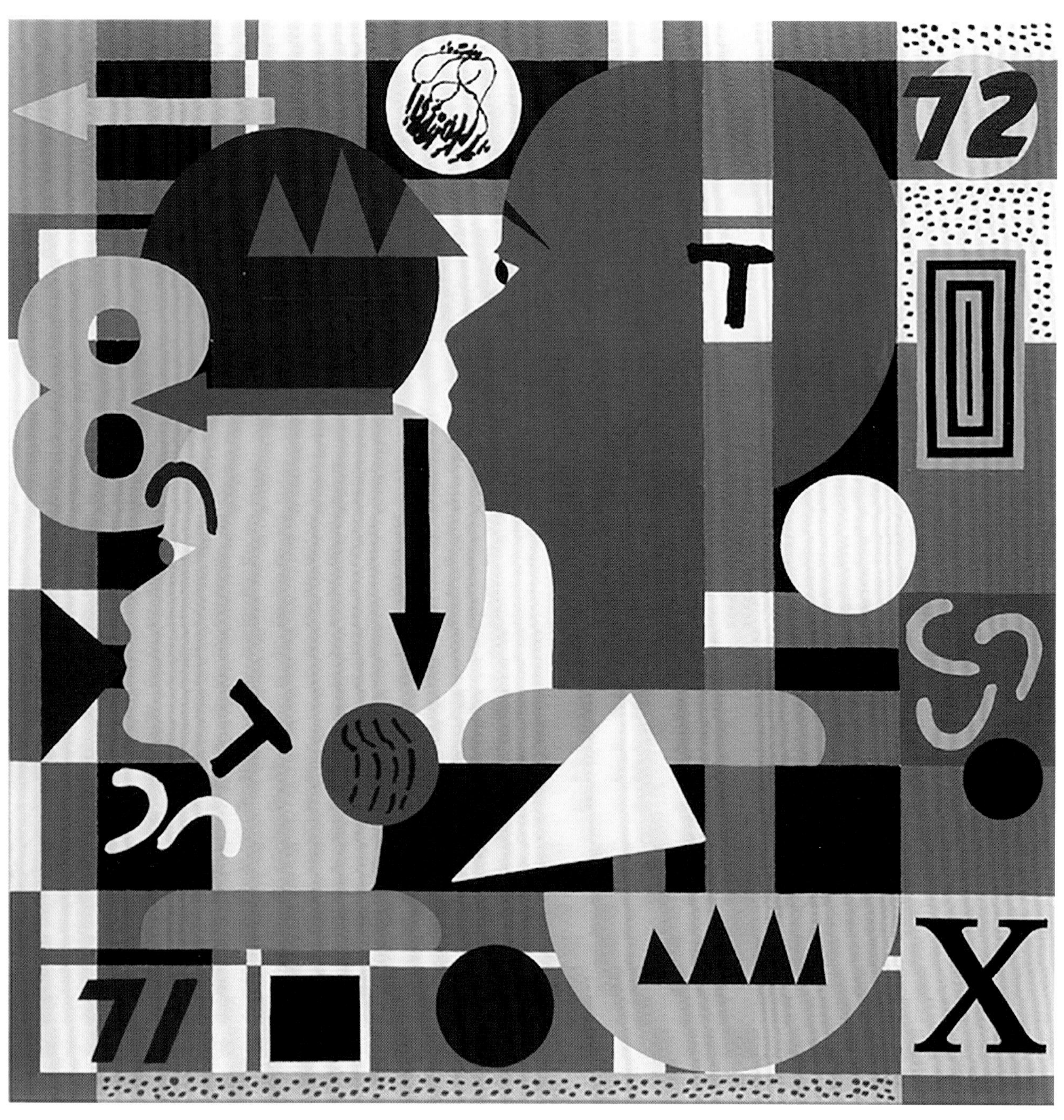

Untitled (Mannequins), 2013

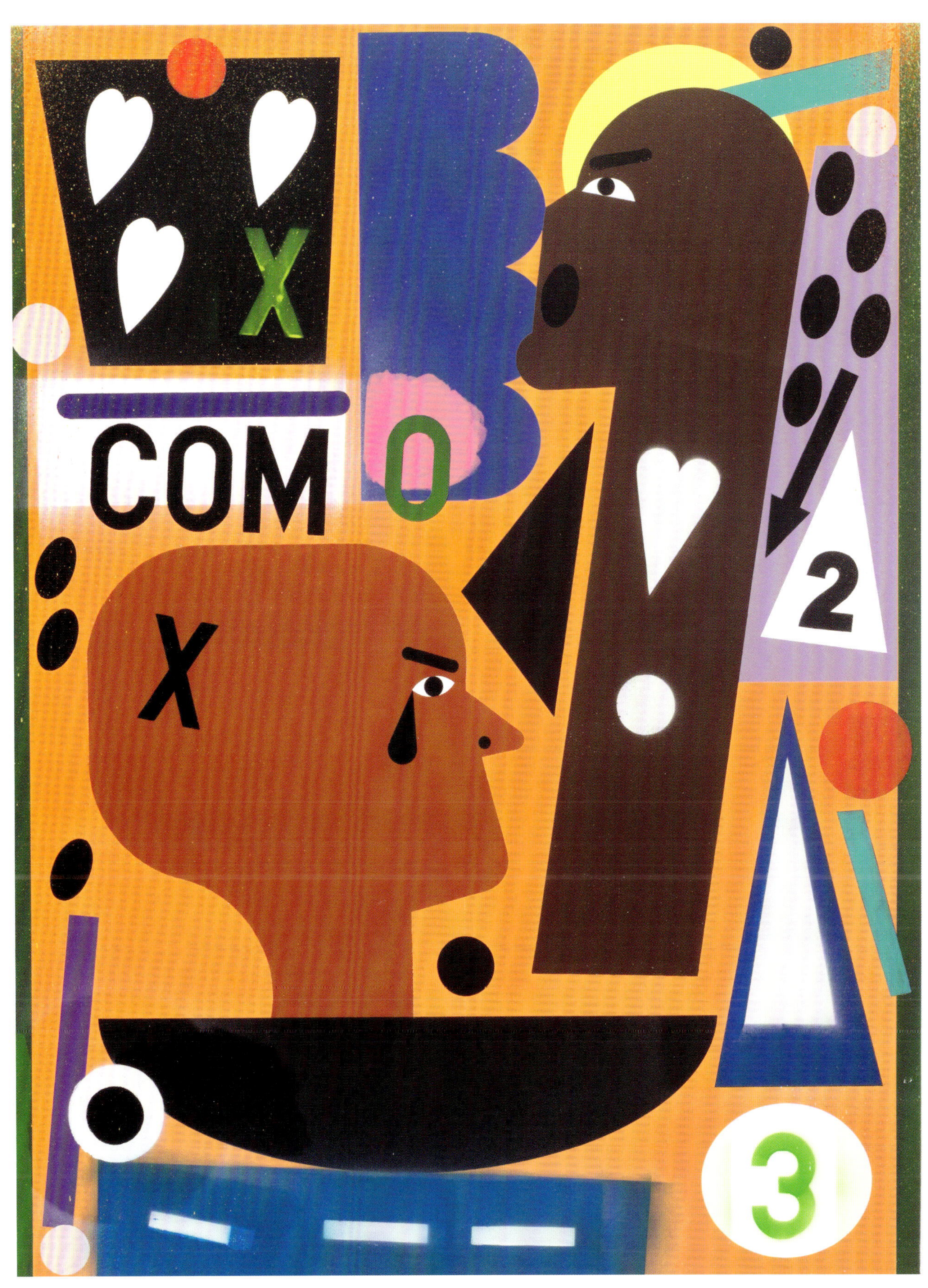

[ABOVE] Incite (COM), 2015
[OVERLEAF] Untitled (FUCK T*E *OP), 2014

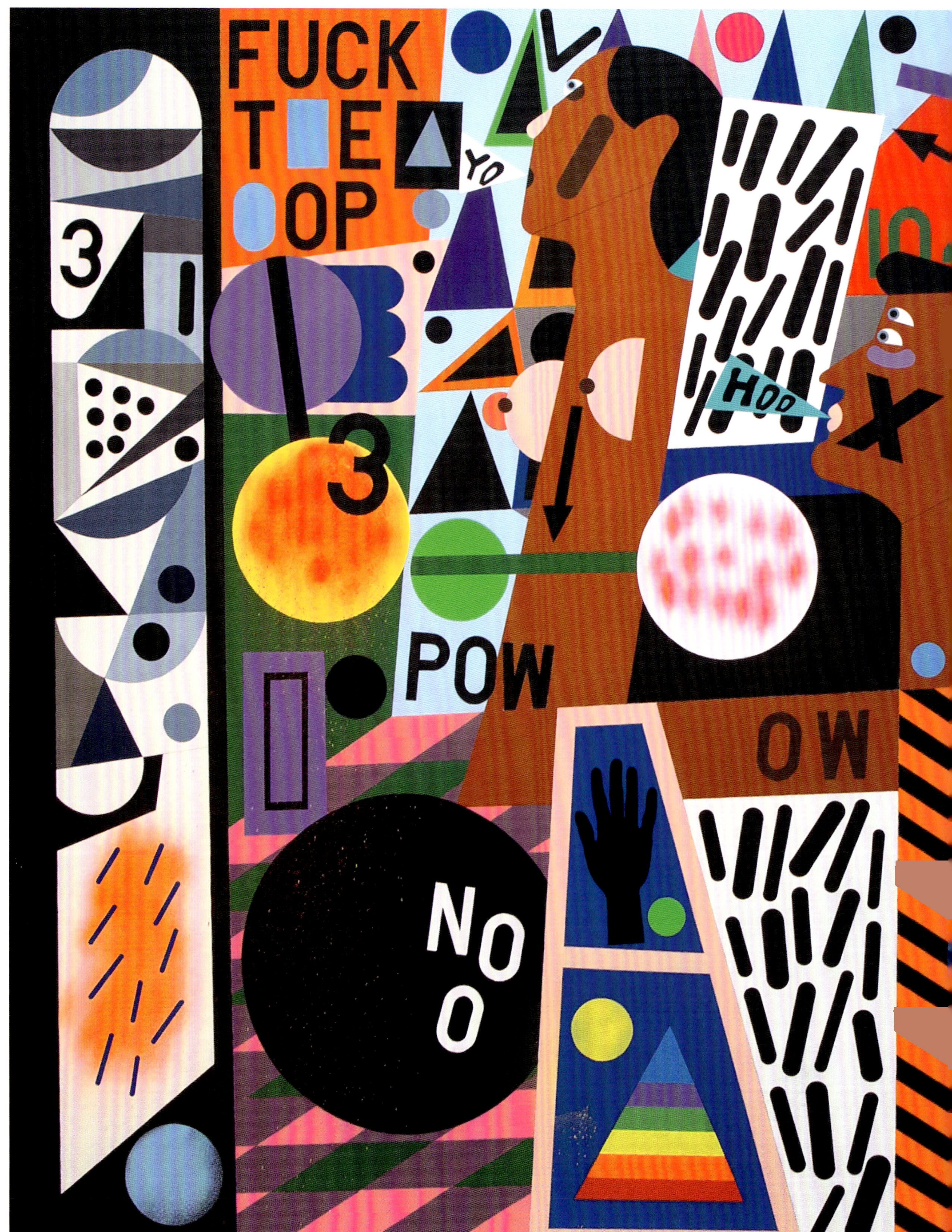
FUCK
T E
OP
YO
3
3
HOO
X
POW
OW
NO
O

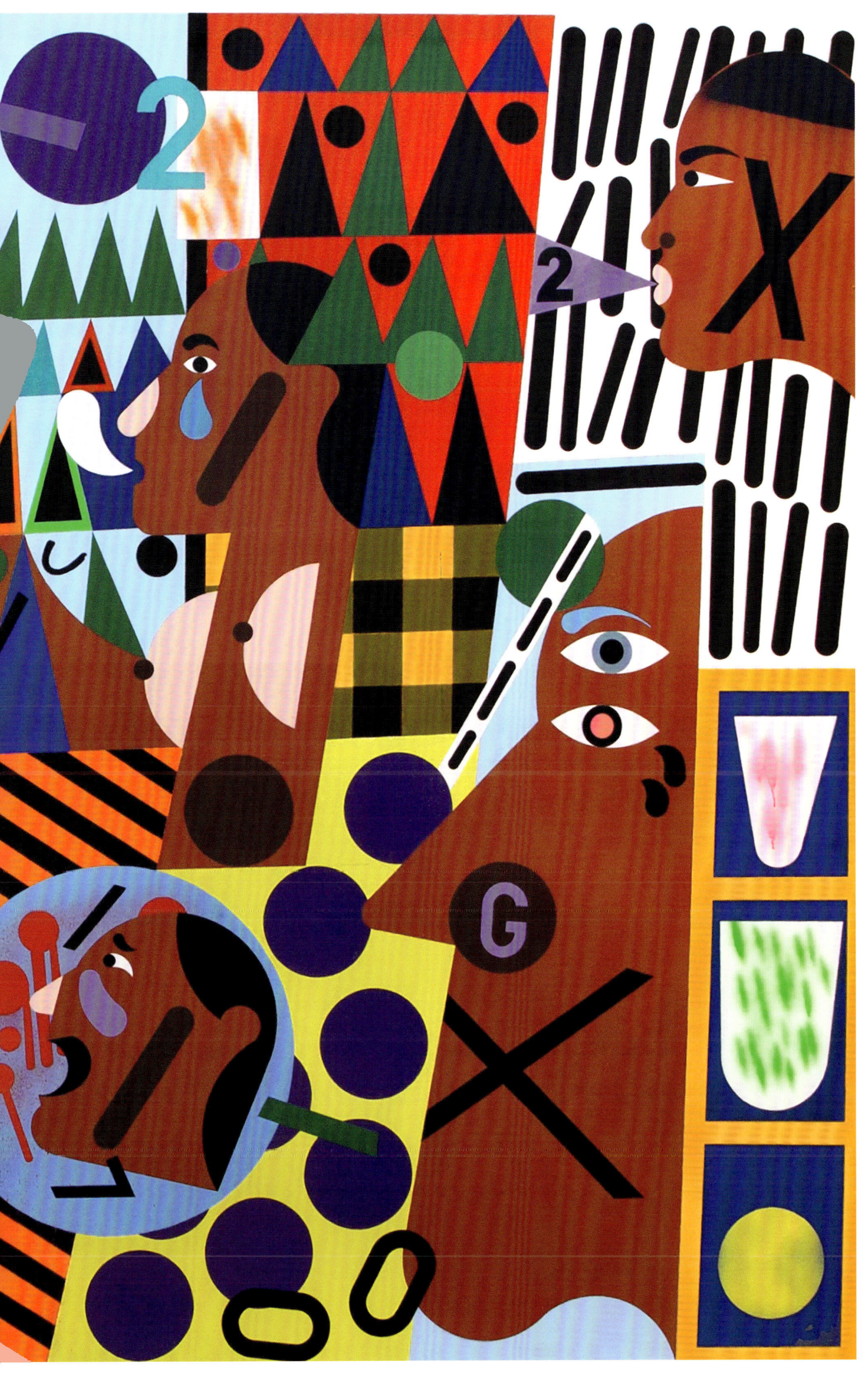

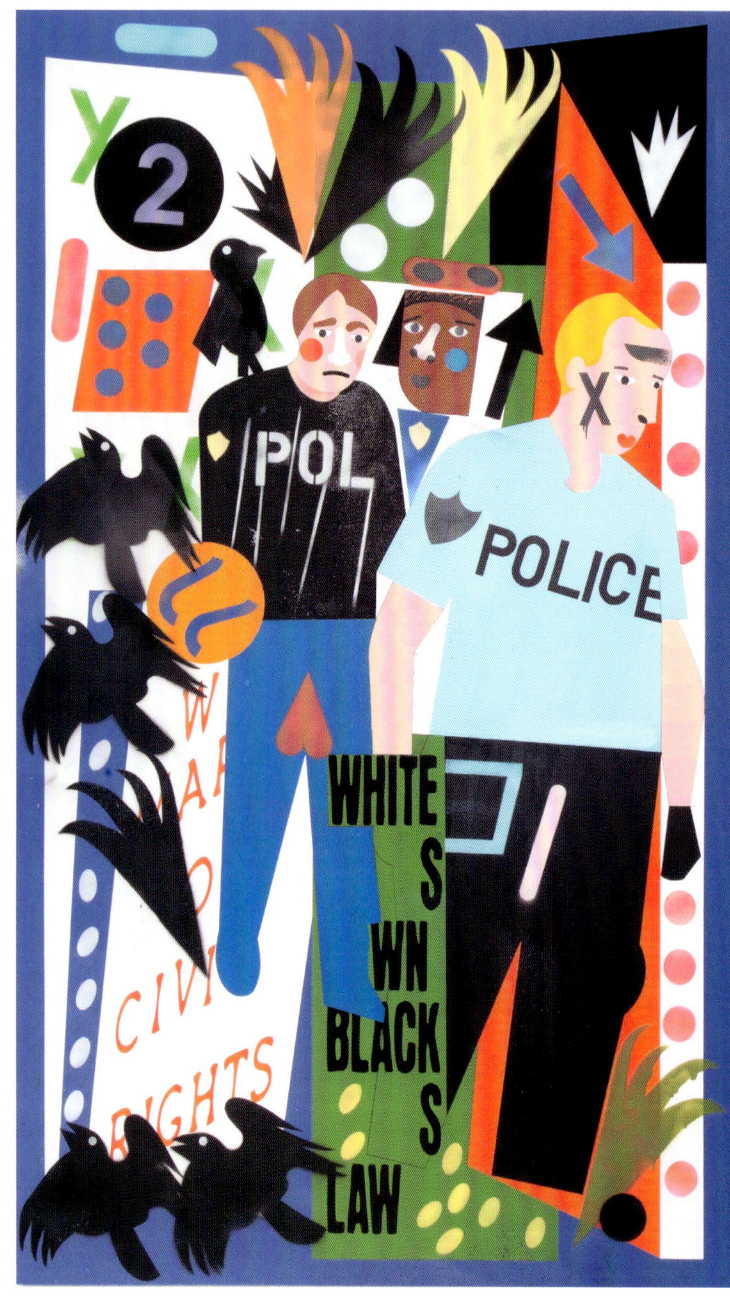

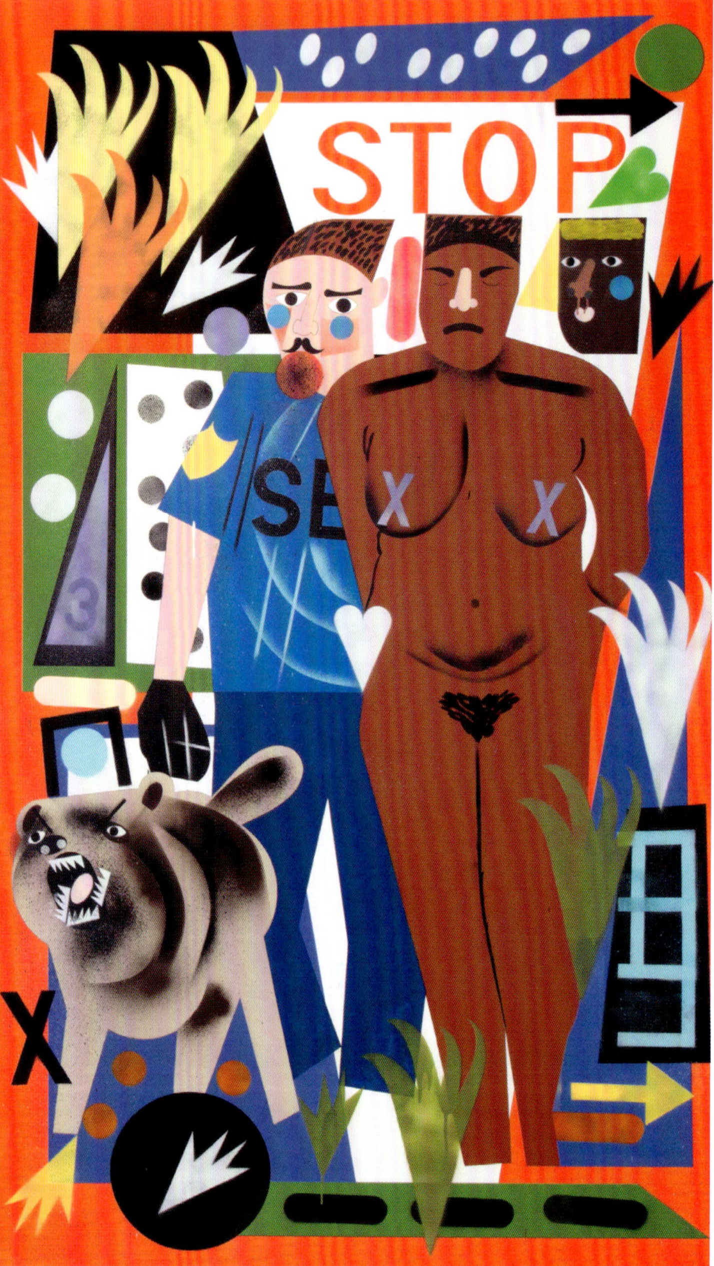

Who, 2015

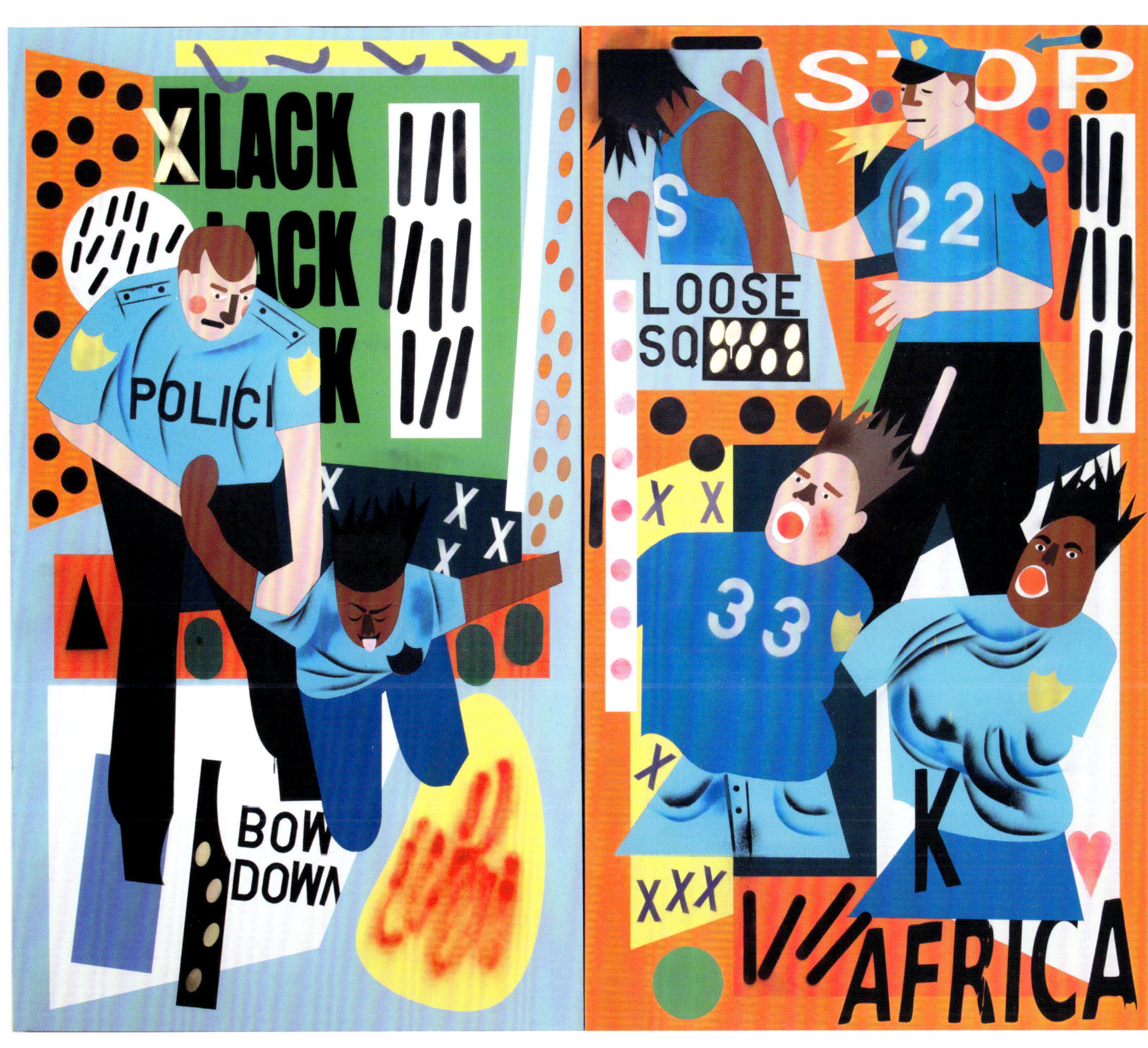

What, 2015

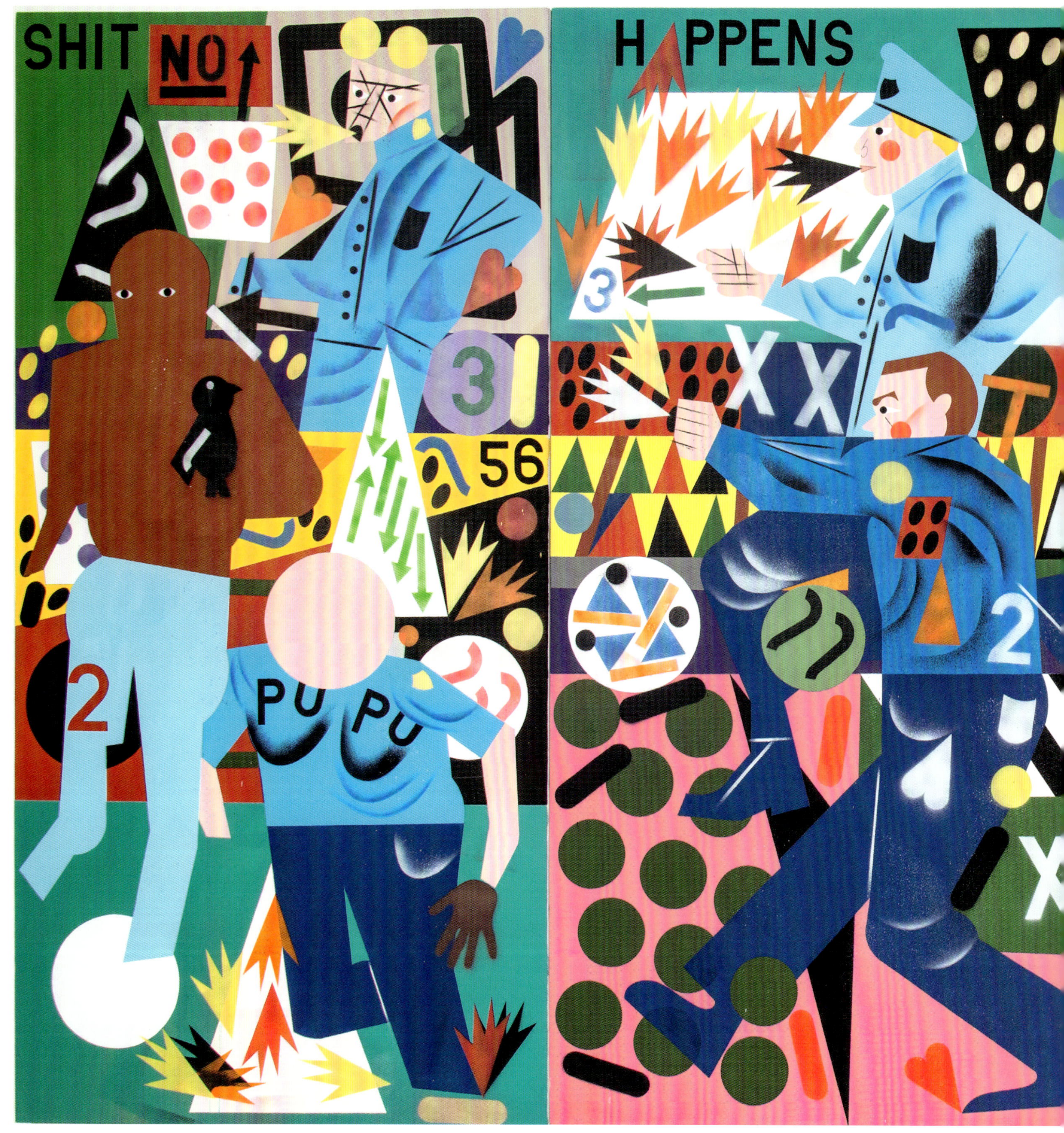

Why, 2015

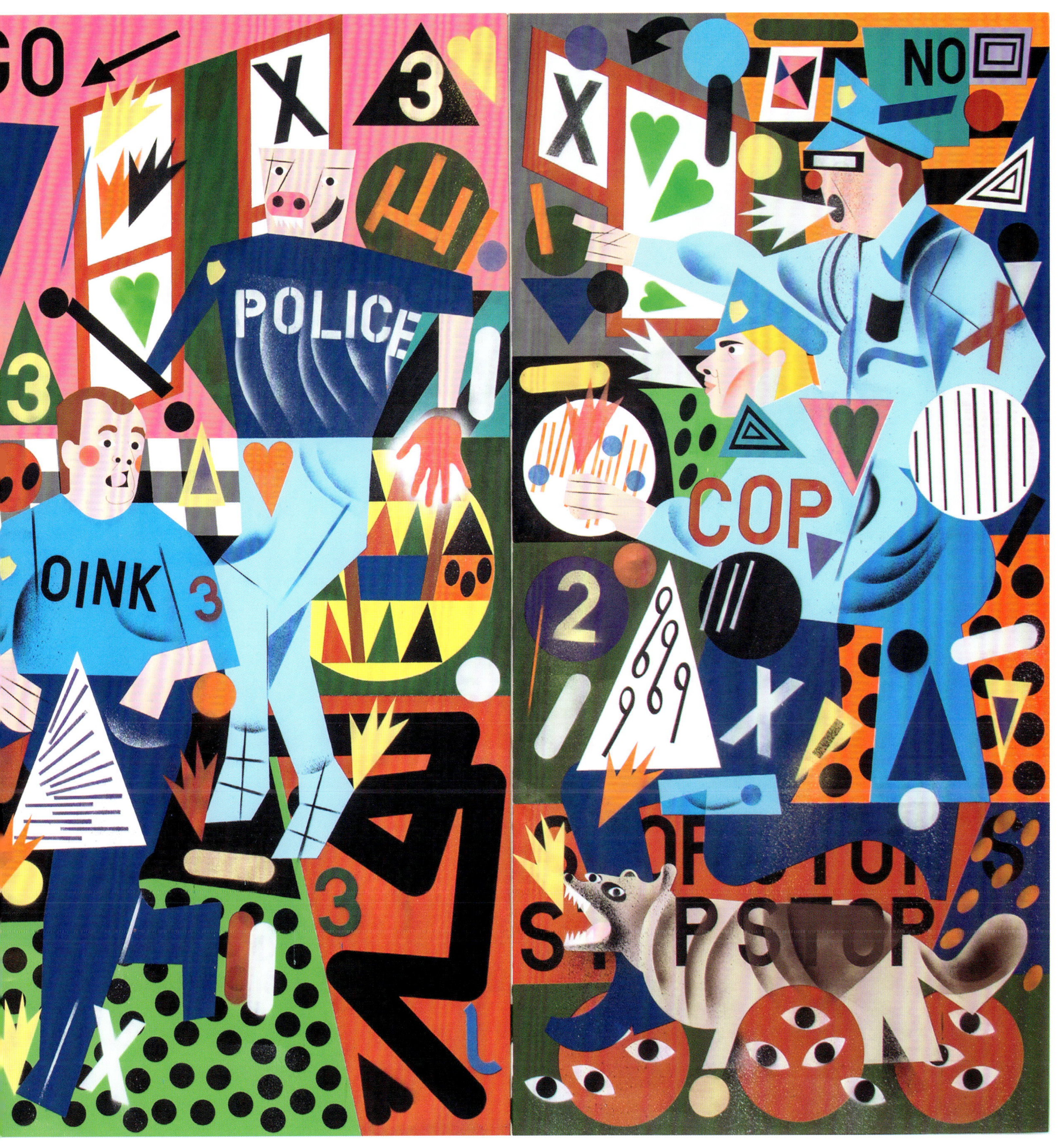
GO
X
3
POLICE
3
OINK
3
3
X
X
NO
COP
2
X
STOP

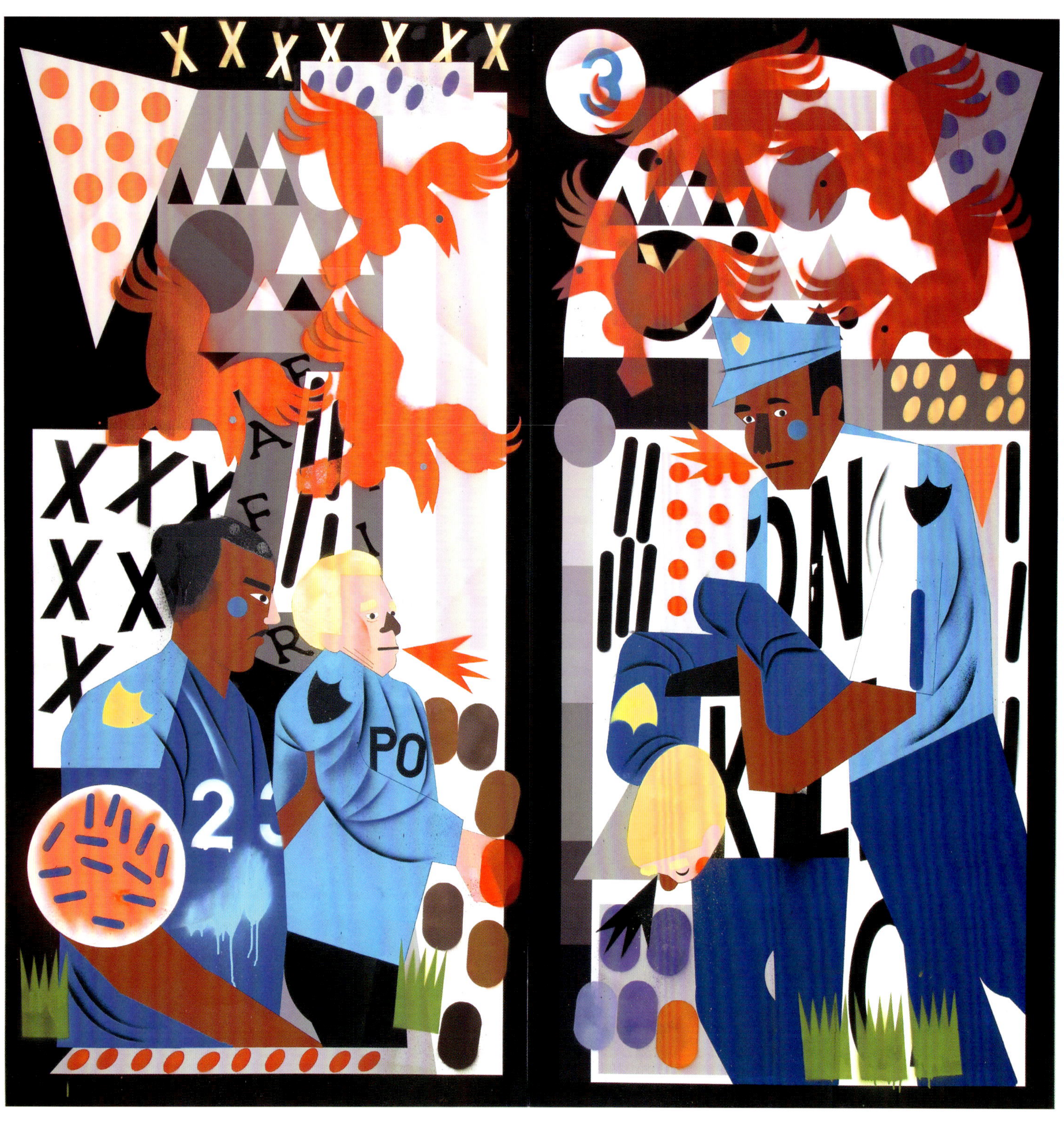

Where, 2015

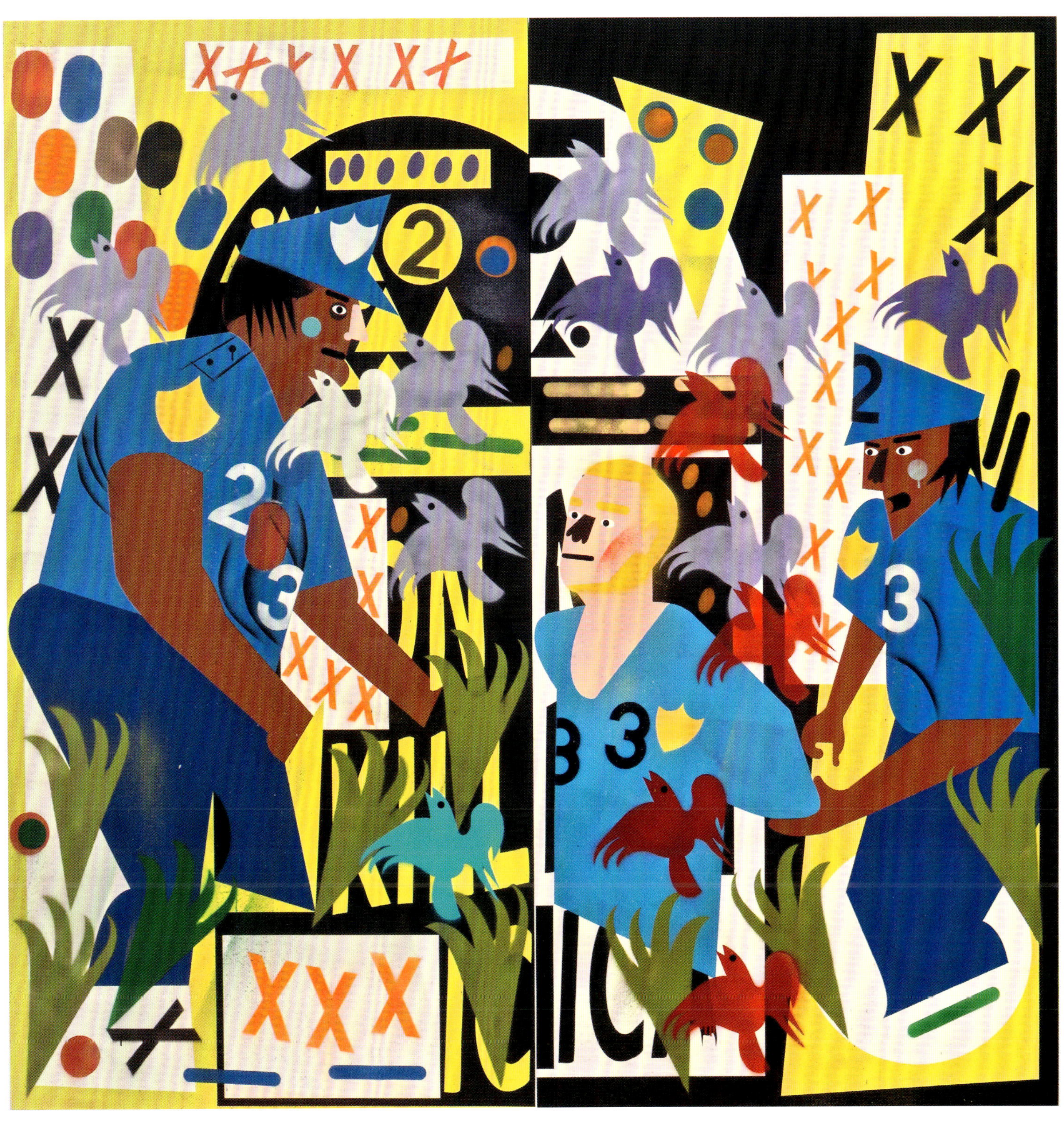

Untitled, 2015

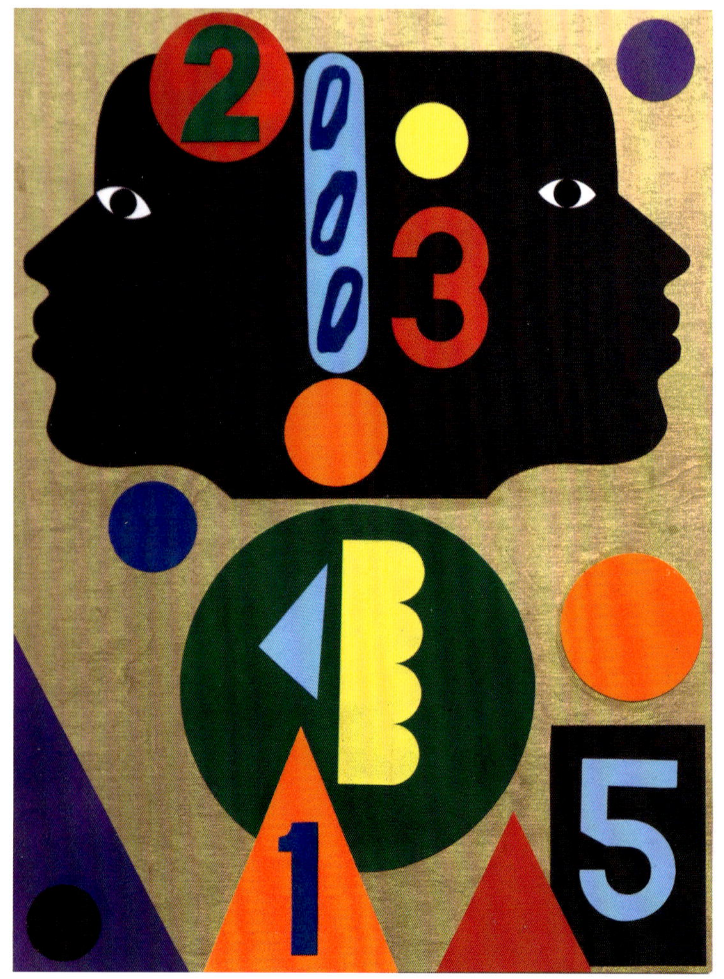

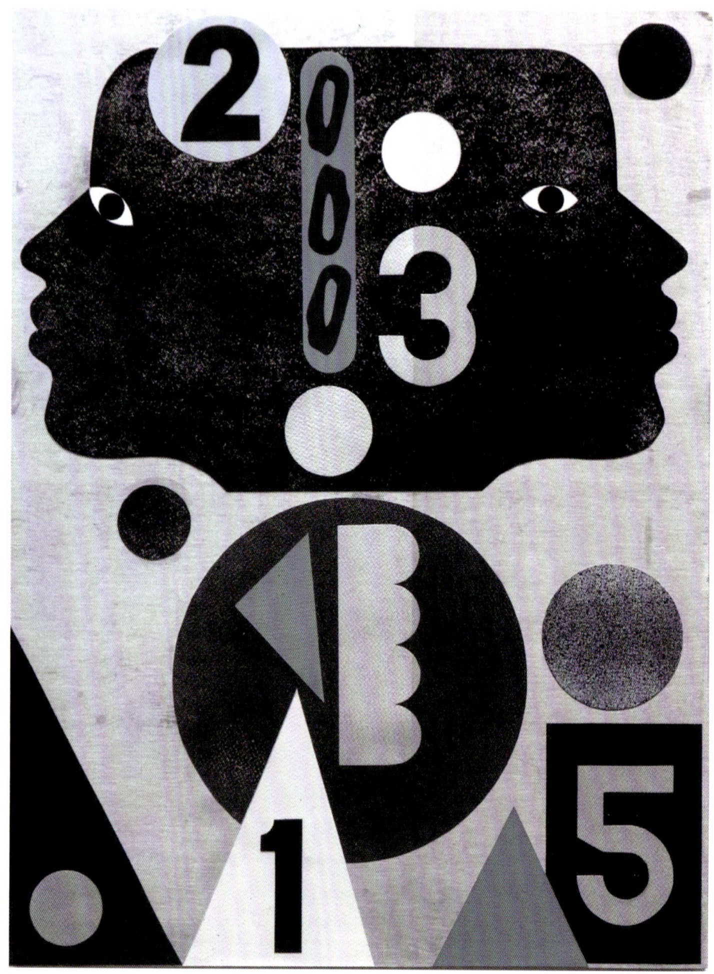

[ABOVE] Untitled, 2015
[OPPOSITE] Brazil -4, 2016

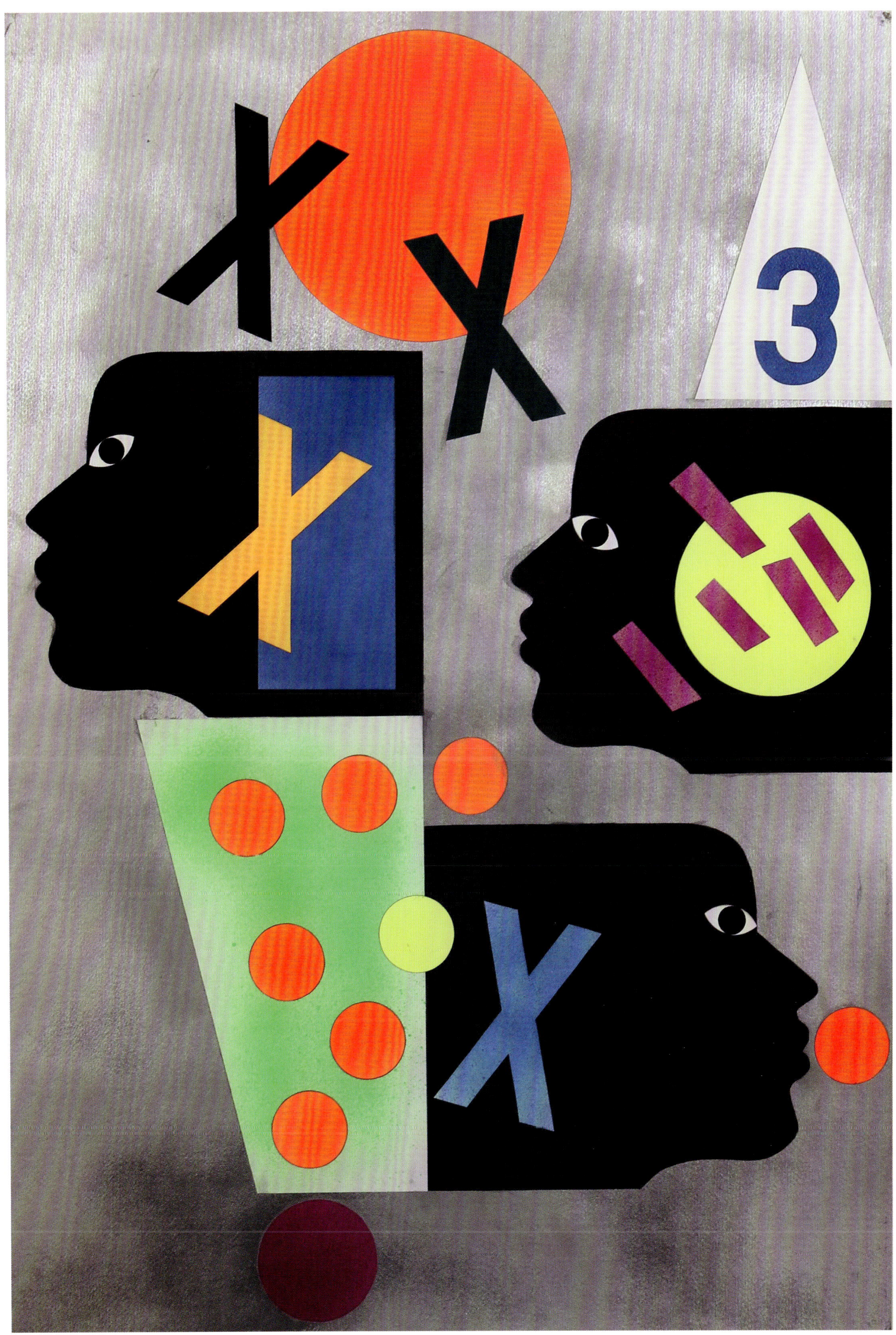

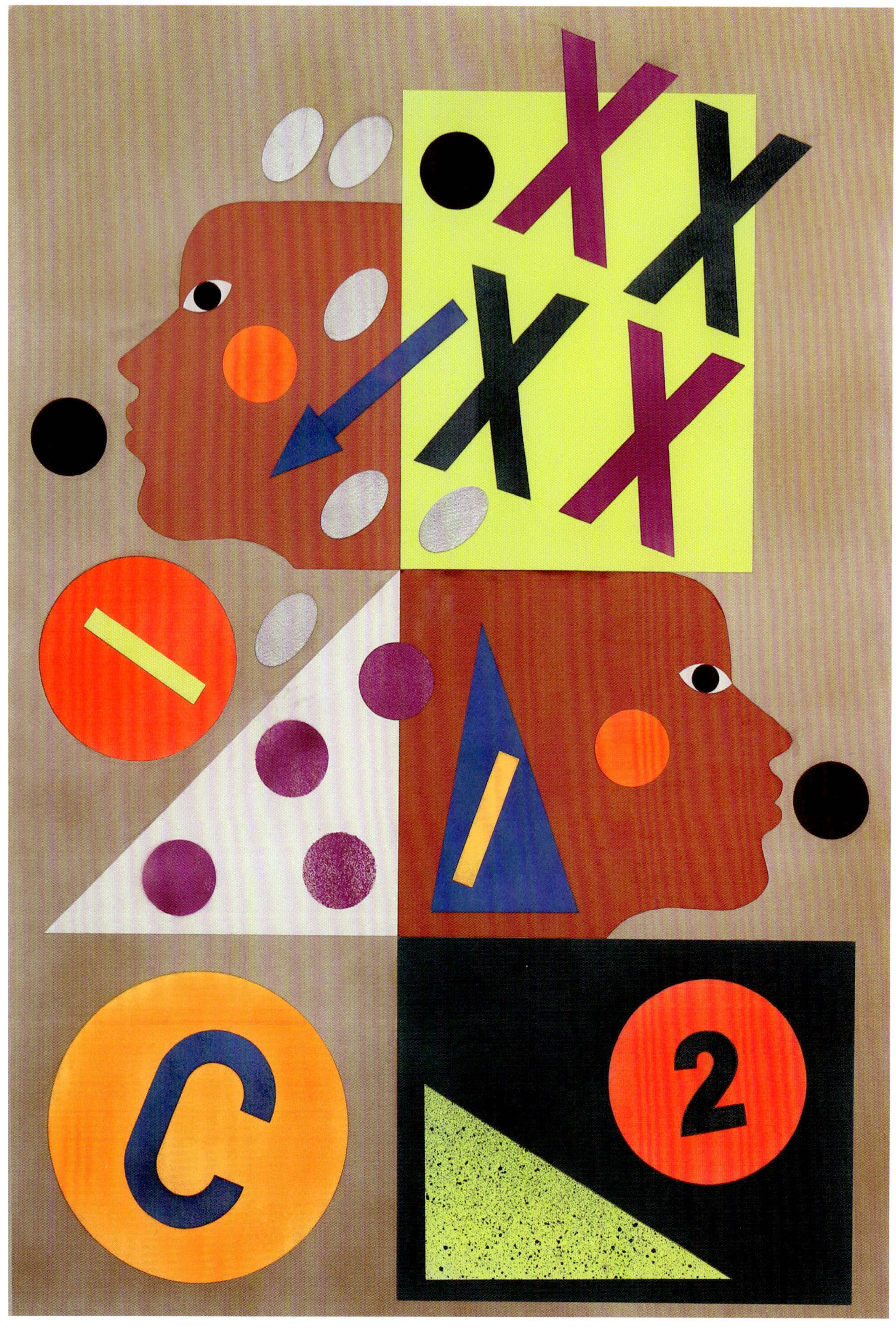

Brazil -3, 2015

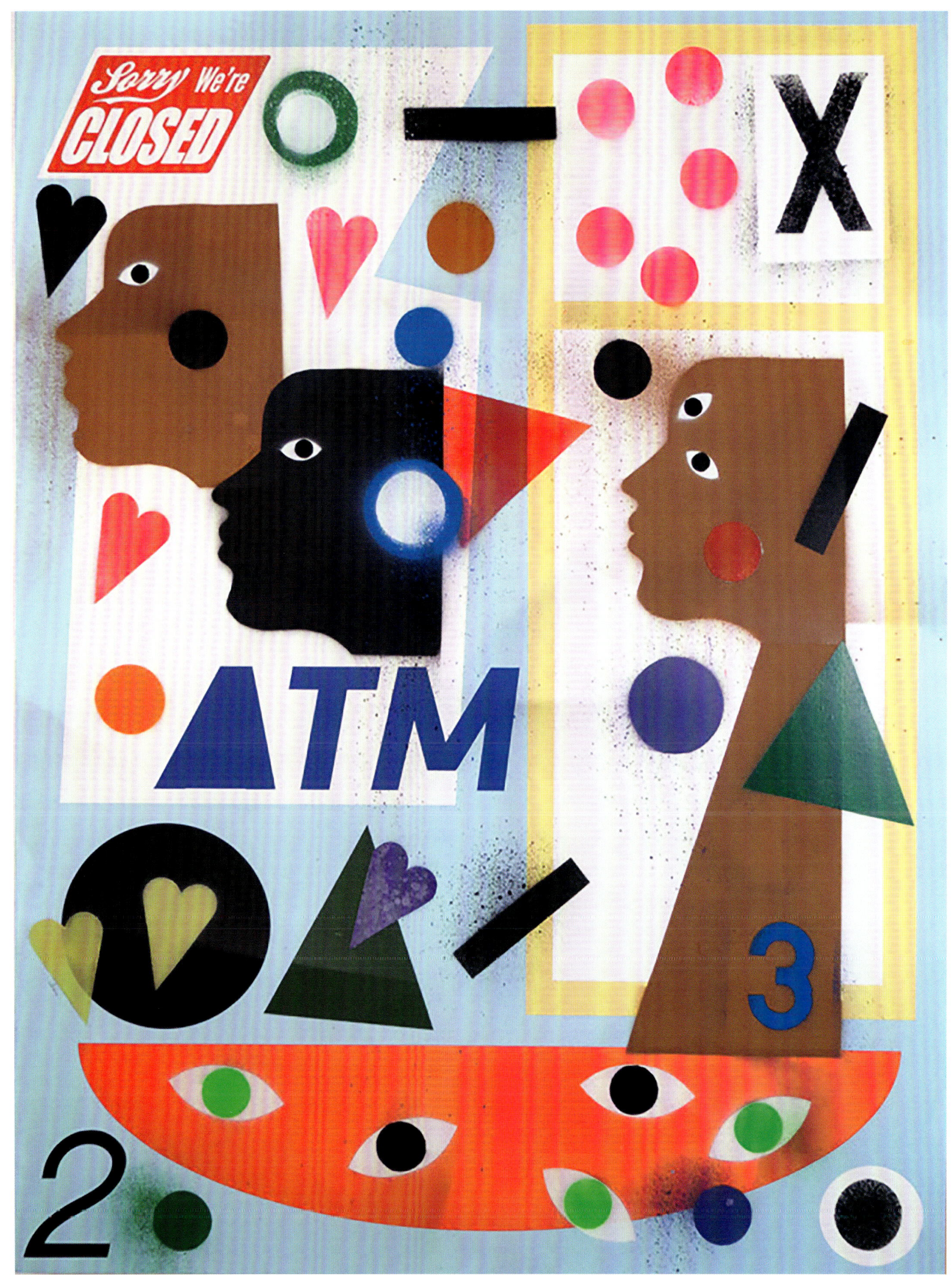

Sorry We're Closed, 2015

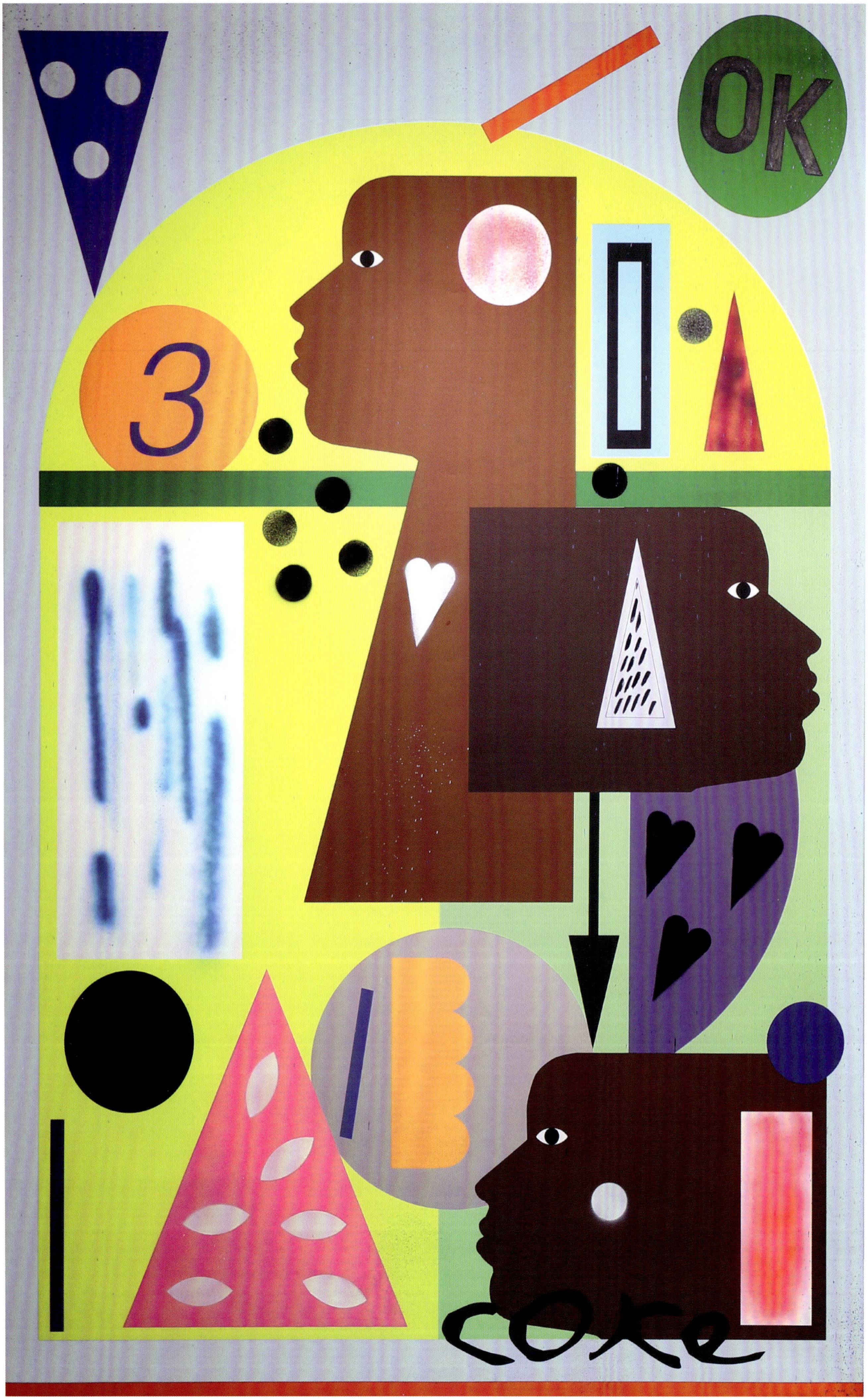

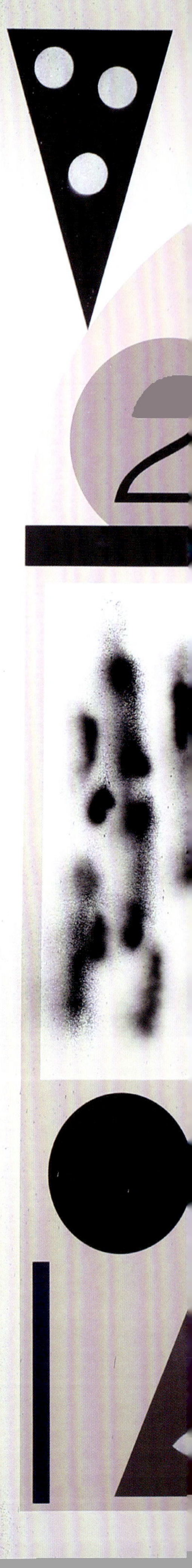

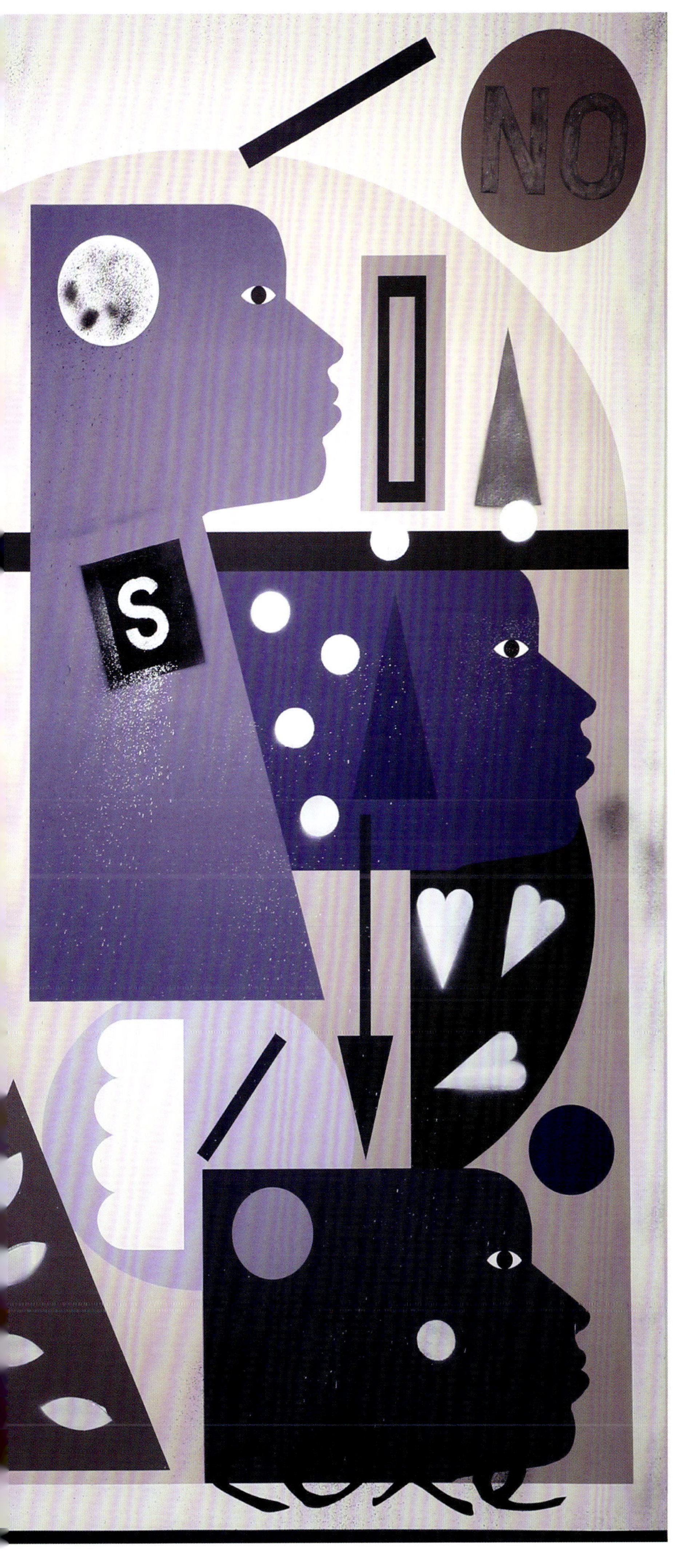

Potato, Potata, 2015

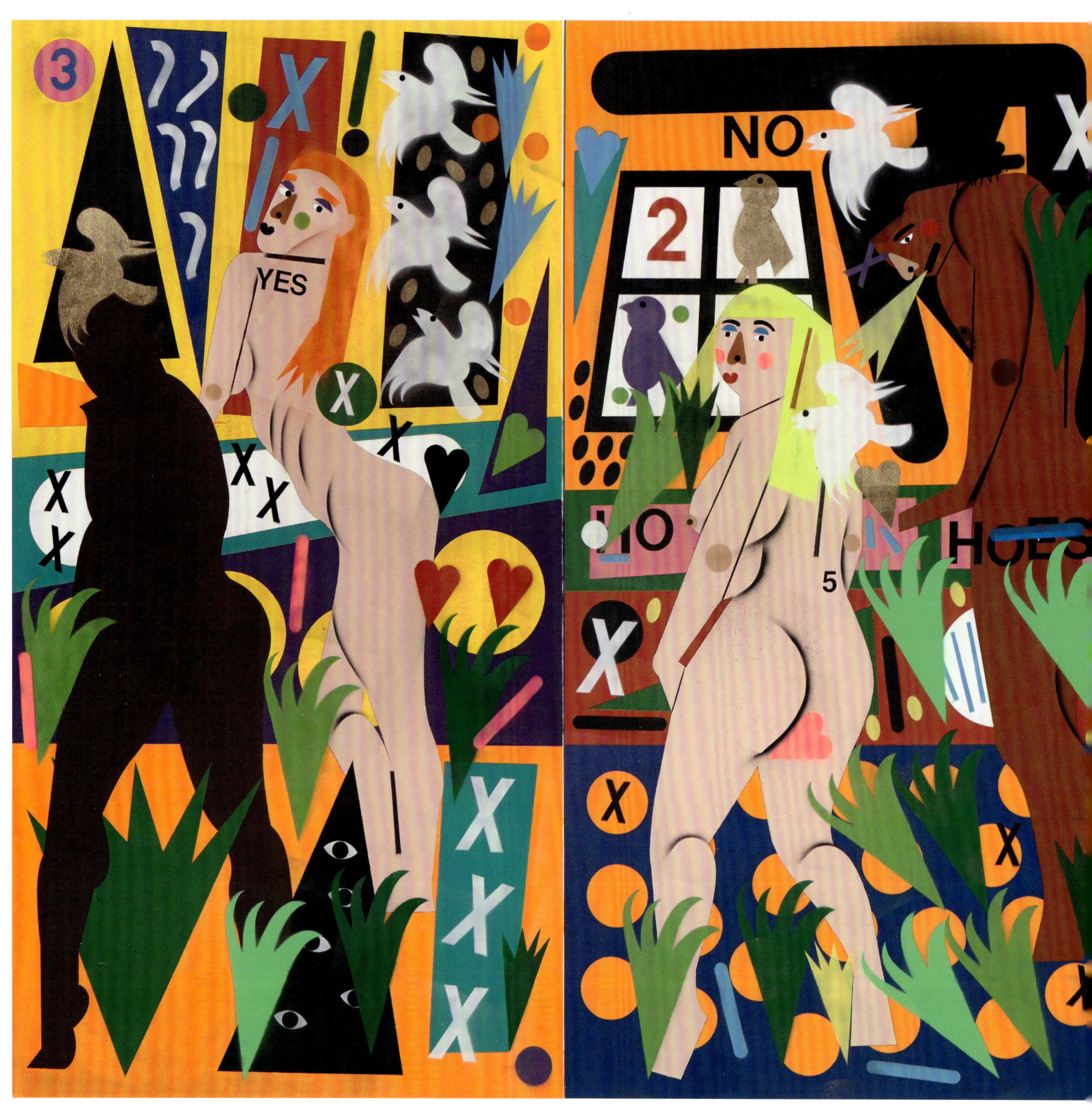

Hothouse, 2016

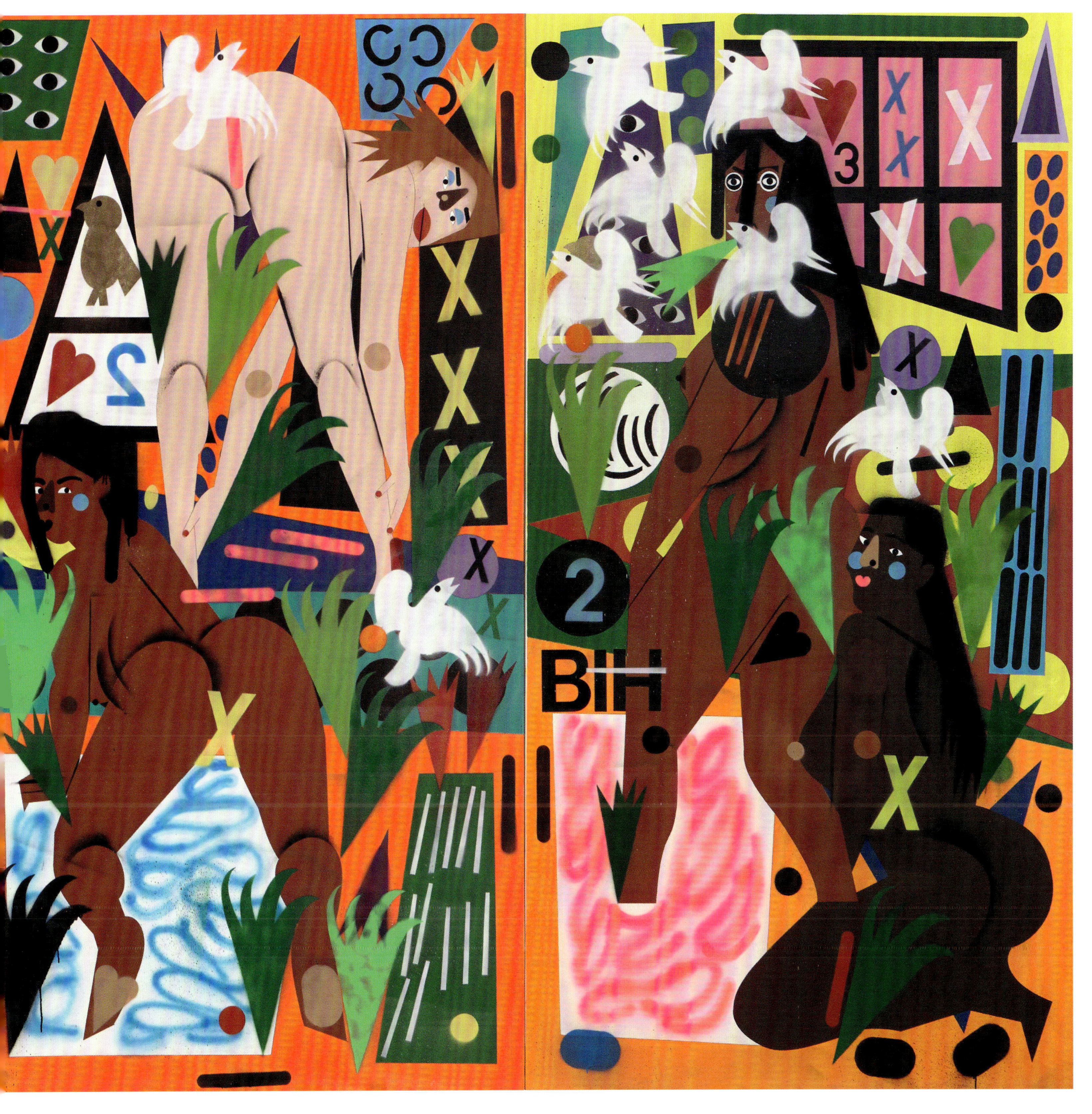
BIH

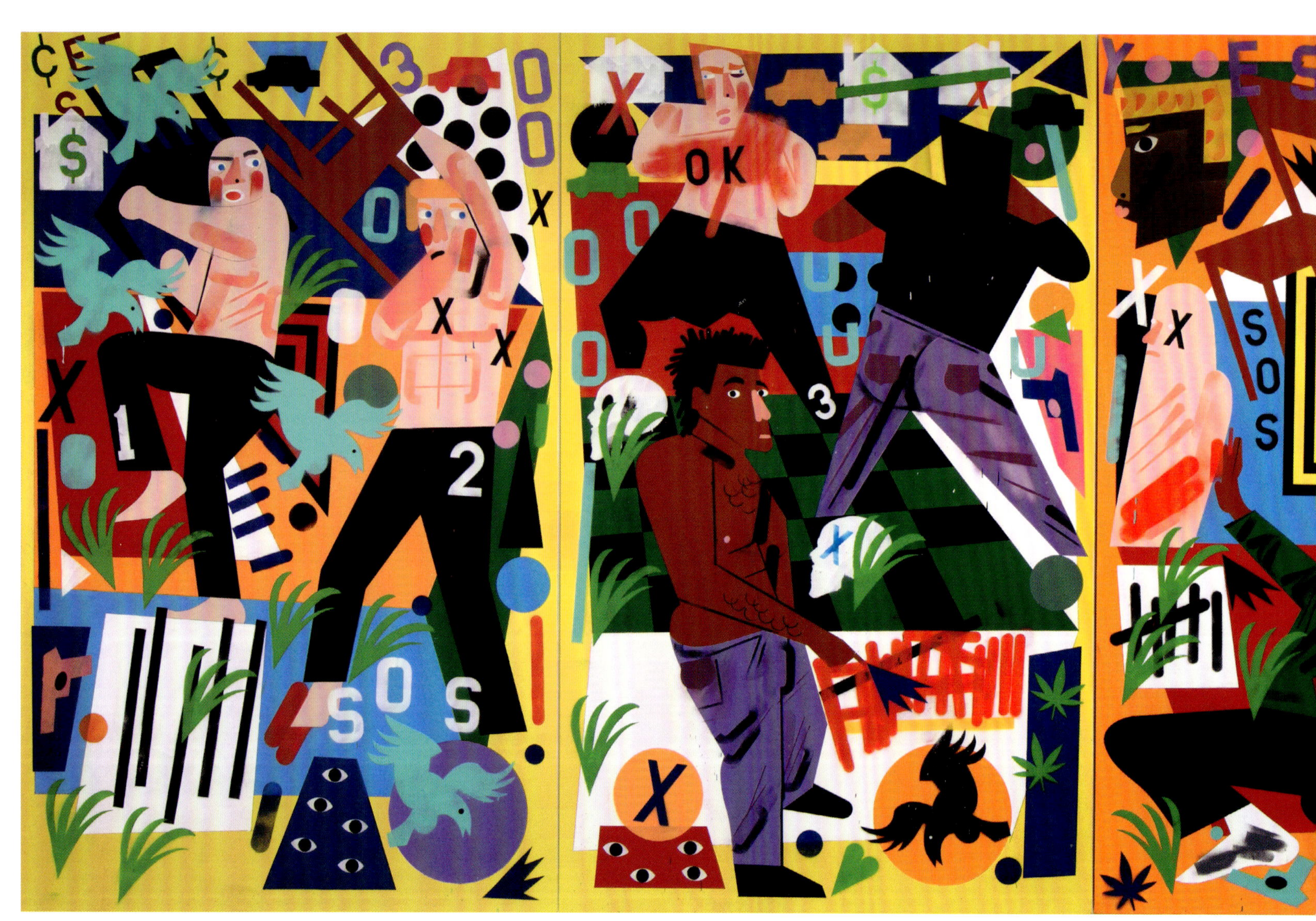

Catch Me If You Can, Catch 22, 2017

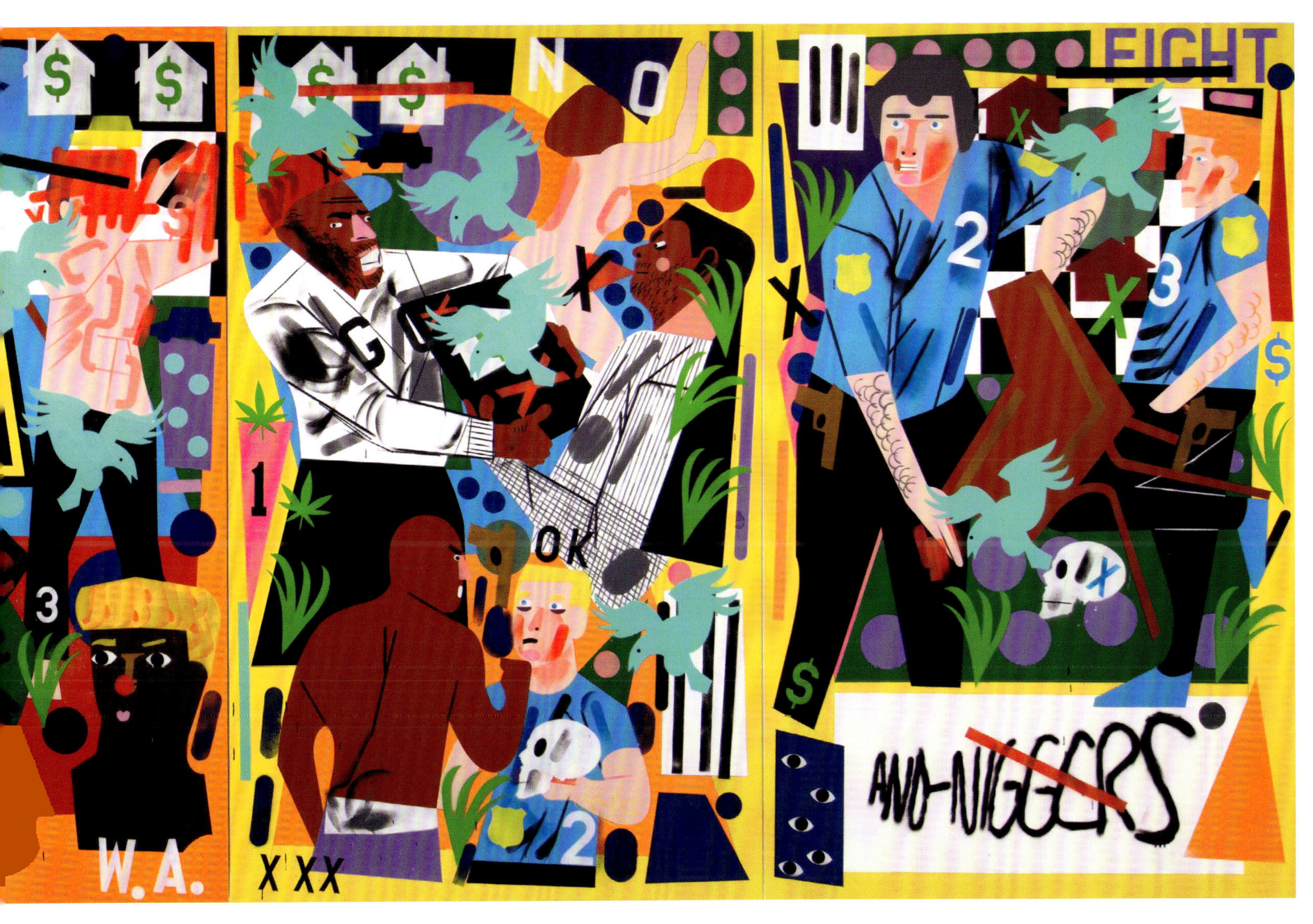
NO
FIGHT
OK
AND NIGGERS
W.A.
XXX

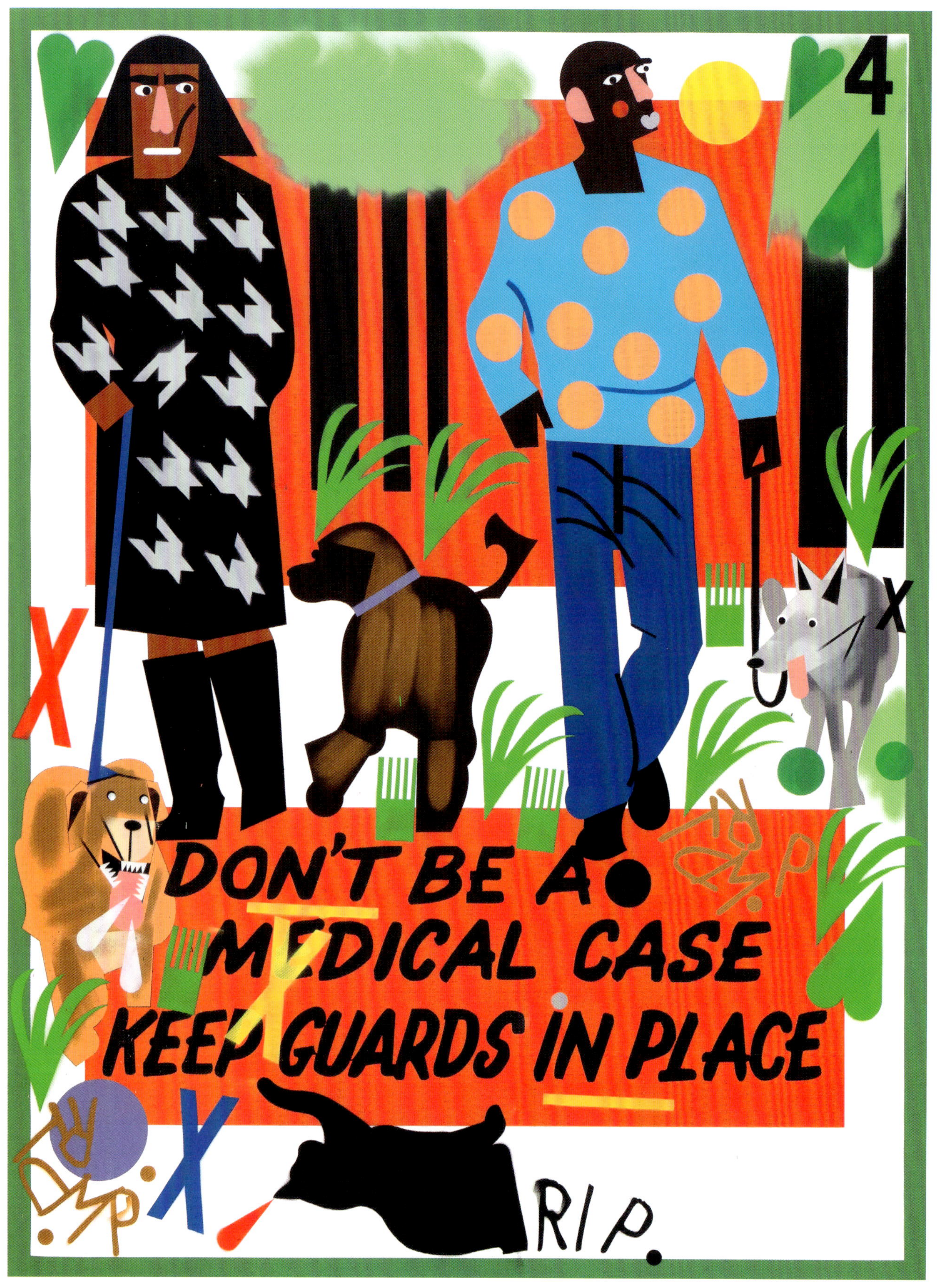

Pooh-Pooh, 2017

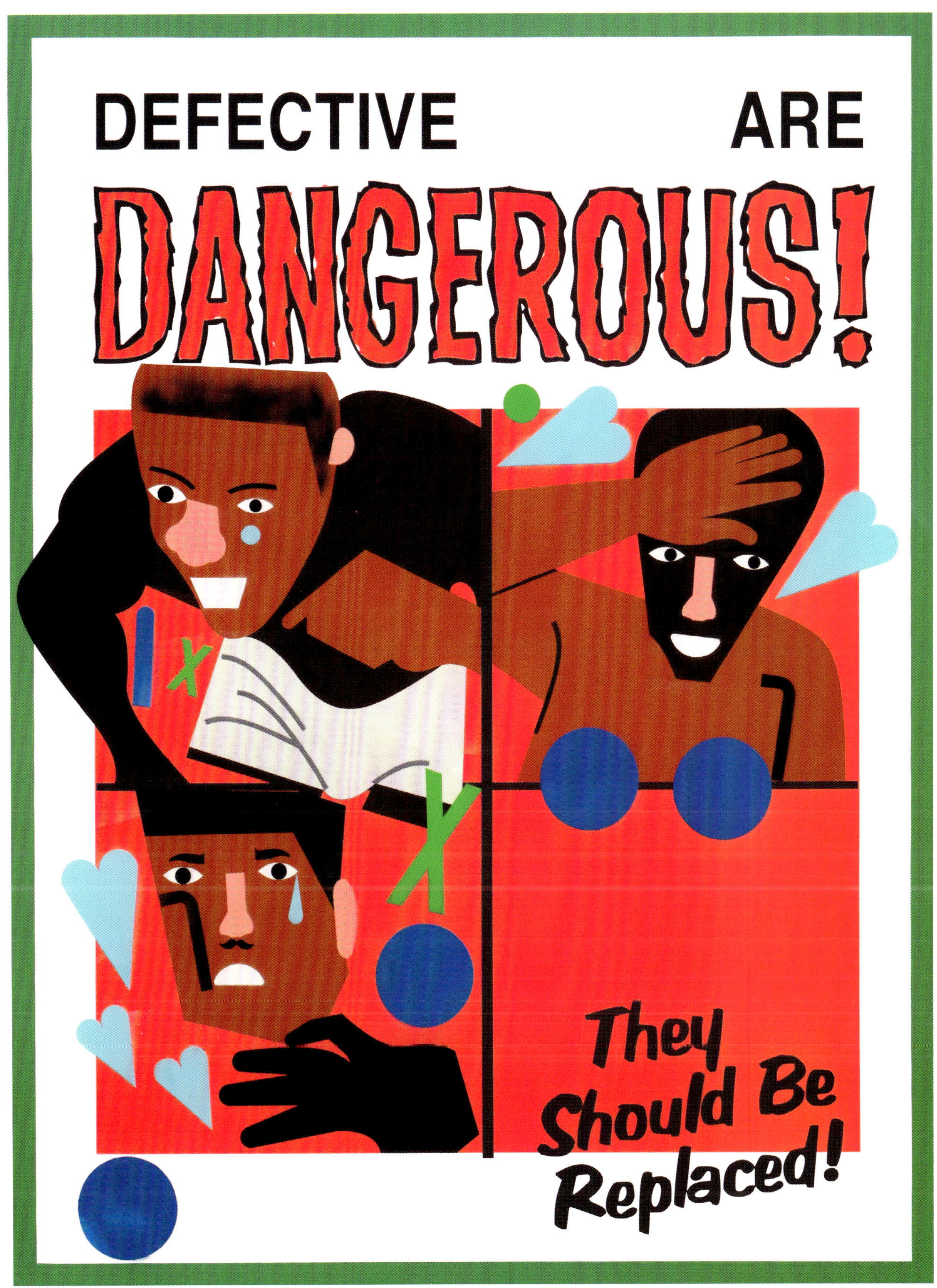

Non Action Satisfaction, 2017

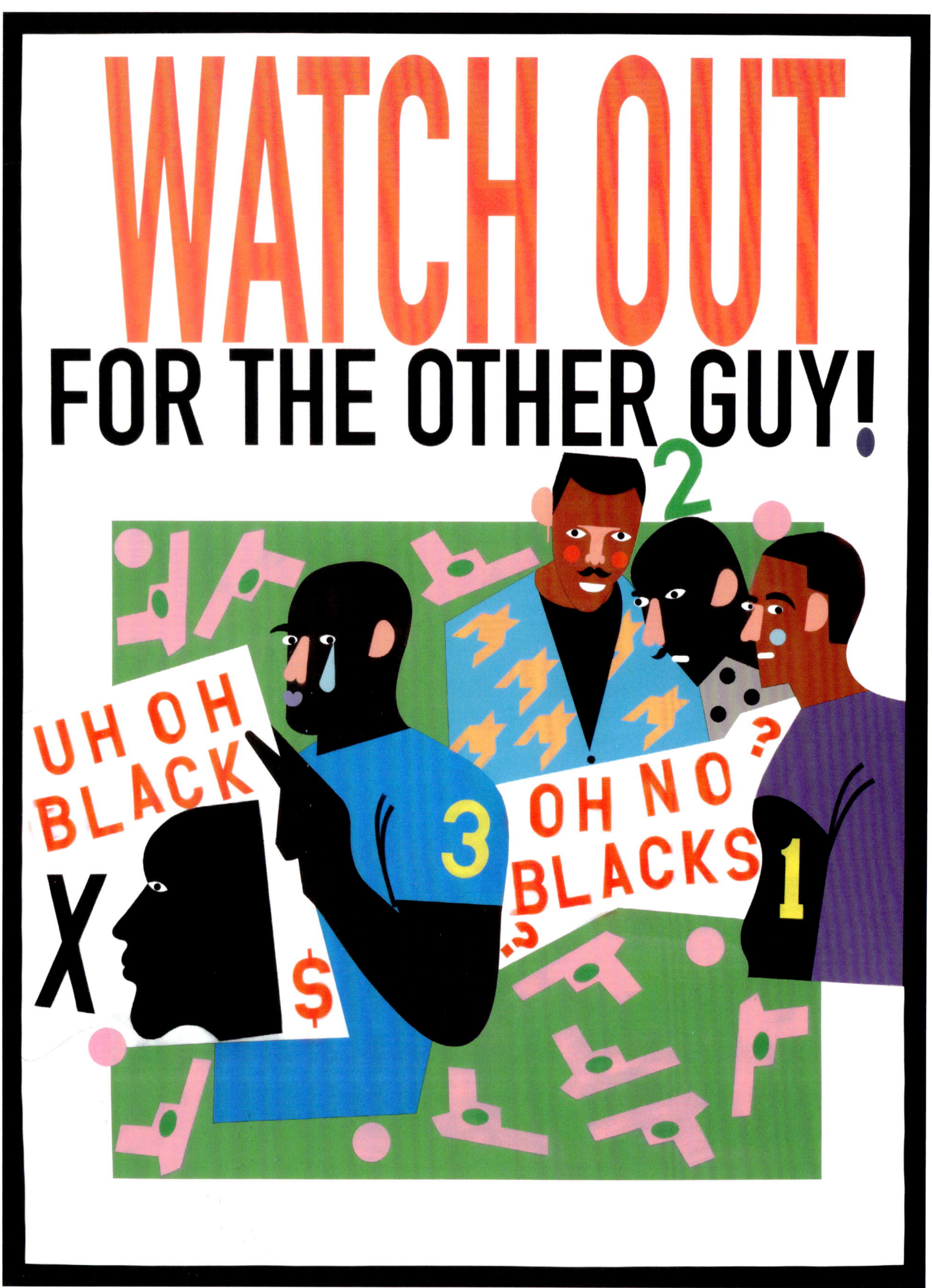

Guns and Butter, 2017

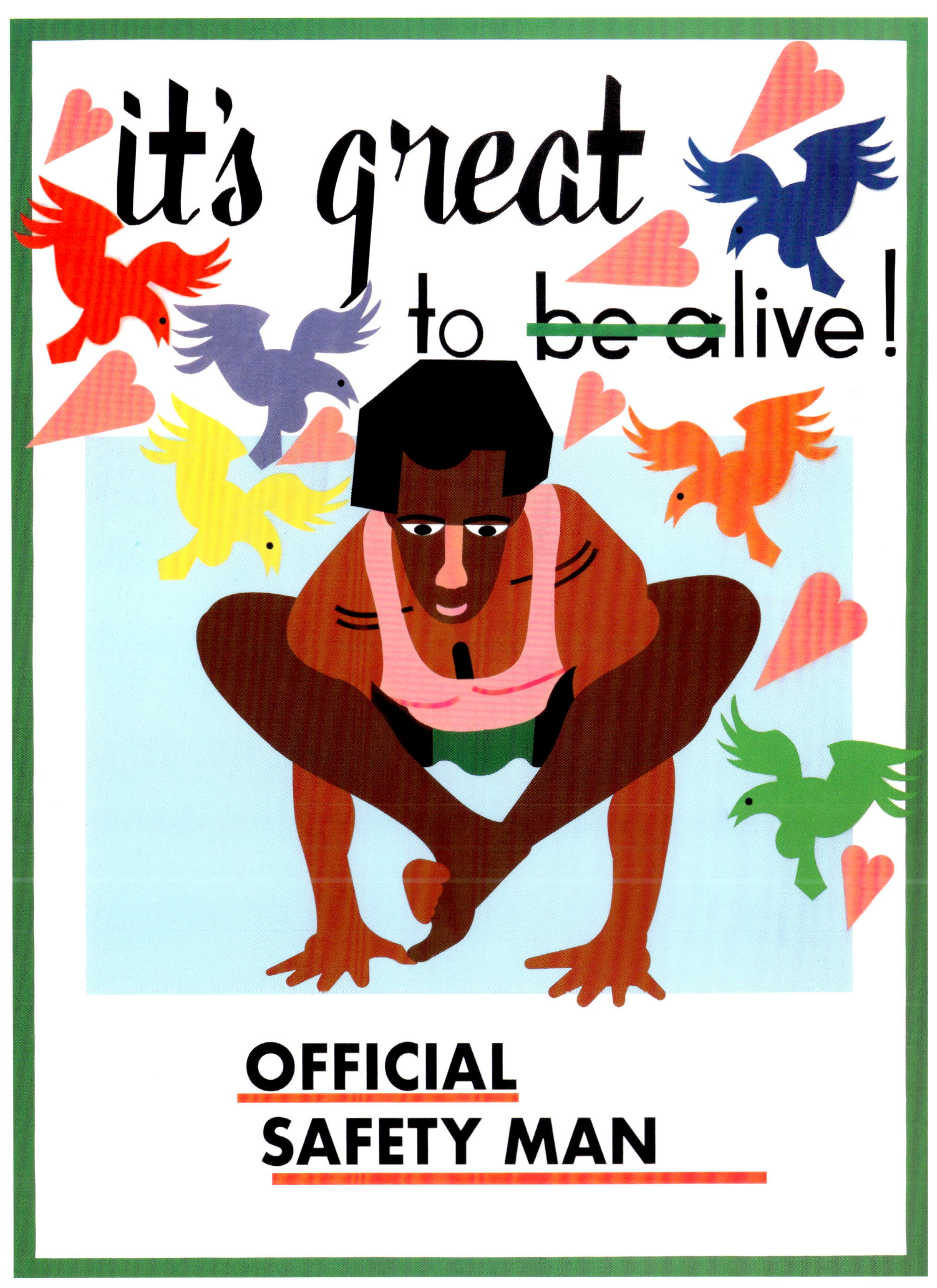

In The Land Without Feelings, 2017

PUBLIC

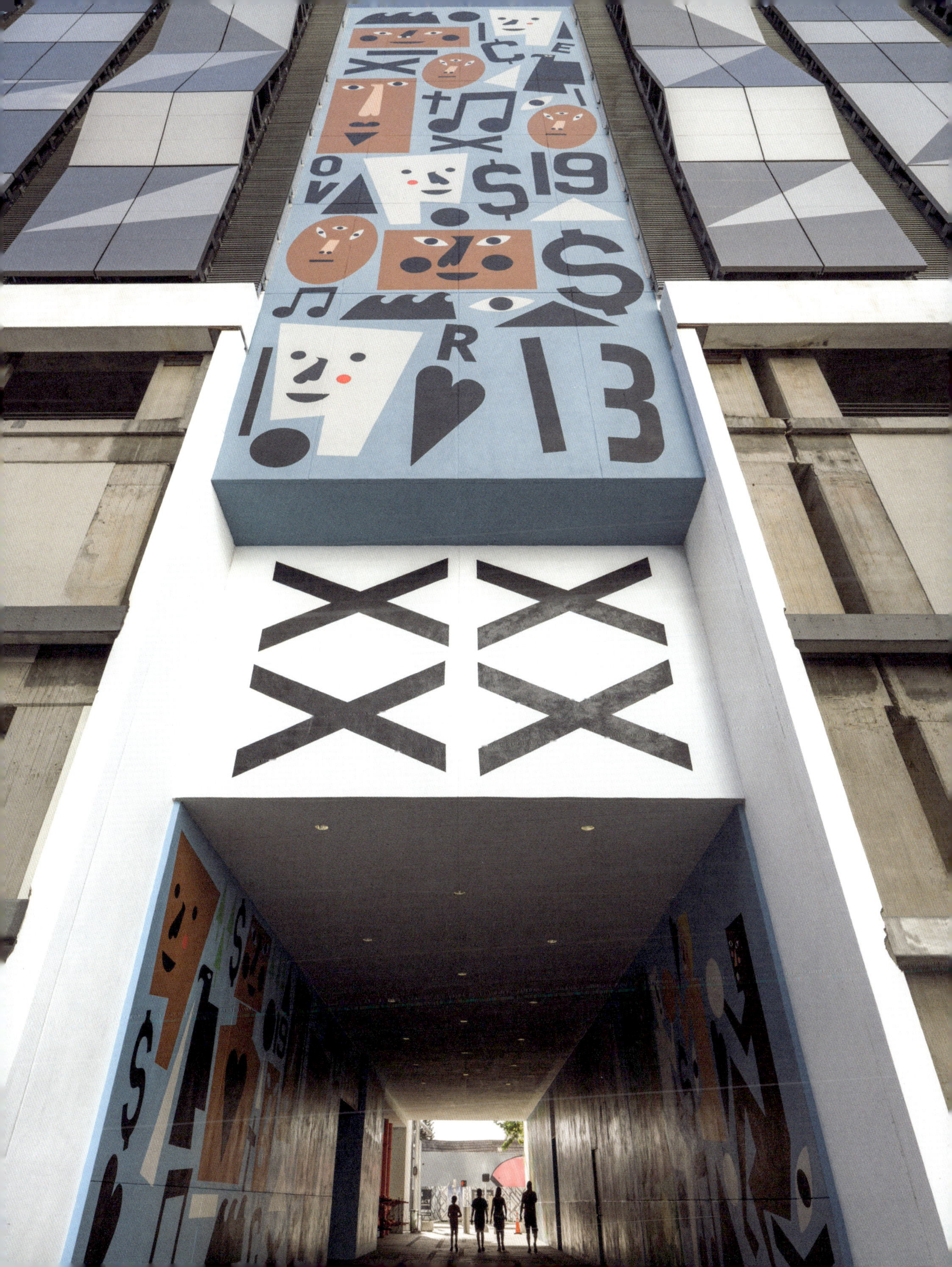

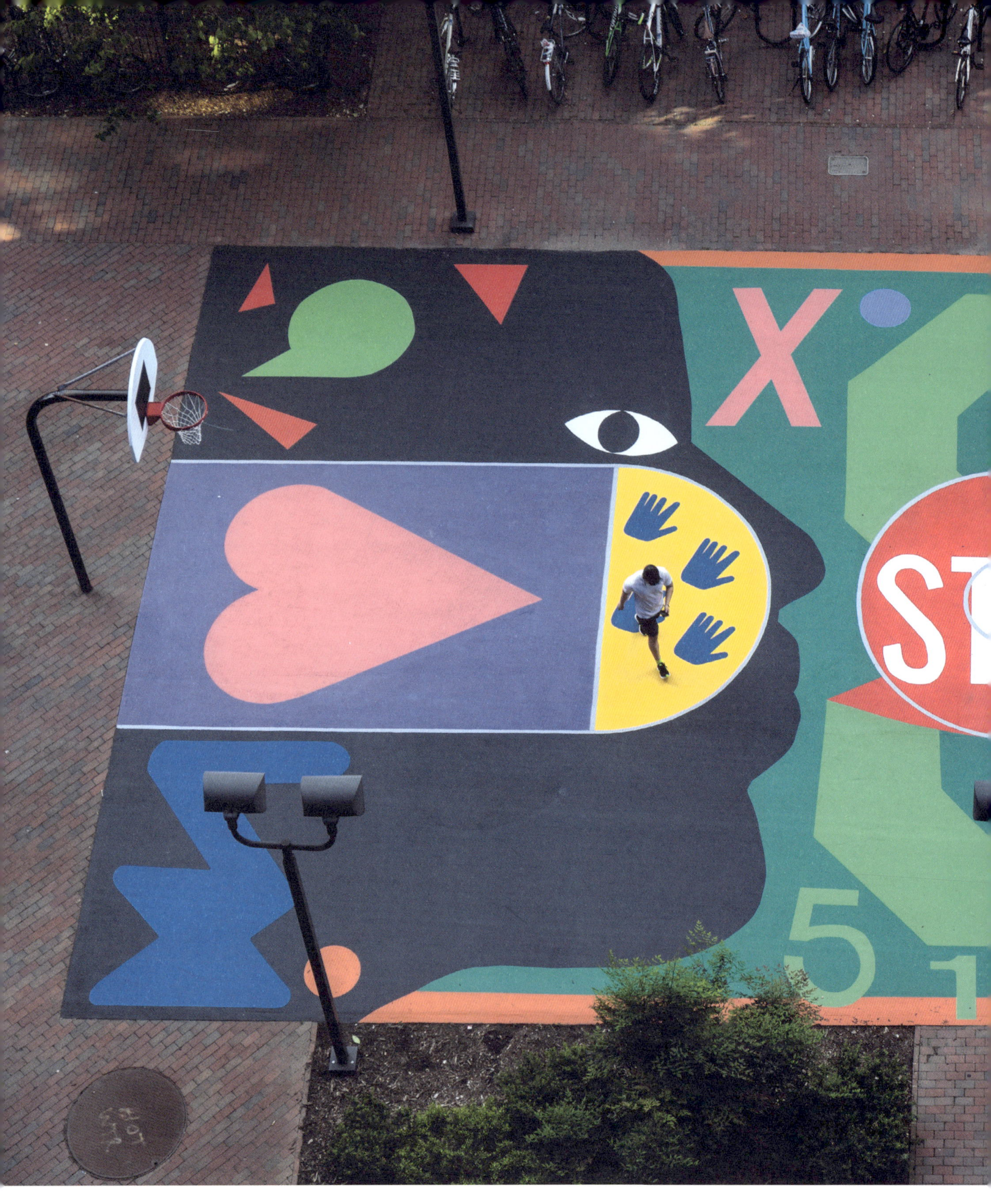

[PREVIOUS] R&R, 2022
Miami Worldcenter, Miami, FL

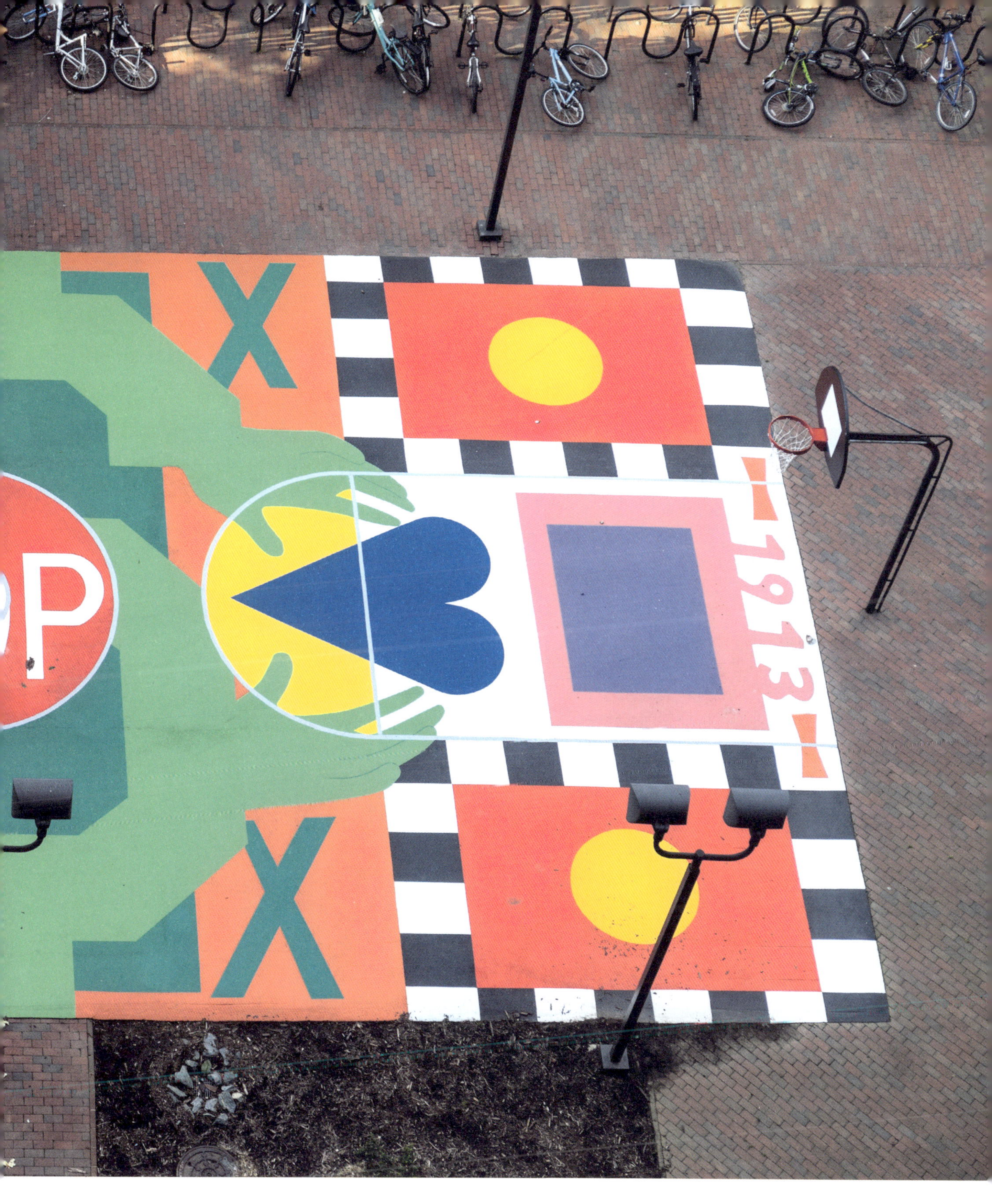

Mural for the Morrison Residence Hall basketball court, 2018
University of North Carolina at Chapel Hill

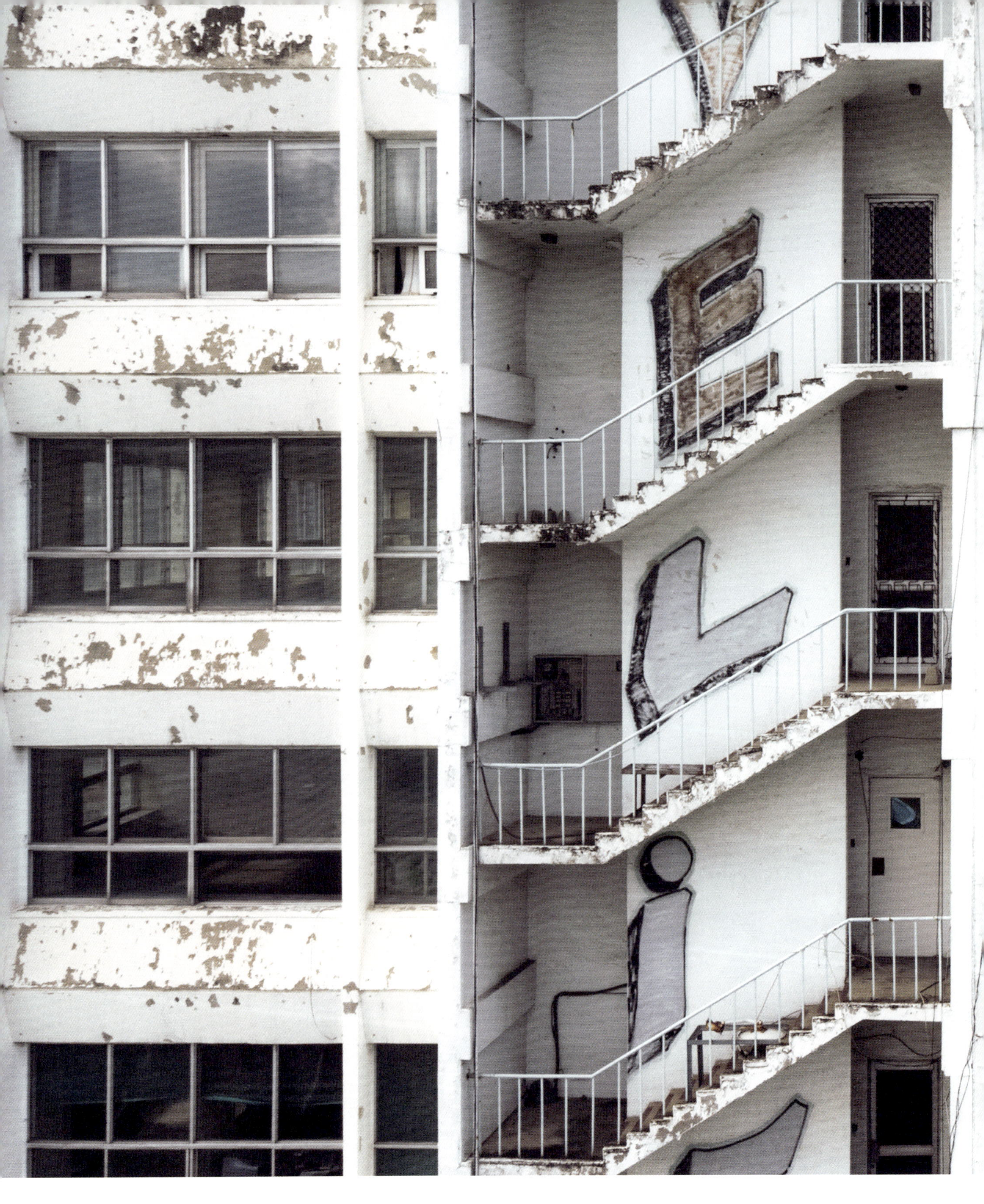

Untitled, 2018
Imagined Borders: Gwangju Biennale, Gwangju, South Korea

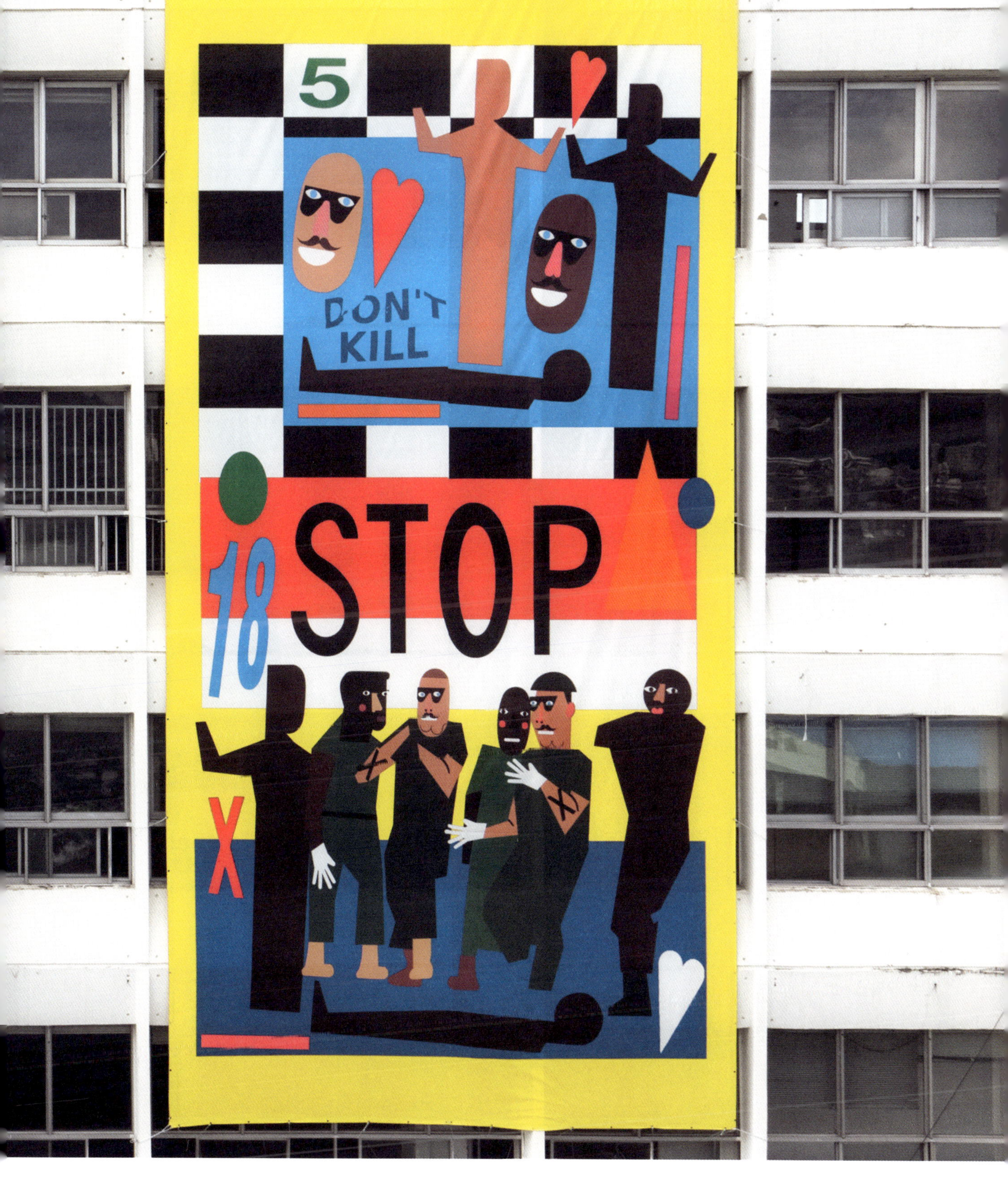
5
DON'T
KILL
18
STOP
X

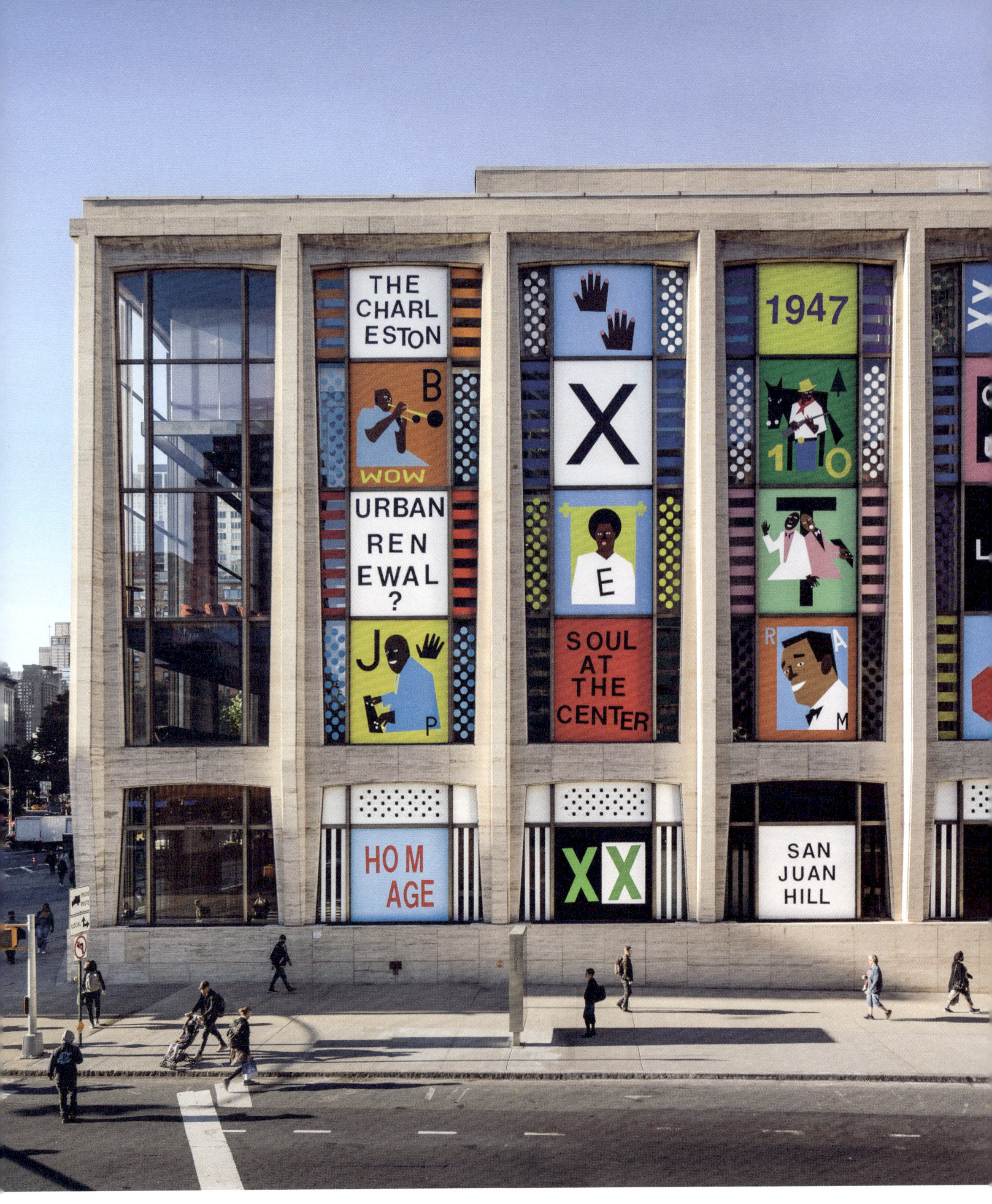

San Juan Heal, 2022
Facade of David Geffen Hall, Lincoln Center, New York, NY

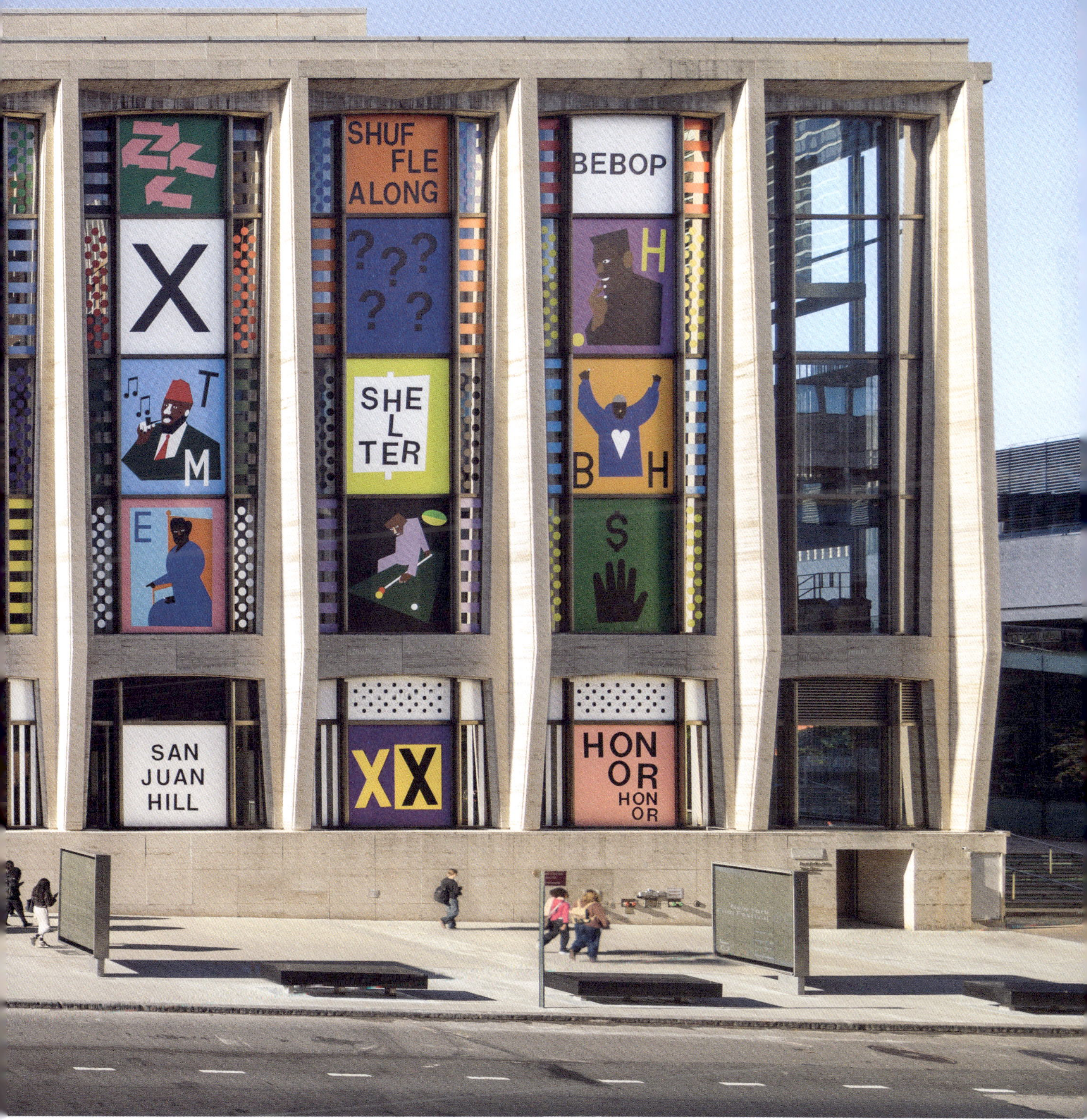

X
T
M
E
SHUF FLE ALONG
? ? ? ? ?
SHE L TER
BEBOP
H
B H
$
SAN JUAN HILL
XX
HON OR
HON OR

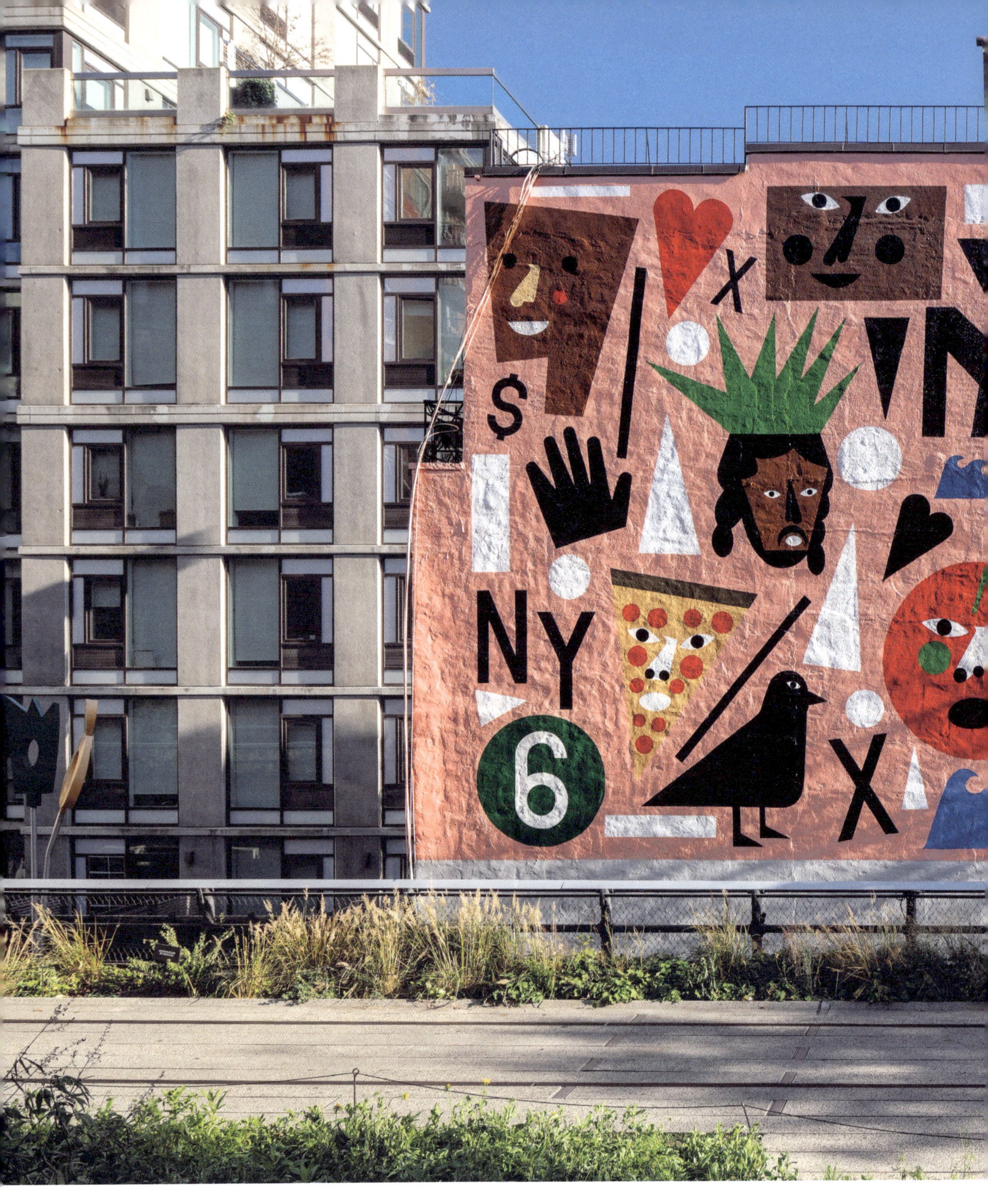

NYC LOVE, 2022
The High Line, New York, NY

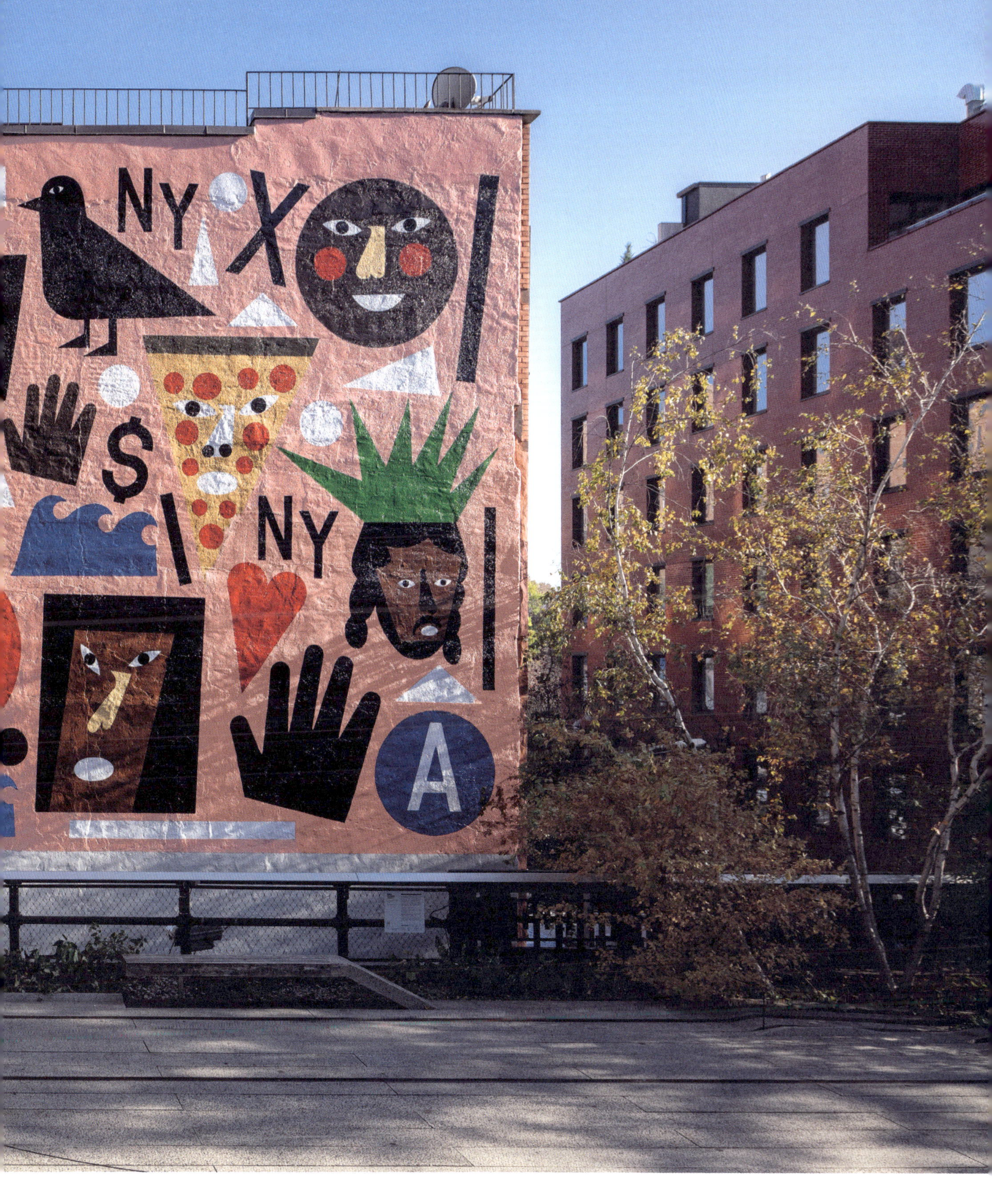
NY
$
NY
A

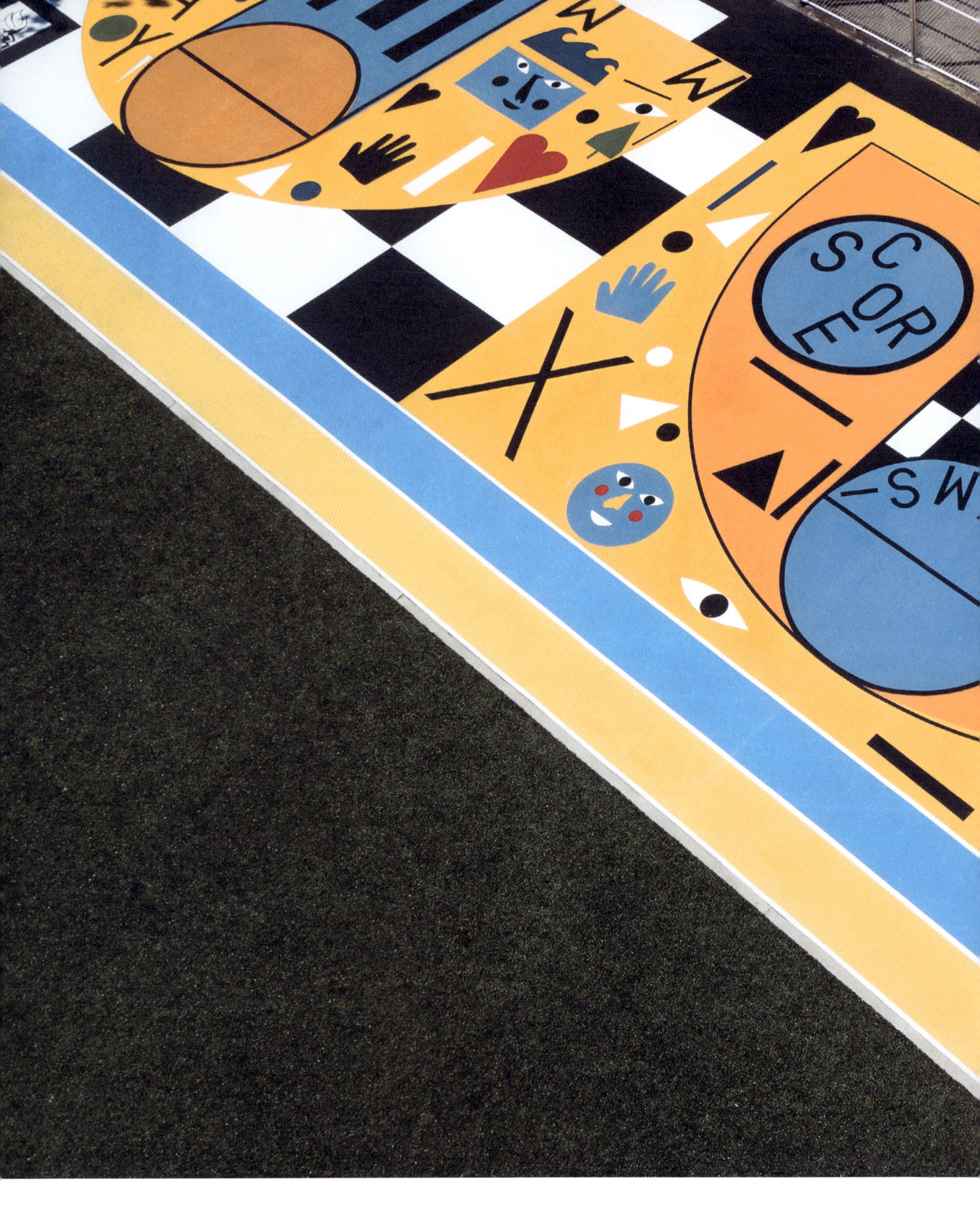

Schoolyard basketball court, 2022, Juan Morel Campos Secondary School, Brooklyn, NY

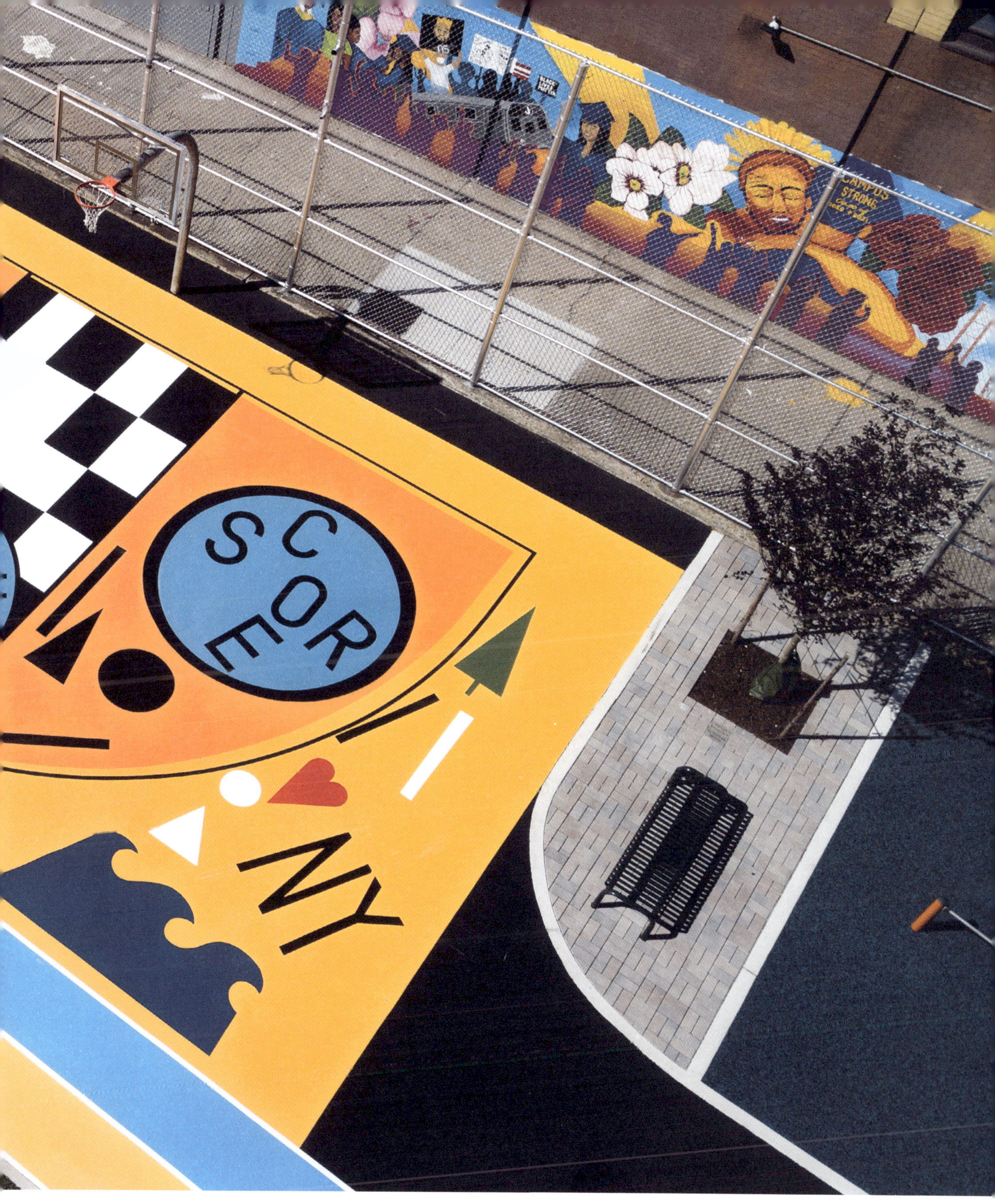
CAMPUS
STRONG
NY

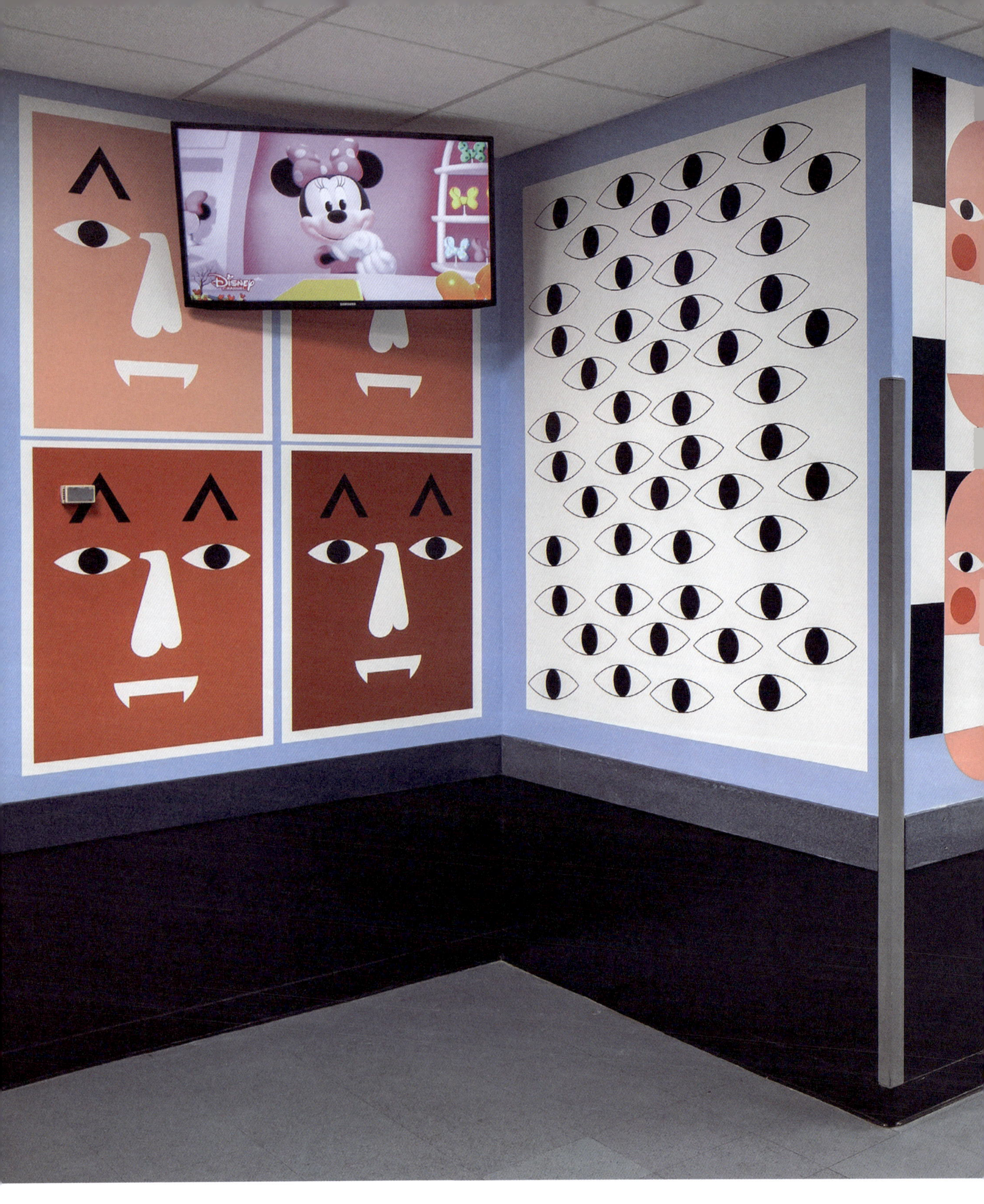

Fun #1, 2022
Pediatric Ambulatory Clinic at NYC Health + Hospitals/Elmhurst, Queens, NY
In collaboration with RxART

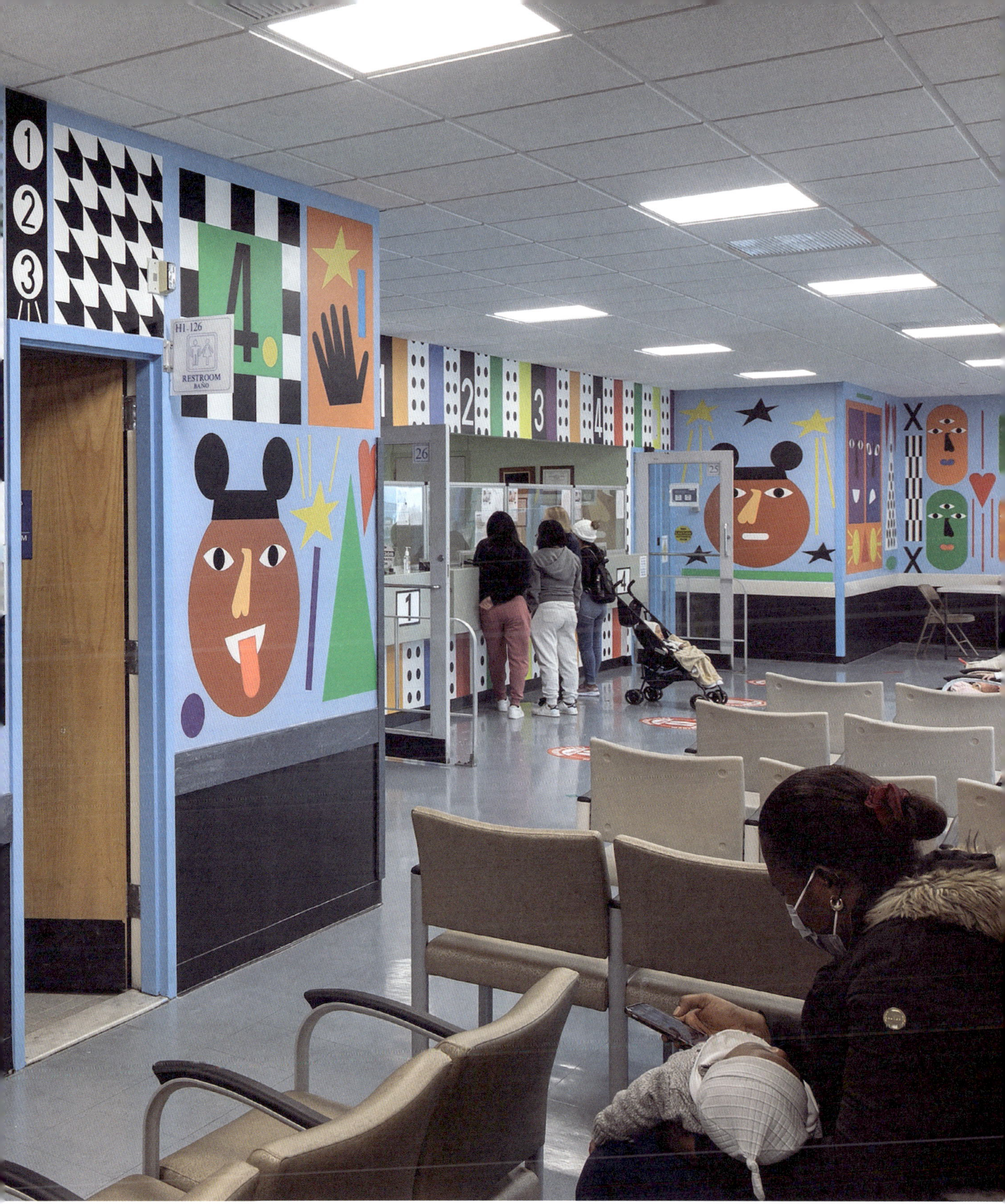
H1-126
RESTROOM
BAÑO

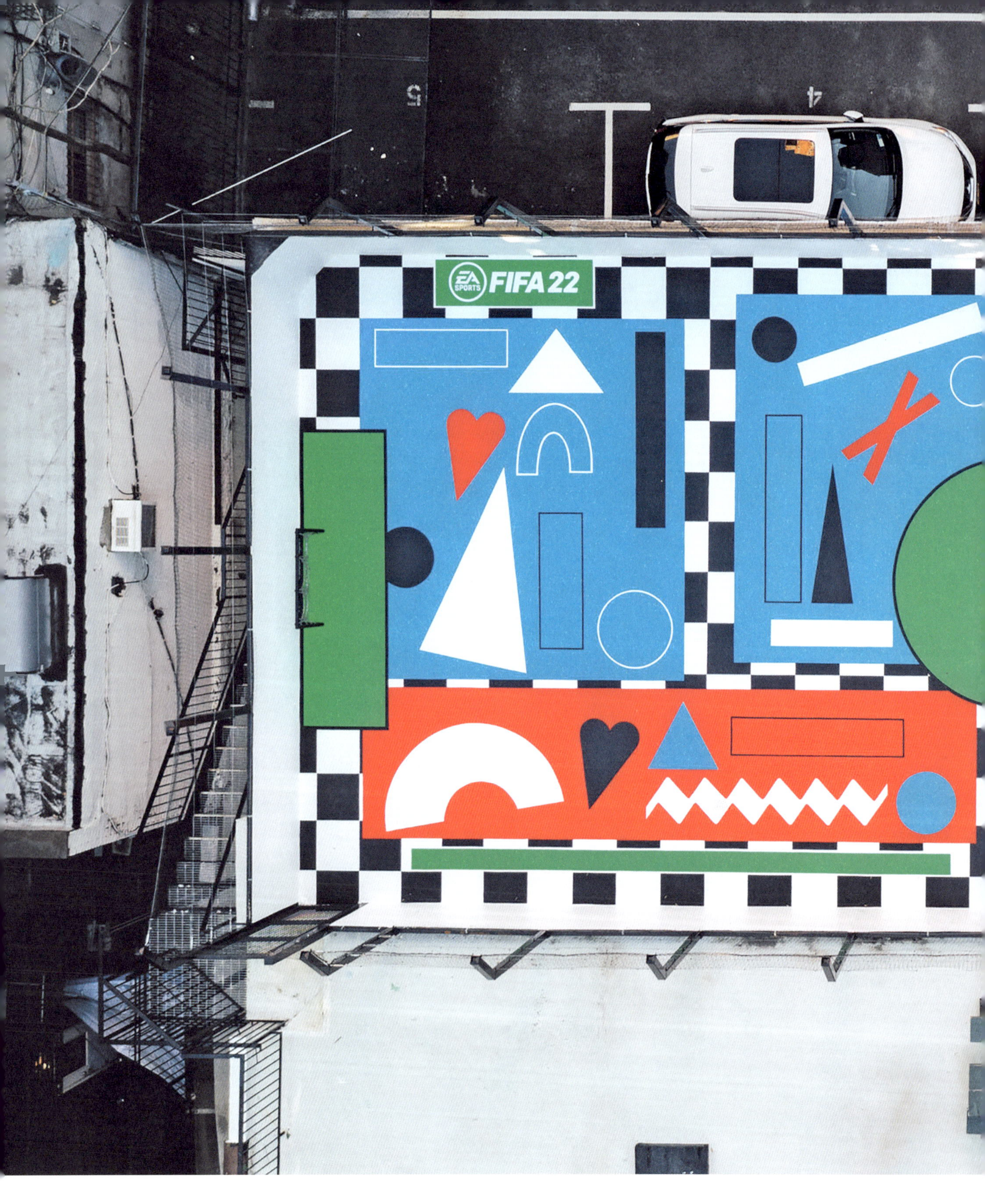

Mural for the launch of FIFA 22, 2022
In collaboration with EA Sports, at the Ground, New York, NY

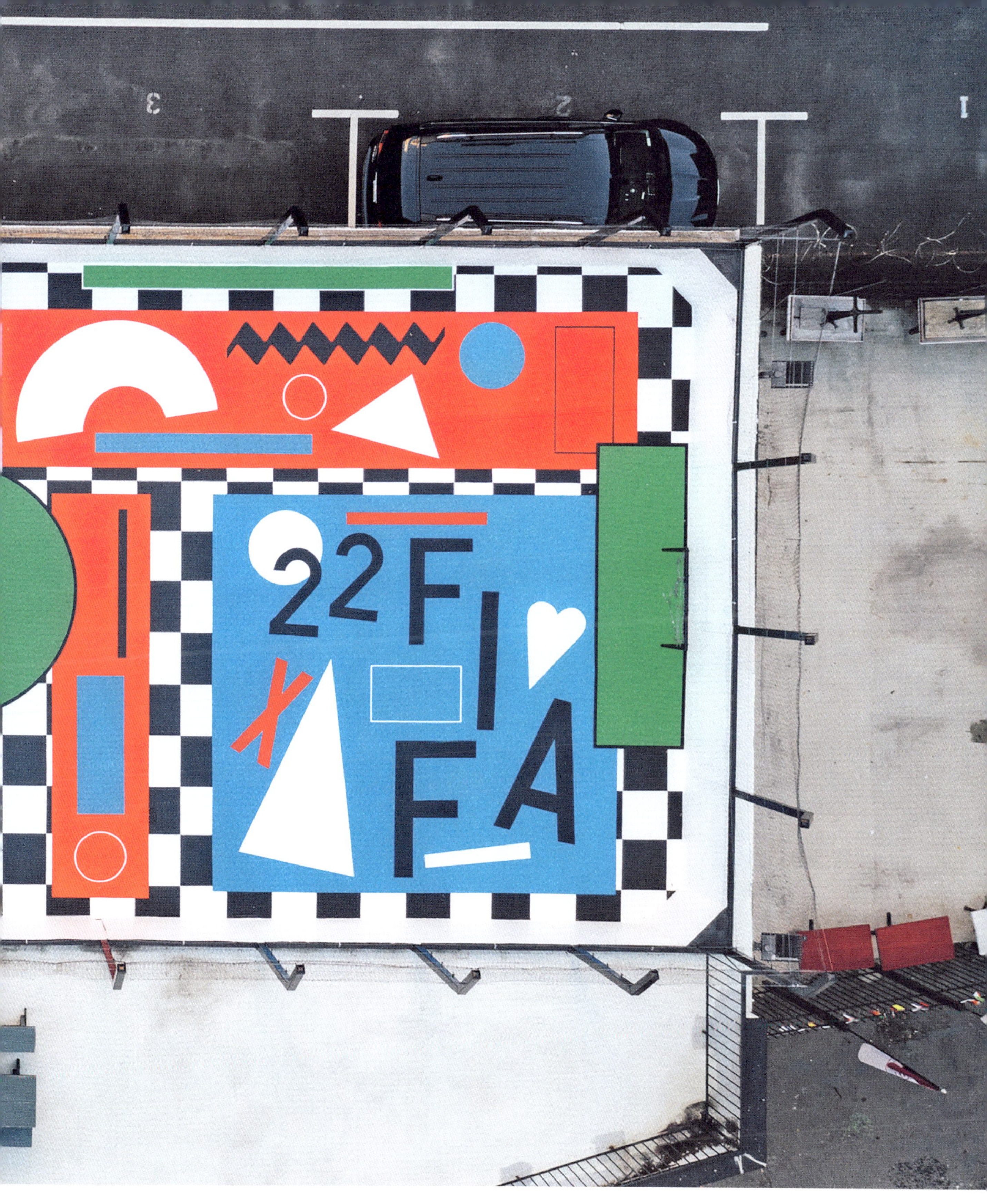

[OVERLEAF] Mull it Over, 2021
Mural for OZ Art NWA, Bentonville, AR

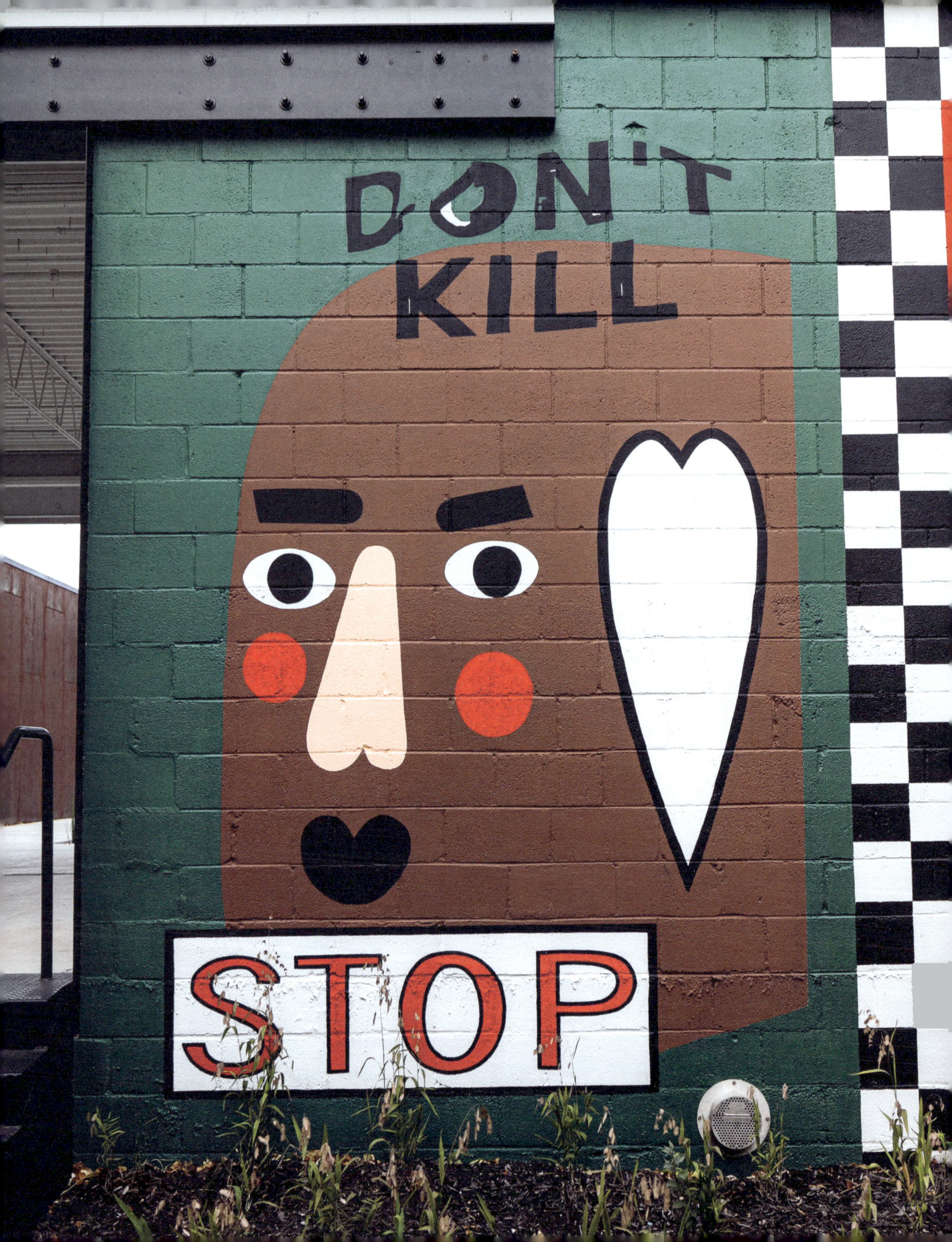
DON'T
KILL
STOP

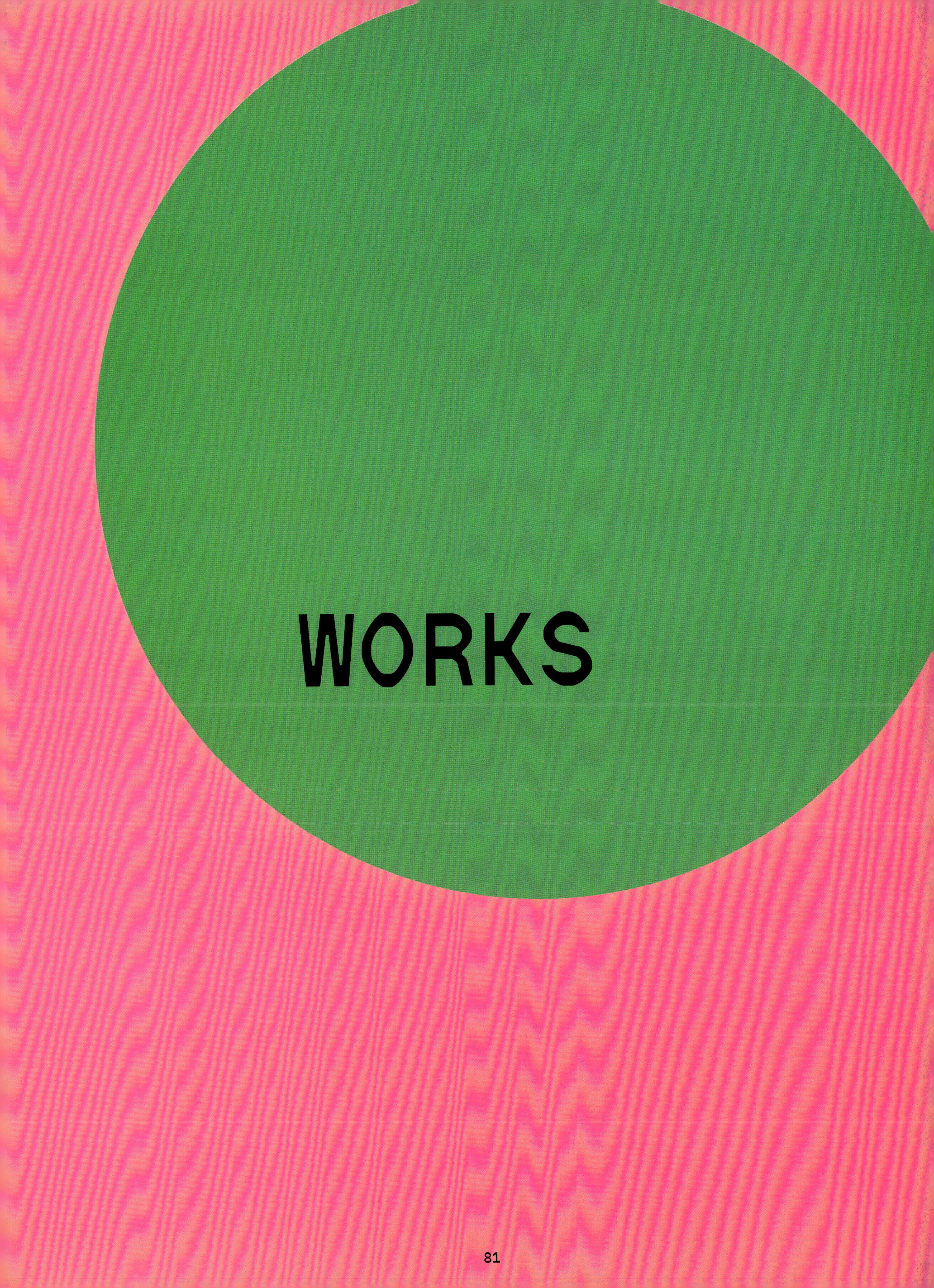

WORKS

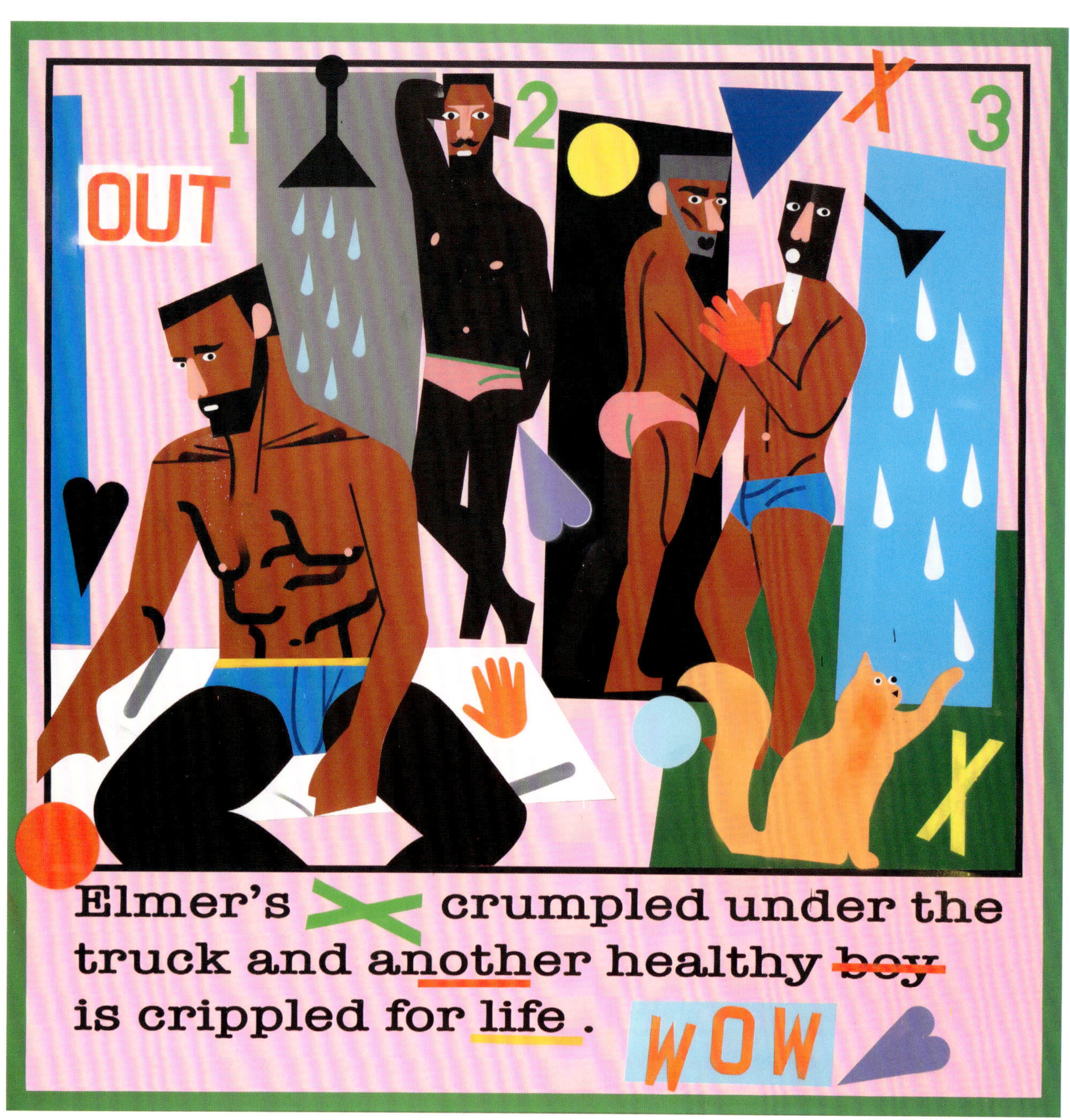

Fruit of the Womb, 2017

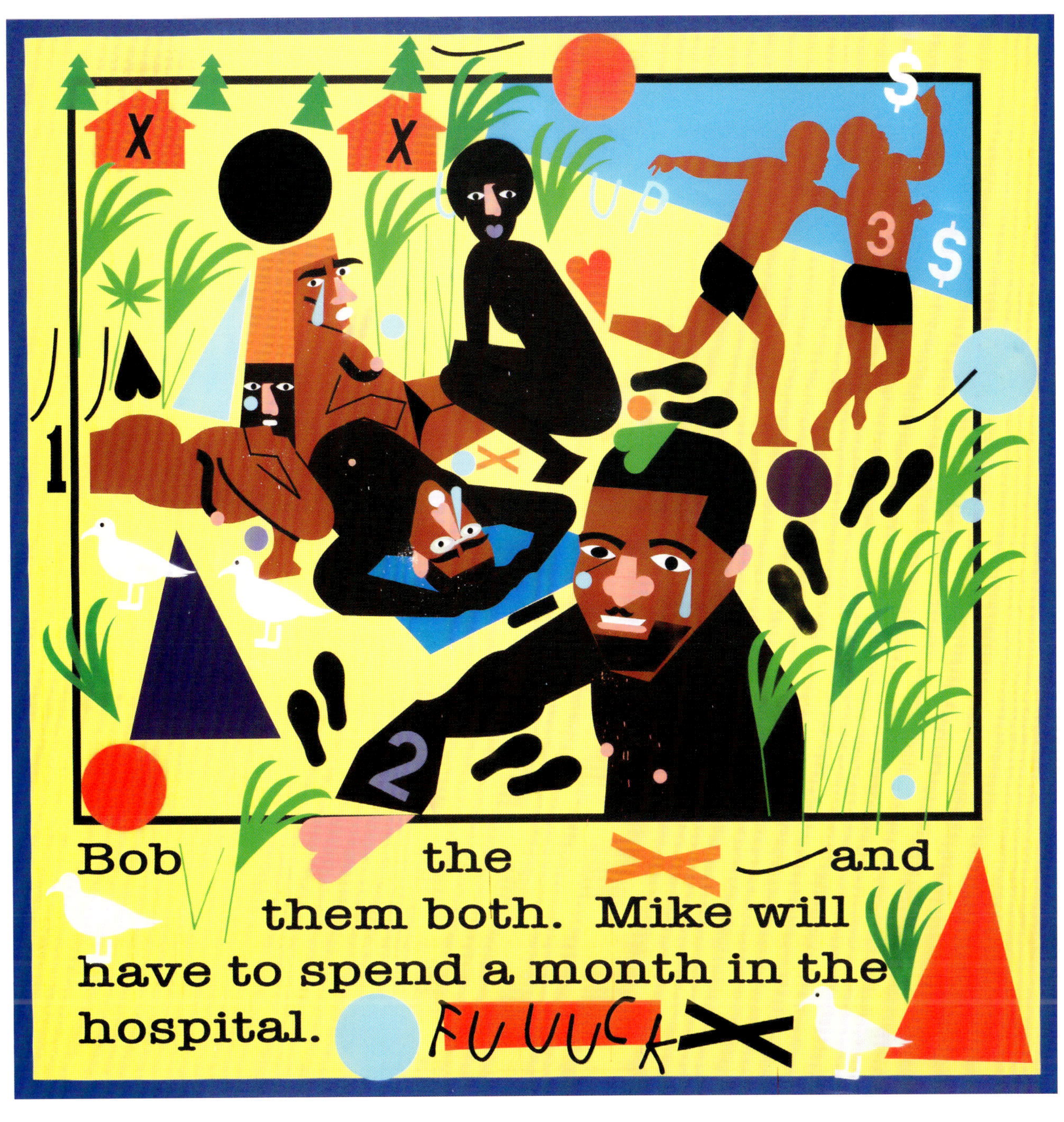

People at Peoples Beach, 2017

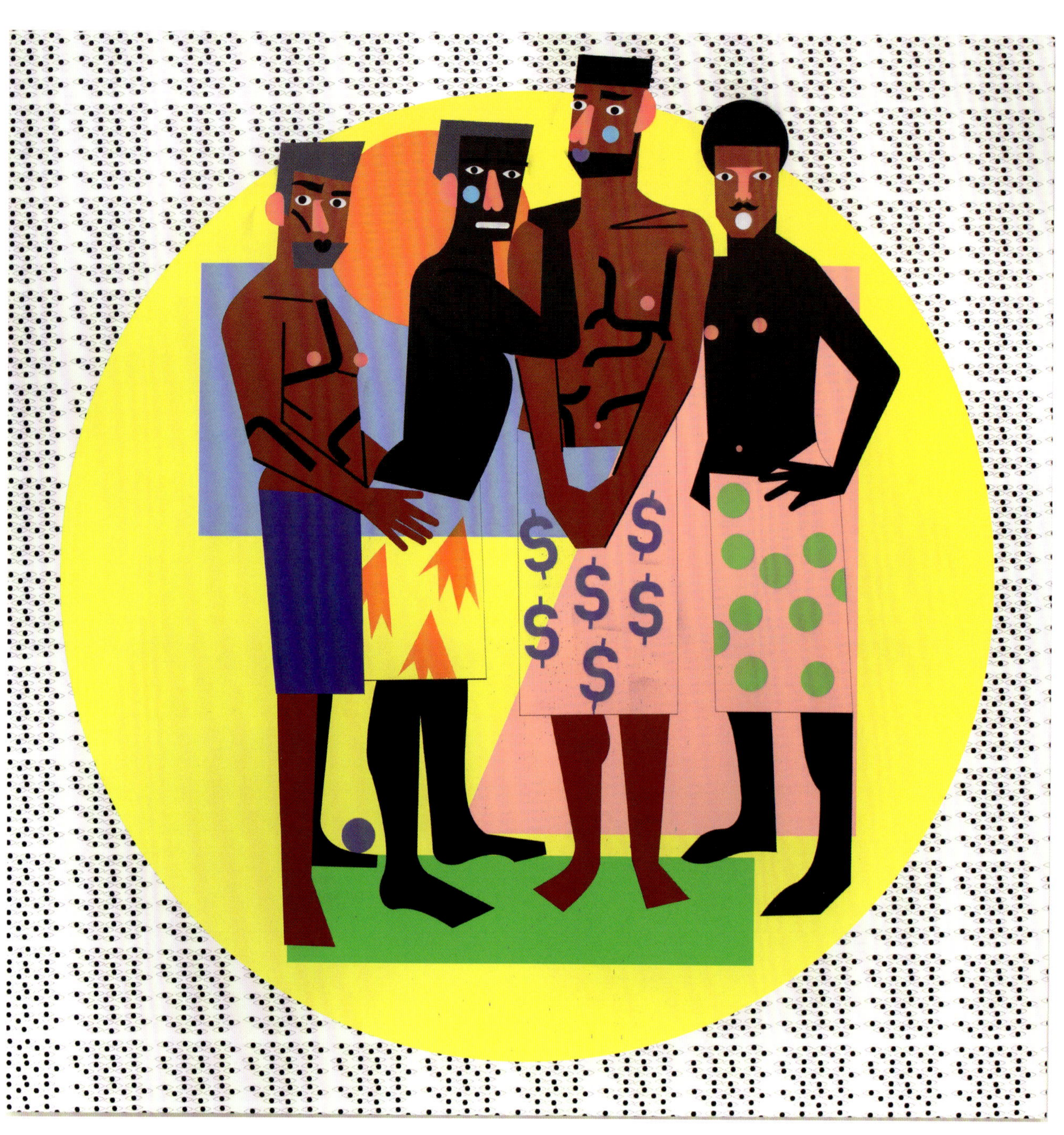

All These Flavors and You Choose to be Salty, 2017

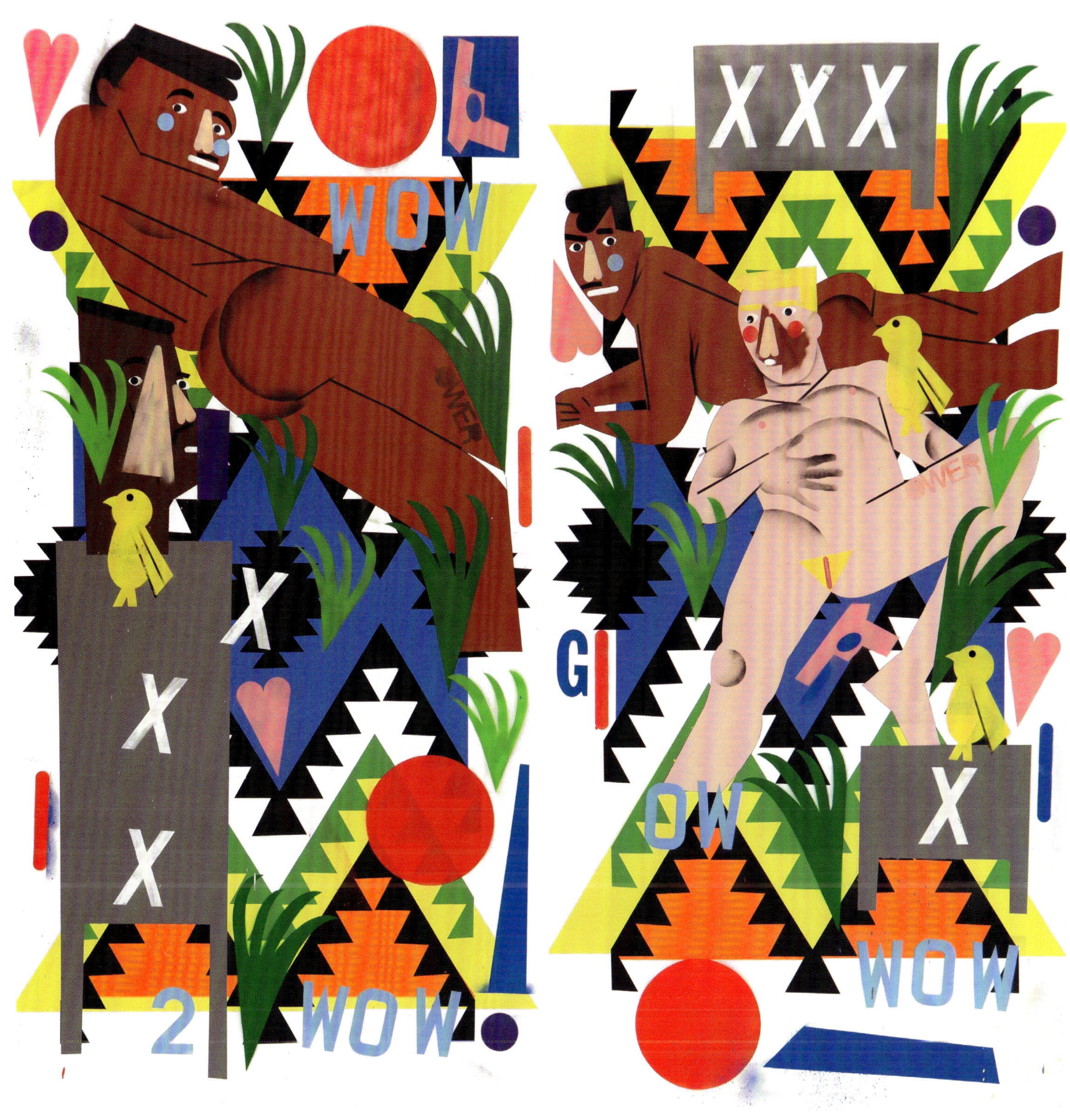

Si, Mister, 2017

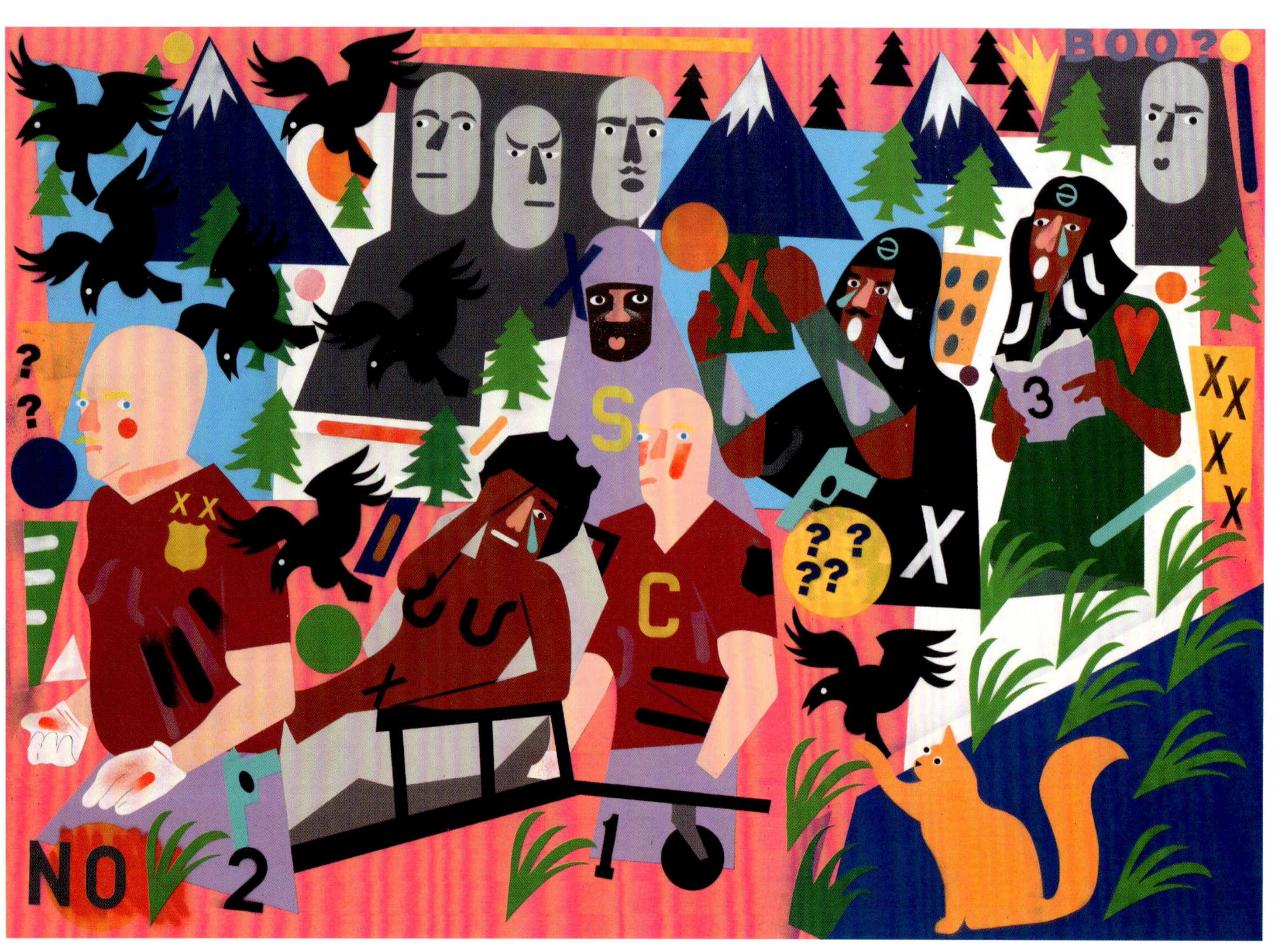

Black and Blues, 2017

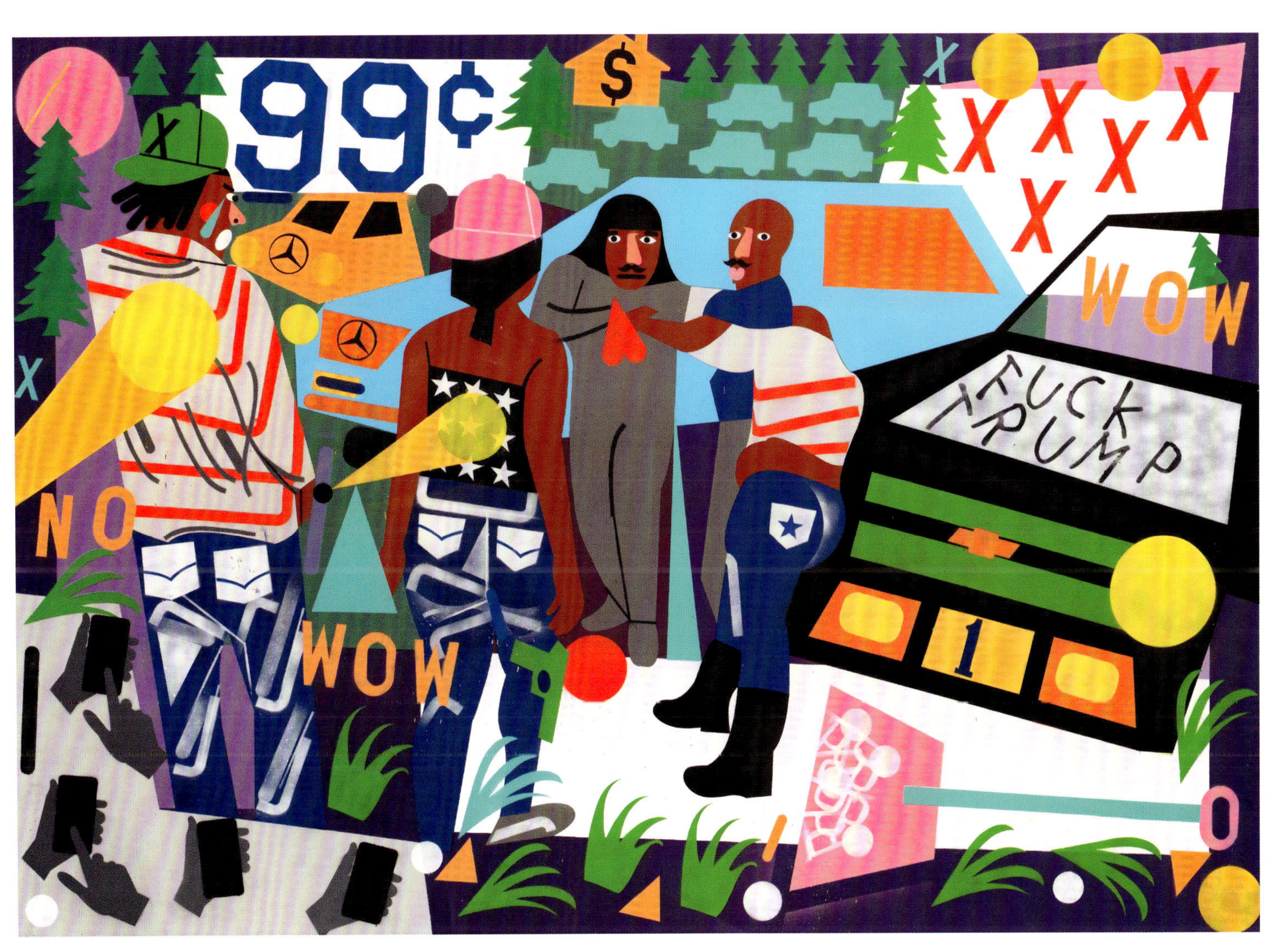

Penny Dreadful, 2017

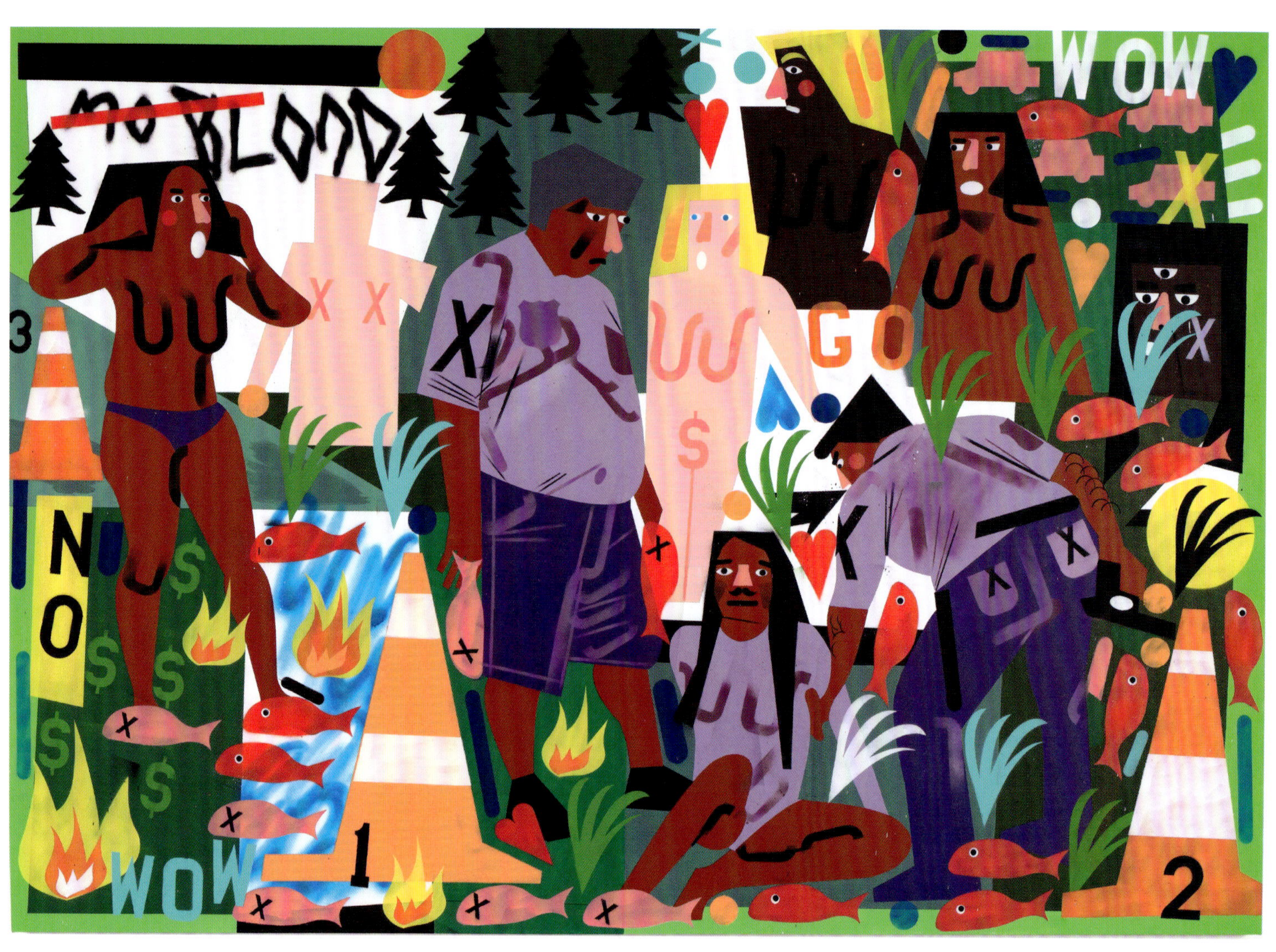

White River Fish Kill, 2017

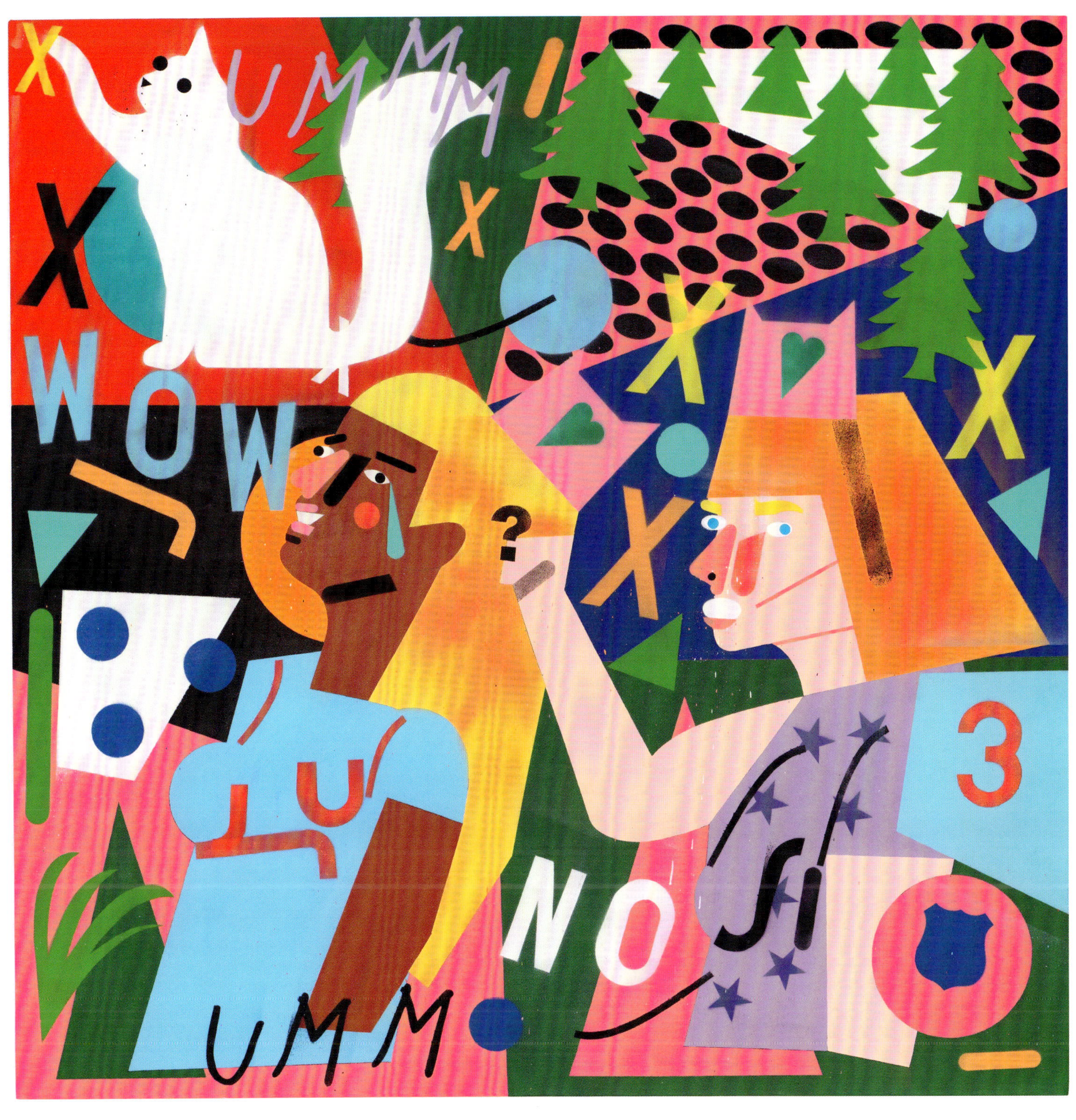

Whet, 2017

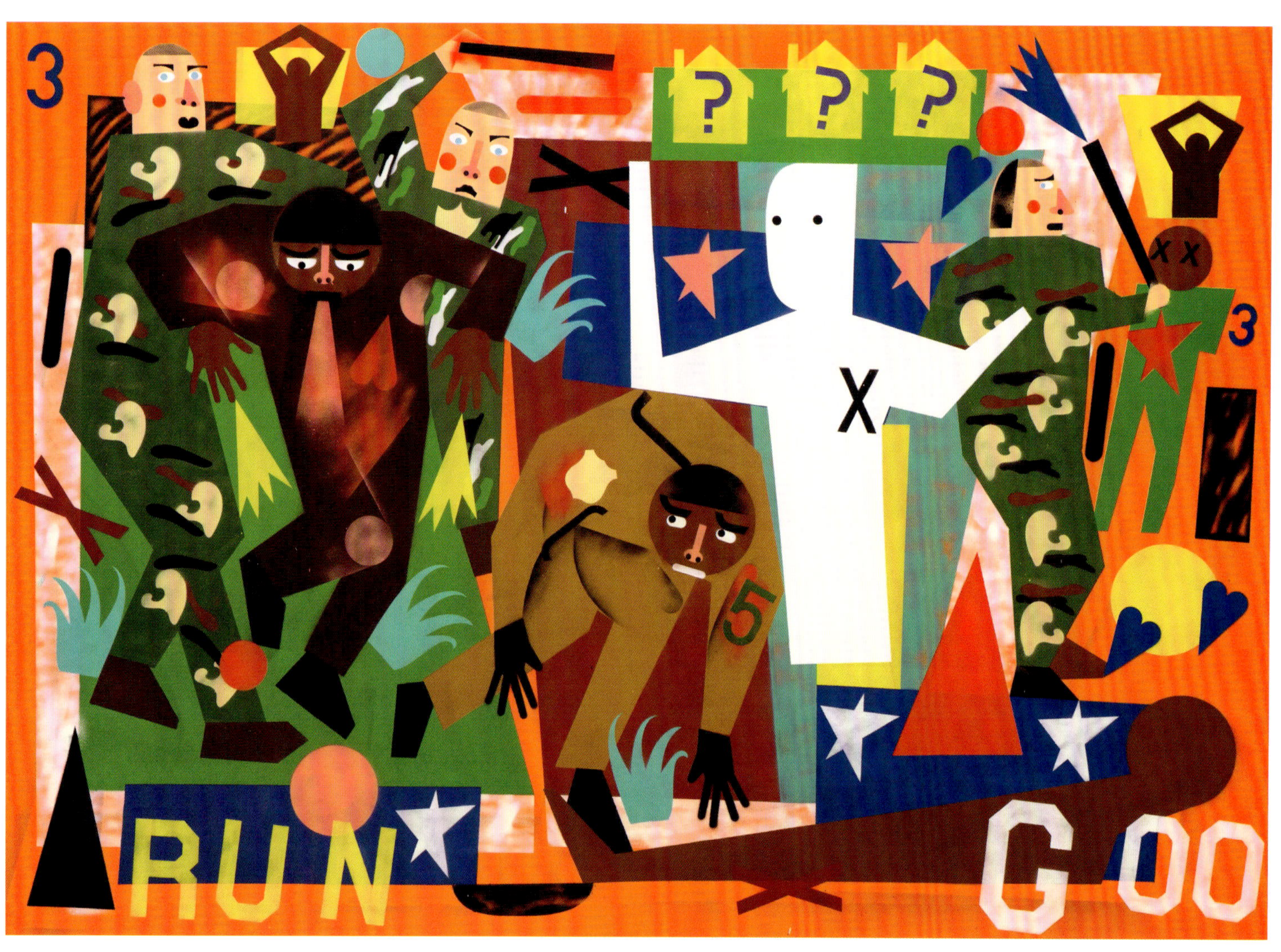

Always Ready, Always There, 2018

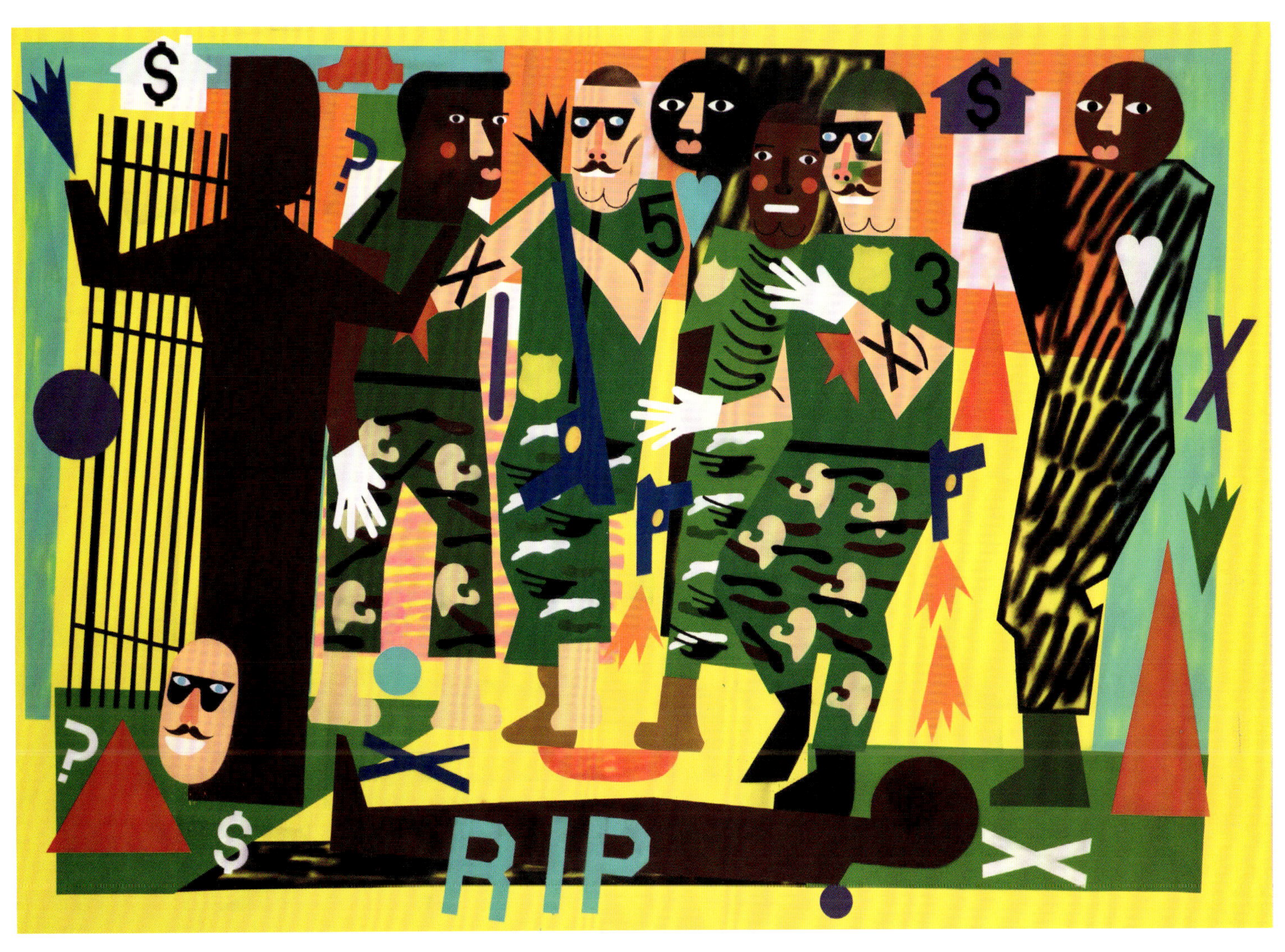

Anytime, Anyplace, 2018

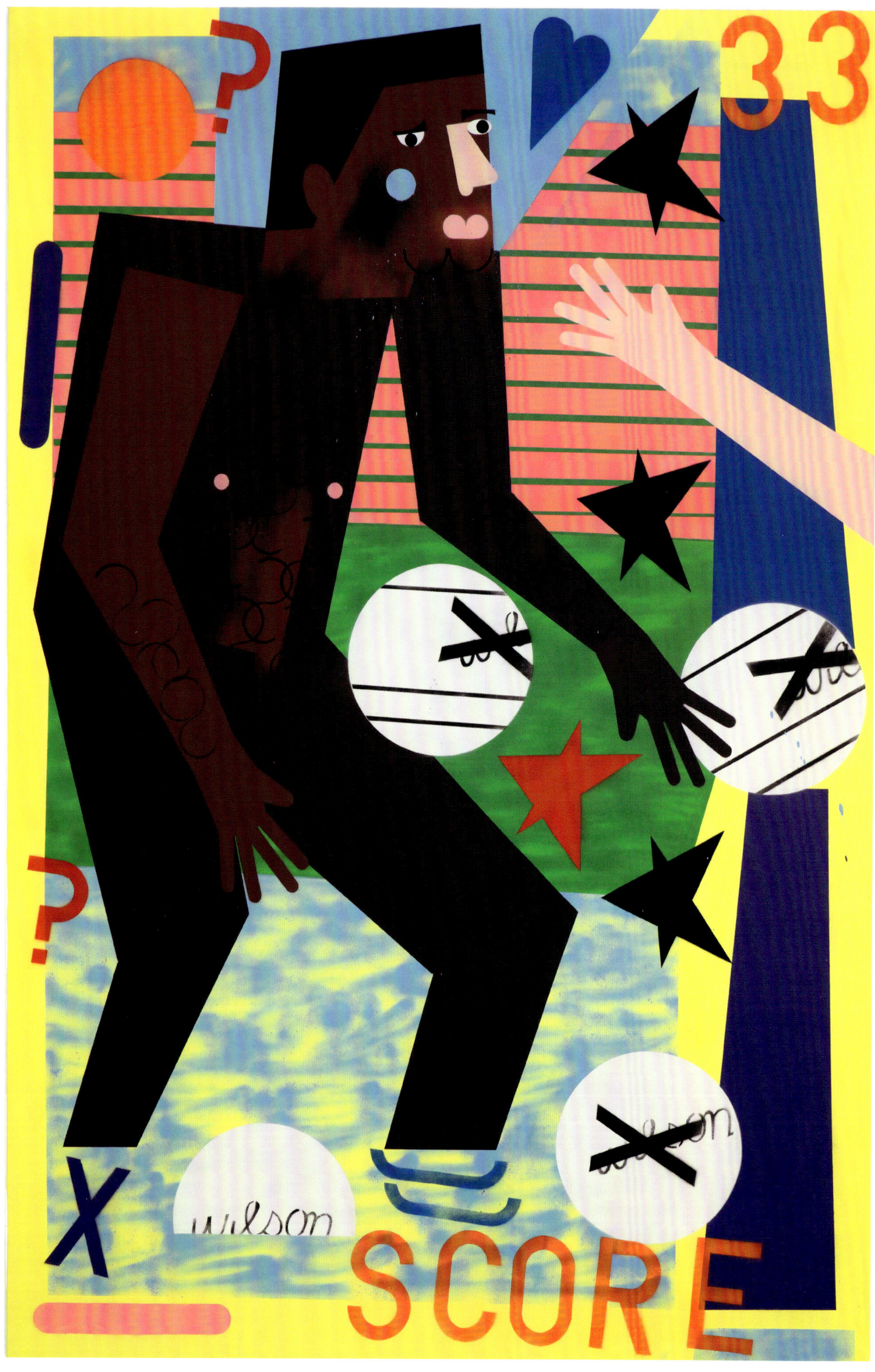

#33, 2018

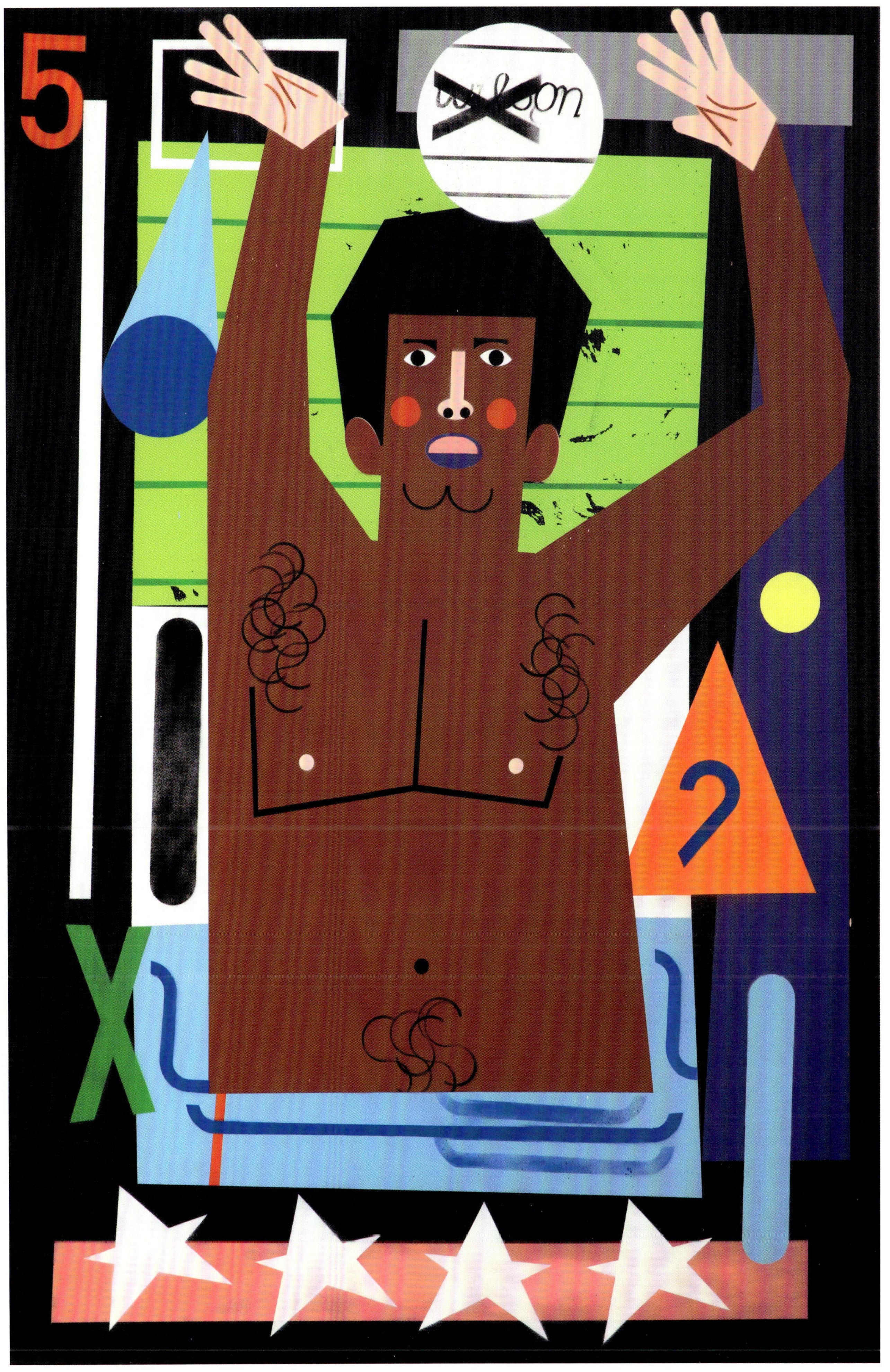

#5, 2018

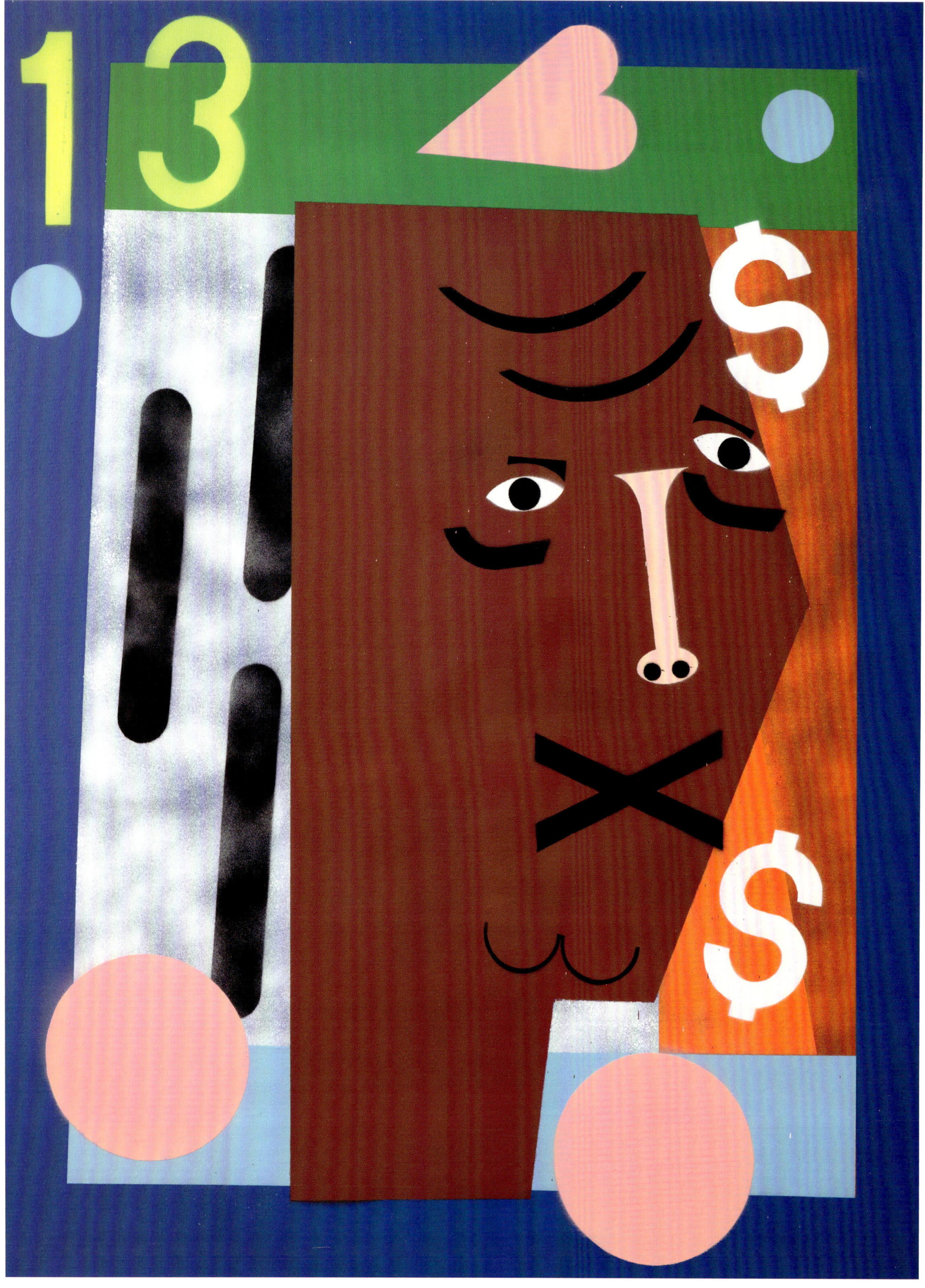

#13, 2018

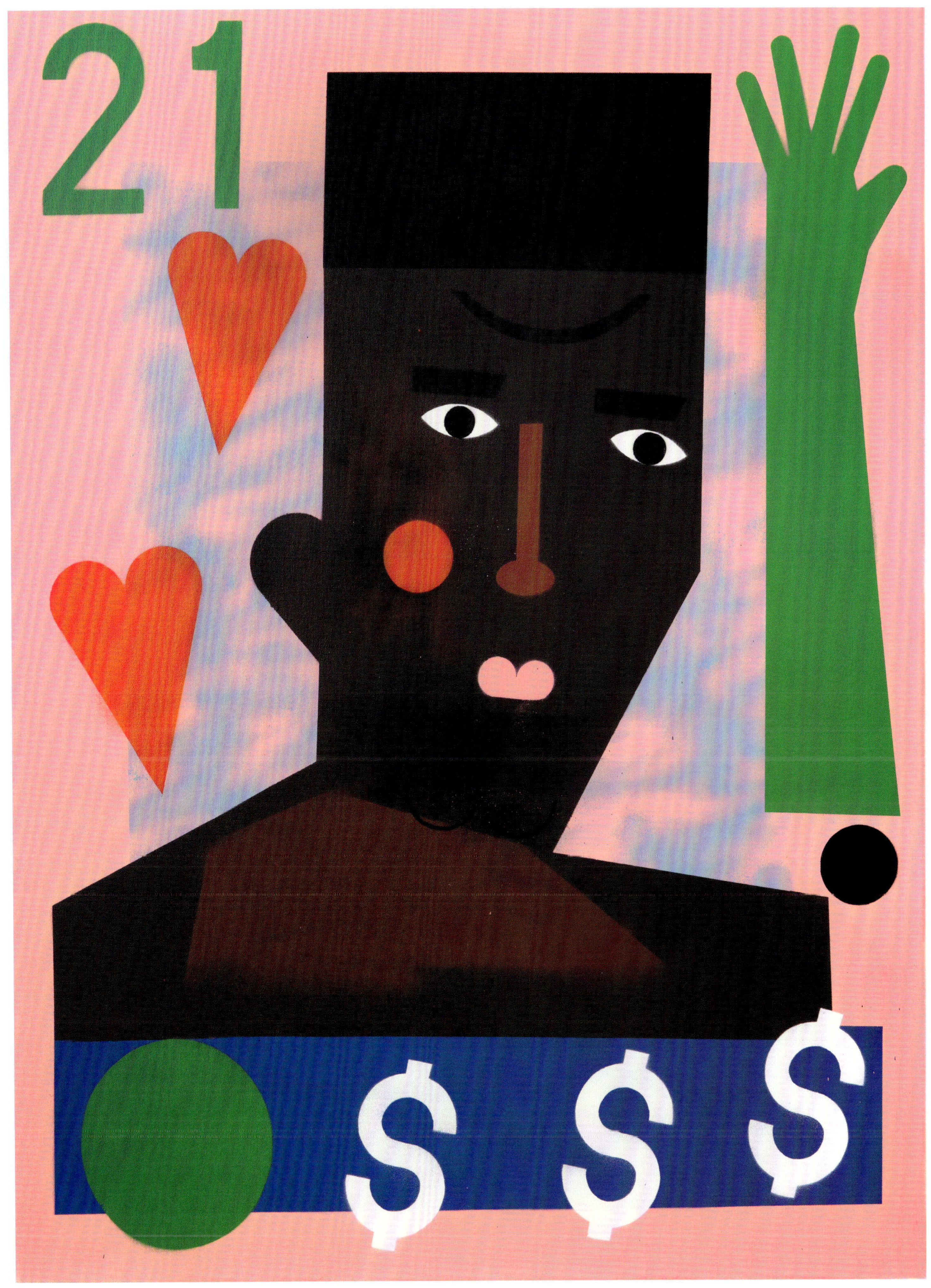

#21, 2018

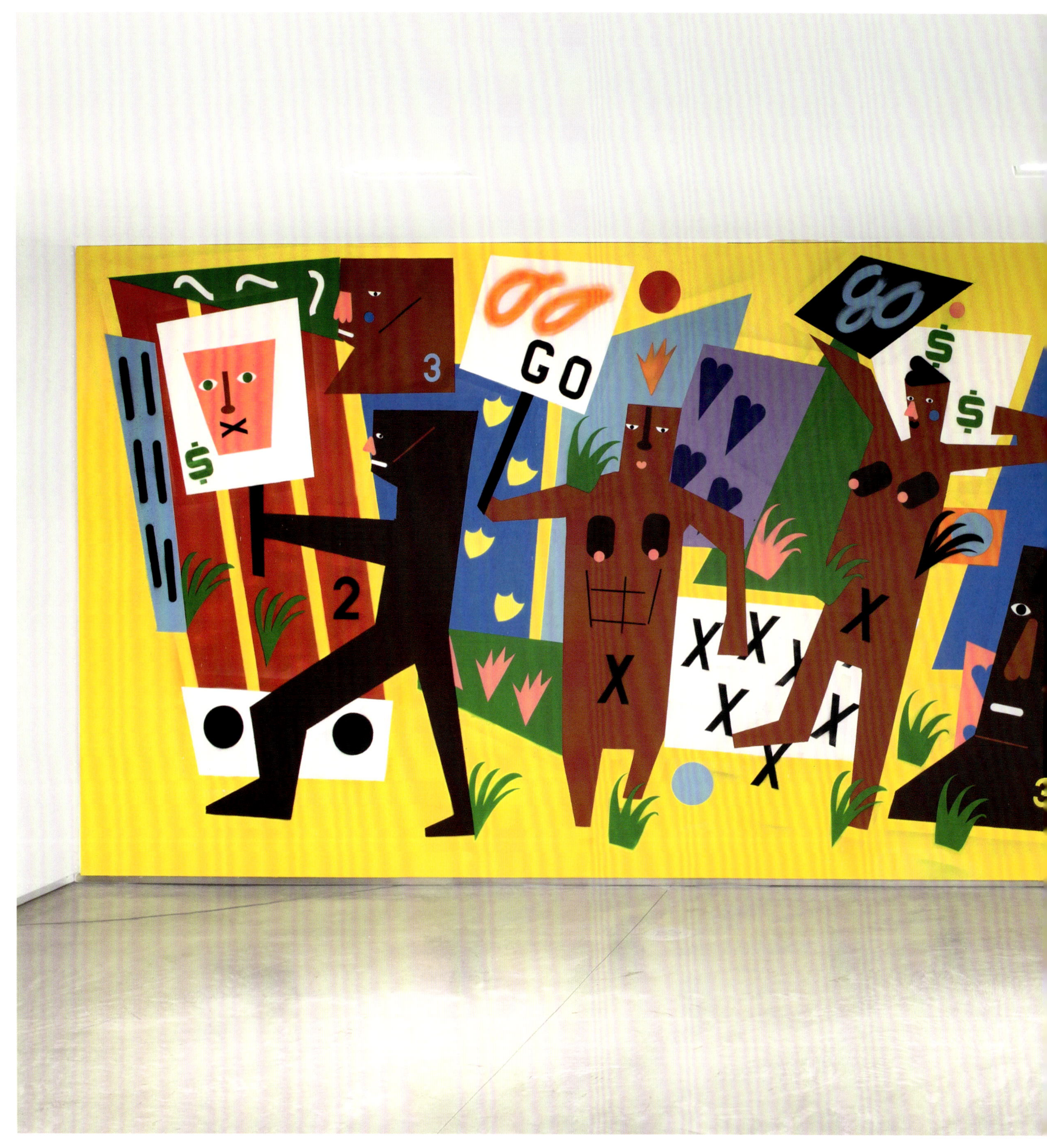

Untitled, 2018

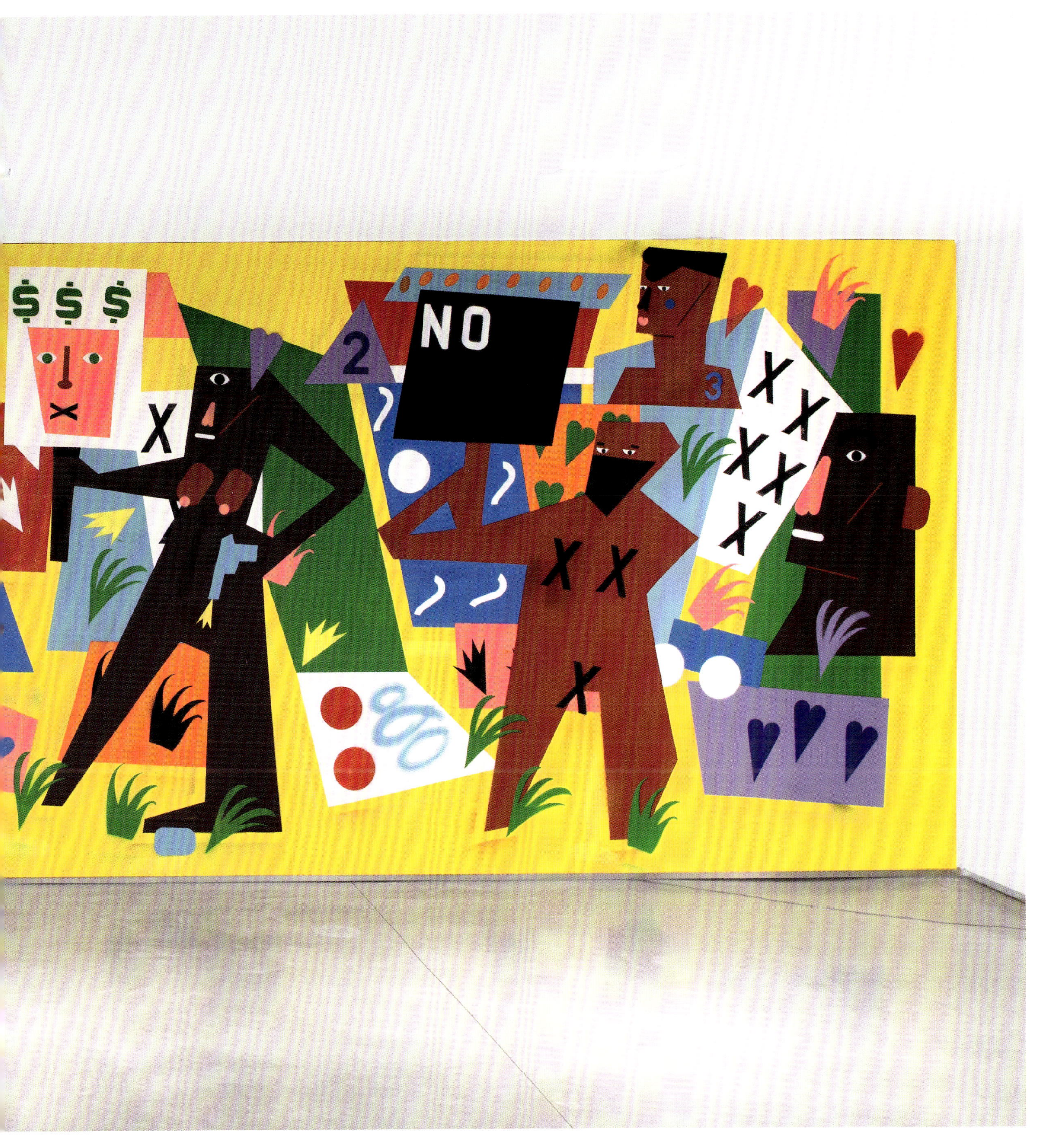
$ $ $
X
2
NO
3

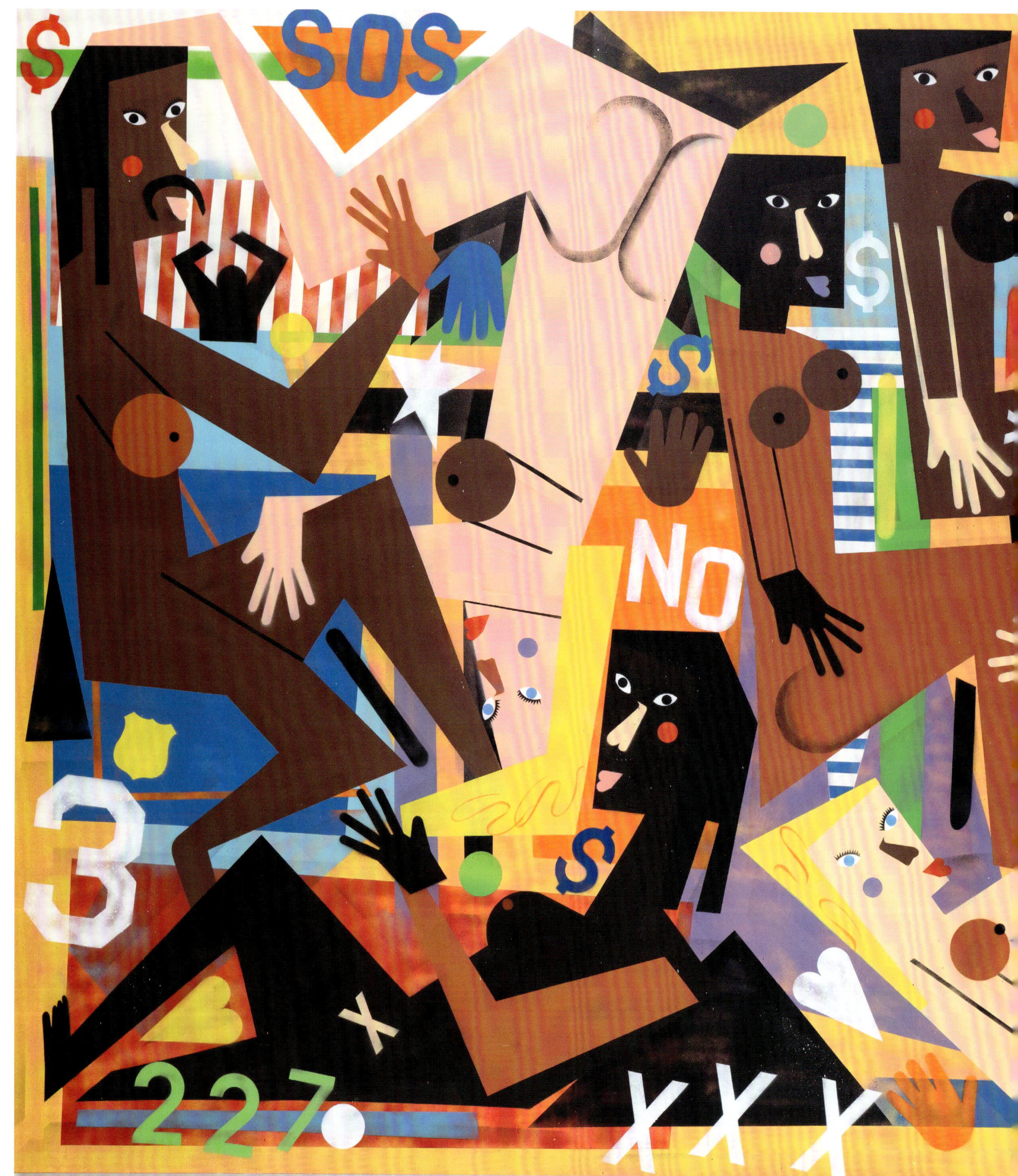

Junk Mail Scribble, 2019

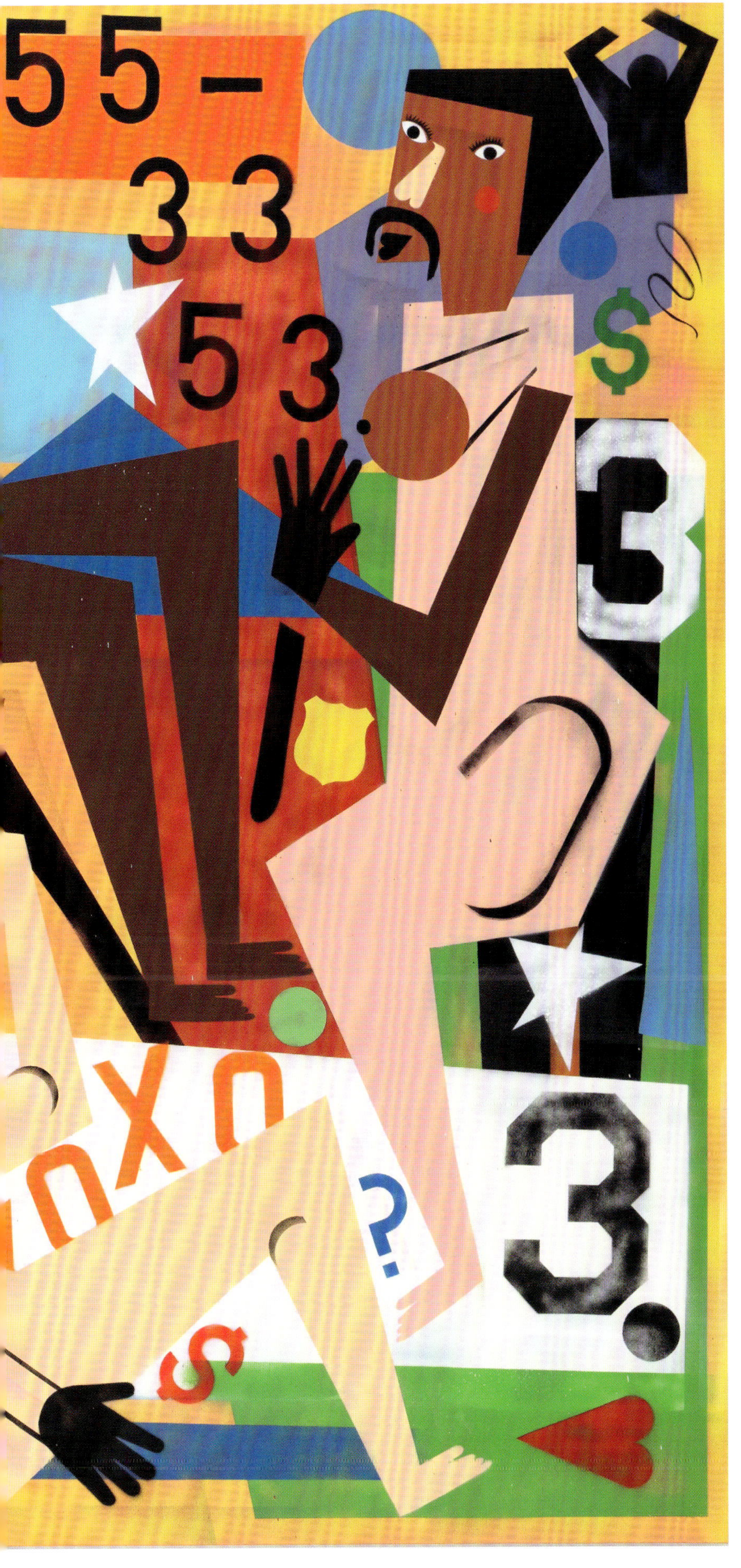
55-
33
53
3
3.

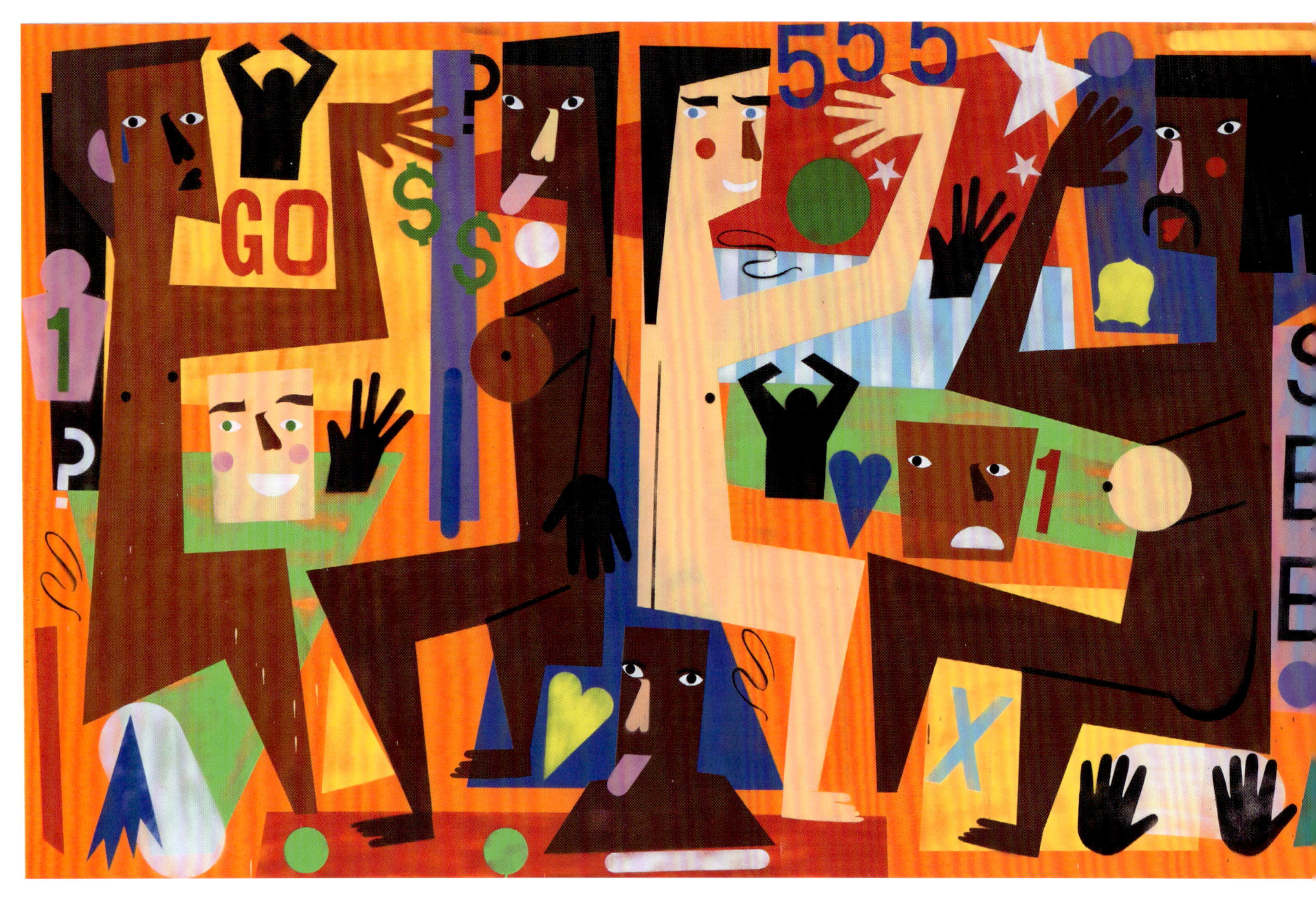

Junk Mail Scribble #2, 2019

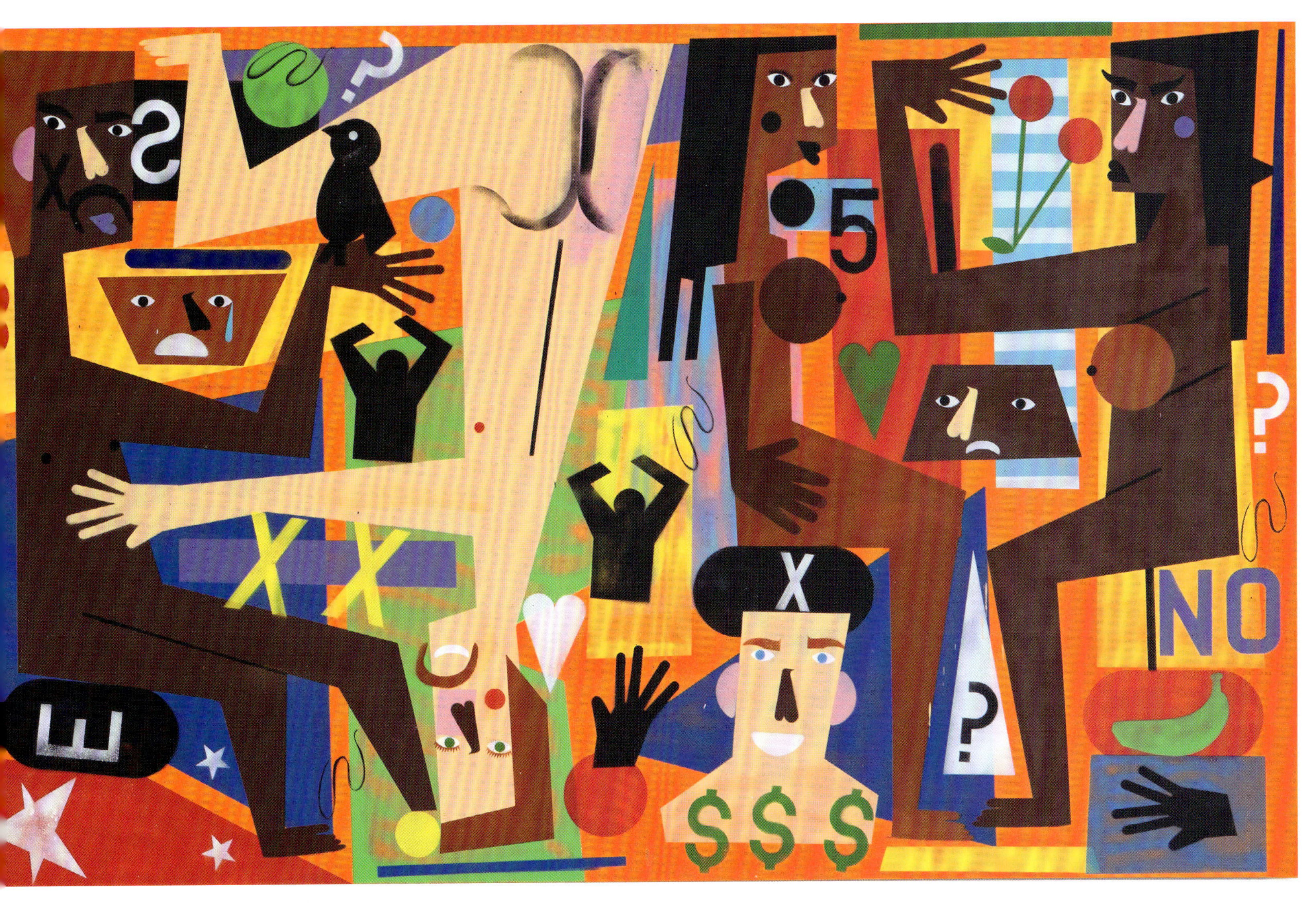
5
X
NO
$ $ $

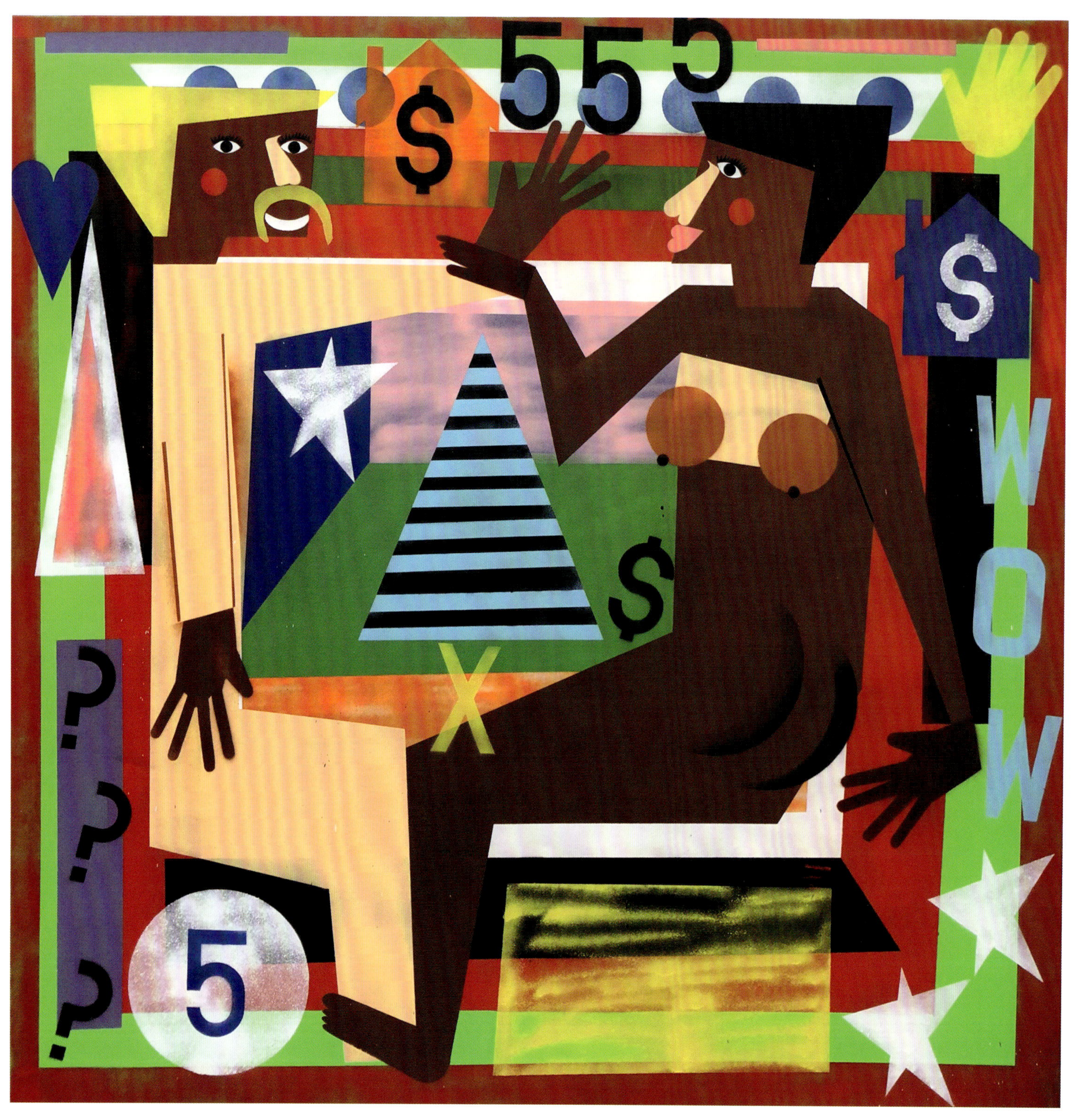

555 Wow, 2019

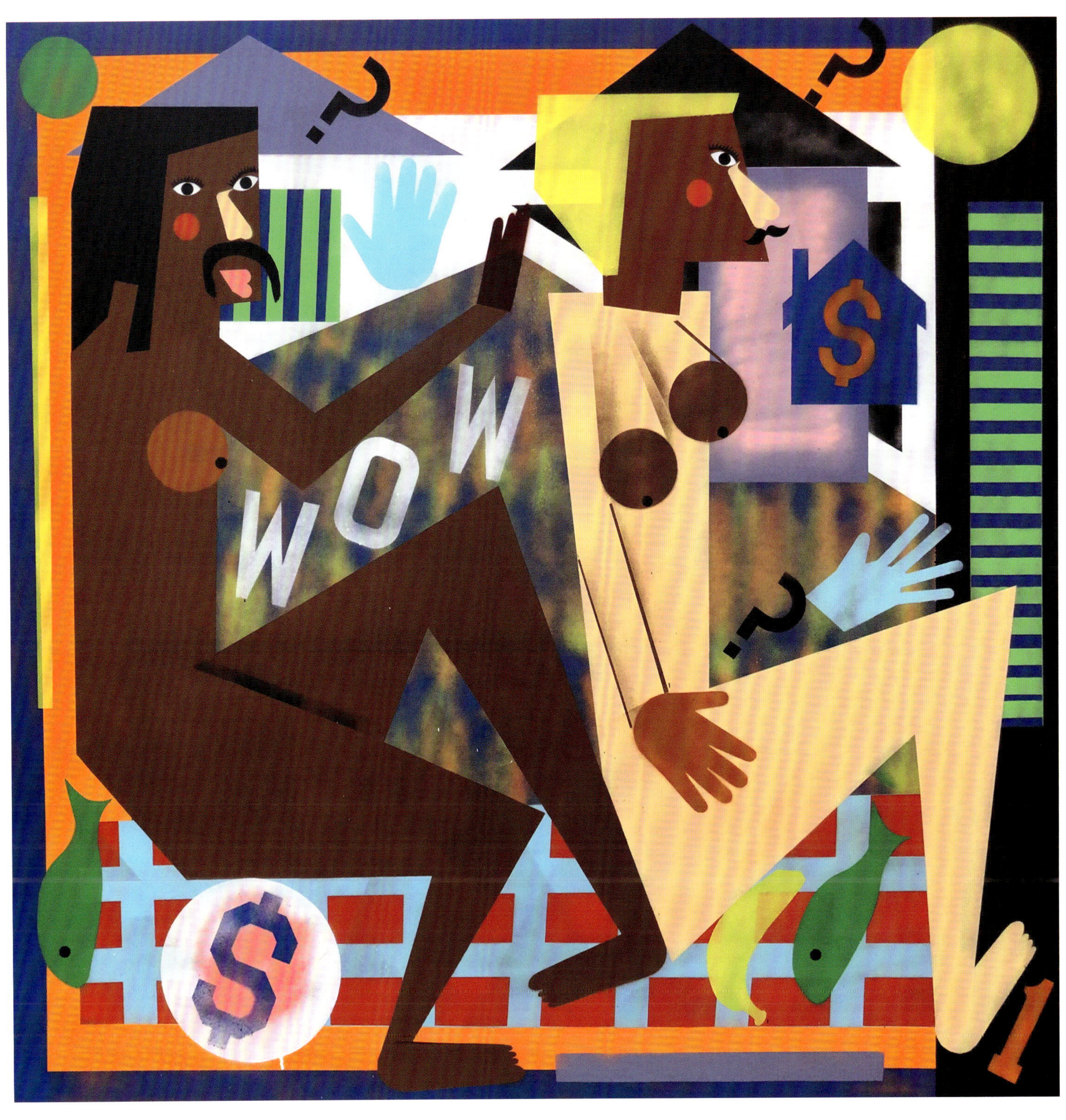

Wow Money, 2019

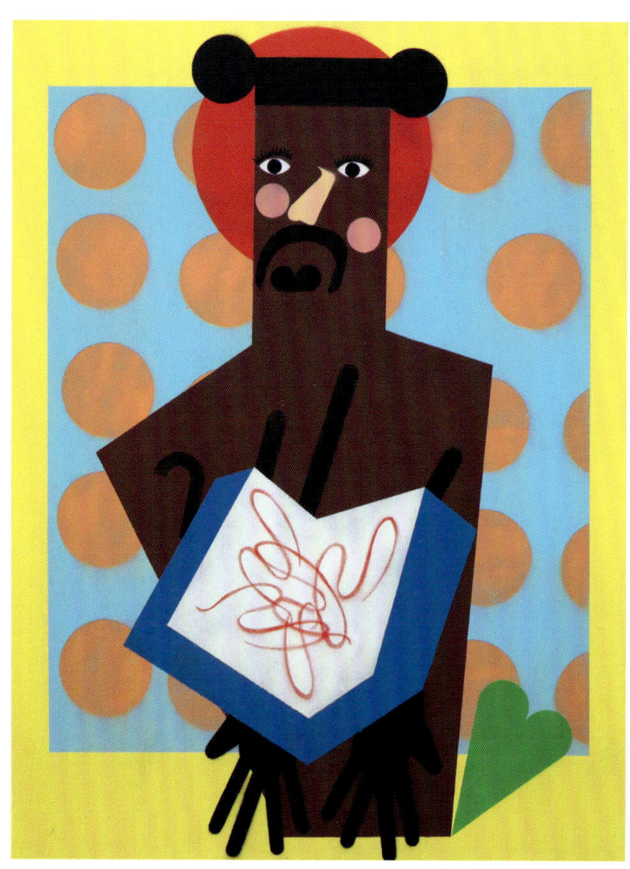

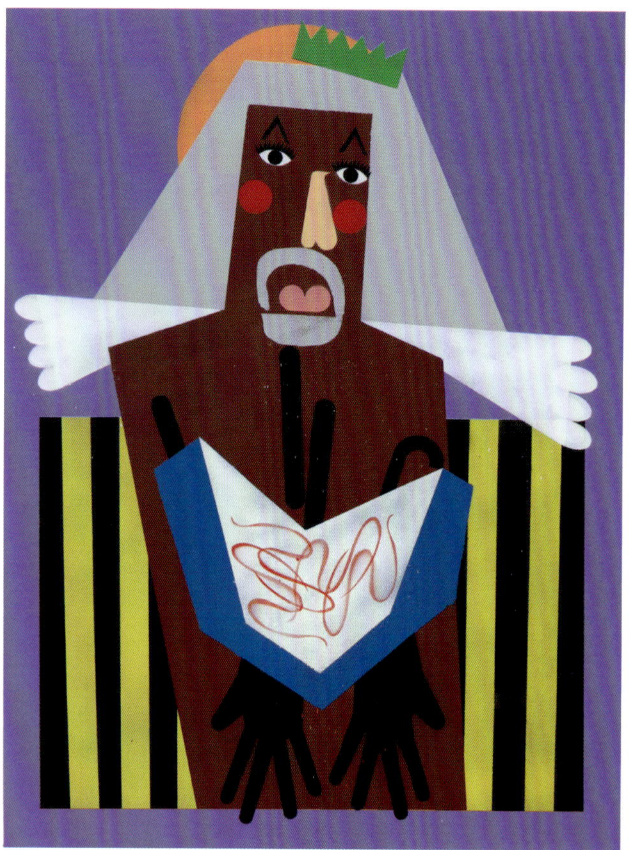

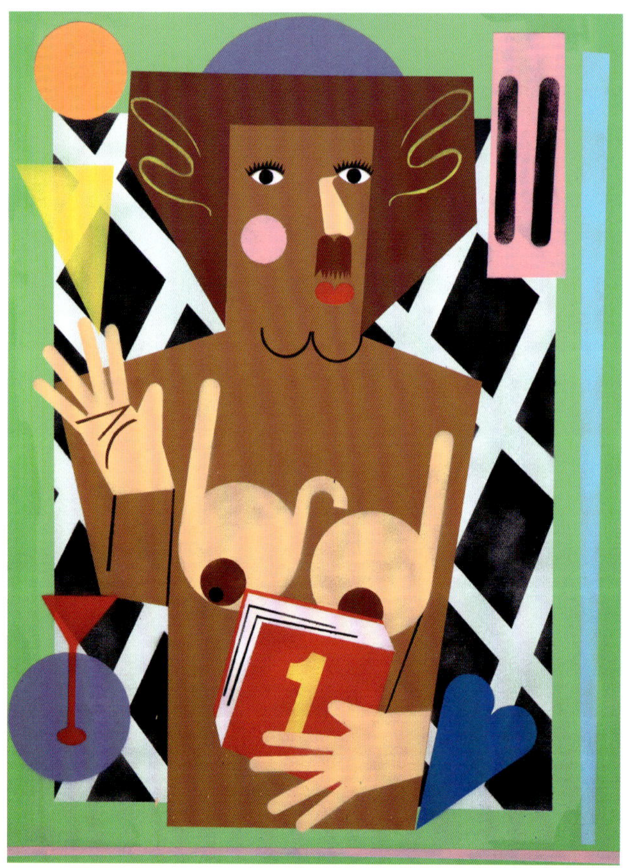

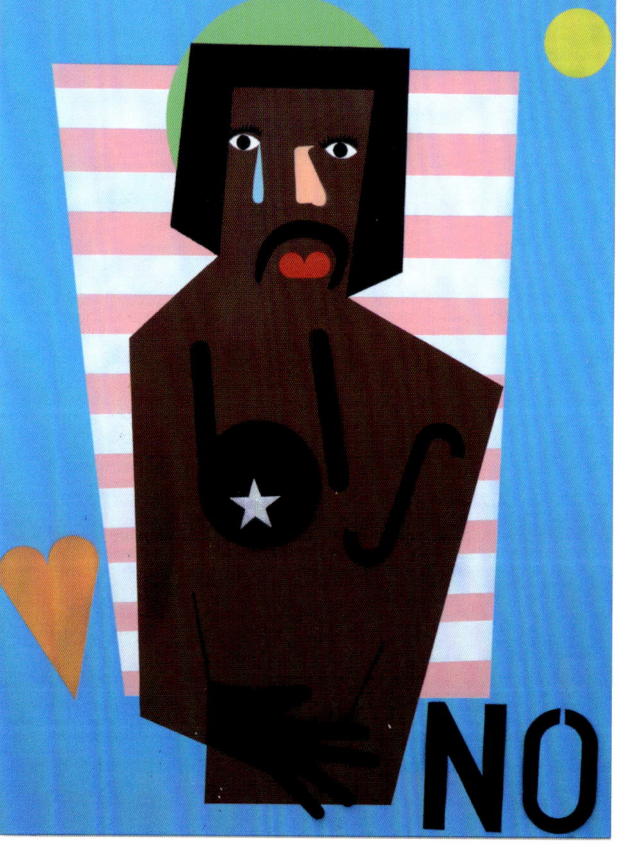

[LEFT & RIGHT] A Vanilla Position, 2019

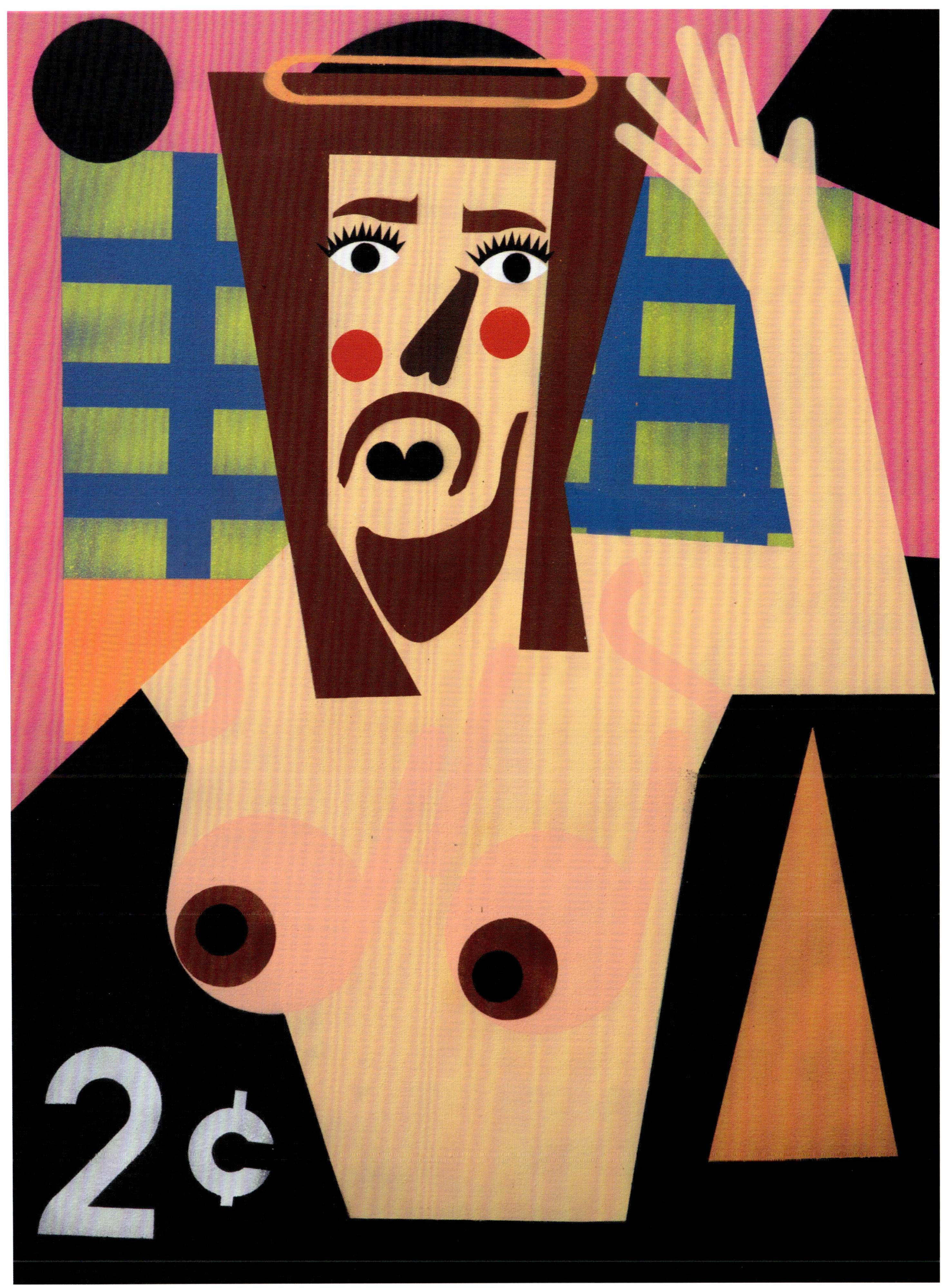
2¢

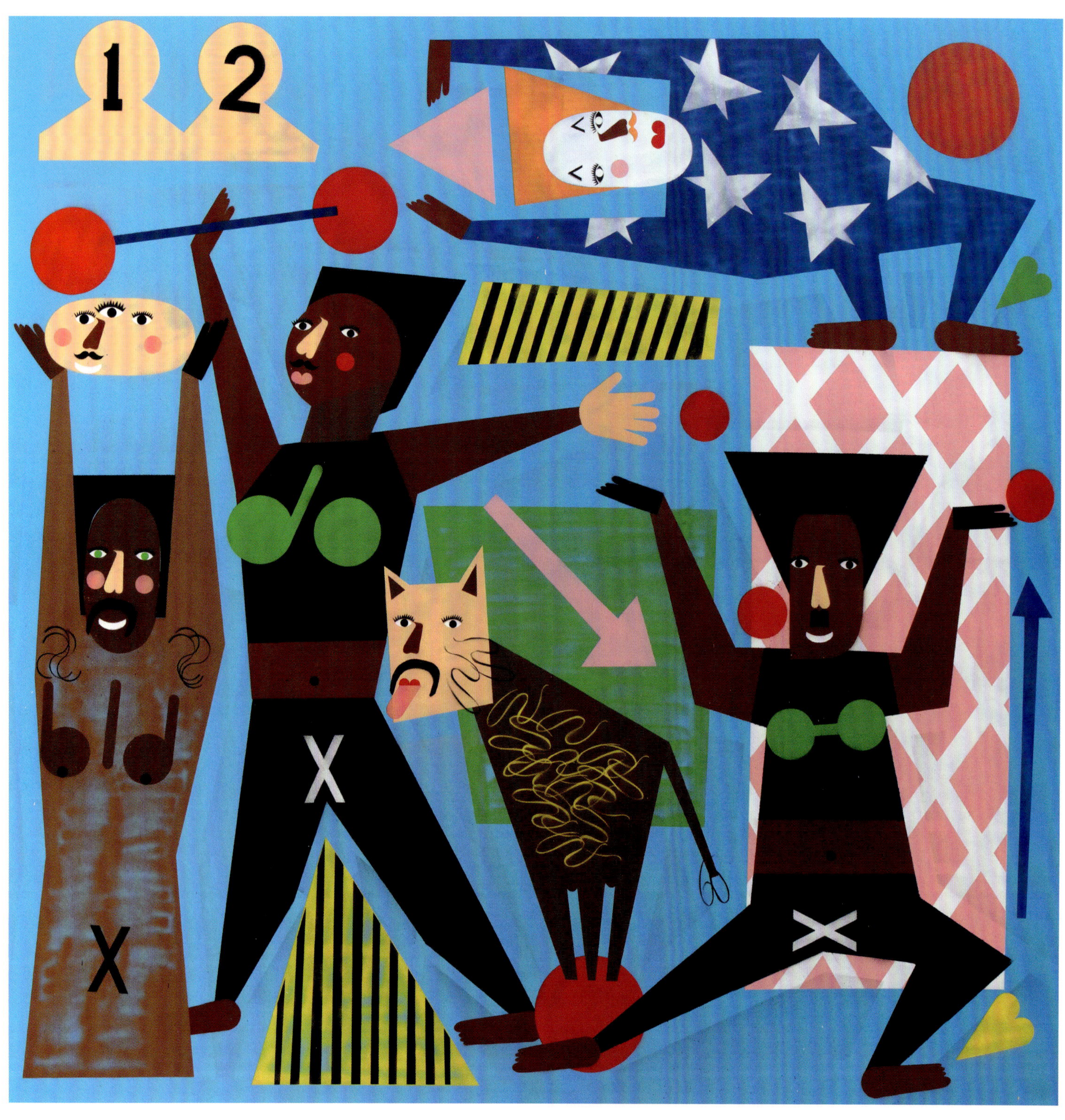

Bizarre Blazaar, 2019

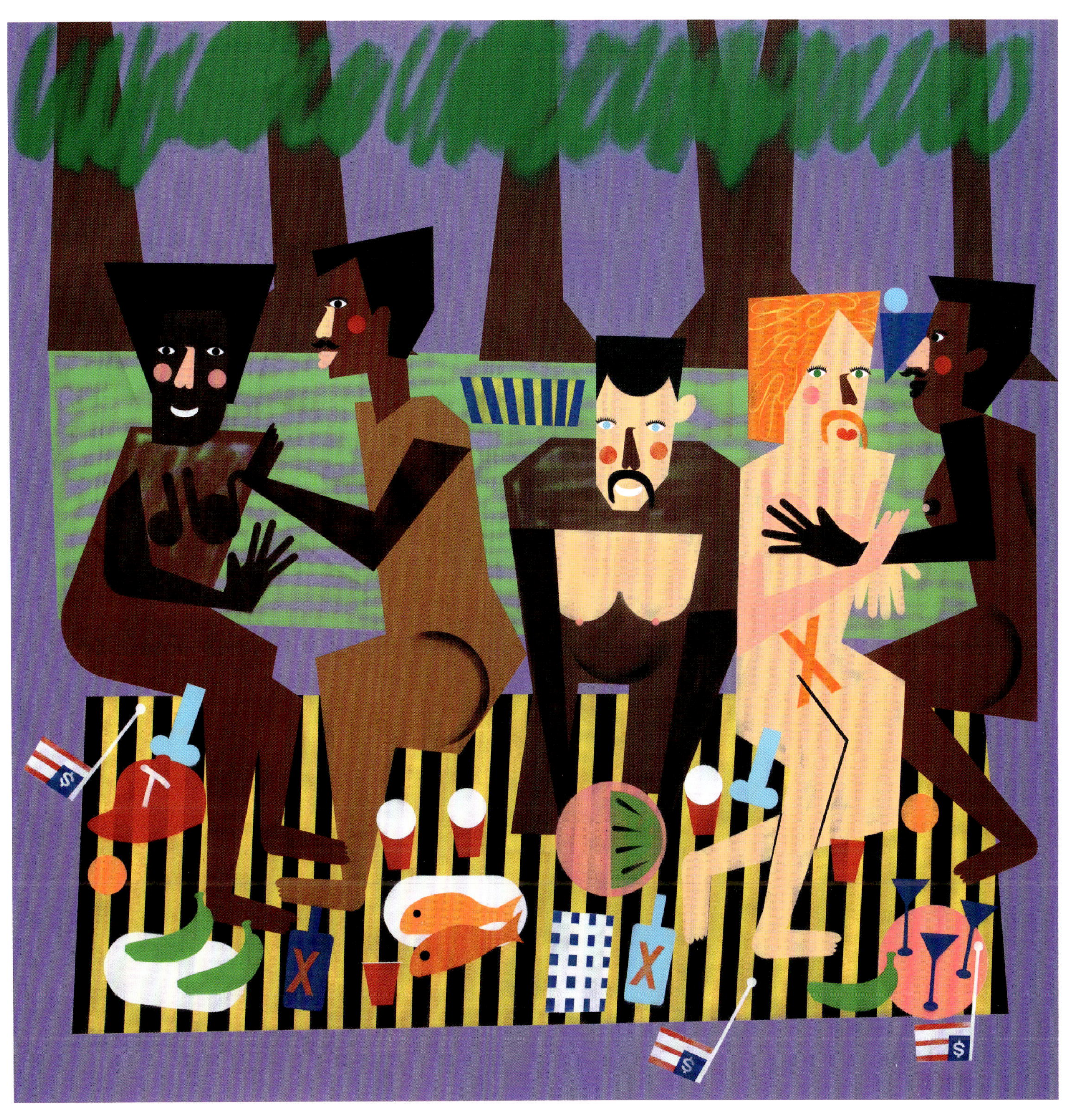

Issa Saturday (Study), 2019

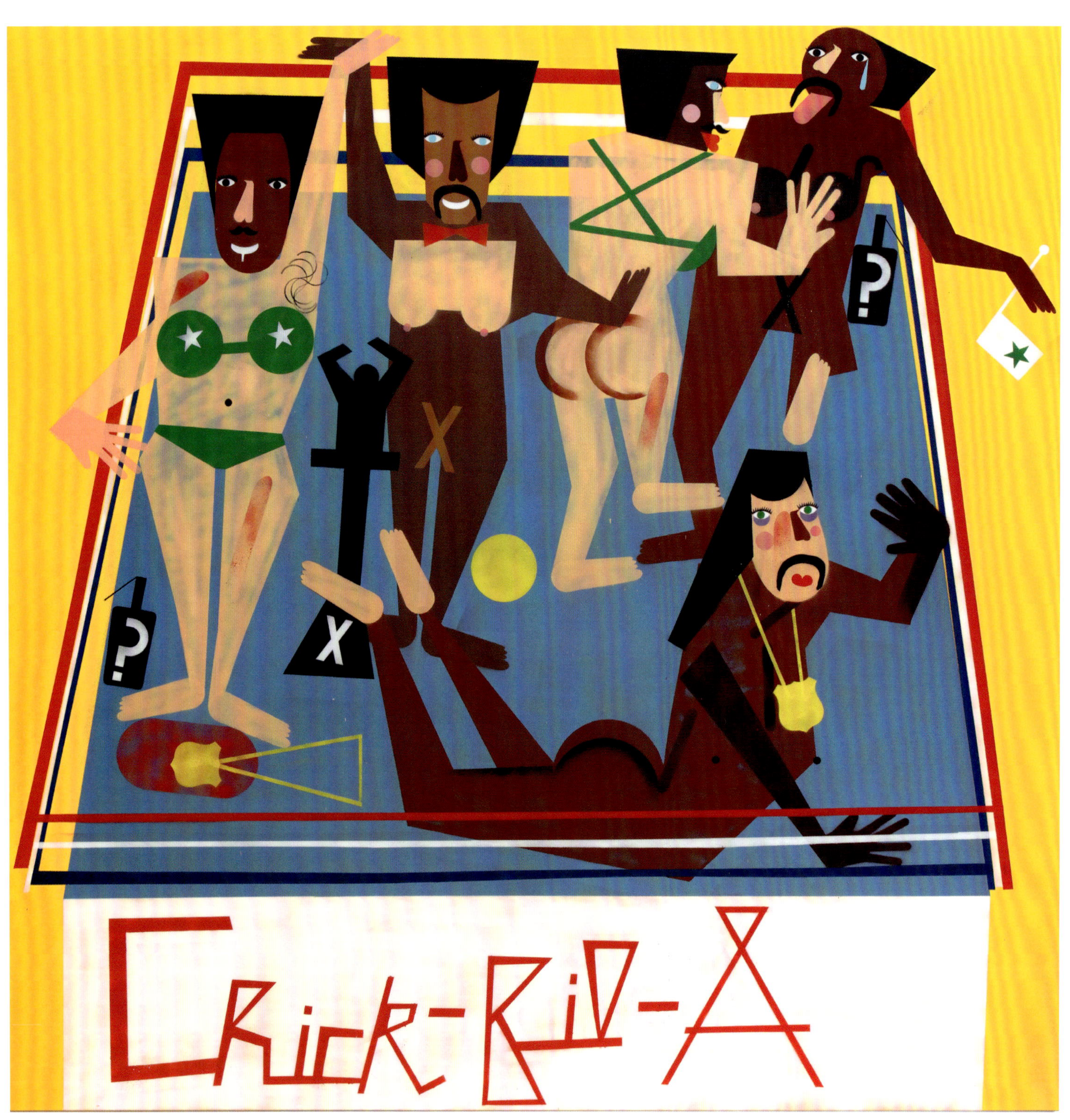

Explicit Bias, 2019

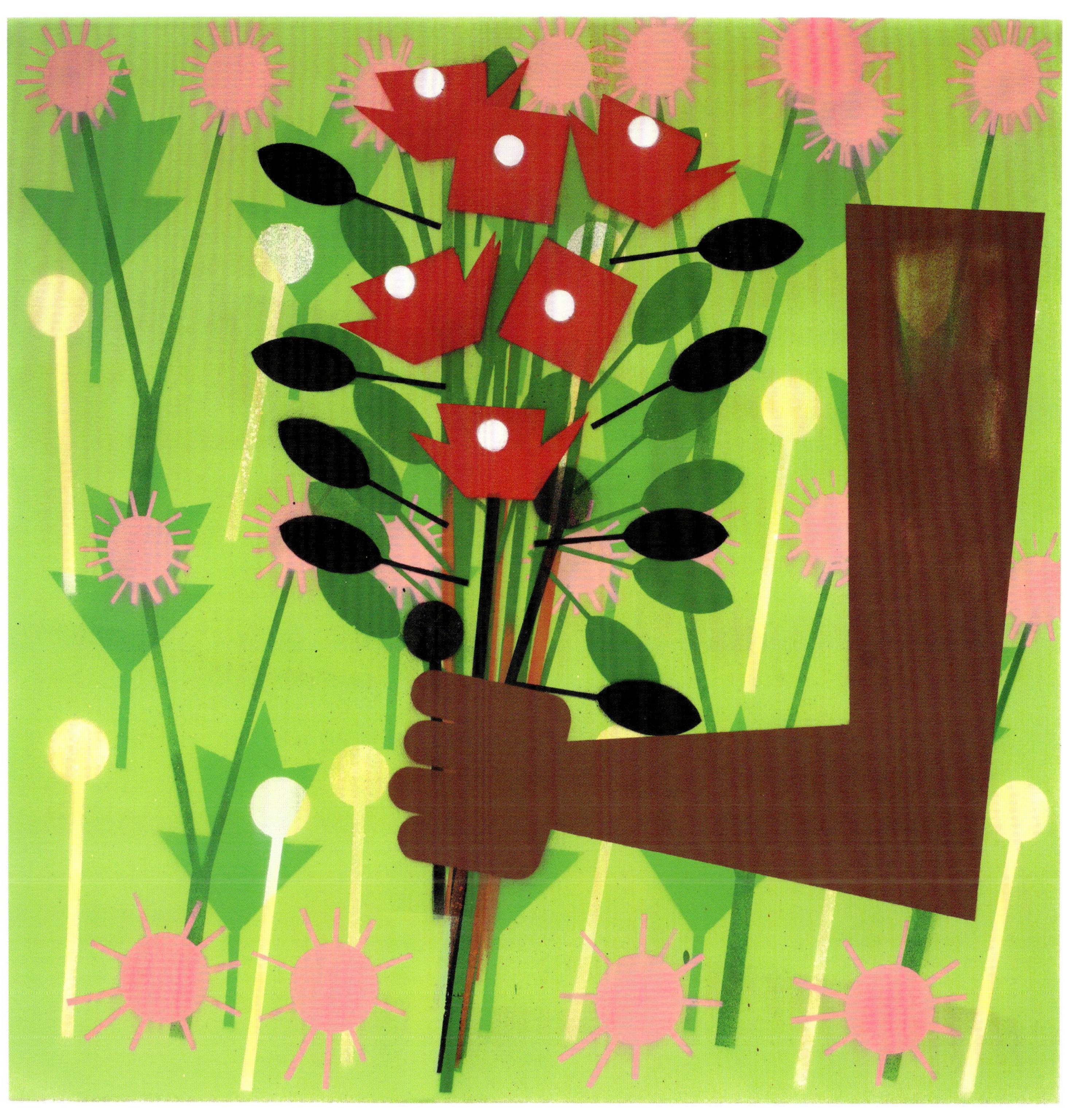

Taking My Flowers, 2020

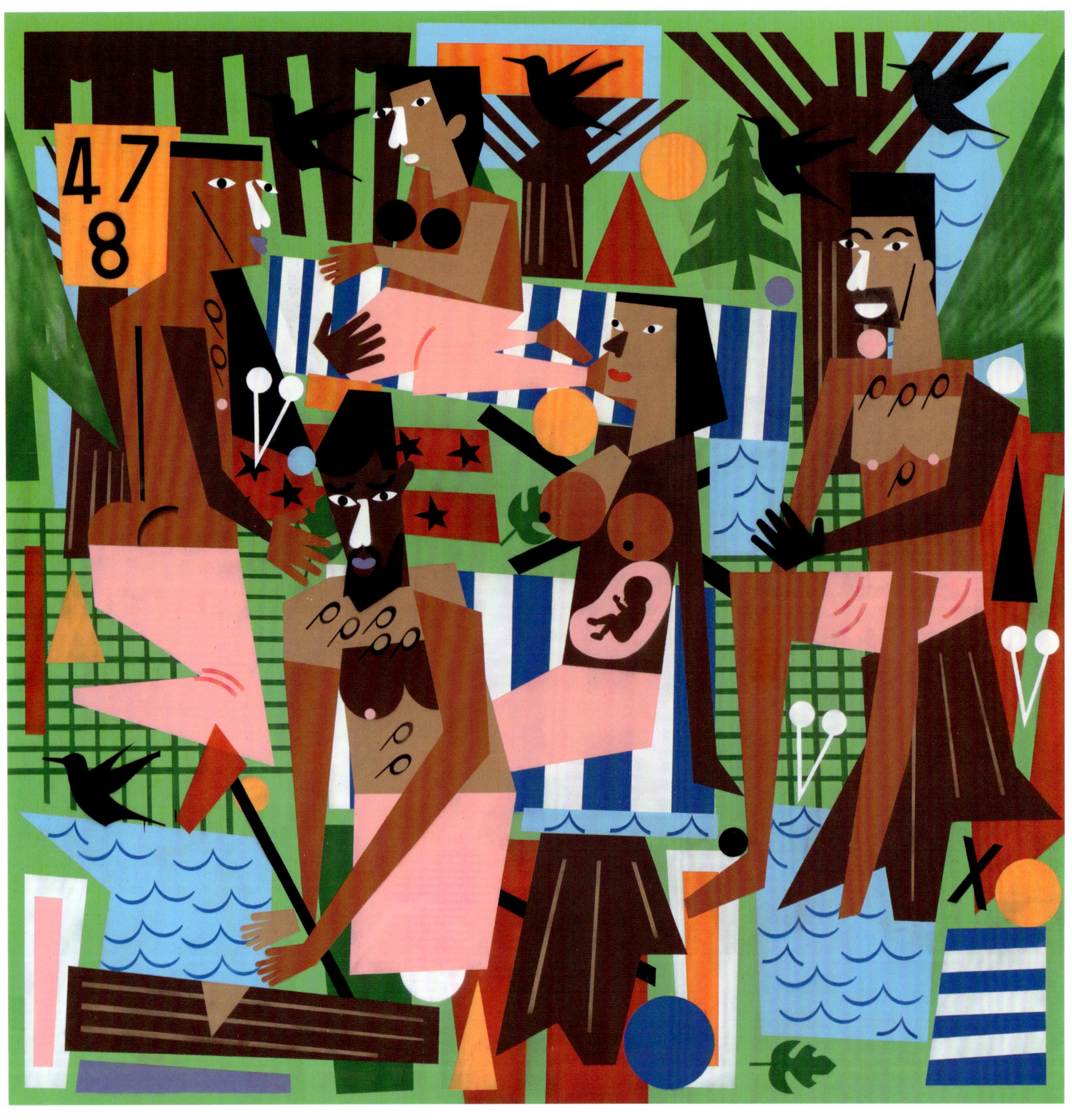

Femme Games, 2020

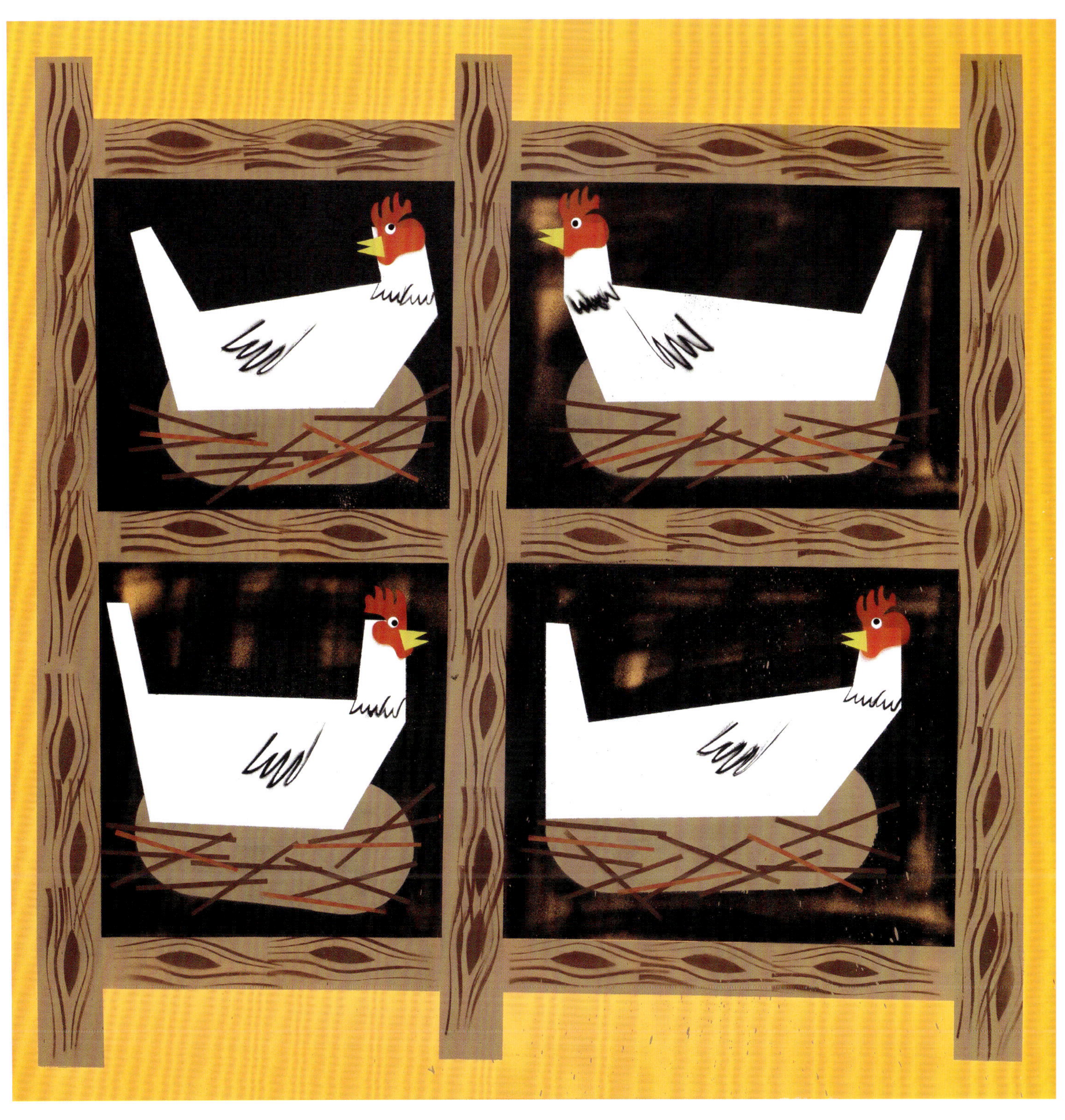

Bird Talk, 2020

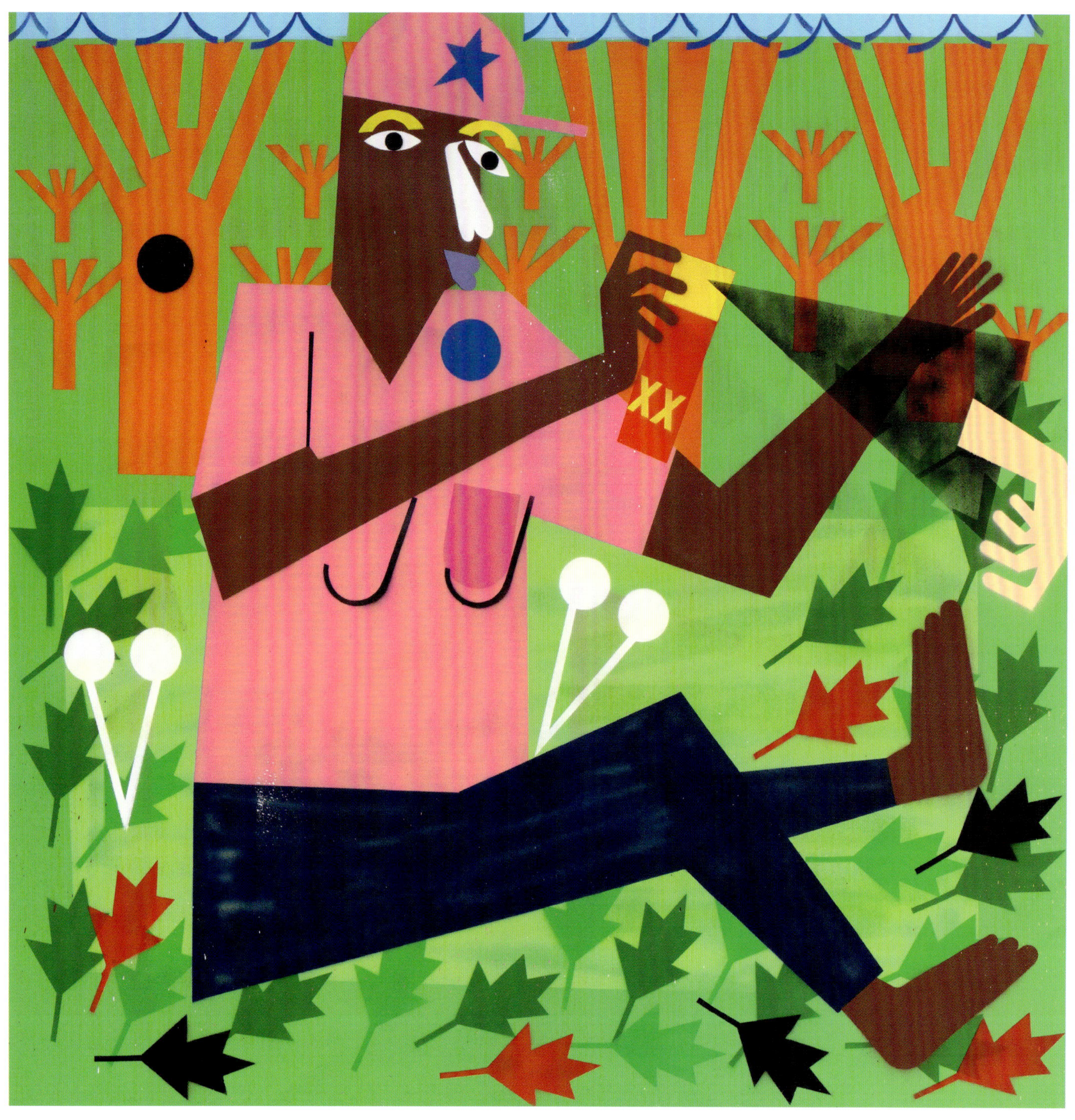

Off, 2020

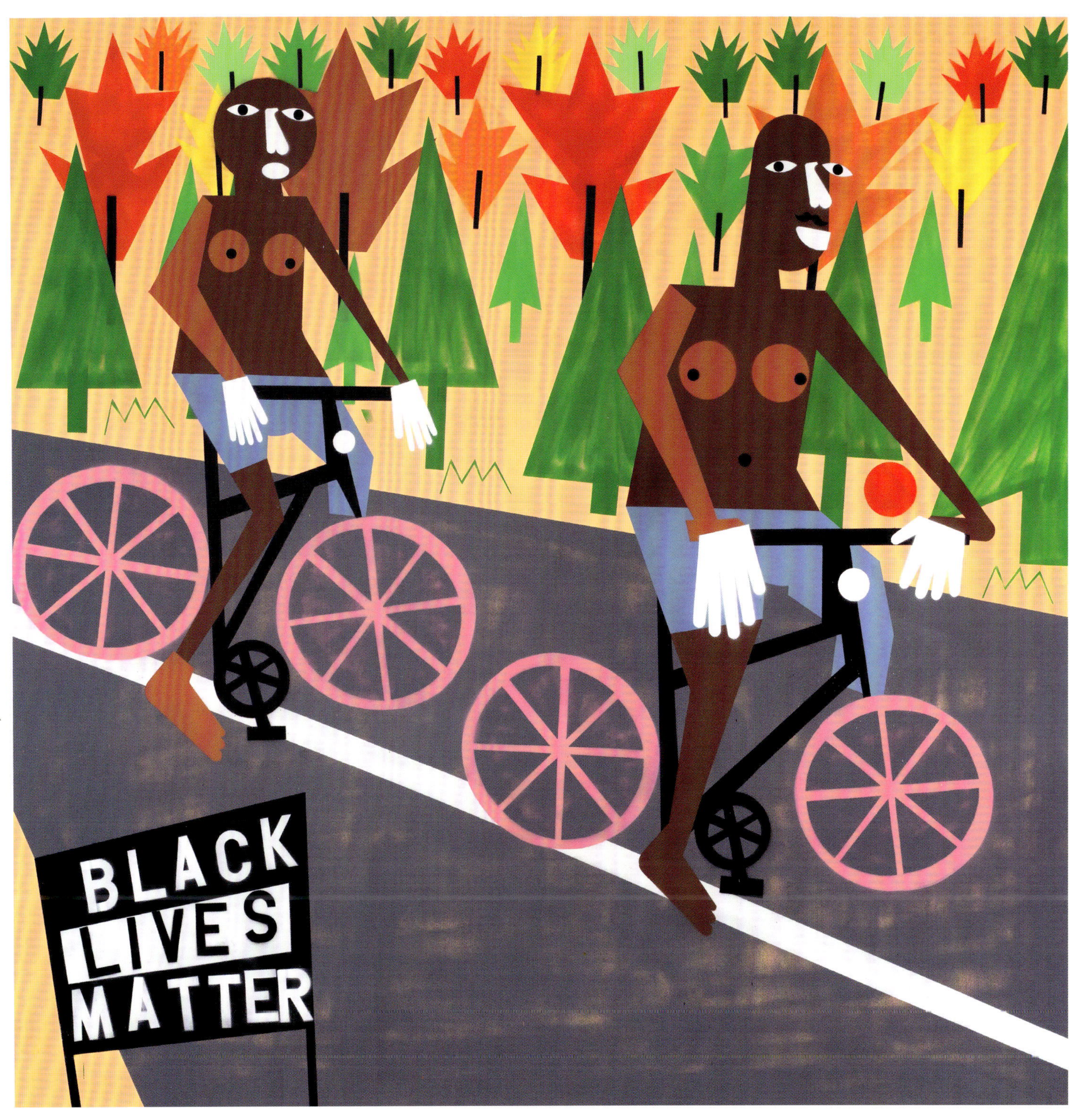

Being Mixie with My Fixie, 2020

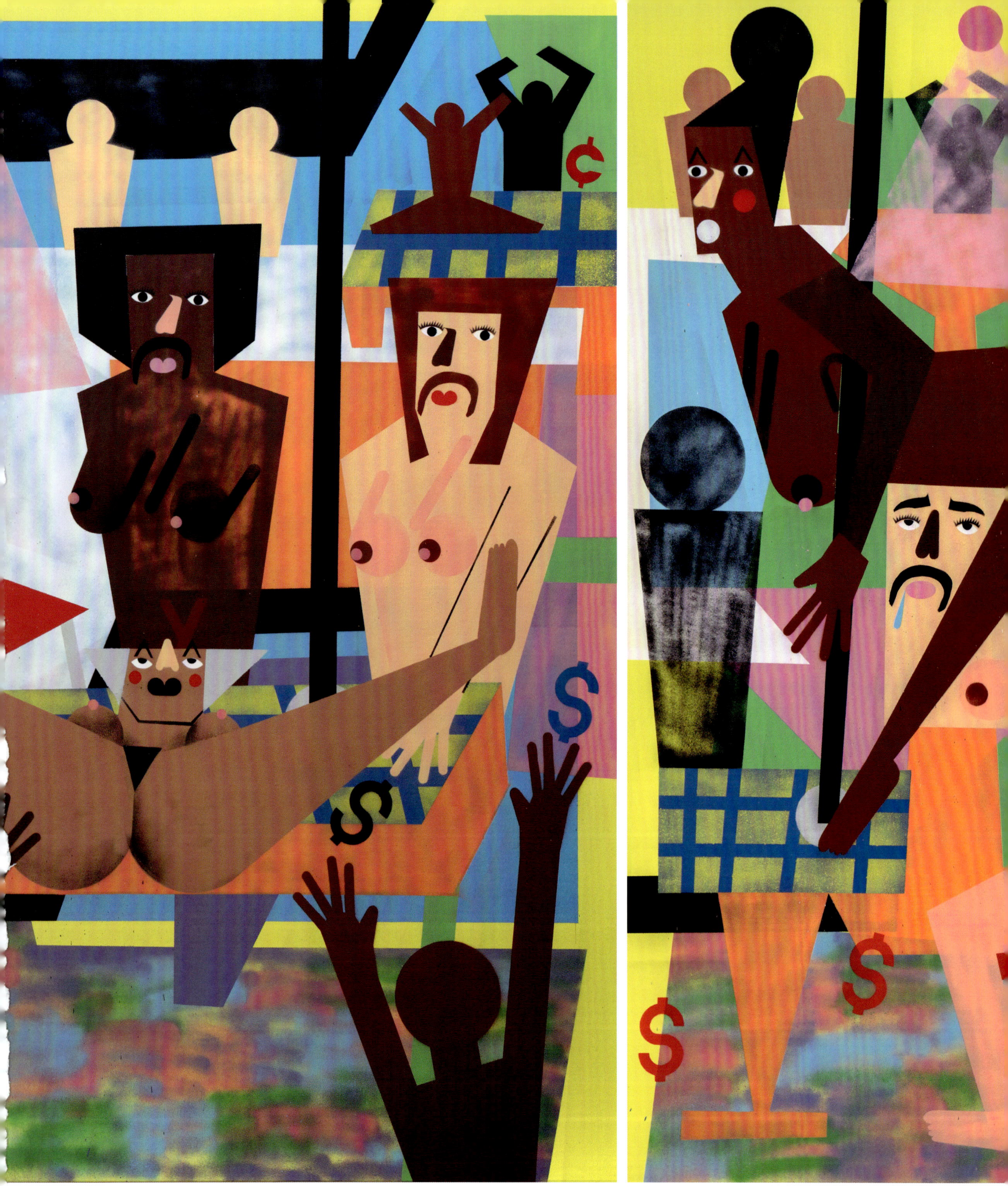

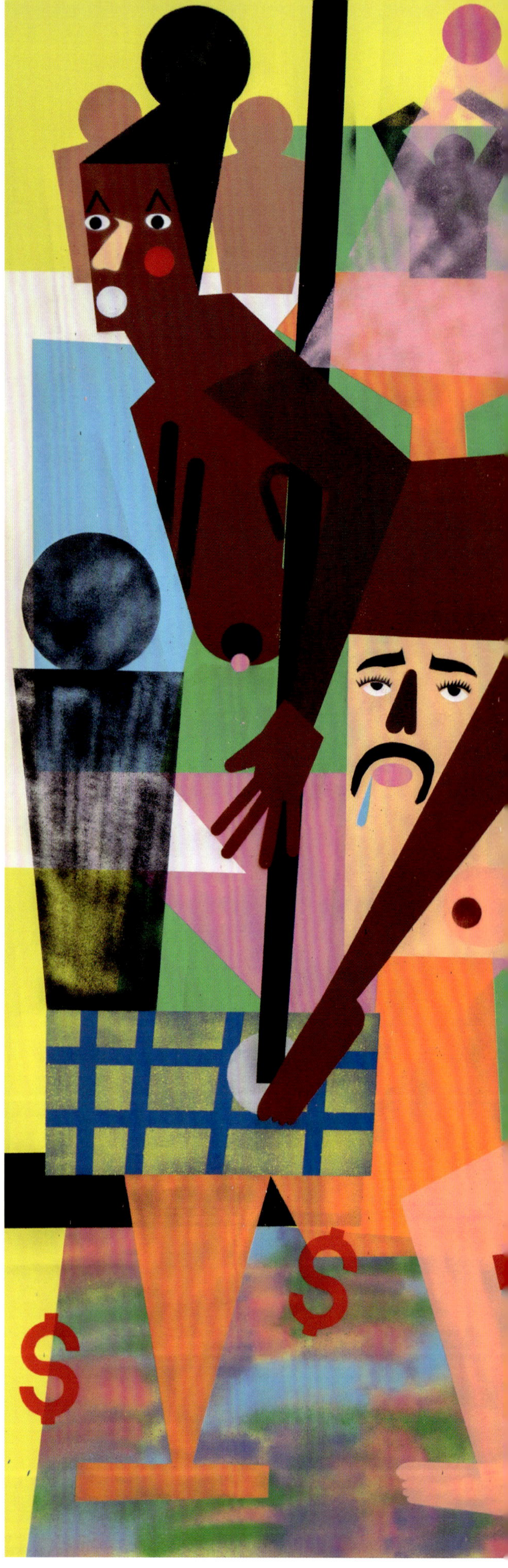

Peep, 2019

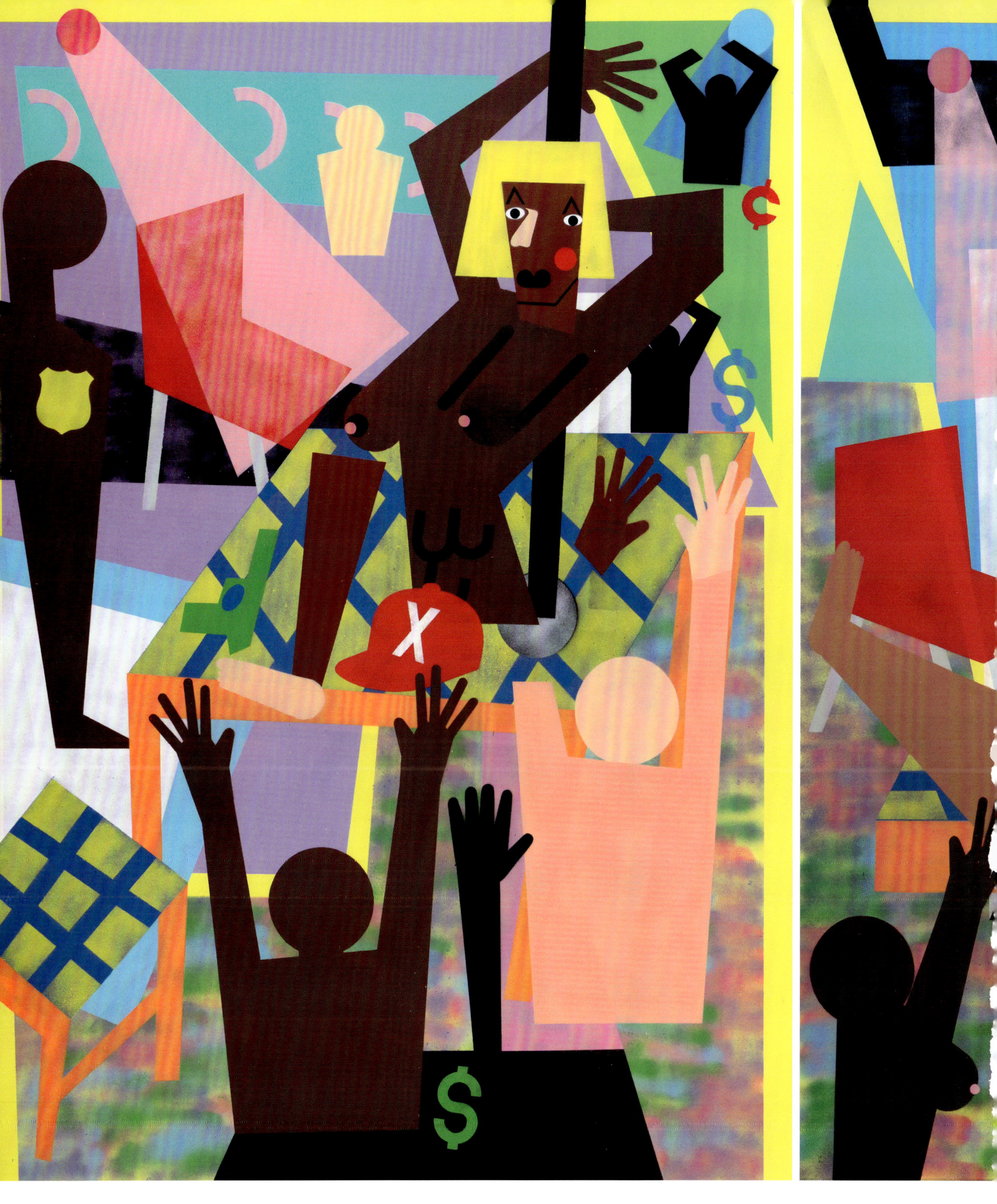

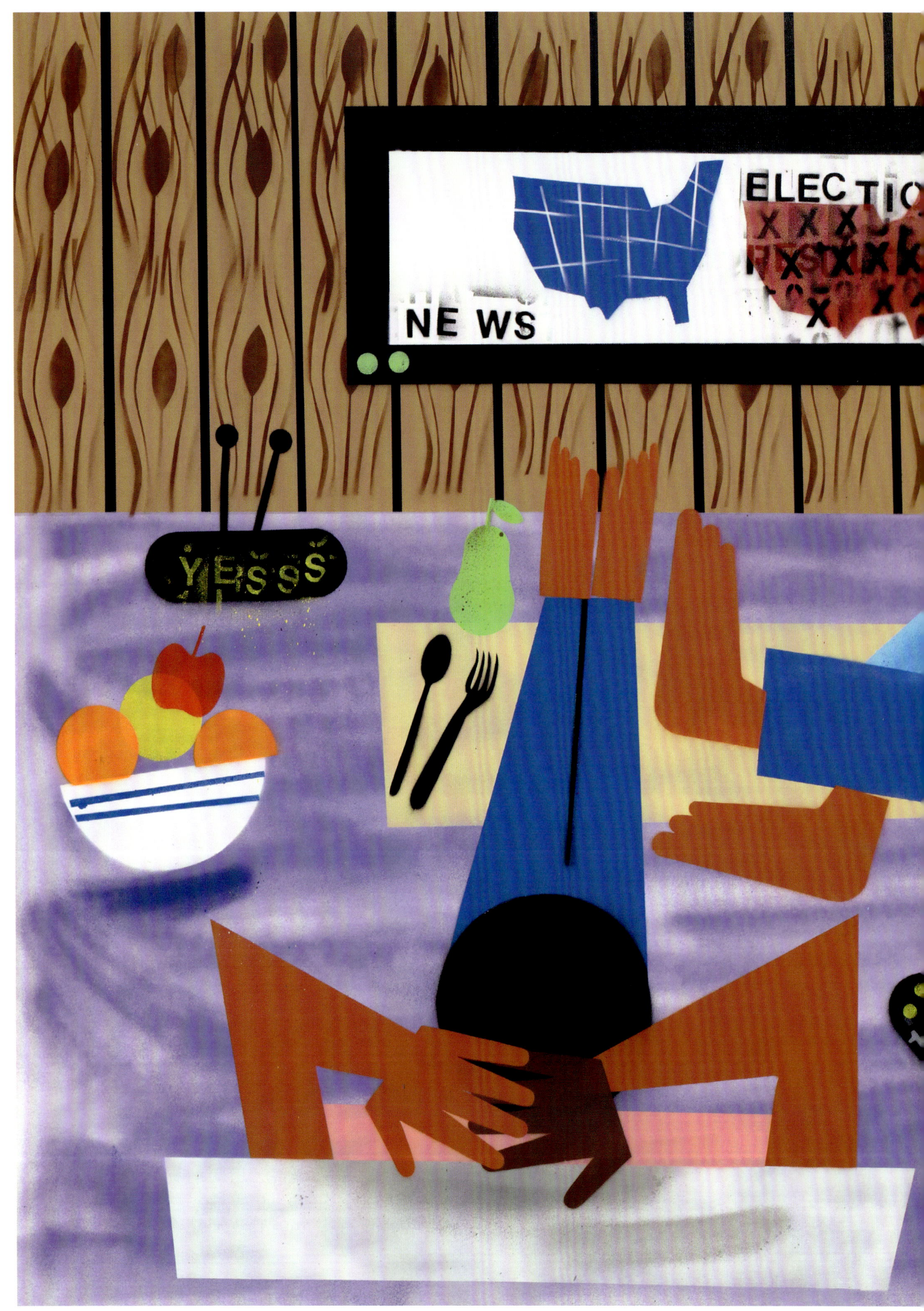

Where's the Remote, 2020

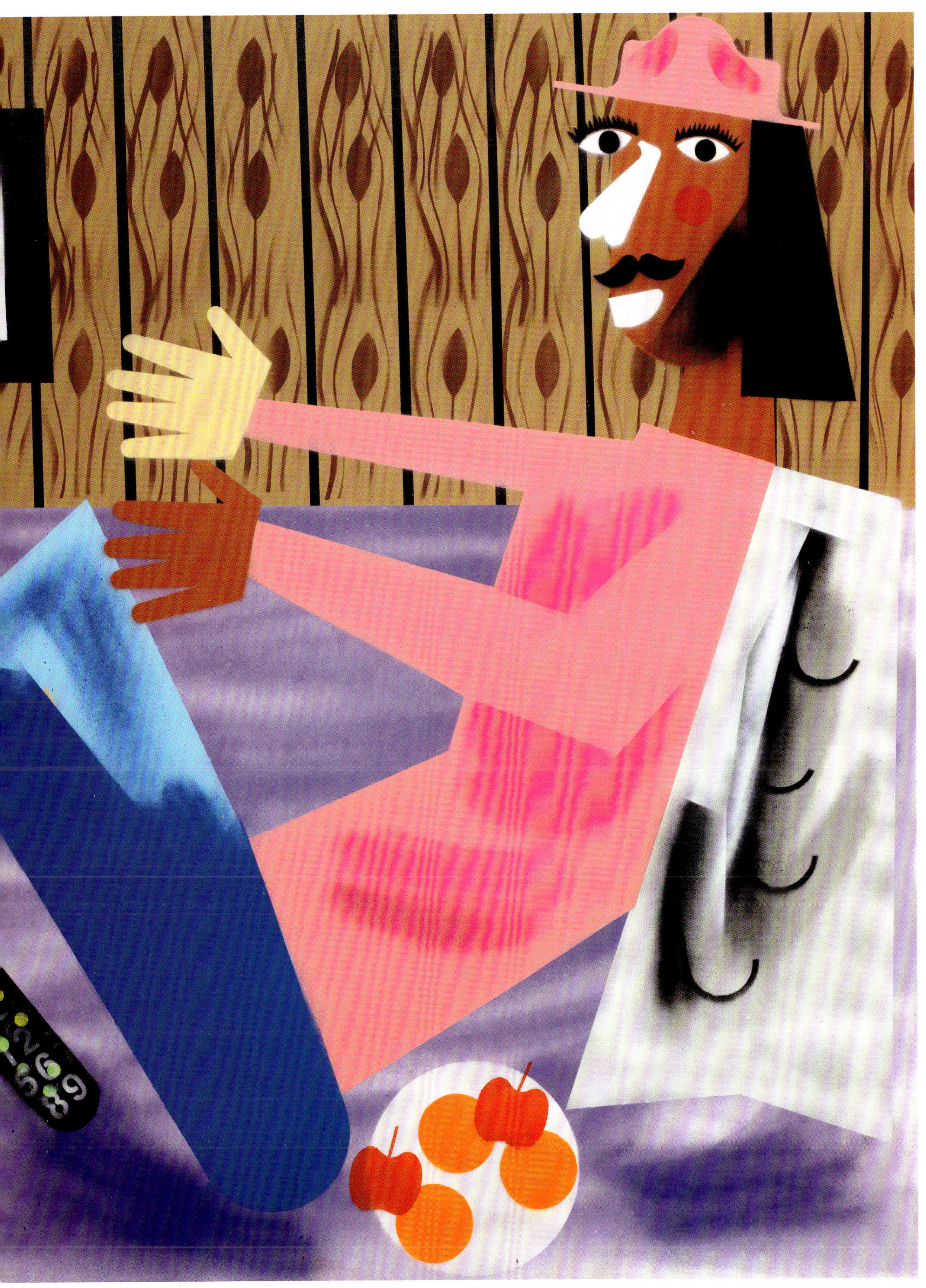

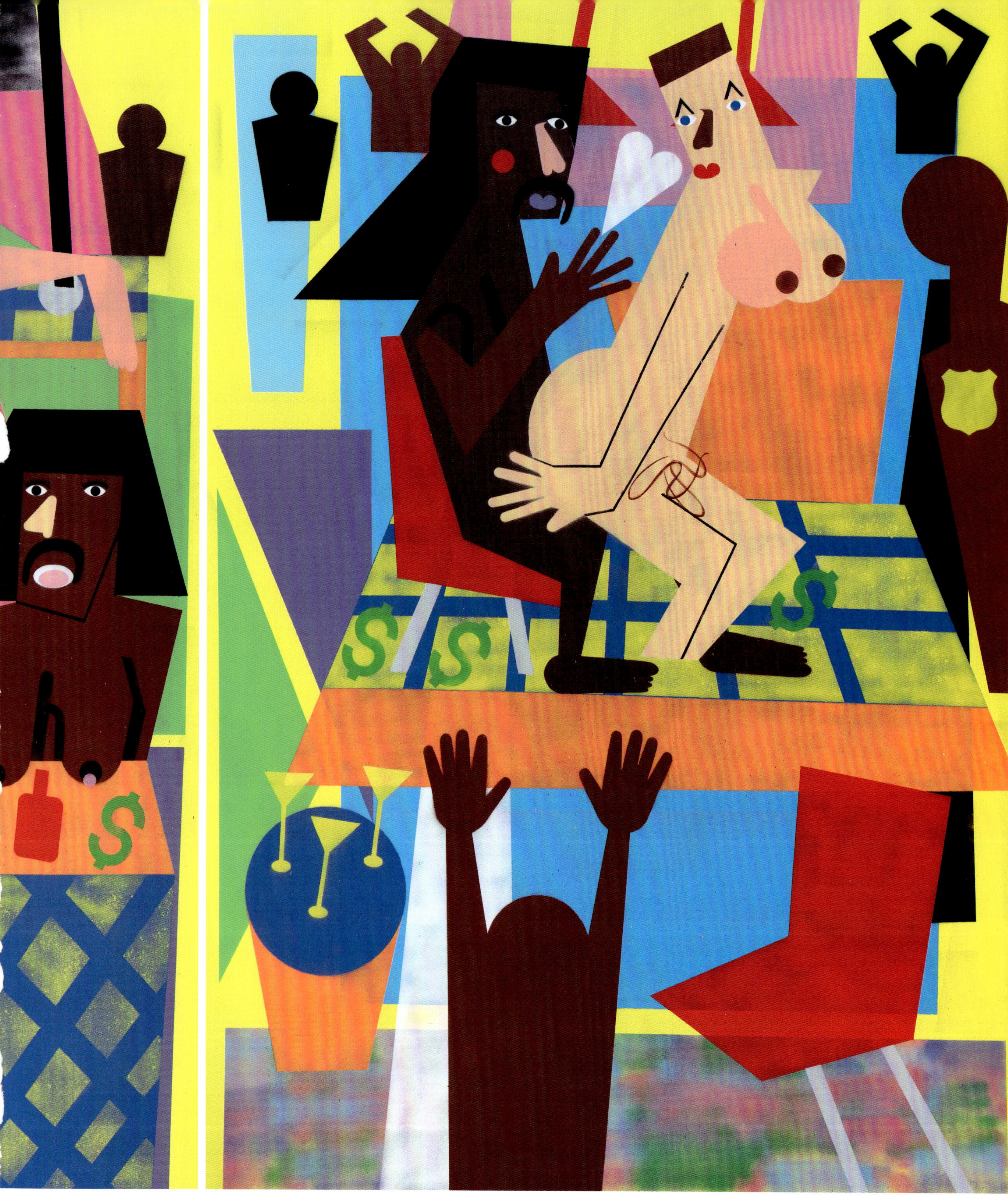

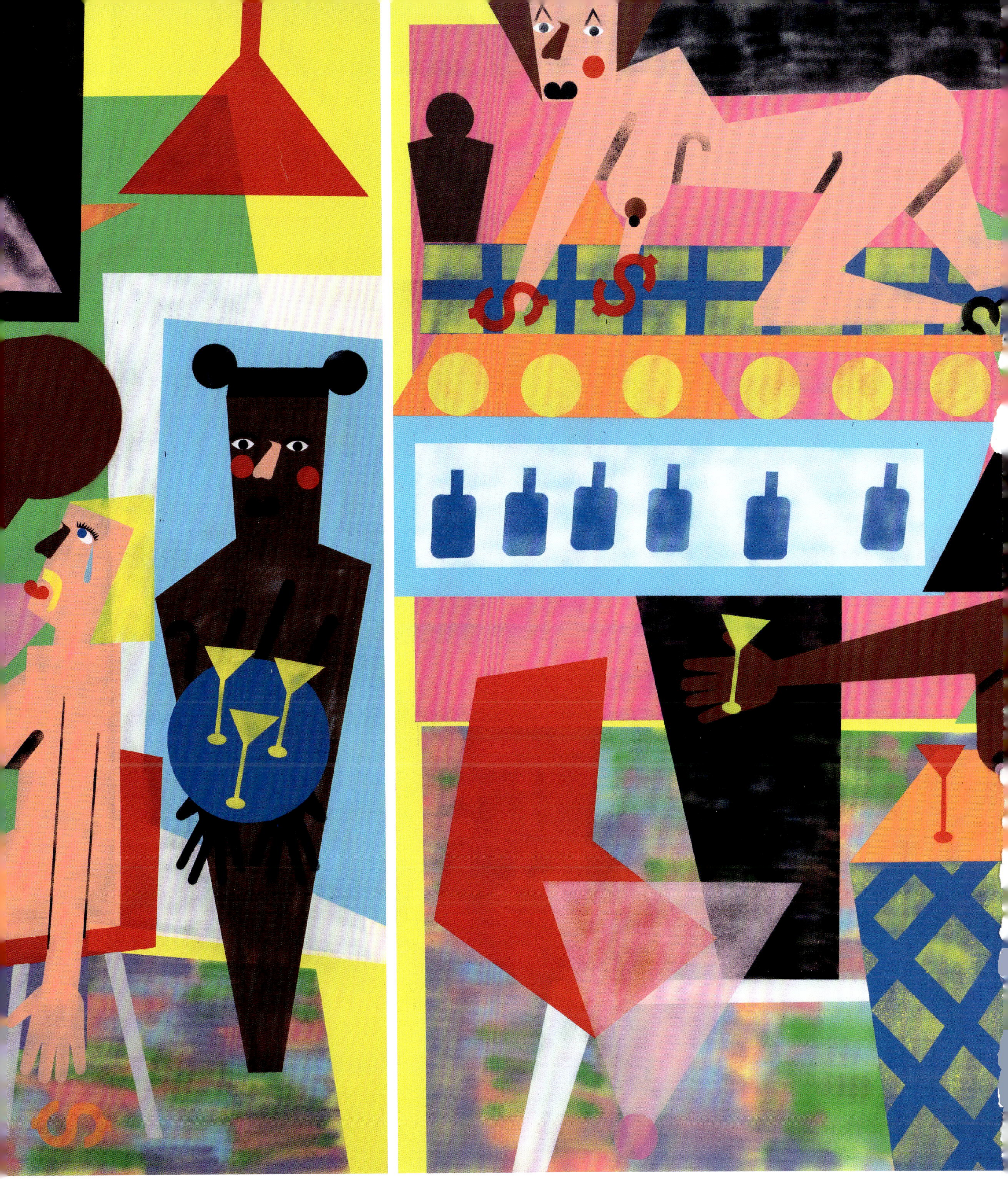

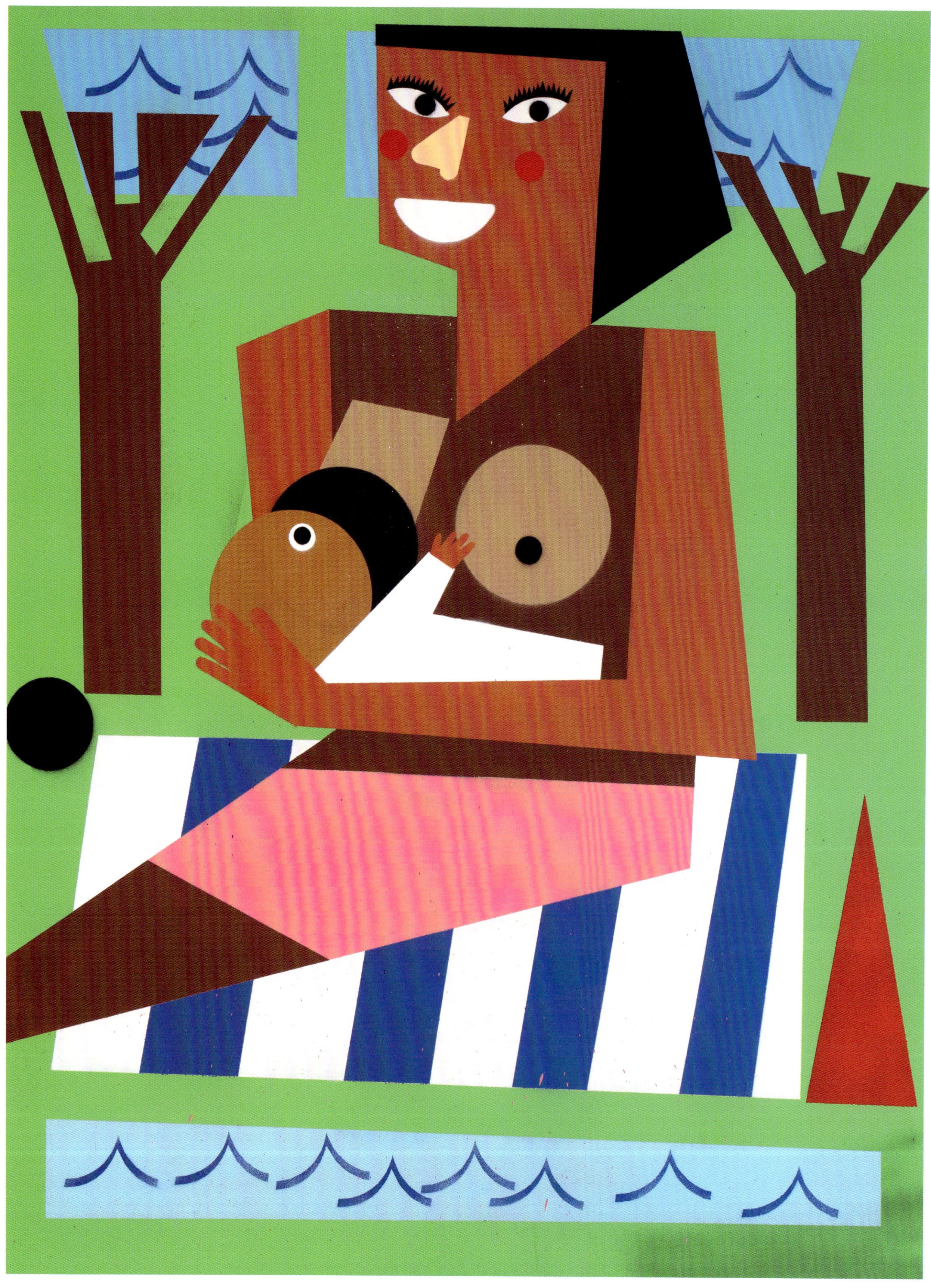

Thirsty, 2020

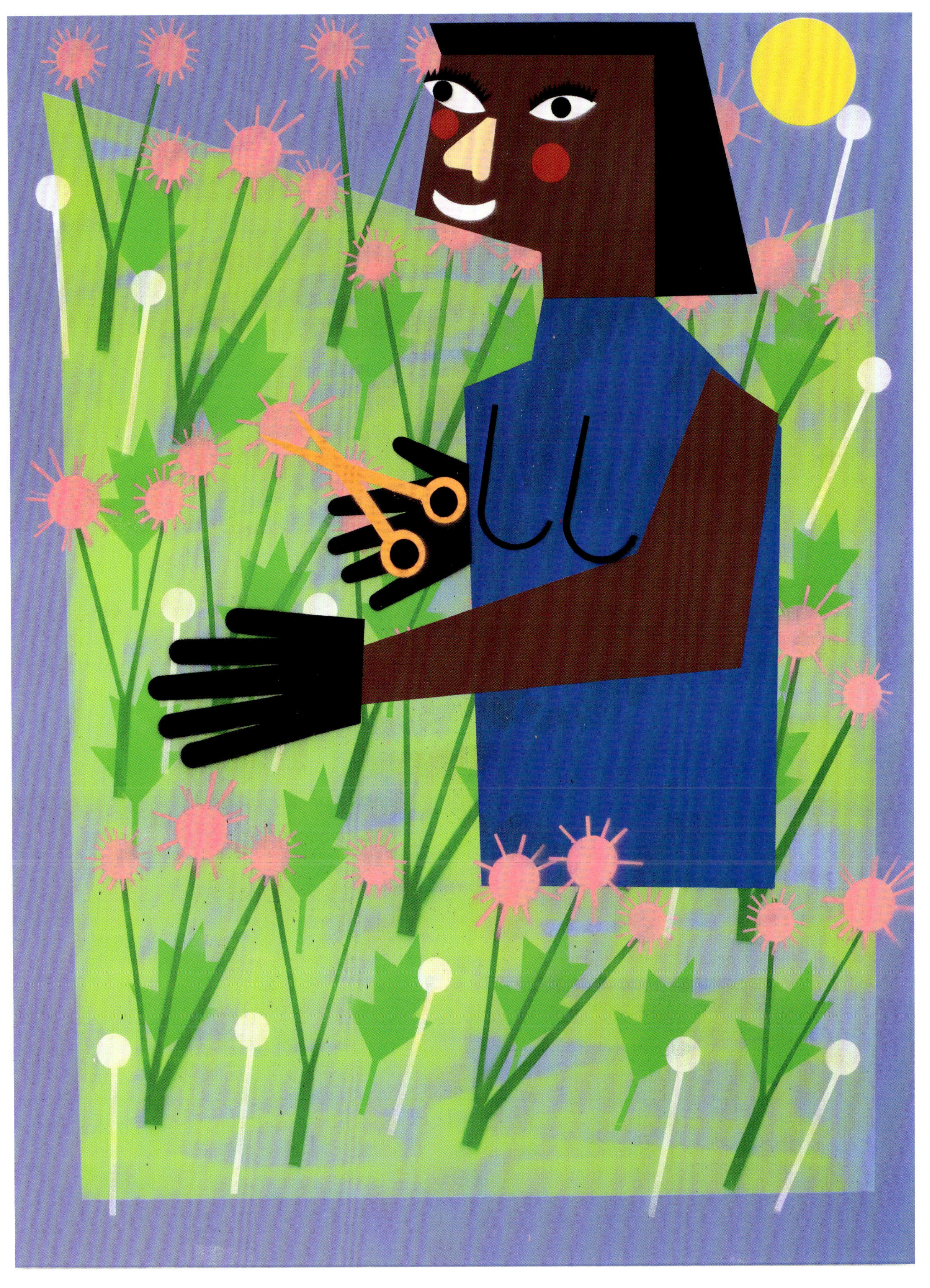

Cut Em' Off, 2020

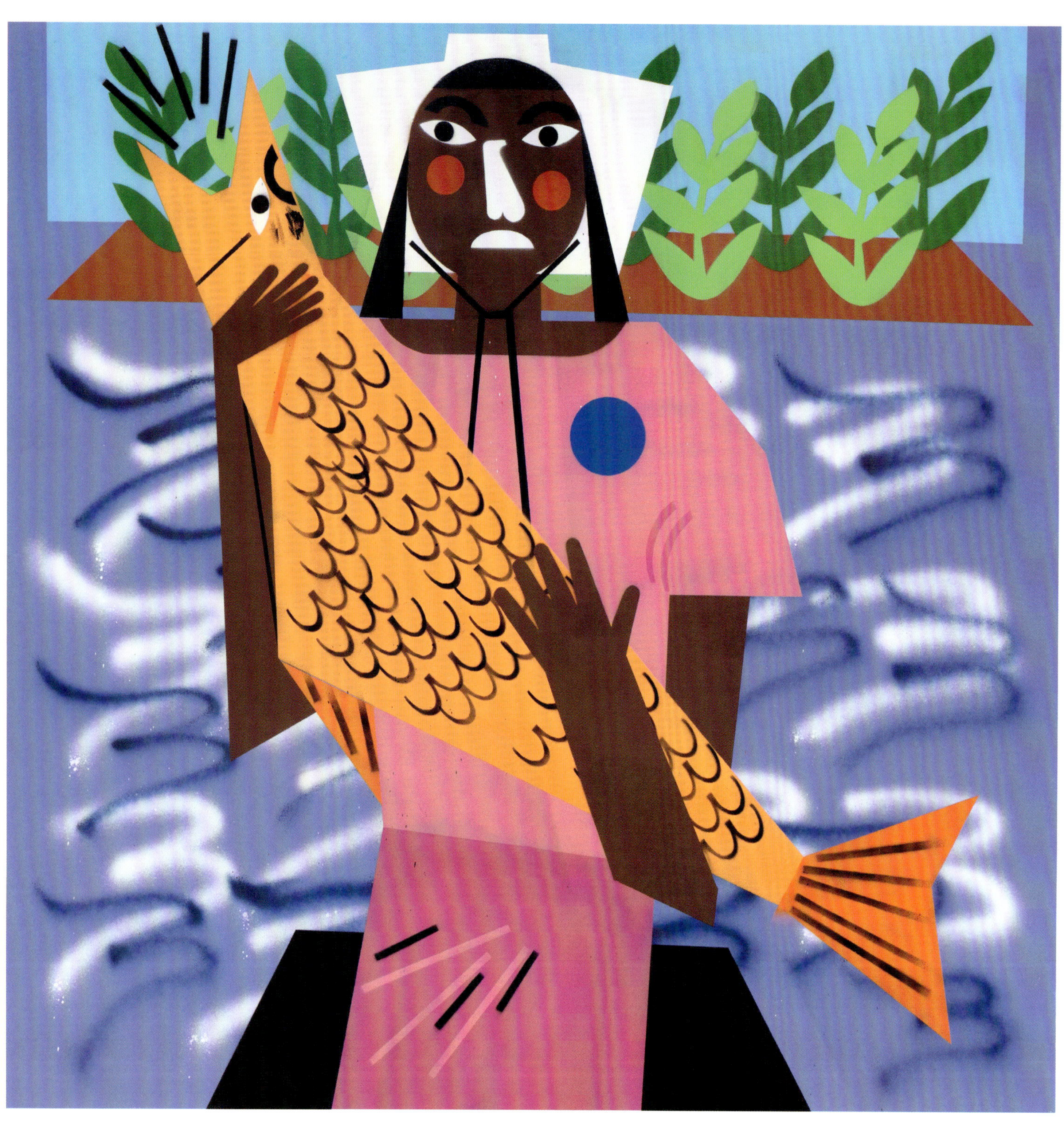

Plenty of Fish, 2020

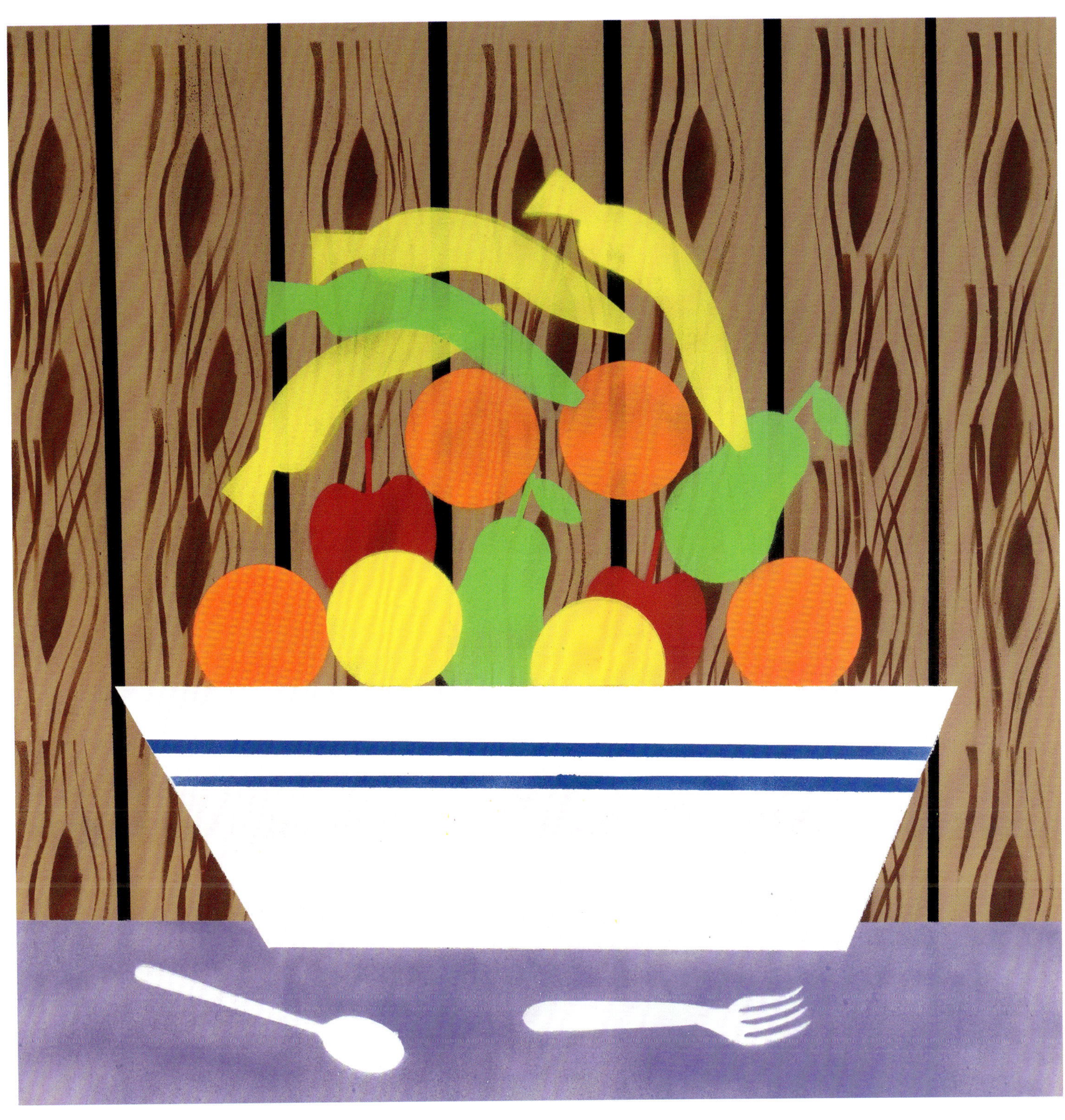

Bring Me A Cutie, 2020

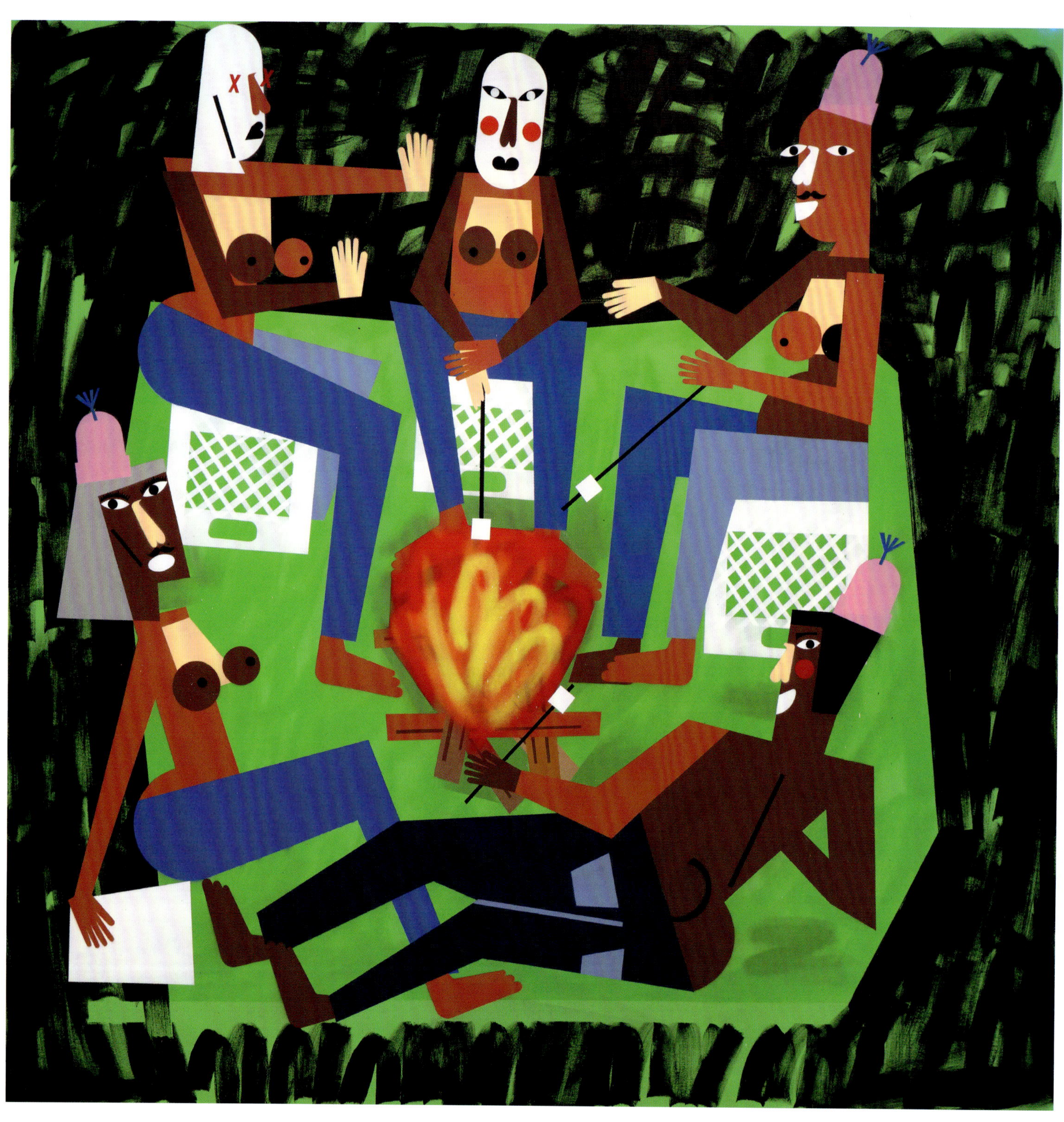

Storytime - Learn How to Read, 2020

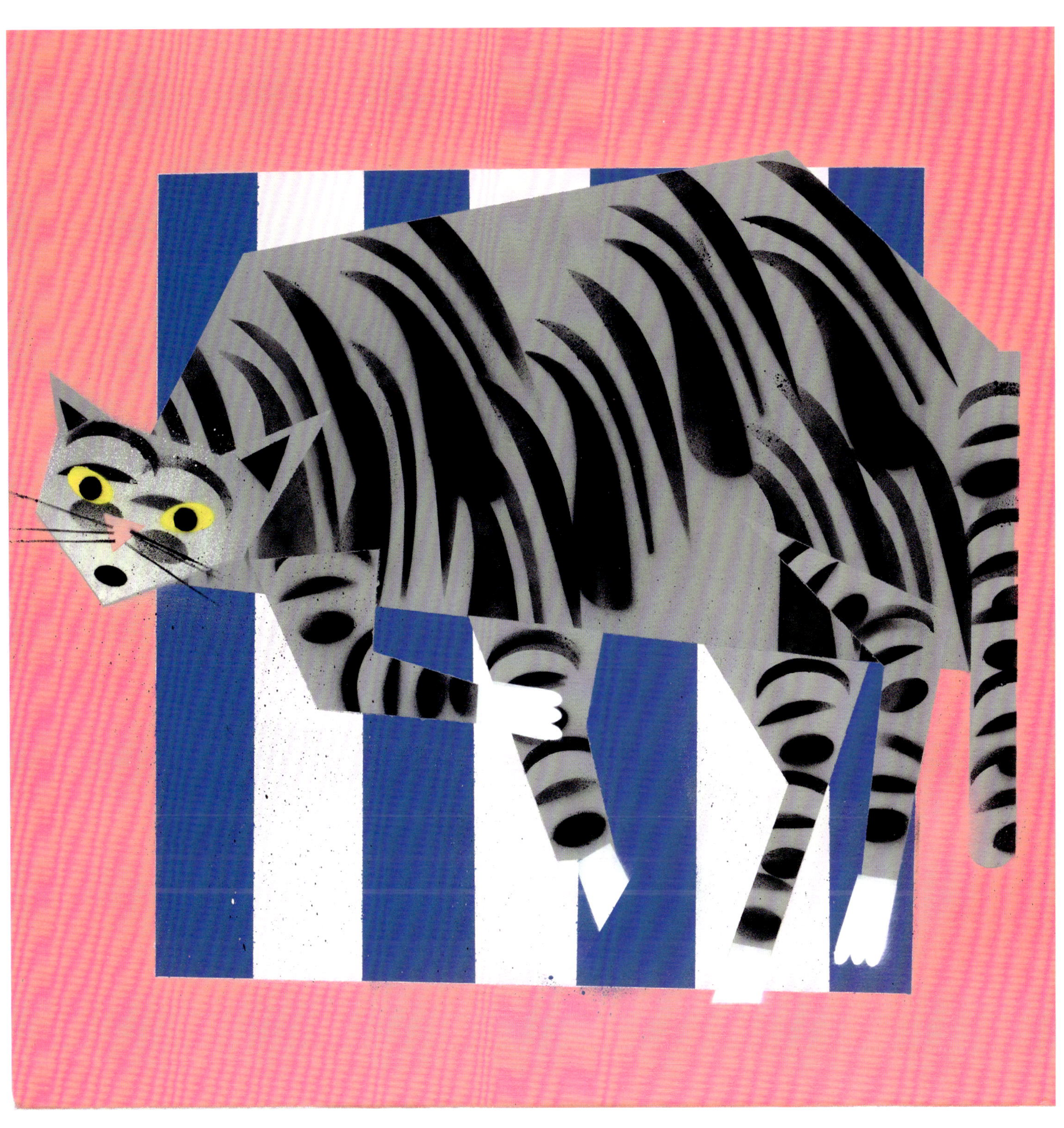

He's Catty, 2020

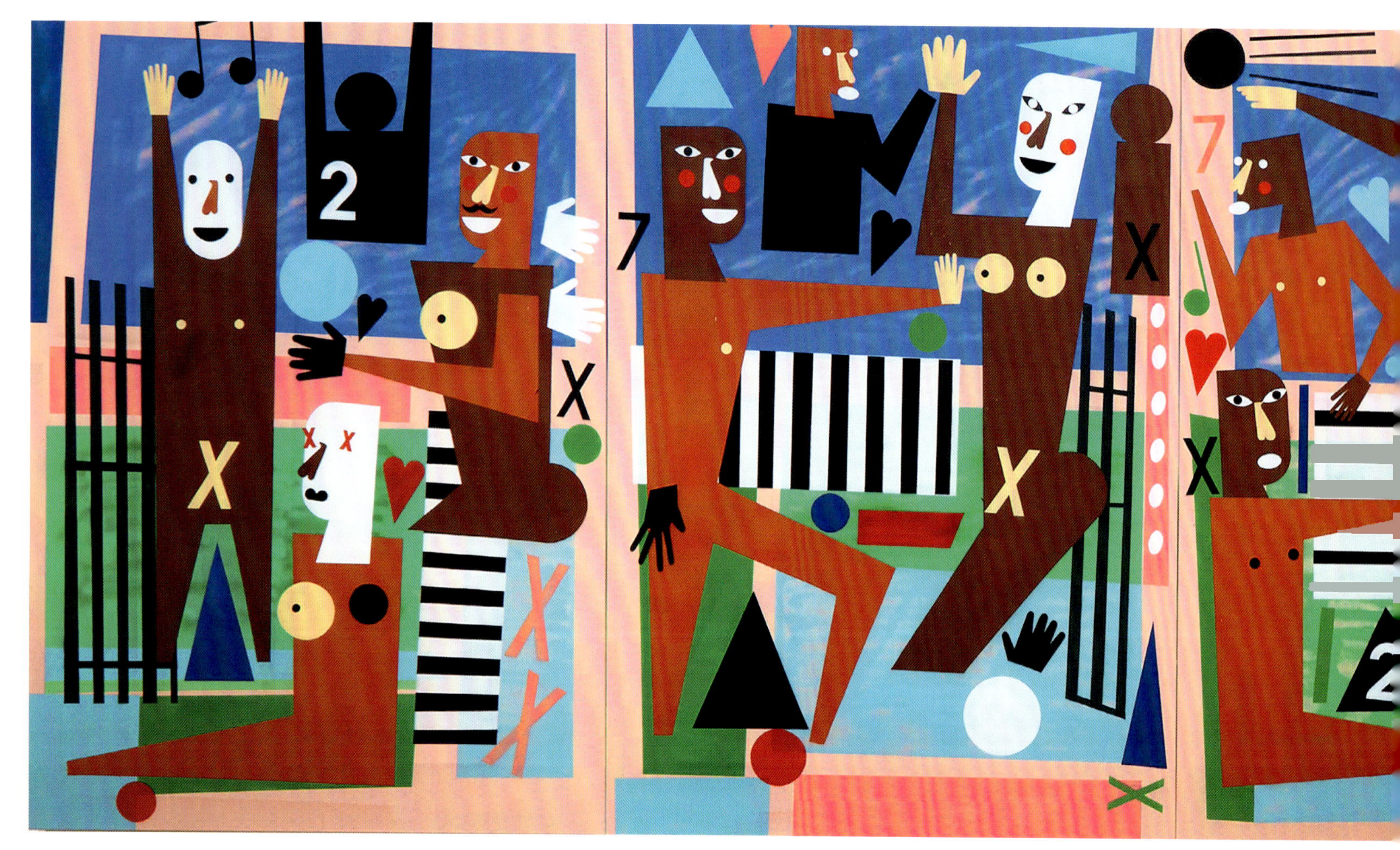

2 Step, 2021

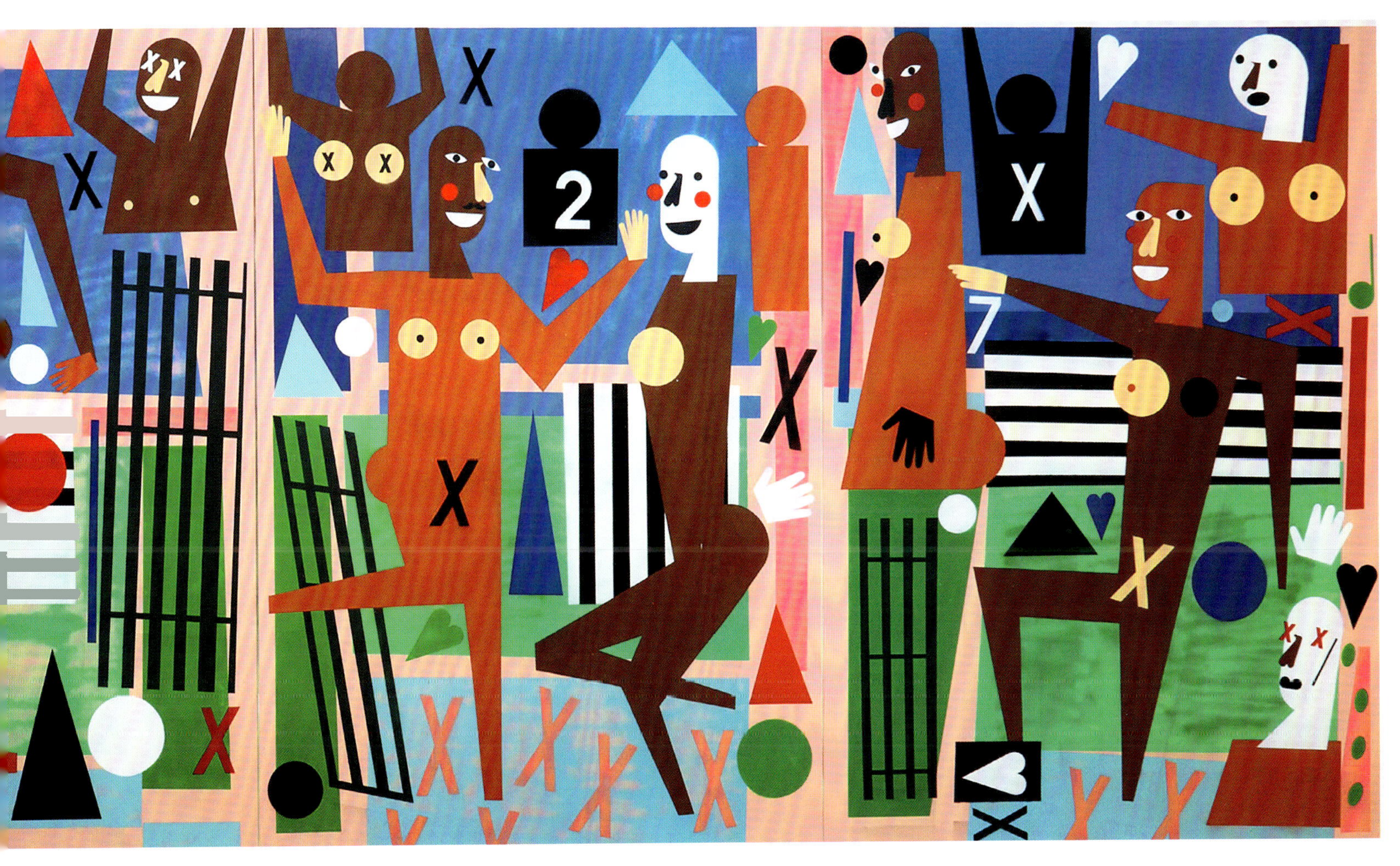

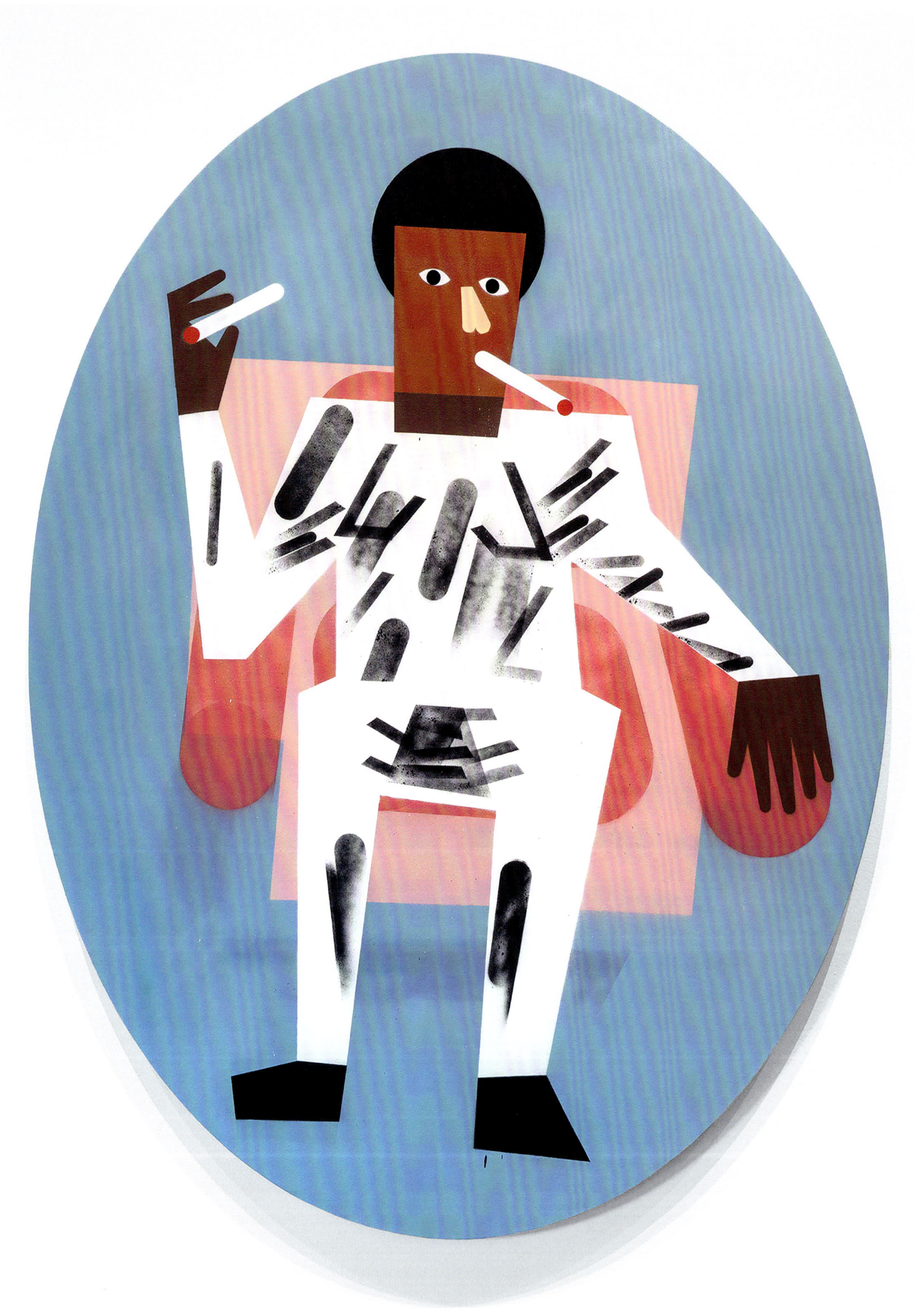

Mary, 2022

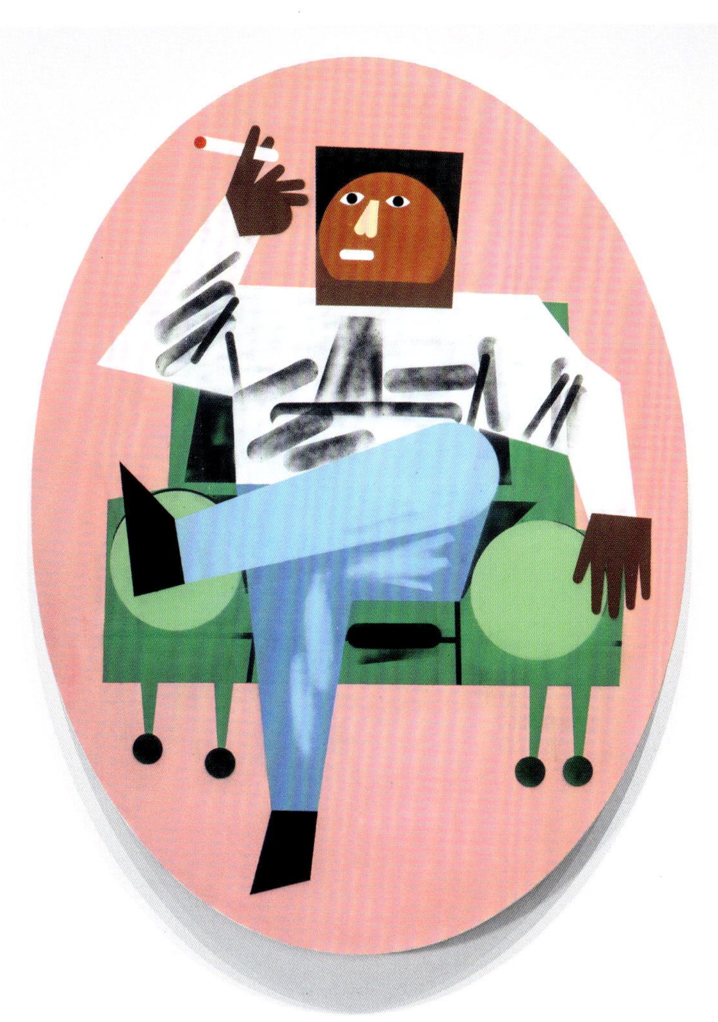

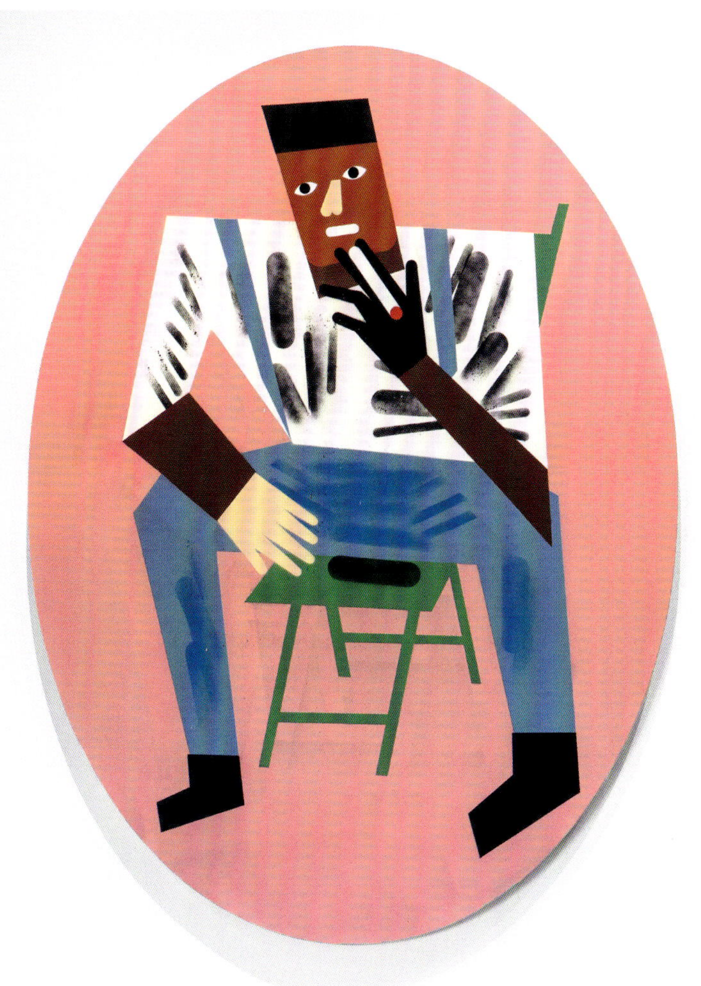

[LEFT] Courtney, 2022
[RIGHT] Jordan, 2022

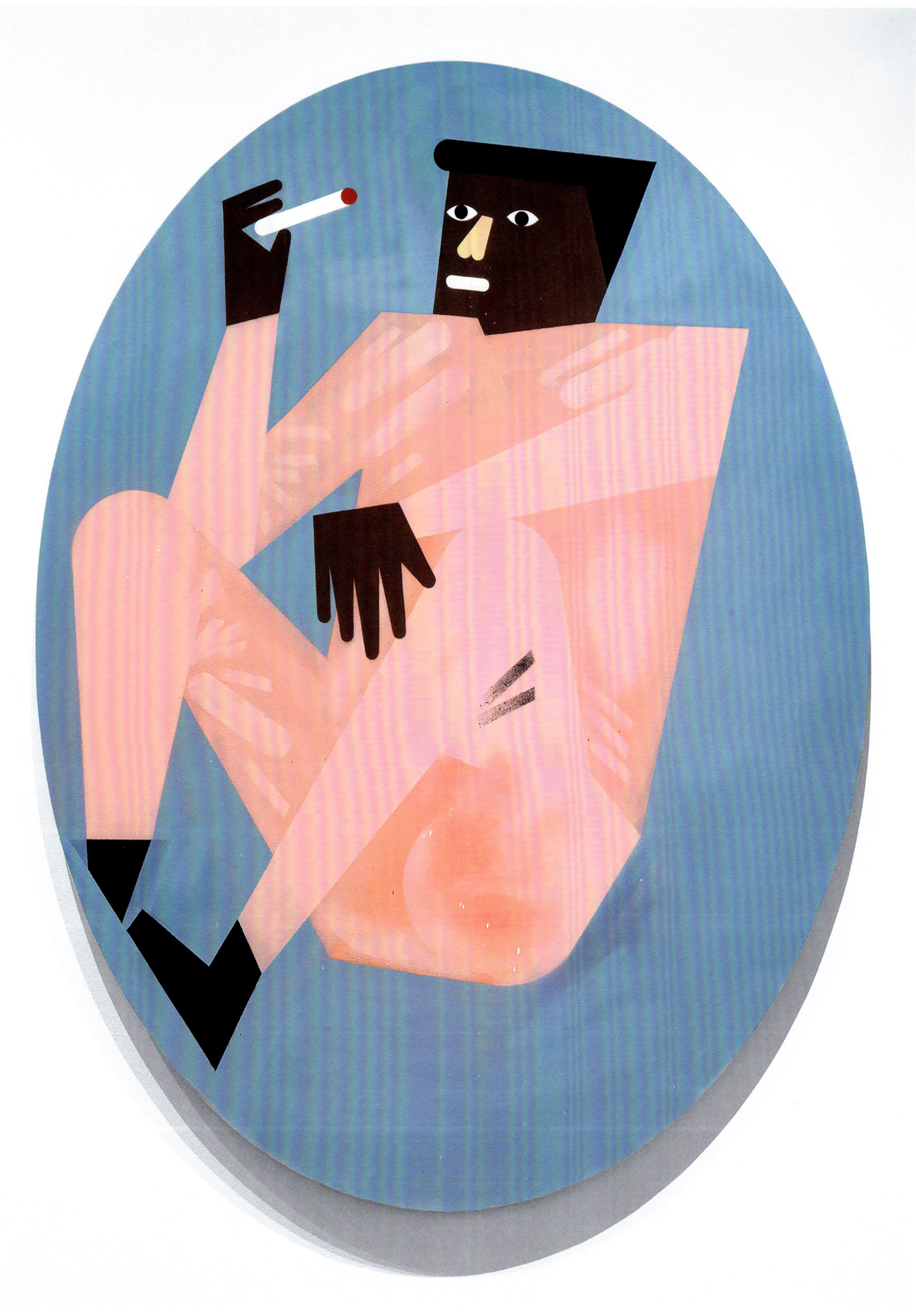

Jackie, 2022

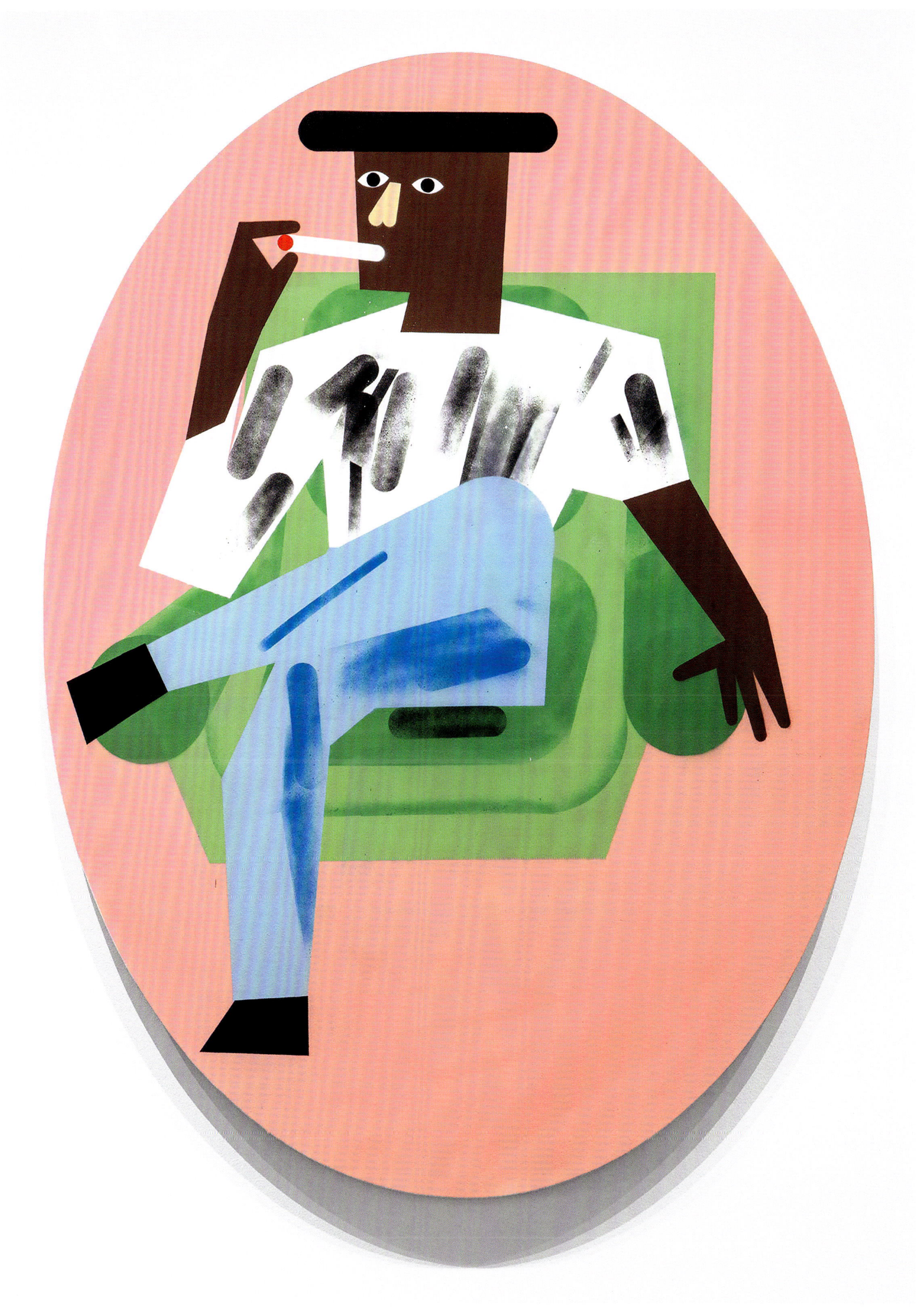

Keisha, 2022

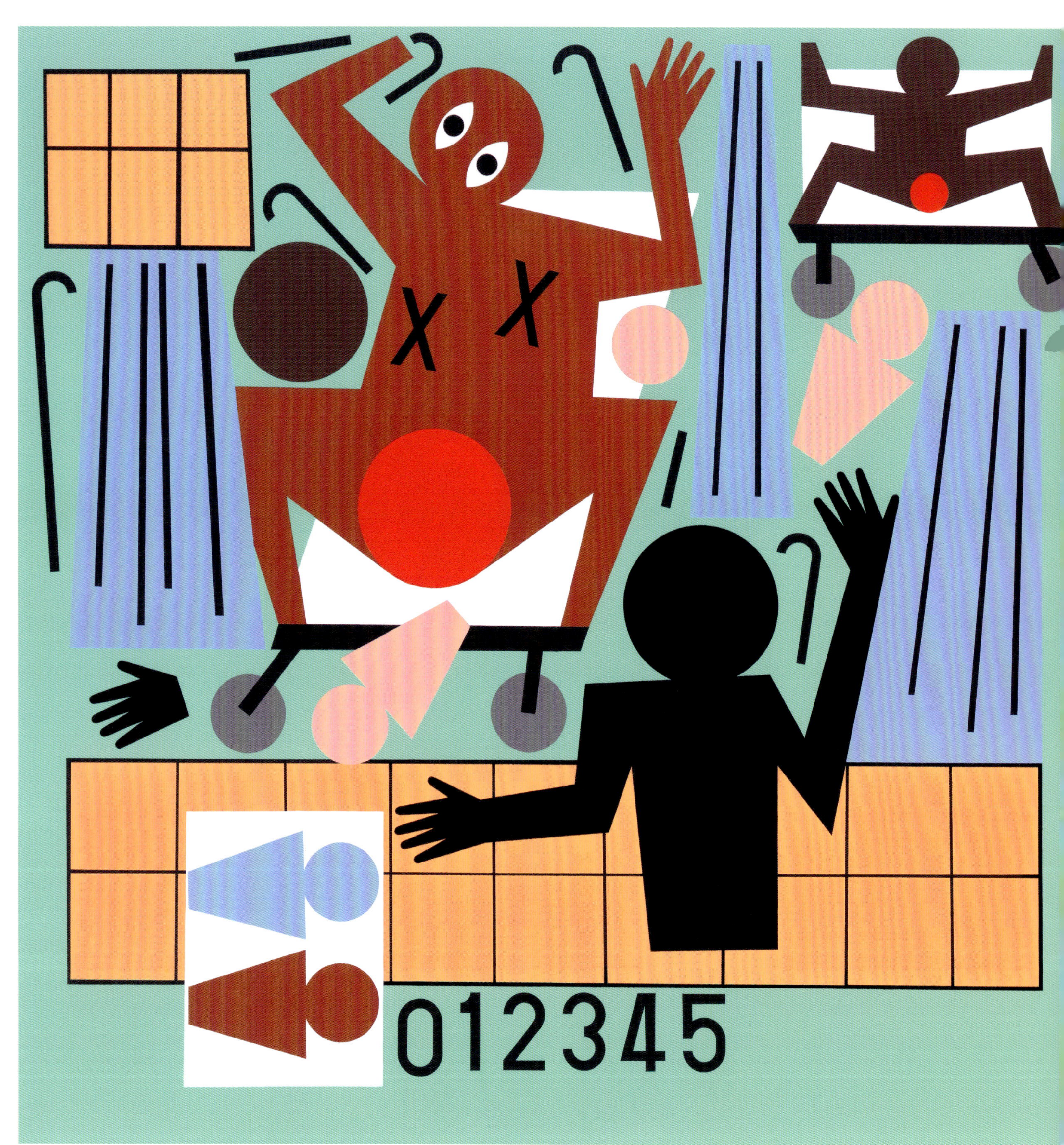

[ABOVE] Marabou, 2024
[OVERLEAF] Miss Opportunity, 2024

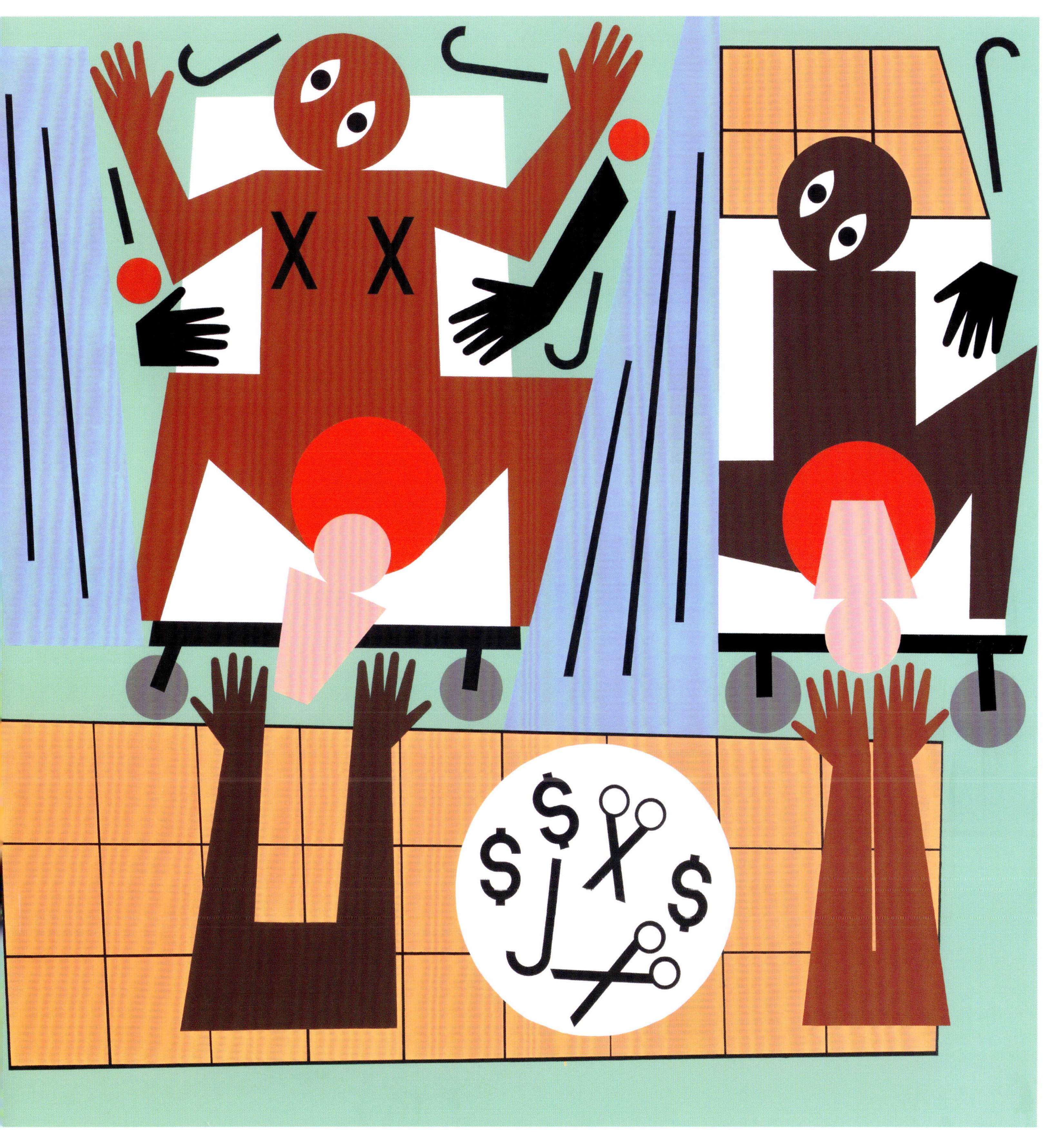

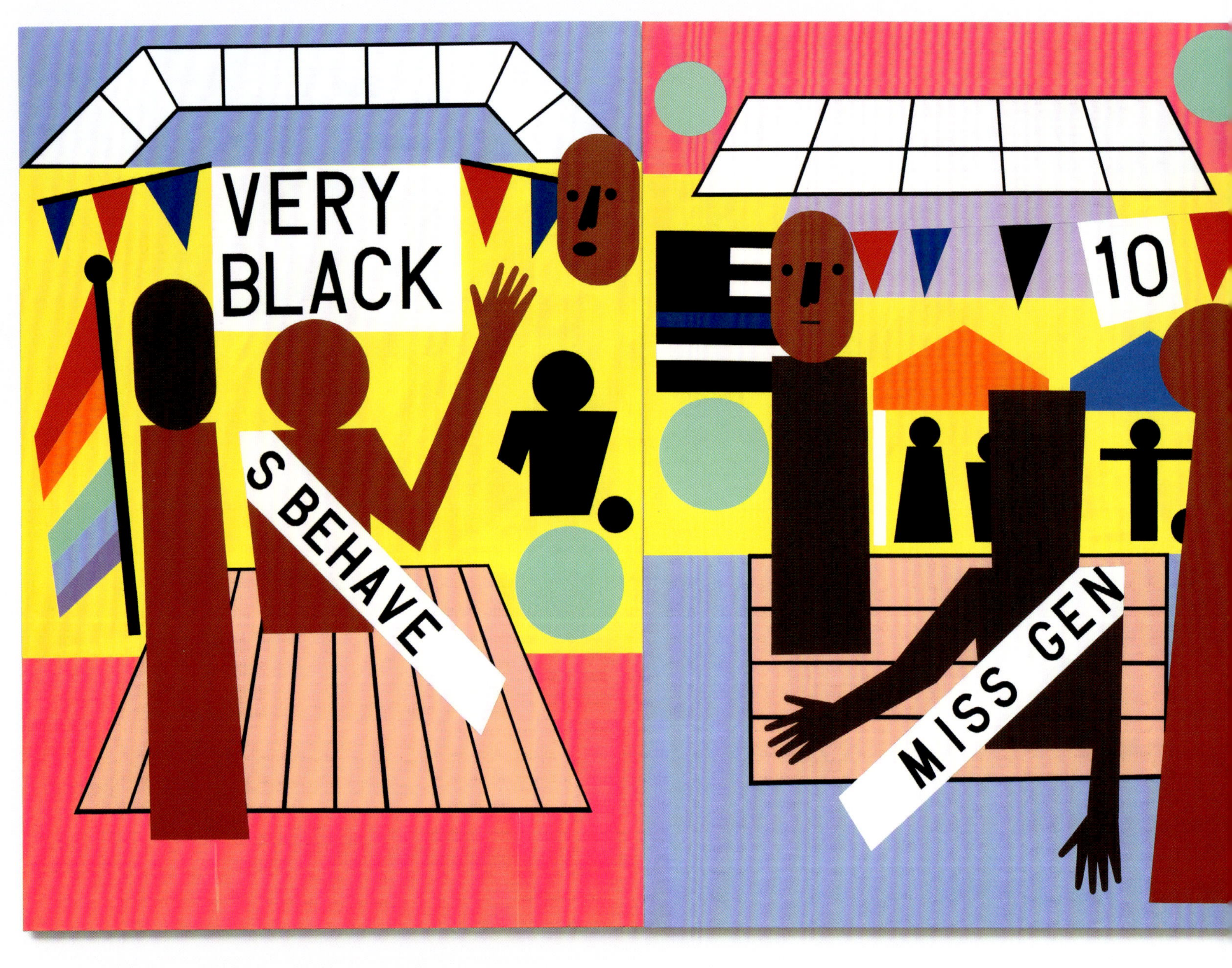
VERY
BLACK
S BEHAVE
10
MISS GEN

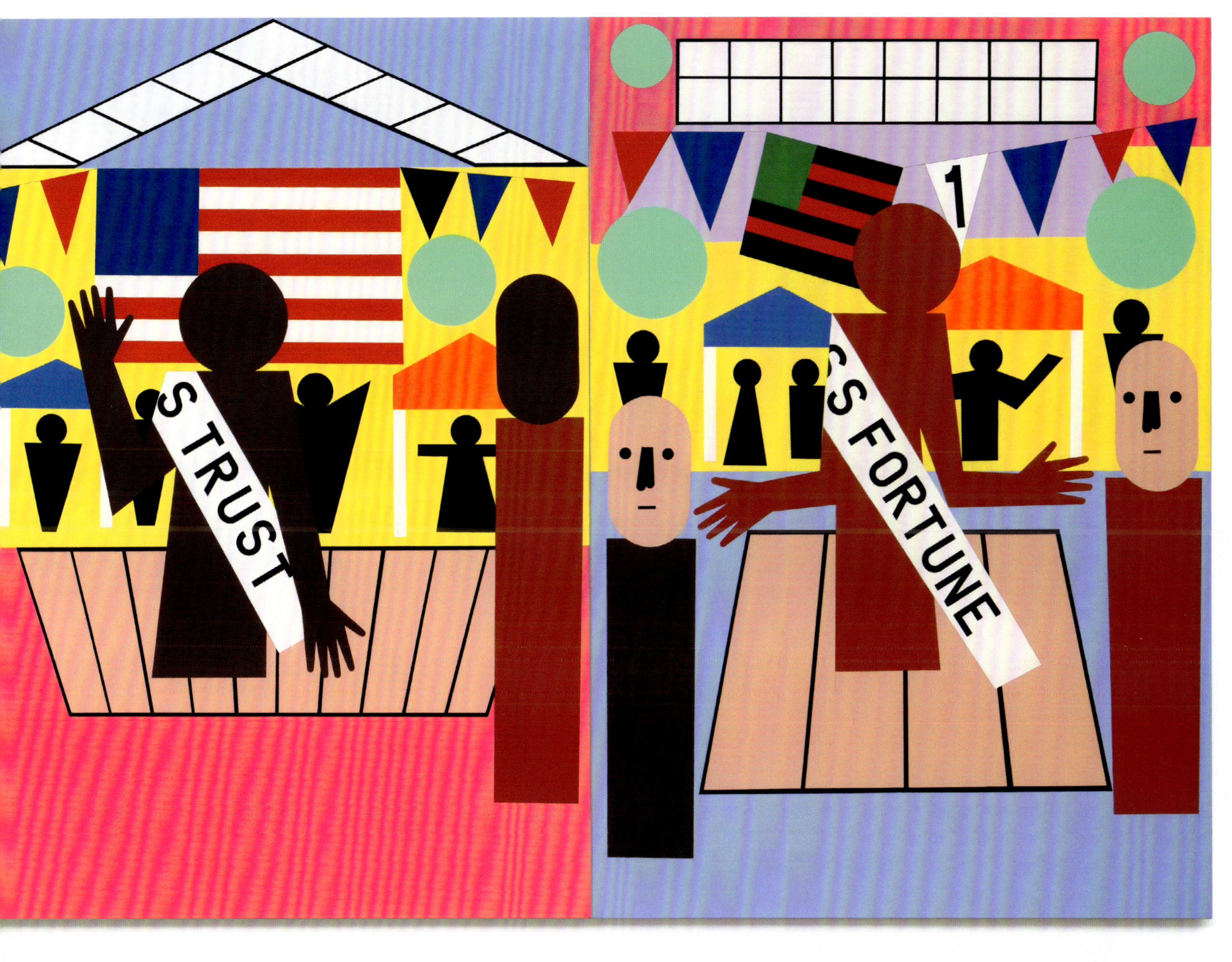
S TRUST
S FORTUNE
1

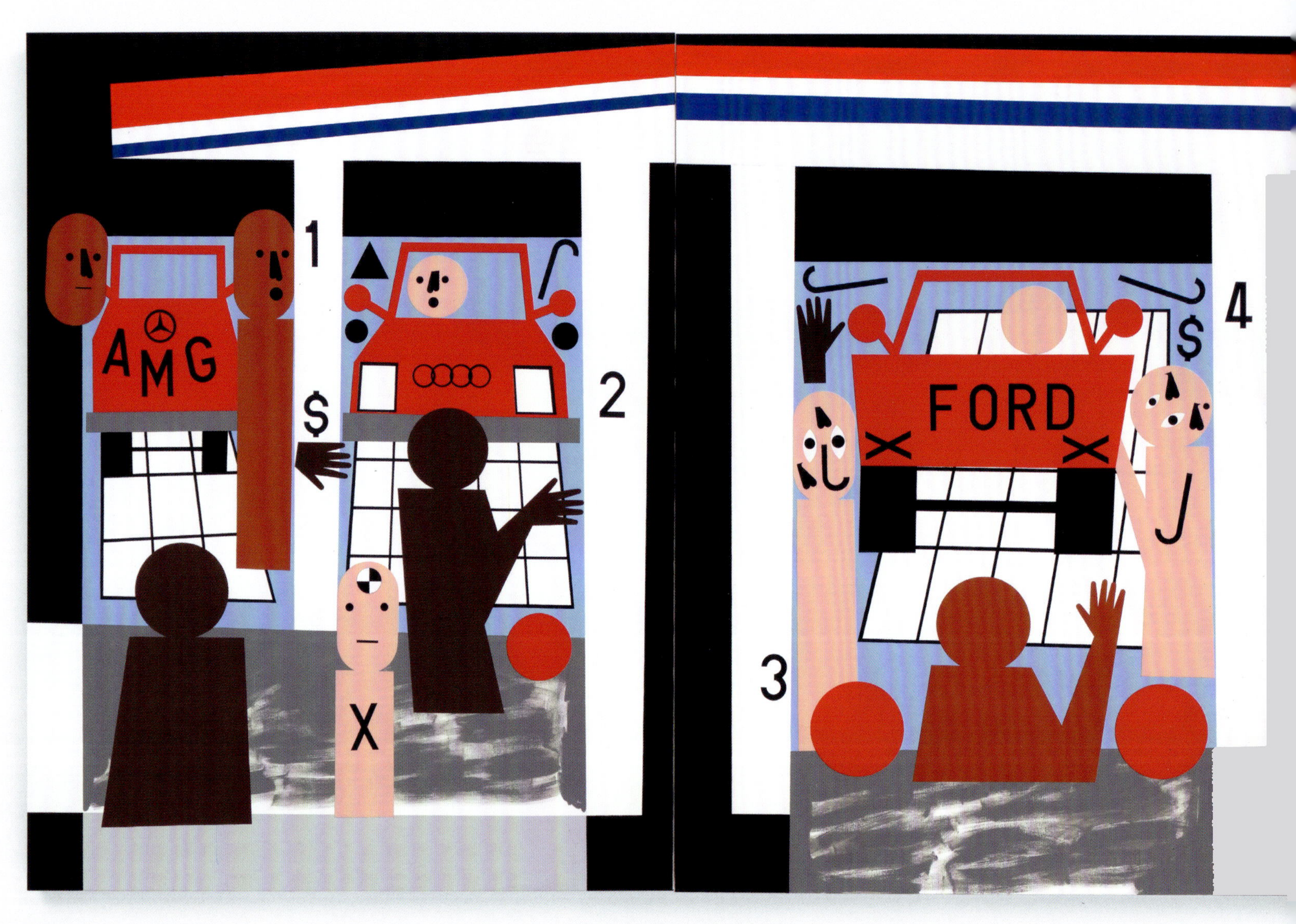
AMG
1
2
3
4
$
X
FORD

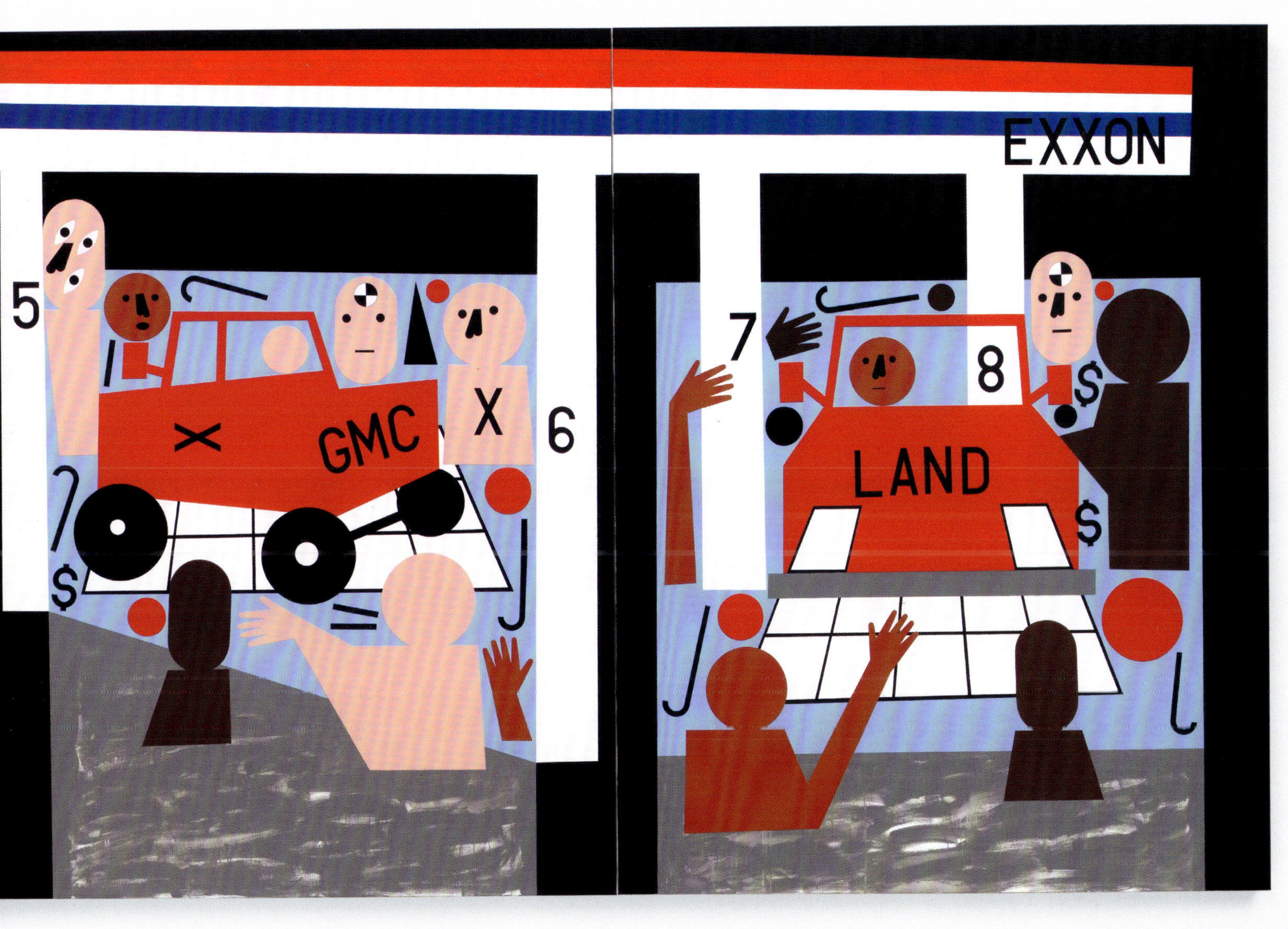
EXXON
5
GMC
X
6
7
8
LAND
$

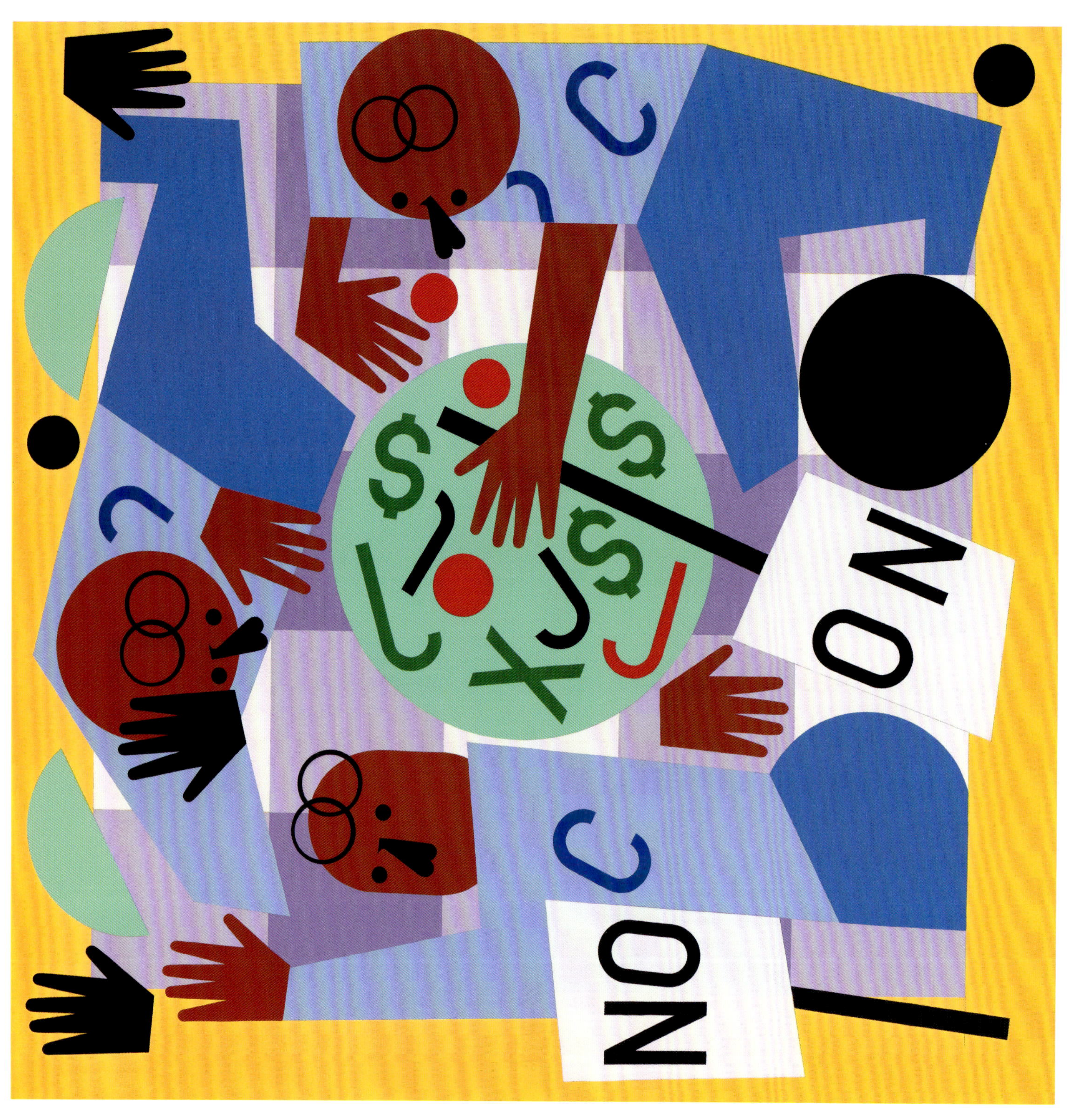

[PREVIOUS] Flint Fuel, 2024
[ABOVE] Picnic at Butler, 2024

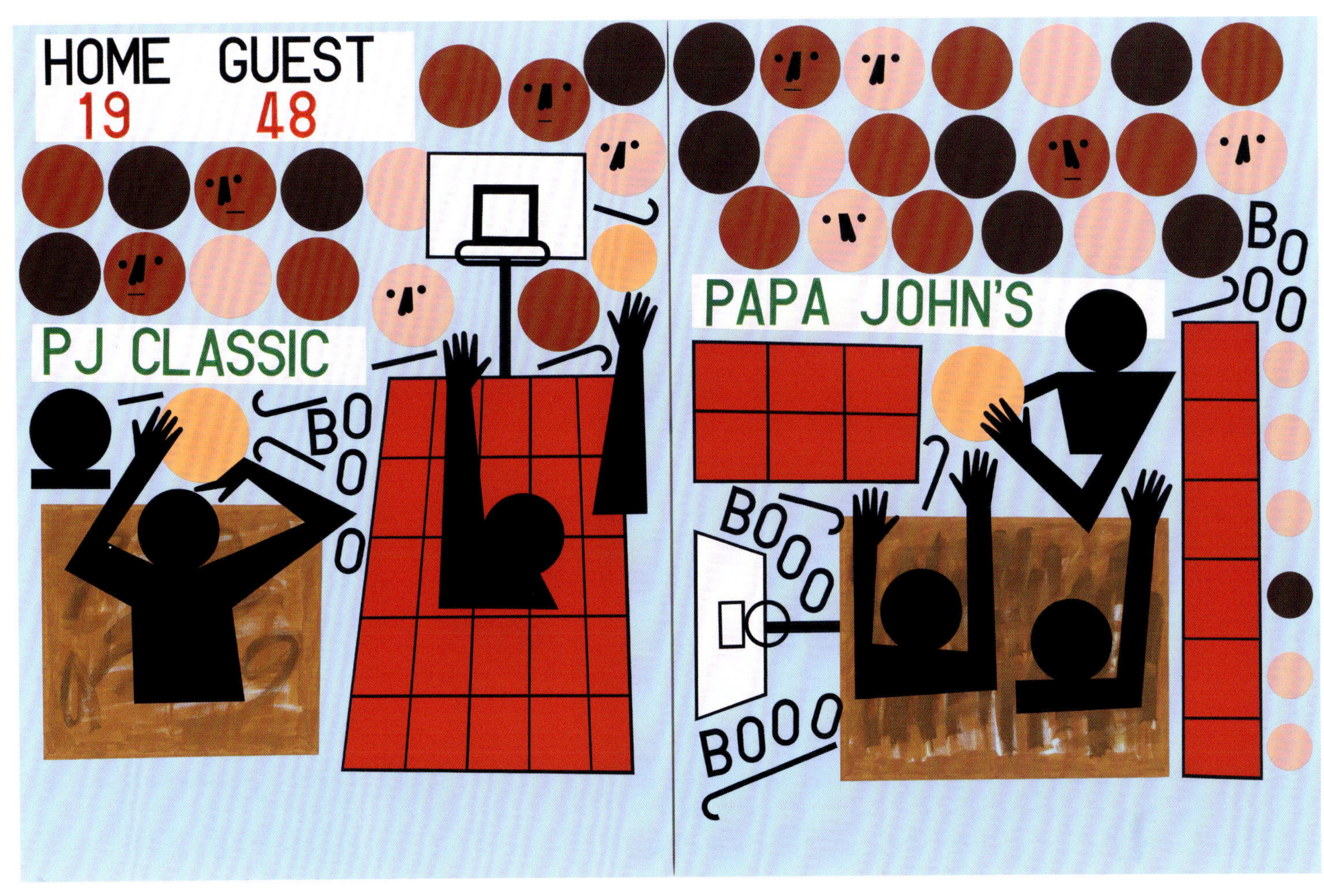

All Fun and Games Until, 2024

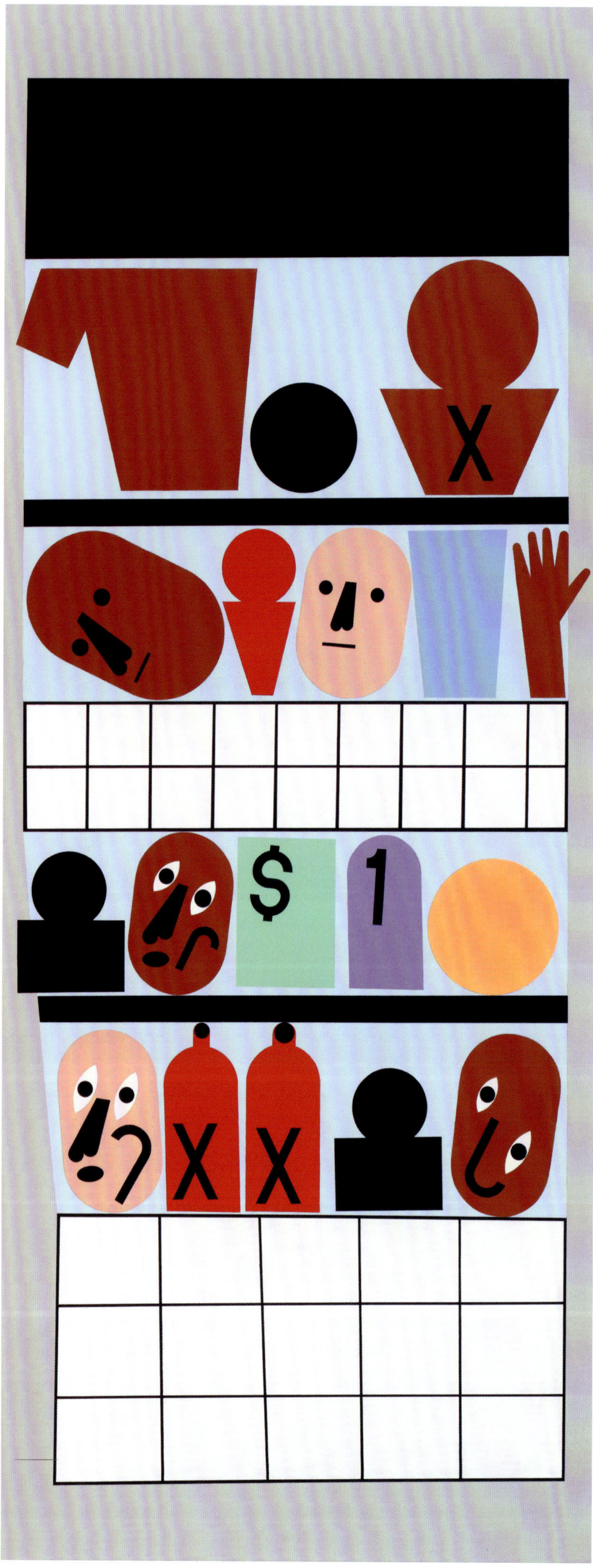

Stock 2, 2024

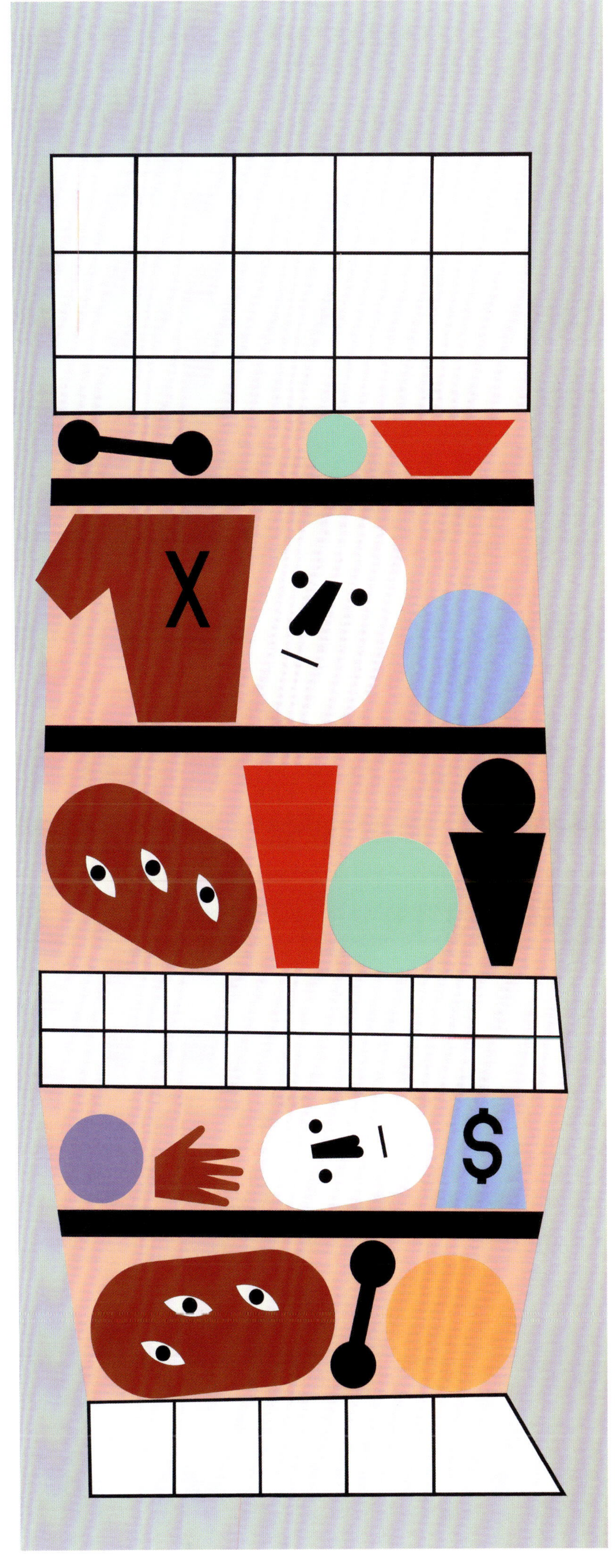

Stock 1, 2024

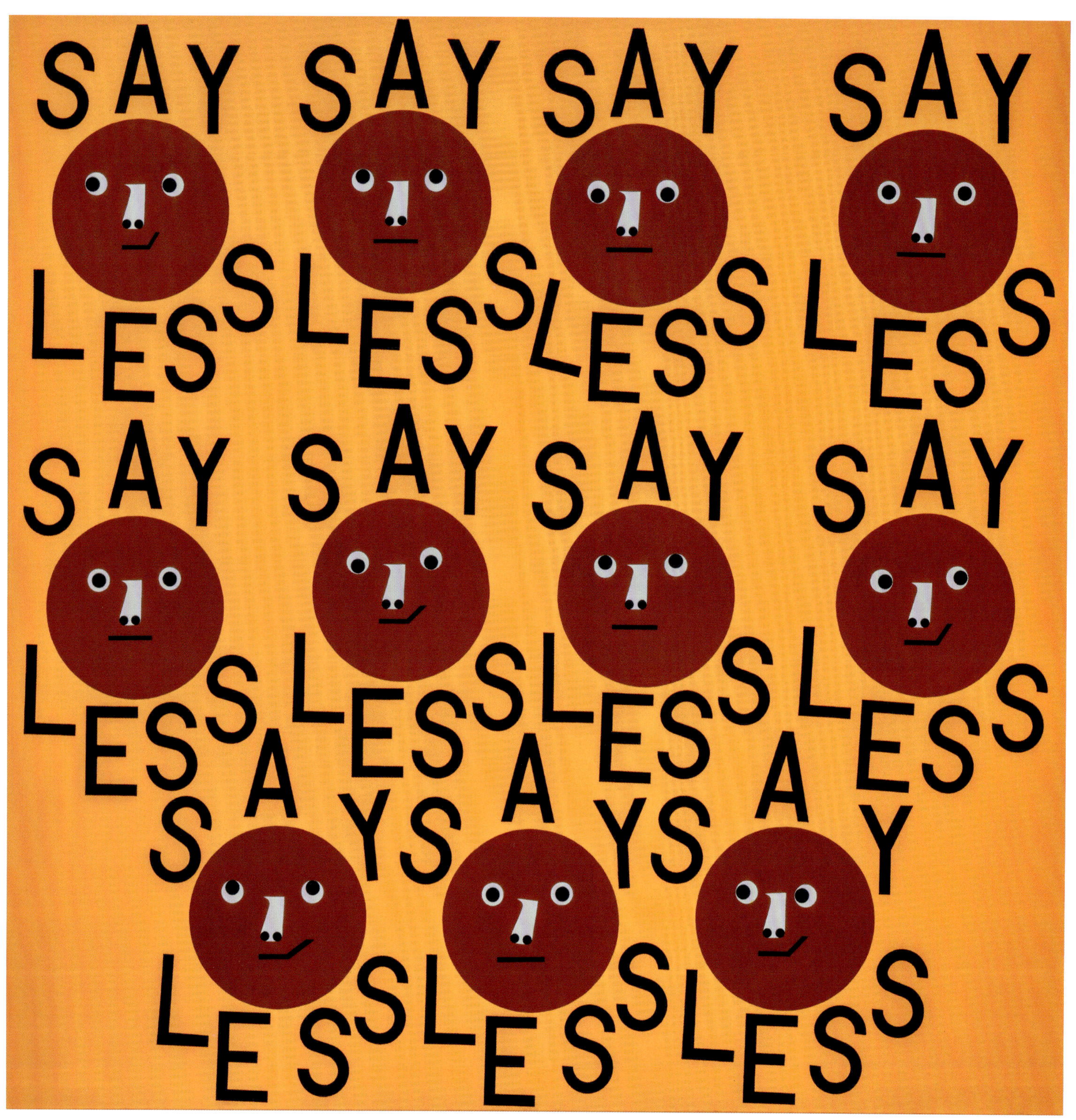
SAY SAY SAY SAY
LESS LESS LESS LESS
SAY SAY SAY SAY
LESS LESS LESS LESS
SAY SAY SAY
LESS LESS LESS

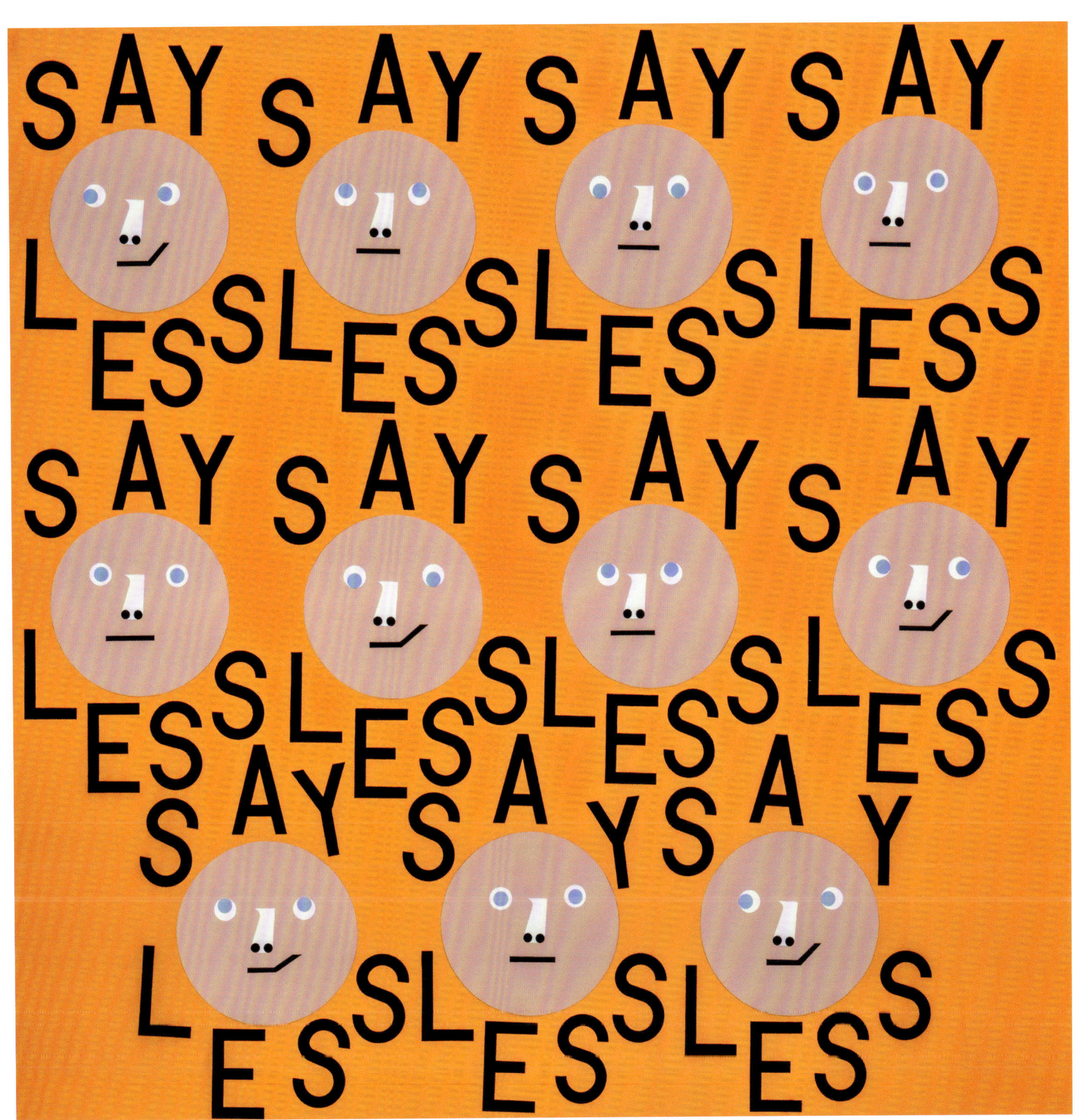
SAY SAY SAY SAY
LESS LESS LESS LESS
SAY SAY SAY SAY
LESS LESS LESS LESS
SAY SAY SAY
LESS LESS LESS

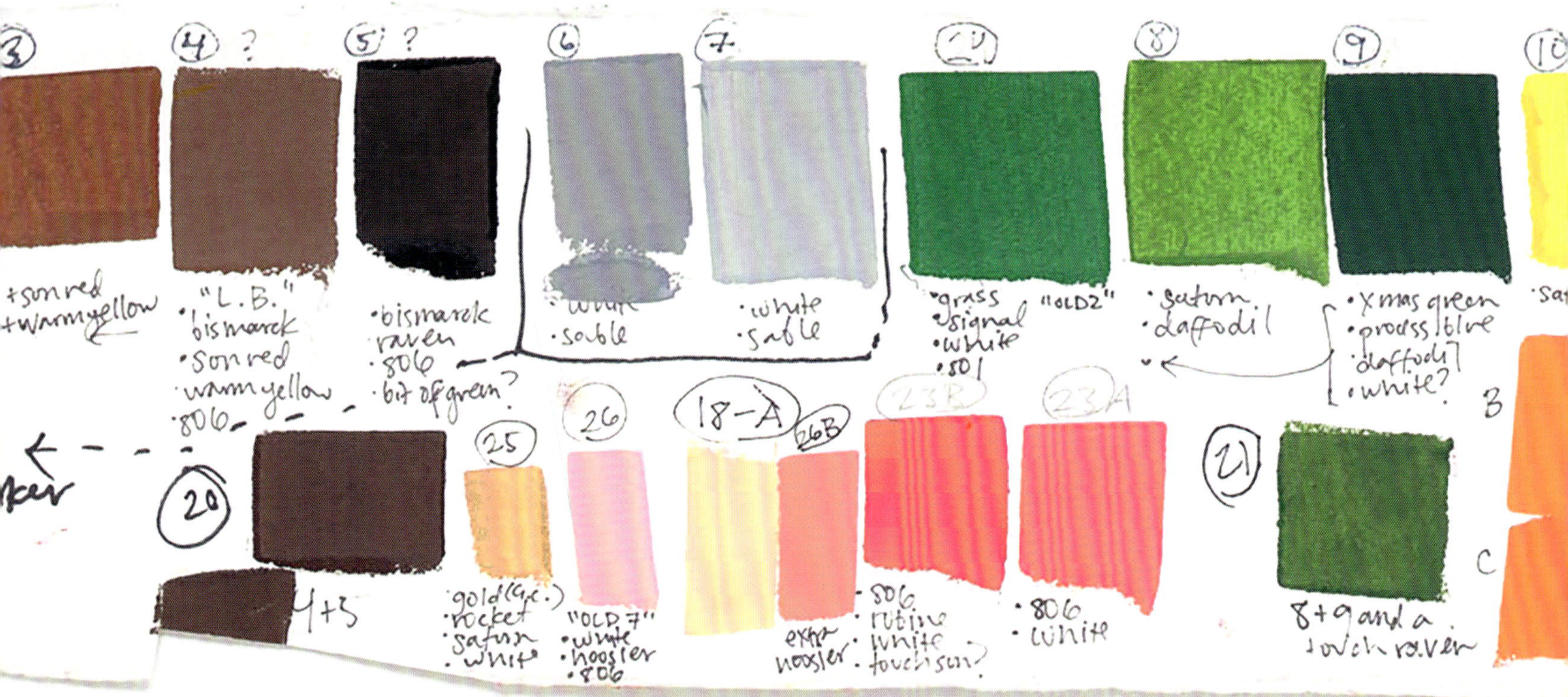
3
4 ?
5 ?
6
7
8
9
+son red +warm yellow
"L.B." ·bismarck ·son red ·warm yellow ·806
·bismarck raven ·806 ·bit of green?
·white ·sable
·white ·sable
·grass ·signal ·white ·801
"OLD2"
·saturn ·daffodil
·xmas green ·process blue ·daffodil ·white?
20
25
26
18-A
26B
23B
23A
21
B
C
4+5
·rocket ·saturn ·white
"OLD 7" ·white ·hoosier ·806
extra hoosier
·806 ·rubine ·white ·touch sun?
·806 ·white
8+9 and a touch raven

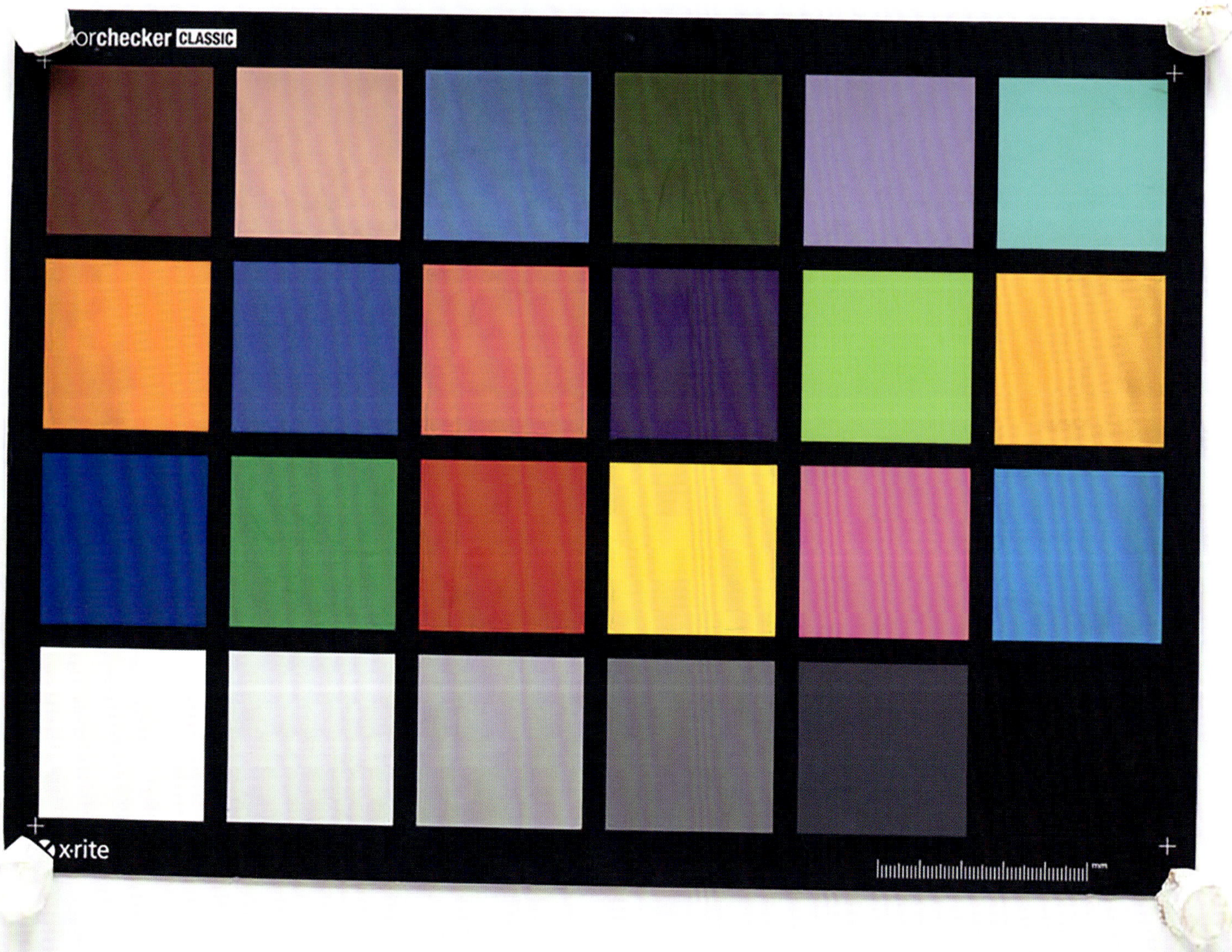

WORKS ON PAPER

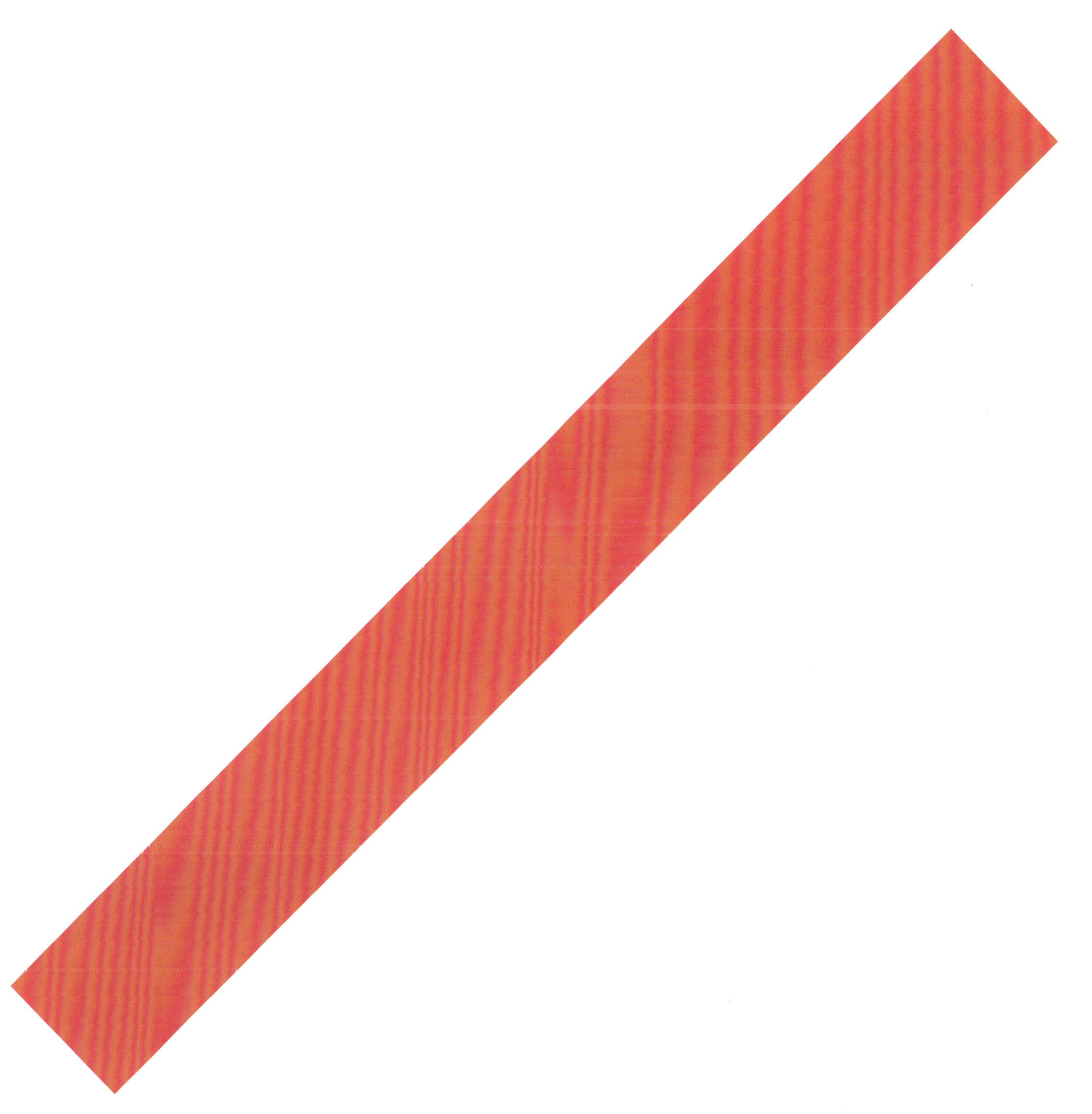

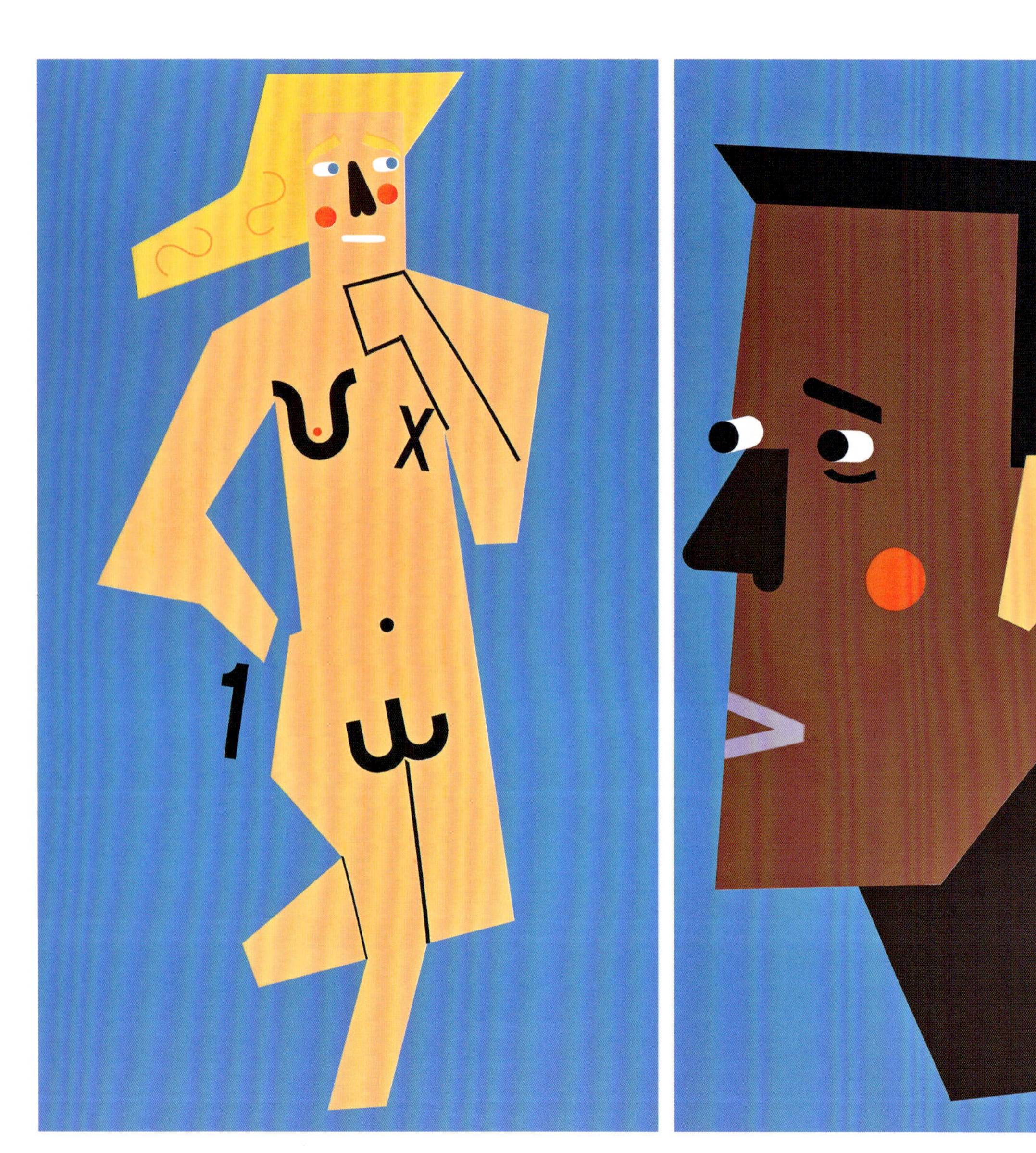

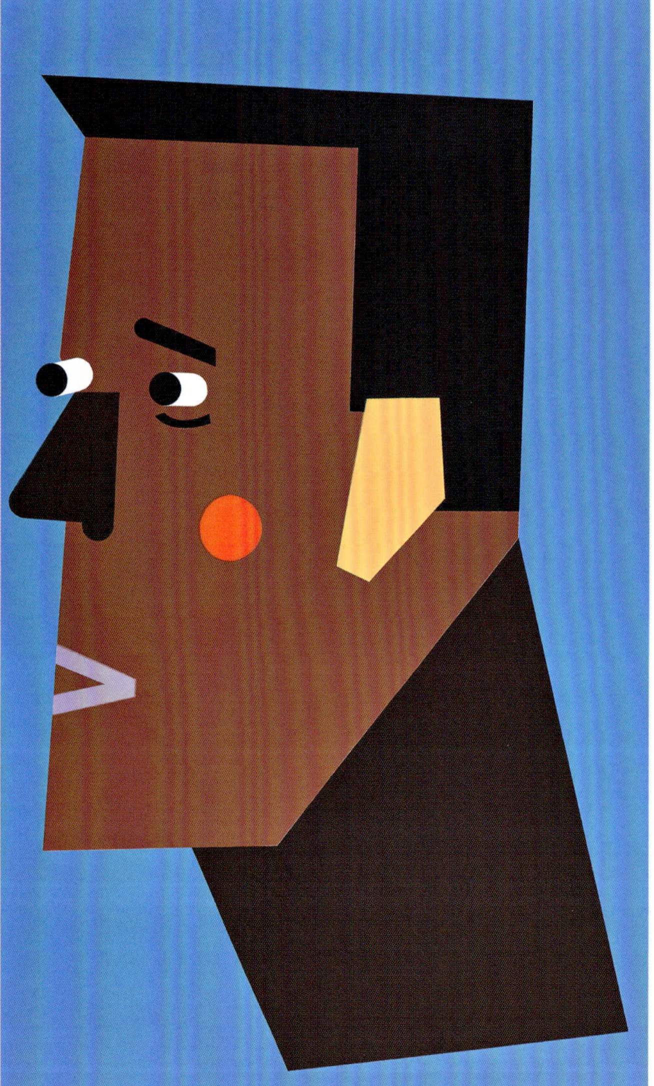

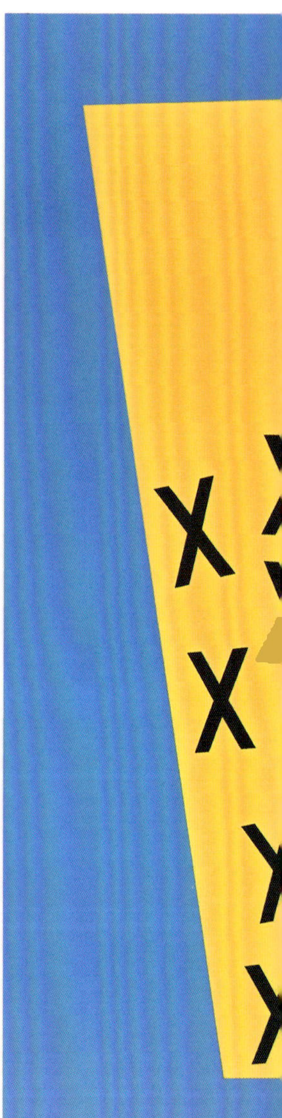

Ooh La, La, 2018

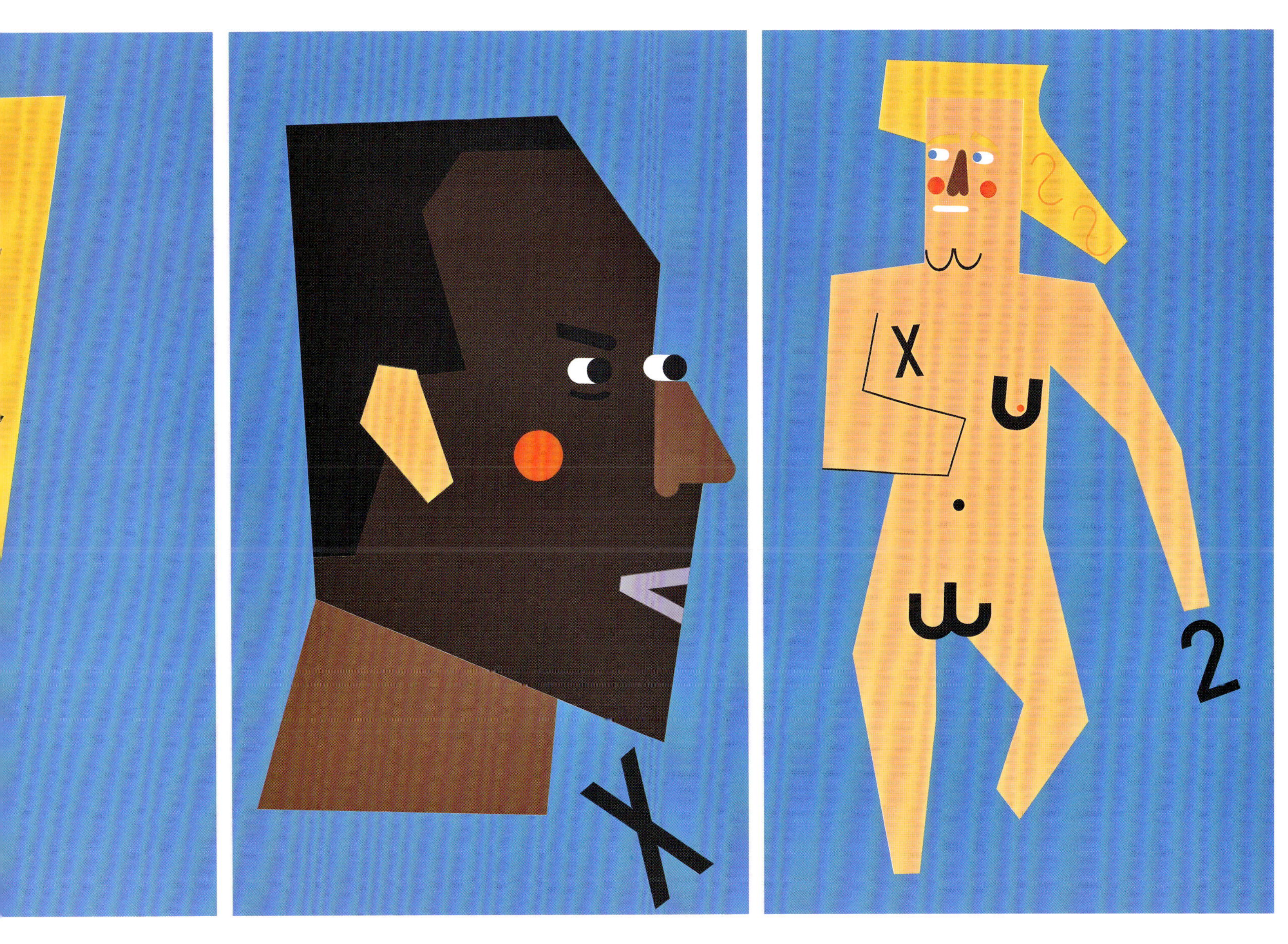

Third Time's the Charm, 2018

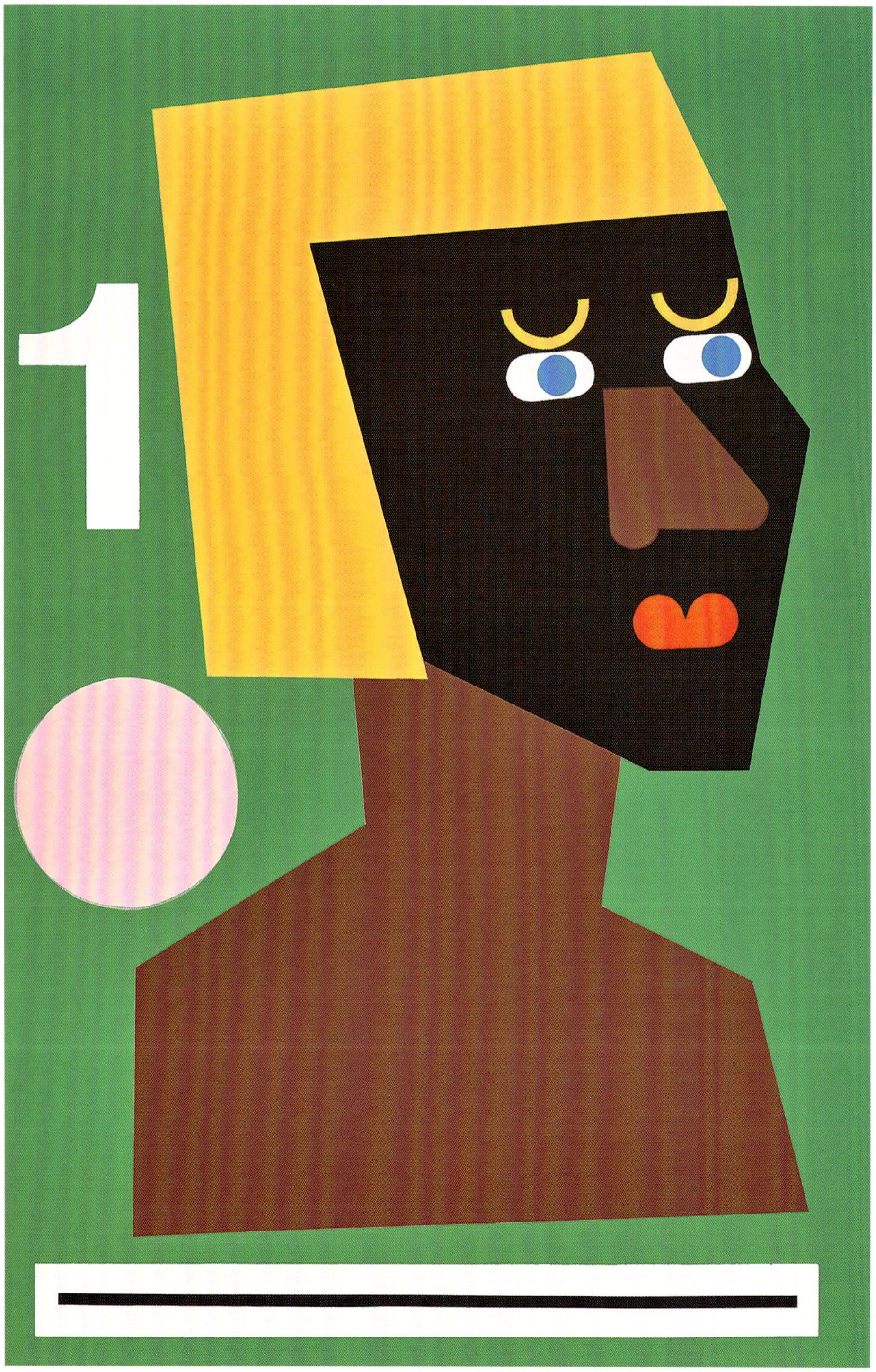

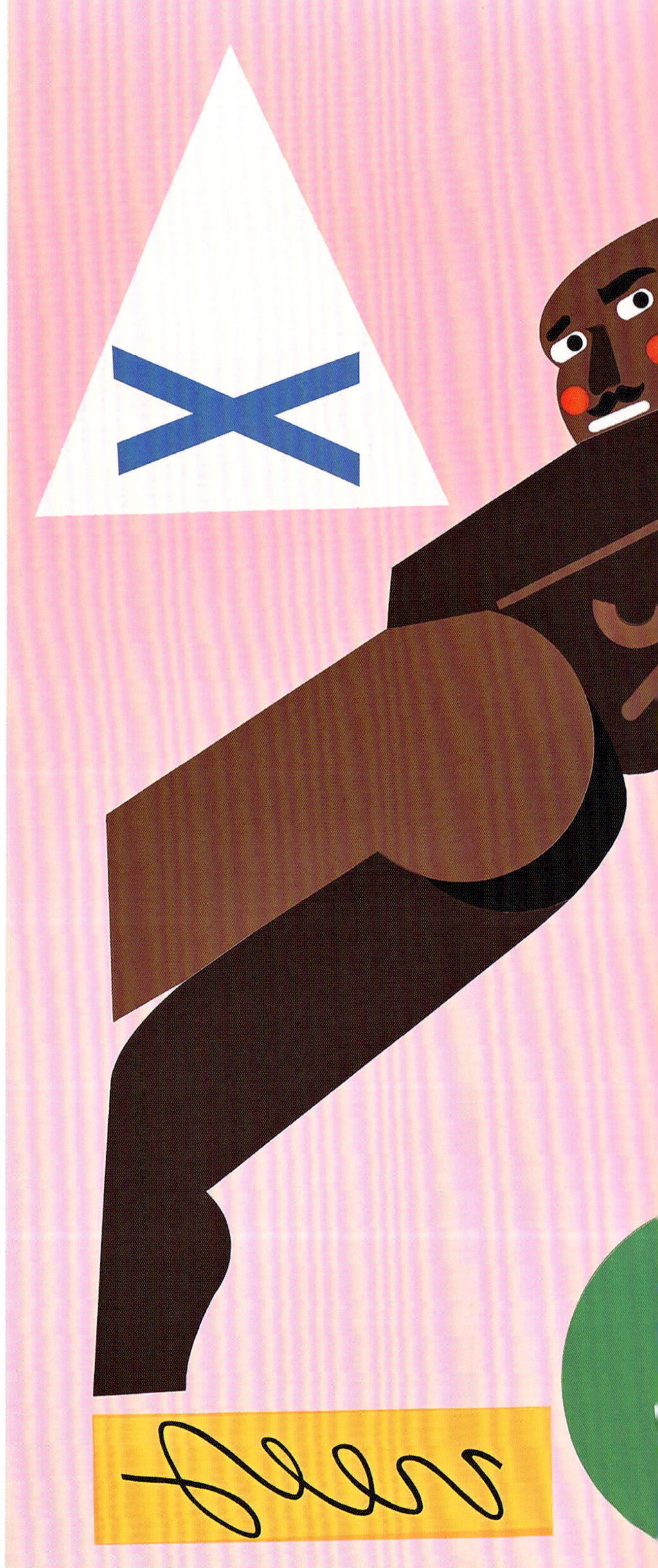

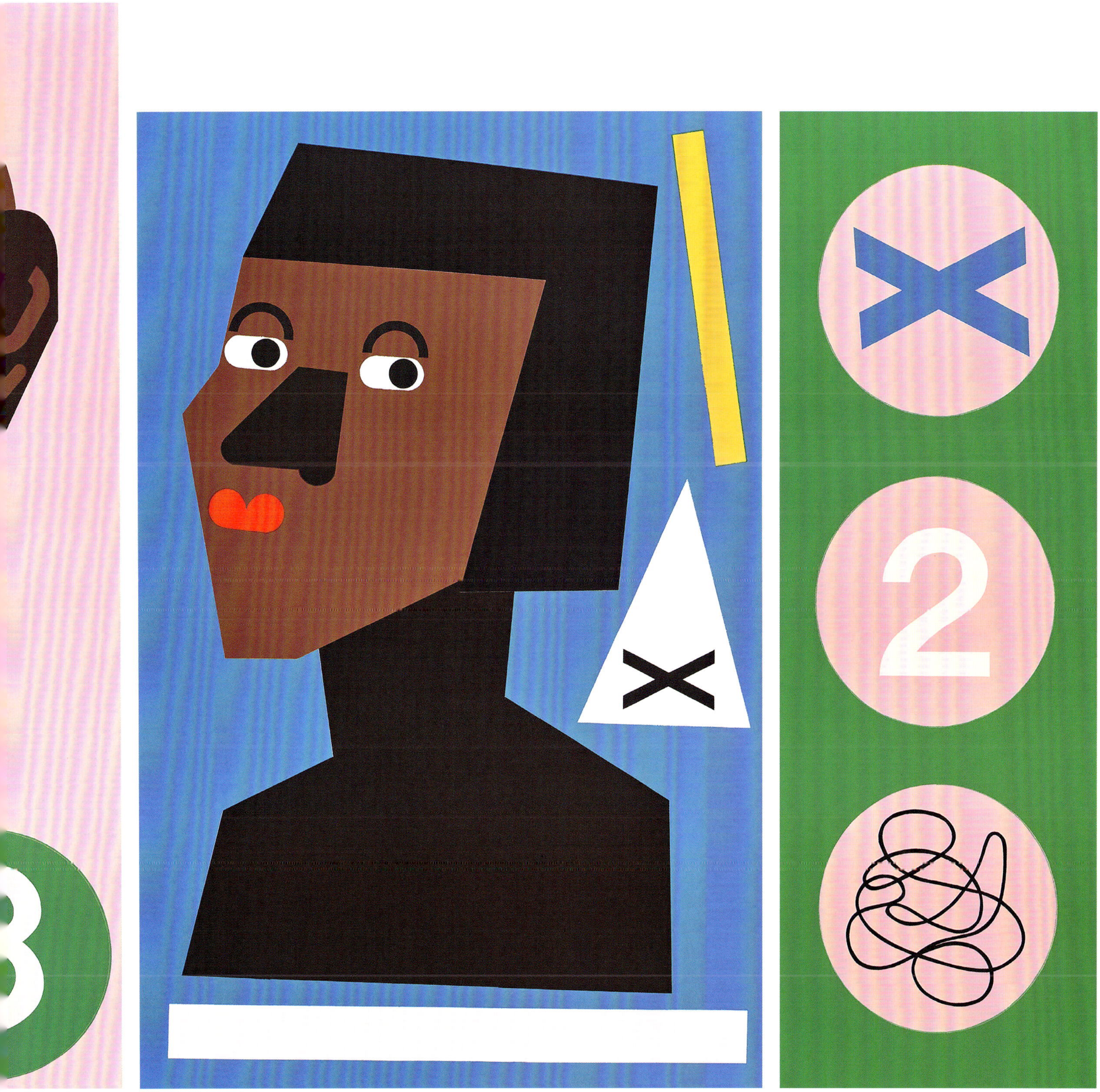

2

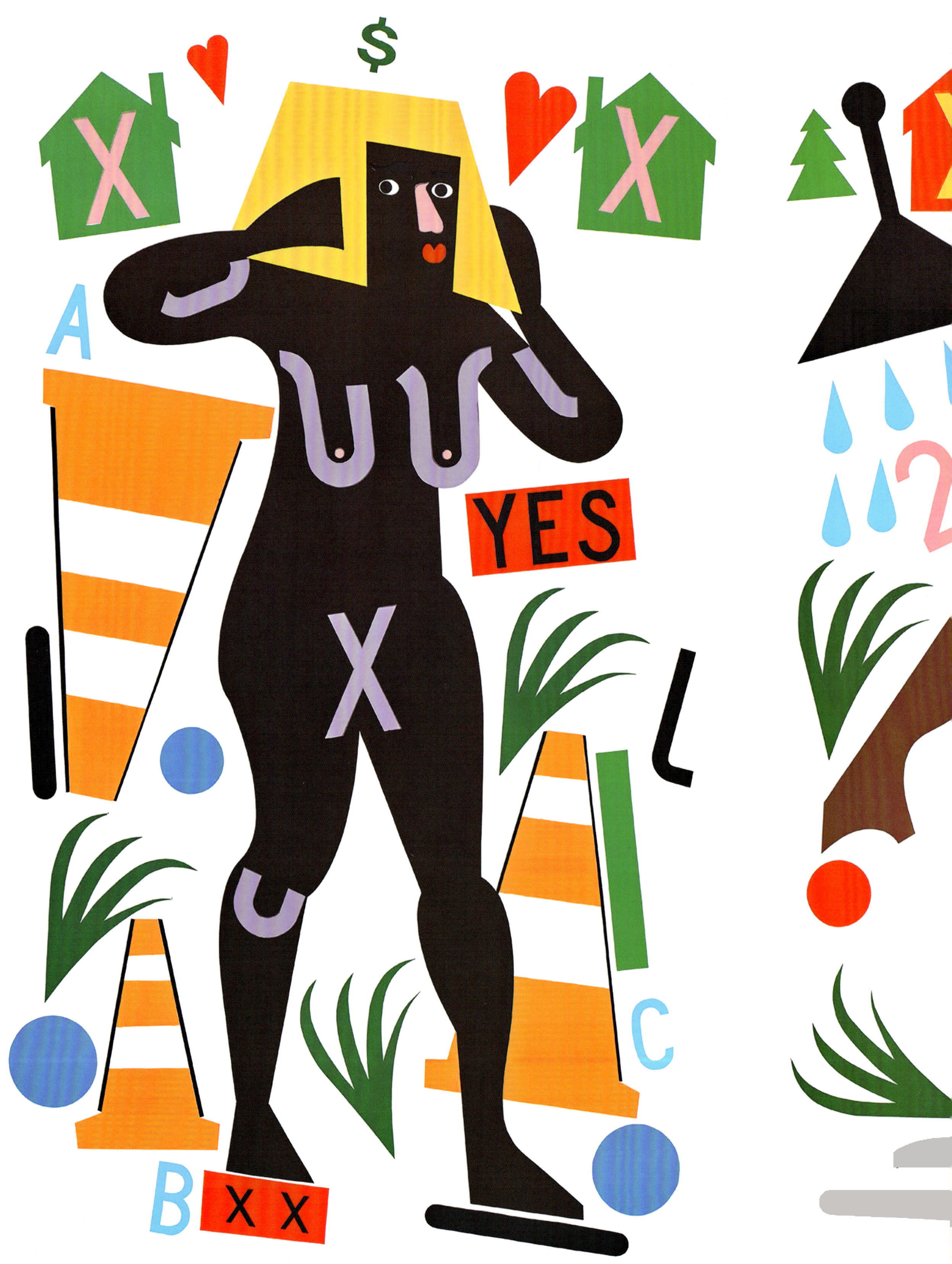
$
X
X
A
YES
X
C
B
XX

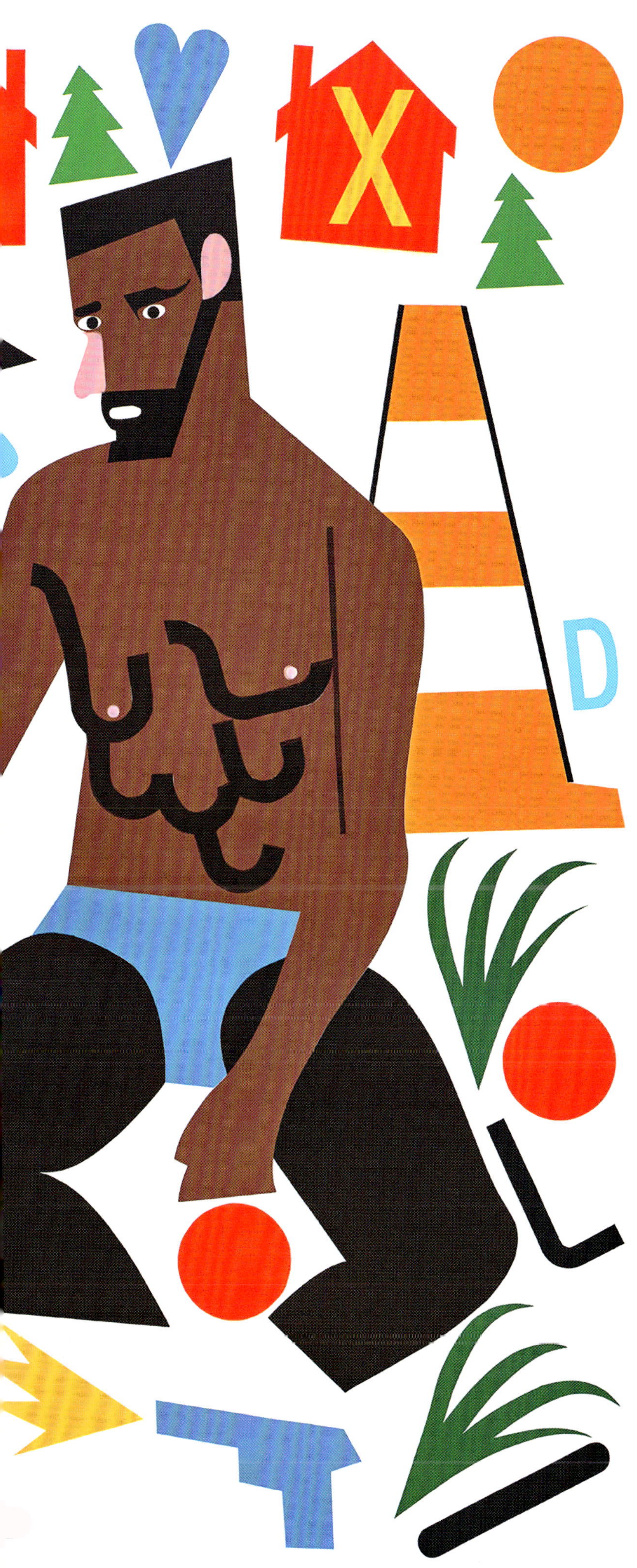

Let's Work, Let's Play, Let's Live Together, 2018

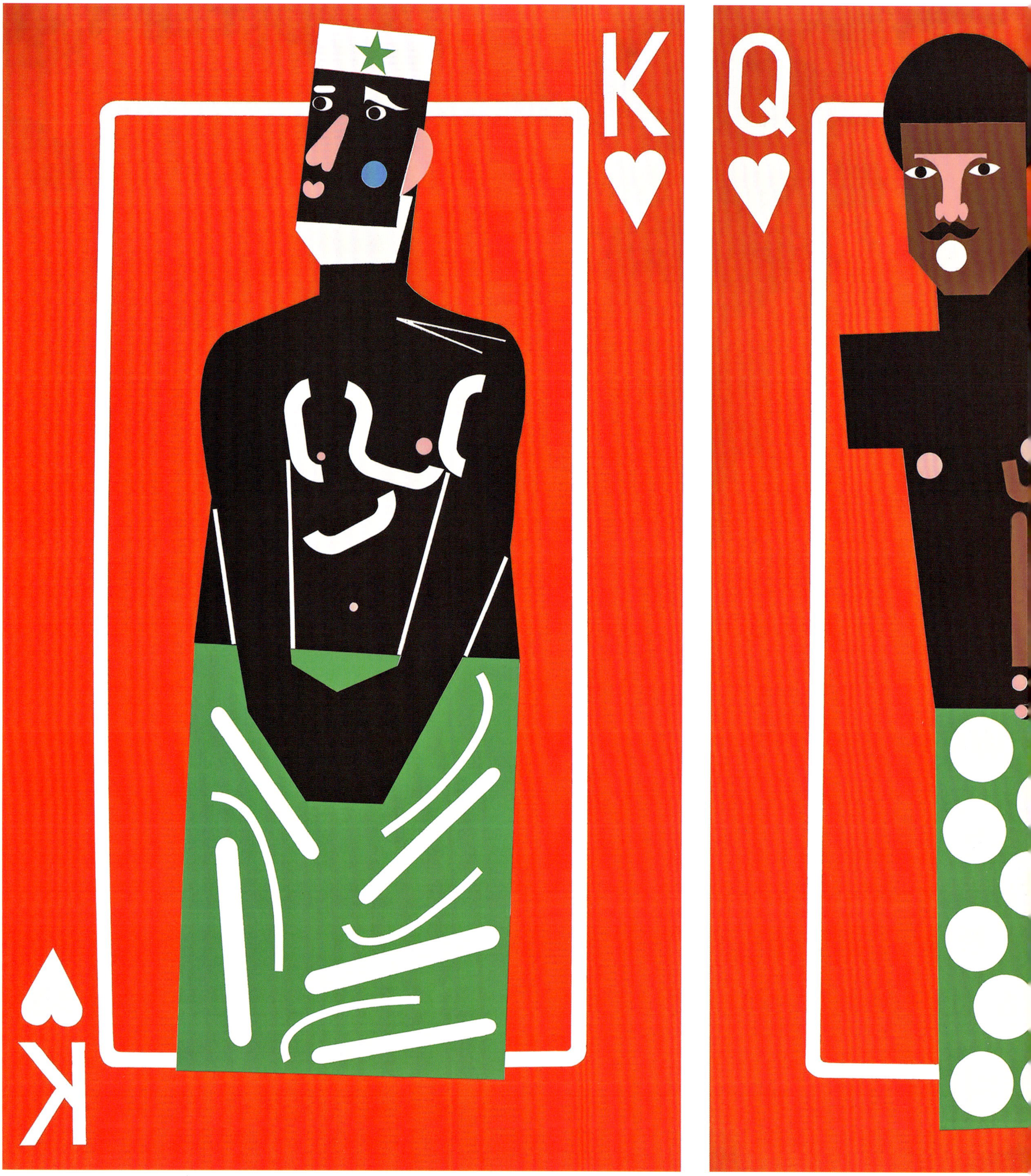

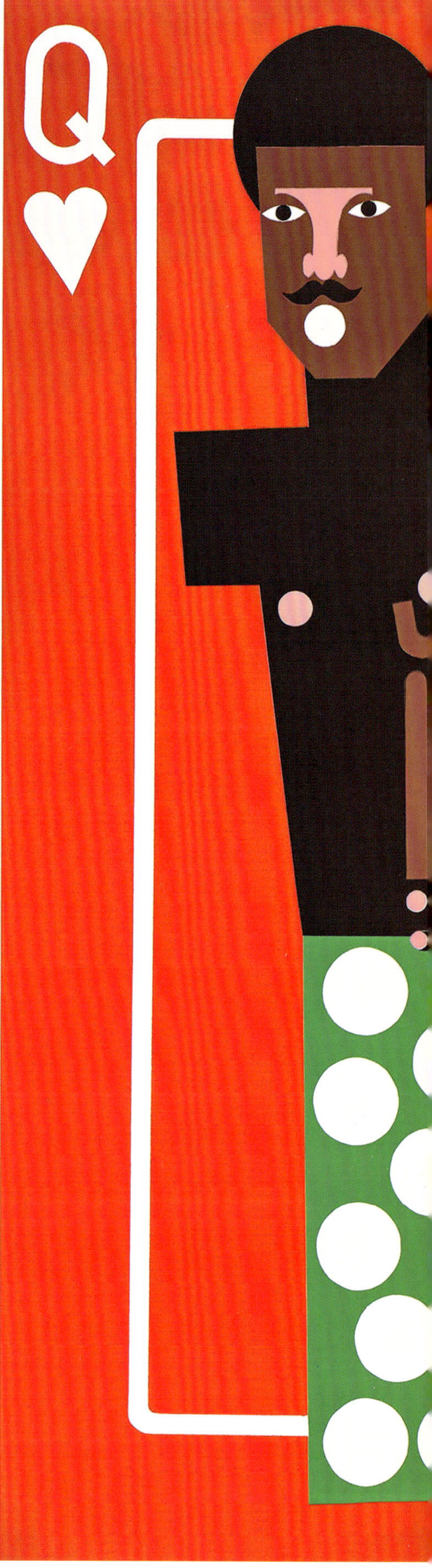

What Beats What, 2018

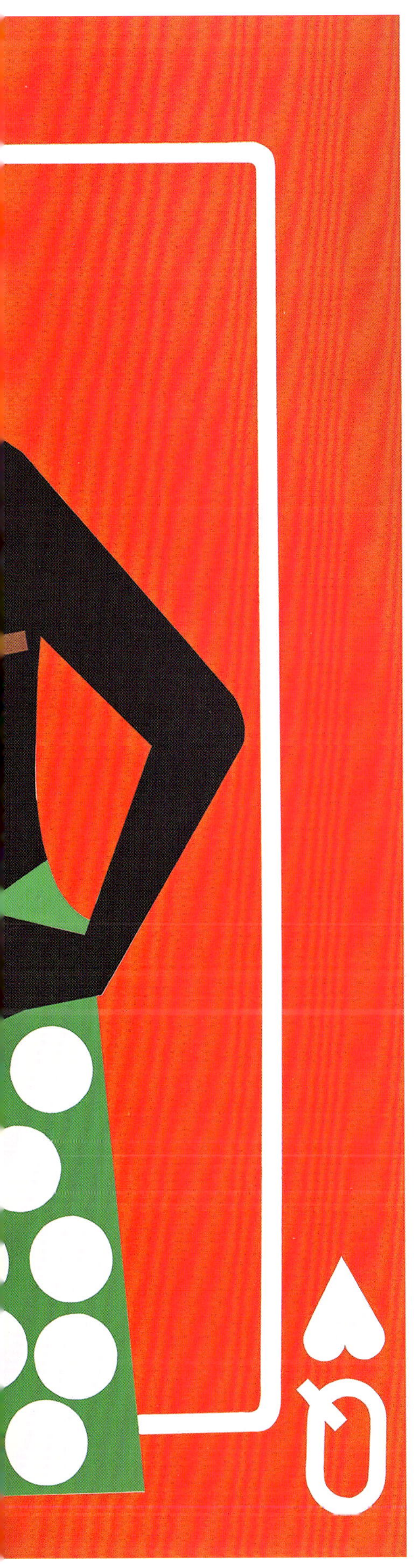

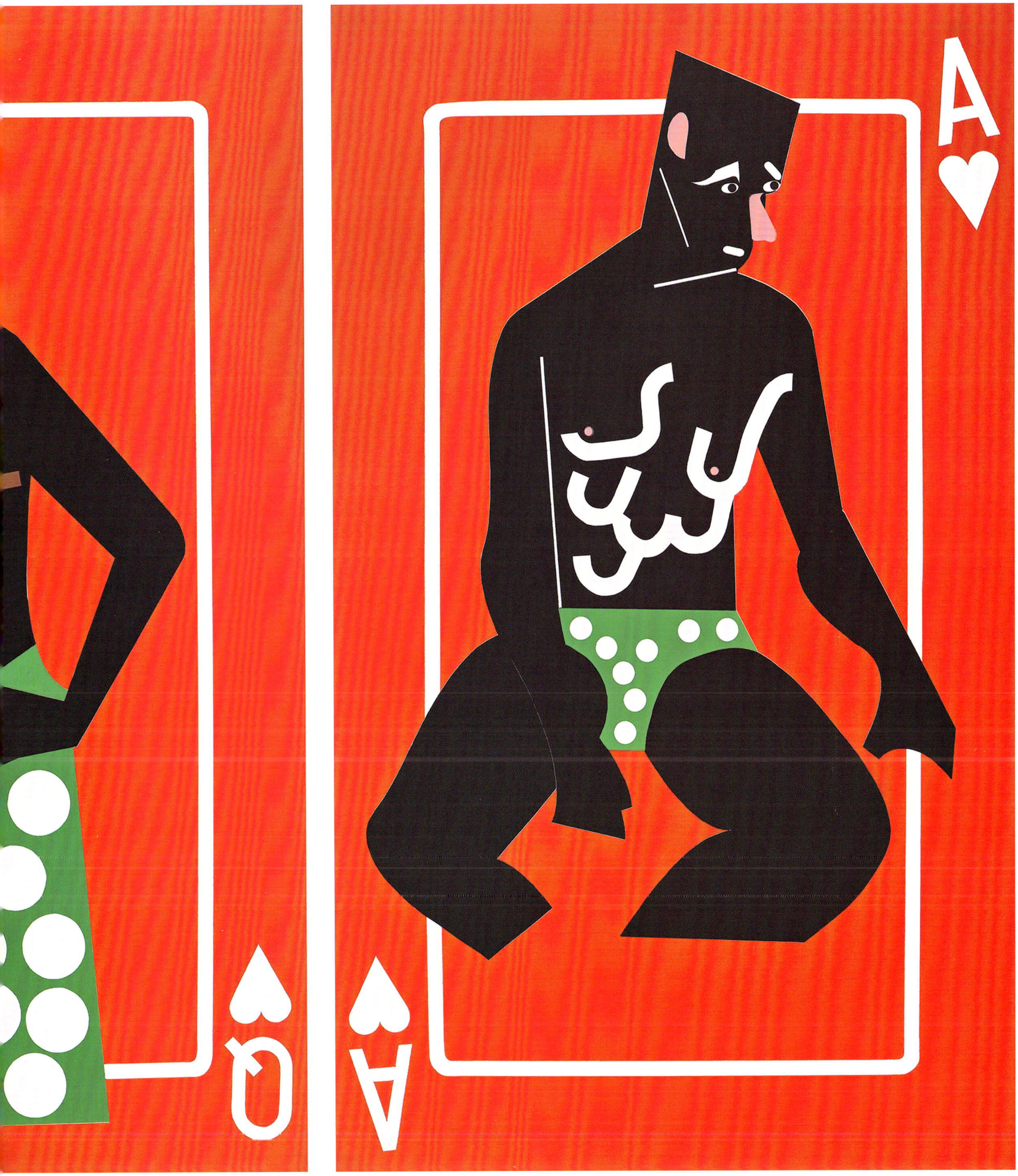

Being Mixie with My Fixie, 2020

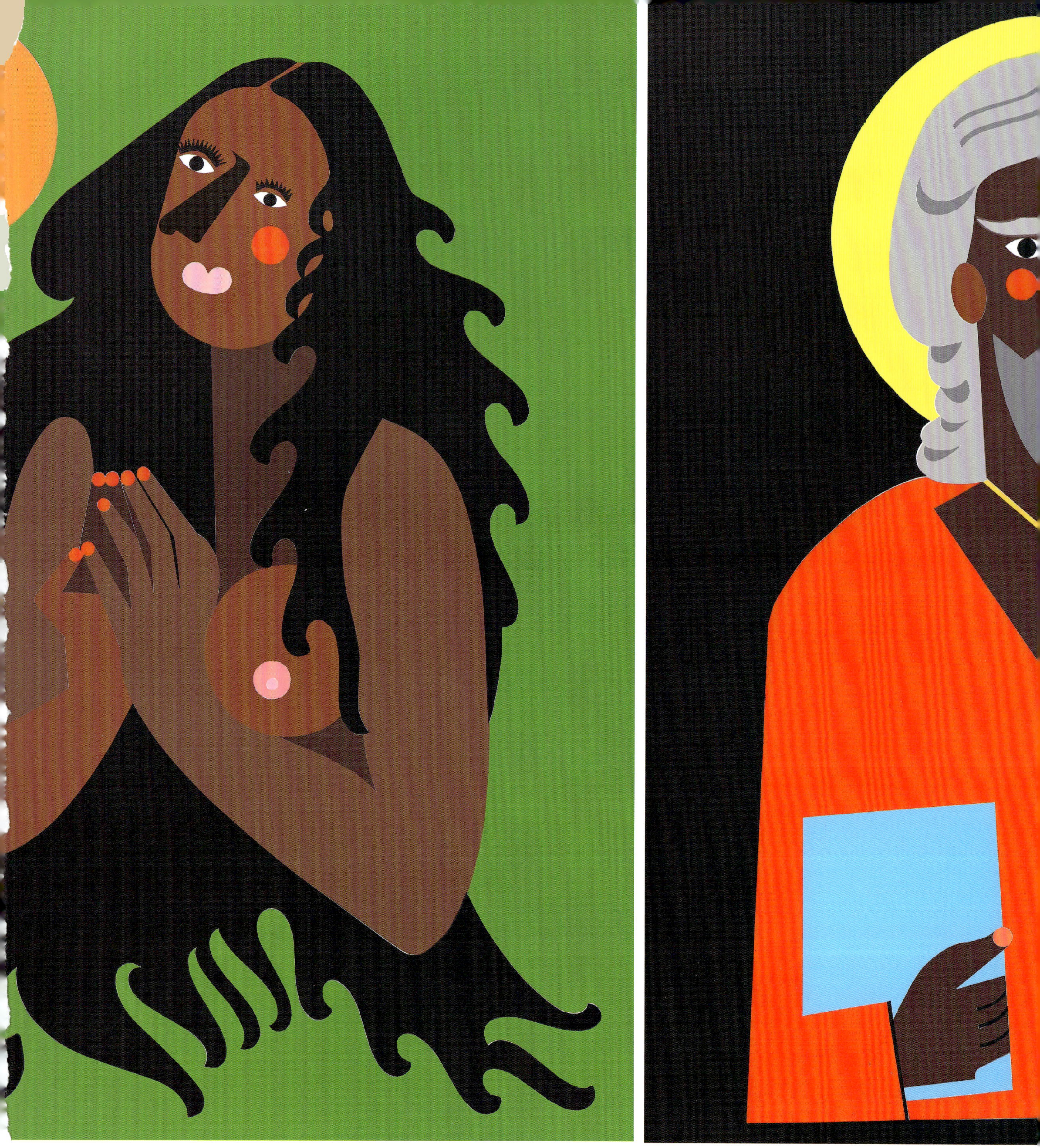

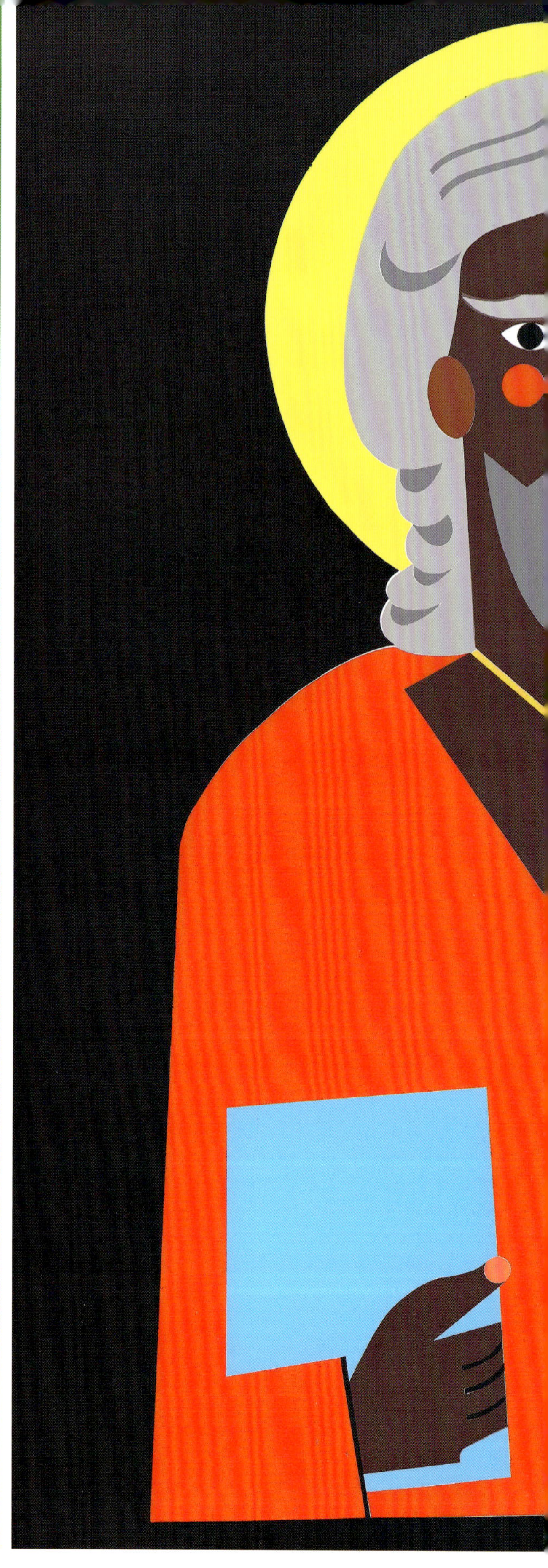

Temporary Friends, 2019

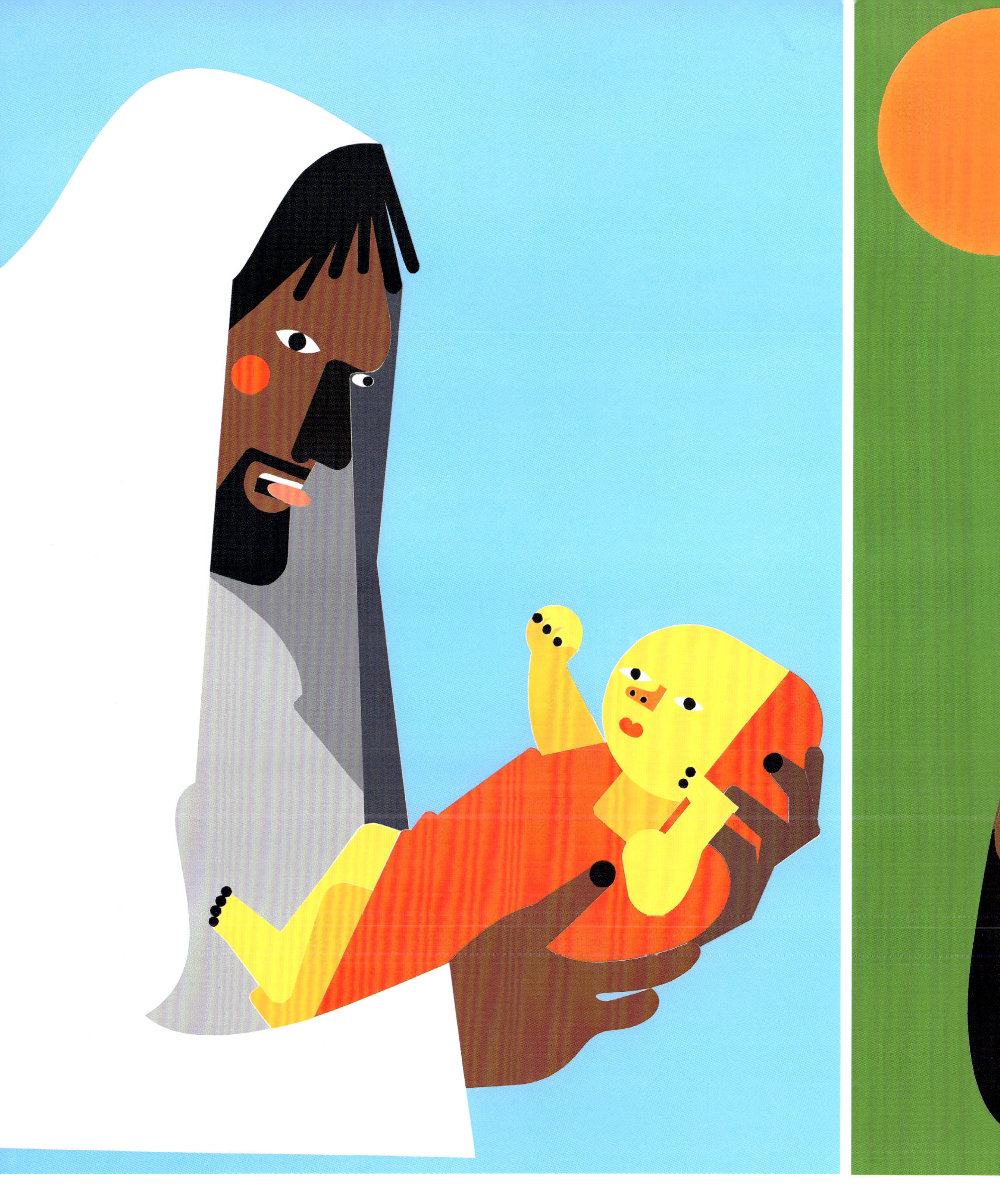

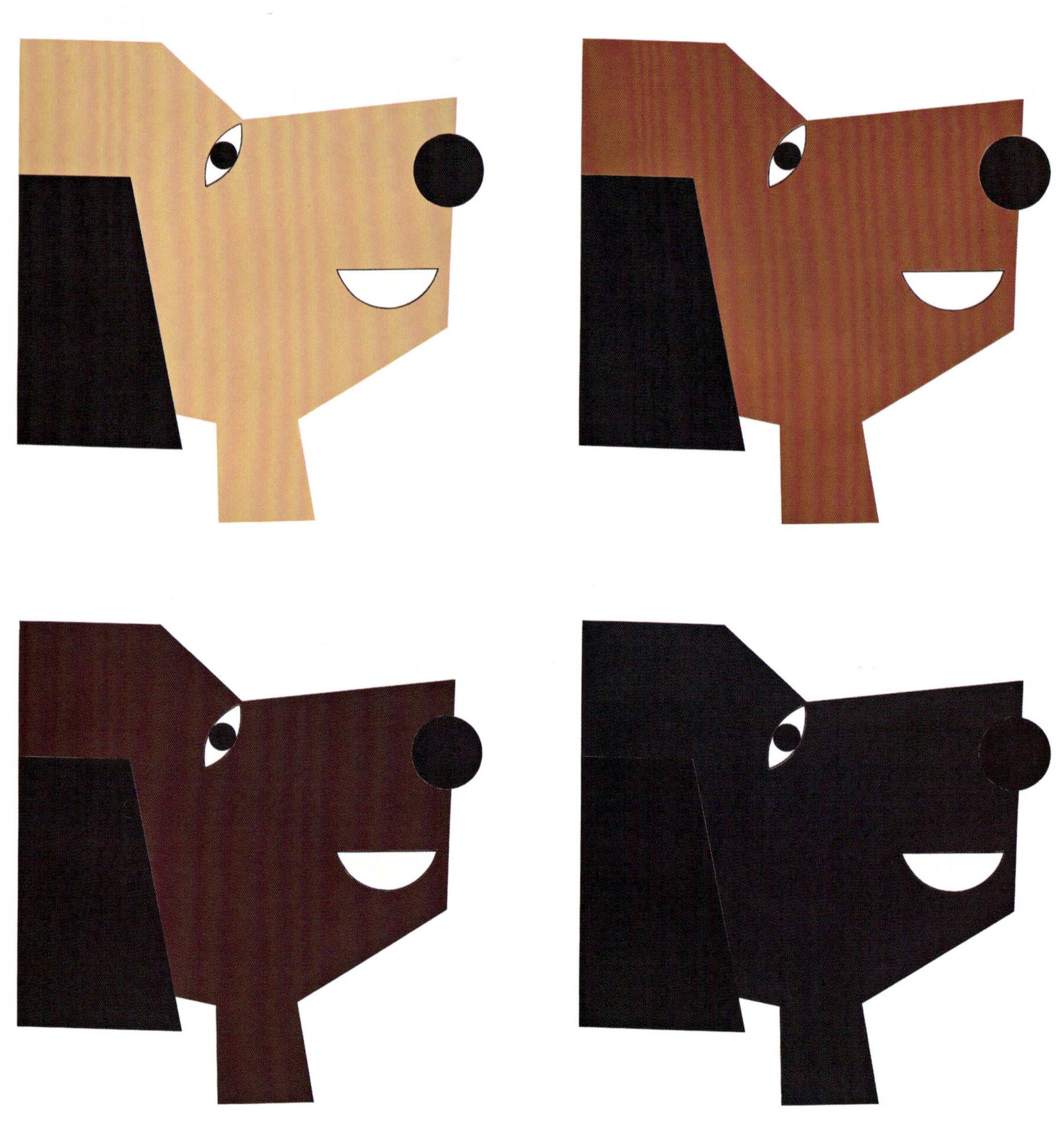

Snoops, 2018

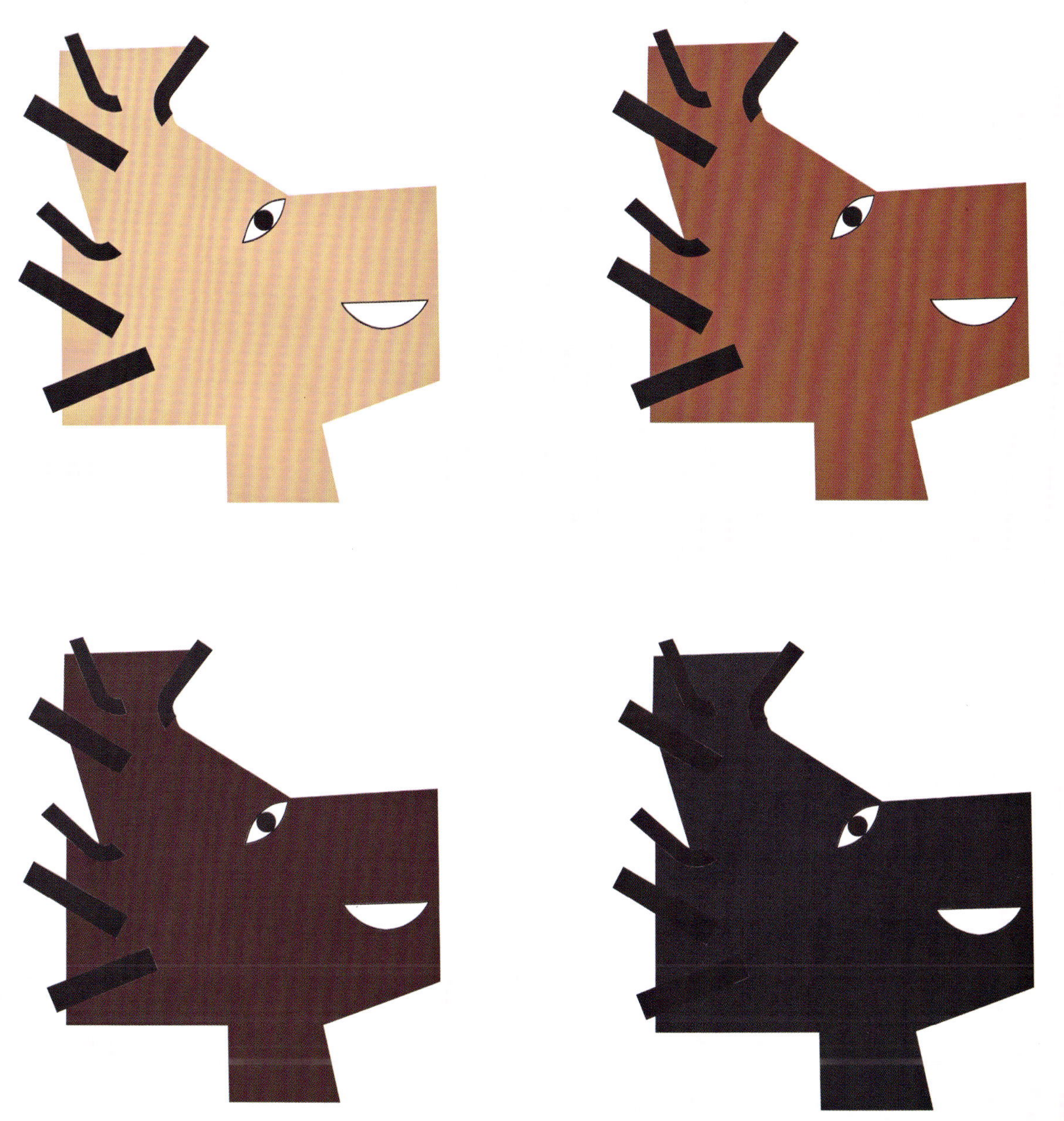

Snoops' Friend, 2018

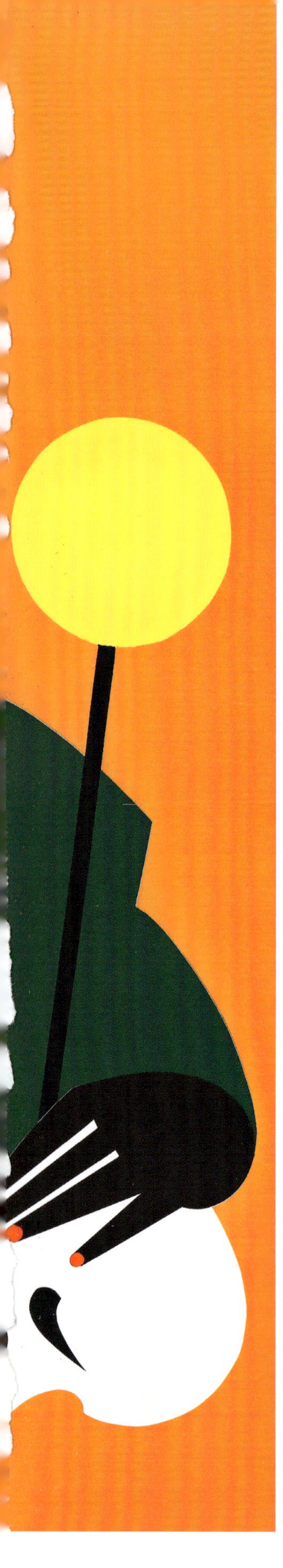

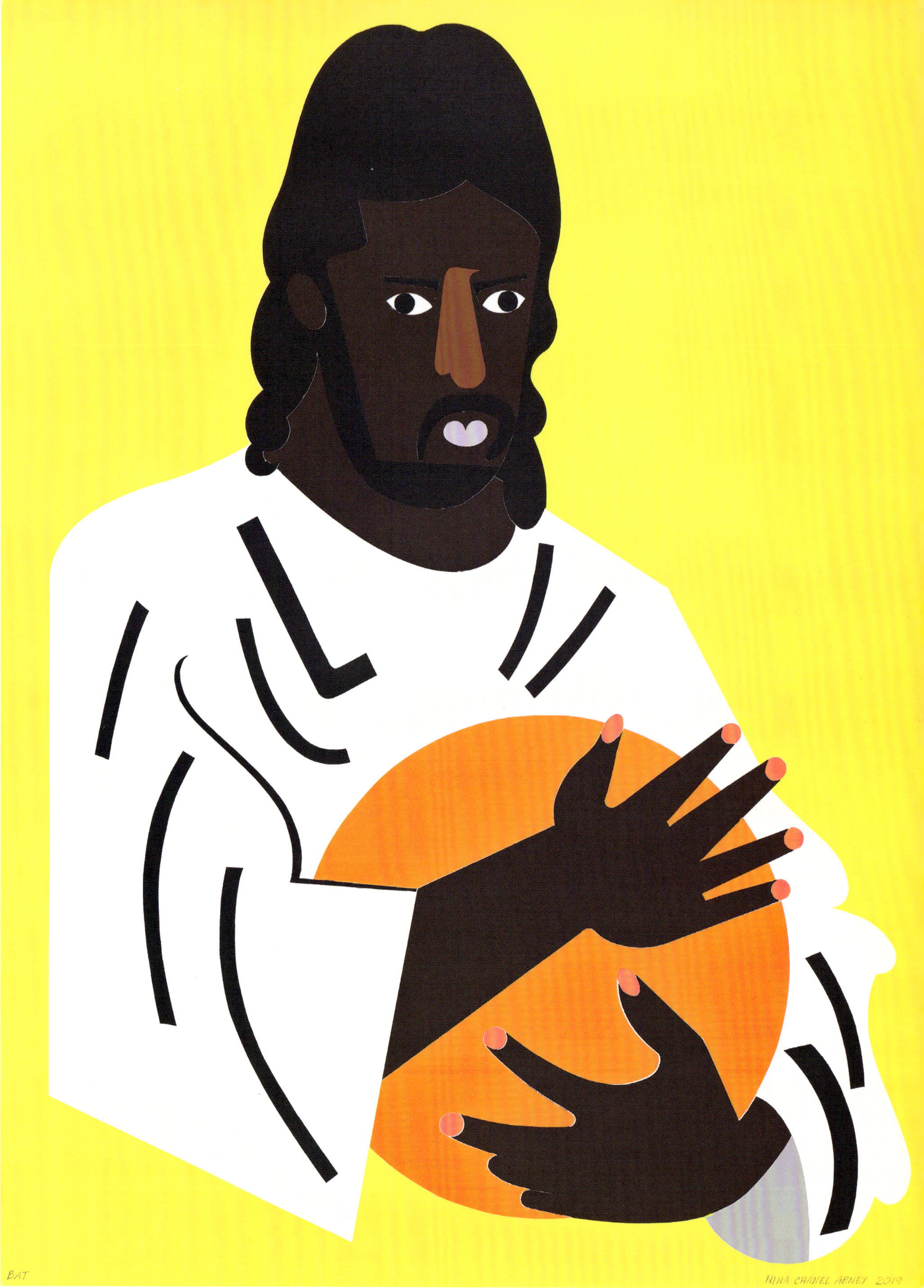

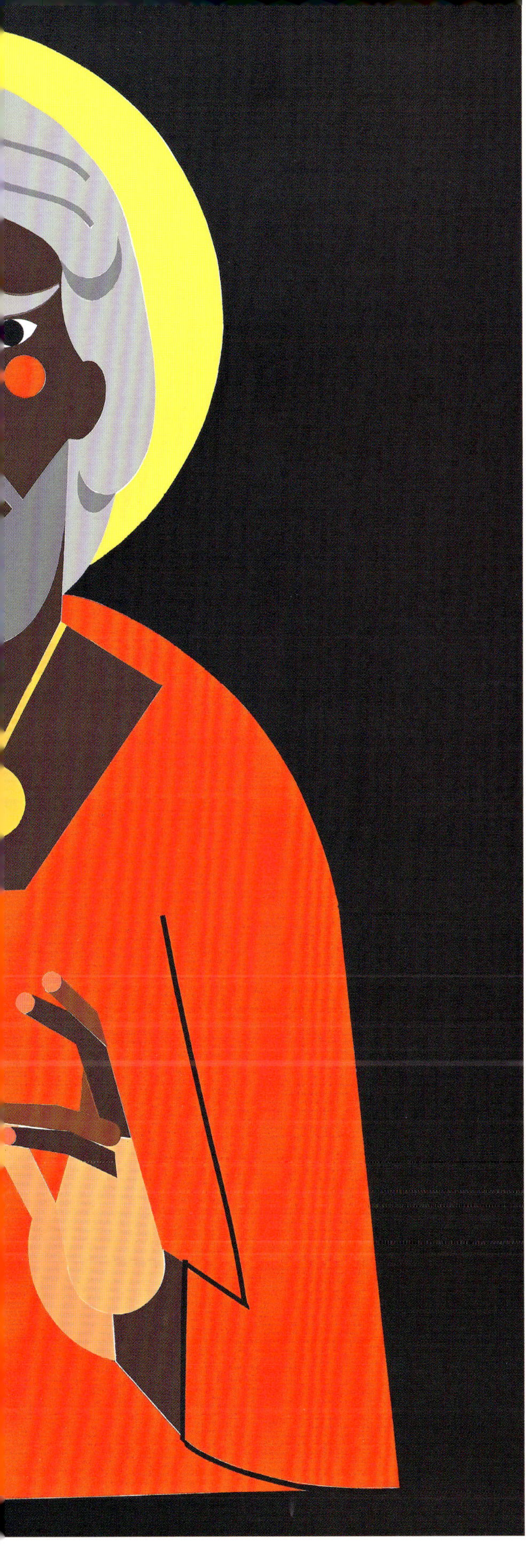

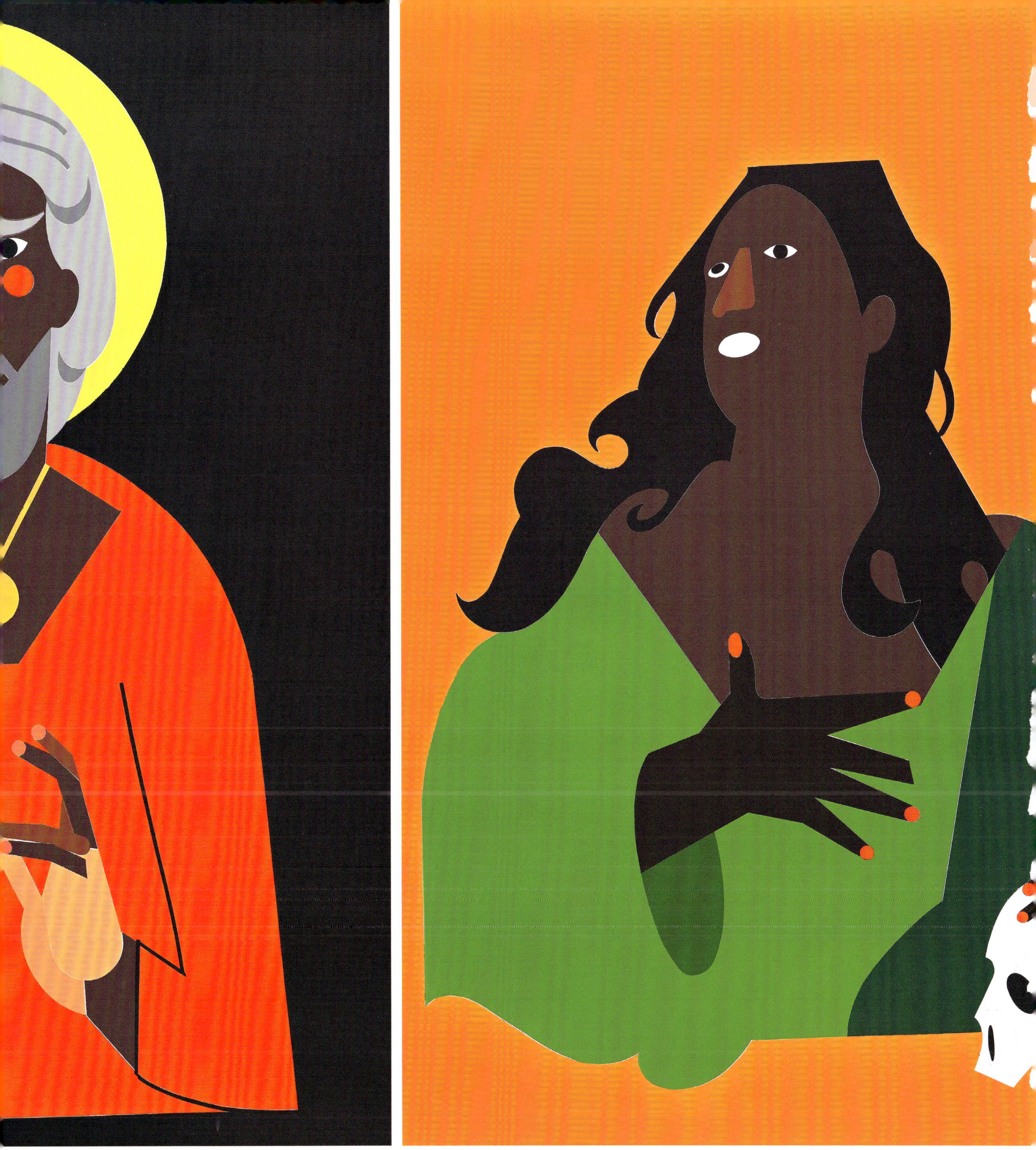

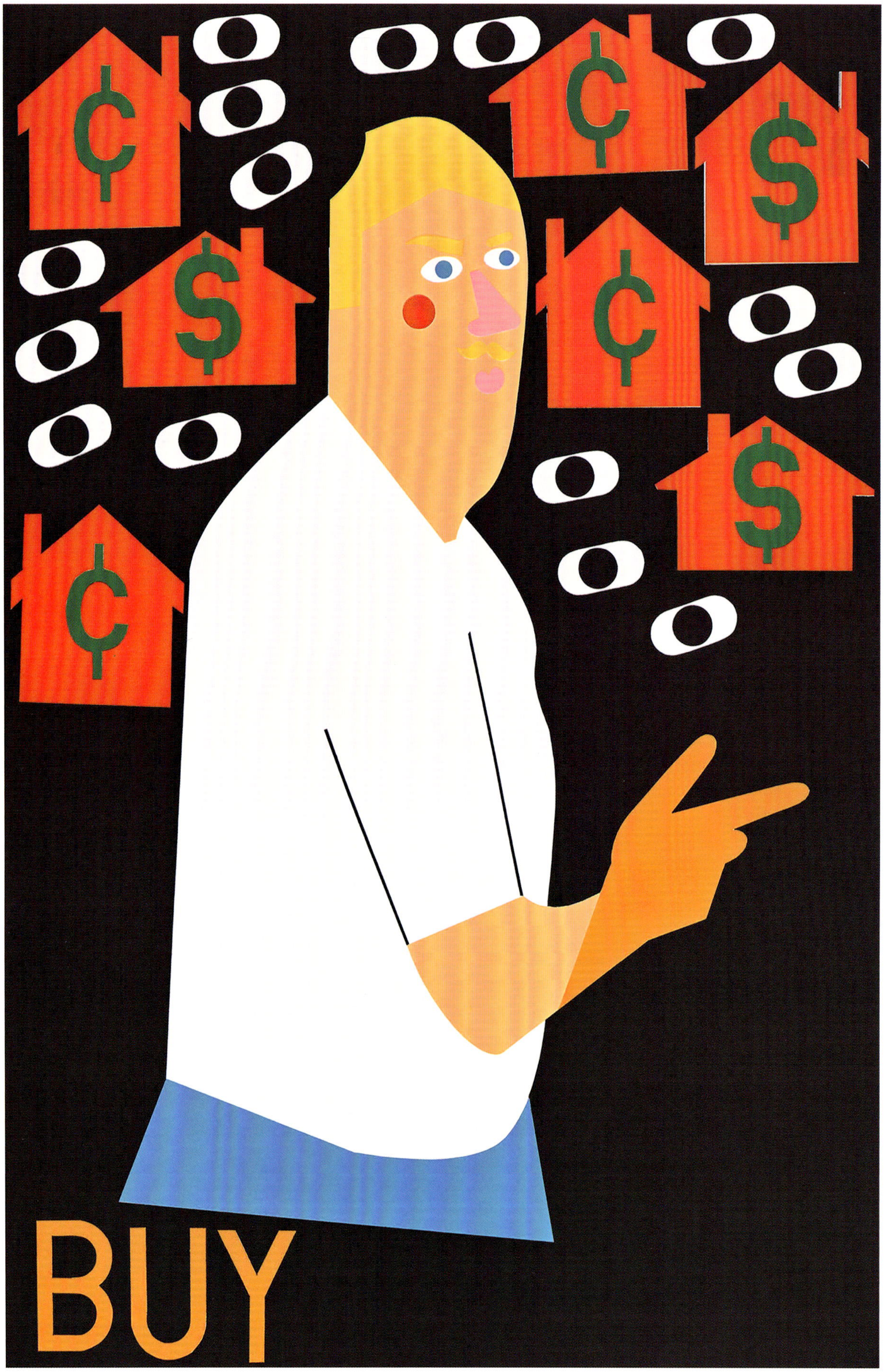

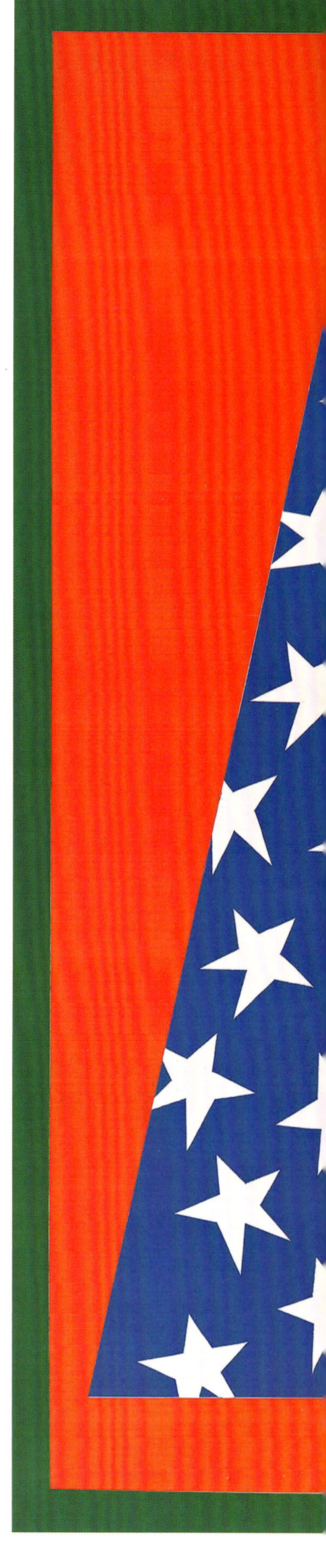

Fast Draw, 2018

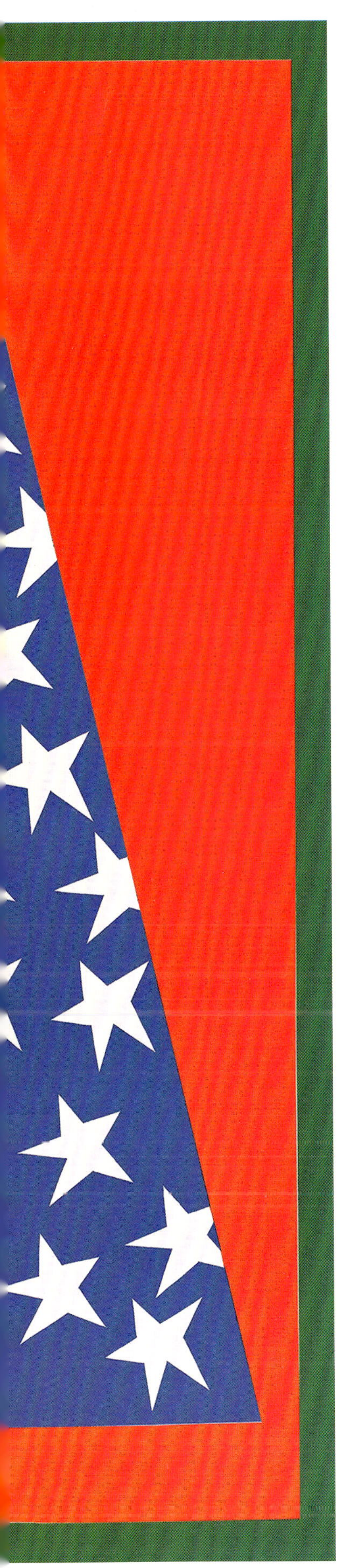

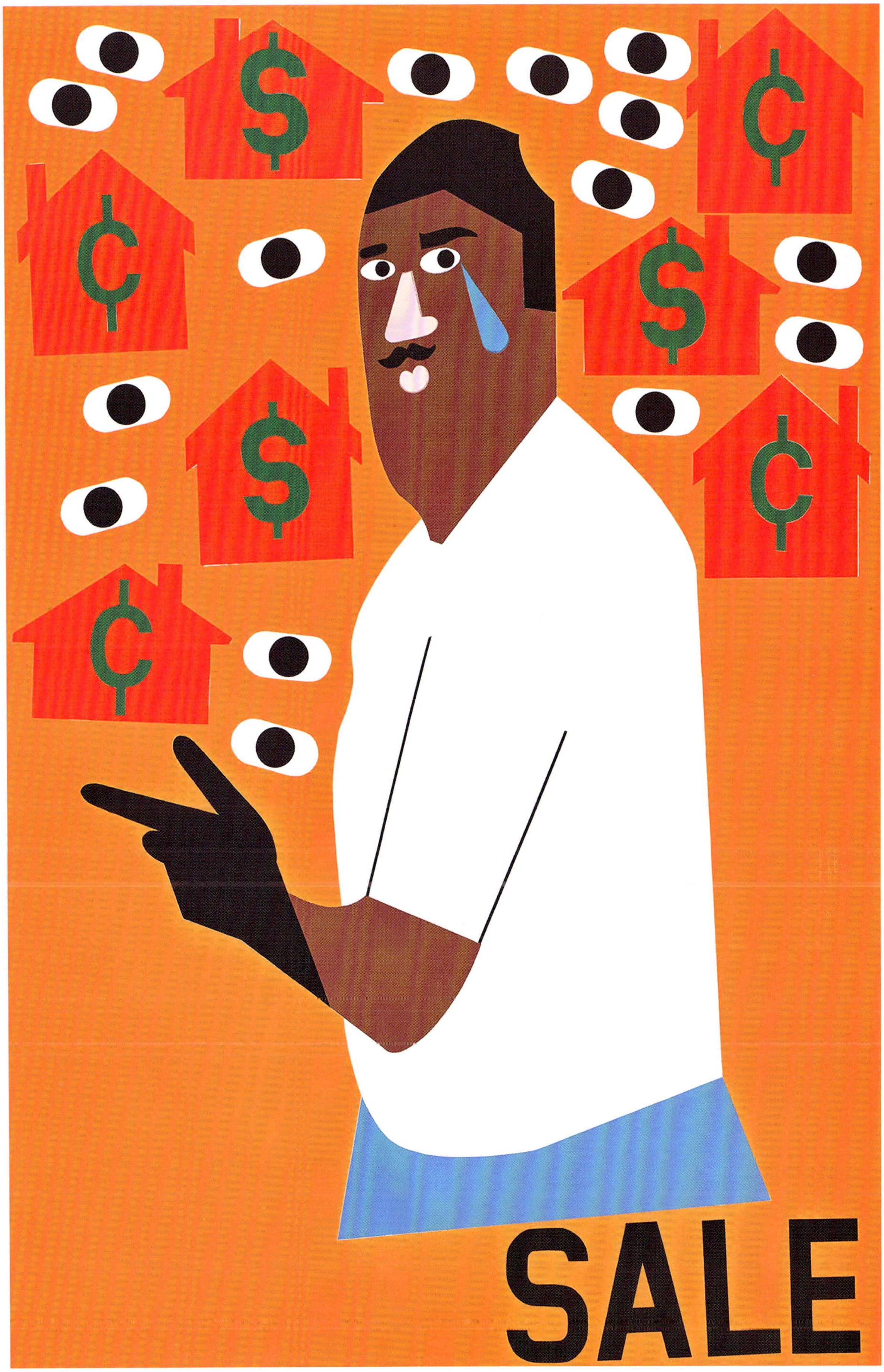

SALE

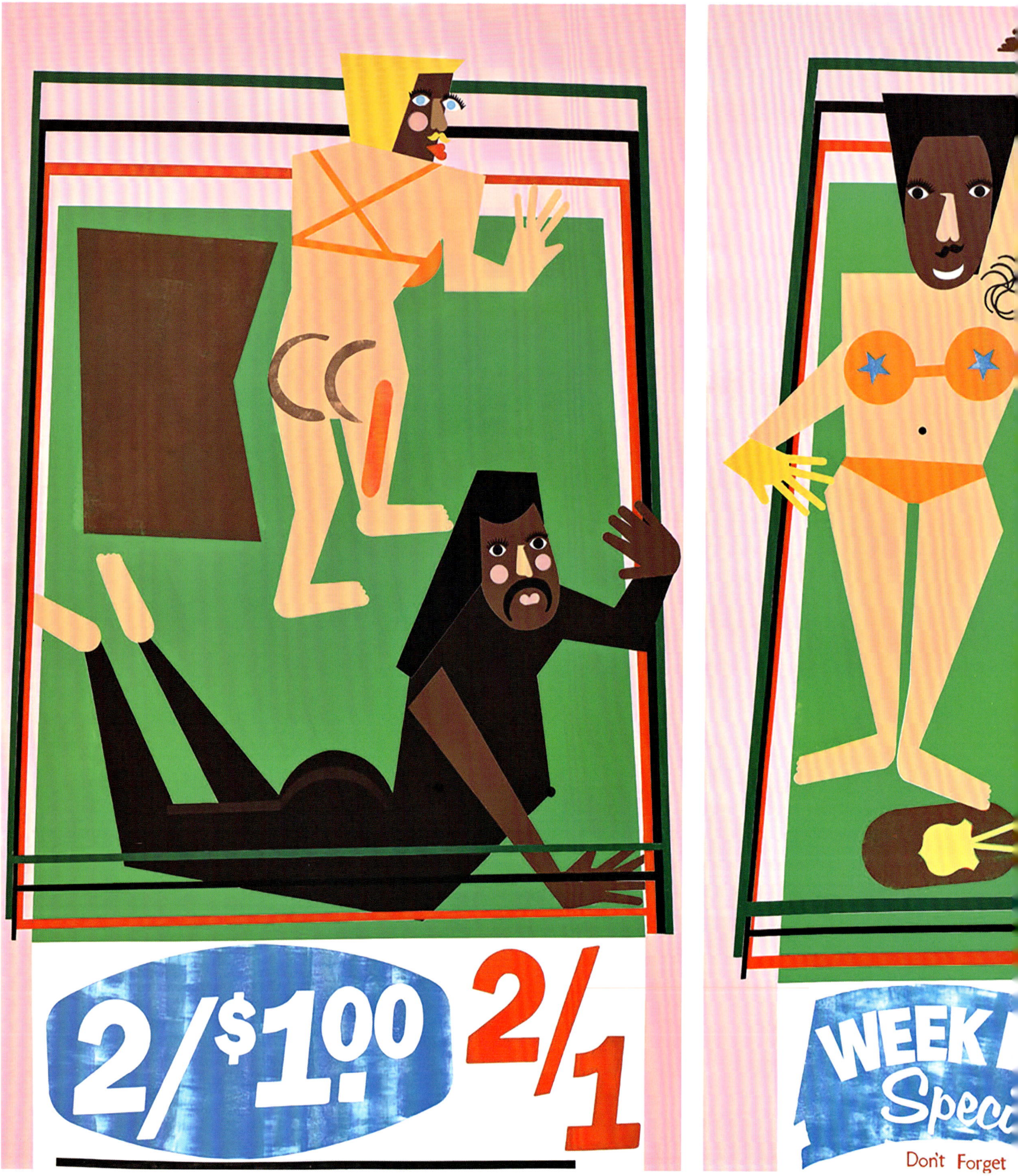

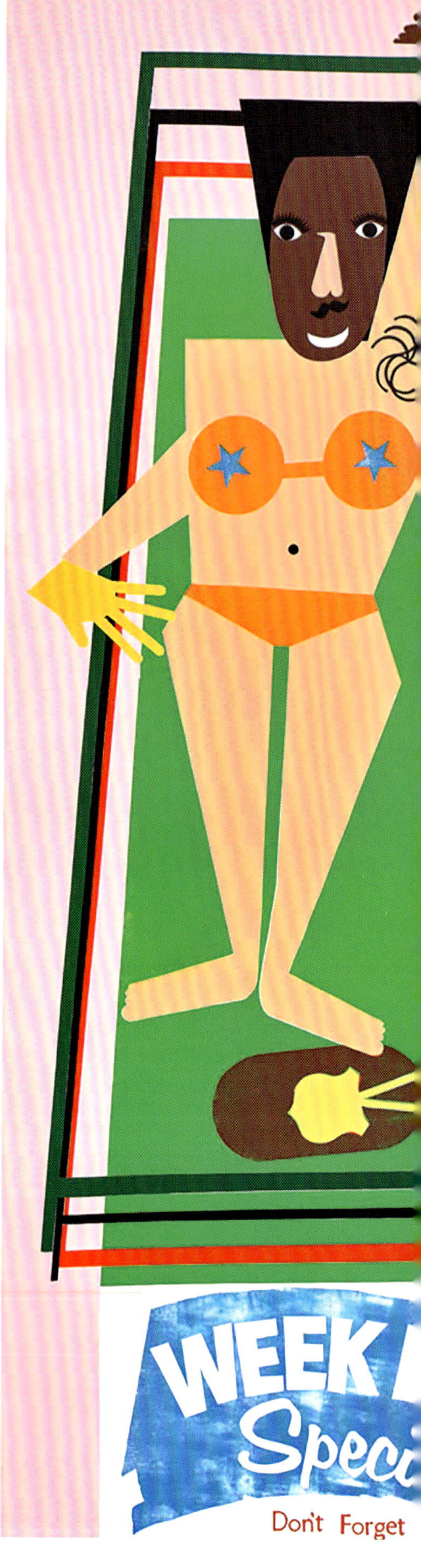

Untitled, 2019

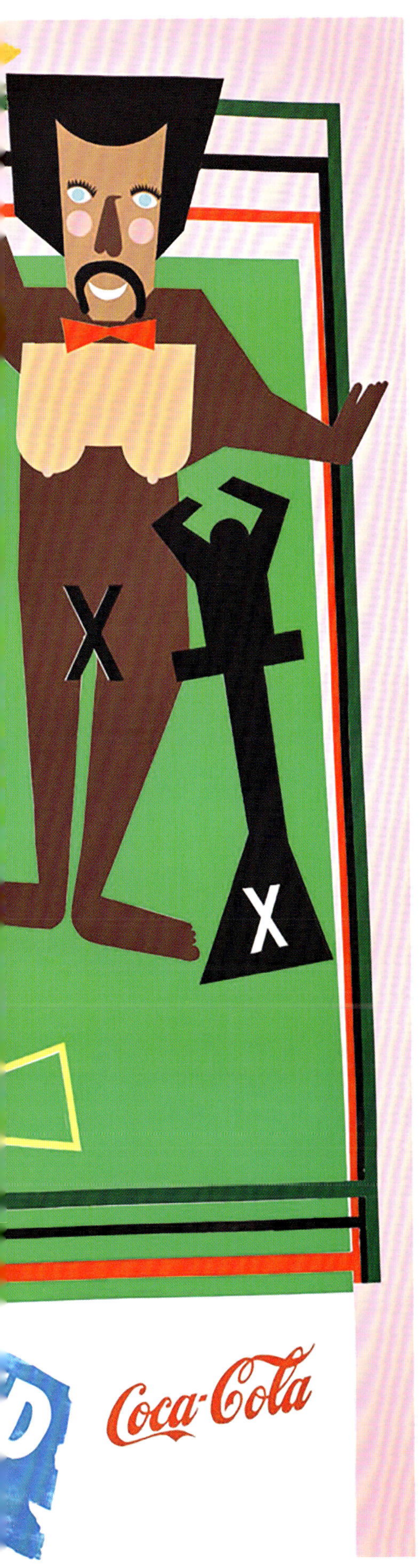

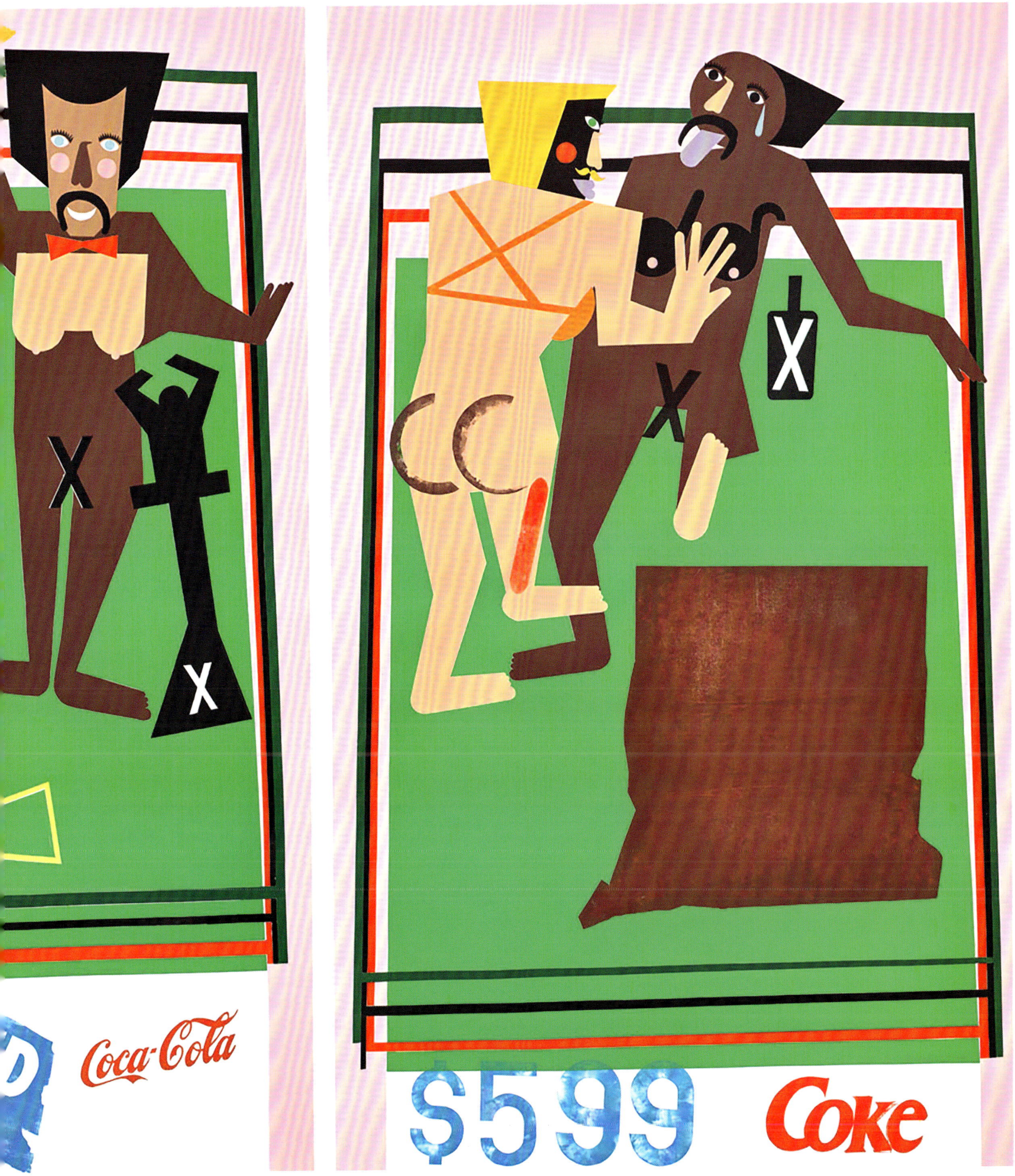

$599
Coke

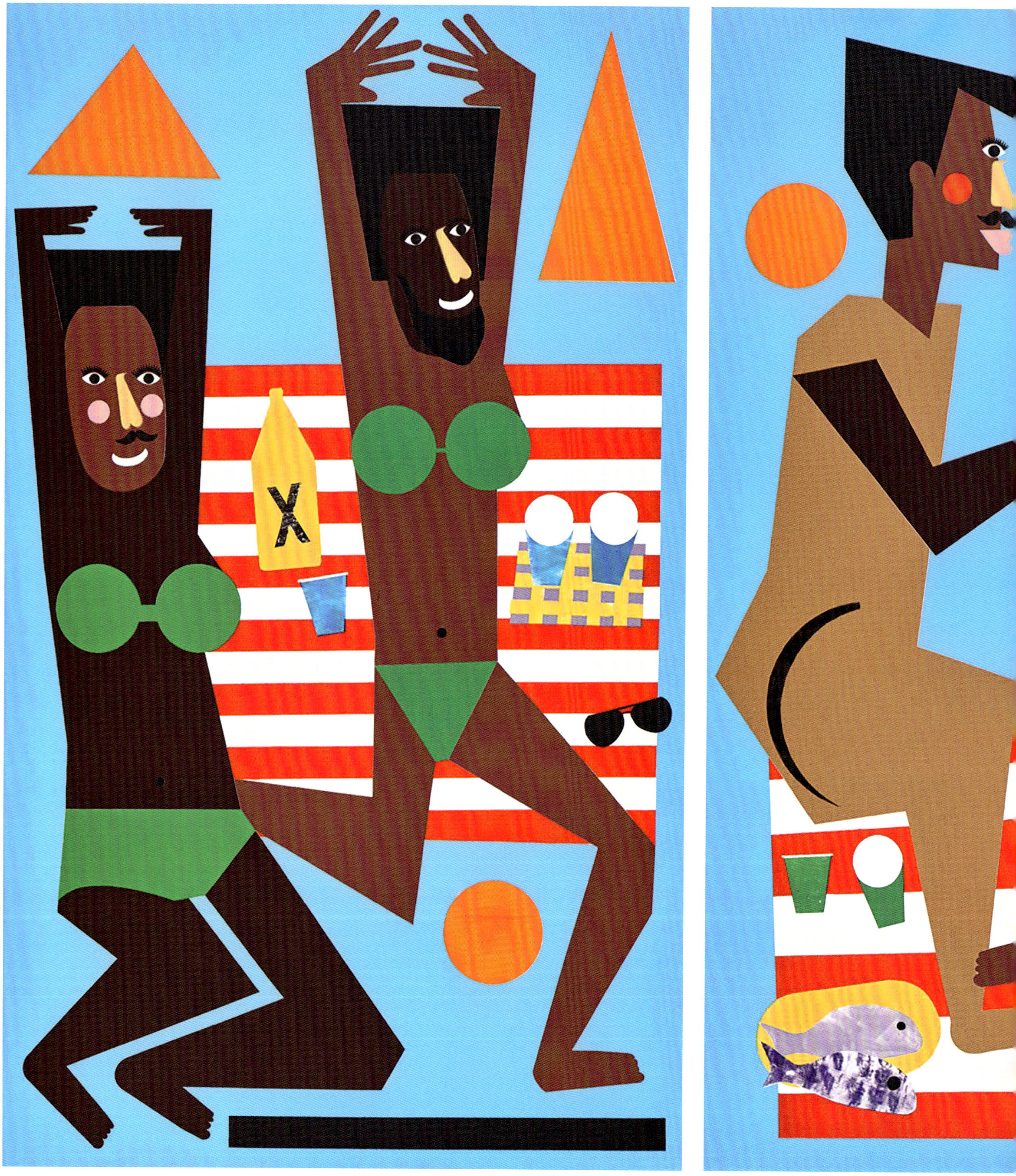

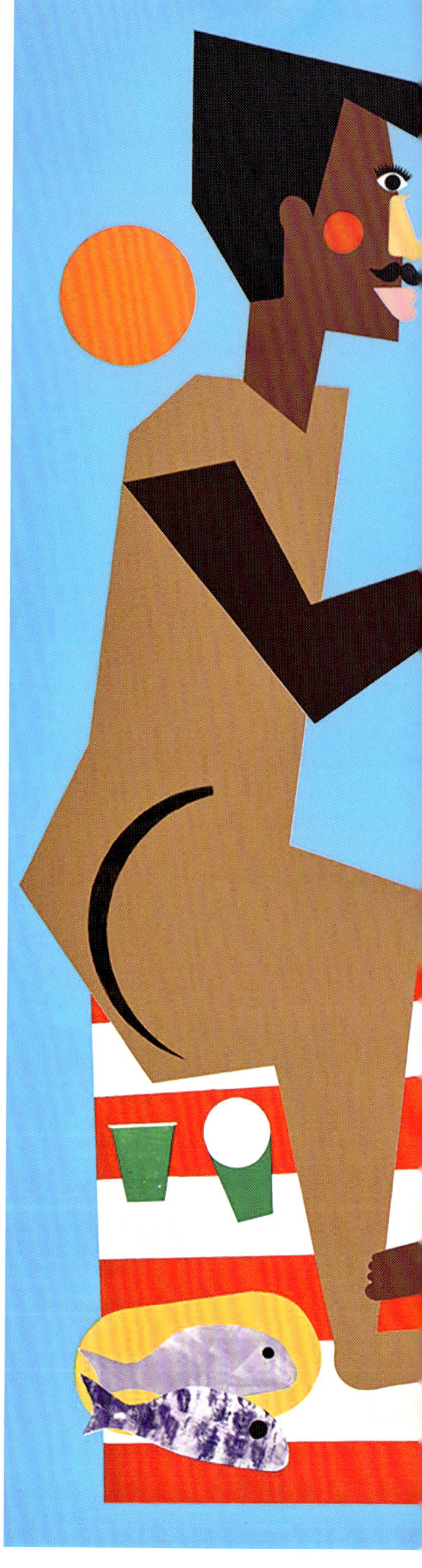

Untitled, 2019

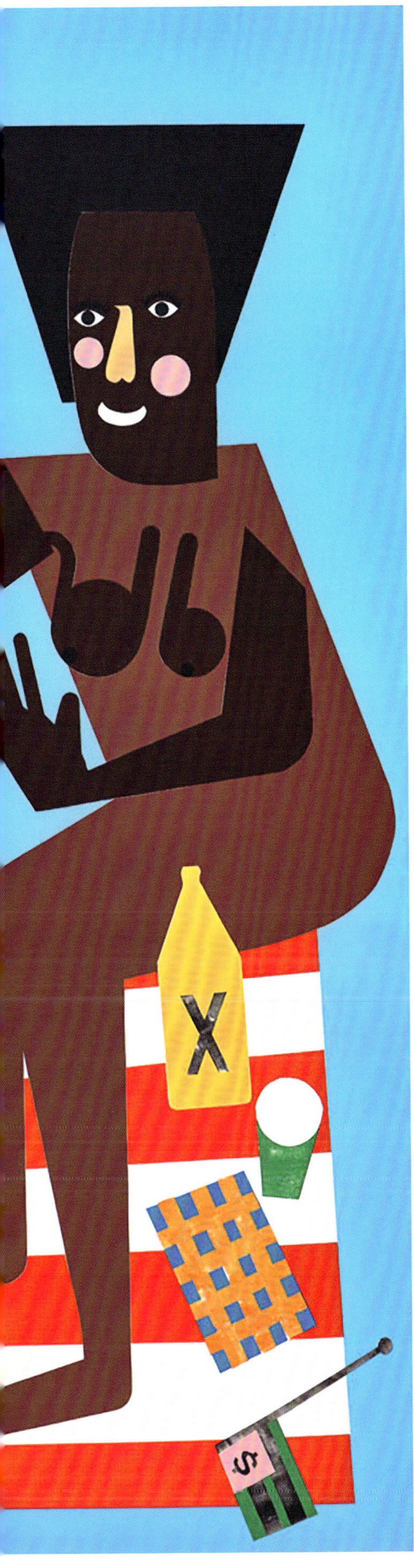
X
$

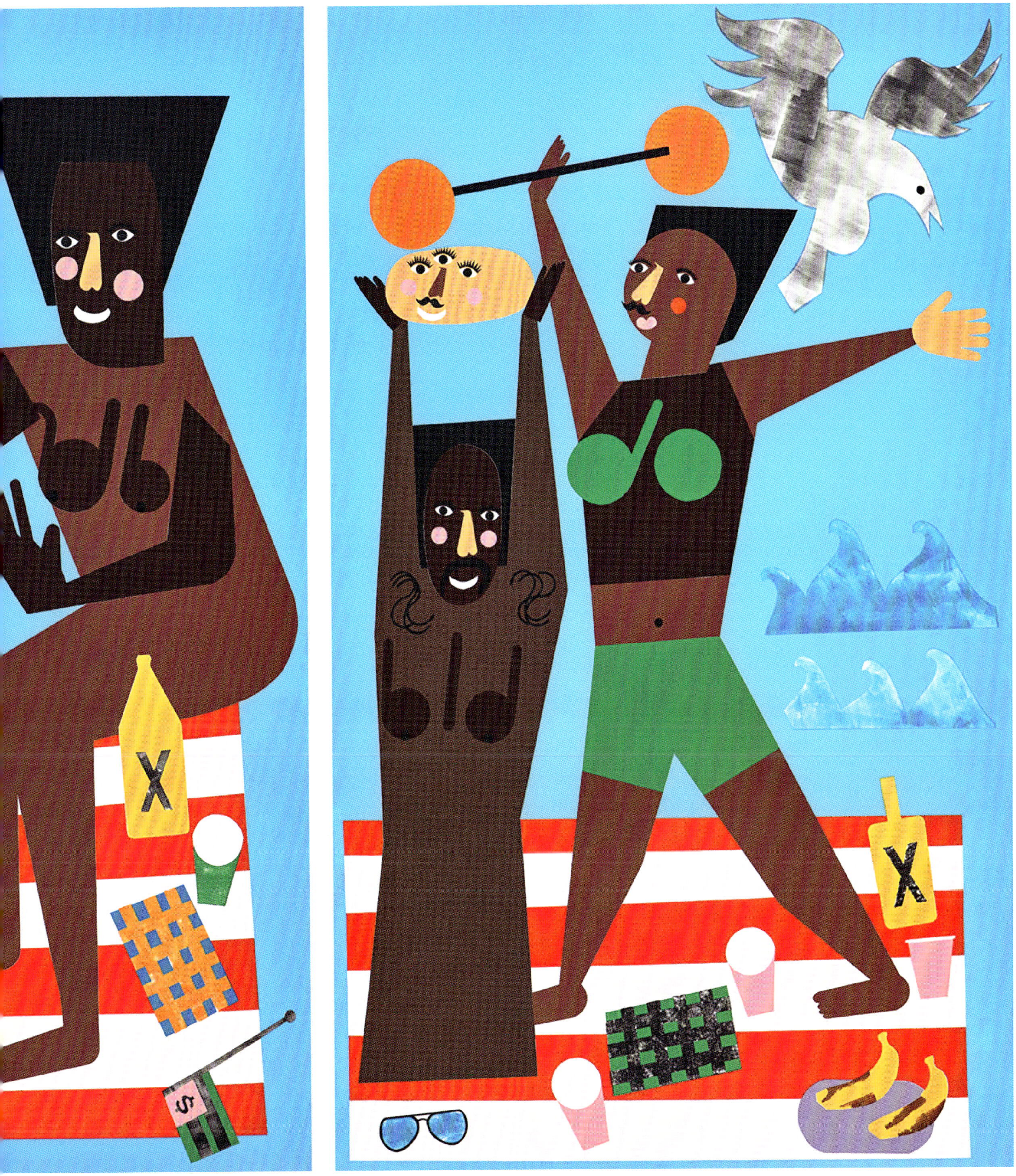

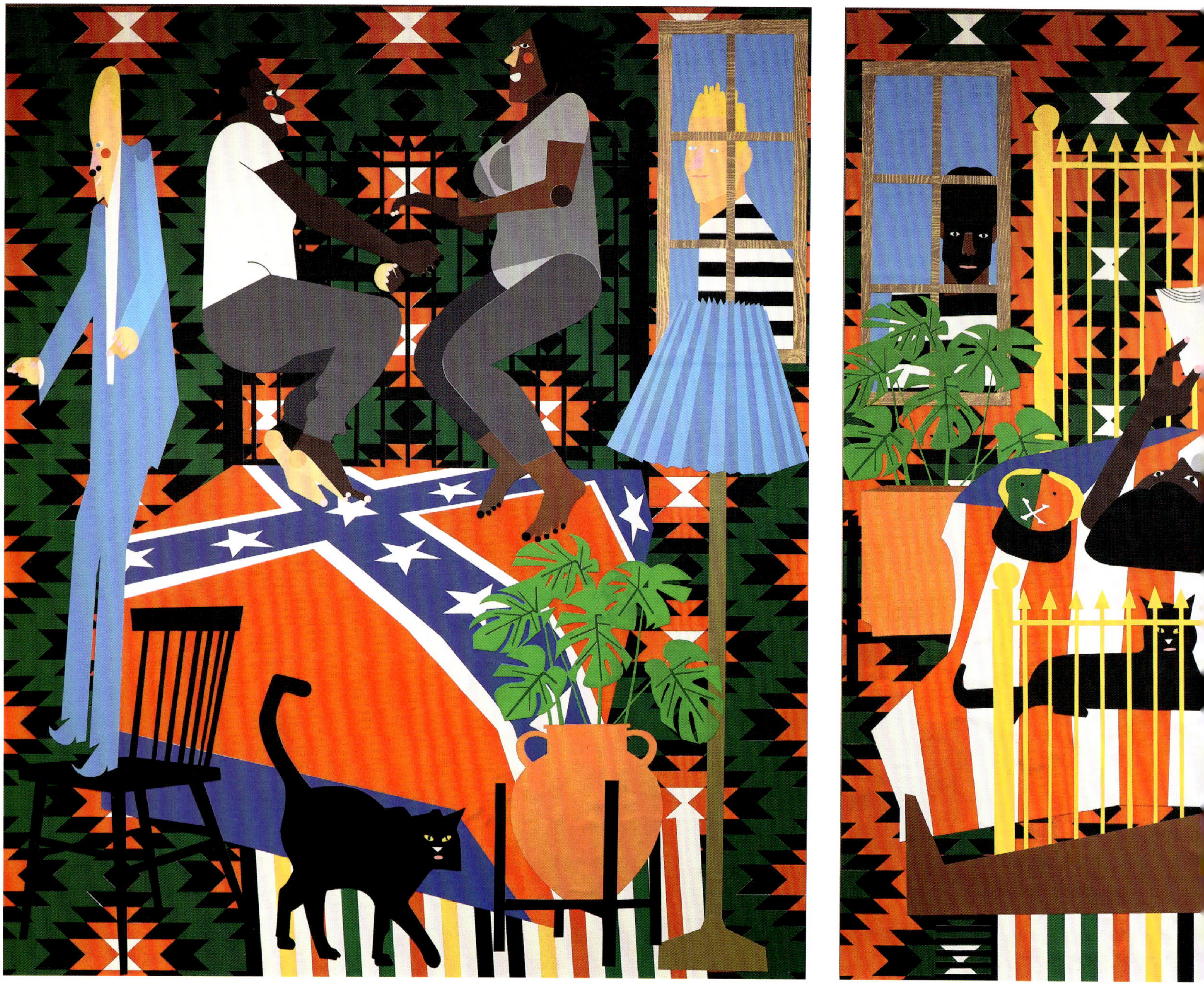

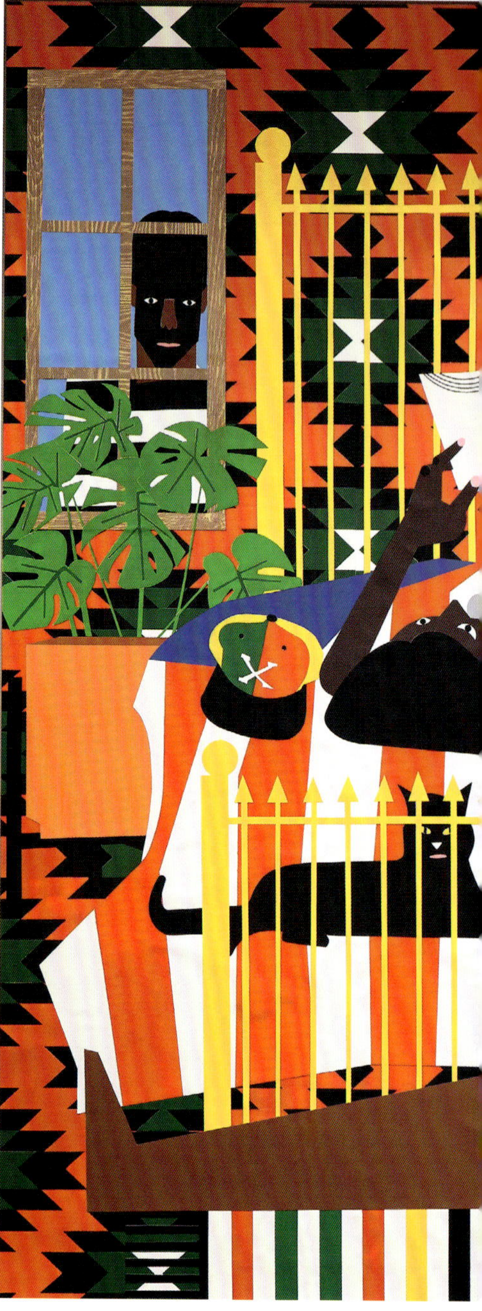

House of Reps, 2020

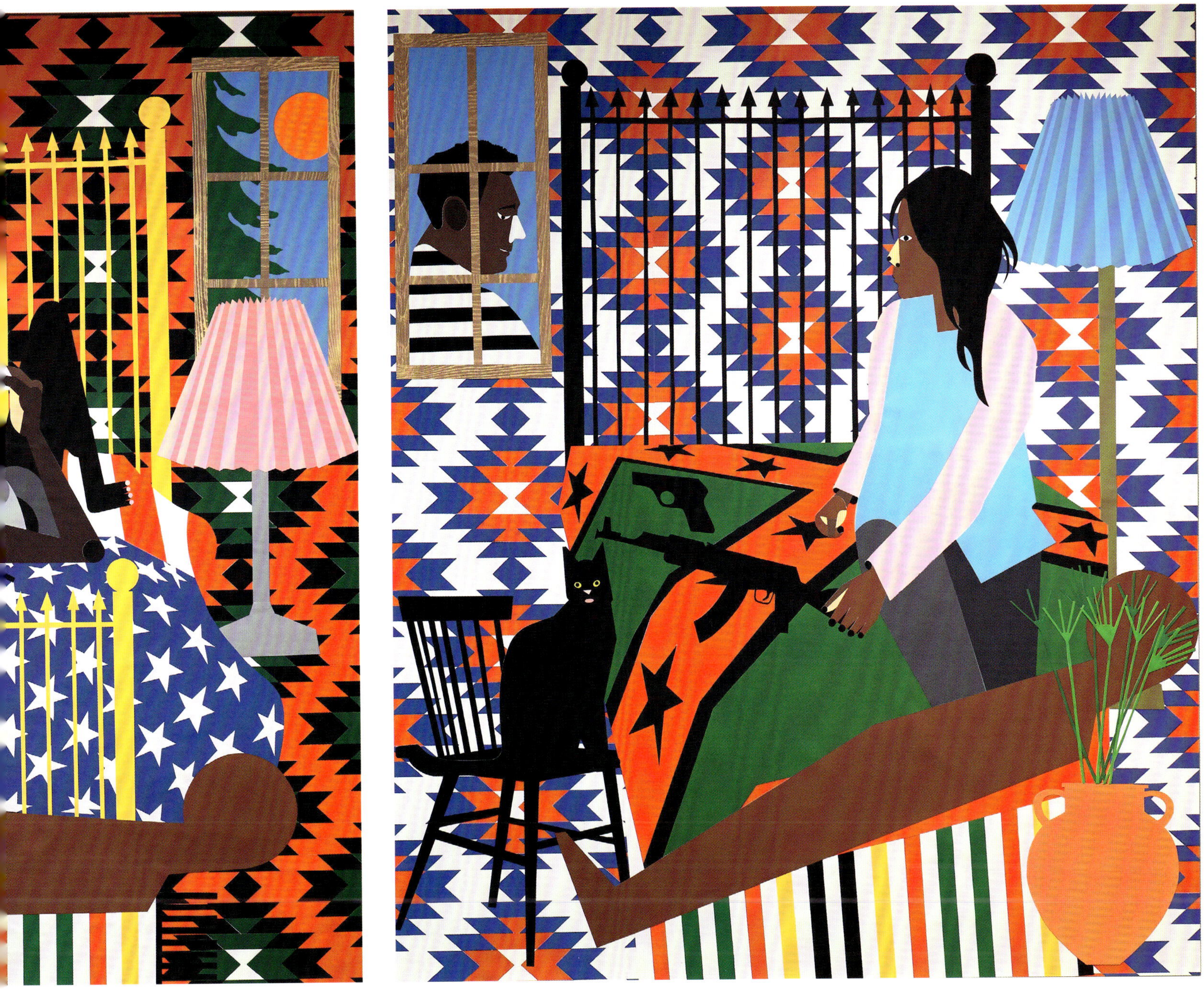

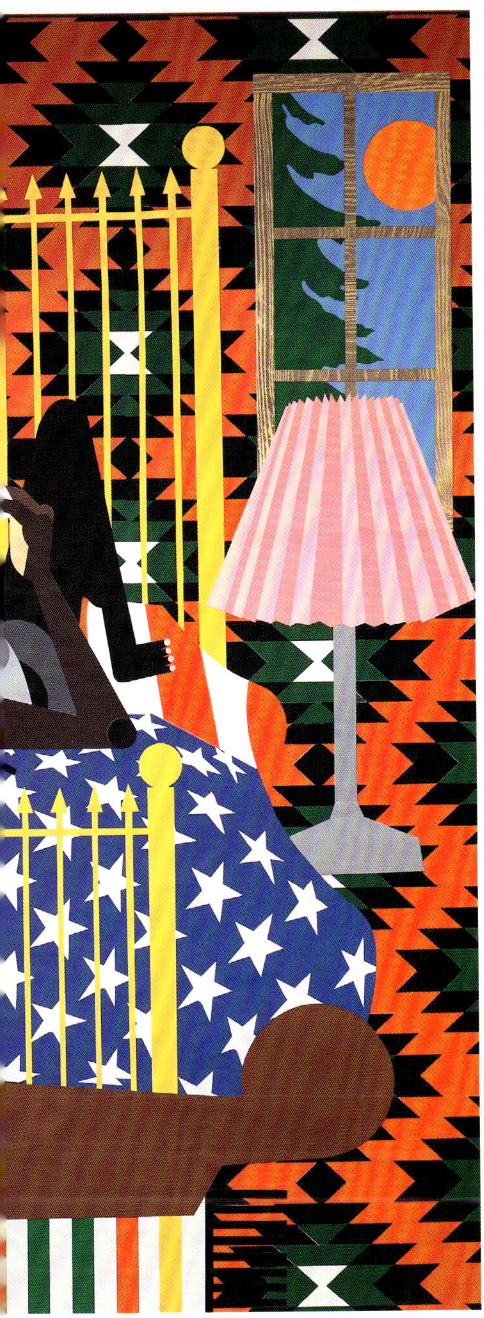

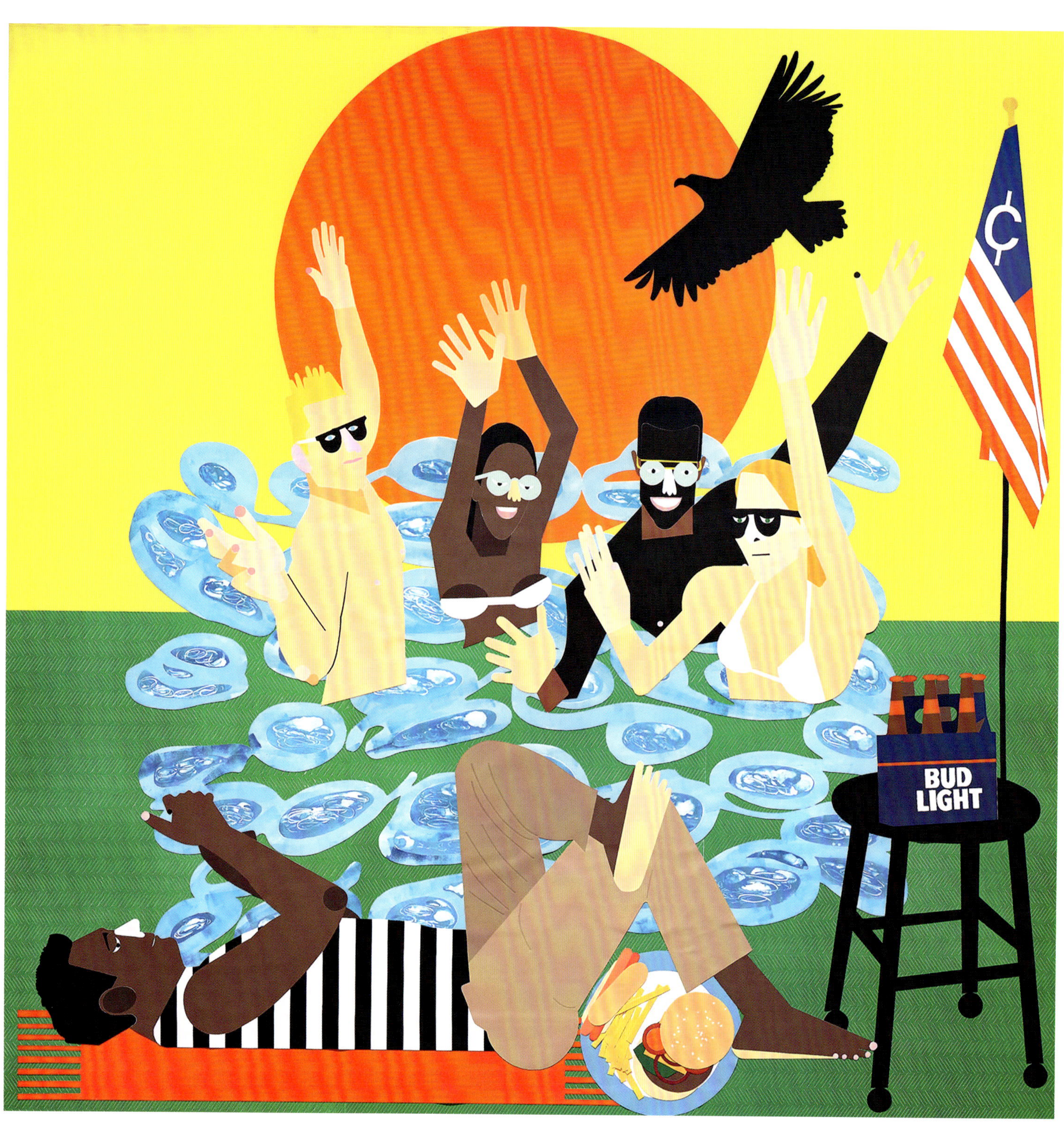

WA and Up for Whatever, 2020

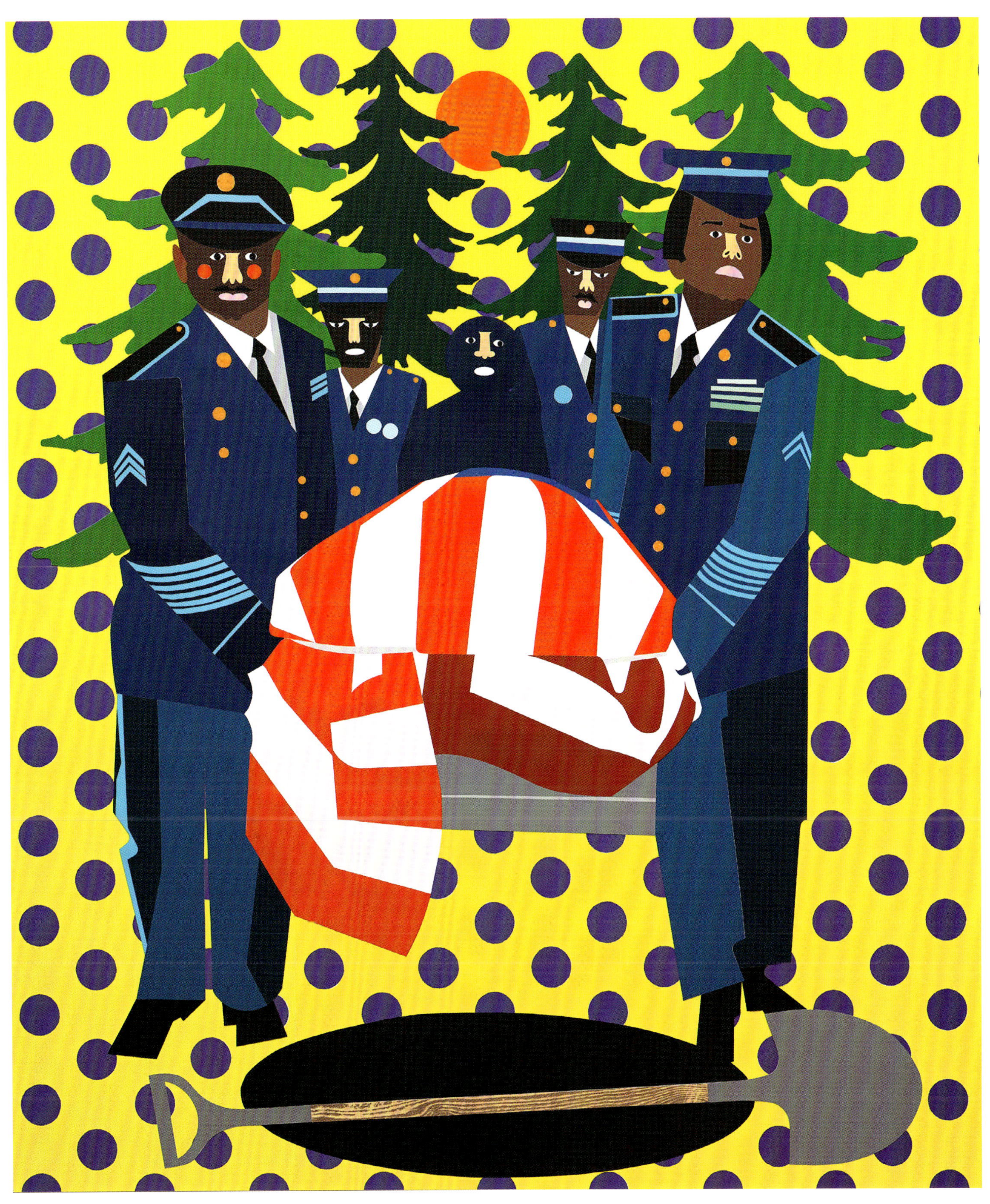

She Was a Real Trouper – Acts of Service, 2020

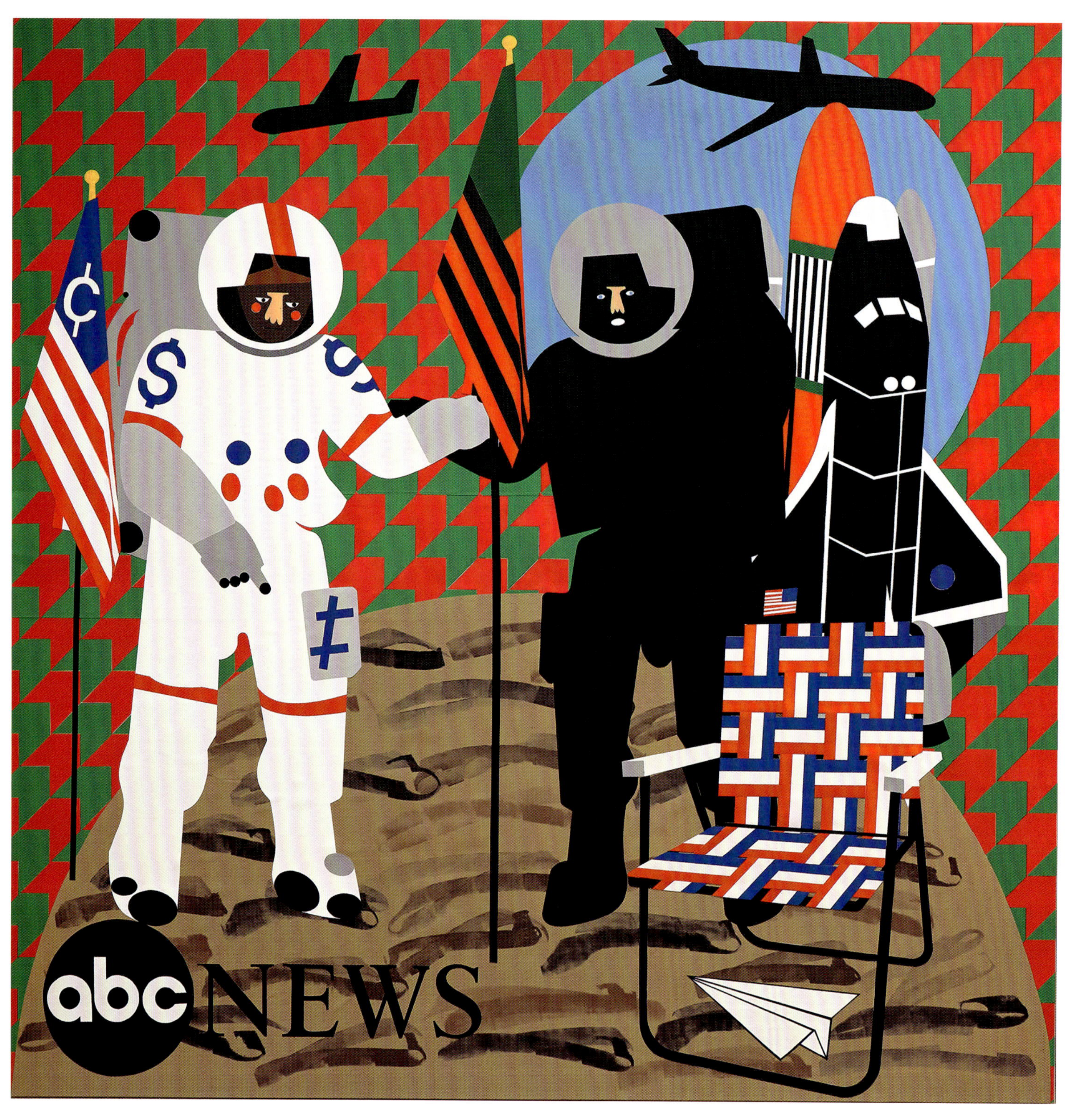

Outer Space, Inner Circle, 2020

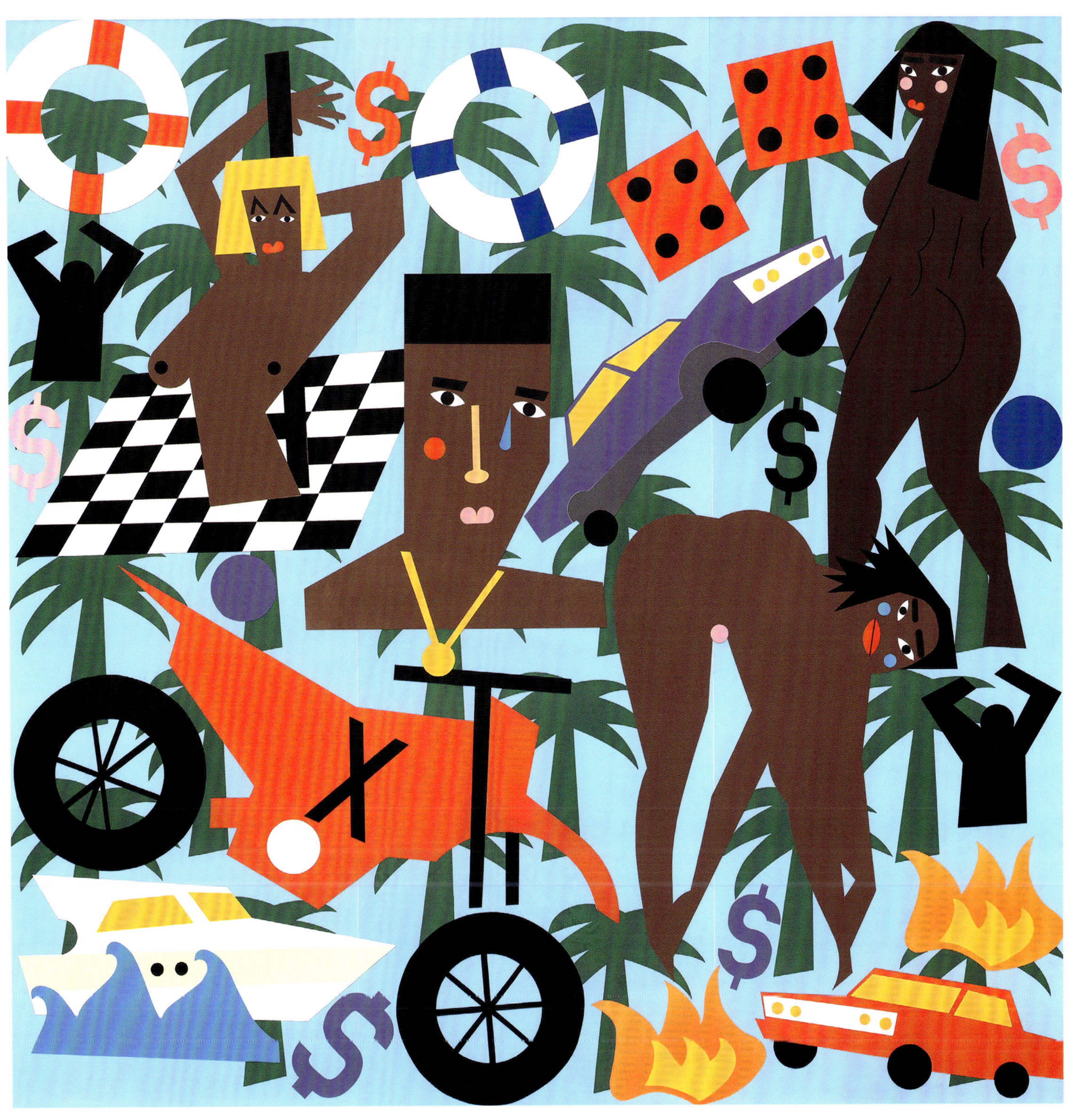

Untitled, 2021

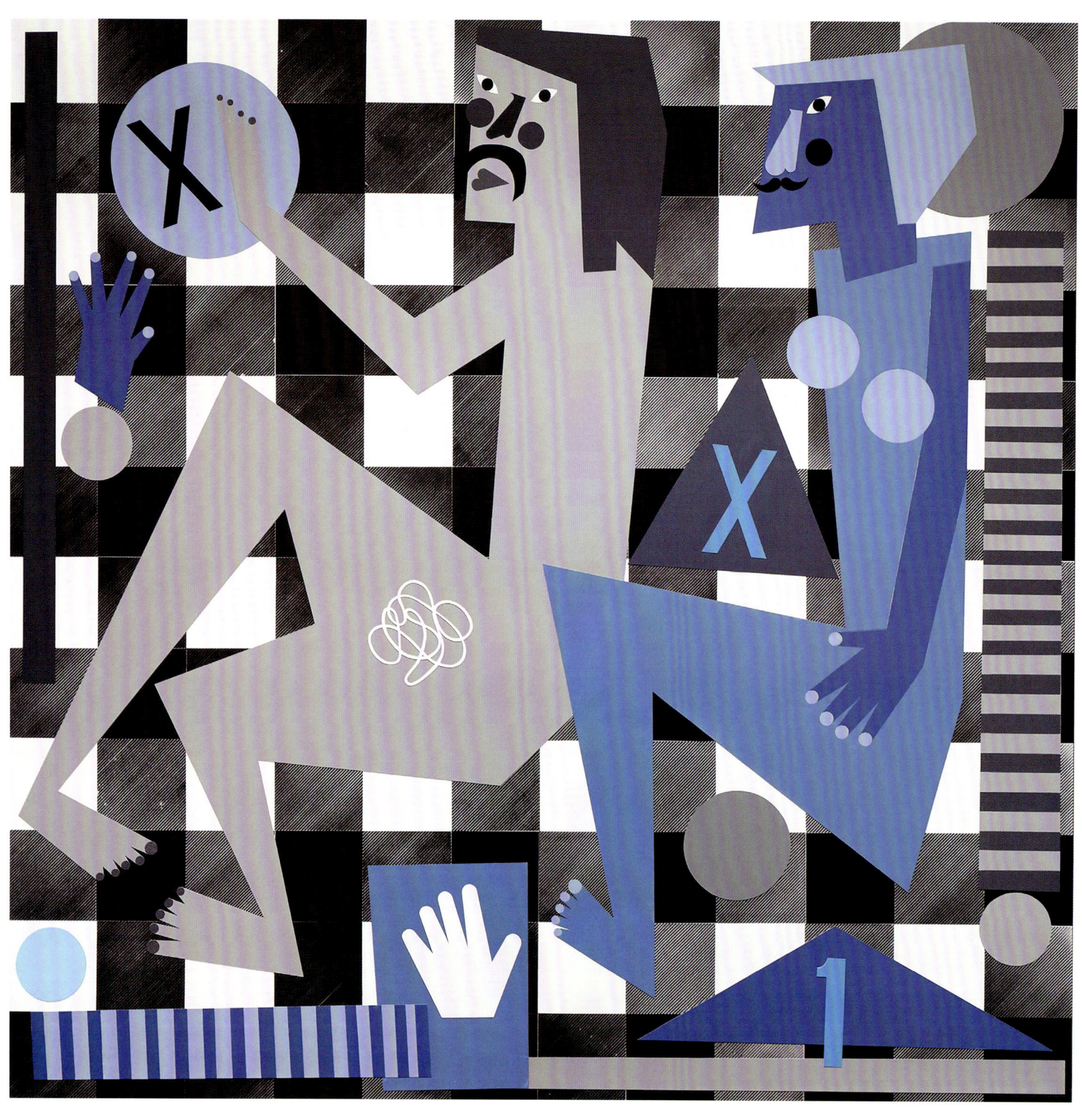

White, 2021

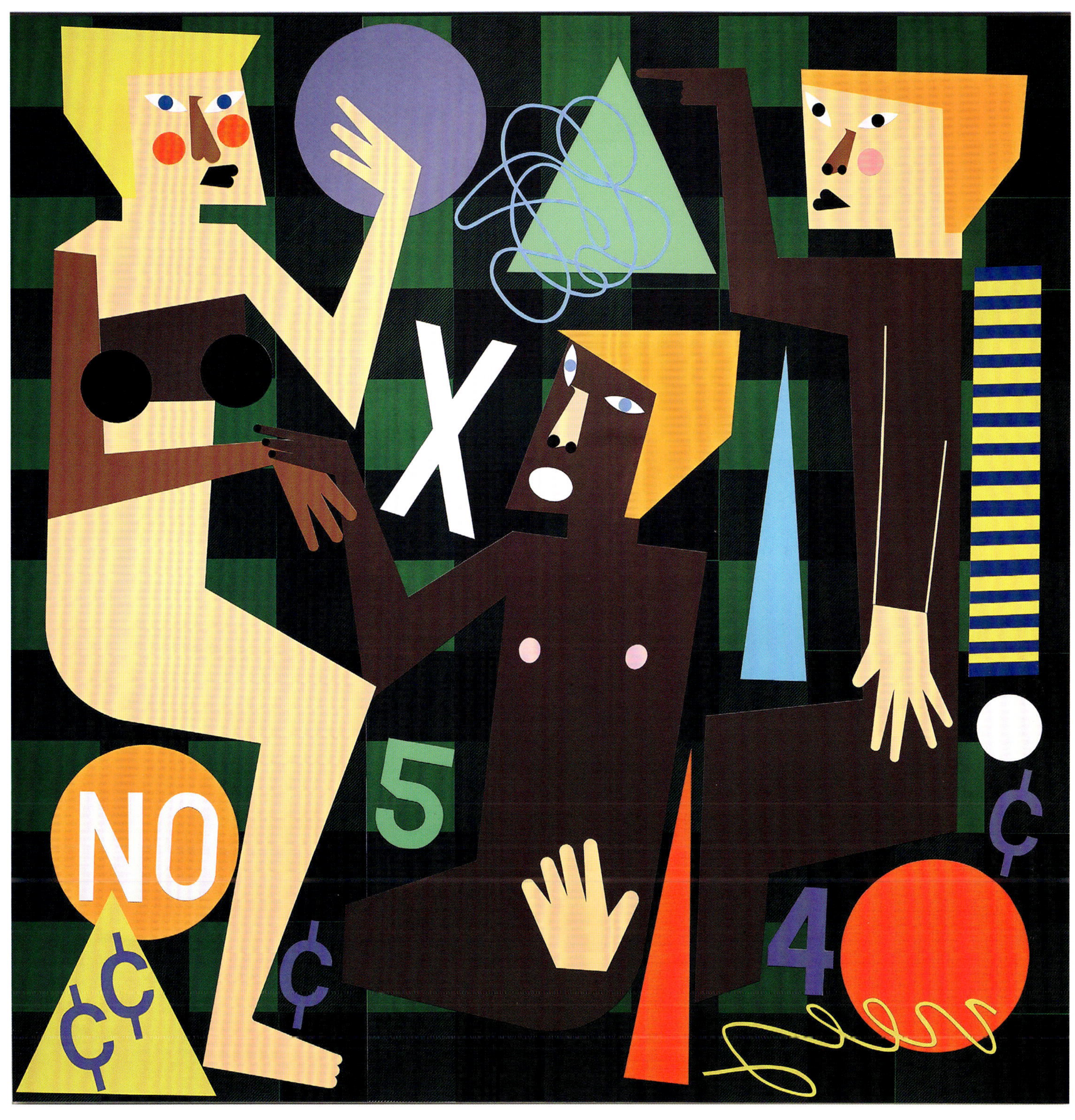

Green, 2021

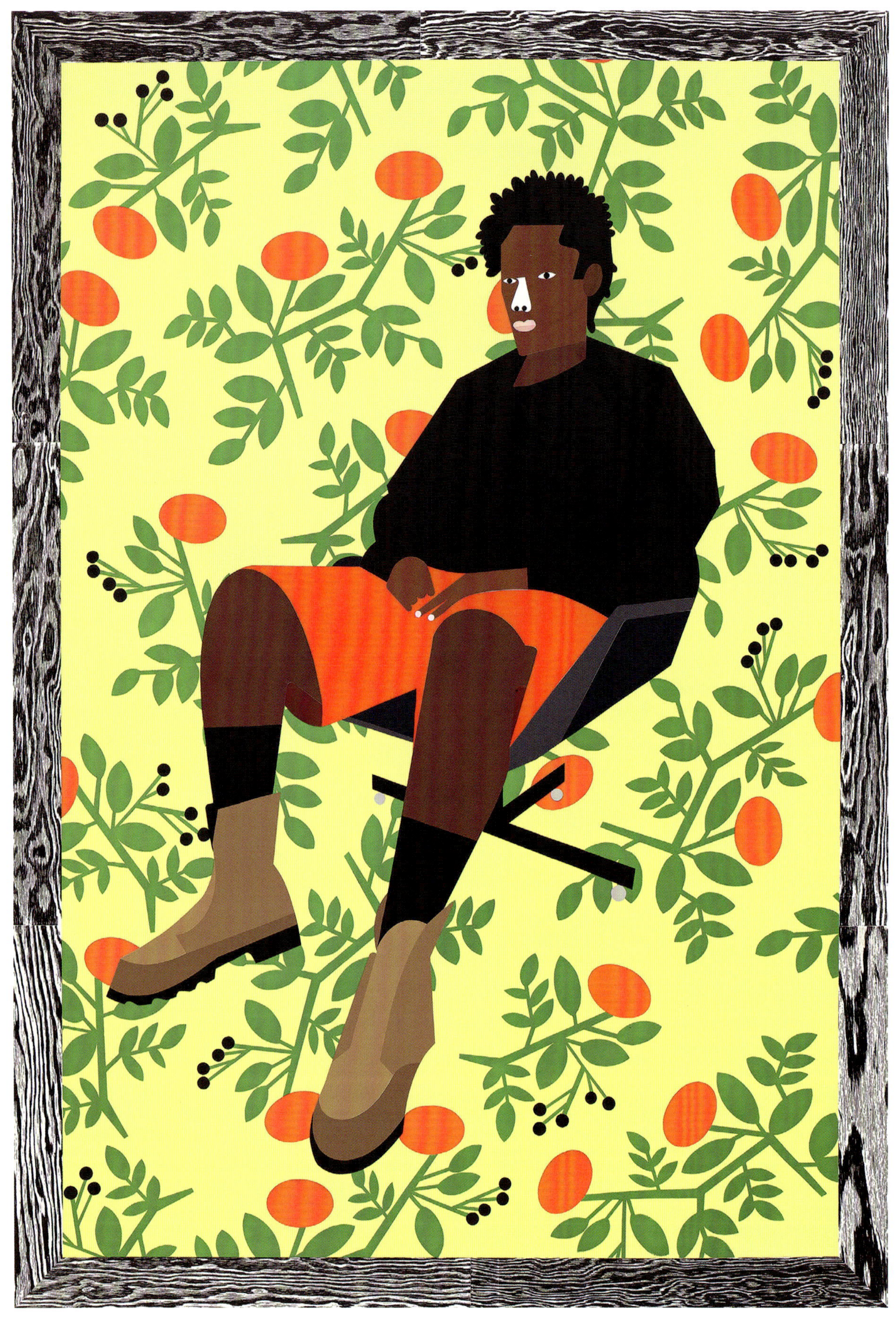

CREW, 2021

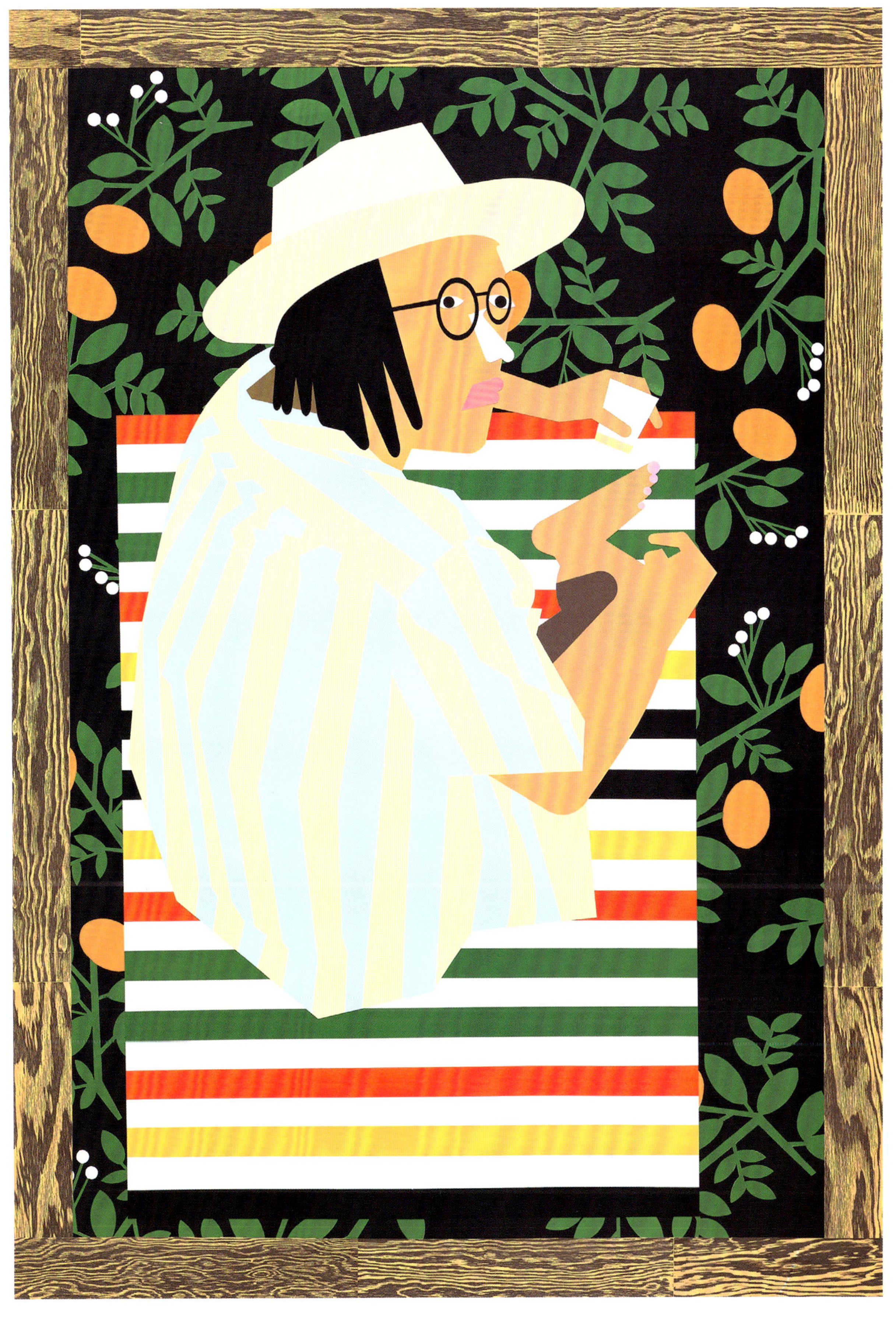

CREW, 2021

ARTIST

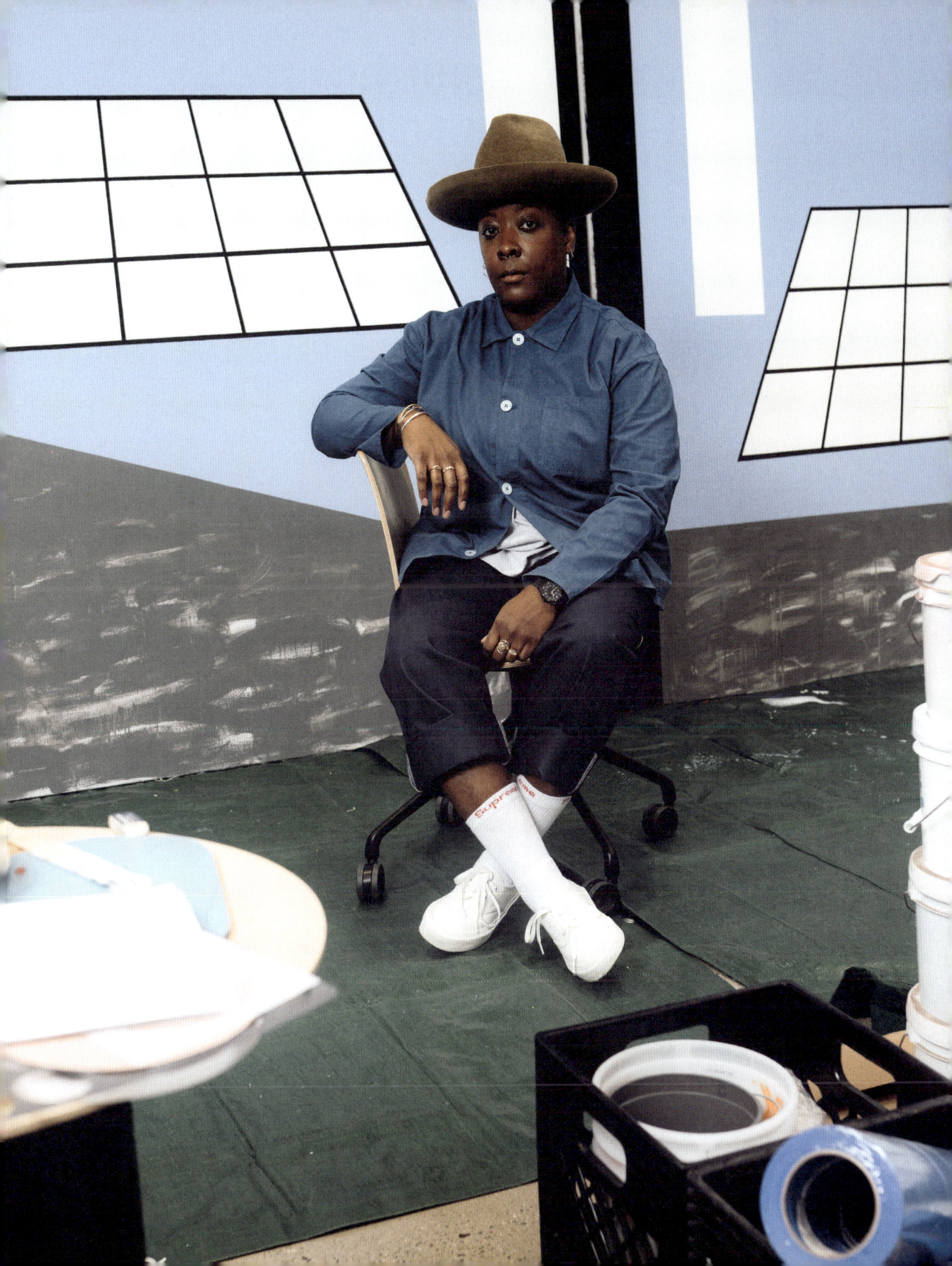

ART IS A CONVERSATION, NOT A LECTURE

JAZMINE HUGHES

Nina Chanel Abney paints in her own dialect, a language all her own. There are the words—*Yum! Tasty! Yay!*—that regularly slice through her scenes, as familiar as a recurring guest star. There is the iconography—dollar signs, *X*'s, hands, numbers—that appears in many of her paintings that are less floating through the picture than hanging in the balance. And there is, of course, the desire to make sense of it all, to crack the code of creativity. Do the *X*'s mean we should avert our eyes? Should we consider the circles to be portals? Or mirrors? Are the dollar signs intended to call to our attention the haunting specter of capitalism?

"Everyone's like, *Oh, what does it mean*?" Abney said one afternoon, in her home studio in Cold Spring, New York. It was December and the snow was indiscriminate—clinging to roads, branches, and windshields. Inside, it was as warm as a pocket. Fitful trumpets and brassy saxophones blared through the studio's speakers; smiley emoji pillows and a Supreme blanket covered the couch. Abney was preparing for three upcoming shows, so a half dozen neon-bright canvases filled the room. Against the studio backdrop, Abney was mellow and fly, dressed in all black, symmetrical tattoos on each forearm. The studio demands soft shoes—that day, she wore socks and slides—but behind a closed closet door, she told me, is her sneaker collection. Around us were the boxes of all the pairs that hadn't made it to the shoe closet yet. (When I asked Abney how many pairs of Jordans she owns, she declined to answer on the record.)

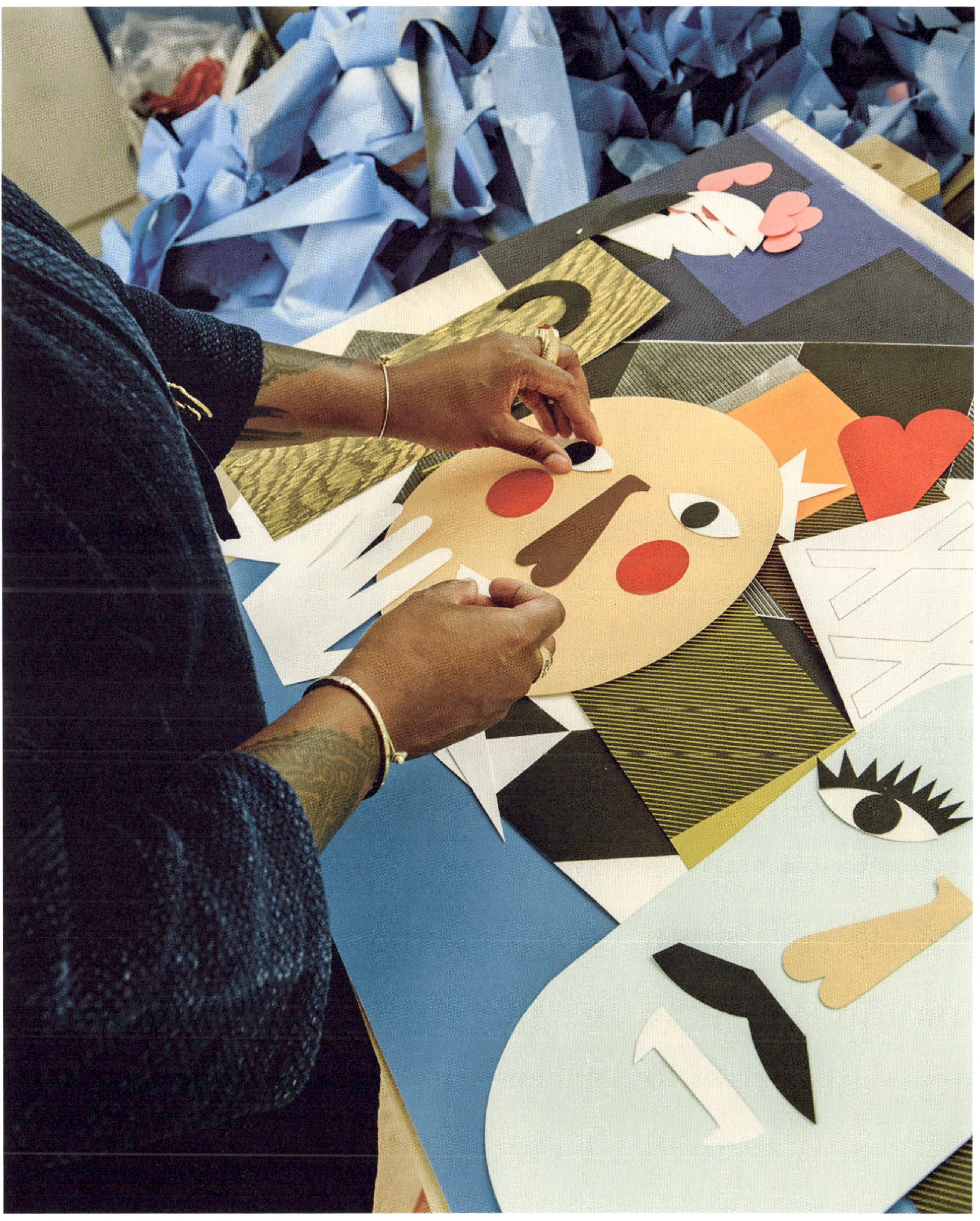

To be asked about the significance of the art squeezes out all the fun. In Abney's mind, art is a conversation, not a lecture. "That question annoys me a little bit," she said, from the second step of a ladder. She stood before an oversized canvas, dipping a slim brush into a vat of paint the color of an egg yolk. "It prevents someone from having their own relationship with the work; they just want you to tell it to them." She's not here to do the thinking for you. She has led you to the water, and it's up to you whether you will drink.

The symbols are a means of storytelling simplification: what's the visual bare minimum a viewer needs for her to effectively get the point across? "There's a difference between making things intentionally ambiguous versus a work that doesn't mean anything."

For a few minutes, she worked silently. "The work was going faster when I was using spray paint," she admits, by way of apology. "I would make a bunch of stencils, but now that I'm back to painting acrylic... It's a long road." She shook her head wearily. "I think sometimes people weren't thinking about a spray-painted work as a *painting*," she said. "If I'm using a brush, it's more 'artistic,' whereas they don't realize that it takes work to make something [spray-painted] look easy."

What people seem to be asking about Abney's oeuvre, beneath their lazy search for meaning, is whether or not something belongs. It's a question she's been presented with her entire career—including from and to herself. In grad school, at Parsons School of Design, she was thrown against a sharp white background. All the other students were white, with BFAs and art experience; Abney came to the program after a year on the assembly line at a Ford Motor Company factory in Chicago. She spent her first day of classes in tears. Professors discouraged her painting style and pressured her to paint more "realistically." She also gravitated toward a flat painting style that was often generally criticized and deemed lesser. Abney was painting on a small scale, no bigger than the three-by-four-foot canvases she could afford—enough to paint a face, but not a family. She figured she had found her steez: besides, she rarely saw women painters working on a large scale.

But then a friend pointed out that her individual characters might go well in a frame together. Abney bought a massive roll of canvas and stretched a large piece directly onto the wall. This method led to her first monumental paintings. One of them became her senior thesis: *Class of 2007* (2007), a diptych of racial inversion and a remix of the power dynamics that had weighed on her since that first day. Her white classmates are depicted as Black inmates in orange jumpsuits; Abney is a gun-toting blonde corrections officer. Bump belonging; she was running the joint.

Almost twenty years later, Abney presented the monumental exhibition *LIE DOGGO*, a bold, jazzy encapsulation of her work, at The

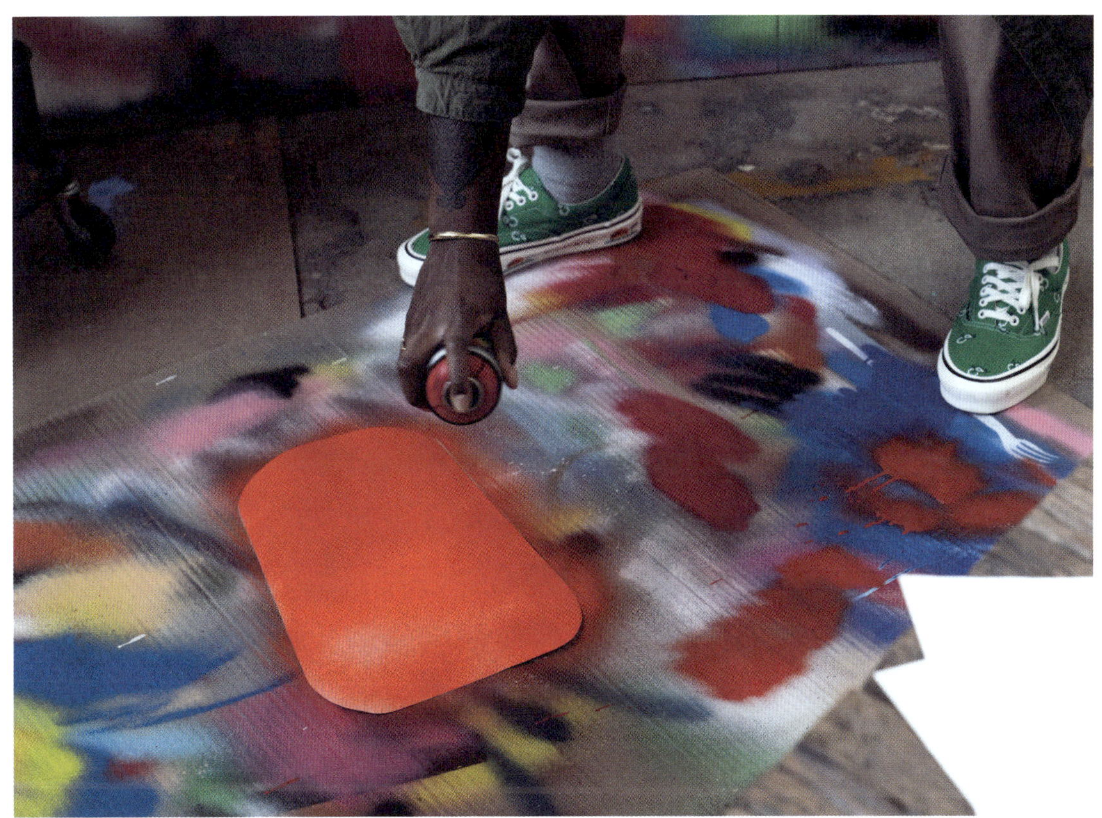

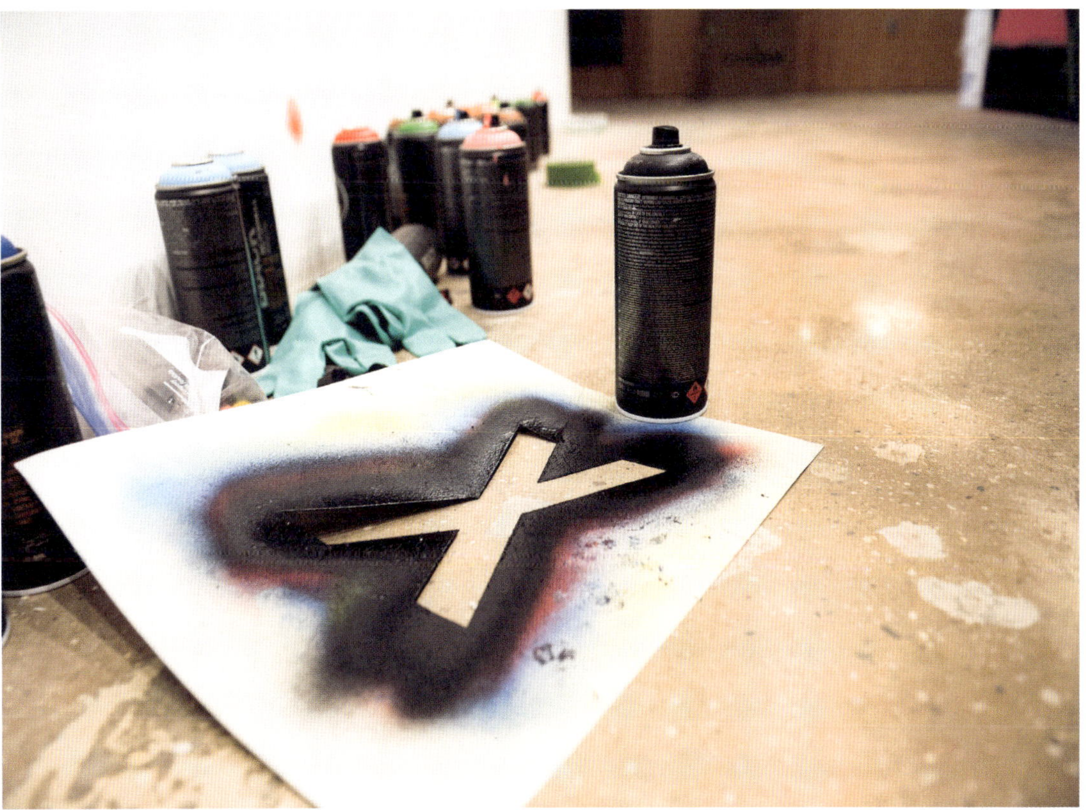

School | Jack Shainman Gallery. It was a fantasia of sculpture, portraiture, collage, digital installation, and mural painting. The title is a peculiar one. I first encountered it in a crossword puzzle, the schematic inverse of Abney's vibrant visual work. "Lay doggo" was a clue for a four-letter word with a "d" in the middle. Nothing came to mind. So like all dedicated cruciverbalists, I cheated, googling the prompt on my phone. The answer, both obscure and obvious, was "hide." Etymologists aren't quite sure where the phrase came from, which thrills me. Abney's show, then, is the biggest stage on which the phrase has played. It feels like hers now. One of the first definitions I found felt uncannily fitting for Abney's work: "'Lie doggo' is an old phrase meaning to lay low, maybe as a process of slyly observing, and with the timing to pounce and make art on consequence." But then I realized it came from a *Times Union* review of her show.

"For me, it represents a commentary on the current social and political climate, in which people often feel the need to lie low to avoid scrutiny or confrontation," Abney has said about the title of her show. Her work is probing, interested not just in the command to conceal oneself but in what it is that we're concealing. "The title also plays with the duality of truth and deception, prompting viewers to consider what is real and what is hidden beneath the surface." Representation is often simply presentation: what glitters is rarely gold.

Abney's work catches your attention and engages with it, making space for a viewer to project oneself onto the scene. Narratives are being played, but we're not beaten over the head with the details; they're roomy enough for us to fill in. "People come to me with their interpretations of the work all the time," she said, sitting at a small desk in the middle of the studio. Take *Flint Fuel* (2024), a four-panel work depicting a legion of cars filling up at a gas station. Figures surround the cars, and a few stand before the vehicles, hands frozen in a wave. I figured they were station attendants, or friends or strangers approaching for a conversation. Abney told me about a friend who saw the painting and thought those figures were drowning, leading them to a thought-provoking conversation about Flint, Michigan, and its decade-long water crisis. "I'm not opposed to hearing other people's perspectives. That's the whole point, to put all these different things together to start a conversation."

And that conversation is, of course, generally about race. Abney has been criticized for making work that's both too much *and* too little about race, a weight that bugs her. While this can have a direct impact on Abney's practice, it certainly isn't unique to her as an artist of color. Black artists, in general, bear the burden of their art having to speak to racial politics, whether they want to or not. "If I paint a black figure, it's automatically going to be about race. If I don't paint black figures, it's going to be about race," said Abney. "[White] artists don't have to do that. They can just paint whatever they want without it being framed in this specific context."

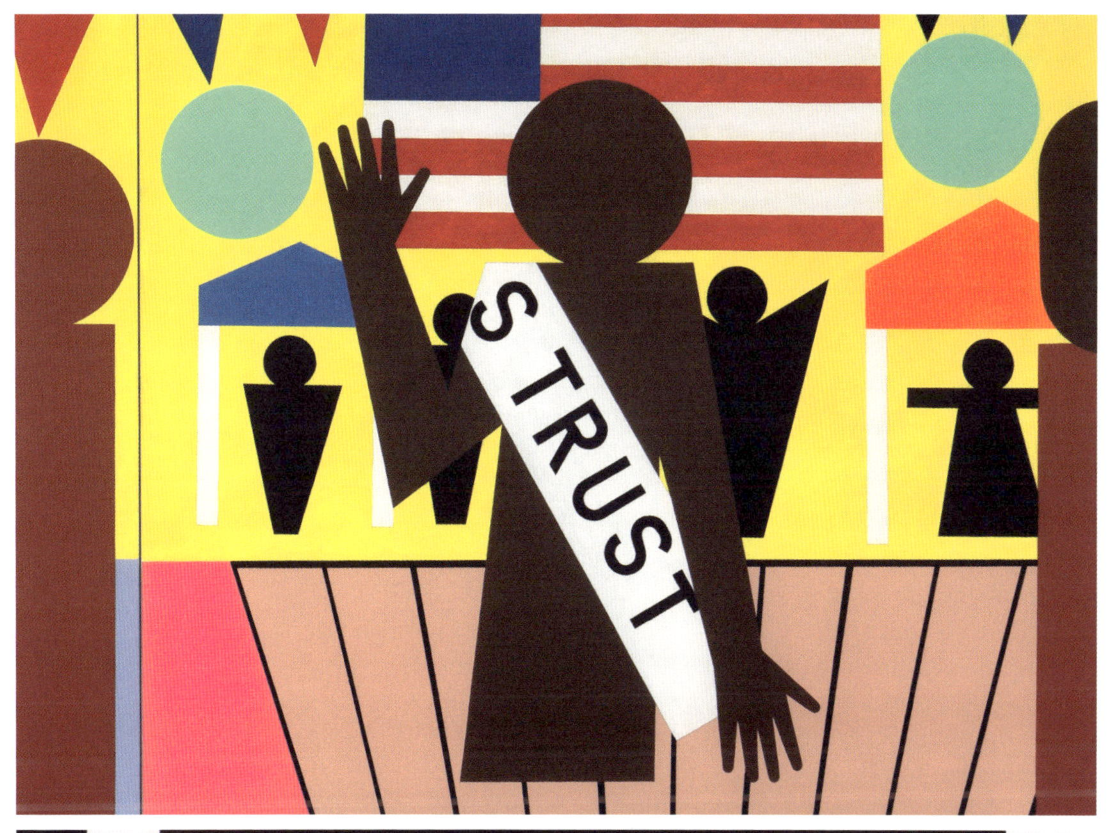

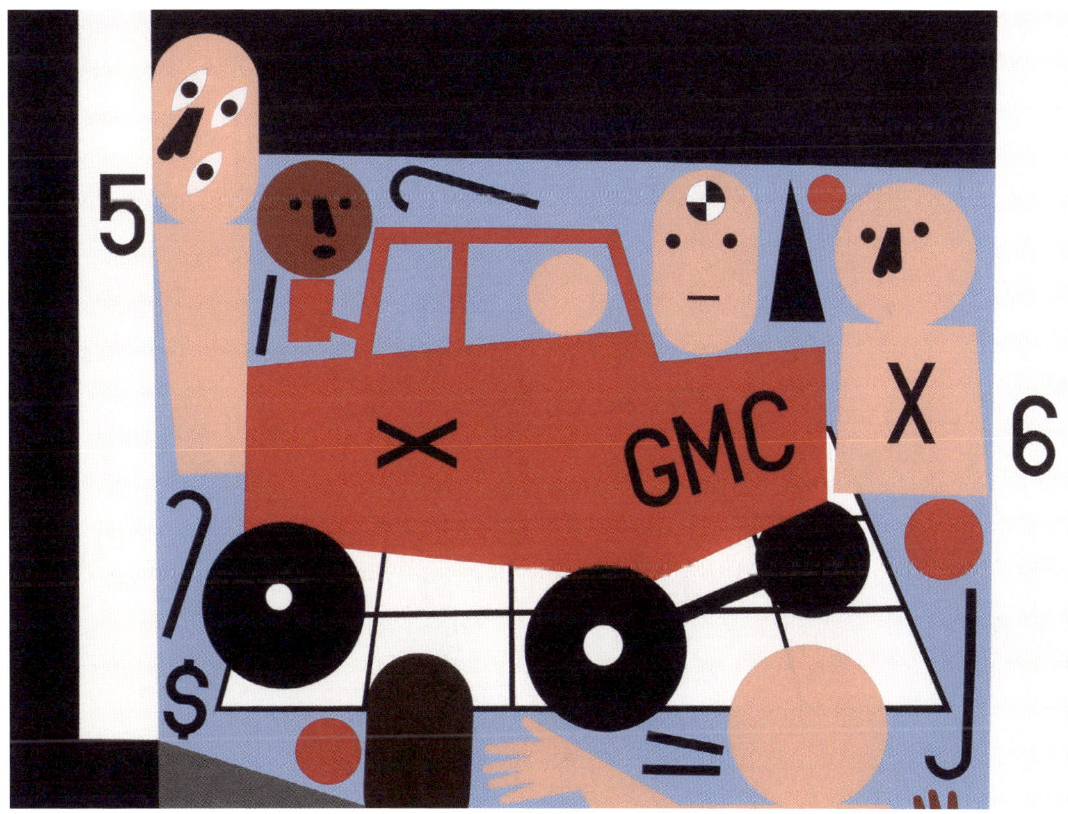

[TOP] Detail, Miss Opportunity, 2024
[BOTTOM] Detail, Flint Fuel, 2024

Even the *LIE DOGGO* banner hung outside the School, a gallery in upstate New York that retained the name of its building's original purpose, insists on ambiguity. Oblong cocoa brown and tawny peach faces float among three simplified American flags, suggesting an image of racial harmony. The grinning, genderless faces are each smiling behind slices of watermelon—our country's most politically charged fruit—providing some healthy speculation. And because this is America, a ghost hovers around the perimeter, a shadow of uncertainty. Do the flags menace or endorse? Is this America's past, present, or future? Why is baring one's teeth both an aggressive and submissive act? Abney and I talked about context—about how, these days, seeing someone proudly wave an American flag is likely to cause more suspicion than solidarity.

Miss Opportunity (2024), a four-panel display suggesting a beauty pageant, is festooned with flags: the Pride flag, the Thin Blue Line flag, the American flag, and the Pan-African flag. The "contestants" are draped in identifying sashes: MISS BEHAVE, MISS GEN[DER], [MISS] TRUST and [MISS] FORTUNE. Their hands are raised in greeting, waving at the crowd like winners do. In her work, Abney remixes her figures' physicality, mismatching the skin tones of faces and body parts. Still, the scene is tagged as VERY BLACK, just as that misbehavior, misgendering, mistrust, and misfortune can all be too. It's realistic, even if it's not lifelike. It's honest and open, even if it's obscured. Abney meets us where we're at: sometimes the mis(s) behavior comes from one of us. The work trusts us enough to resist exclusively perpetuating narratives of empowerment by putting our weaknesses on display. Zora Neale Hurston called an artistic insistence on only uplifting the race a confinement "to the spectacular." More than being delusory, this approach was dishonest. "The realization that Negroes are no better nor no worse, and at times just as boring as everybody else, will hardly kill off the population of the nation," she wrote in a 1950 essay in *Negro Digest*.

What interests Abney most, clearly, is people—specifically the ways in which people perceive each other. Abney places figures in public spaces where they are the center of attention: courtrooms, basketball games, hospitals. The works' vibrancy blares out their messages, an echo affixed to each: NOTICE ME, LISTEN TO ME, SEE ME LIKE I SEE YOU. Abney's characters are consciously conspicuous, looking you straight in the eye. Confidently conspicuous. In meeting the gaze of the figures, the viewer considers them both as individuals as well as participants in a scene. Thus plays out Abney's fascination with the ways we are on display, the ways in which we participate and perform. Even a mundane errand like getting gas, as we see in *Flint Fuel*, is a role in a larger production. The money in my pocket comes from somebody else. The money in my hand belongs to me only briefly. It comes from somewhere bad and goes somewhere worse.

In another work, we see exactly where it goes. *Black People (BP)* (2022) depicts a run-in between fishermen and environmental workers in the

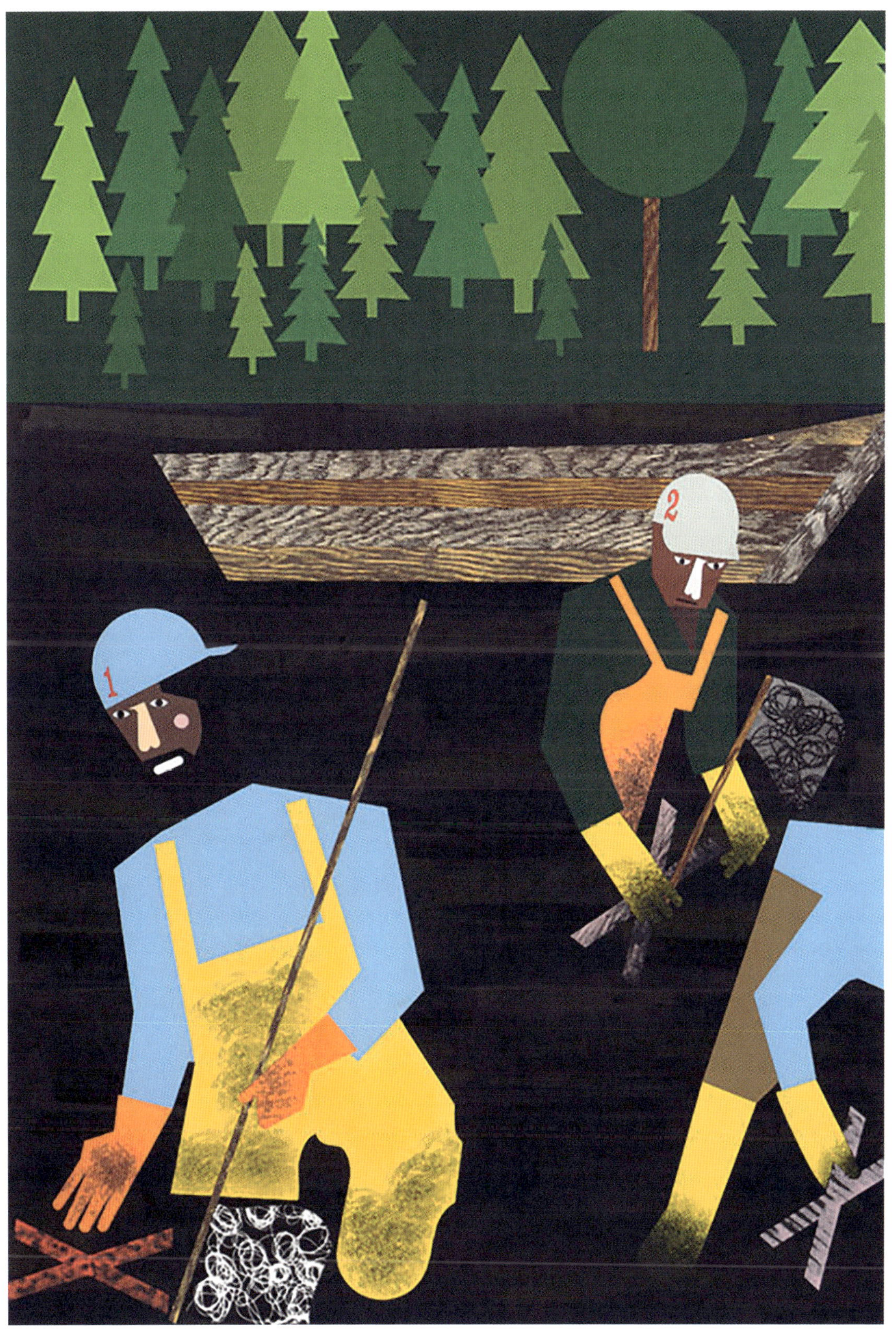

Detail, Black People (BP), 2022

same polluted body of water over three episodic panels. The fishermen's nets sway with anticipation as the workers, in lemon-colored jumpsuits bright against the muck of the water, play their parts. Some pick dirty *X*'s out of the oil. One man takes a selfie with a fish with three eyes, proof of the biochemical havoc. Inspired by Gordon Parks's photographs of the fishing industry during World War II, Abney created *Black People (BP)* in conversation with that series. While Parks mostly photographed white fisherman, Abney does her own thing. Despite being central to the industry, the number of Black fishermen has steadily dwindled since the 1940s, the demographic doubly punished by environmental racism at home and in the workplace. Shrimpers and oystermen along the Gulf Coast were decimated by both Hurricane Katrina and BP's Deepwater Horizon oil spill. Abney imagines narratives of these crucial groups into existence on her canvases, so that they are not forgotten even while they are being erased.

Somewhere in the middle of our conversation, Abney was painstakingly filling in a black stencil, brushing black paint onto a round shape. She told me that I was one of the first people to visit the studio space, which surprised me. Considering her prolific rate of work, I assumed she had plenty of inquiring visitors, as well as a legion of assistants. Instead, she told me that she works completely alone, mostly because other people might not have much to do. "Everything is intuitive," she explained. "I don't know what anything's gonna look like." Procrastination, she swears, is part of the process: hanging out with friends, watching the *Real Housewives*, thumbing through TikTok. All of it is both generative and restorative for her. It's a slog, tying your creativity to your livelihood, only compounding the eternal question about the relationship between good art and suffering.

Abney still gets nervous about premiering her work but wonders if those same fears push her to produce work that, she hopes, is well received. Of course, there's never a guarantee. The pressure is equal parts motivating and daunting. "The goal is to create without anxiety, but it's a vicious cycle," she said, still painting through it. The cycle of creation, steeped in unease and sometimes self-doubt, is still rewarding enough that she reenters the studio and does it again.

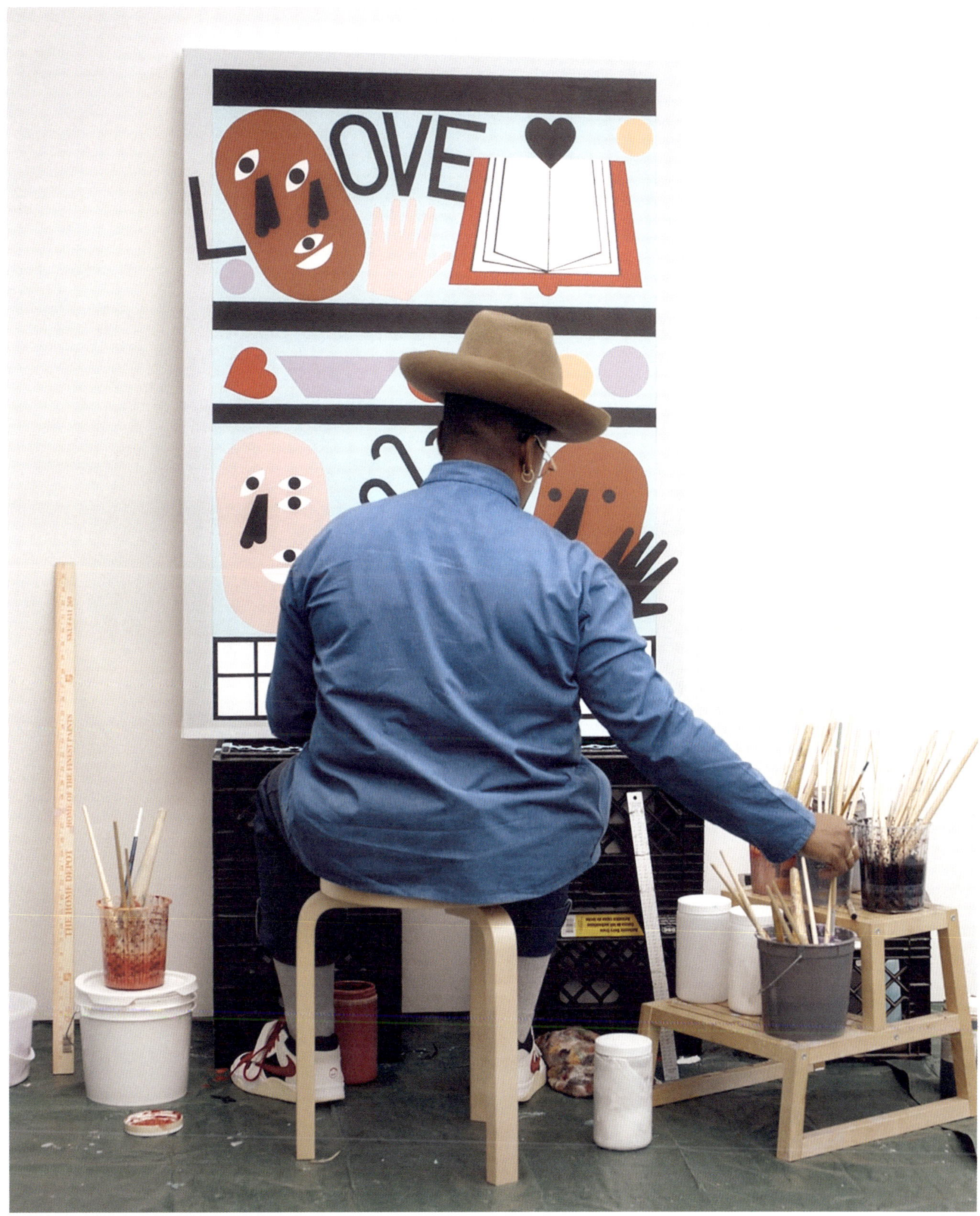

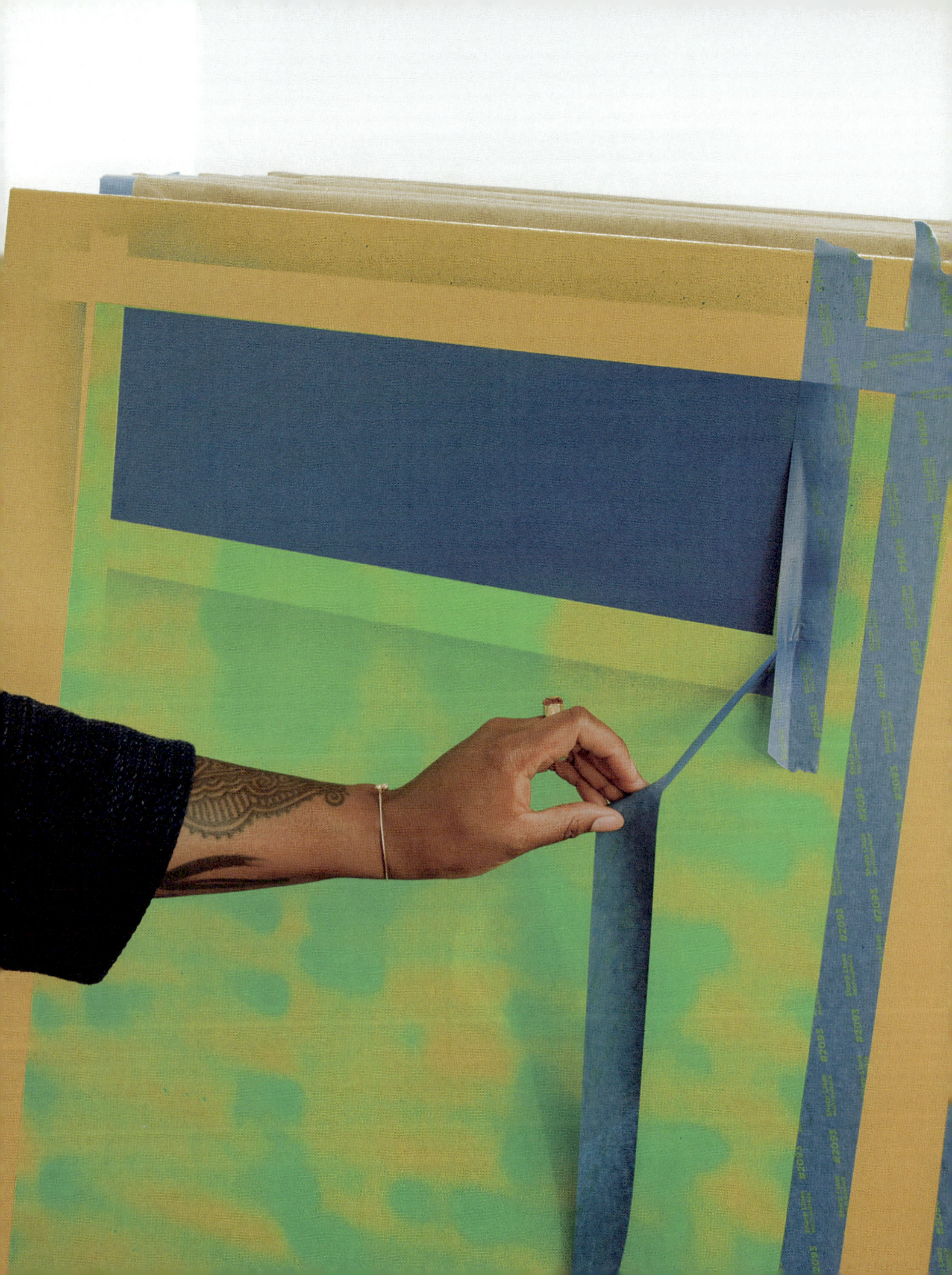

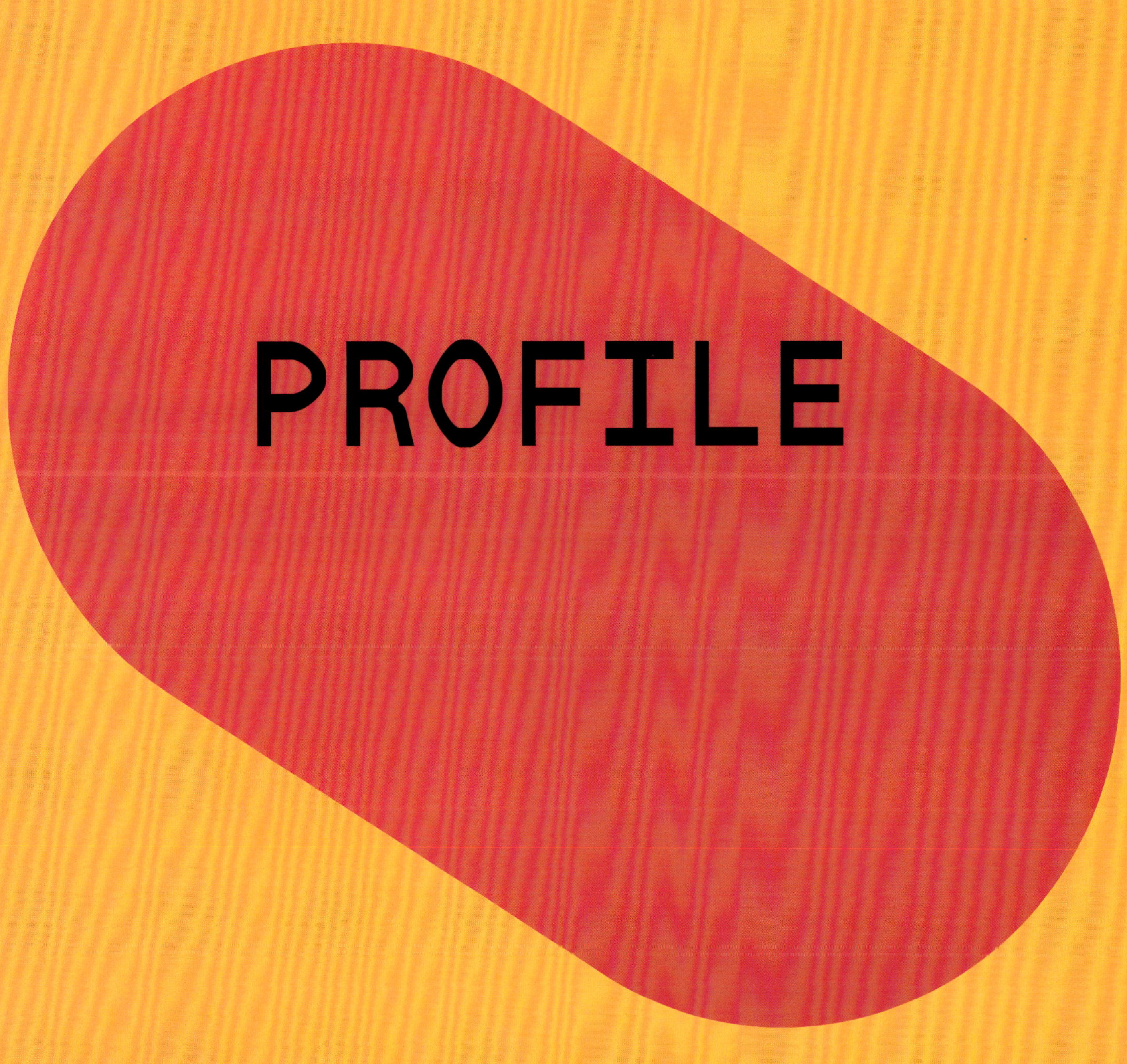

PROFILE

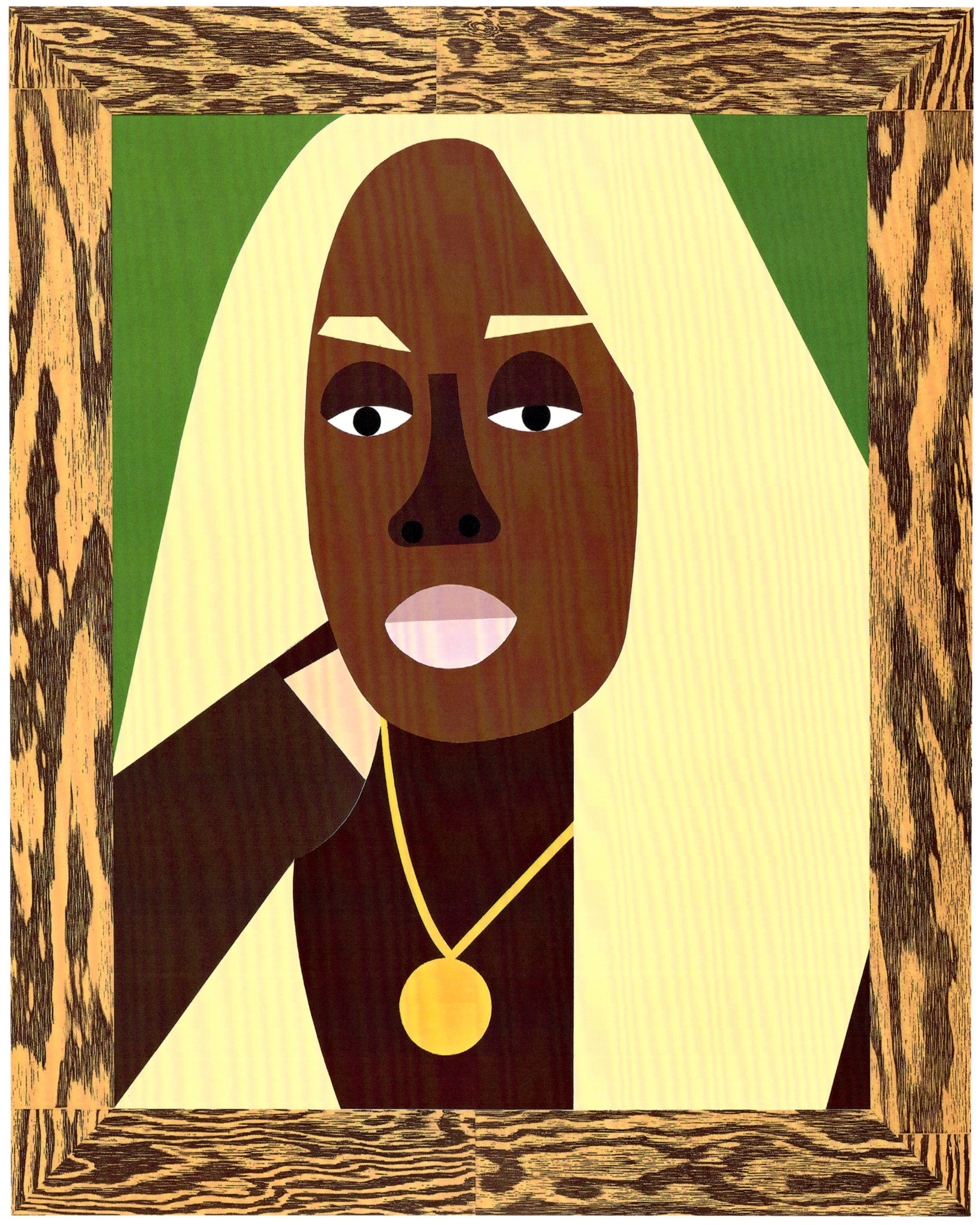

[ABOVE & OPPOSITE] CREW, 2021

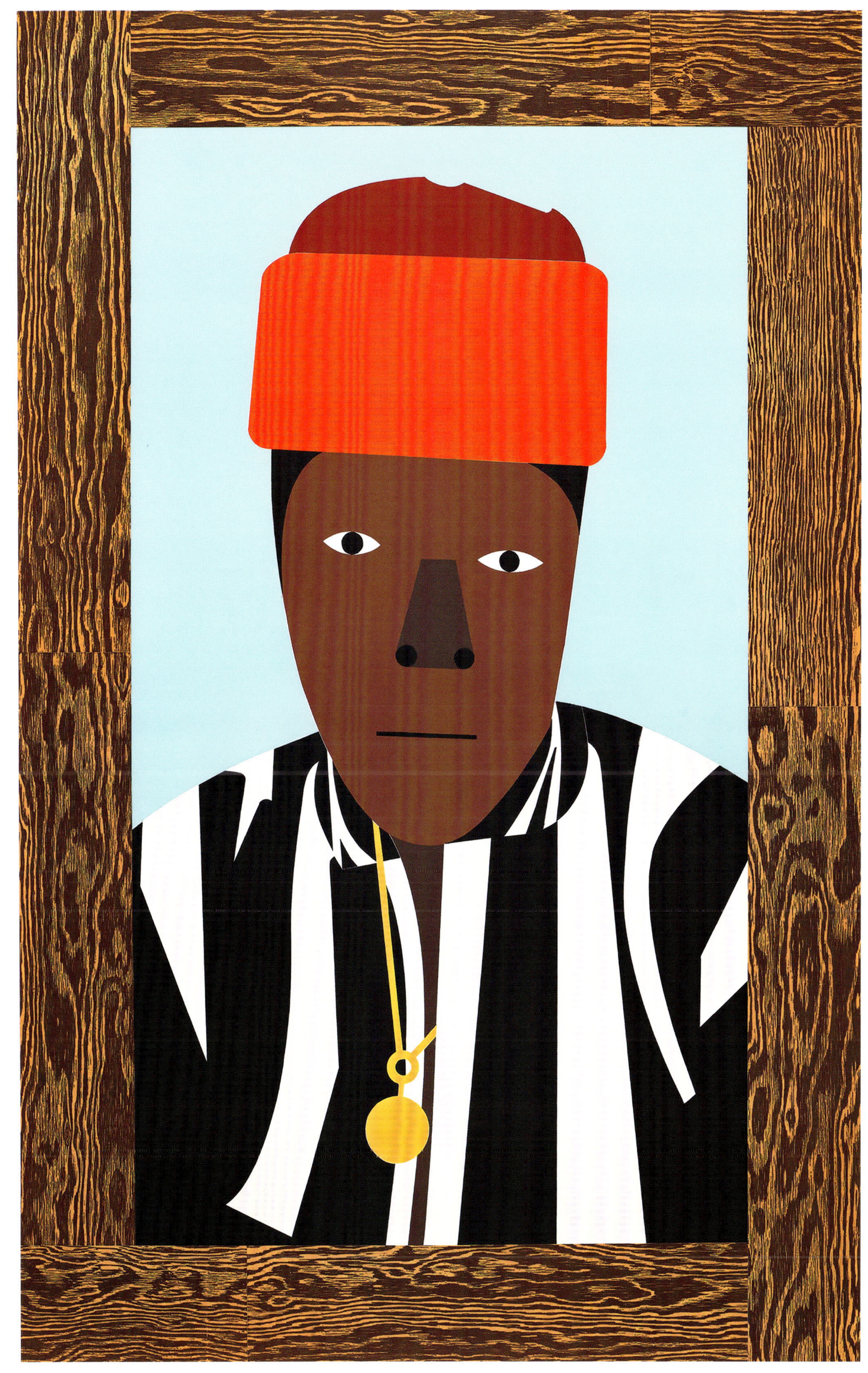

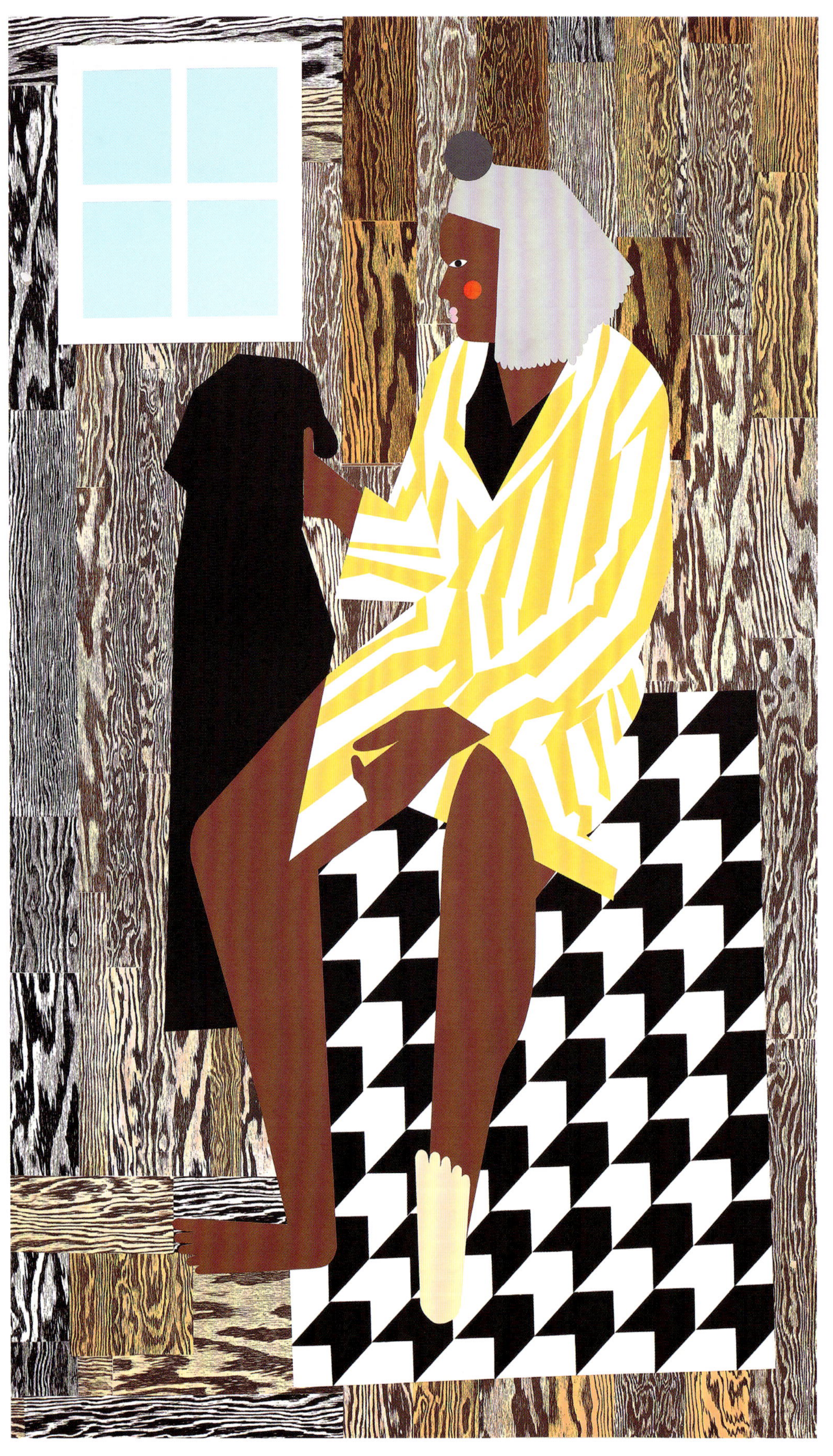

Kiyanna, 2021

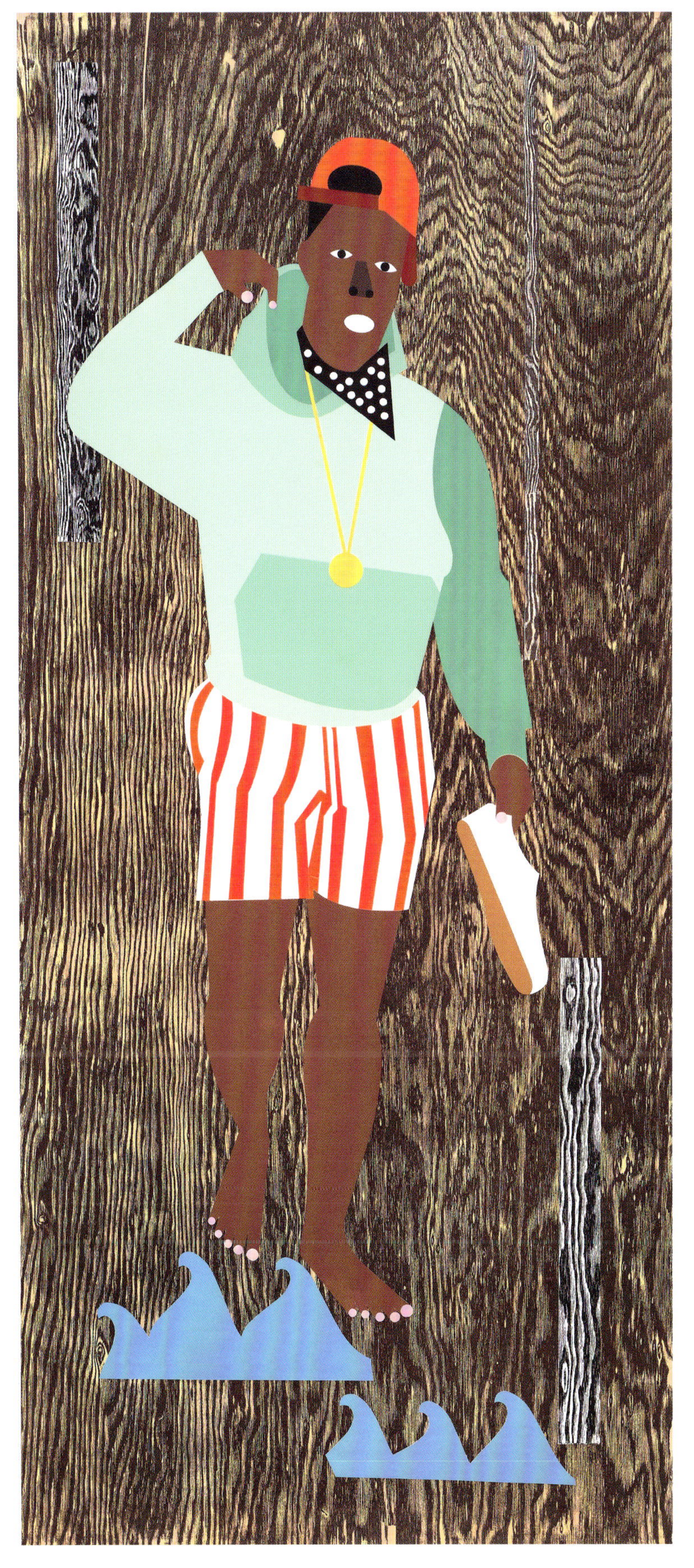

Me, 2021

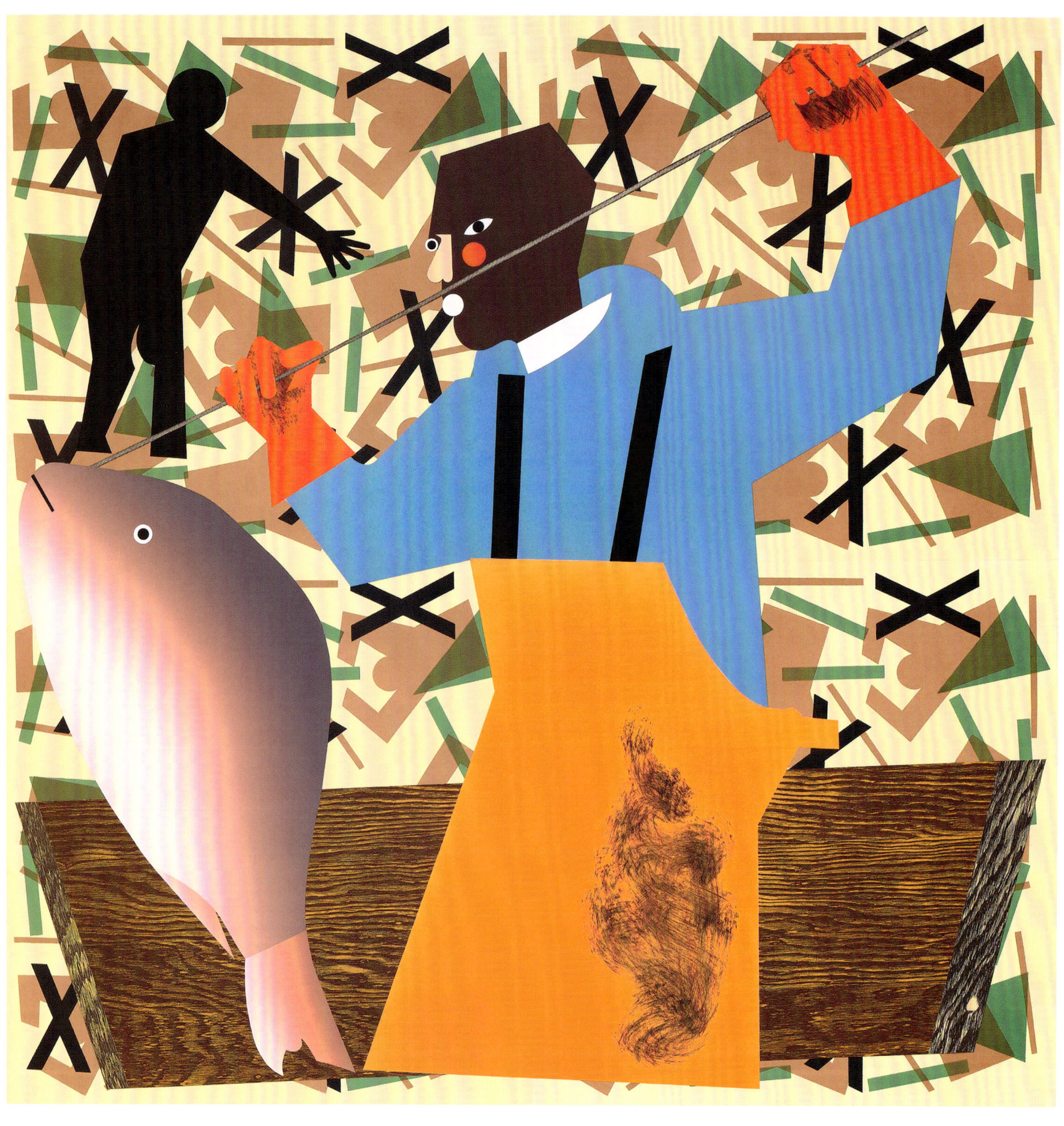

Captain F.M., 2022

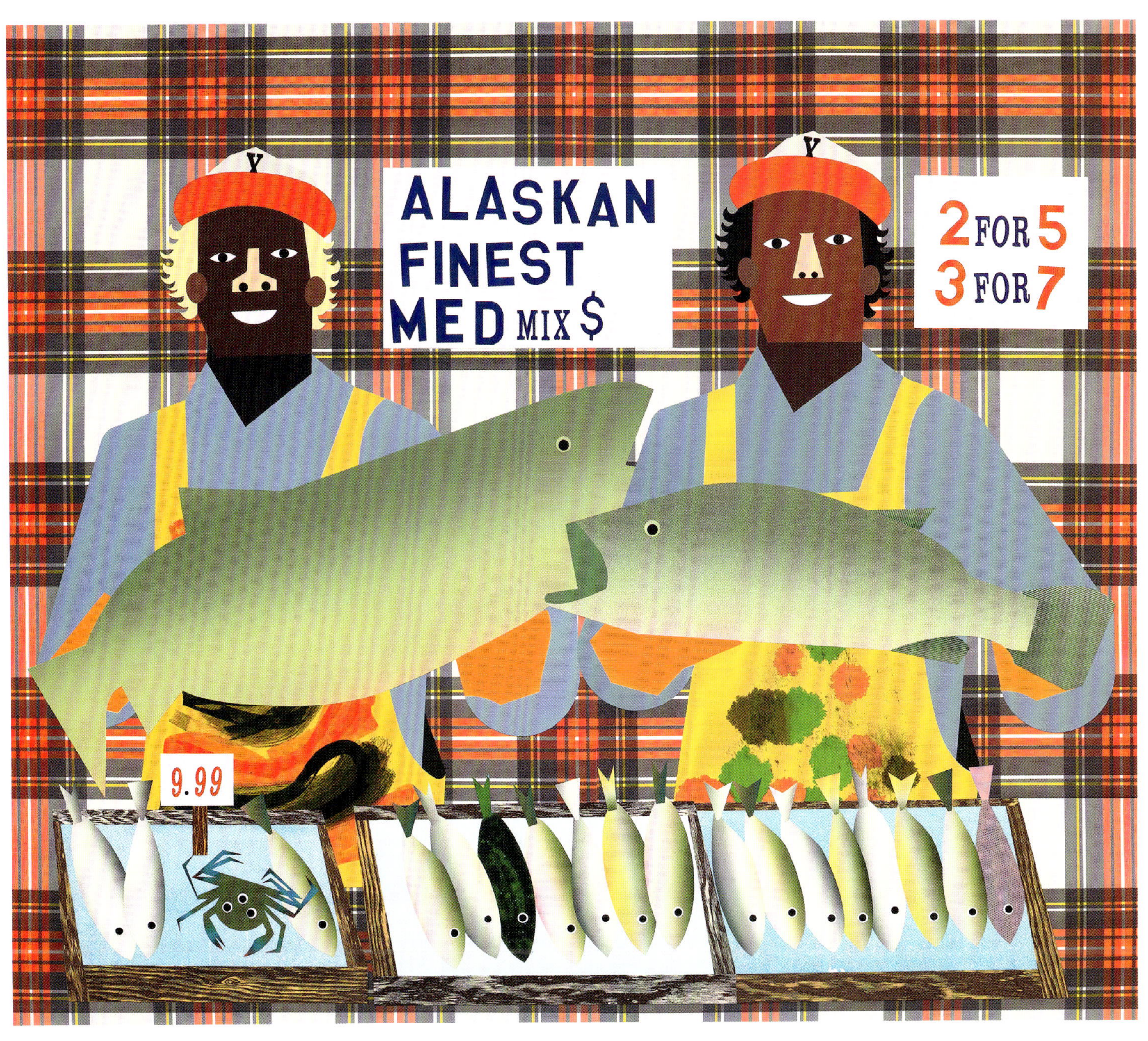

#BRUTHAS WHO #FISH, 2022

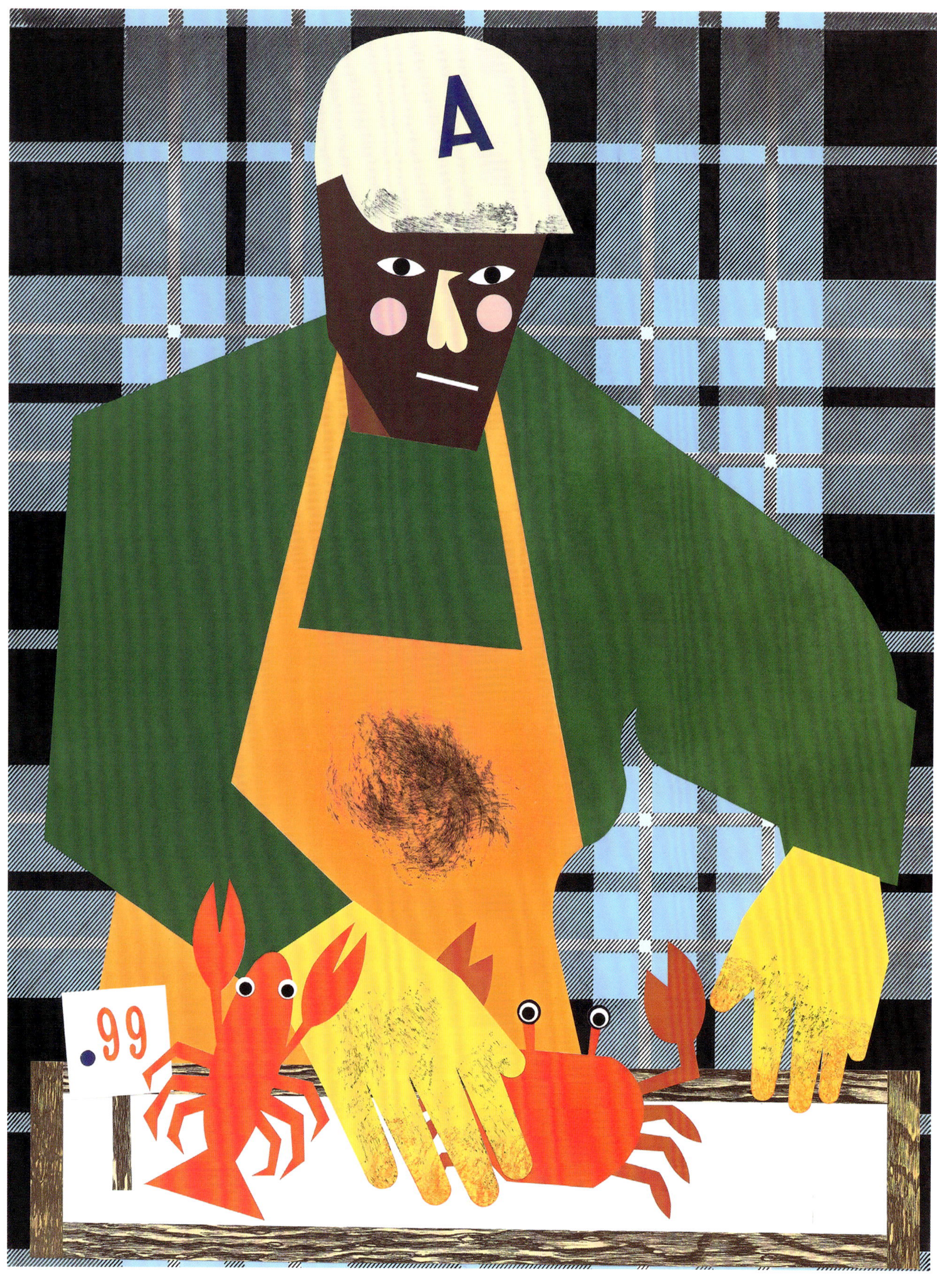

Fish Tales, 2022

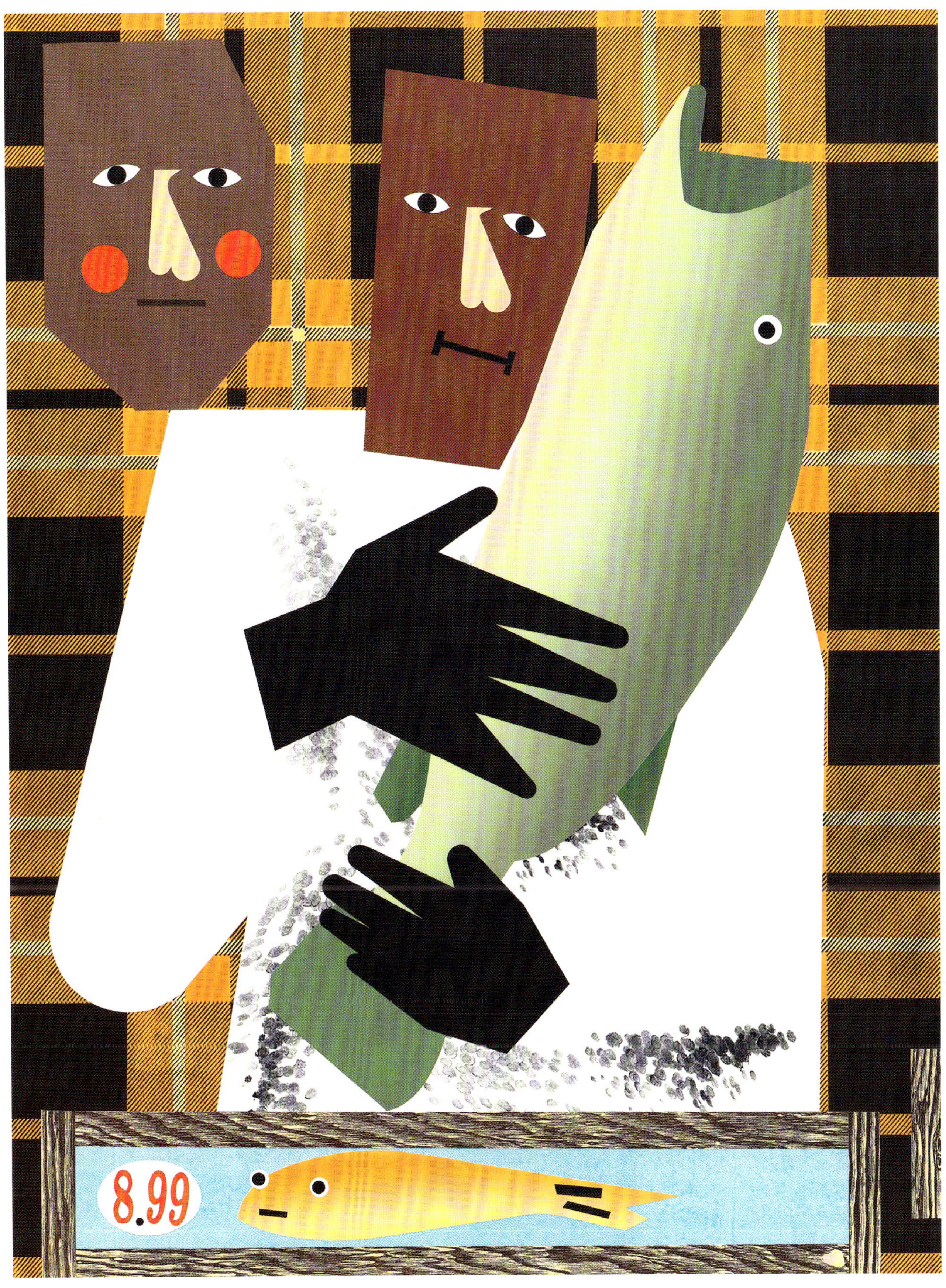

Anthony, 2022

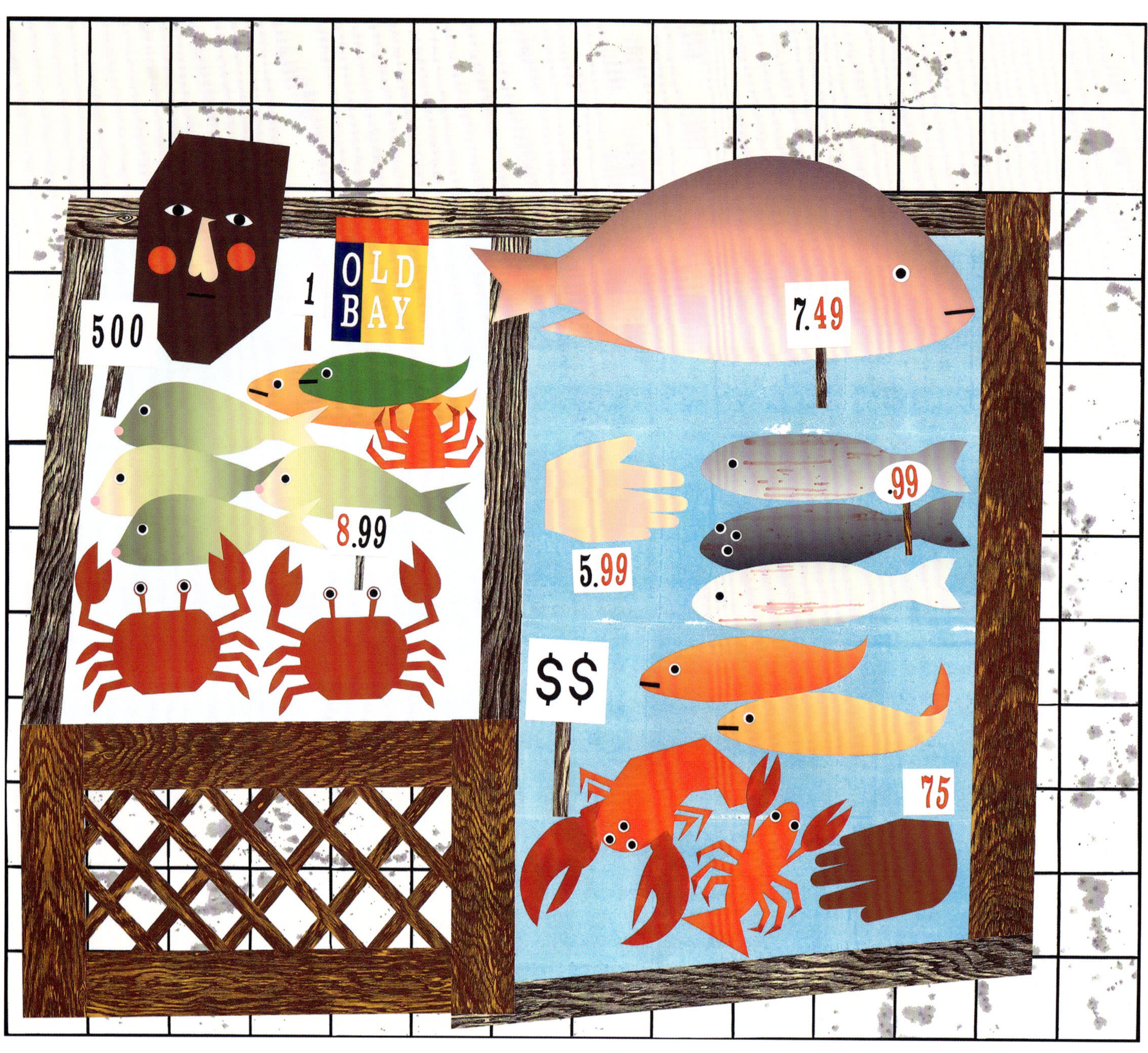

[ABOVE] Sea & Seize, 2022
[OPPOSITE] My Old Bae, 2022

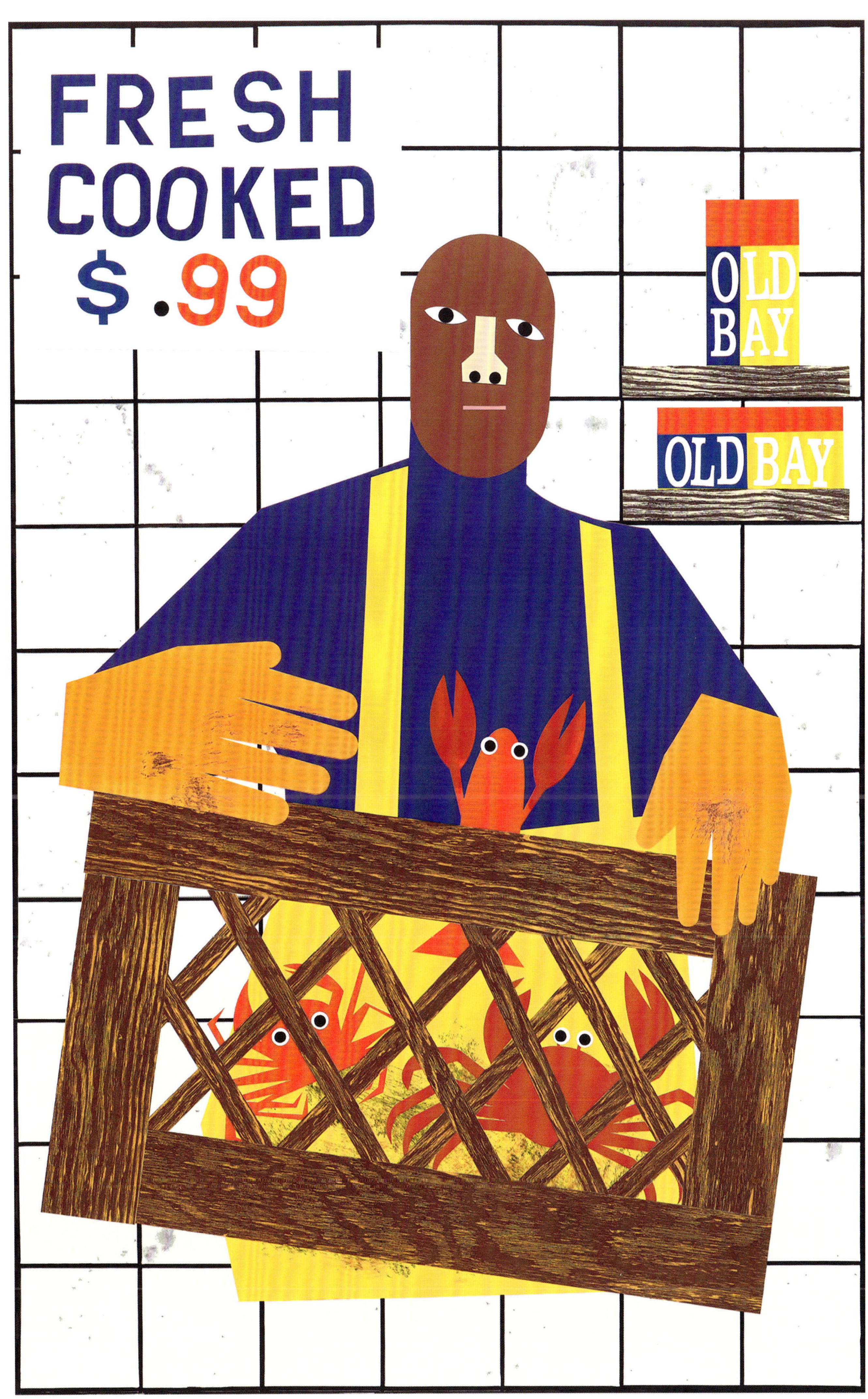
FRESH
COOKED
$.99
OLD
BAY
OLD BAY

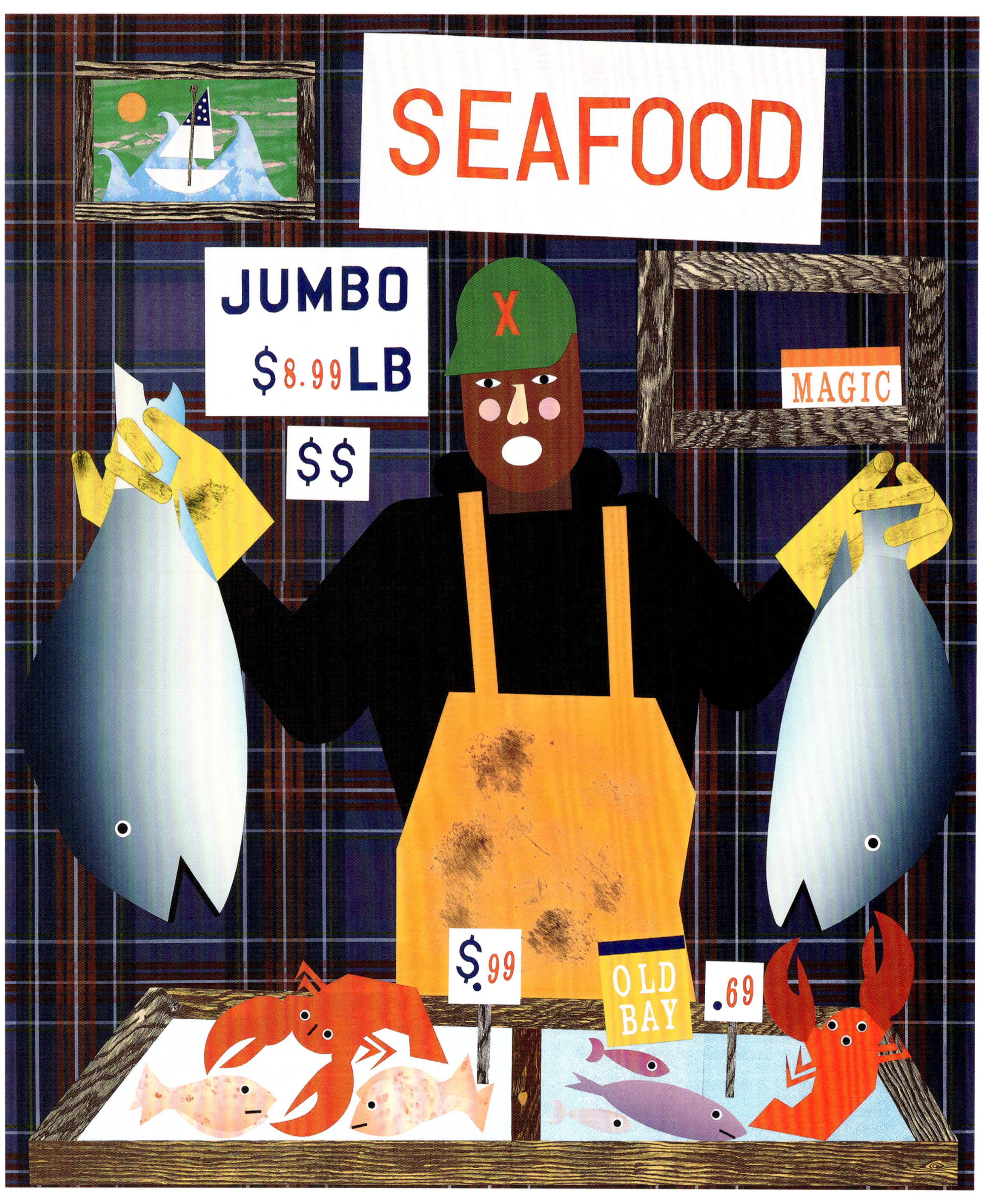

Johnny X, 2022

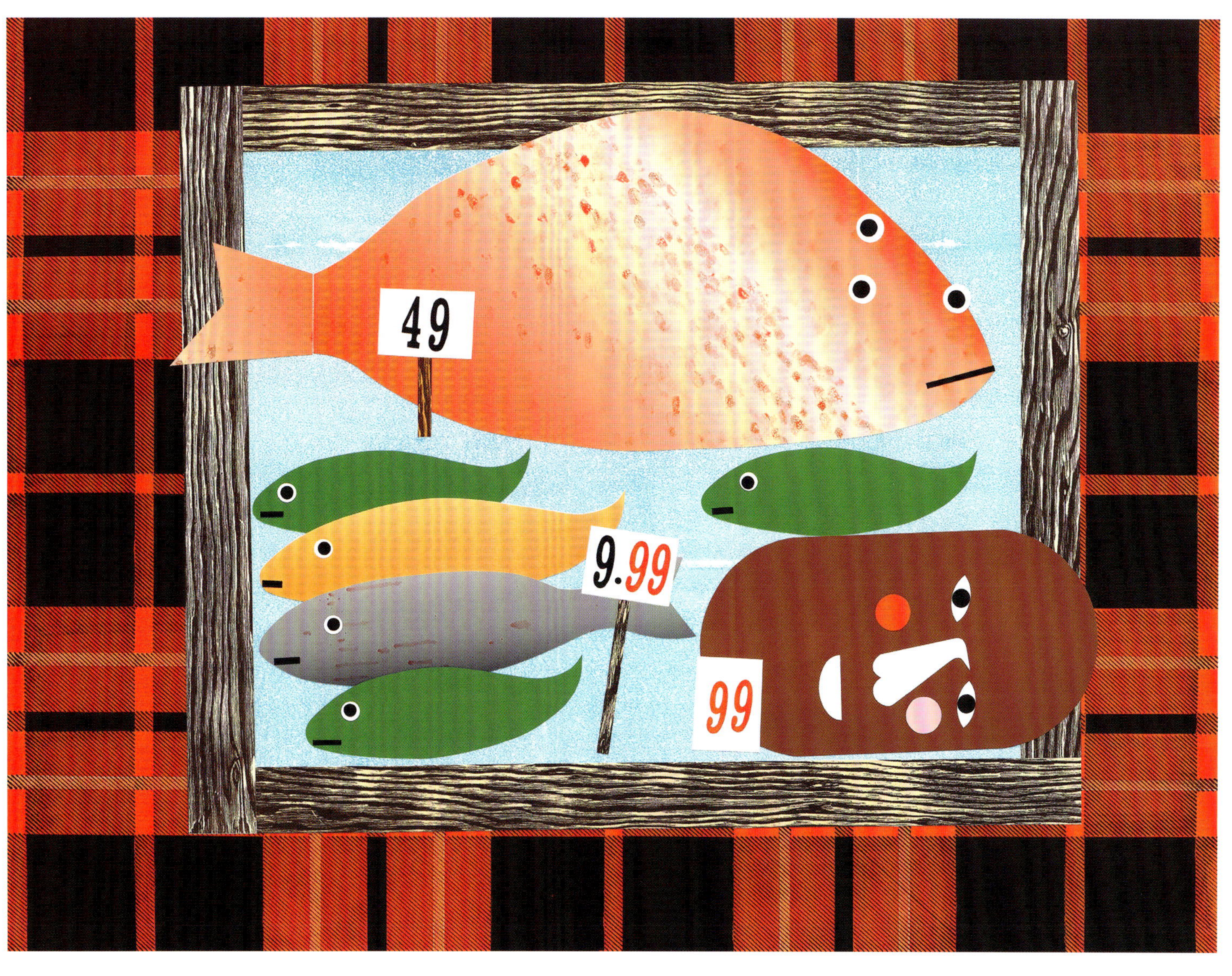

Fish Head, 2022

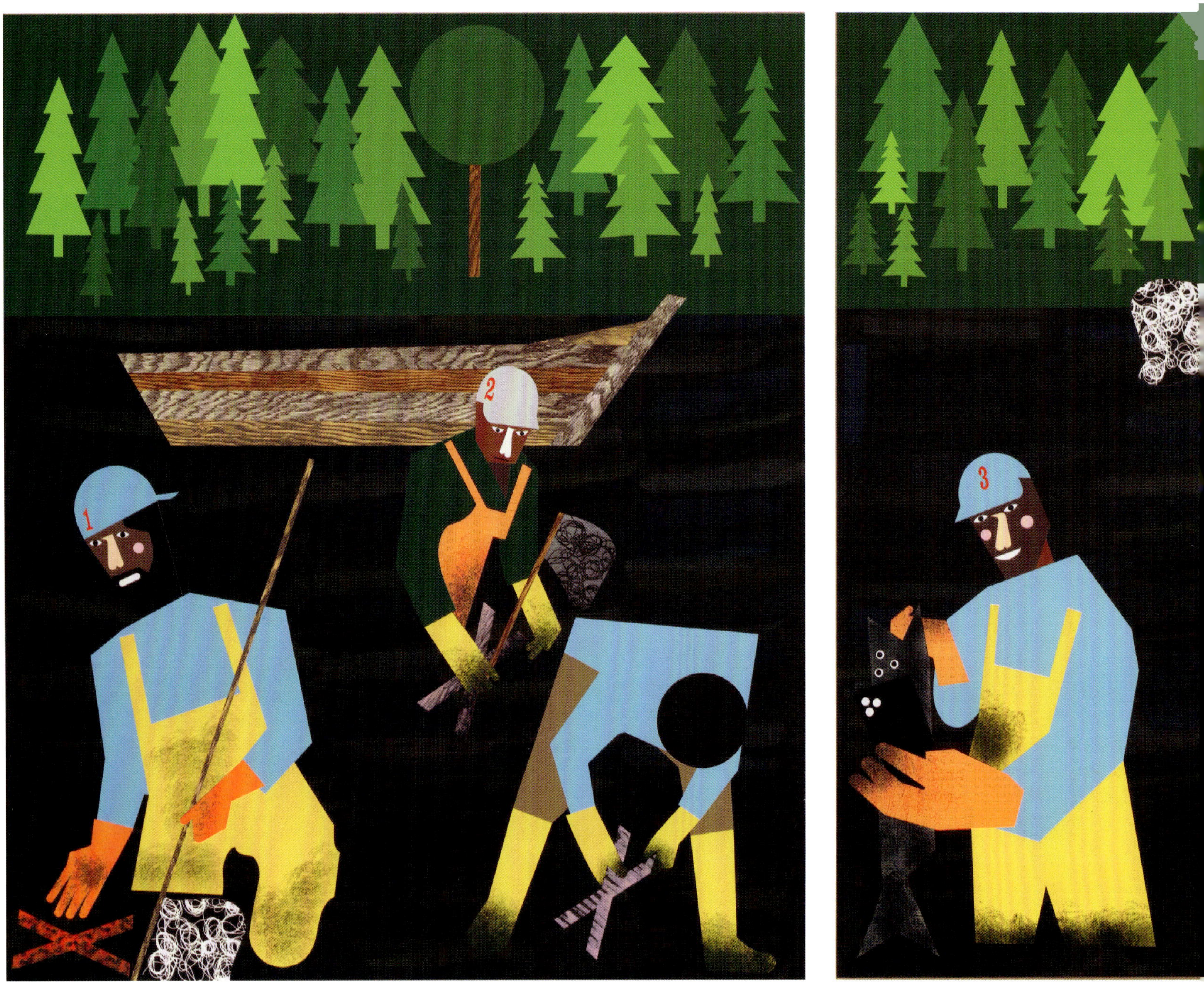

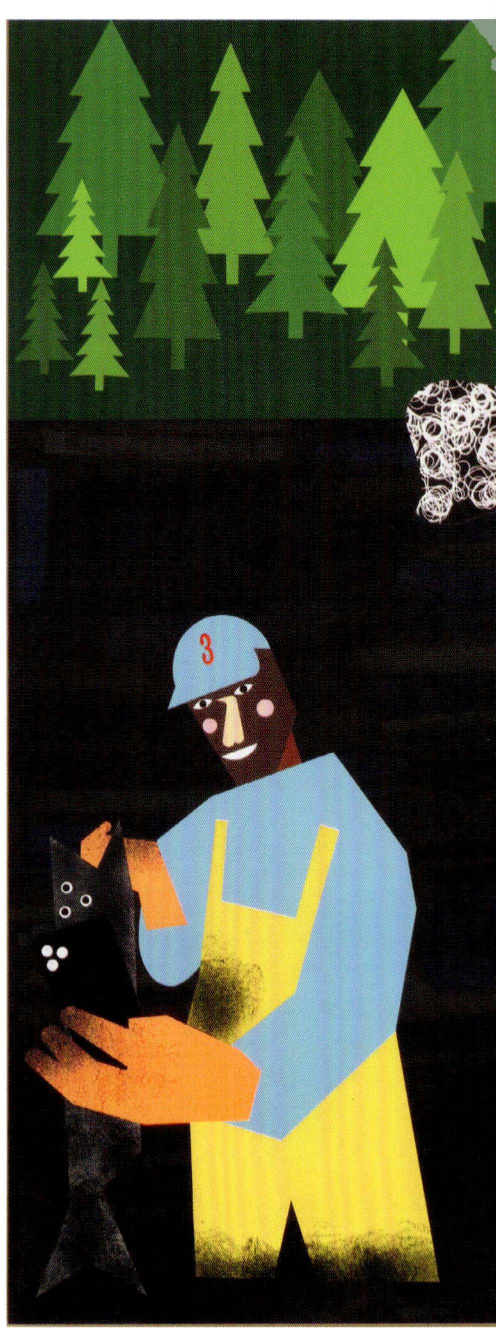

Black People (BP), 2022

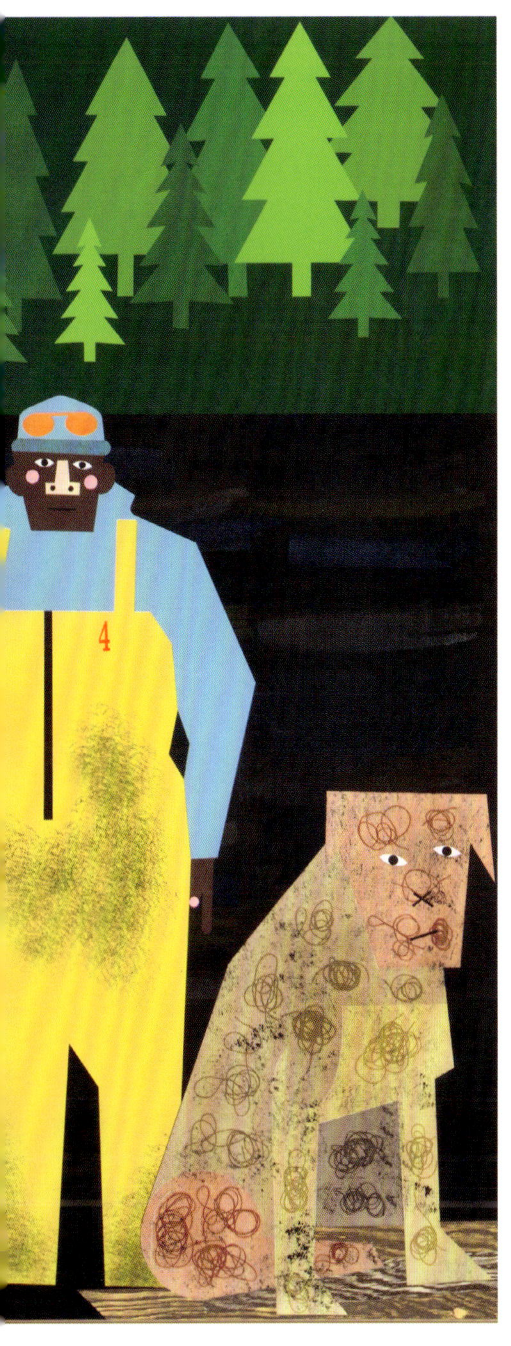
4

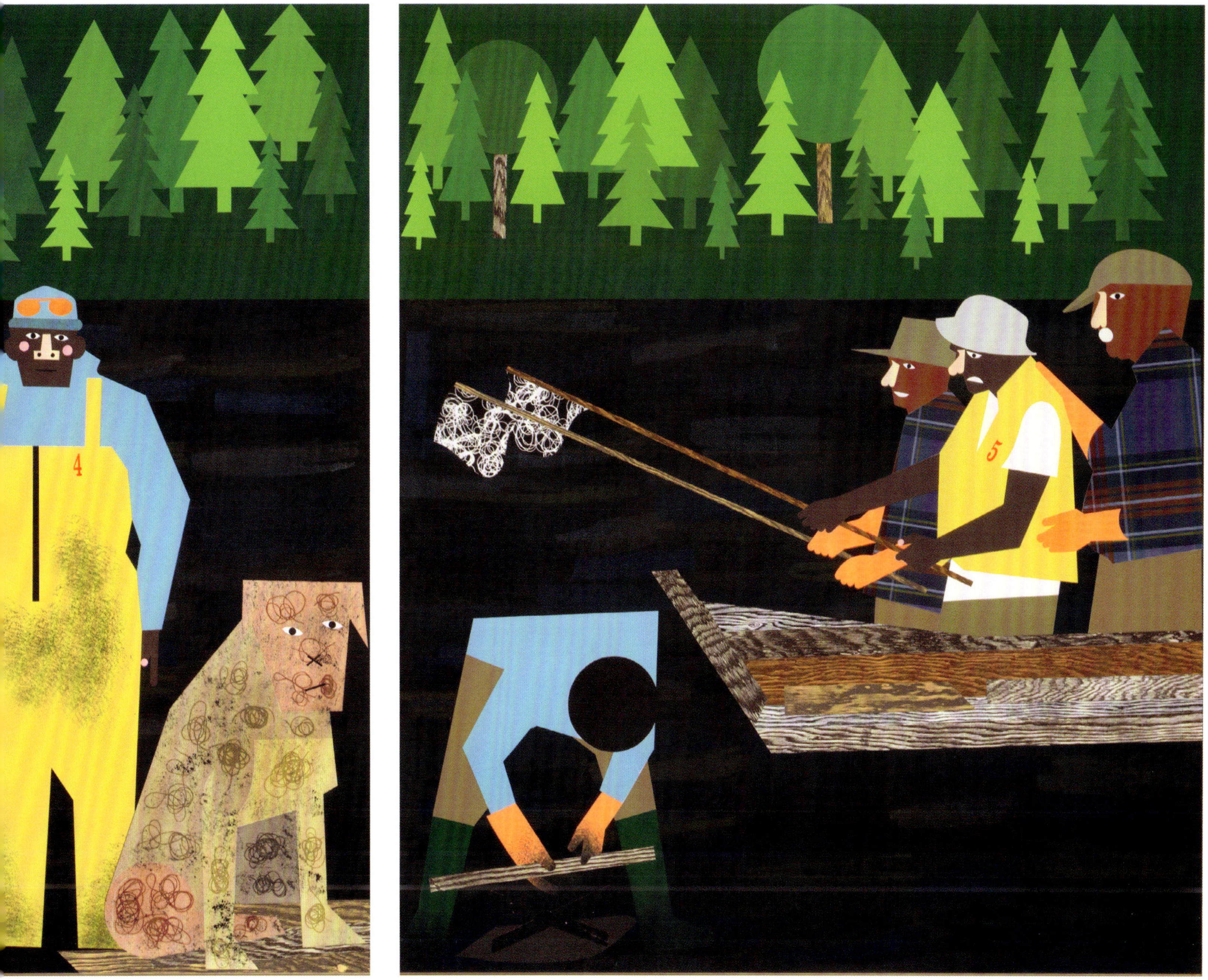

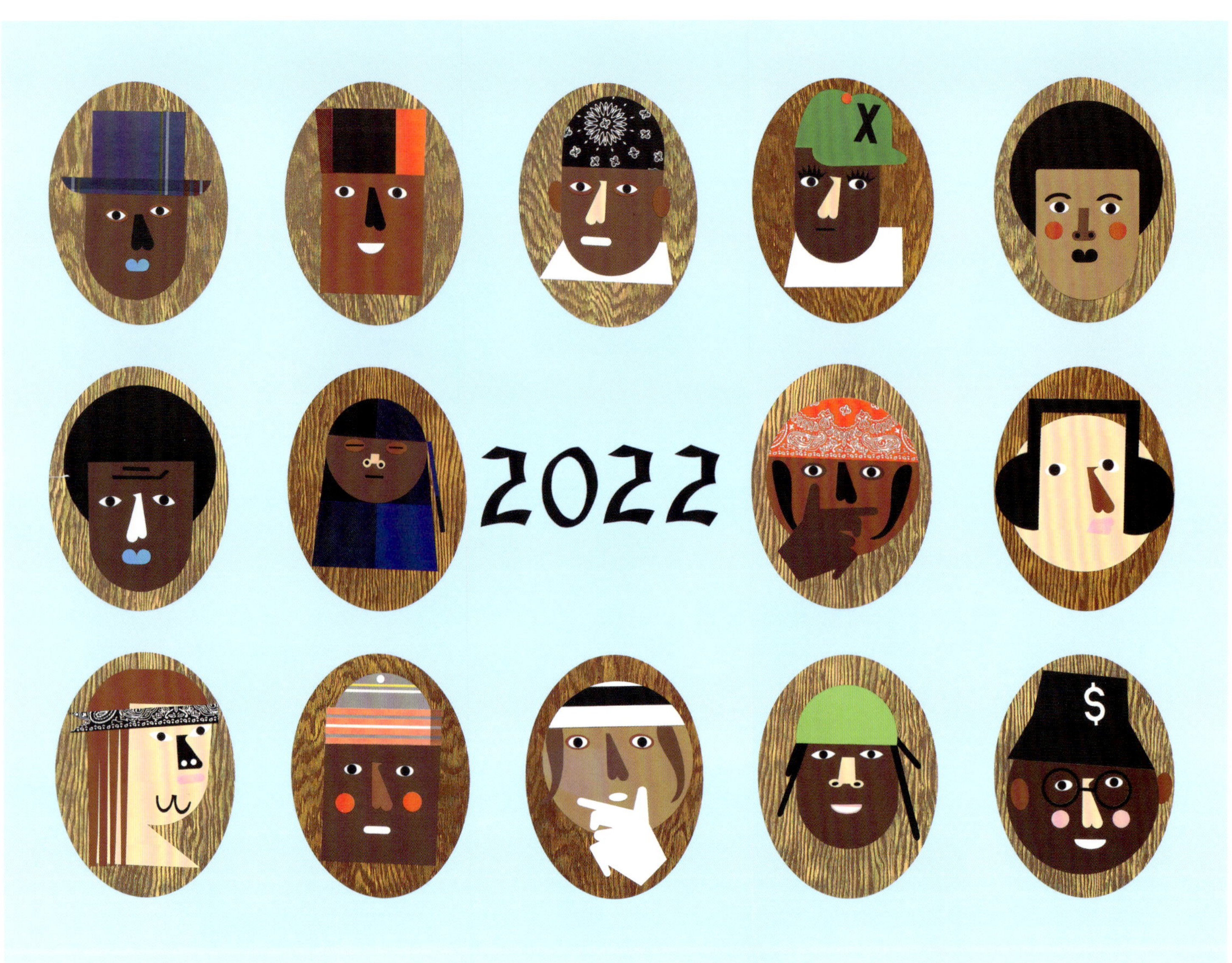

Homiesexuals 1, 2022

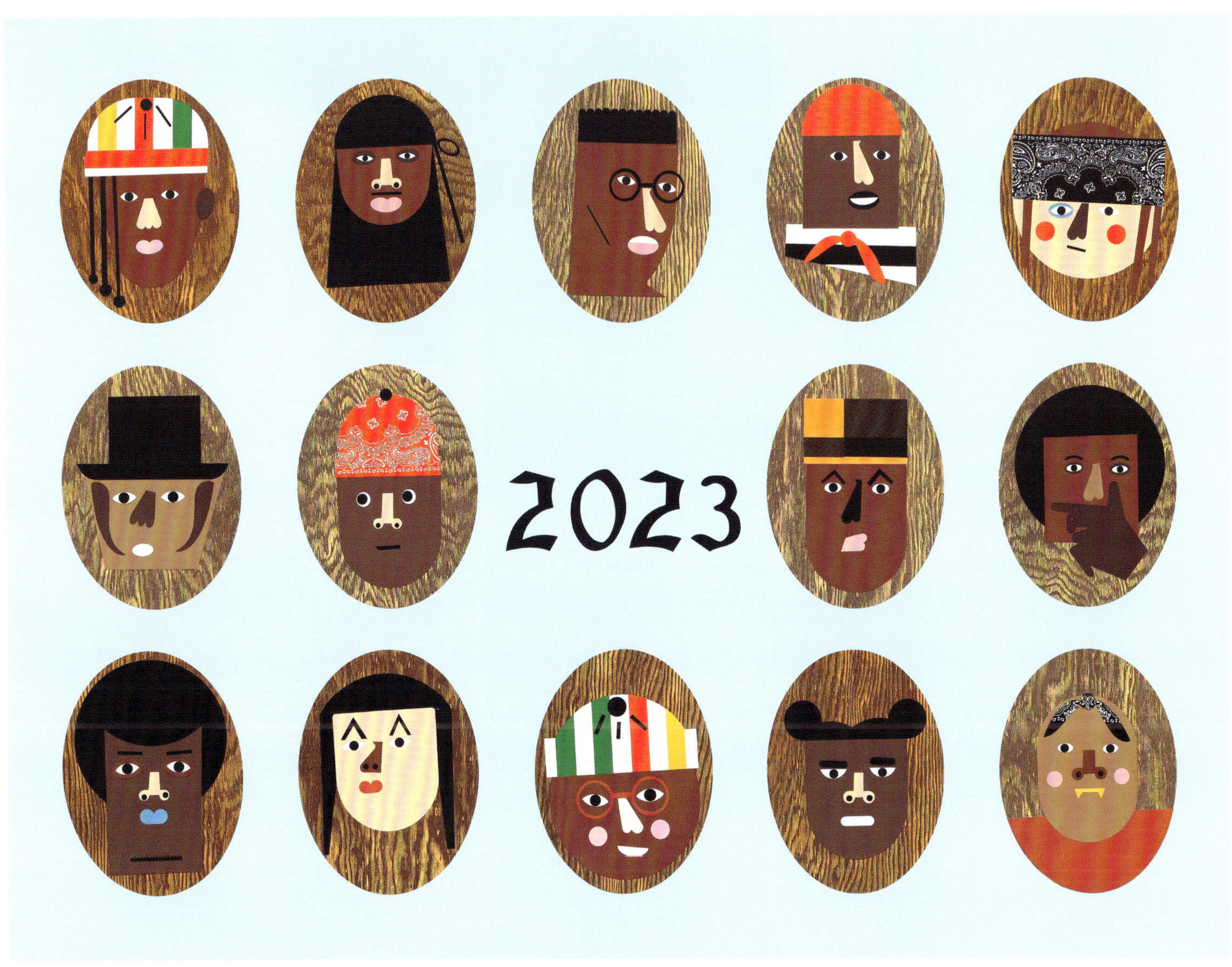

Homiesexuals 2, 2022

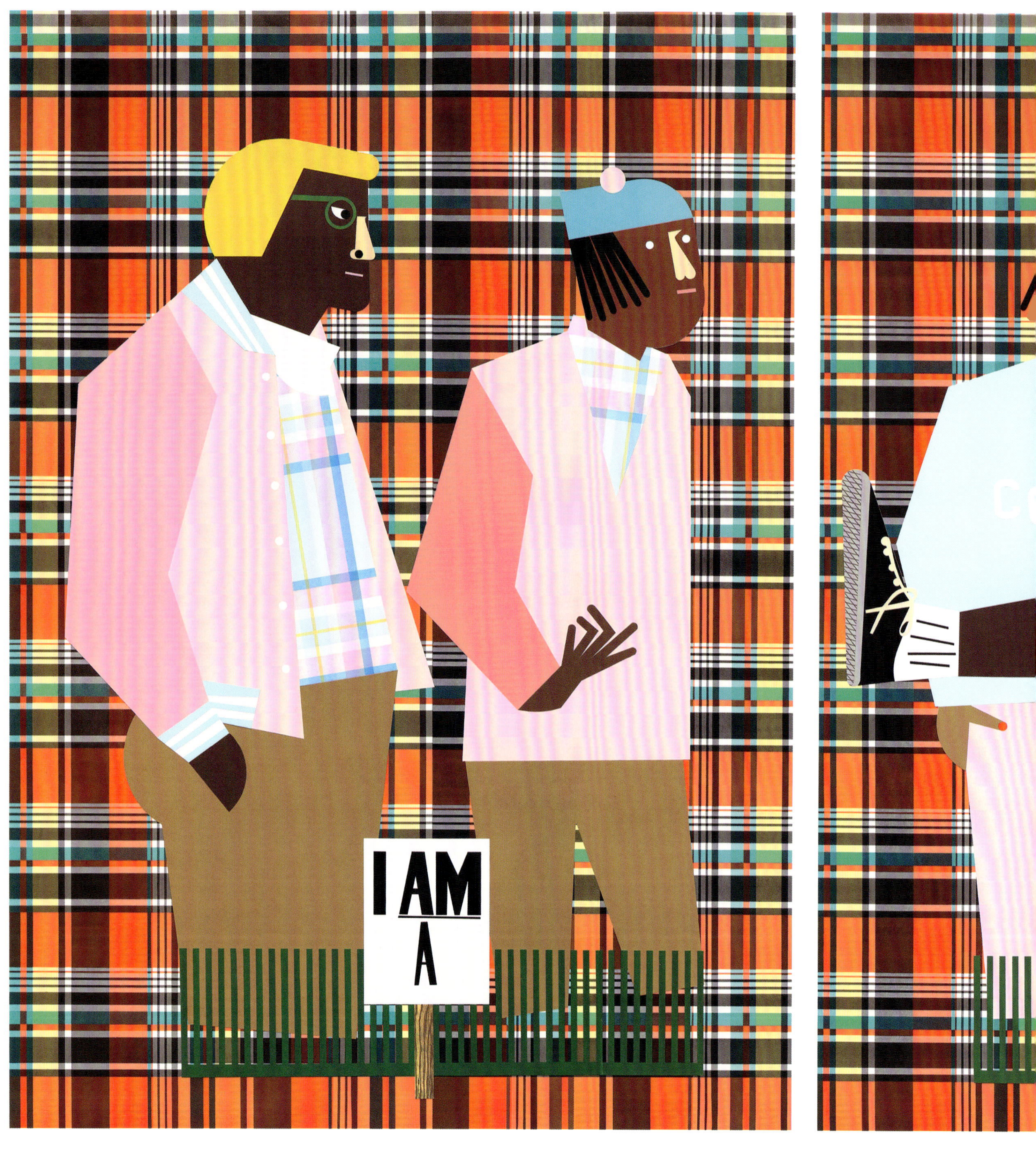

I Am- Somebody, 2022

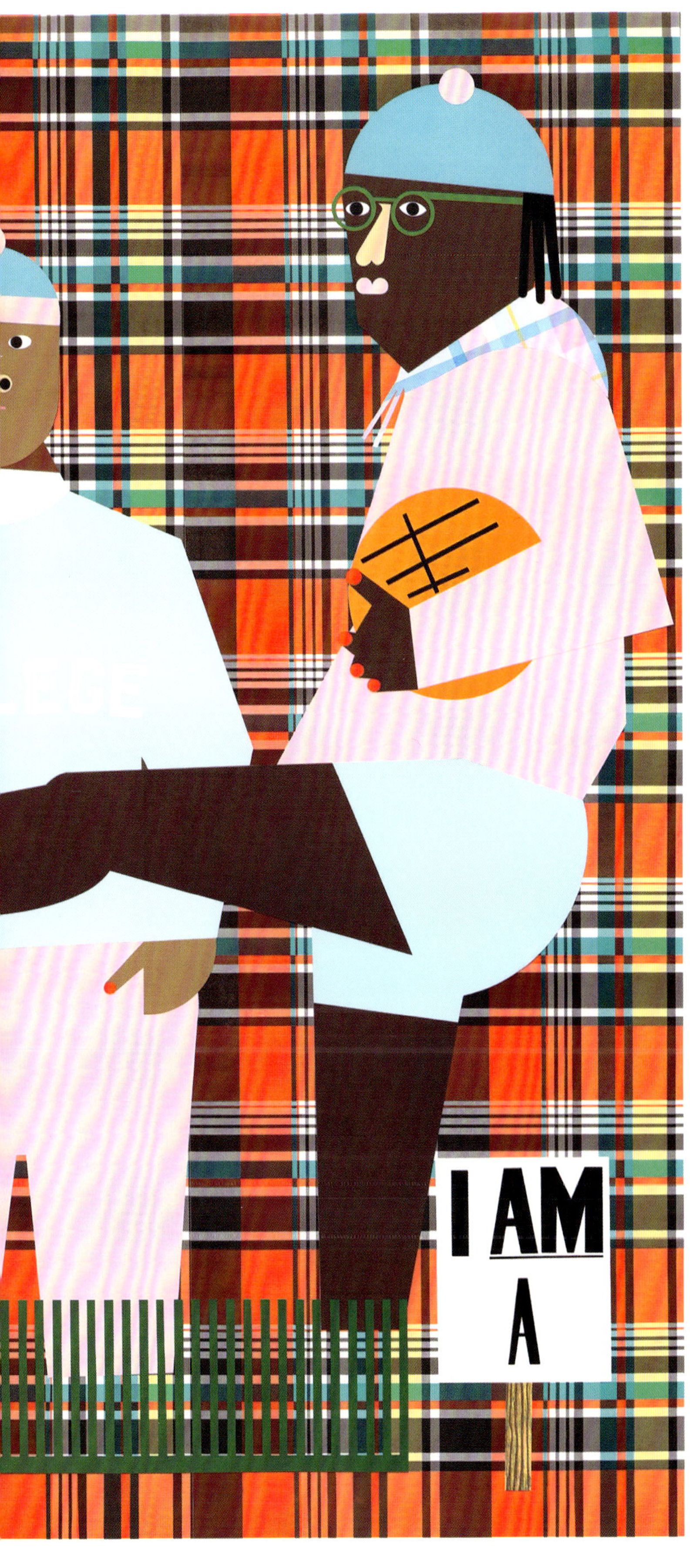
I AM
A

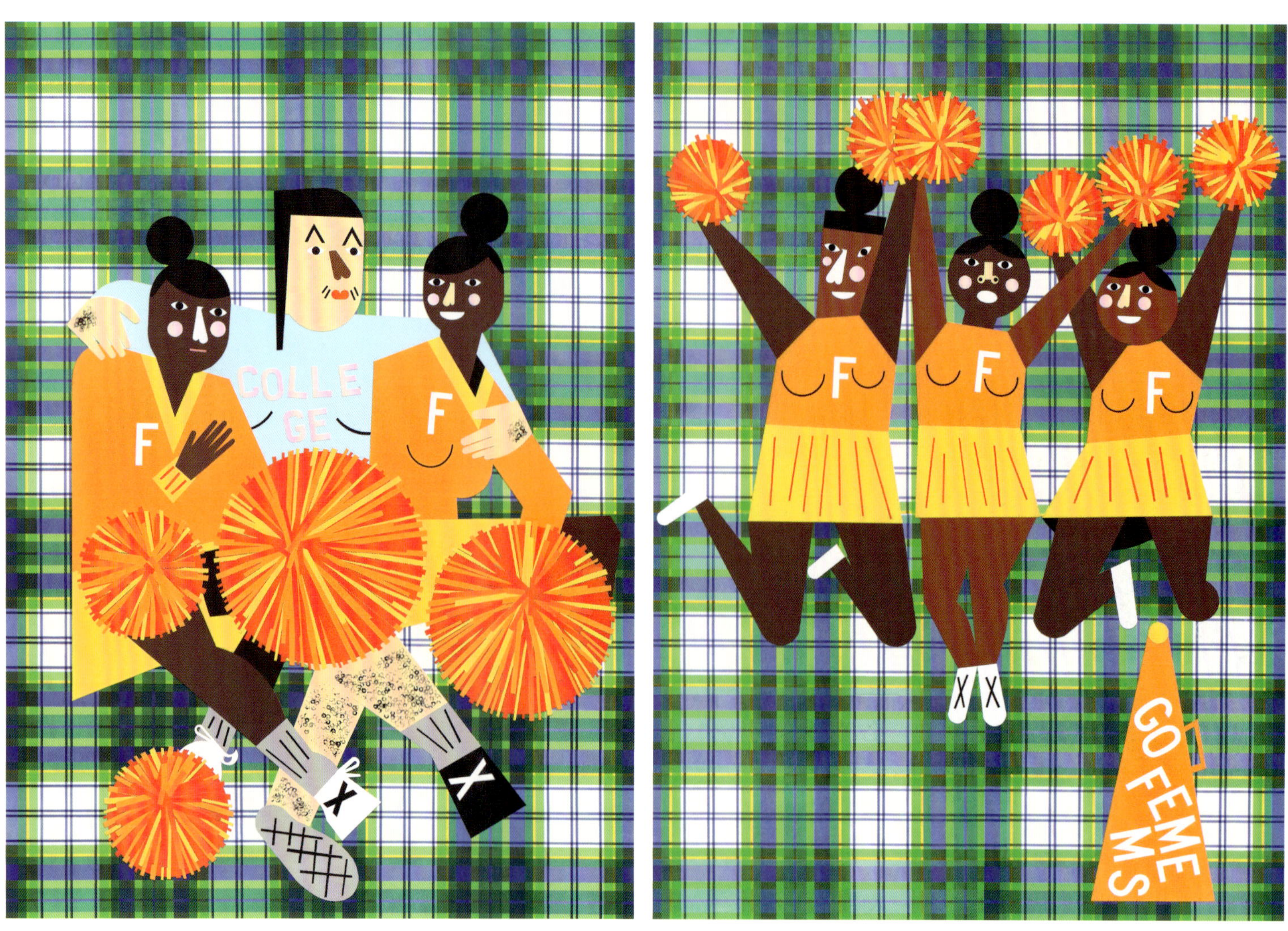

The Light Skinned Comeback, 2022

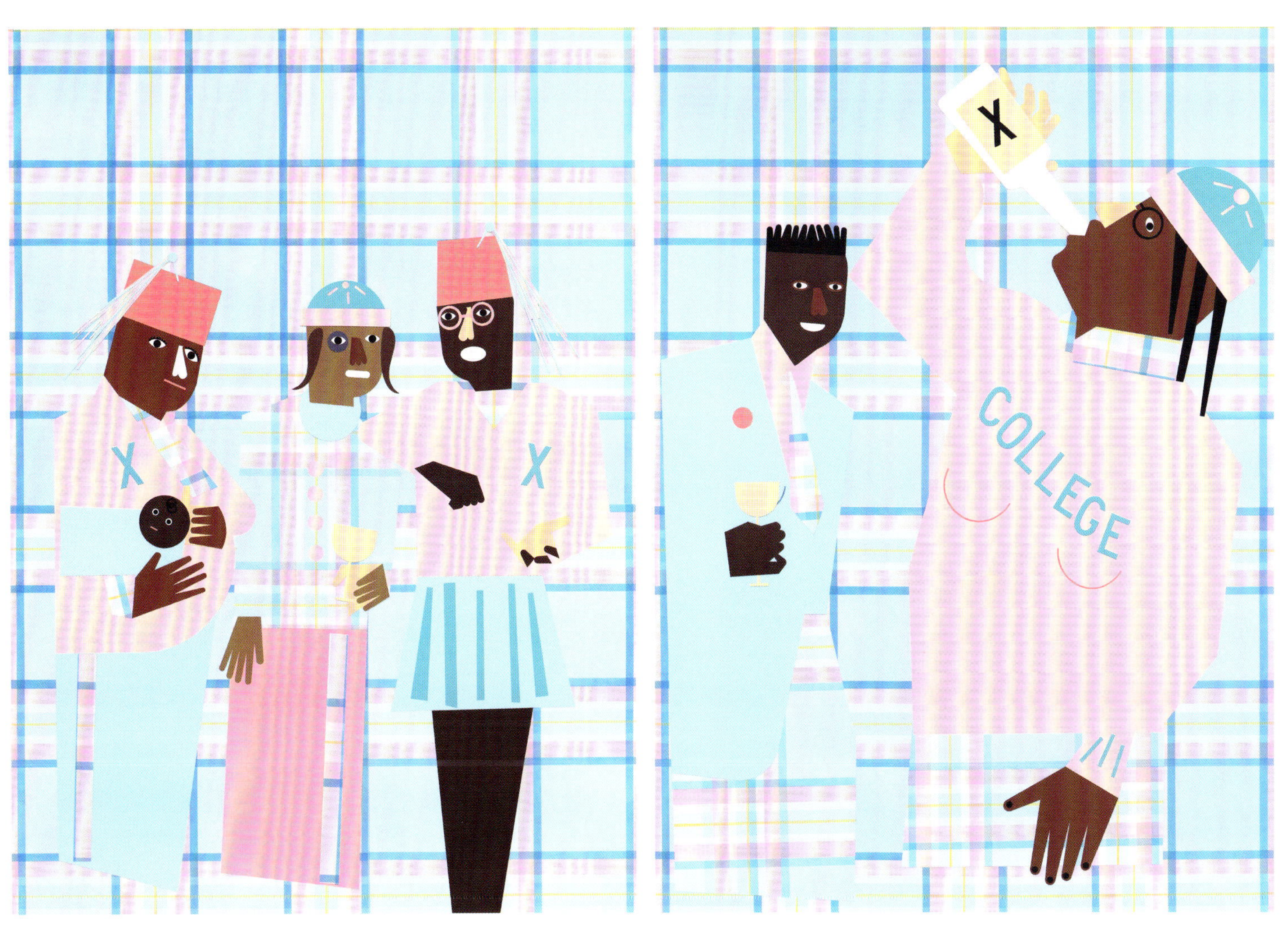

Mama Gotta Have A Life Too, 2022

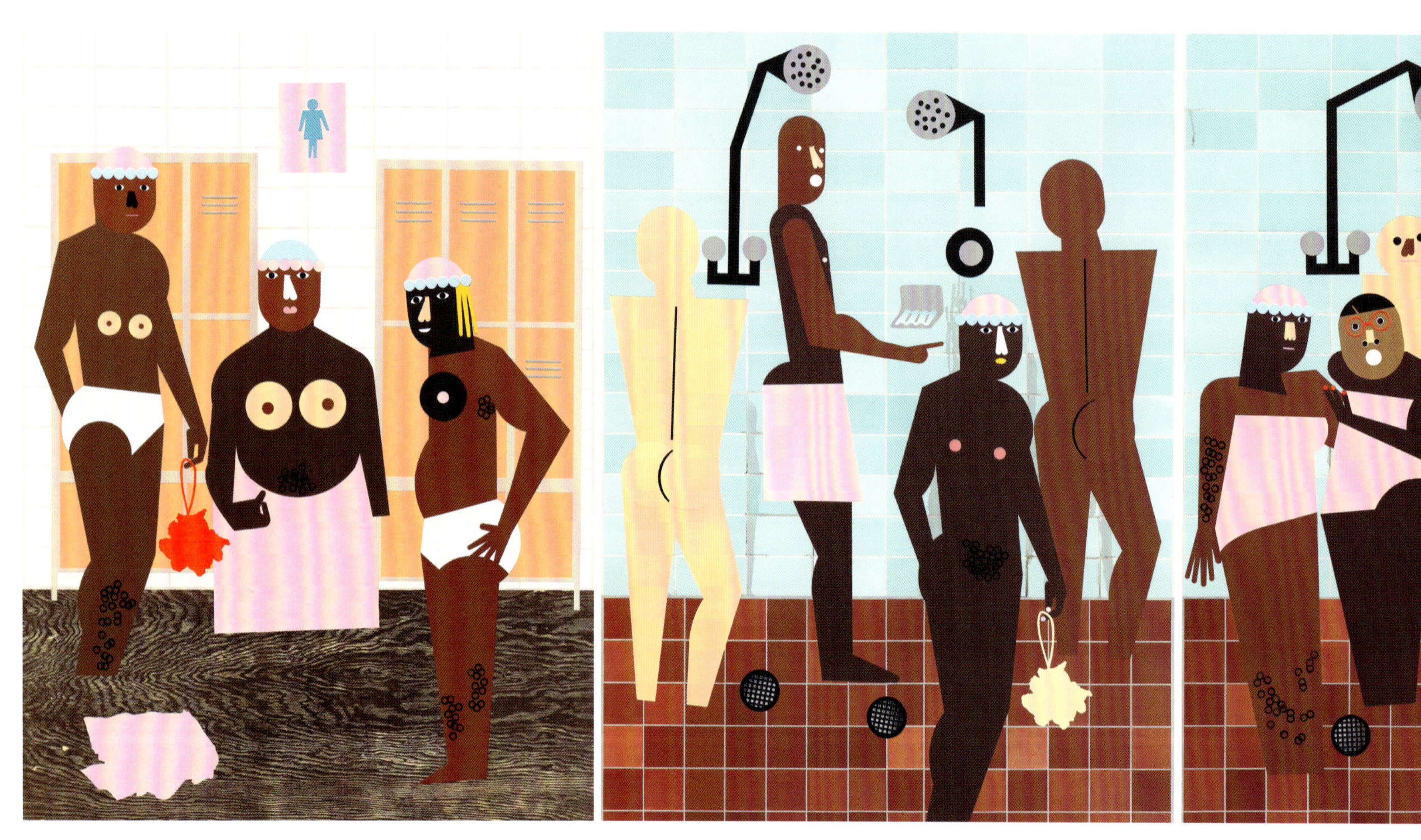

You Spot It, You Got It, 2022

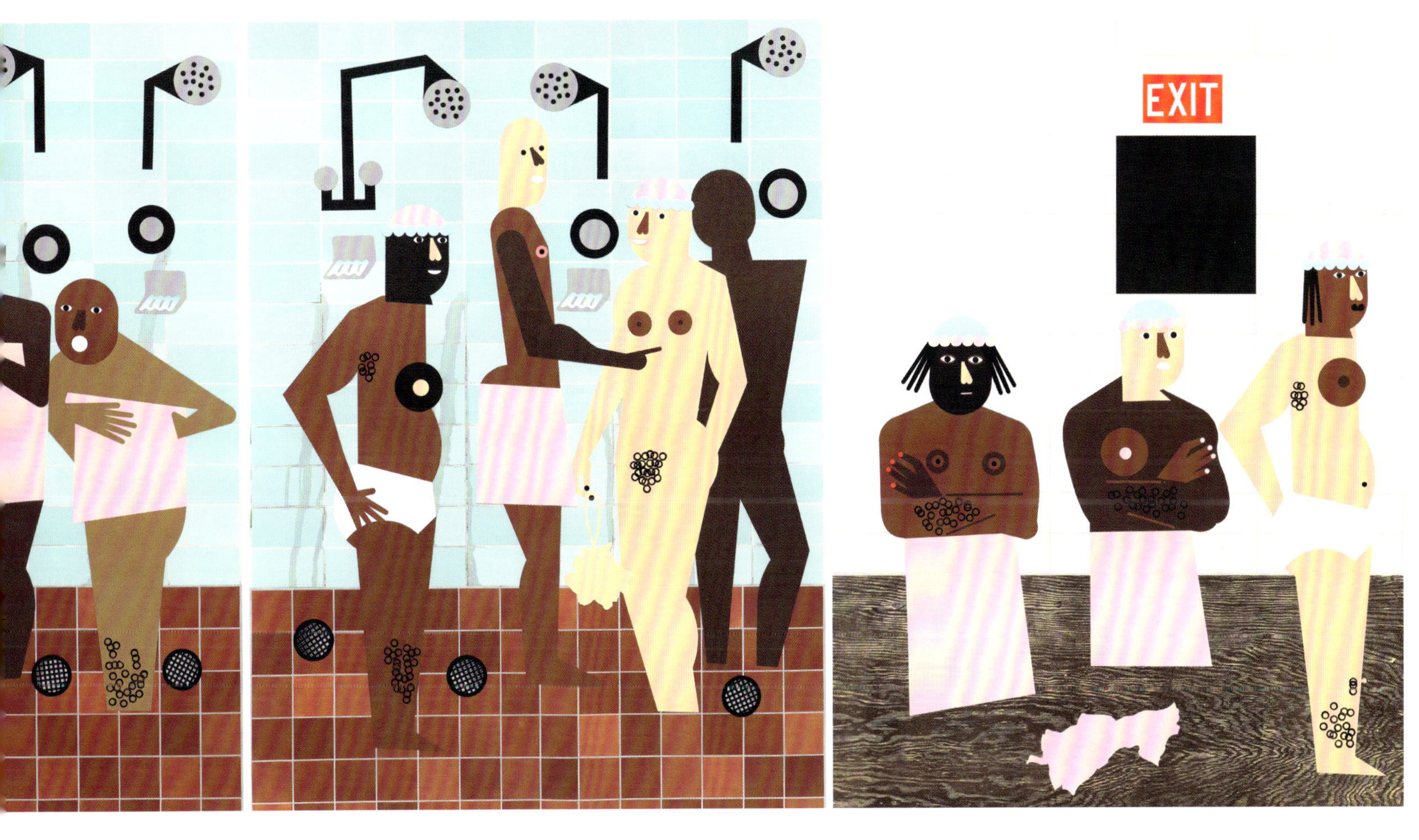
EXIT

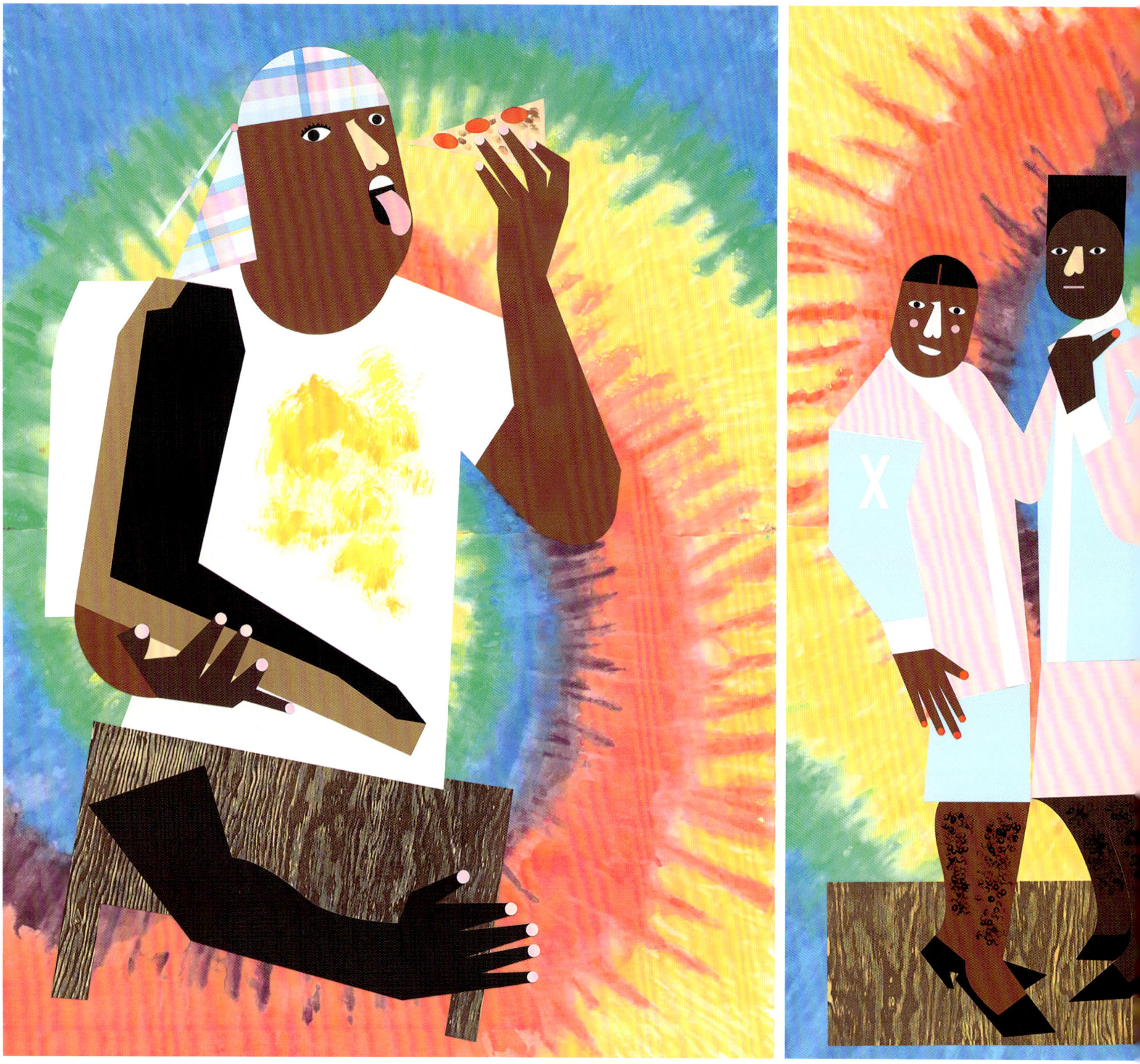

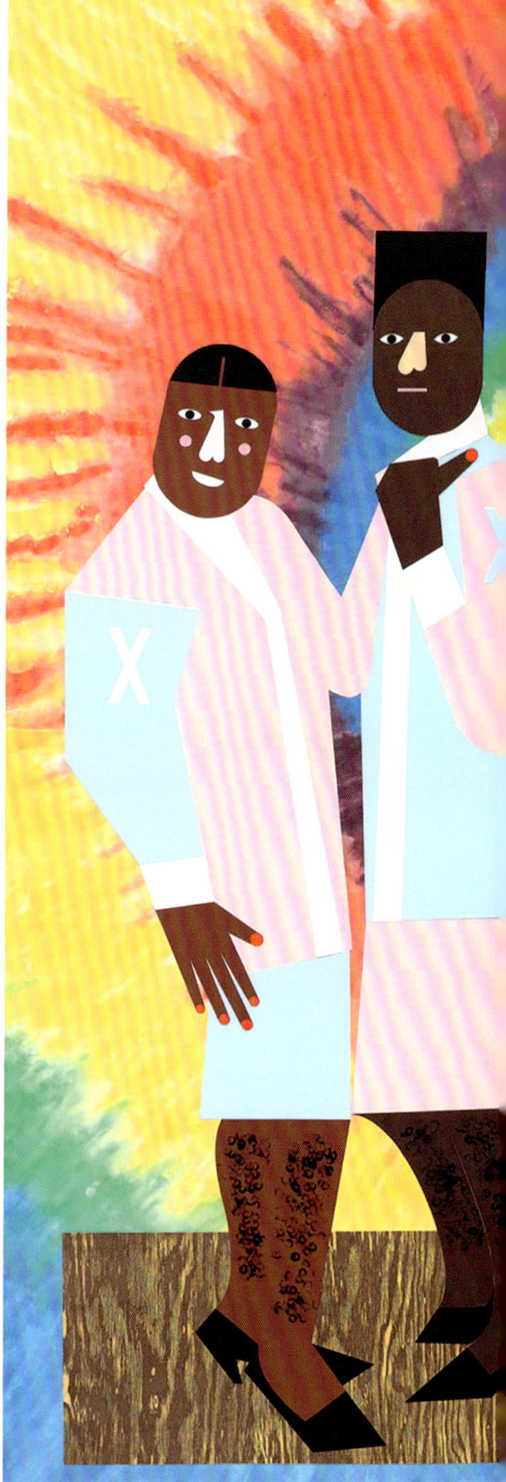

What I Wanted vs. What I Got, 2022

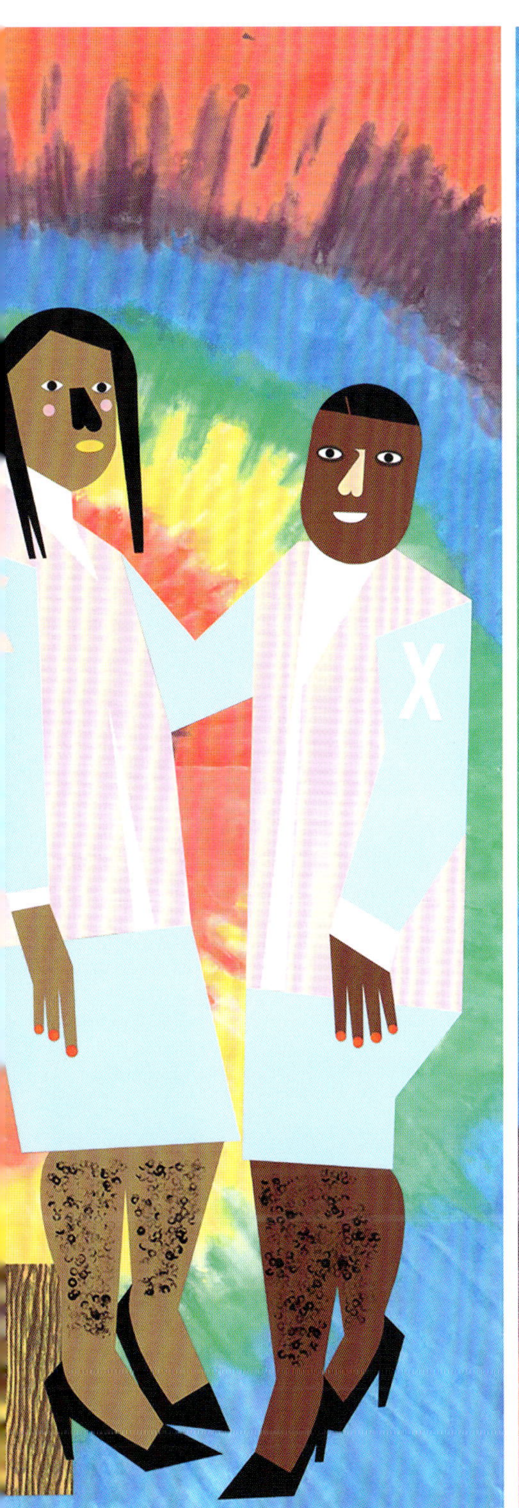

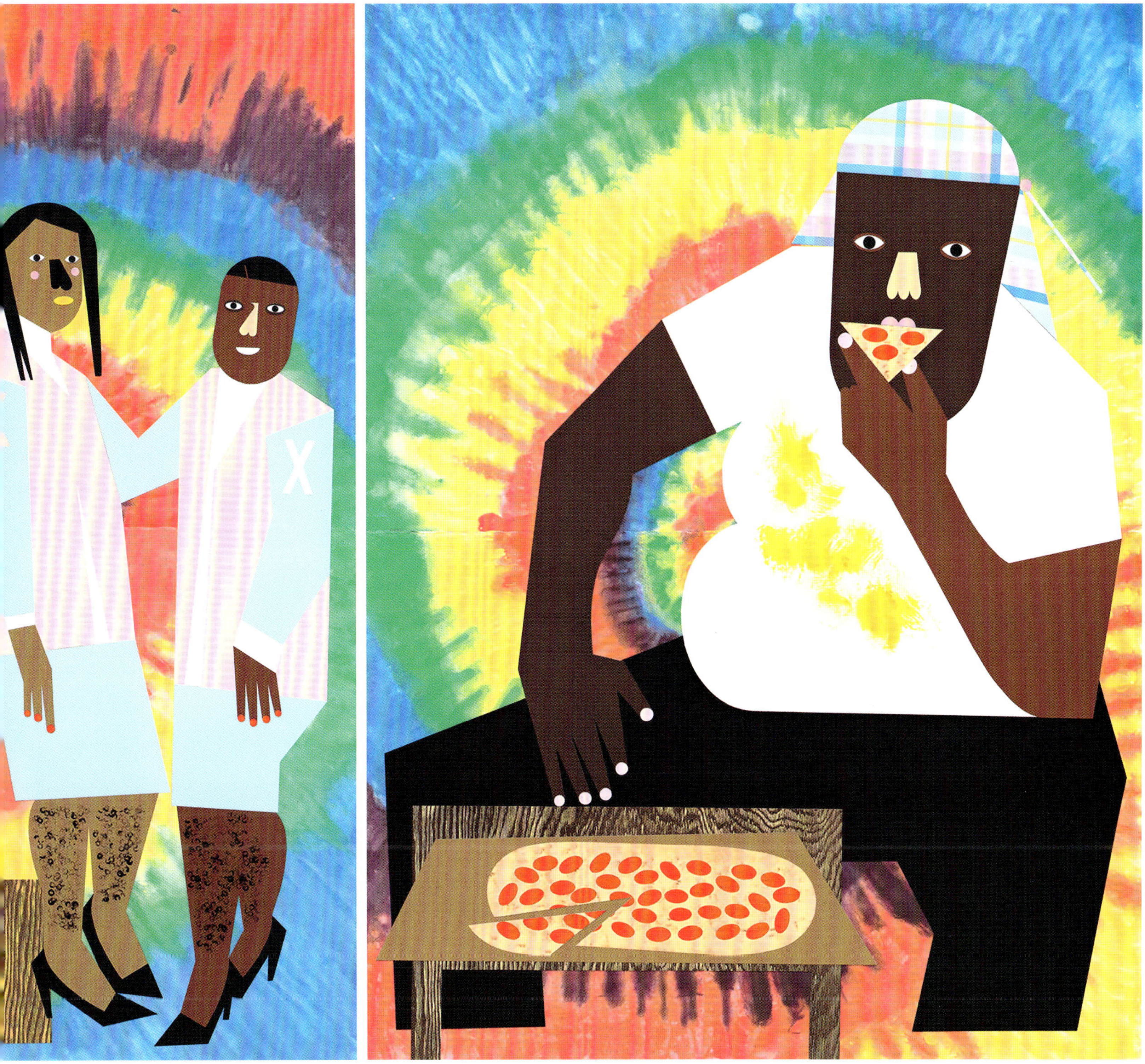

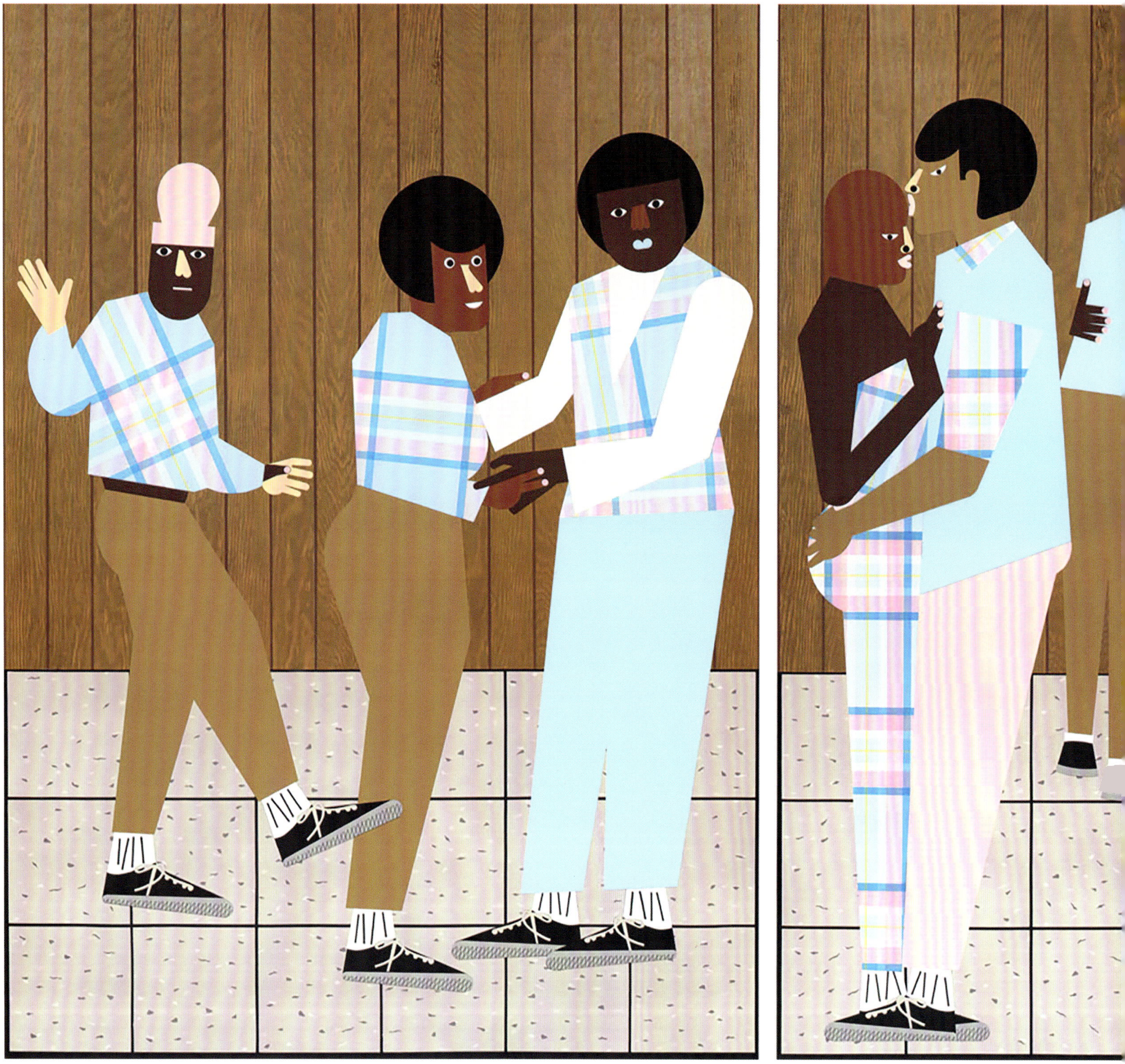

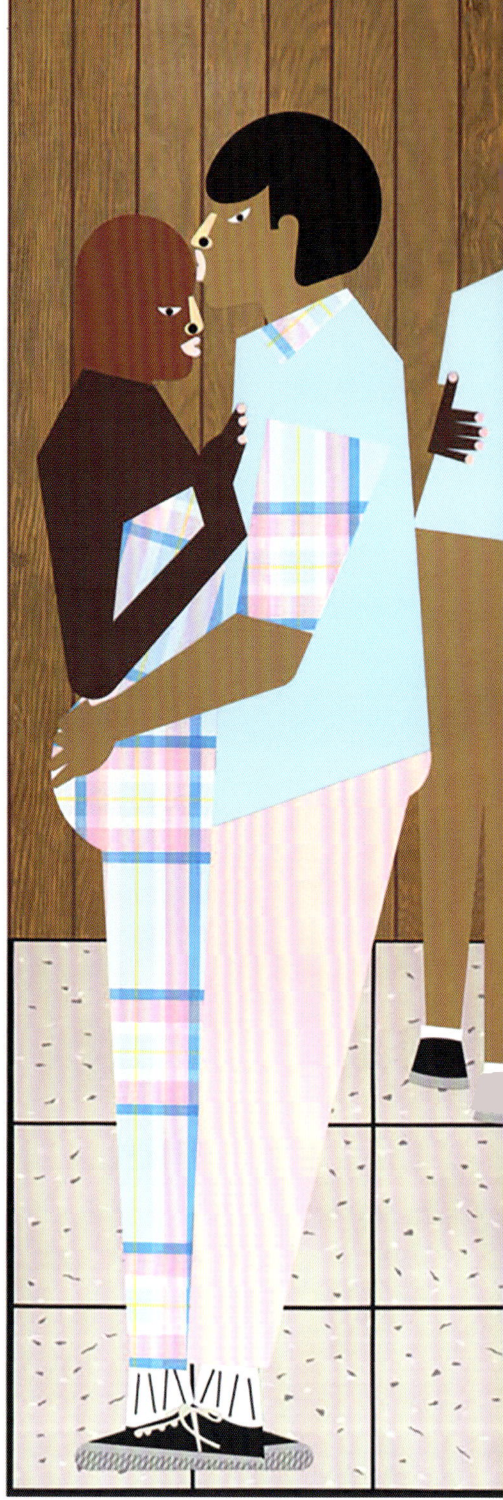

Day Party, Gay Party, 2022

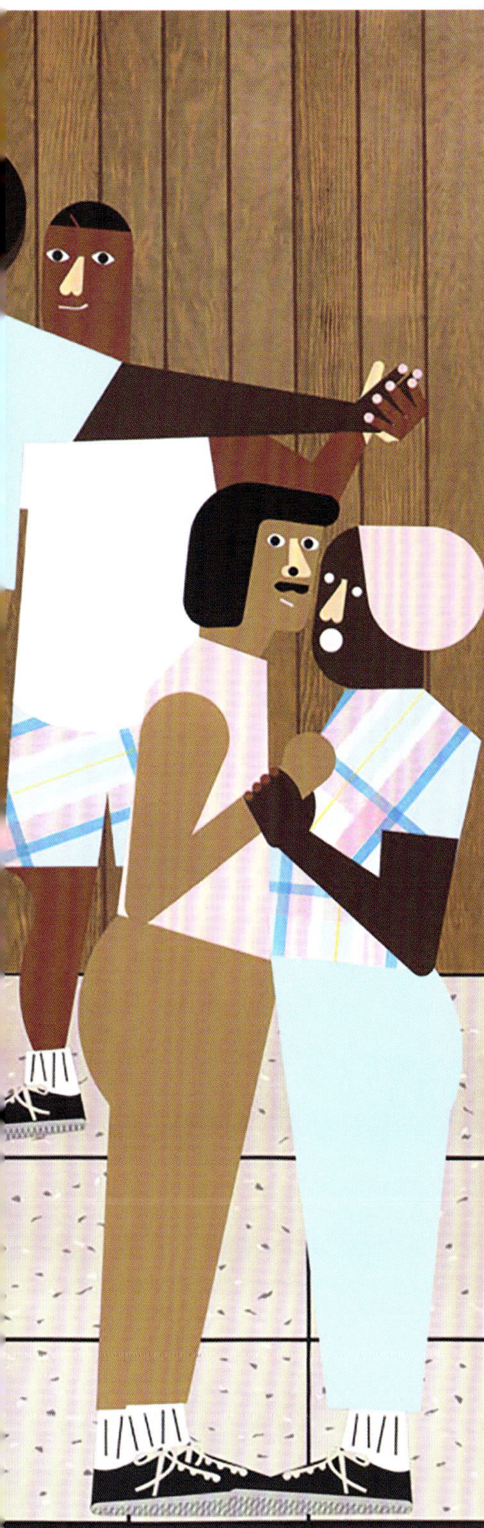

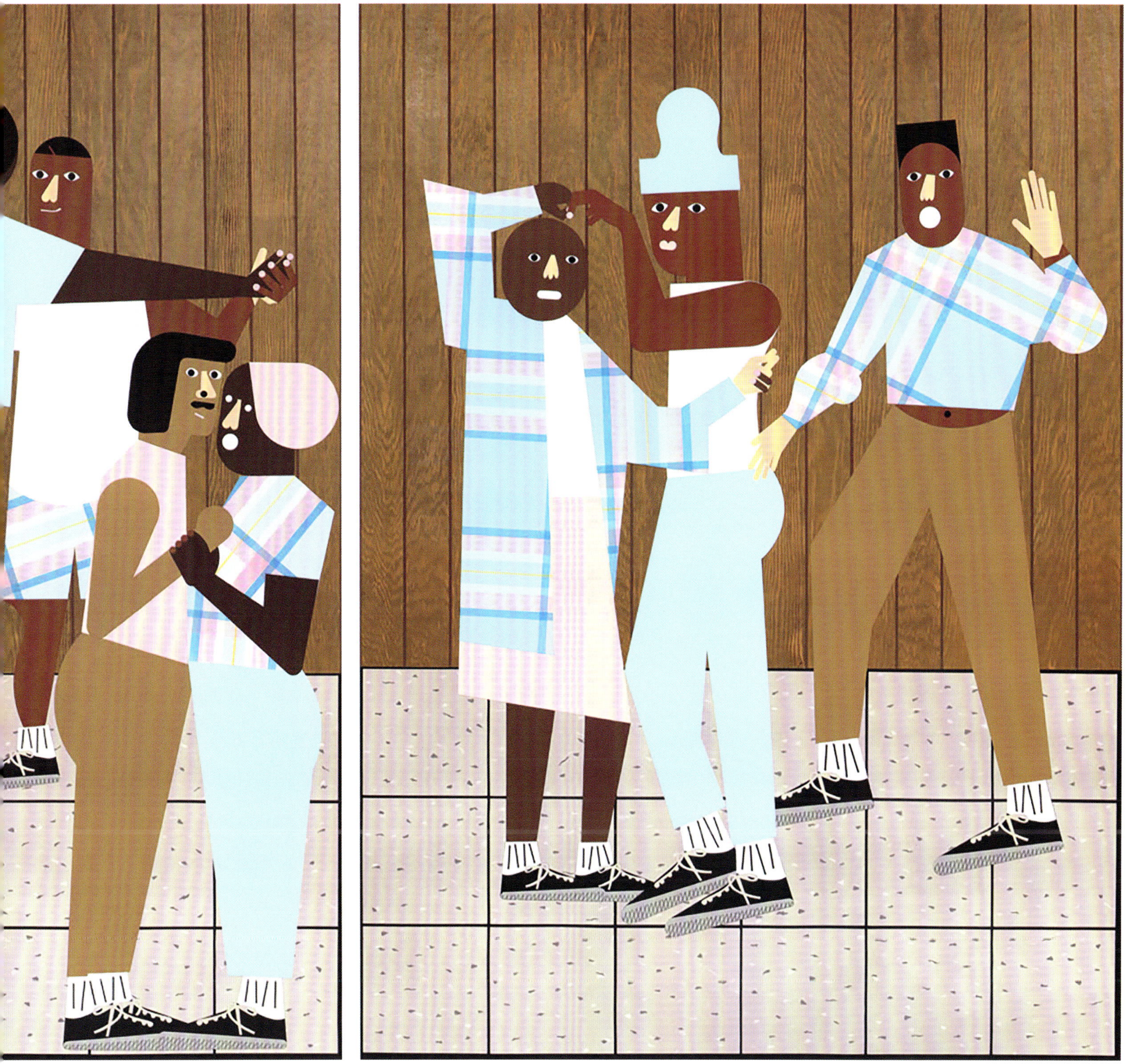

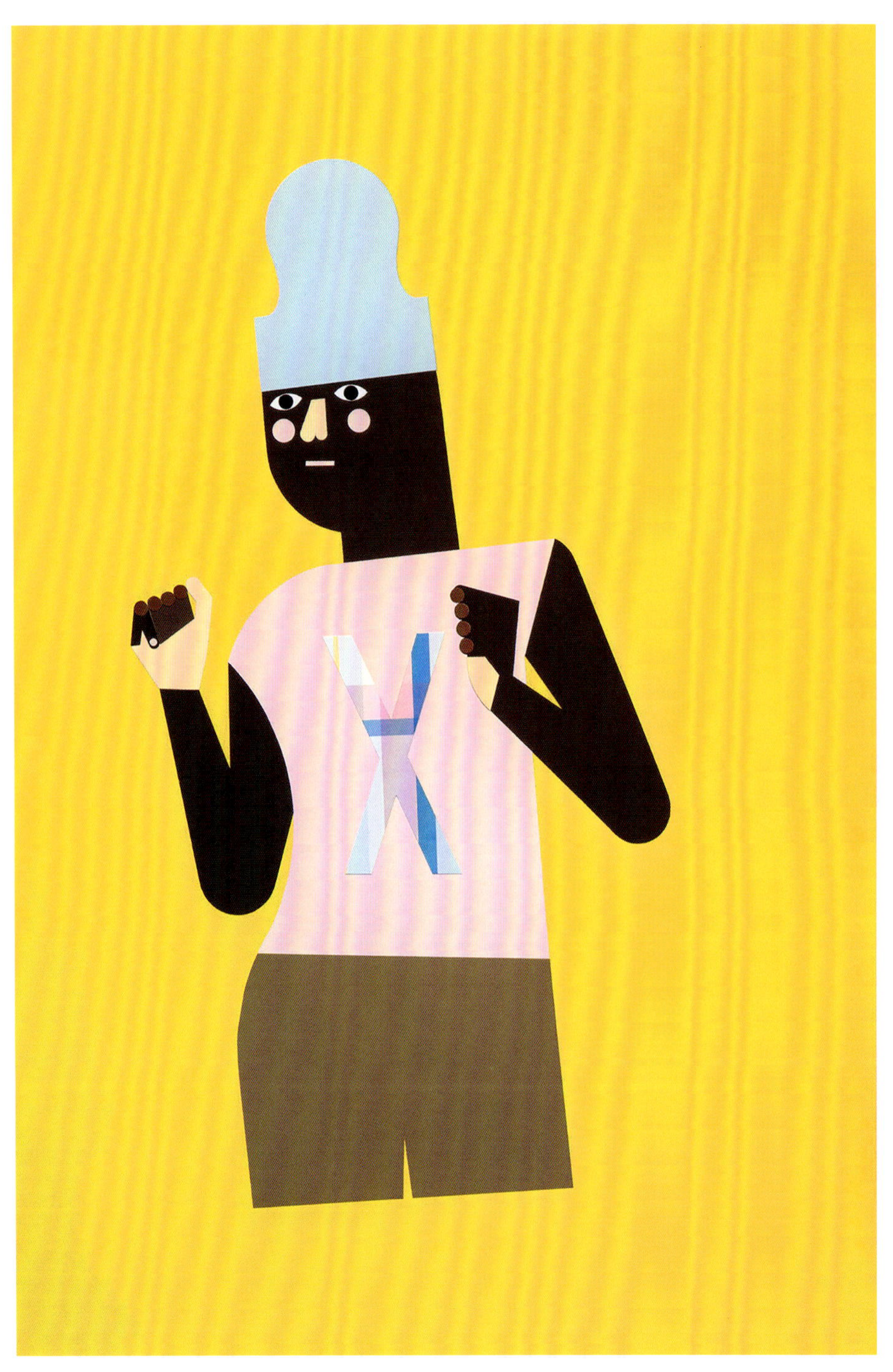

Dance 2, 2022

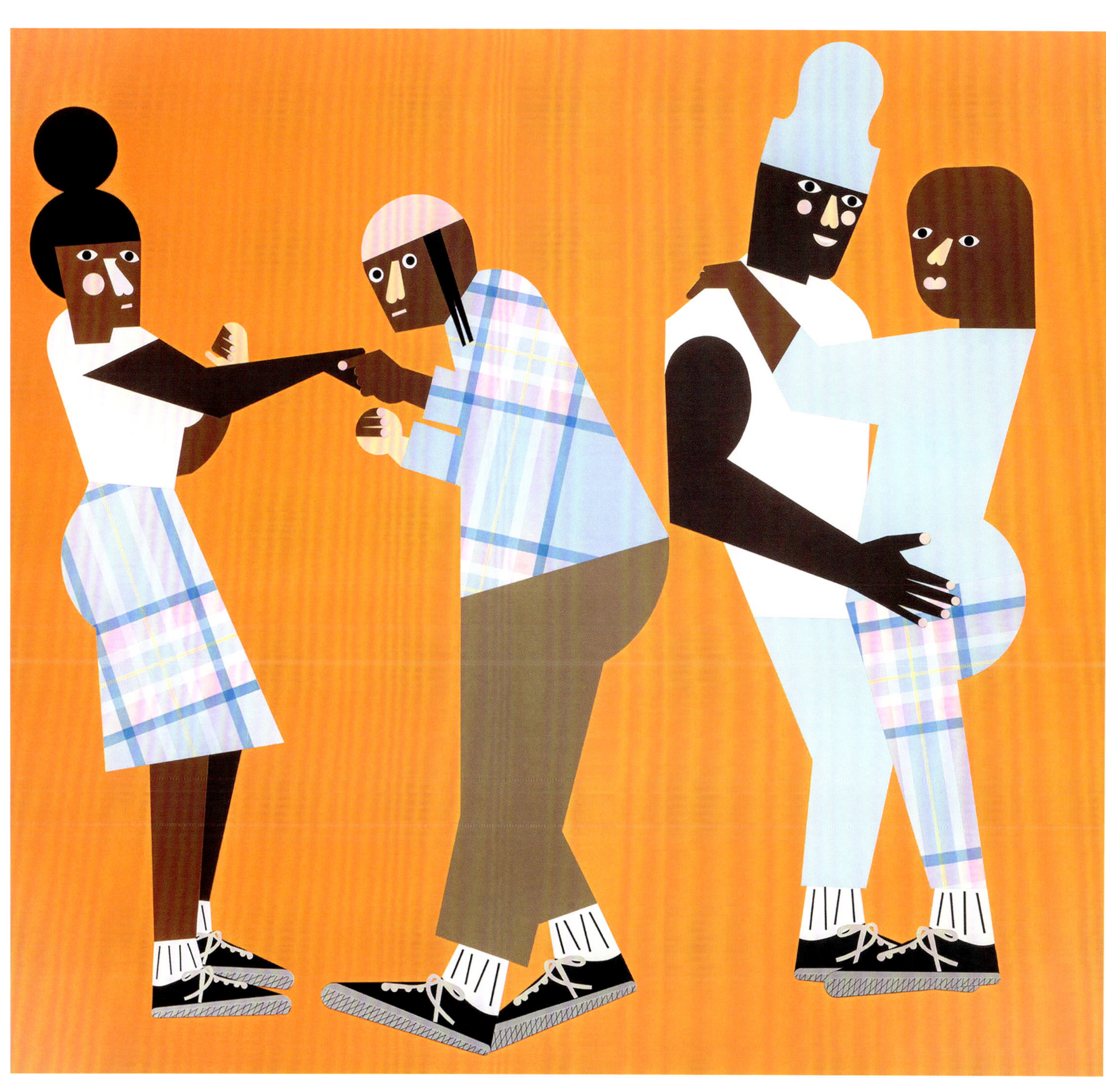

[ABOVE] Light-Footed, 2022
[OVERLEAF] Pump, 2022

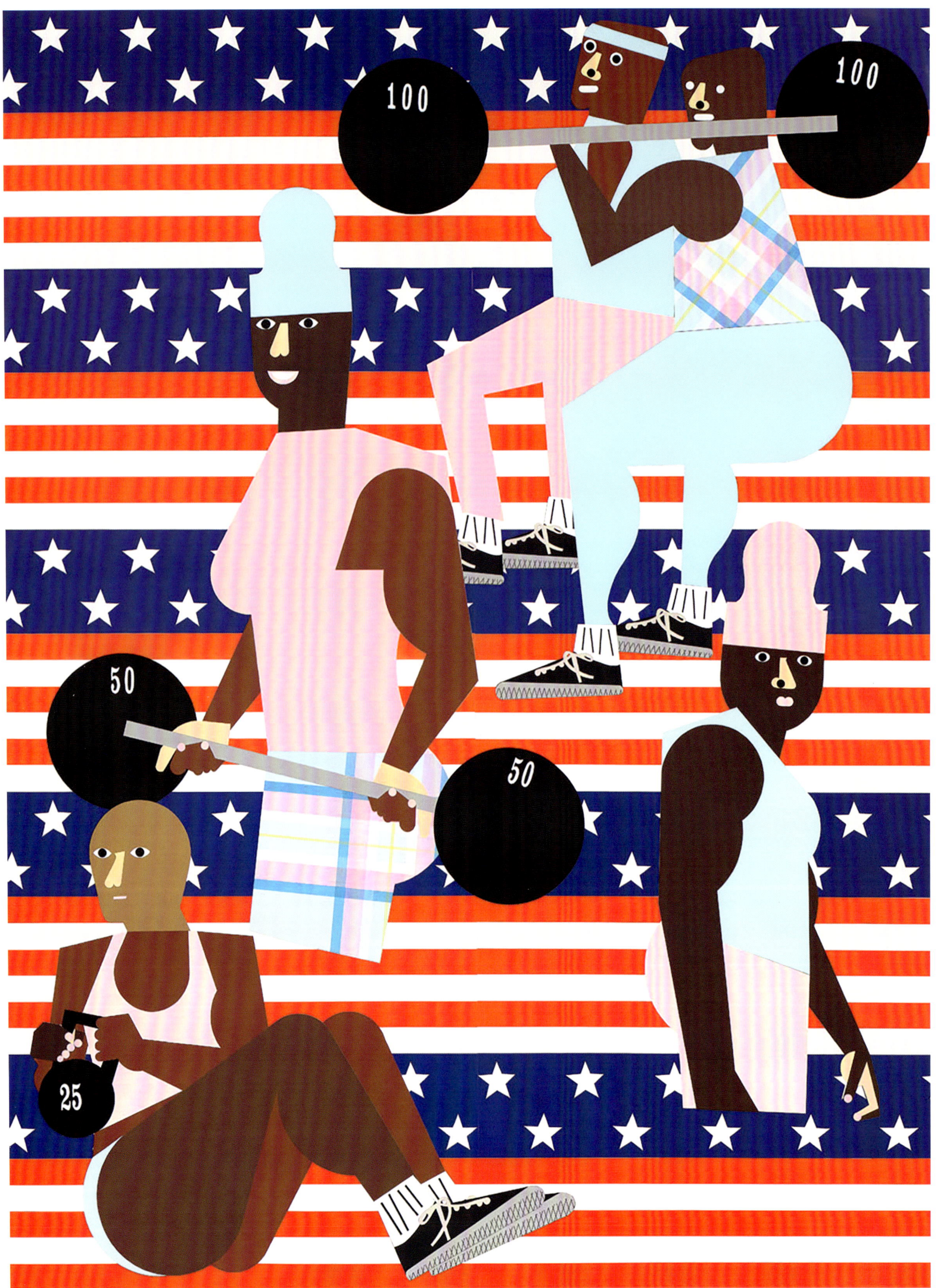
100
100
50
50
25

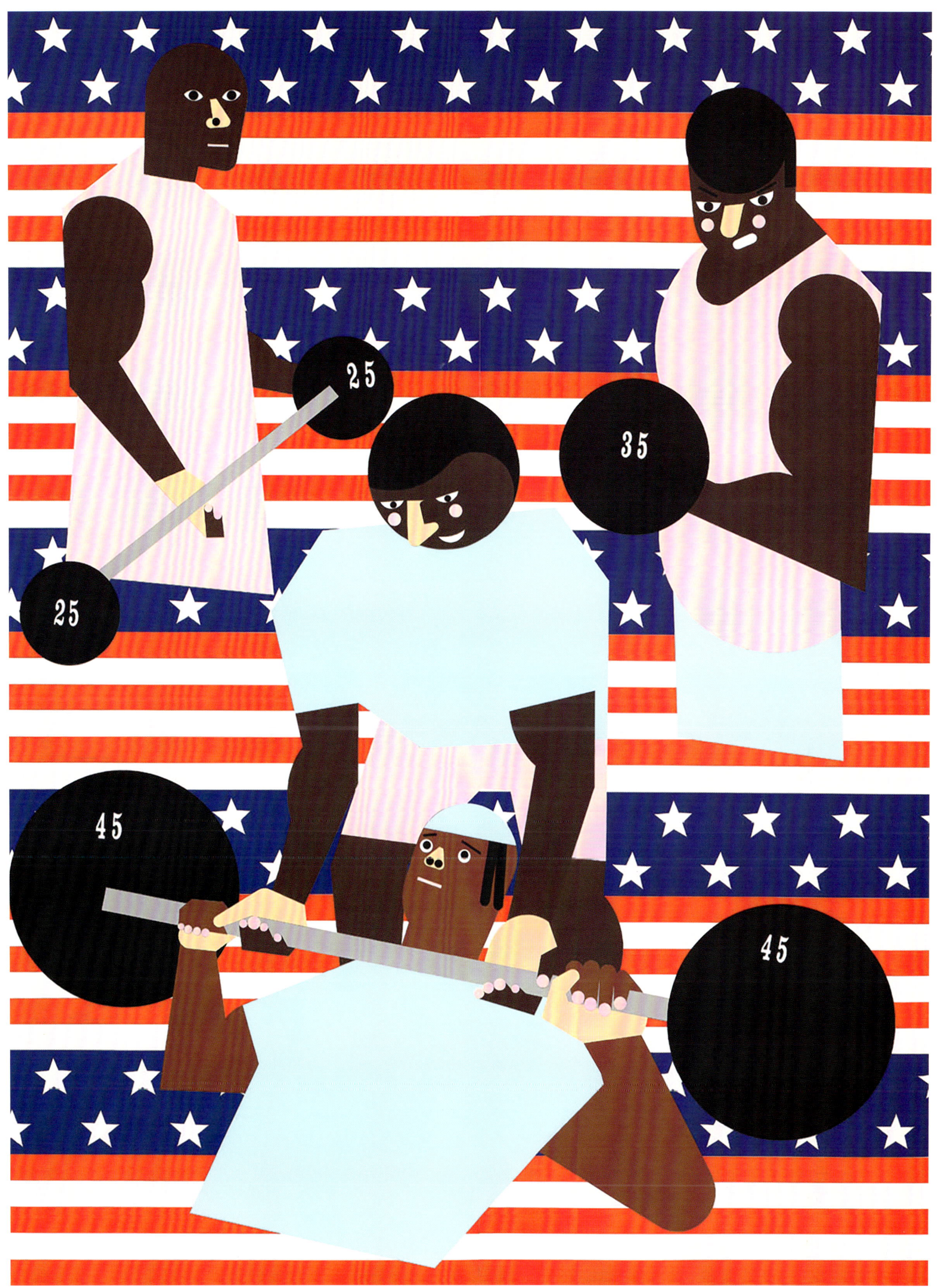
25
25
35
45
45

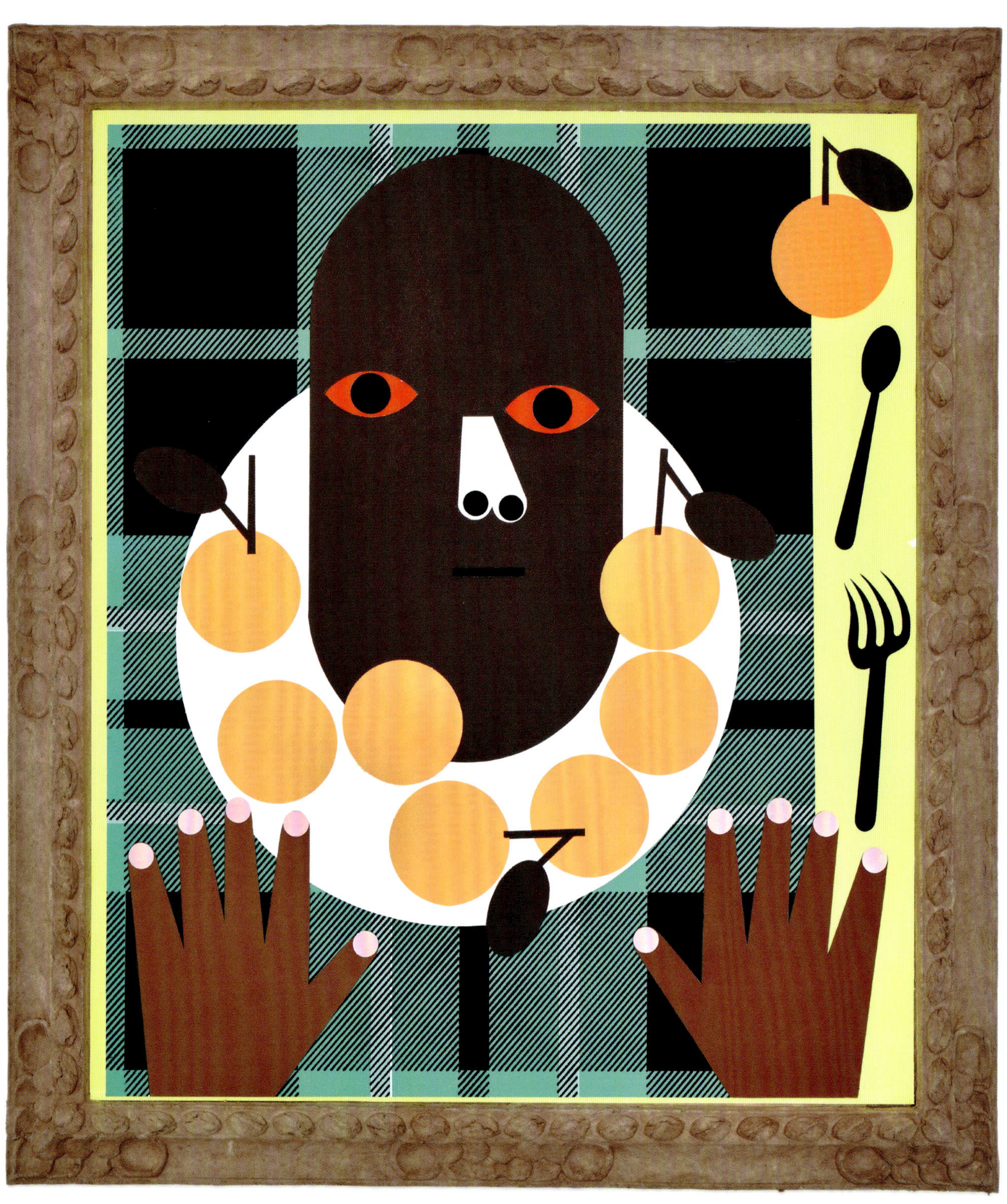

Humble Gifts #12, 2024

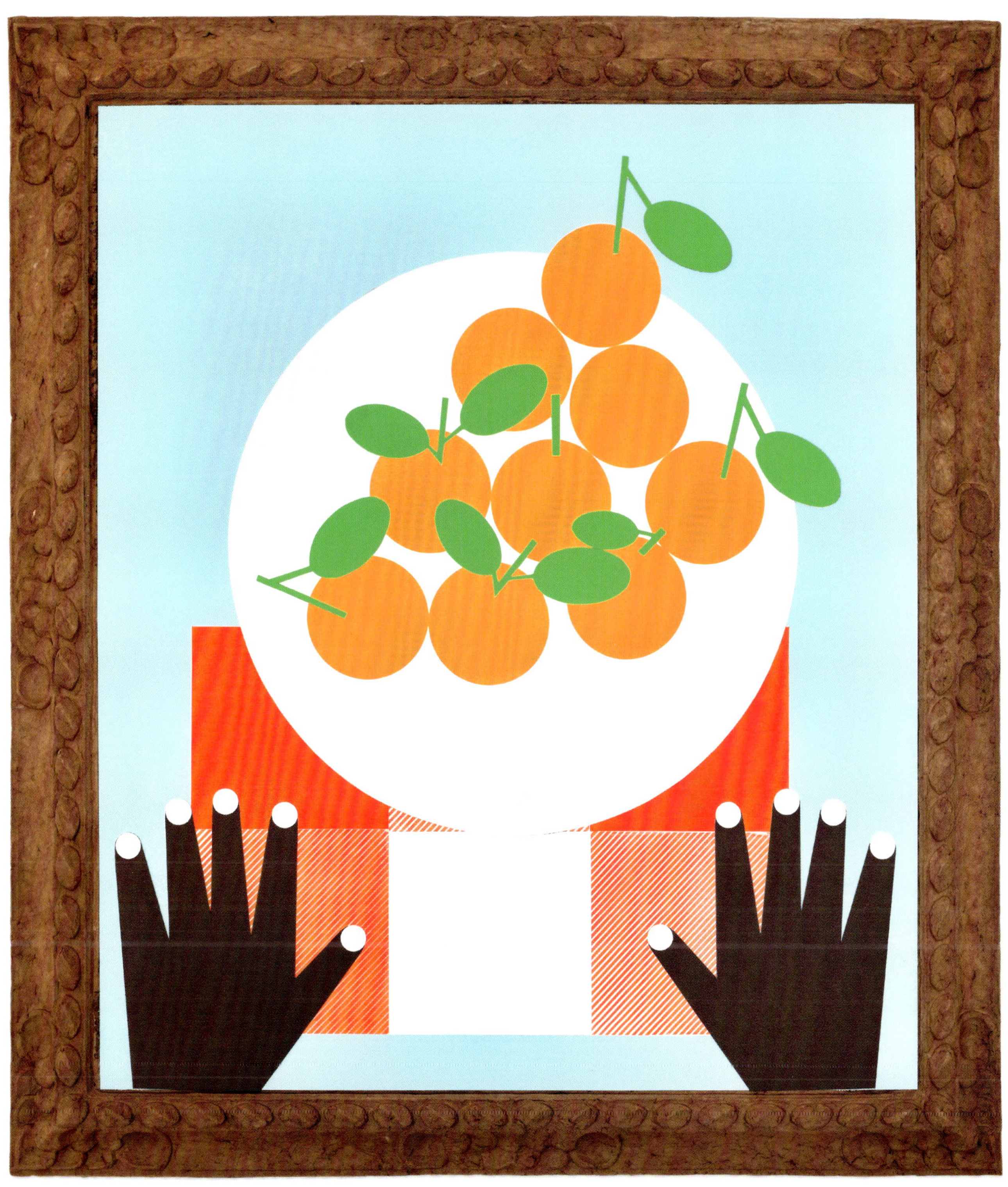

Humble Gifts #7, 2024

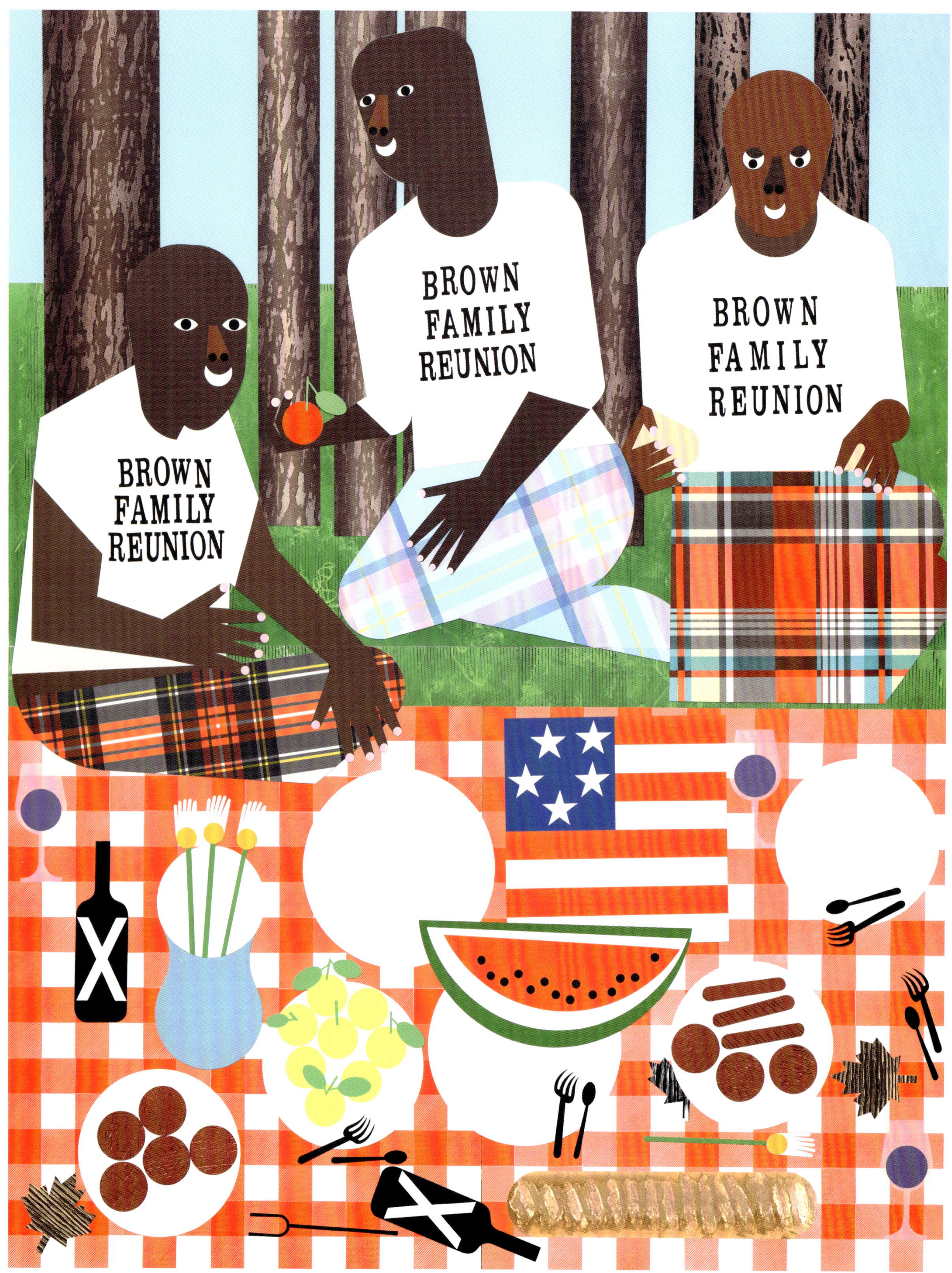

Breaking Bread, 2024

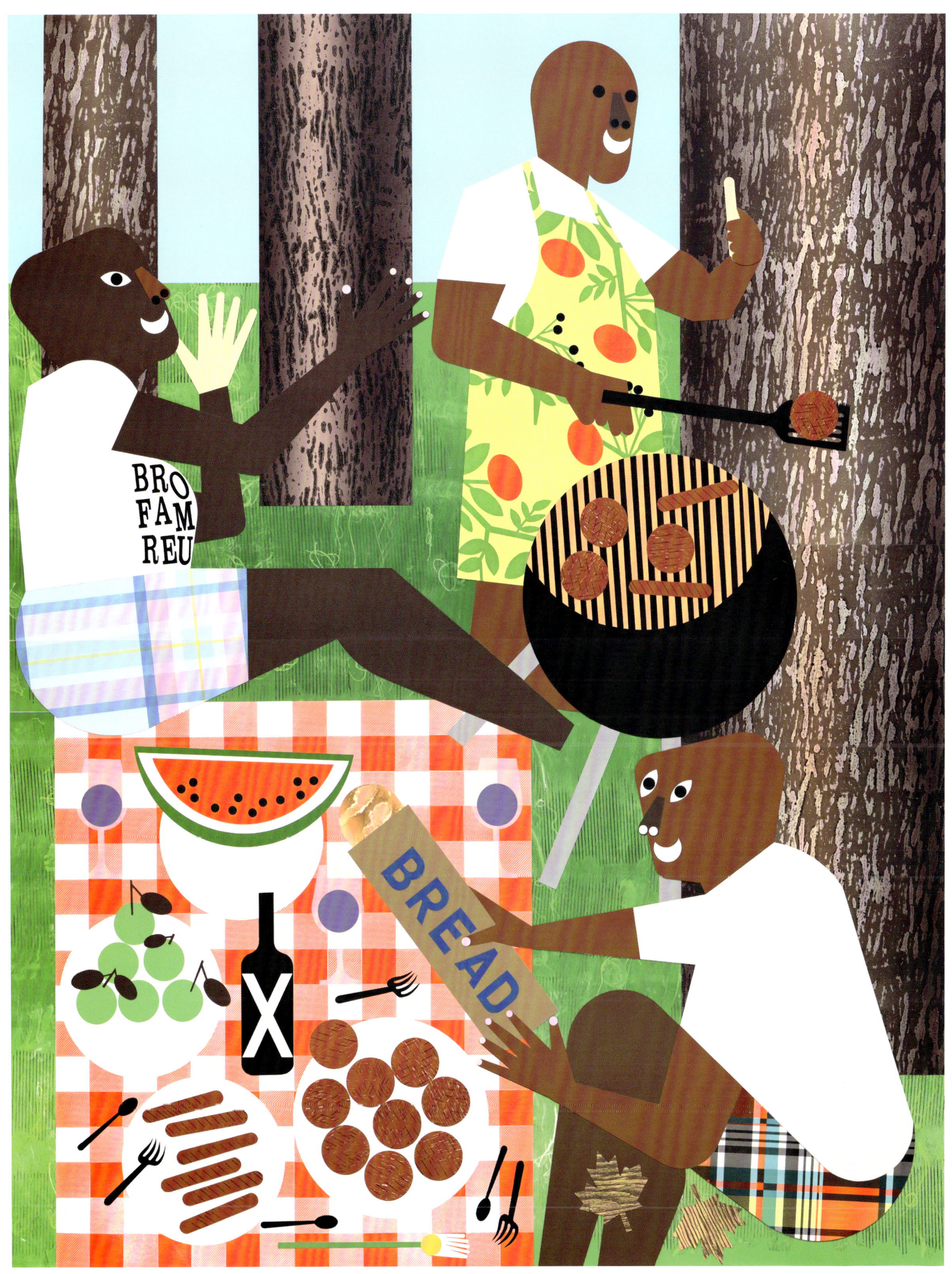
BRO
FAM
REU
BREAD

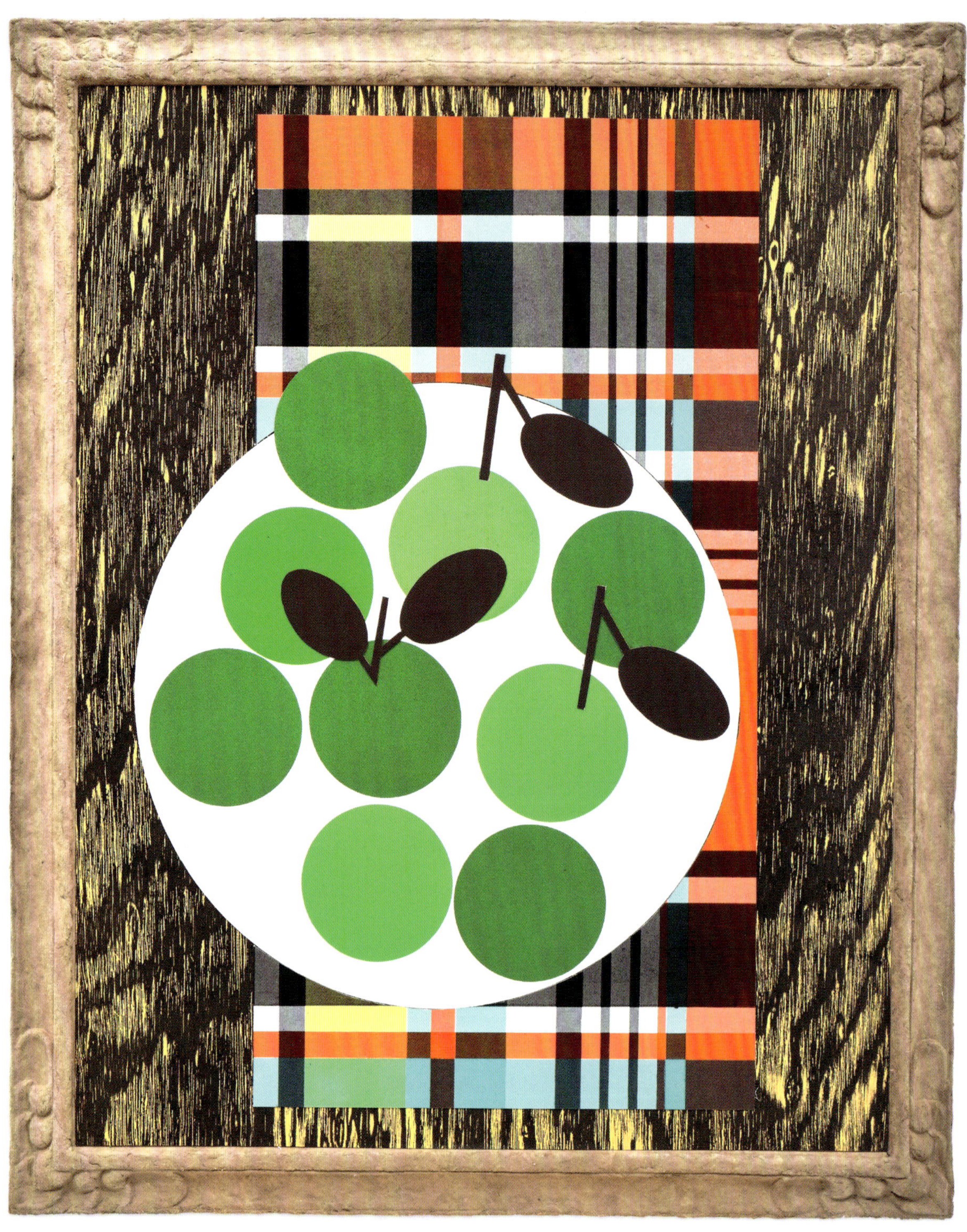

Humble Gifts #9, 2024

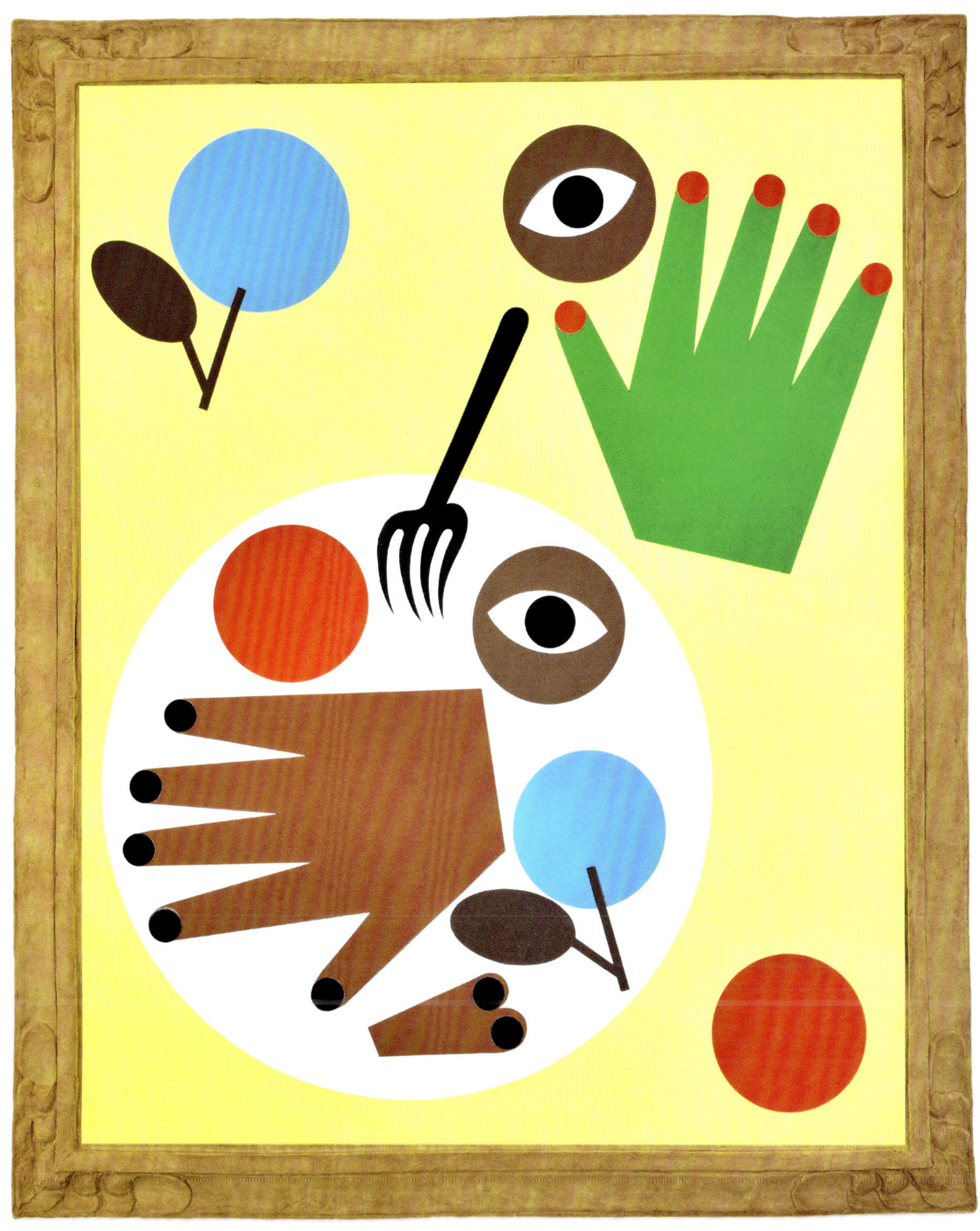

Humble Gifts #11, 2024

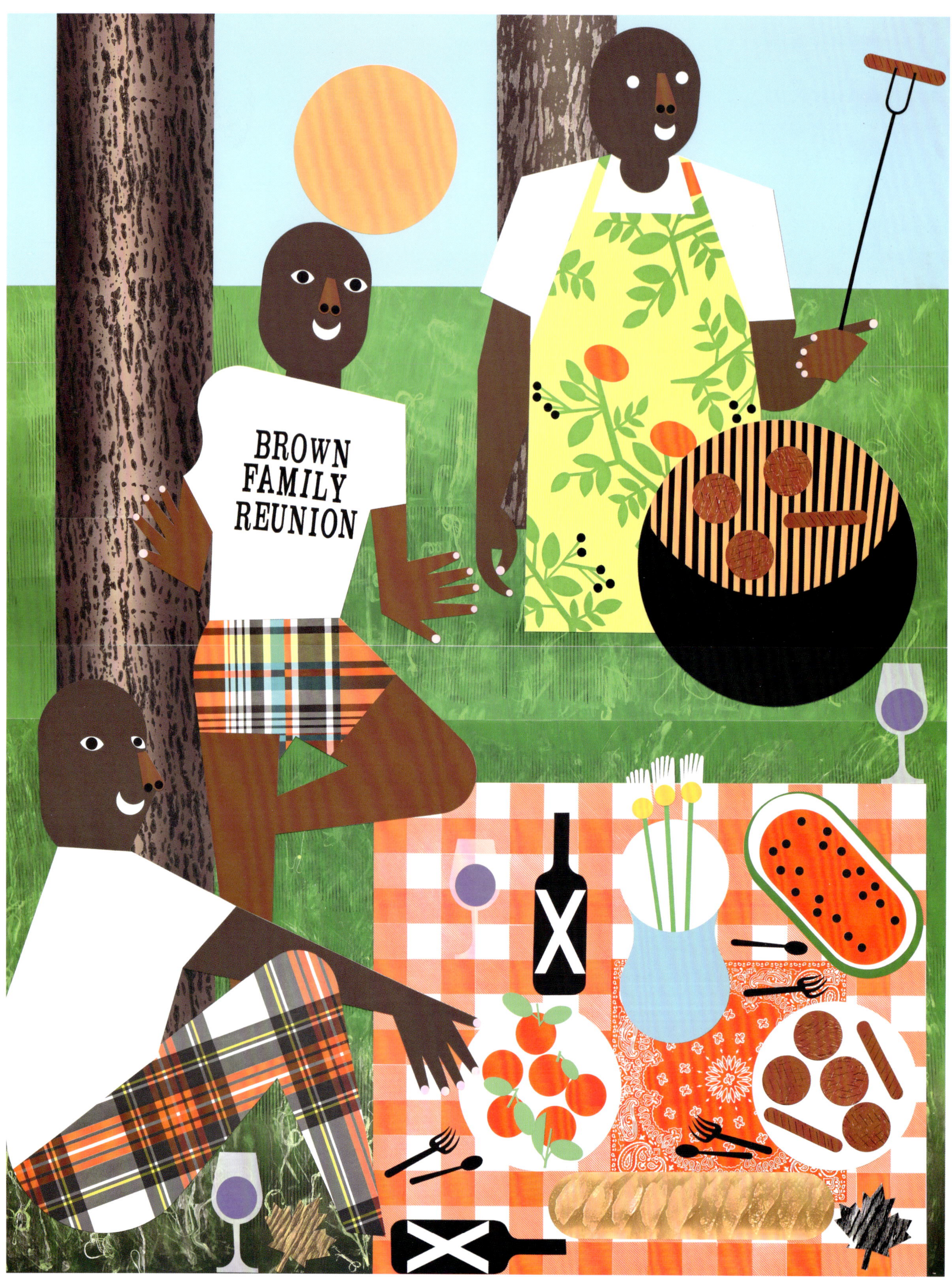
BROWN
FAMILY
REUNION

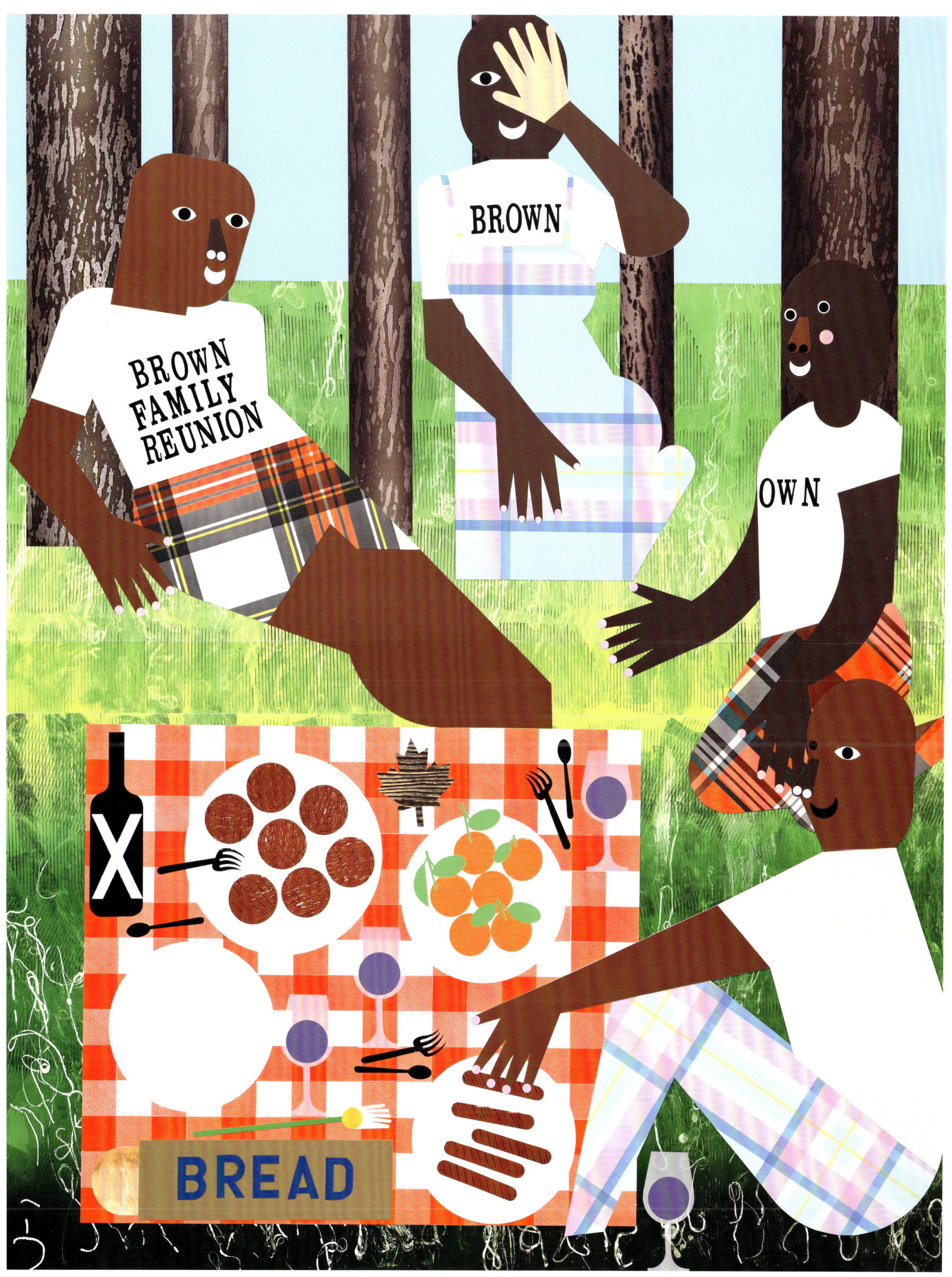
BROWN
FAMILY
REUNION
BROWN
OWN
X
BREAD

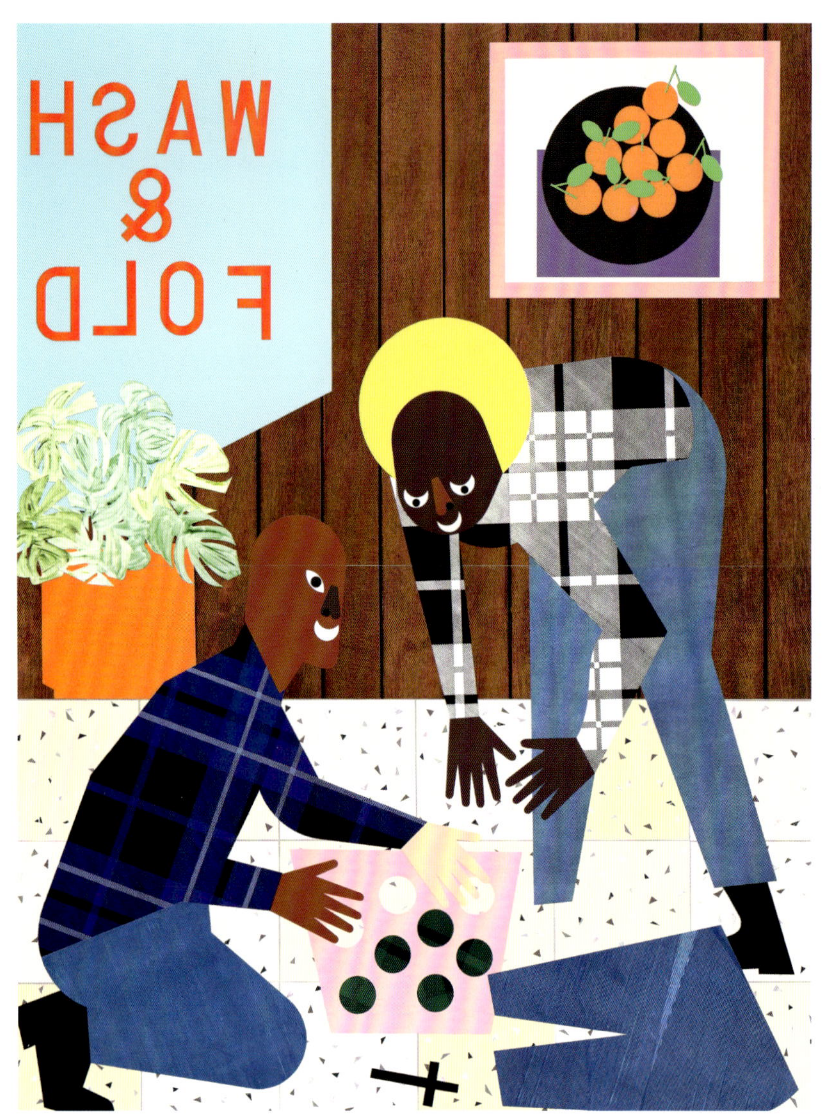

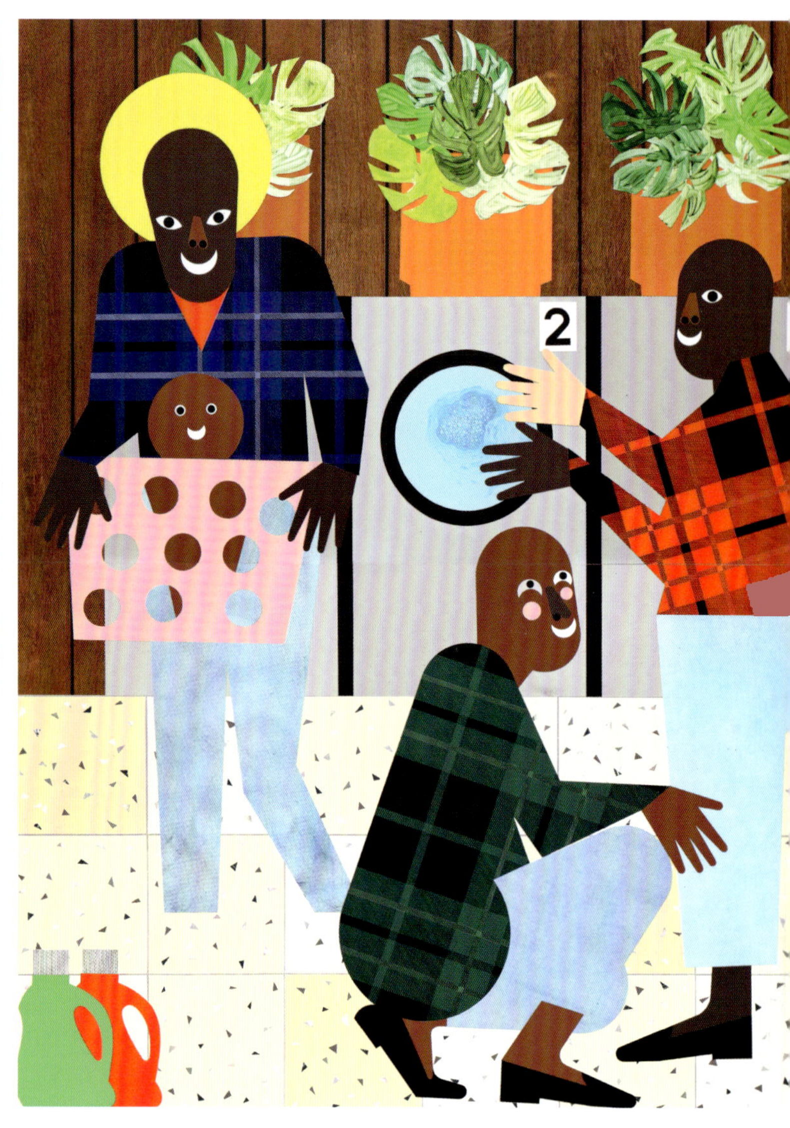

Loads of Grace, 2024

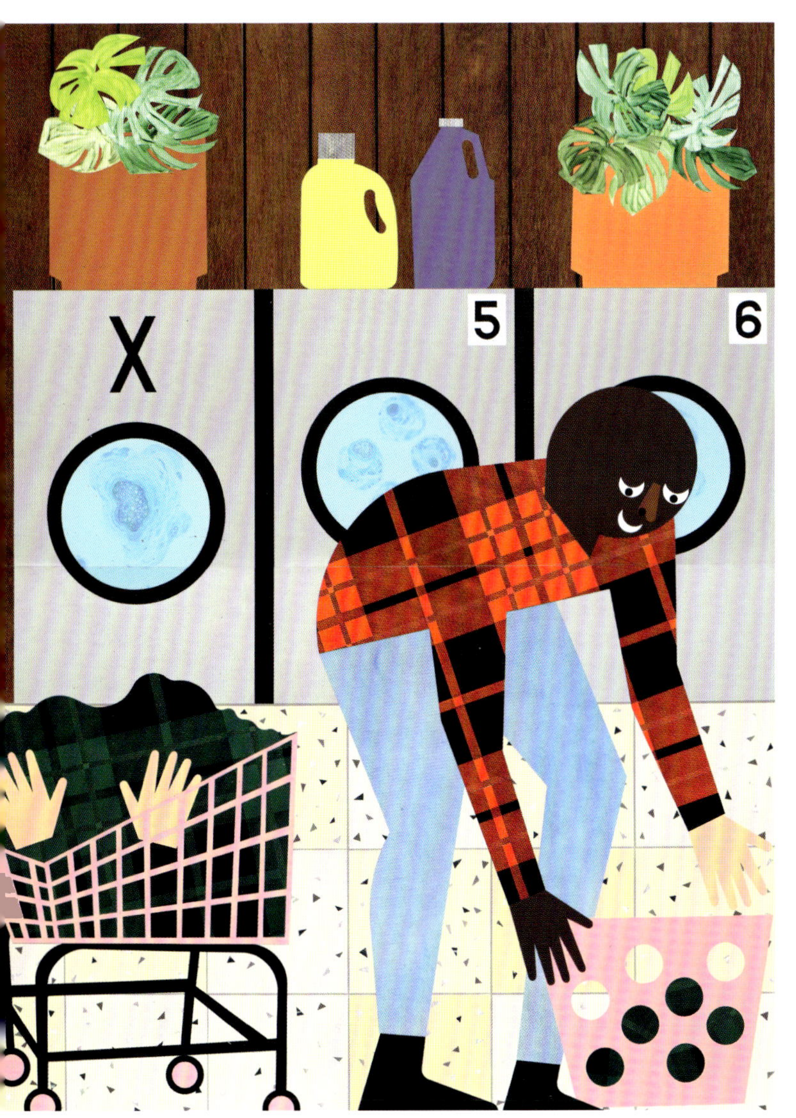
X
5
6

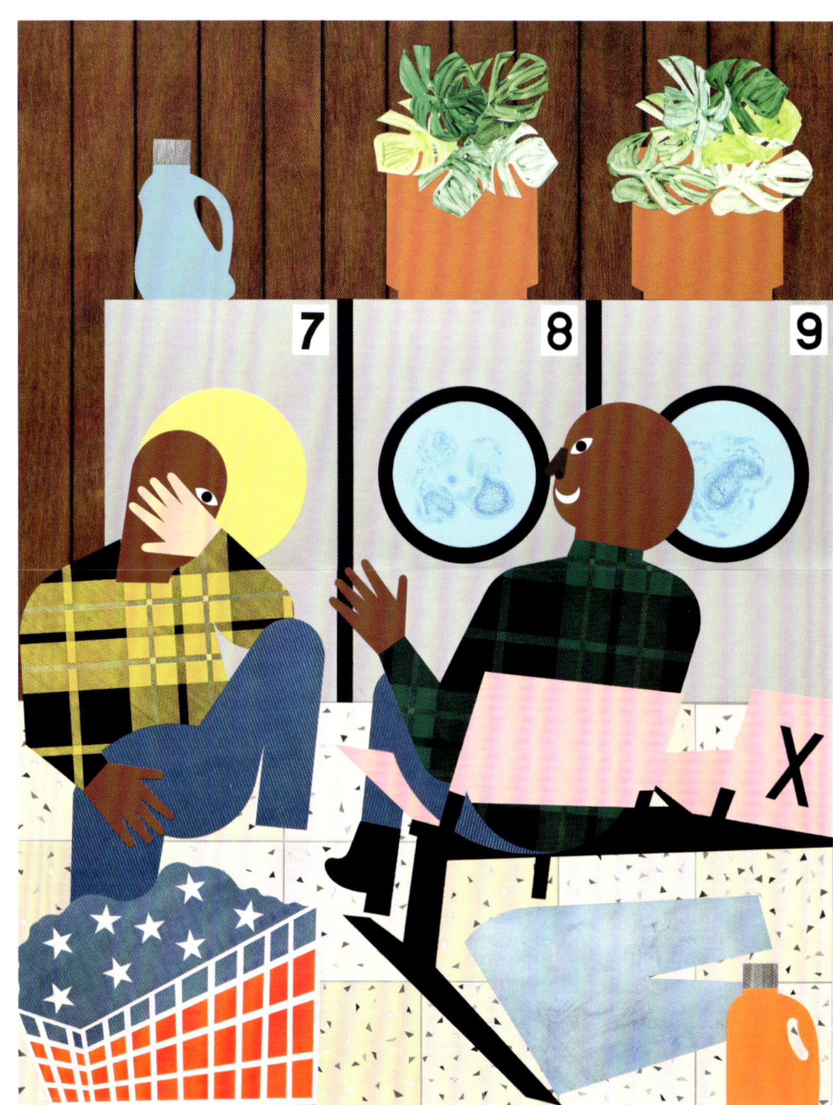
7
8
9
X

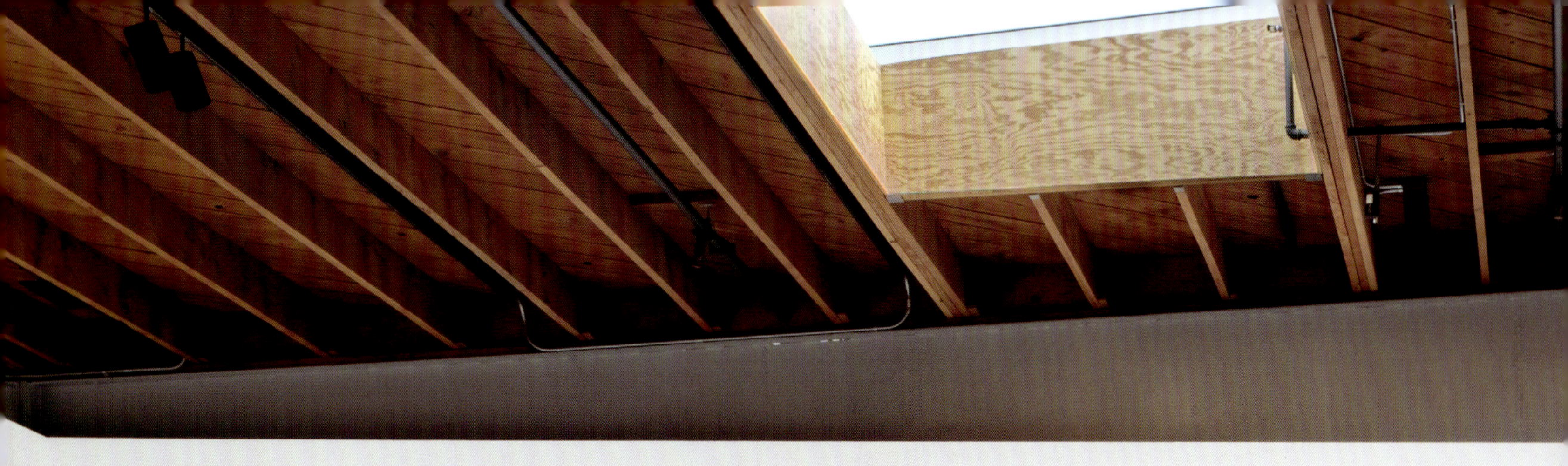

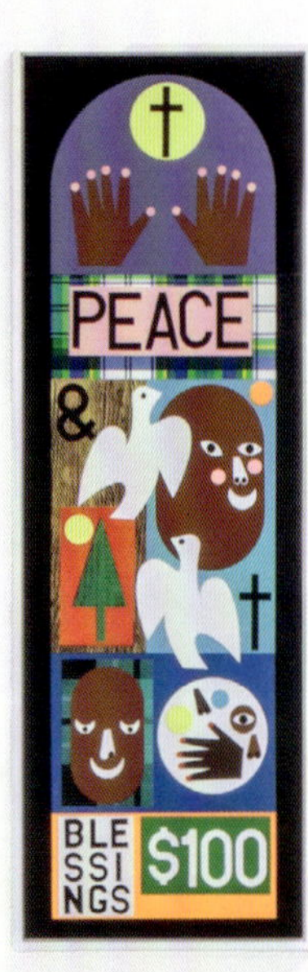
PEACE
&
BLESSINGS
$100

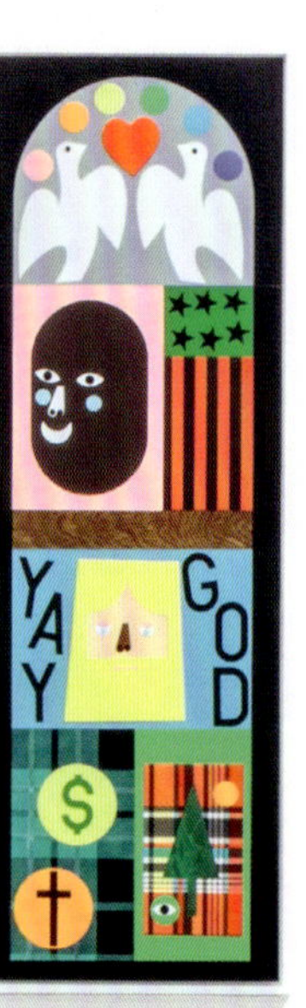
YAY
GOD
$

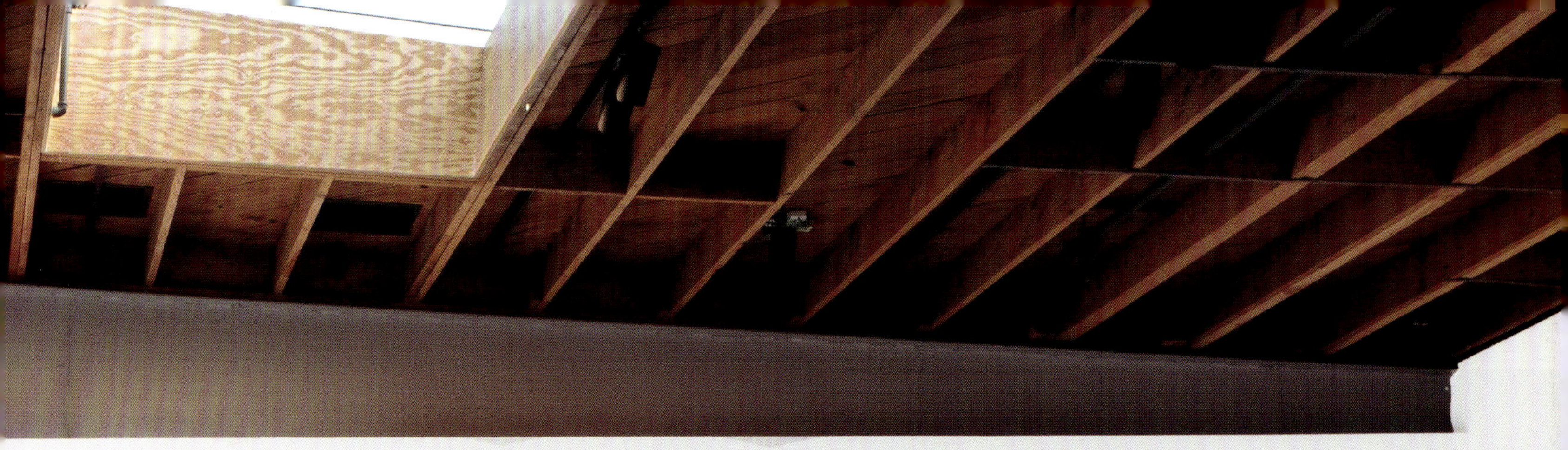

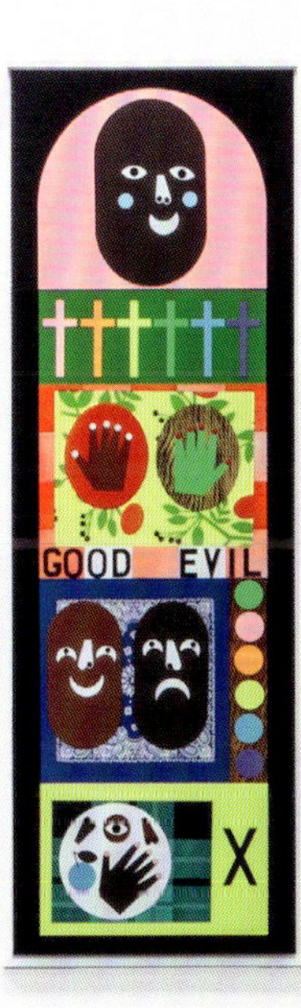
GOOD
EVIL
X

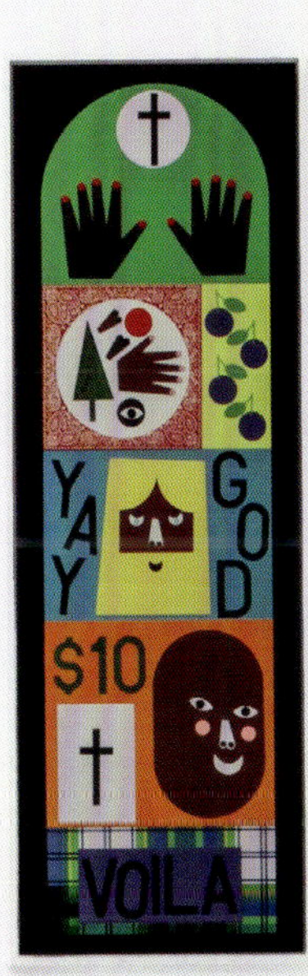
YAY
GOD
$10
VOILA

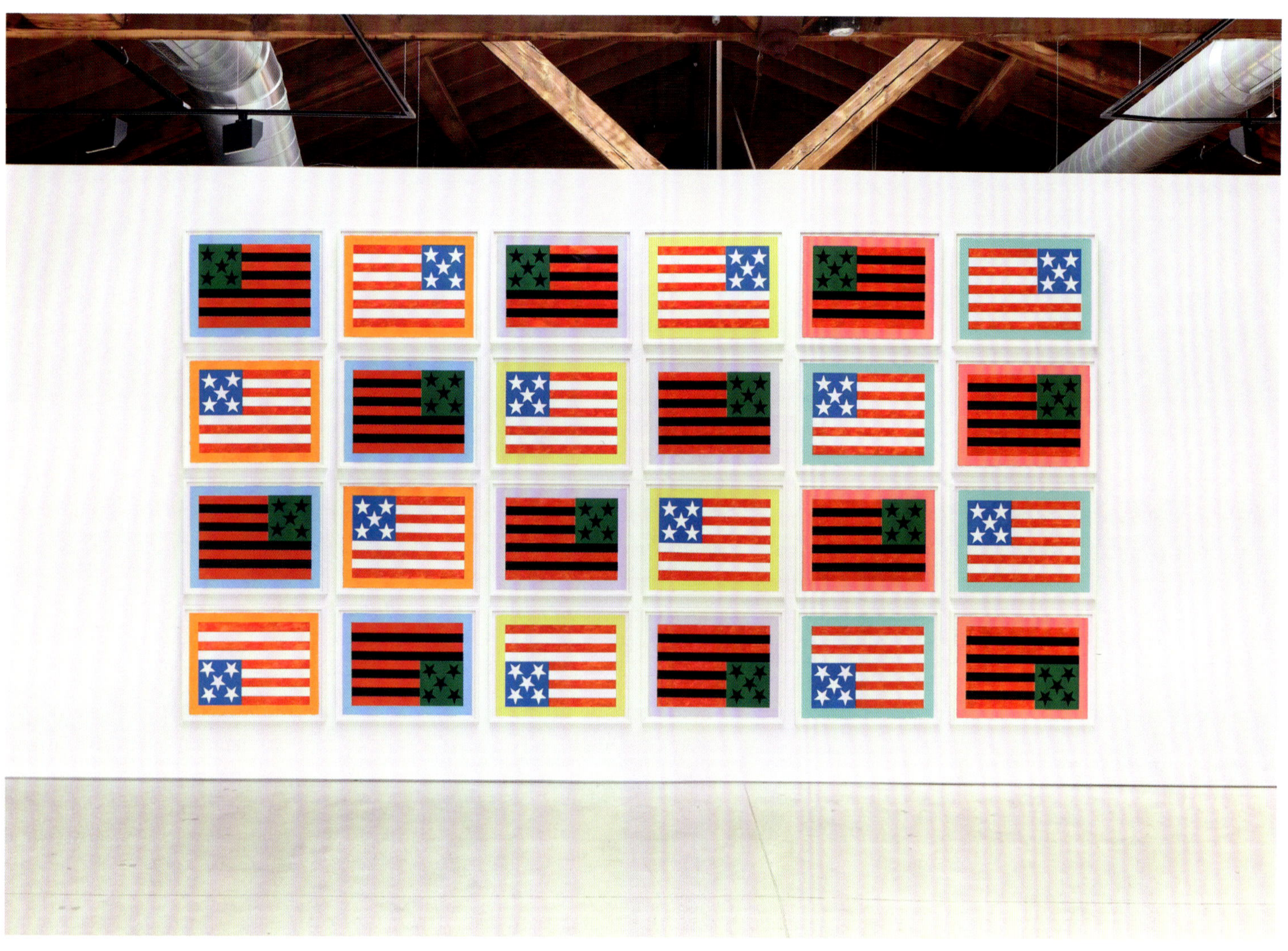

[PREVIOUS] Installation view, Winging It, 2025
[ABOVE] Installation view, Patchwork, 2024

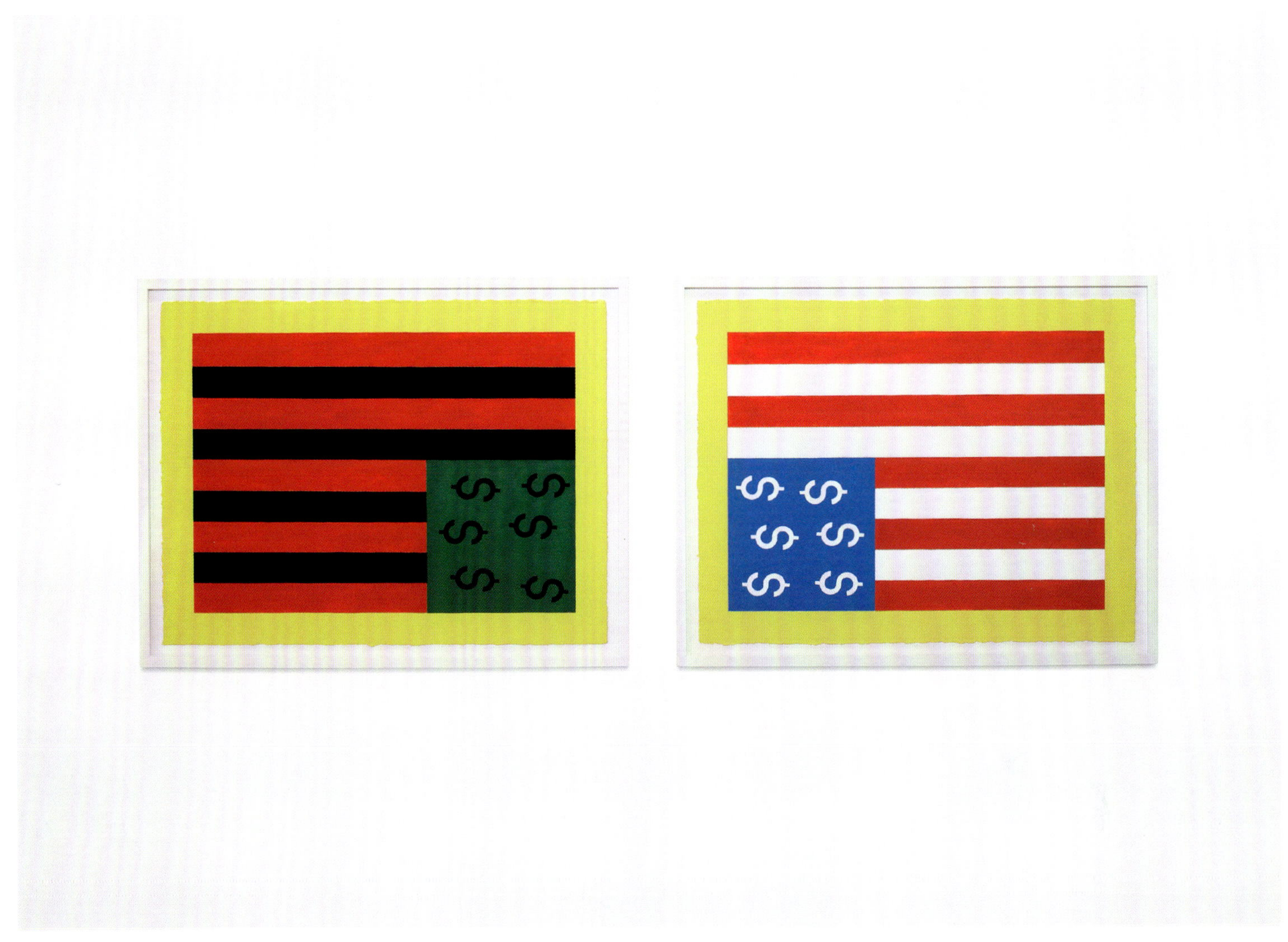

Let the Dollar Circulate #1, 2024

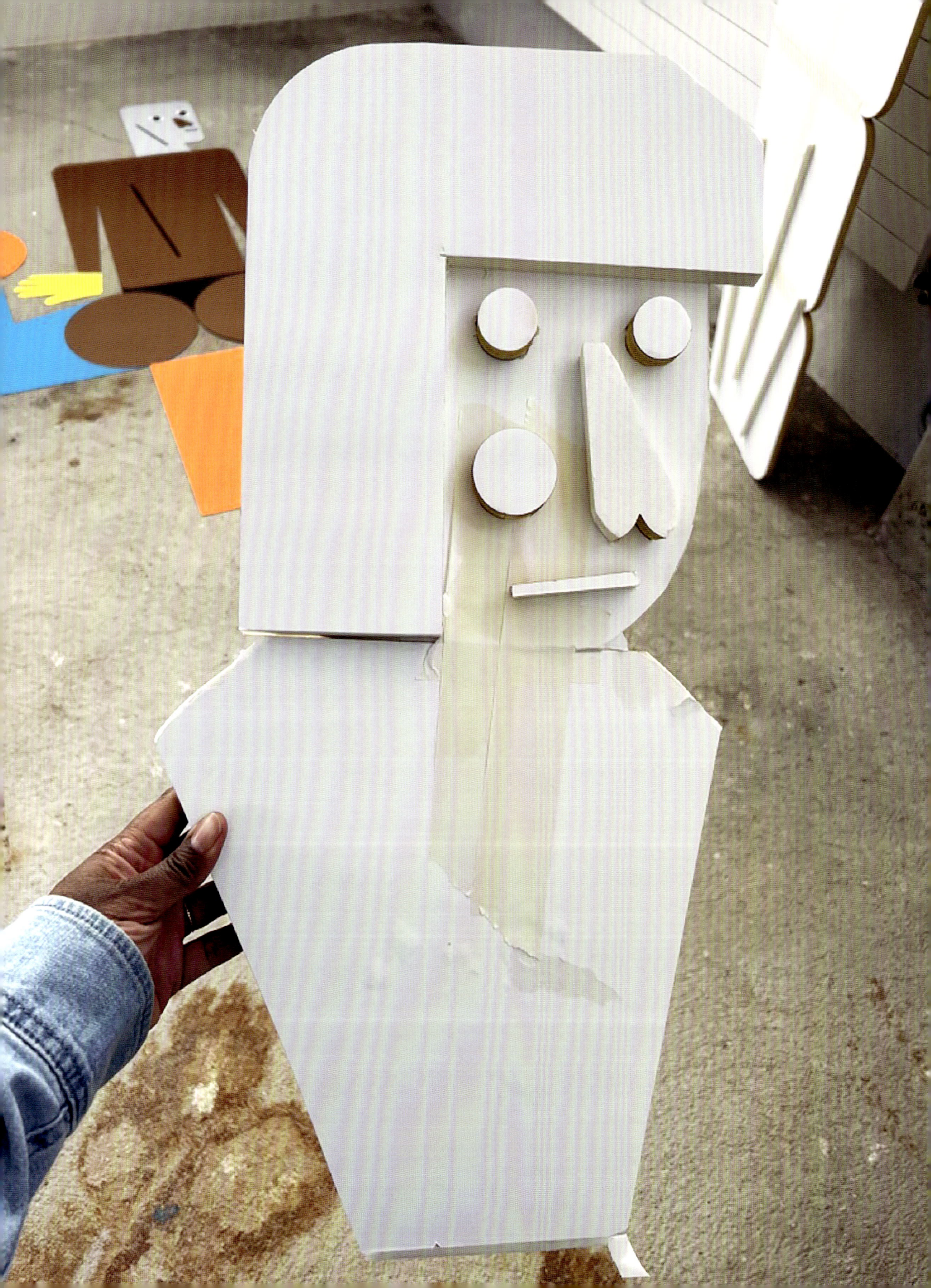

SCULPTURES

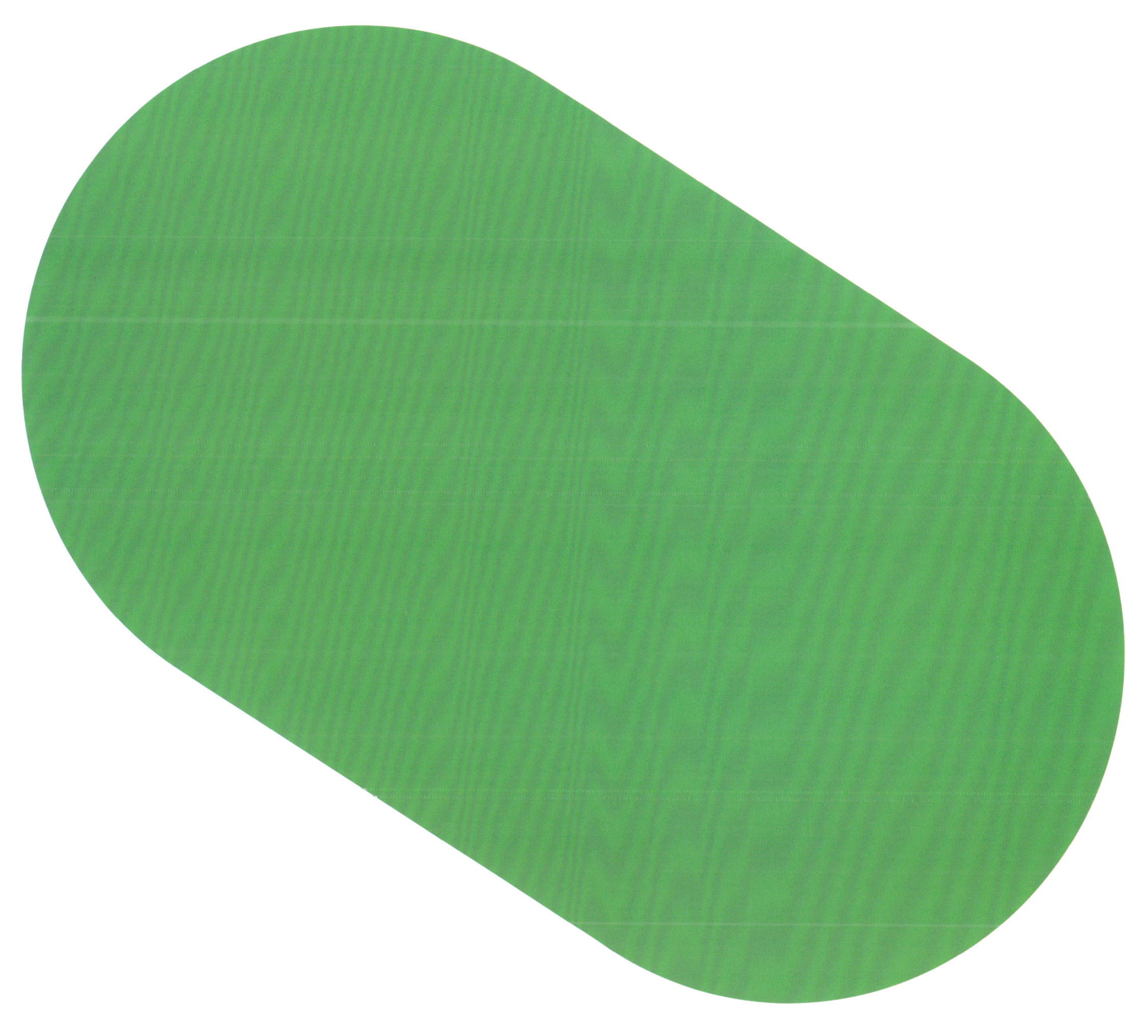

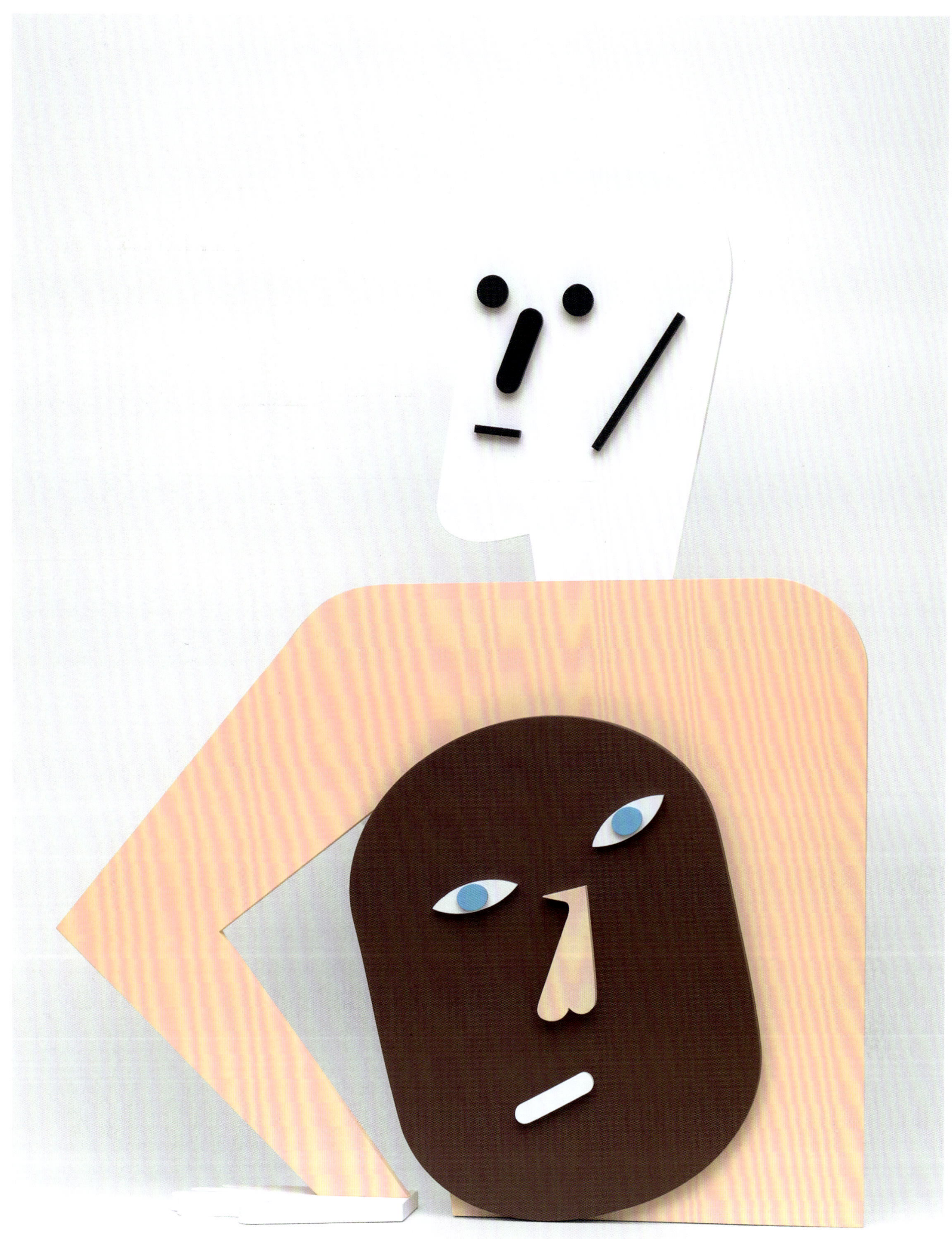

Wrath, 2024

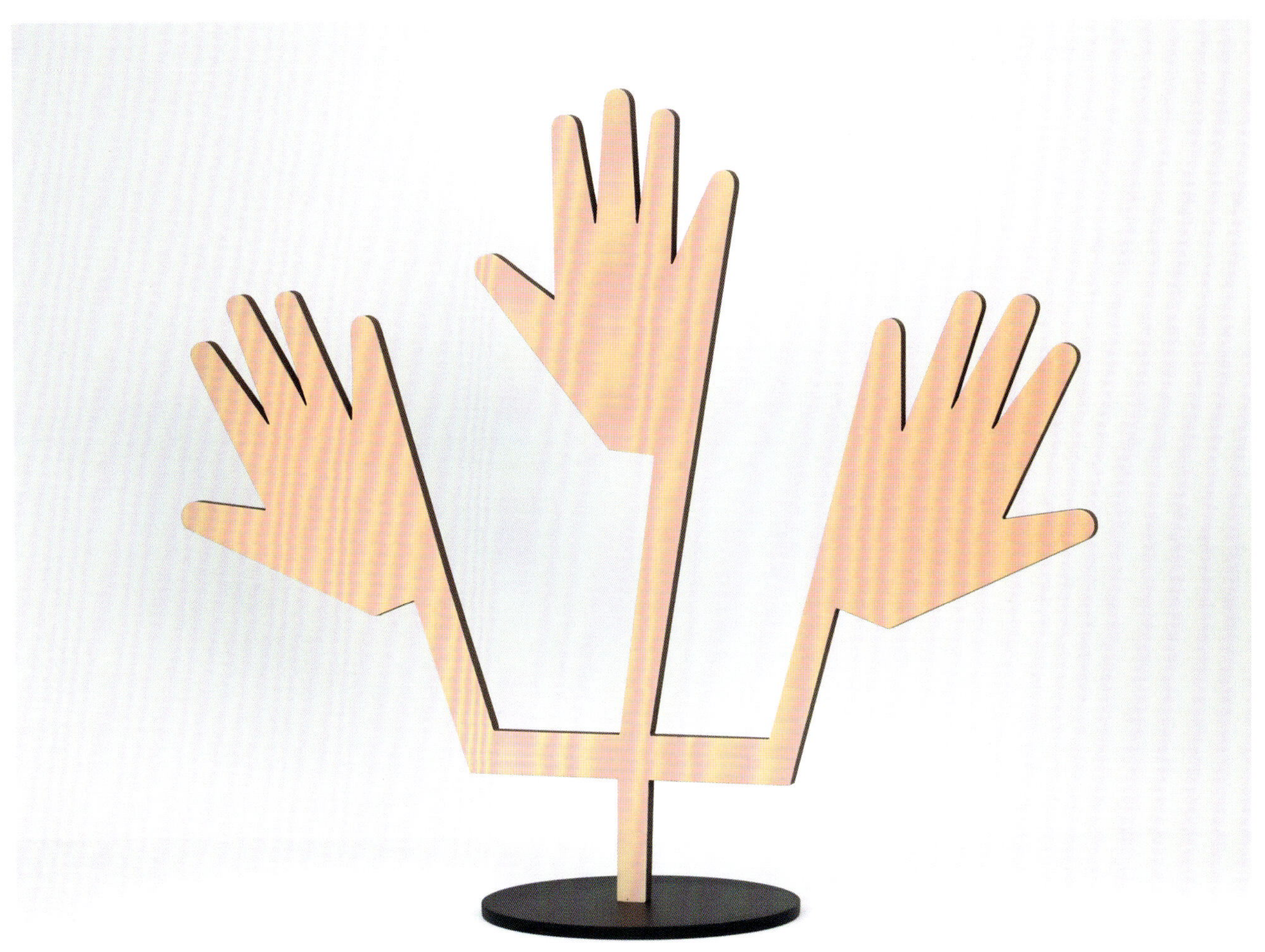

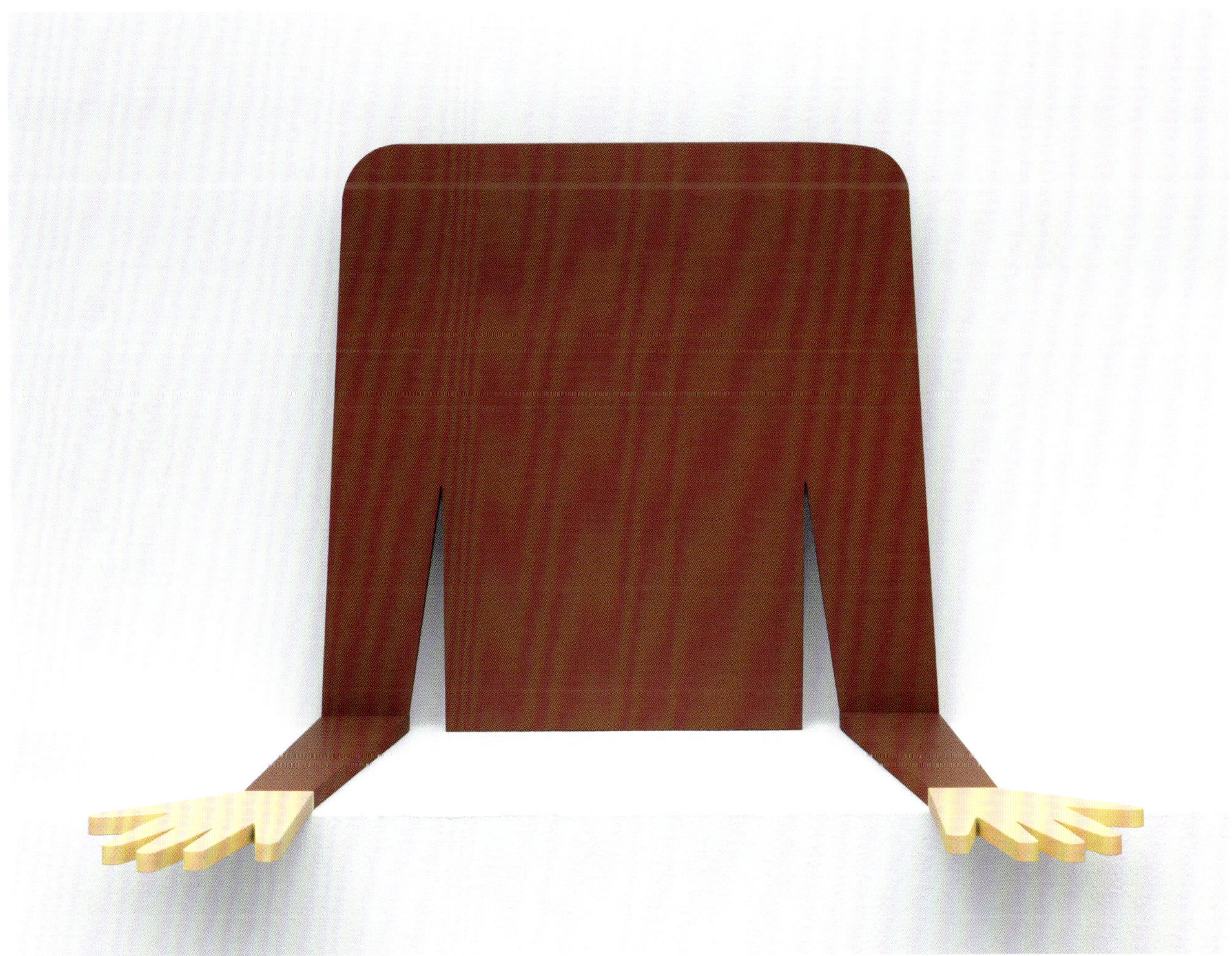

[TOP] Greed, 2024
[BOTTOM] Limbo, 2024

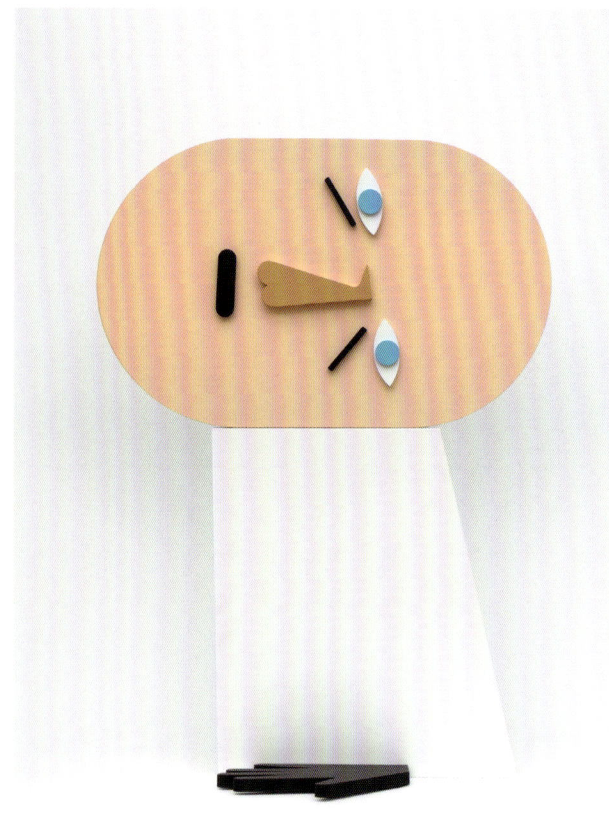

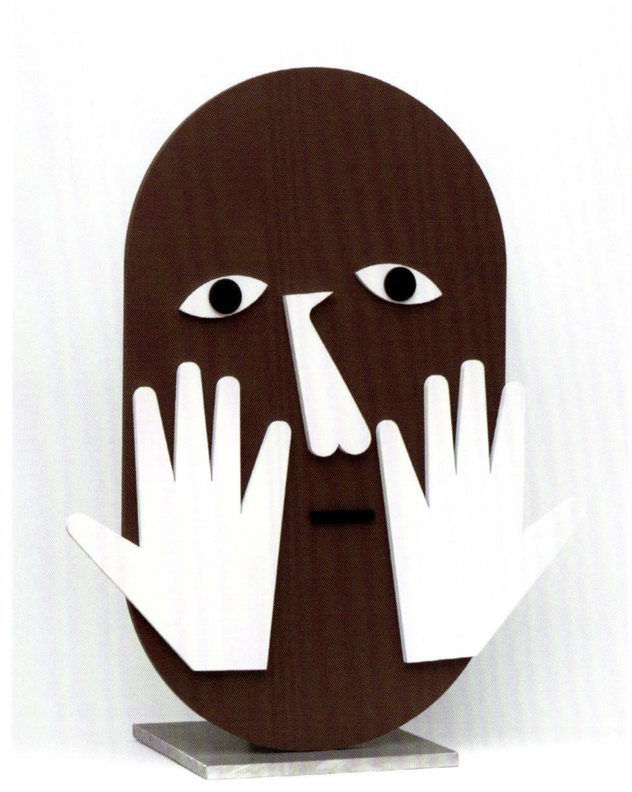

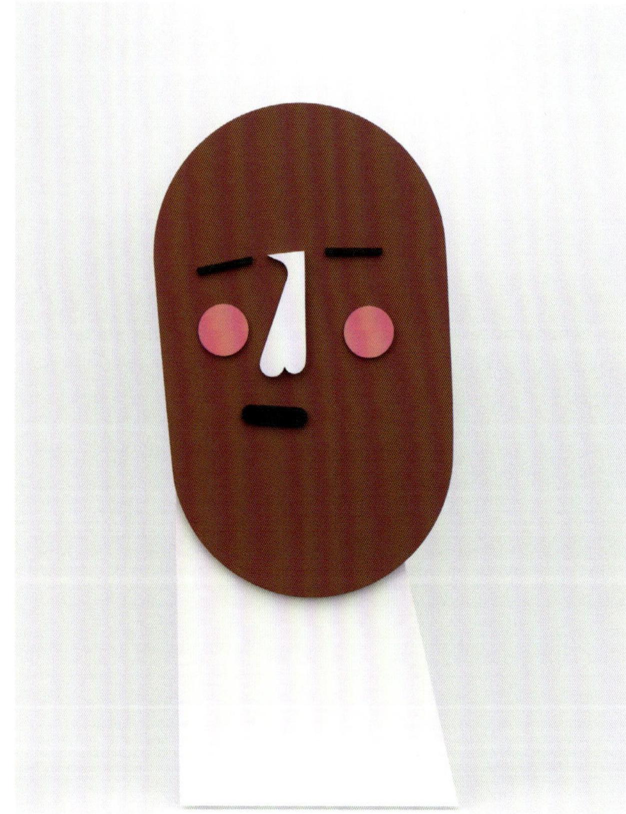

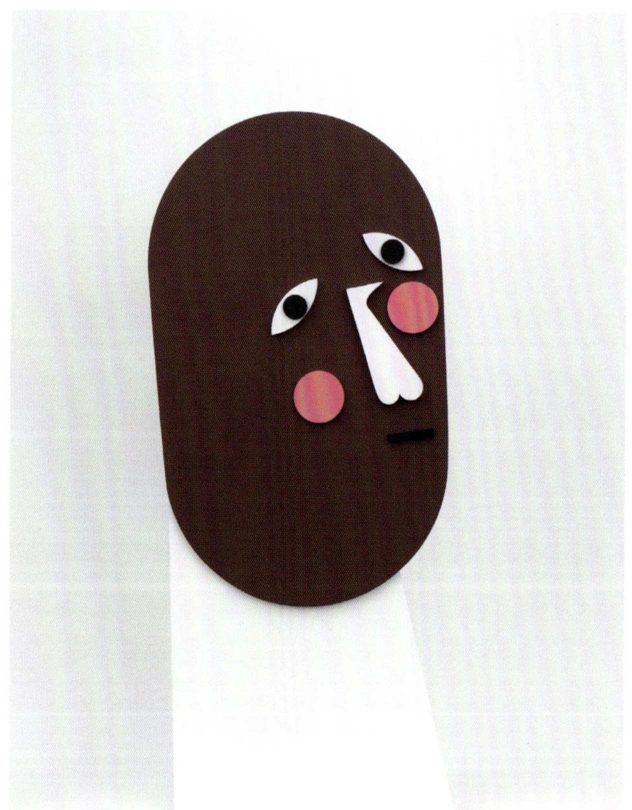

[TOP LEFT] Fraud, 2024
[BOTTOM LEFT] Gluttony, 2024

[TOP RIGHT] Treachery, 2024
[BOTTOM RIGHT] Heresy, 2024

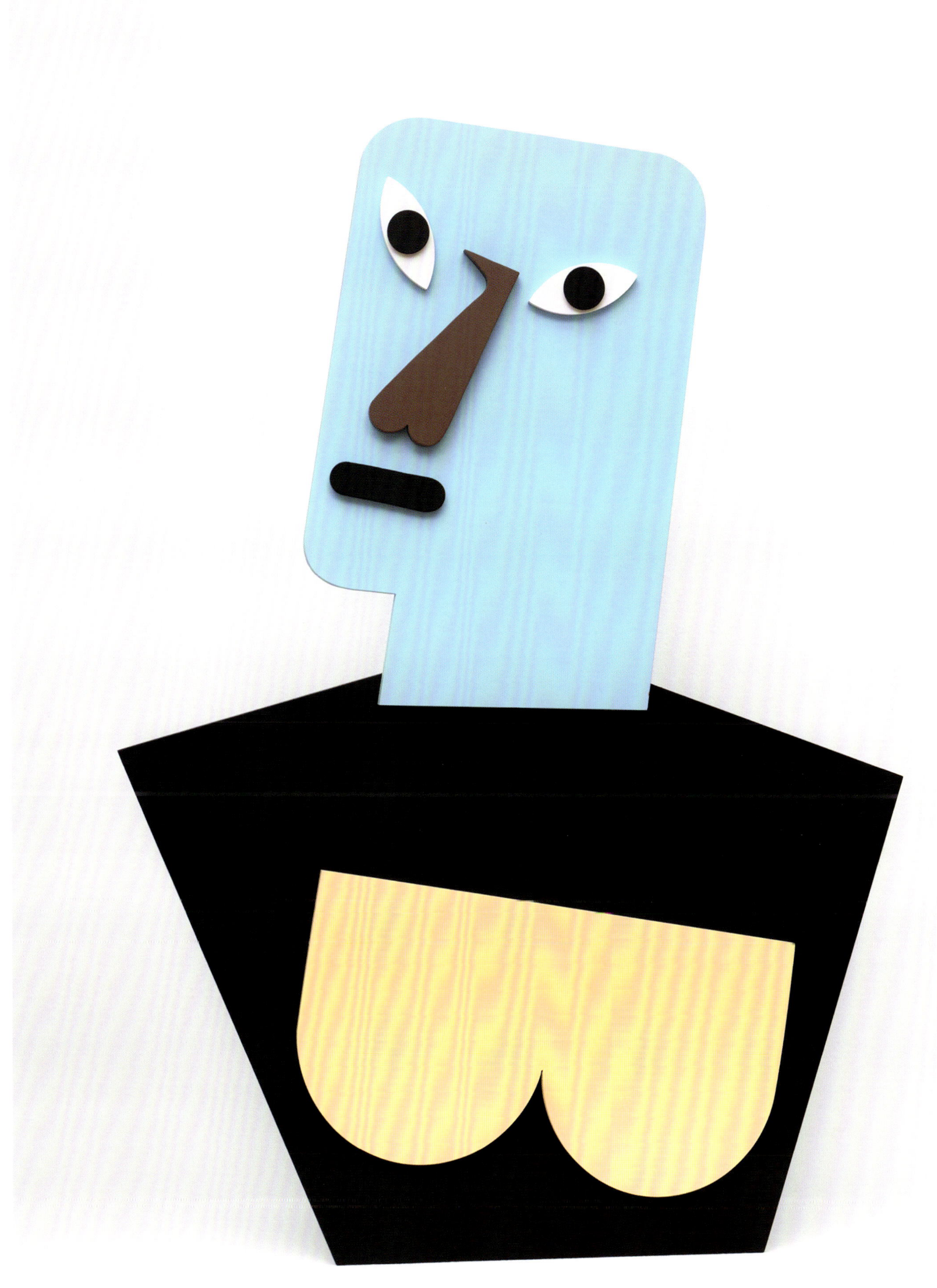

Lust, 2024

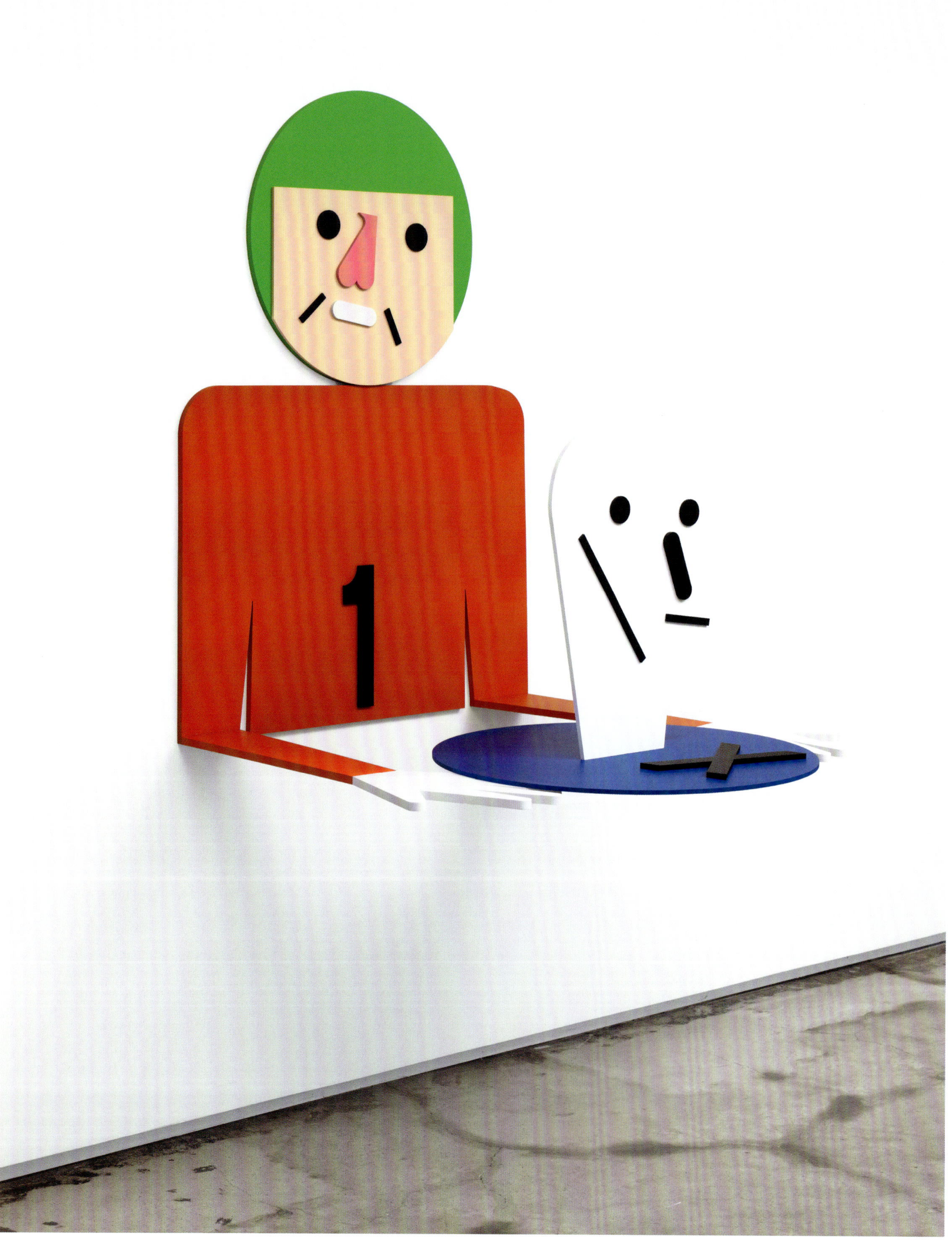

Pig Out 1, 2024

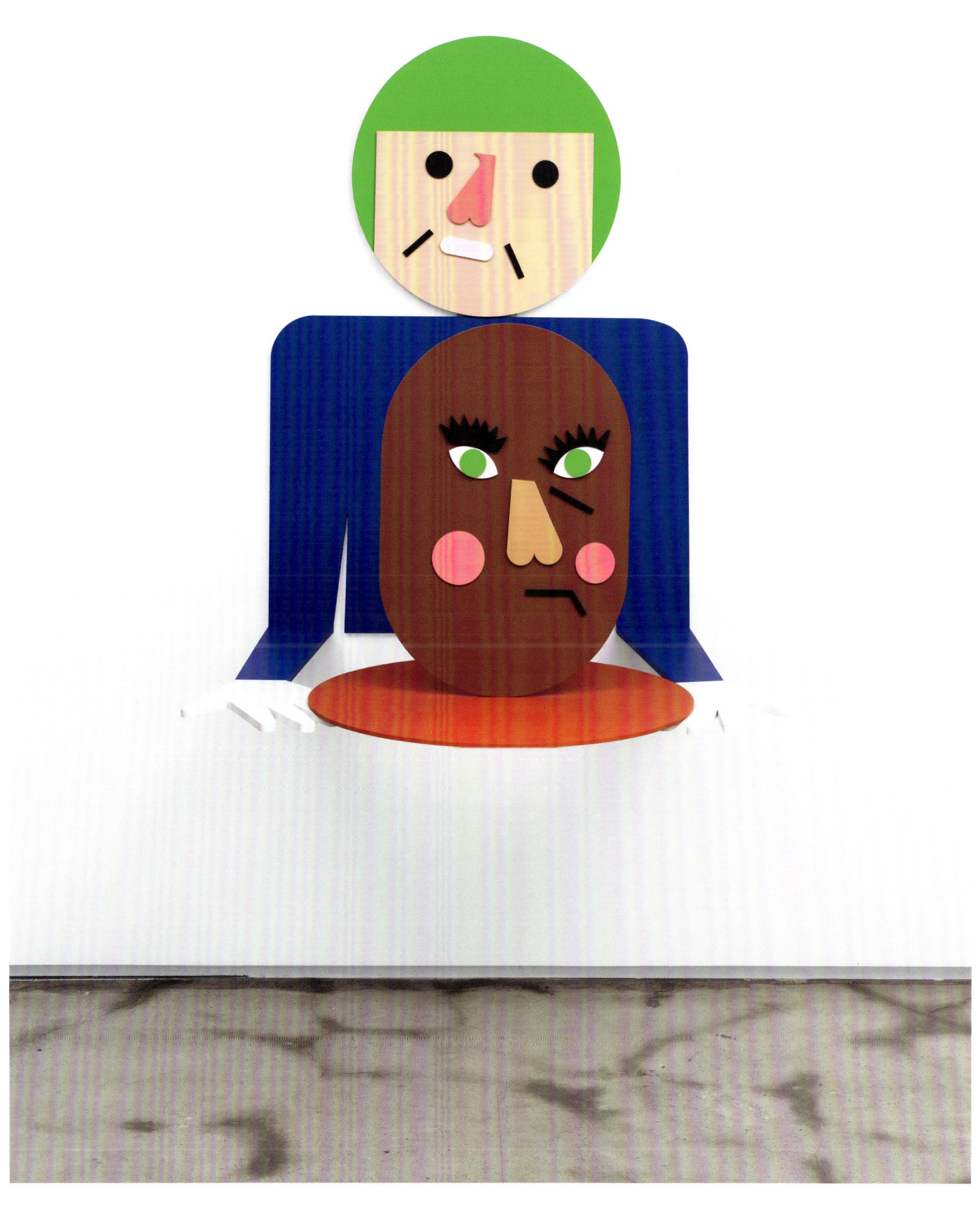

Pig Out 2, 2024

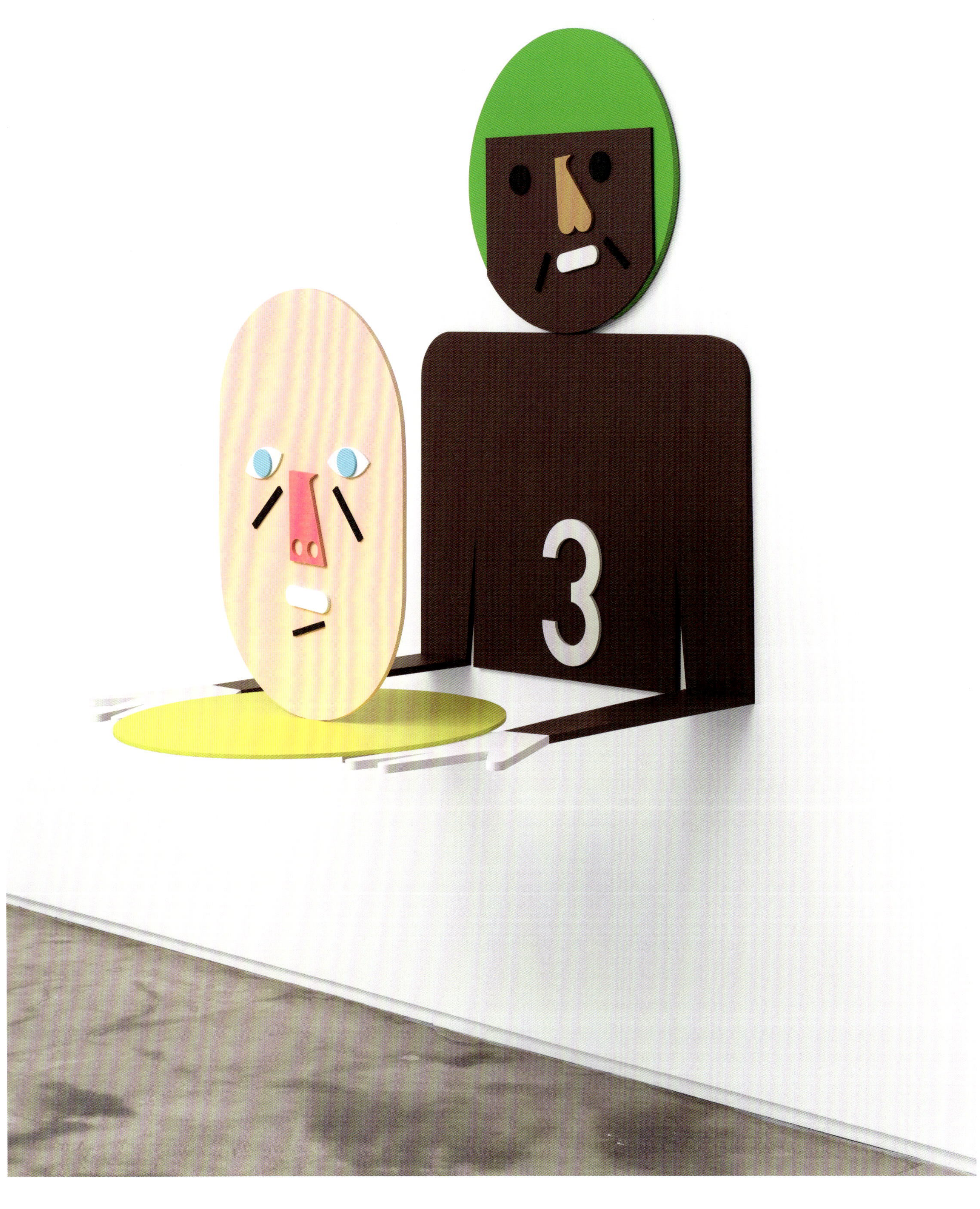

Pig Out 3, 2024

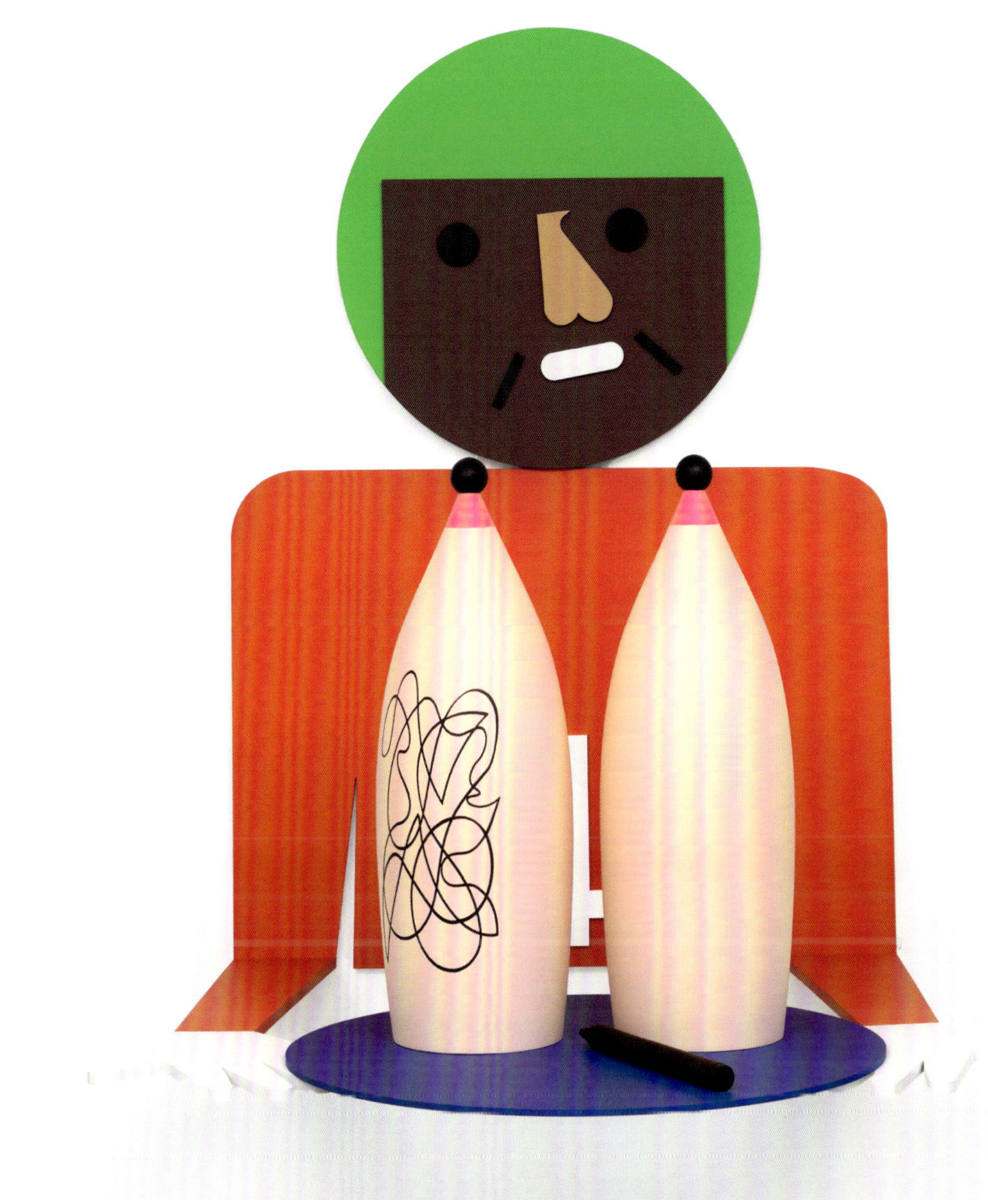

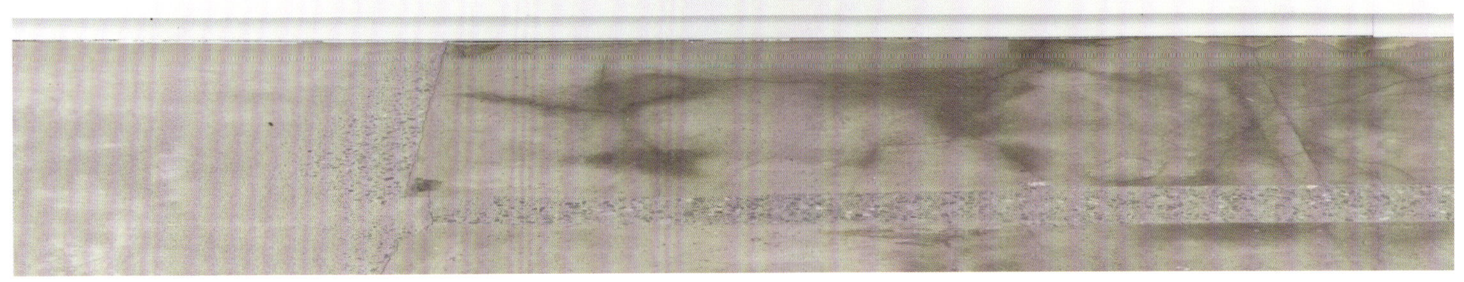

Pig Out 4, 2024

COMMERCIAL

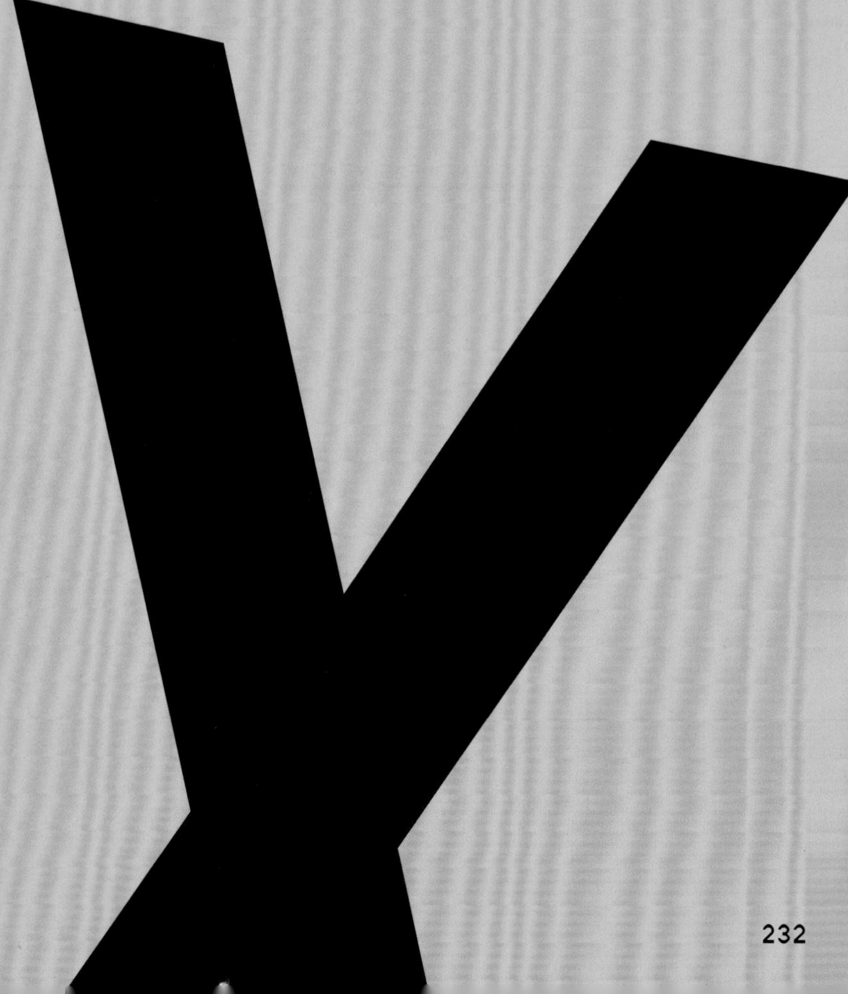

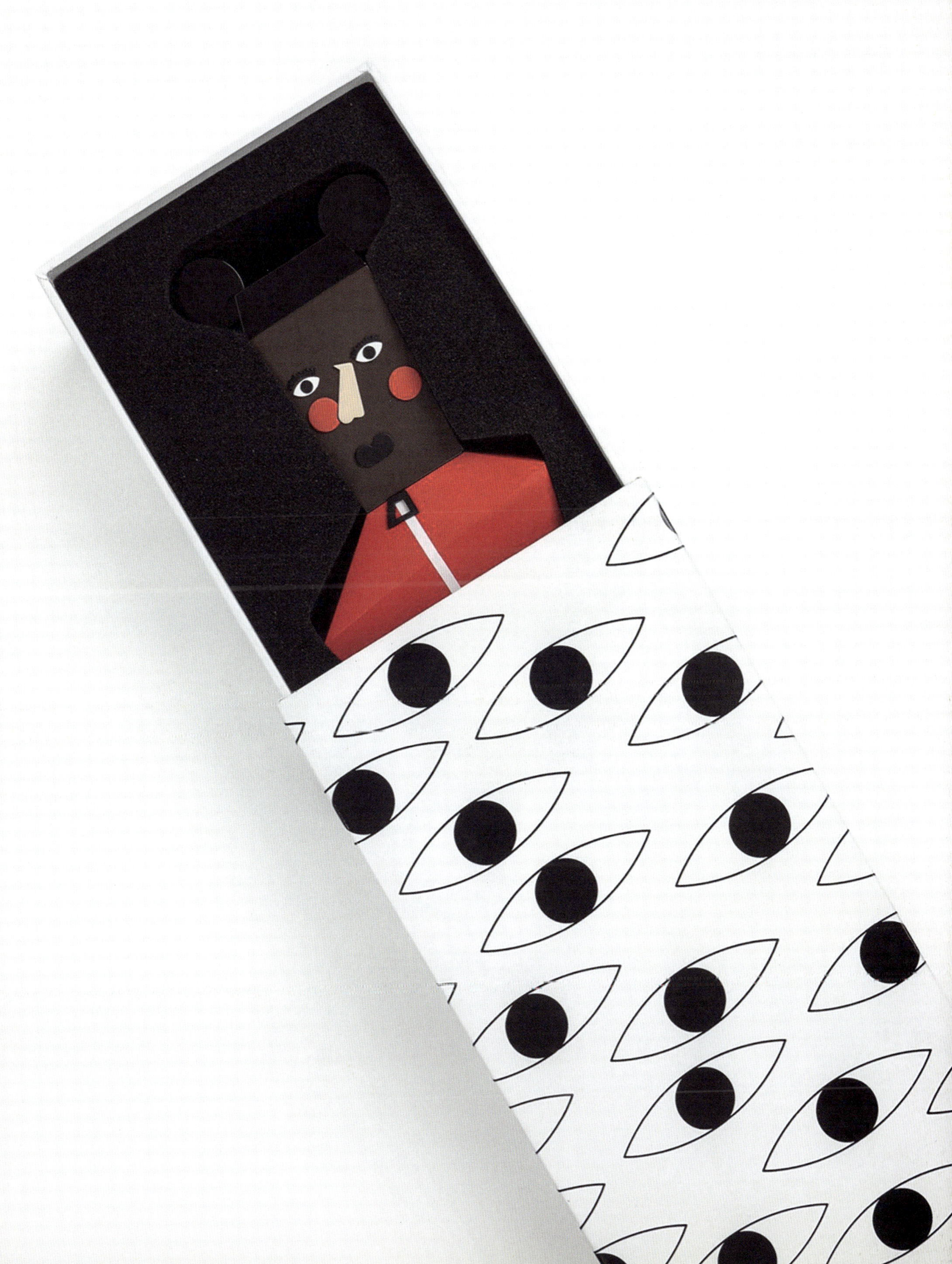

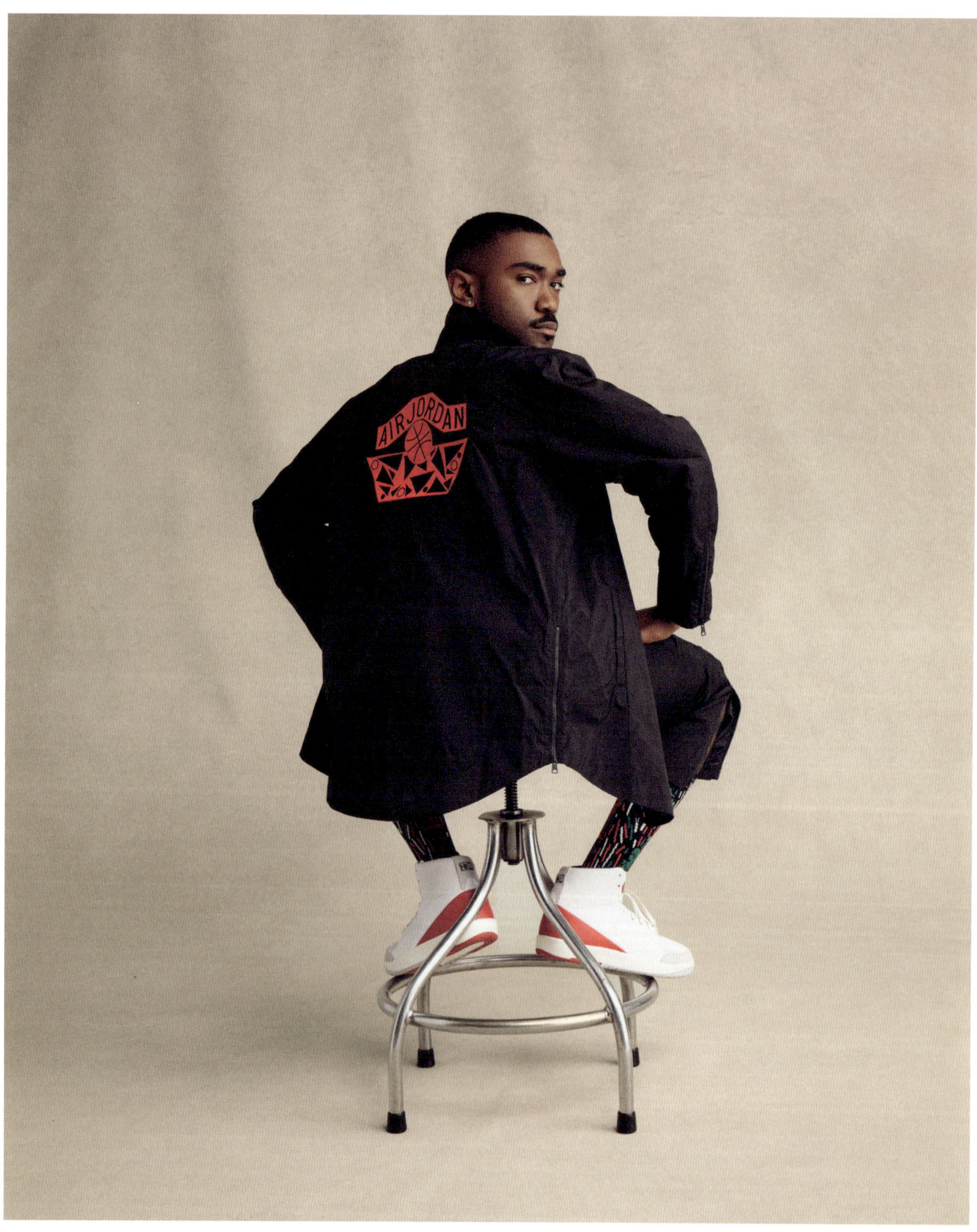

[PREVIOUS] Baby, 2020

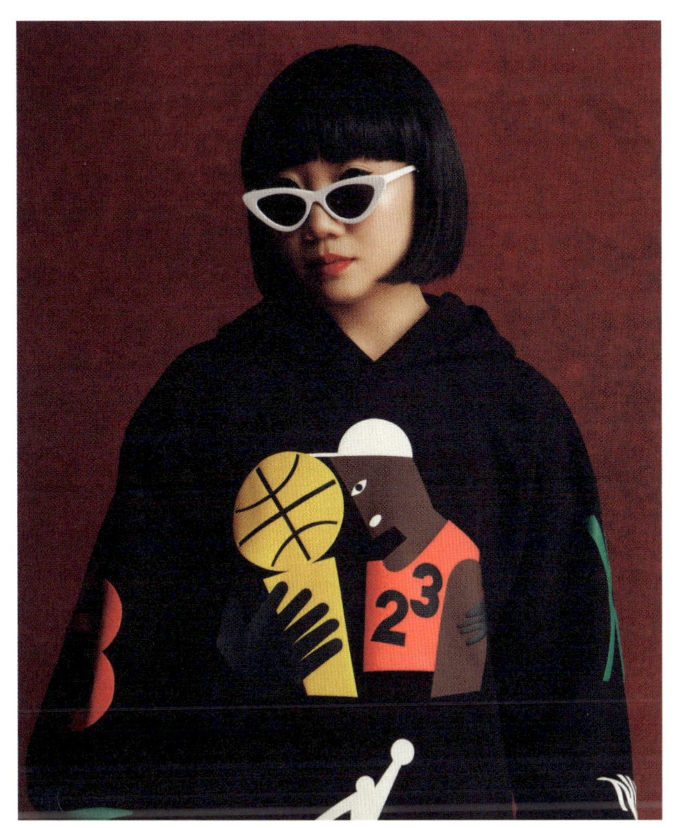

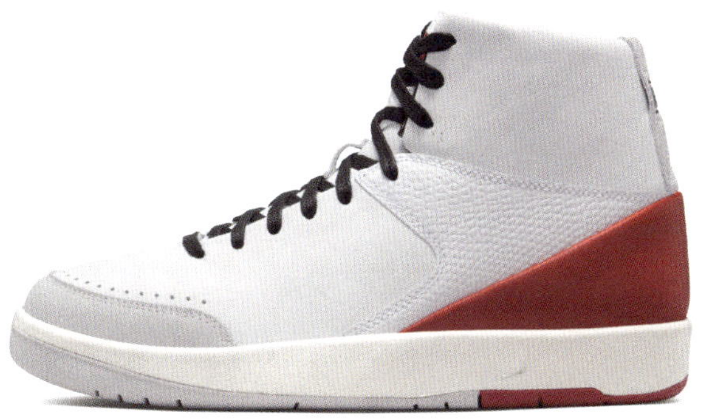

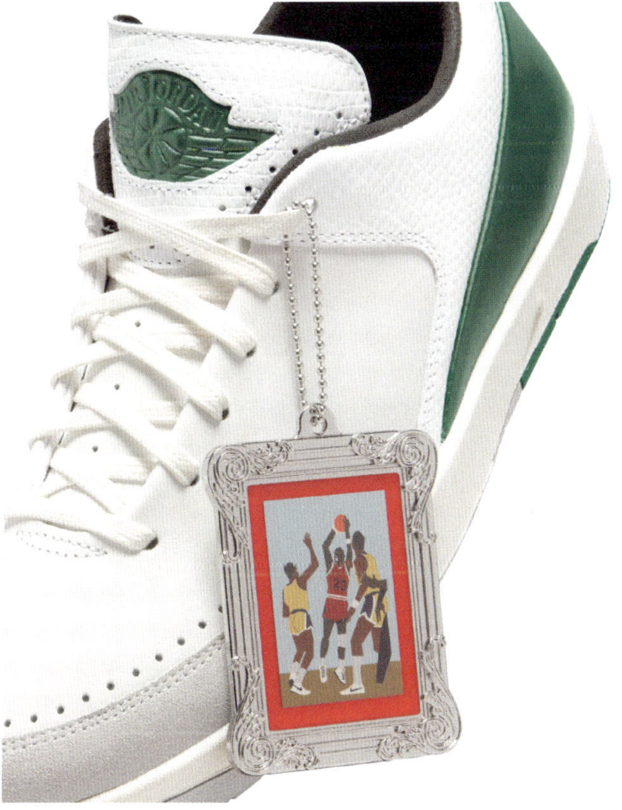

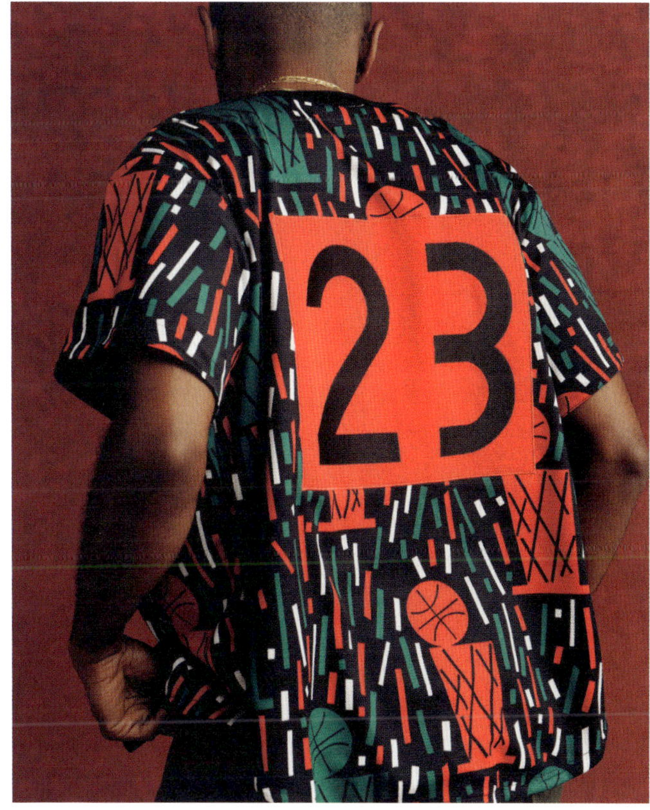

[OPPOSITE & ABOVE] Air Jordan 2 × Nina Chanel Abney, 2022

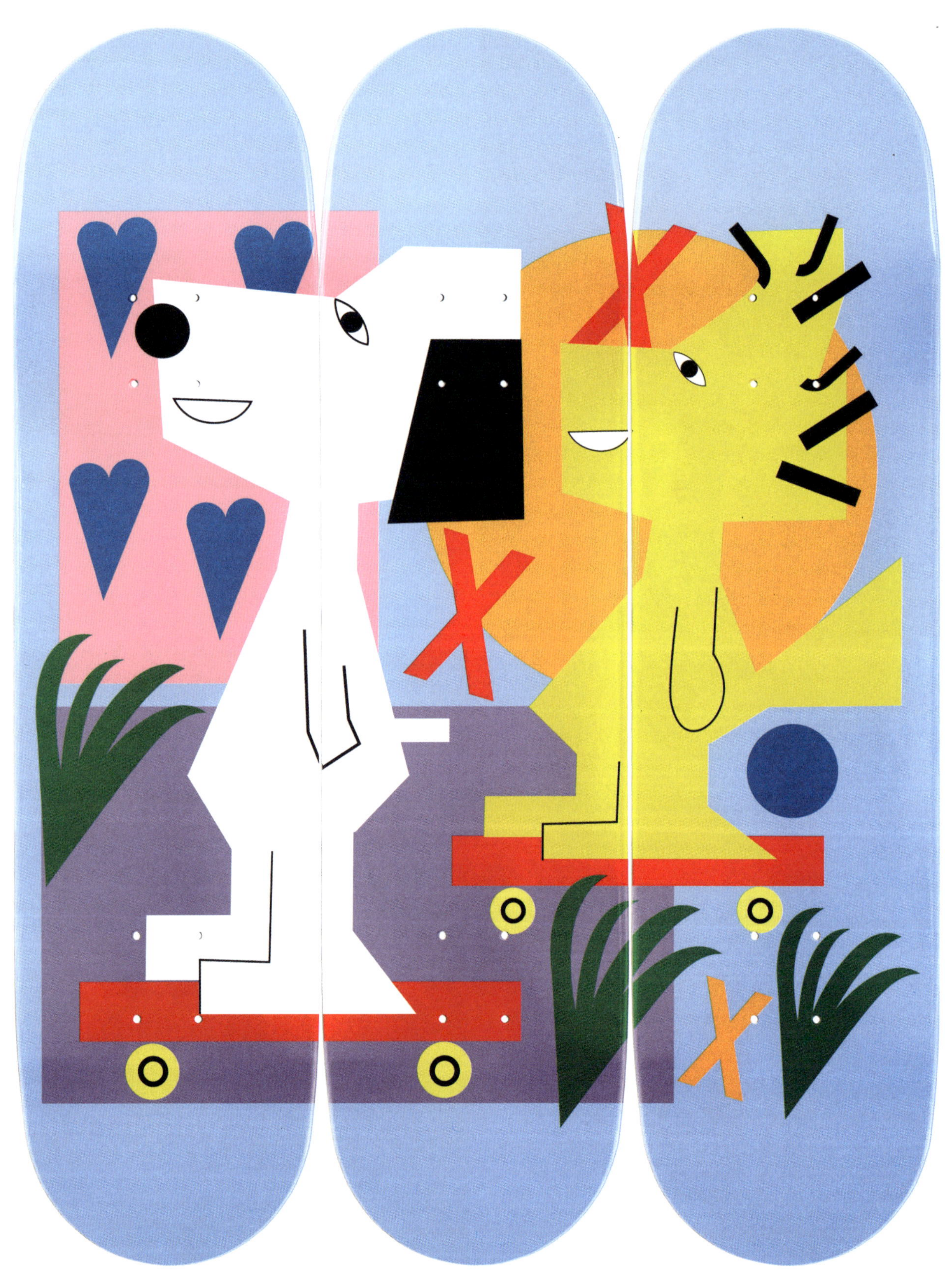

Peanuts (Triptych), 2020, The Peanuts Global Artist Collective, Produced by The Skateroom

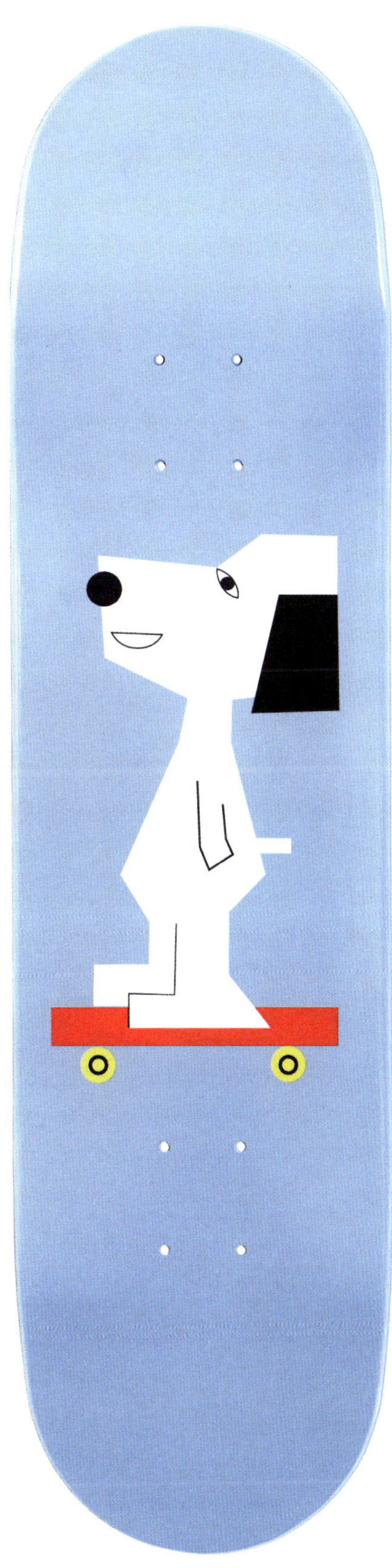

HUF × STORY × PEANUTS × SKATE DECK, 2018

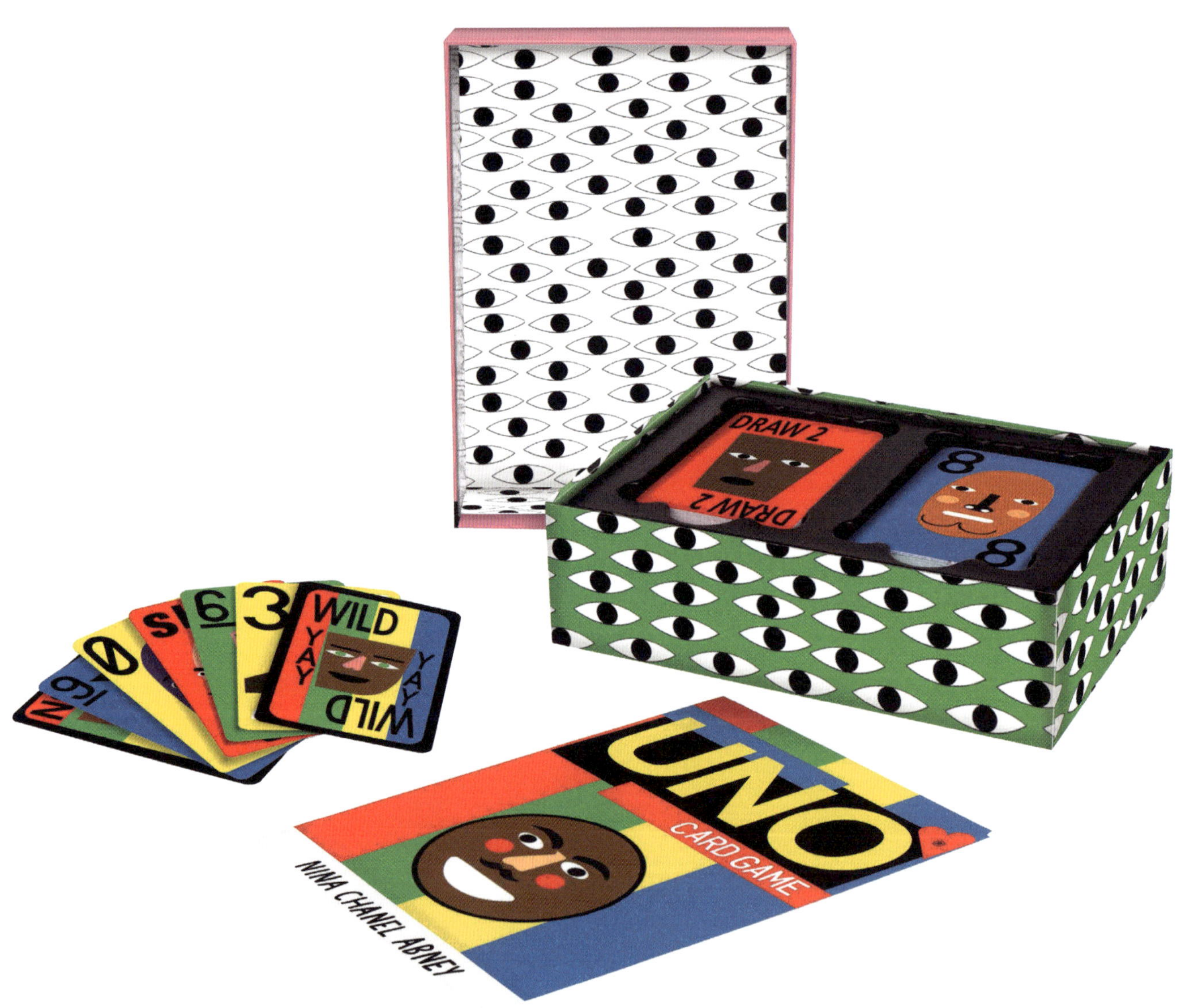

UNO® Artiste: Nina Chanel Abney, 2020

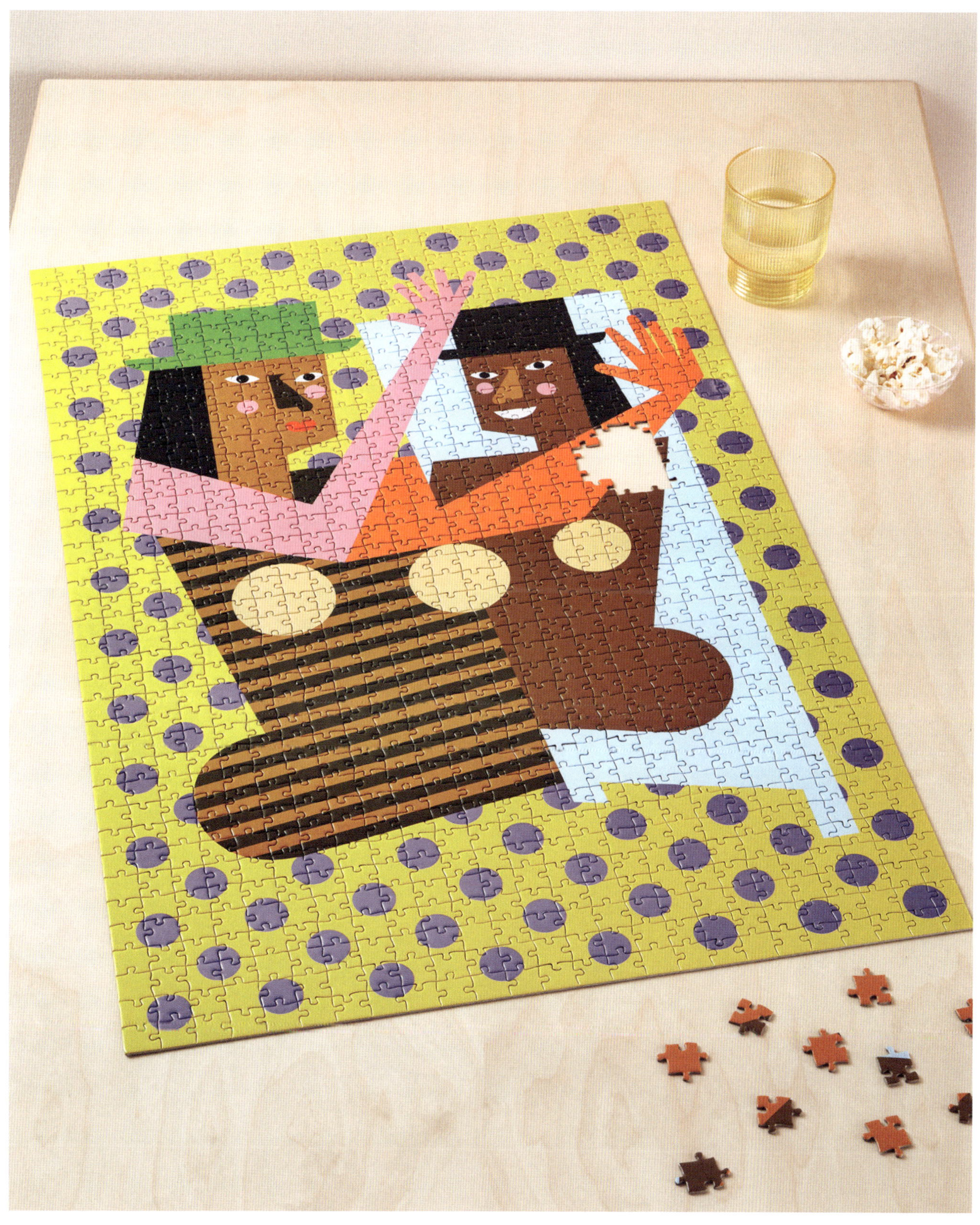

MoMA Exclusive: Nina Chanel Abney Jigsaw Puzzle, 2022

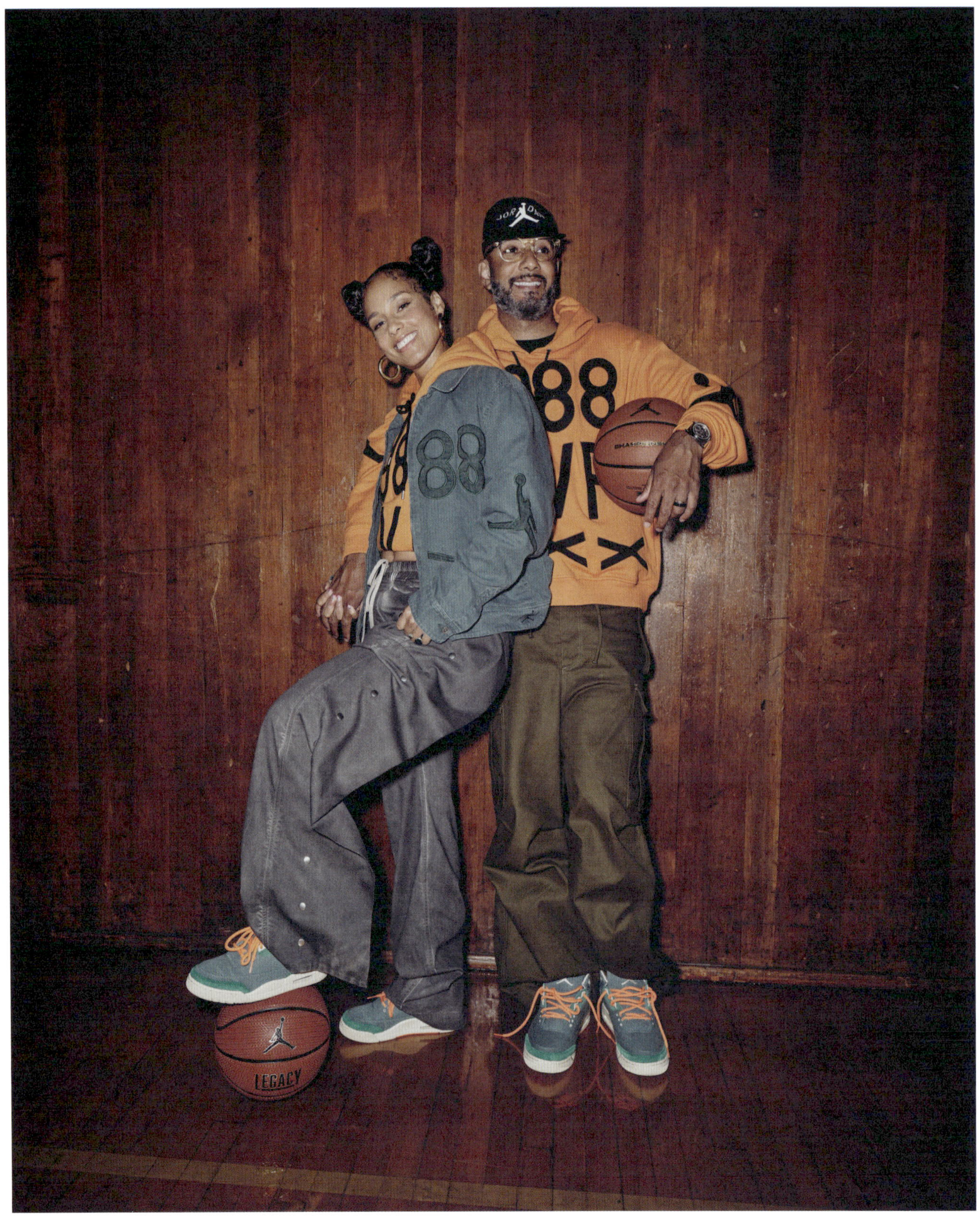

Air Jordan 3 Retro × Nina Chanel Abney, 2024

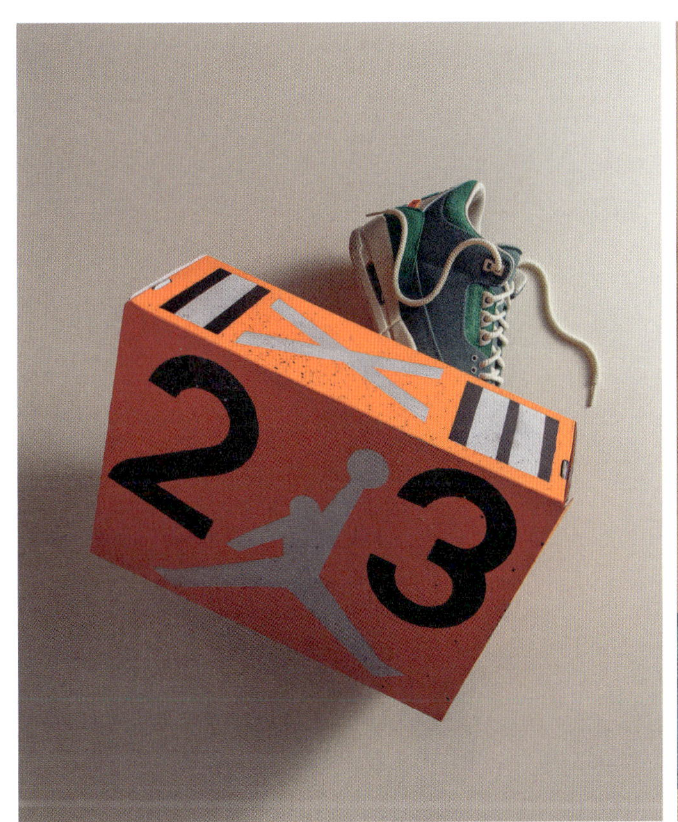
23

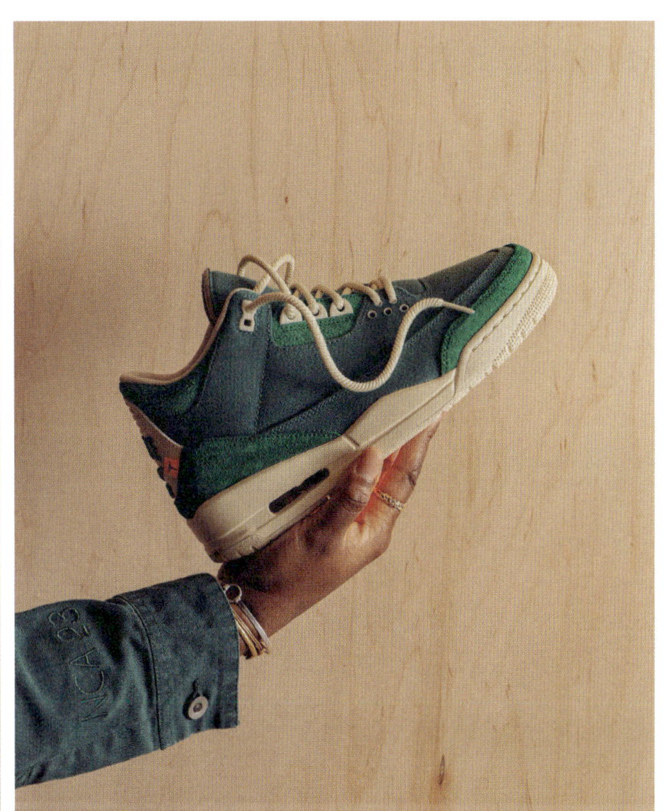

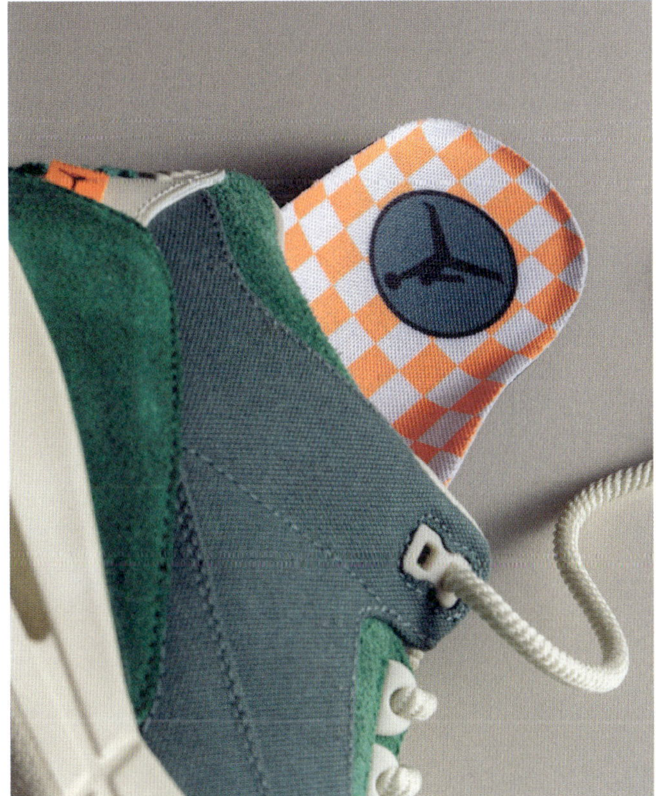

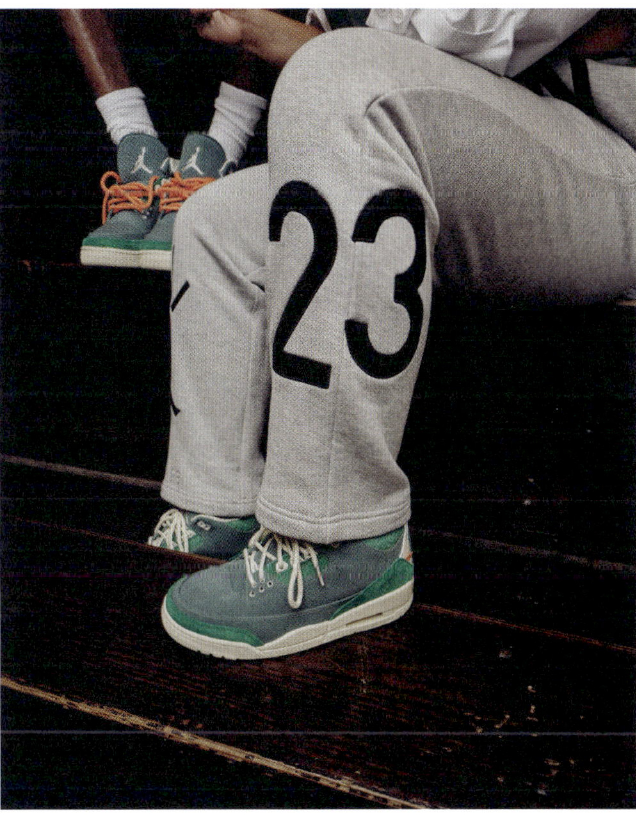
23

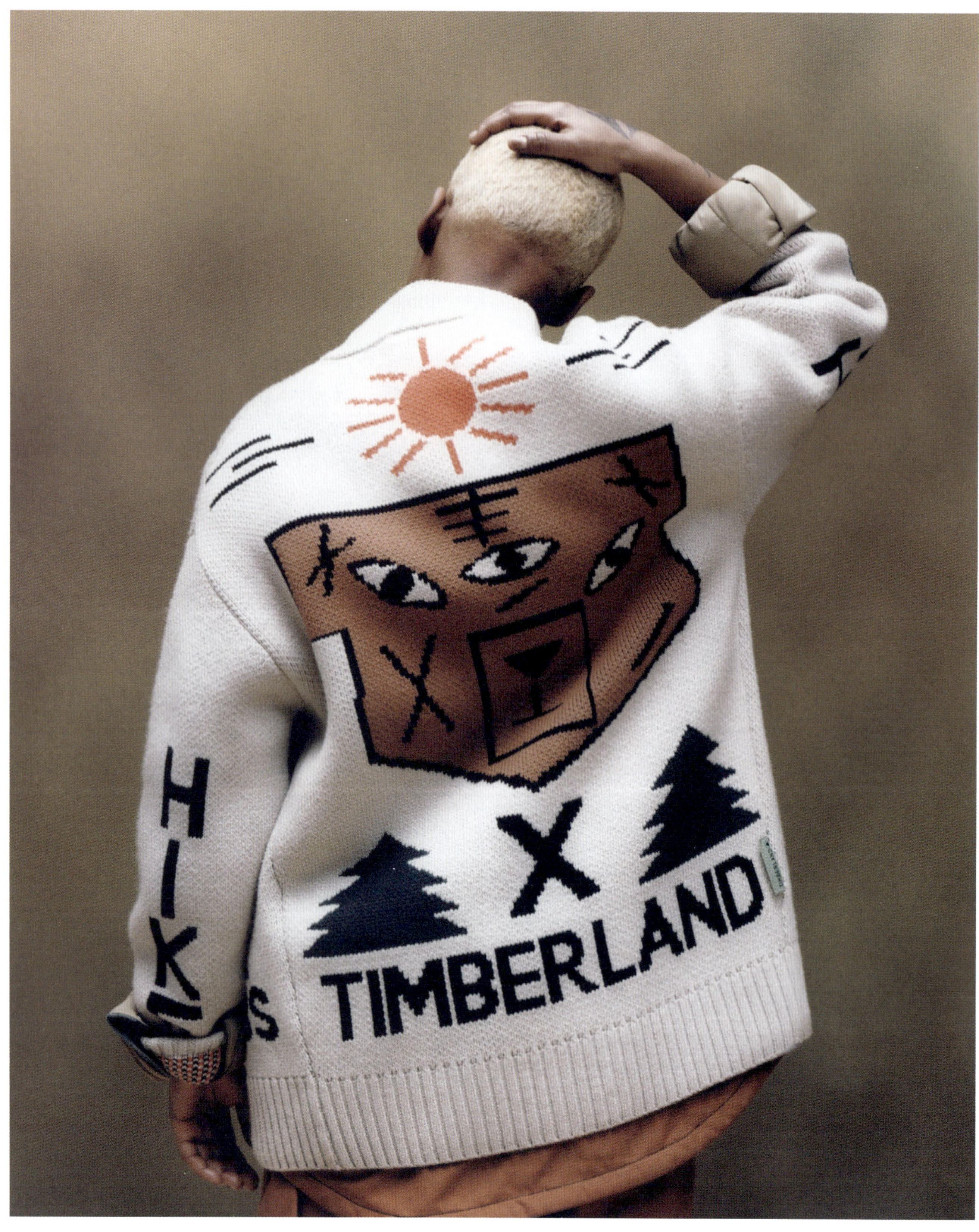

Timberland® × Nina Chanel Abney Future73 Collection, 2023

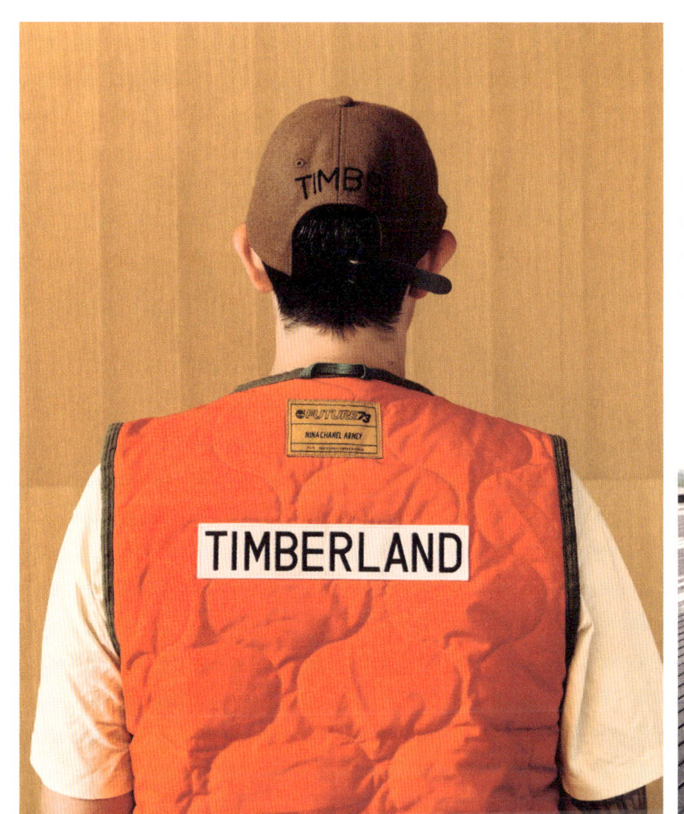
TIMBERLAND

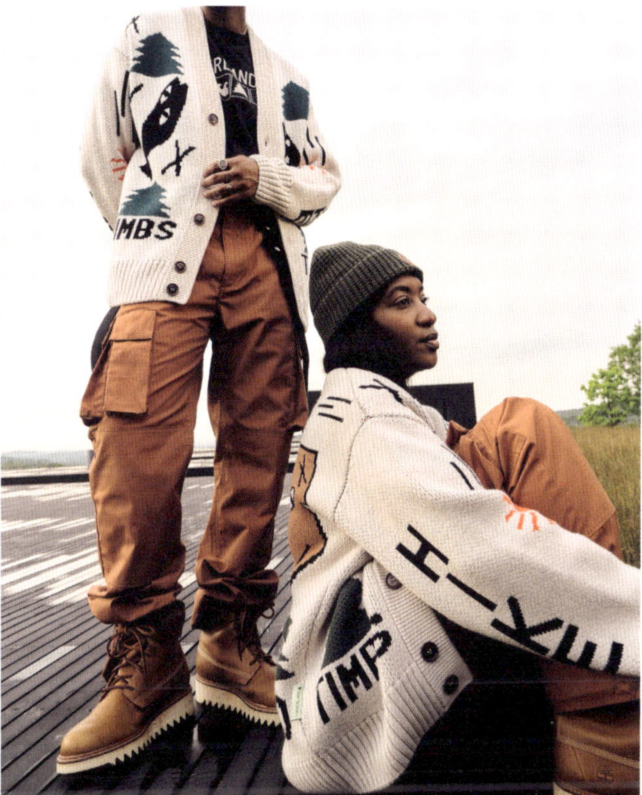

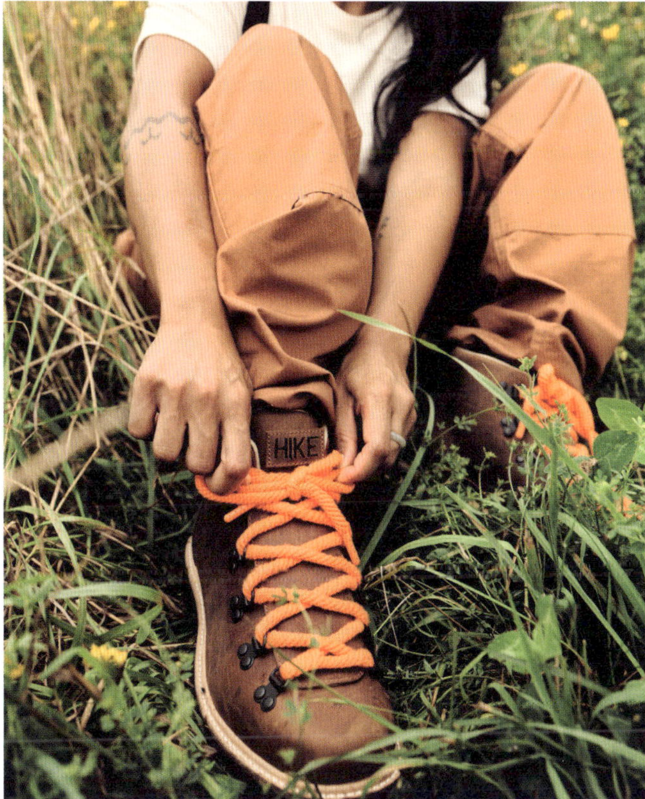
HIKE

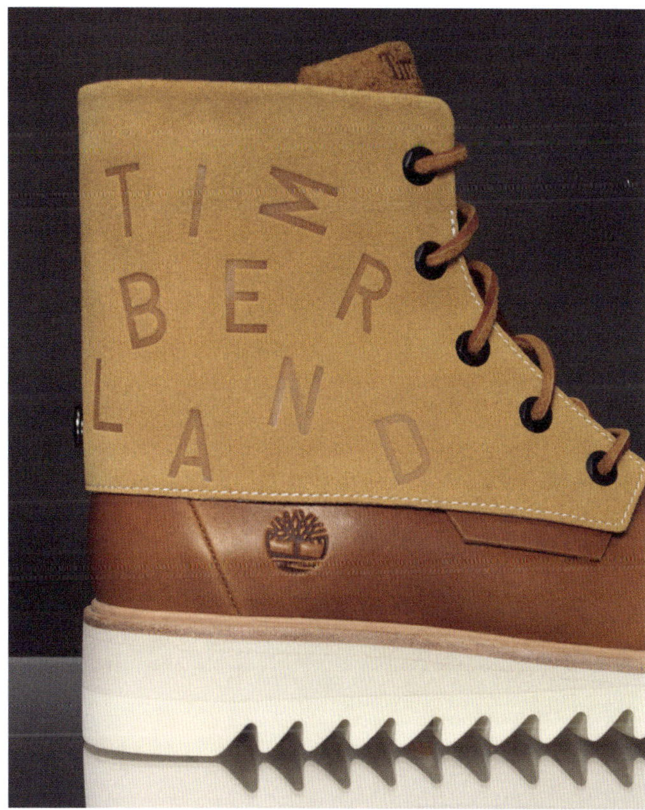
TIM
BER
LAND

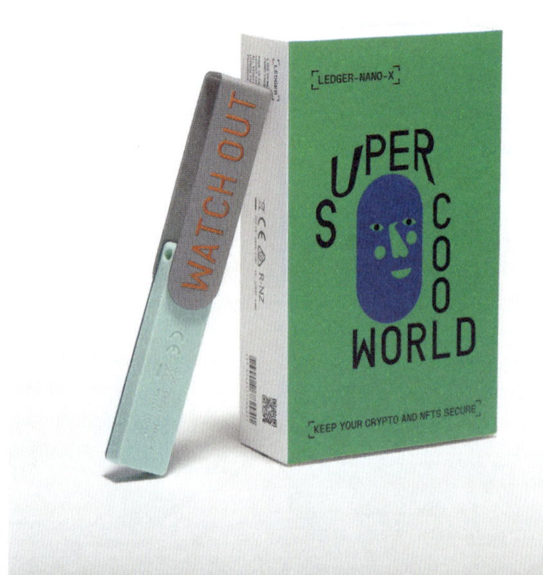

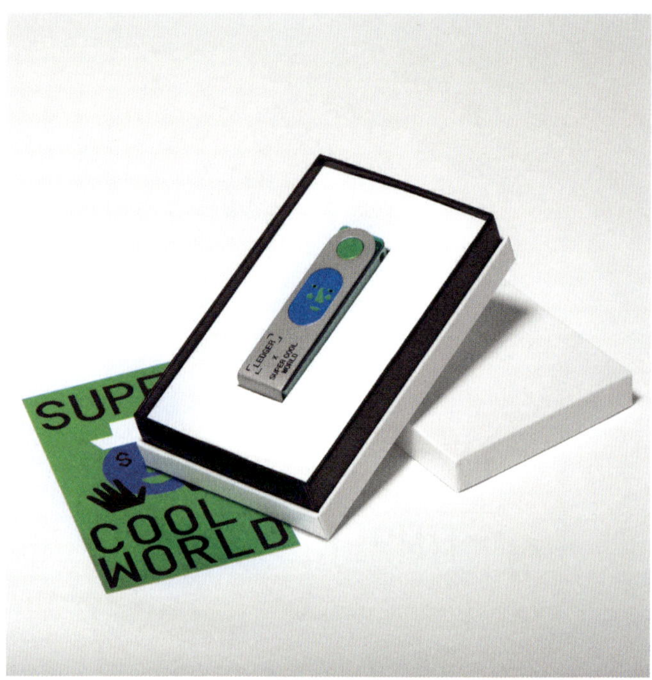

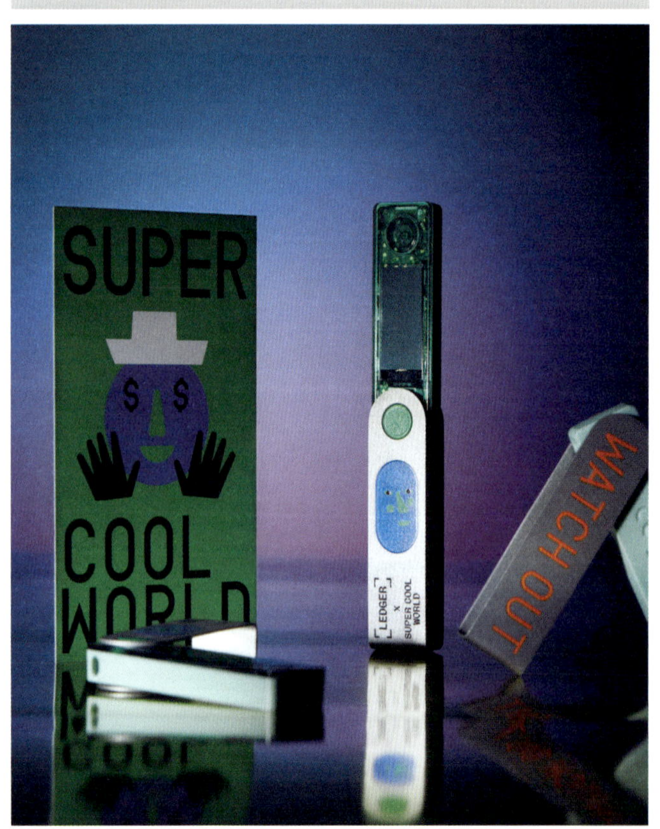

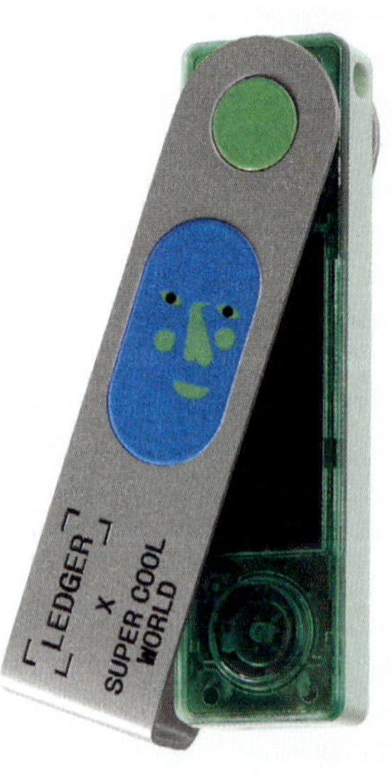

Super Cool World × Ledger Nano X, 2022

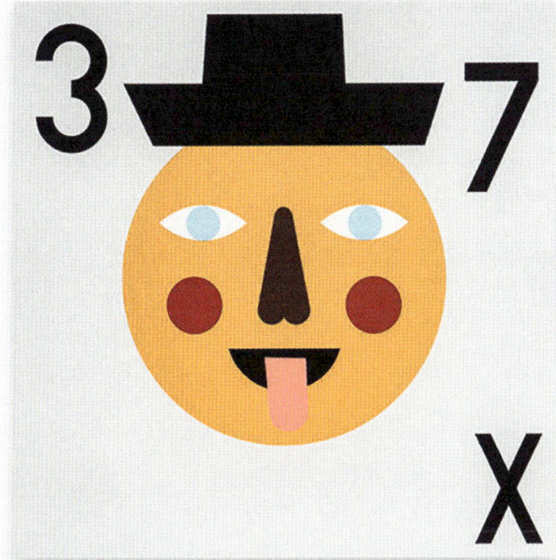

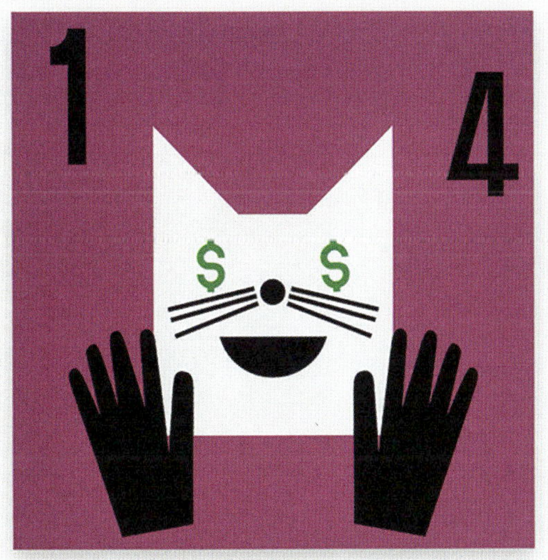

Avante Art, Super Cool World Prints, 2024

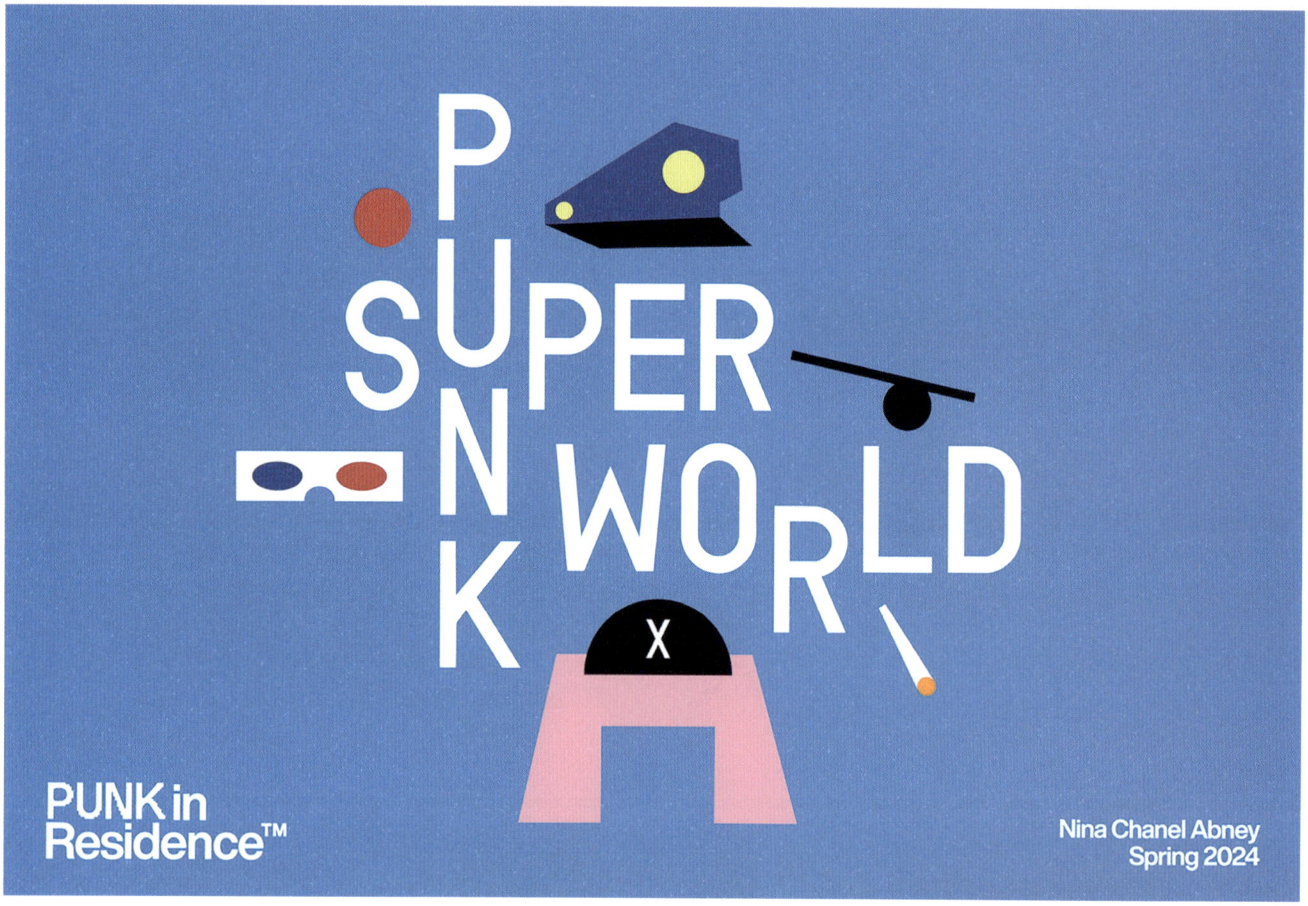

SUPER PUNK WORLD

PUNK in Residence™

Nina Chanel Abney
Spring 2024

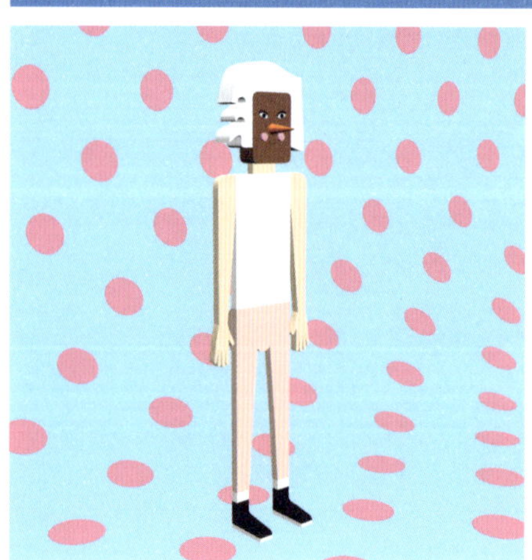

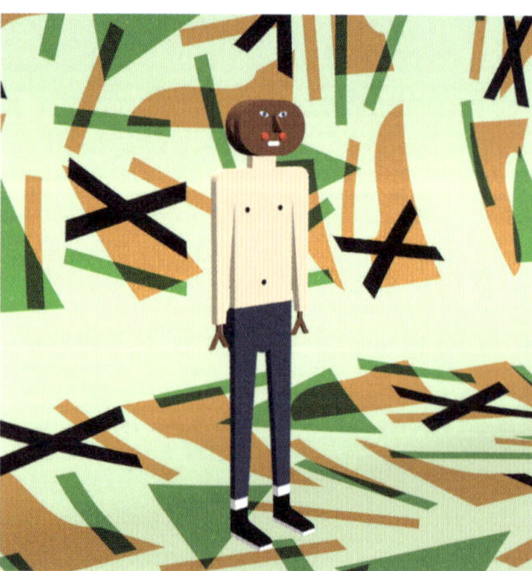

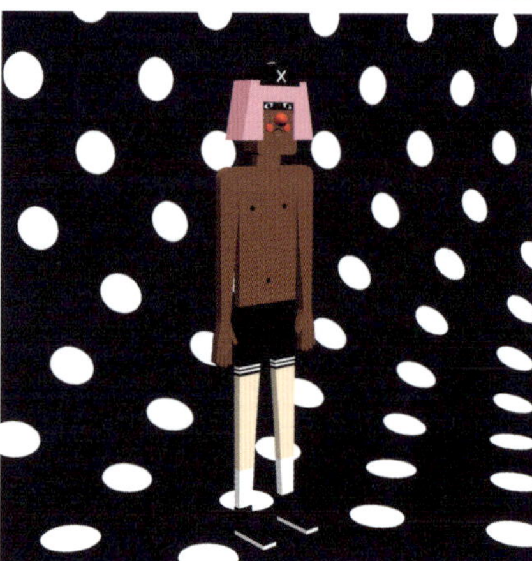

[TOP] Super Punk World logo, 2024
[BOTTOM, LEFT TO RIGHT] Super Punk World #276, #70, #10, 2024

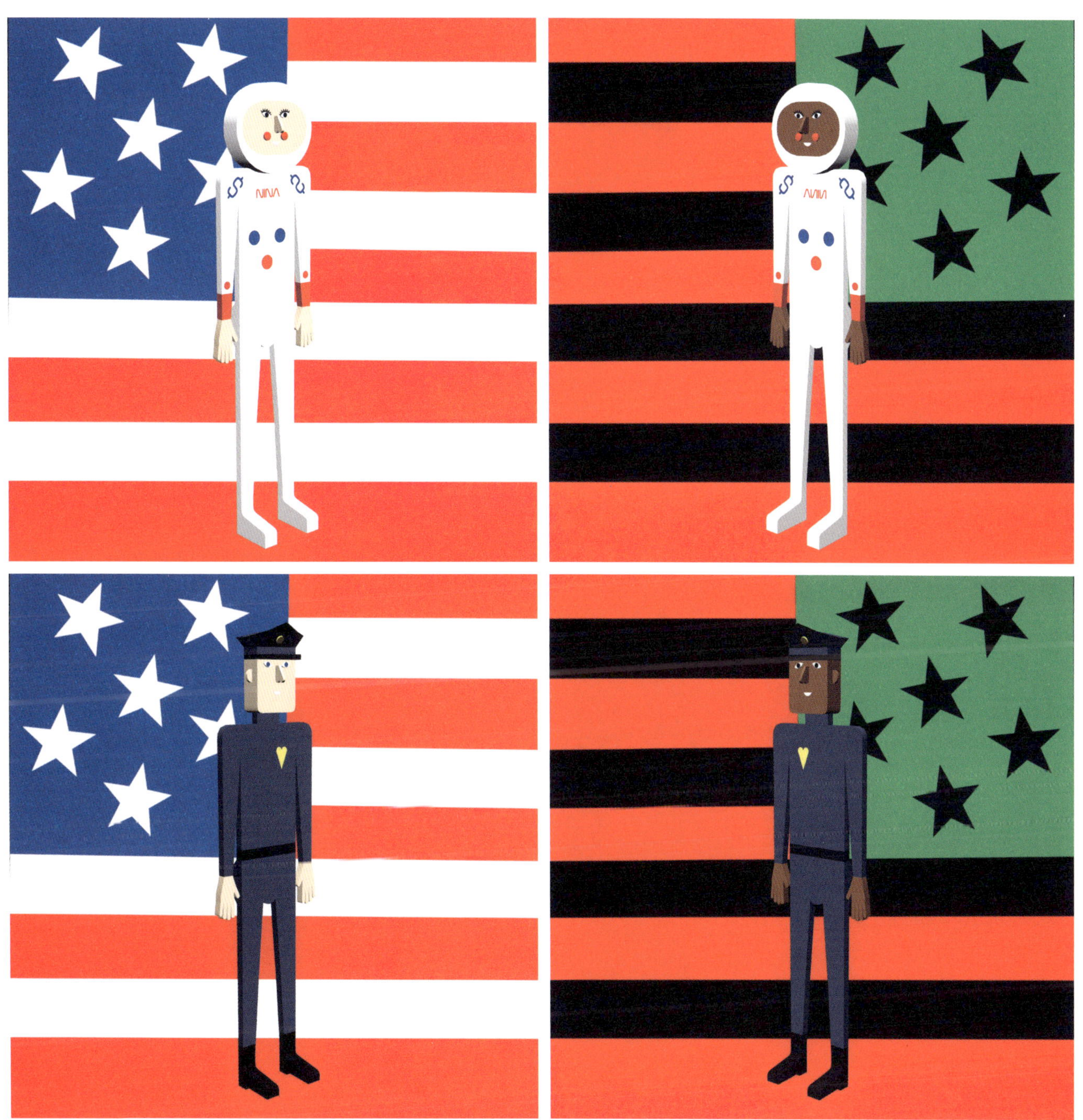

[TOP, LEFT TO RIGHT] Super Punk World Astronaut #1, #2, AP, 2024
[BOTTOM, LEFT TO RIGHT] Super Punk World Cop #2, #1, AP, 2024
[OVERLEAF] Baby, 2020

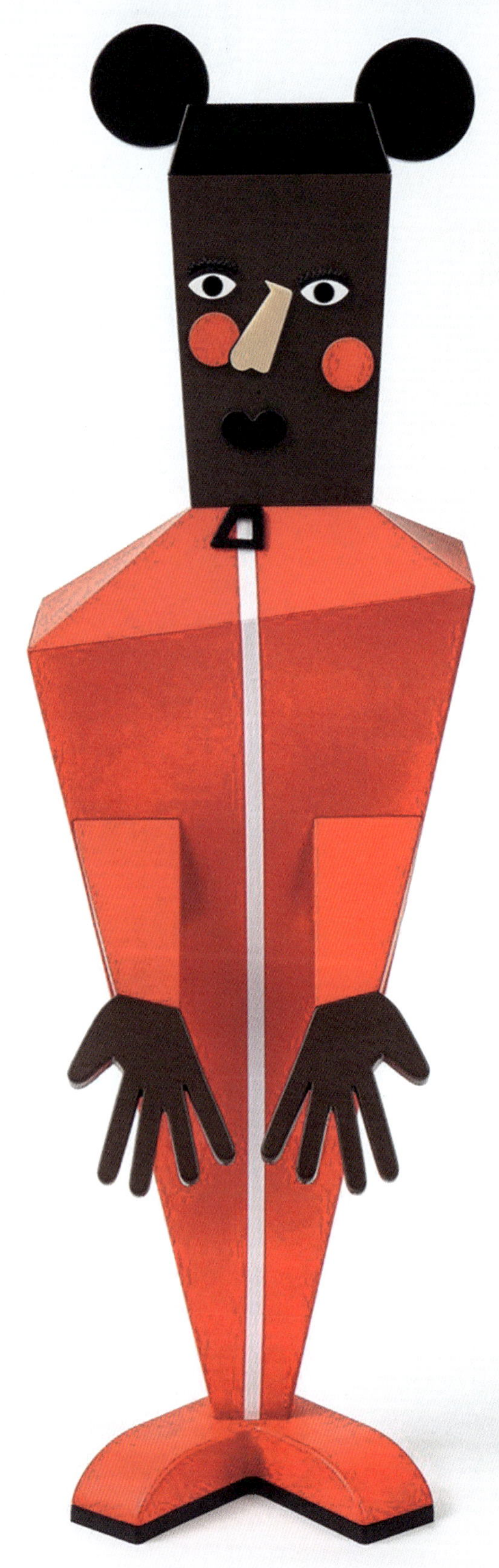

WORKS

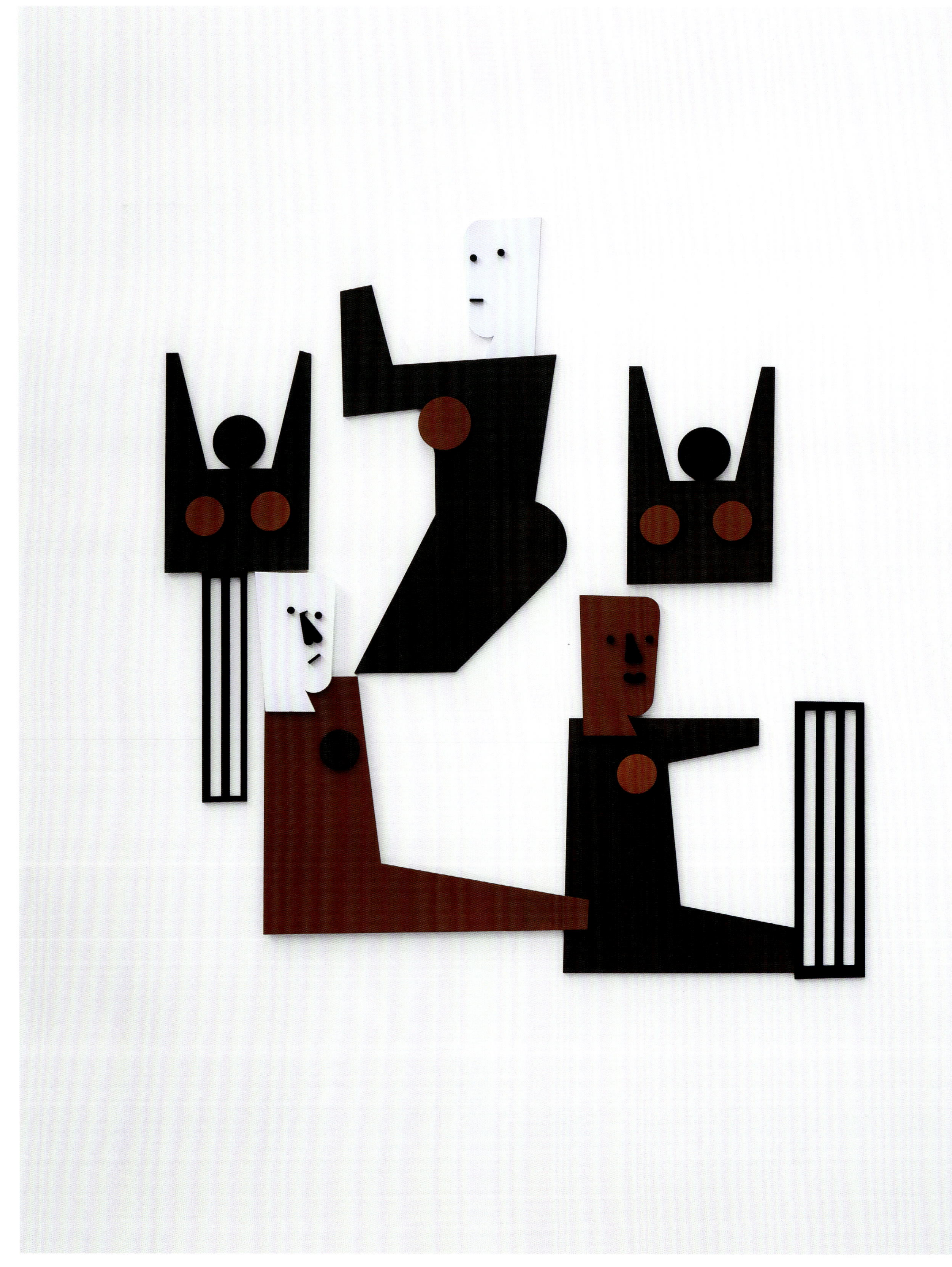

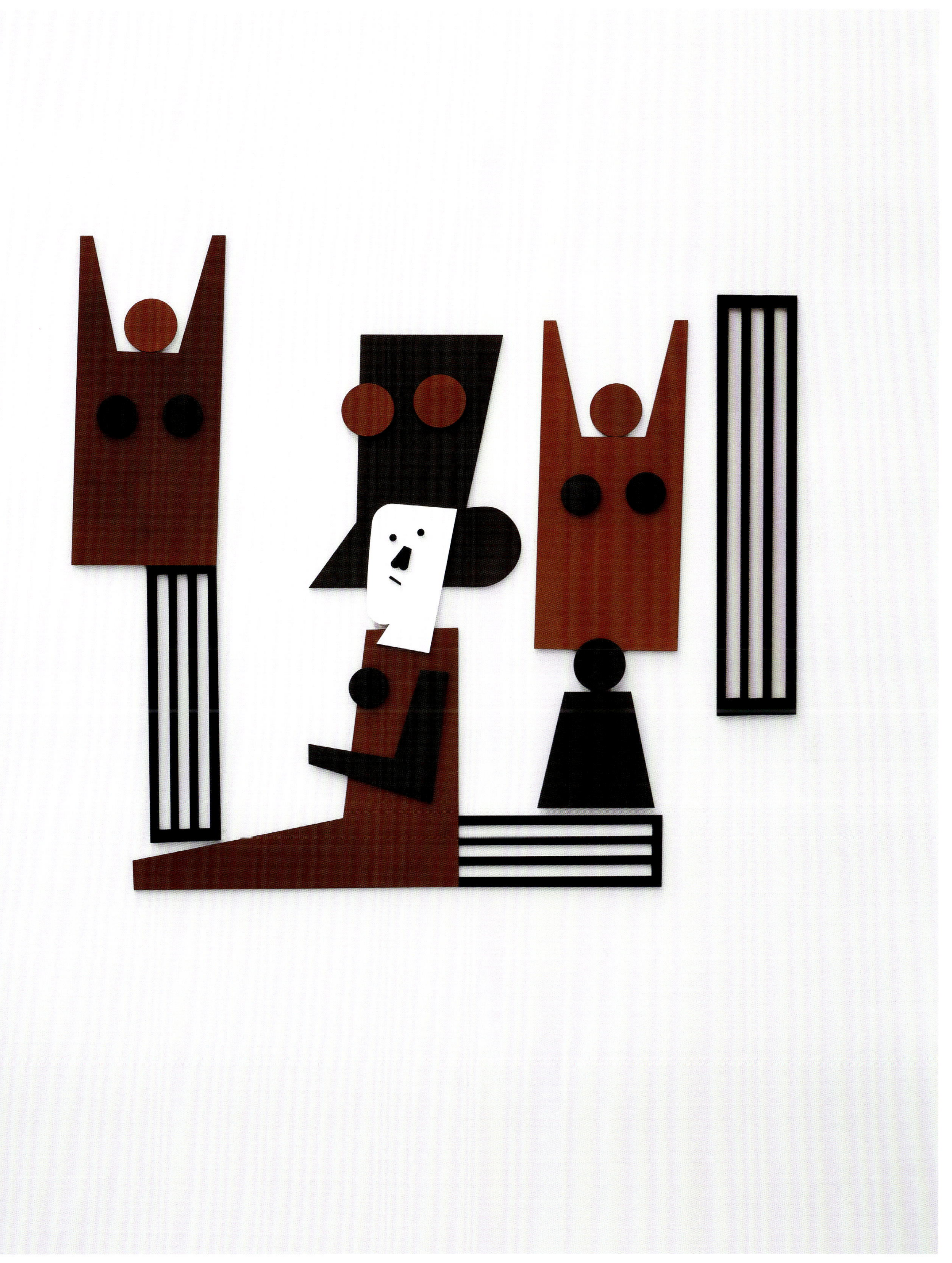

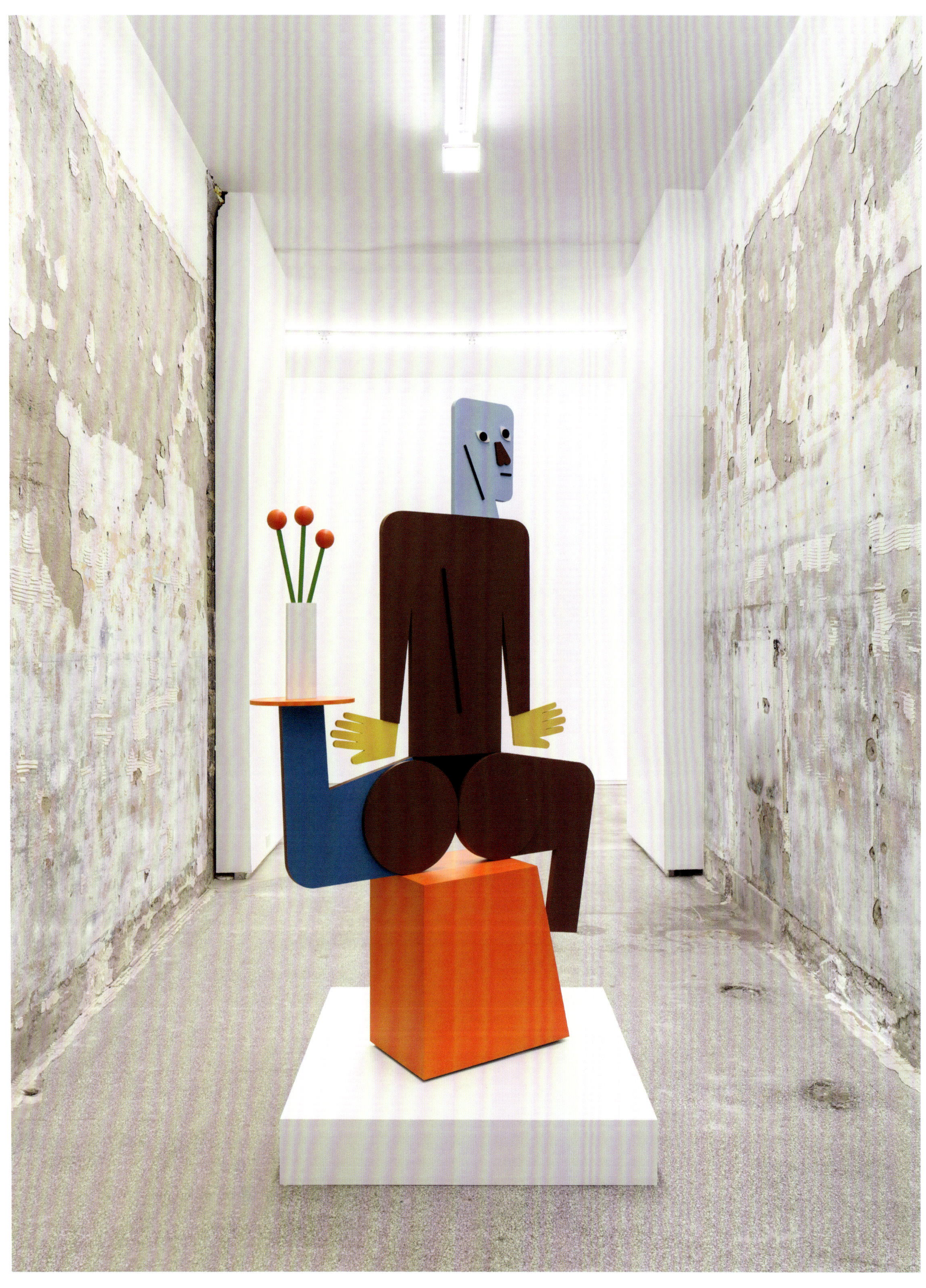

[PREVIOUS] Gated Community, 2024
[ABOVE & OPPOSITE] The Qing, 2024 (multiple views)

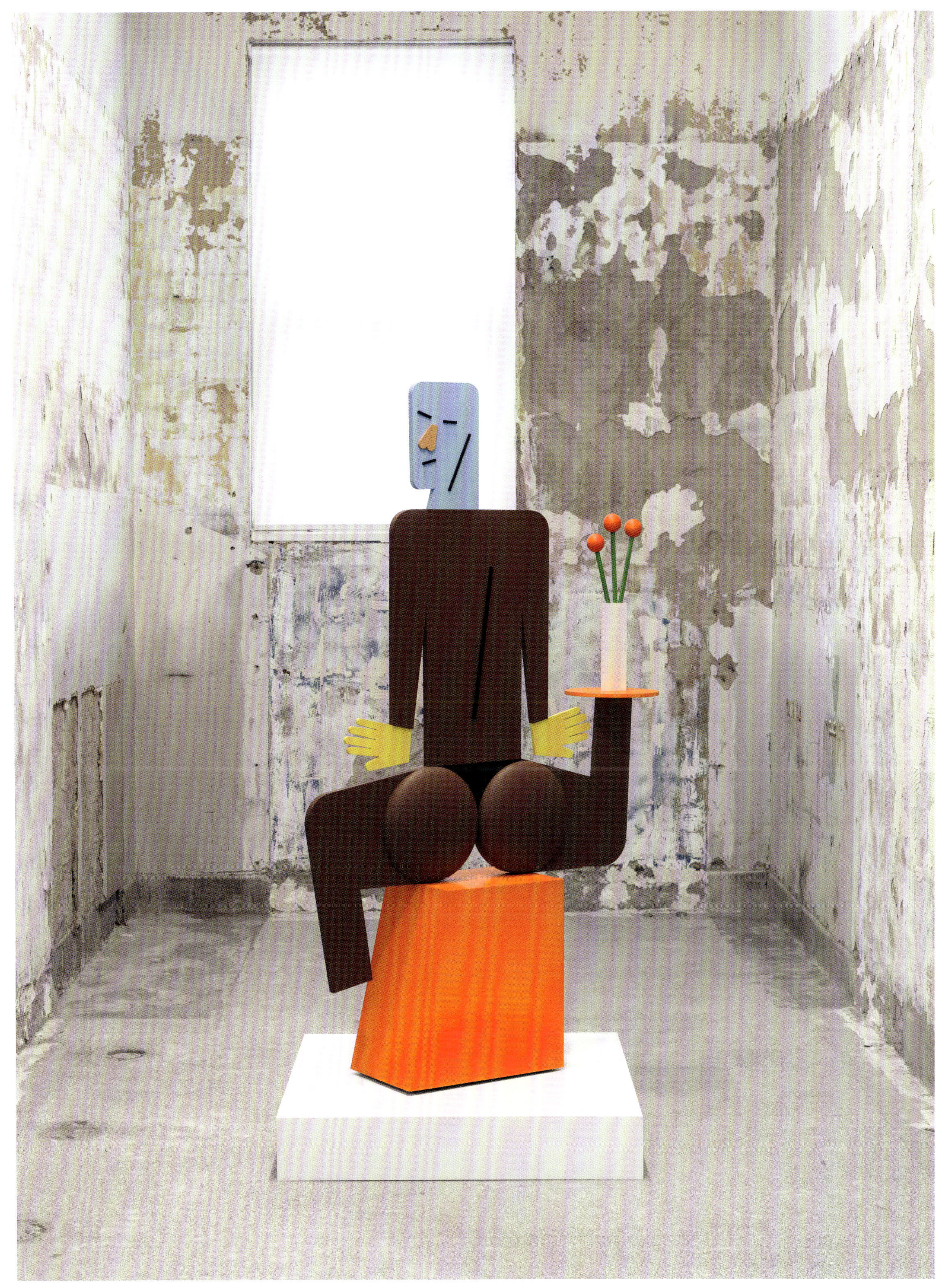

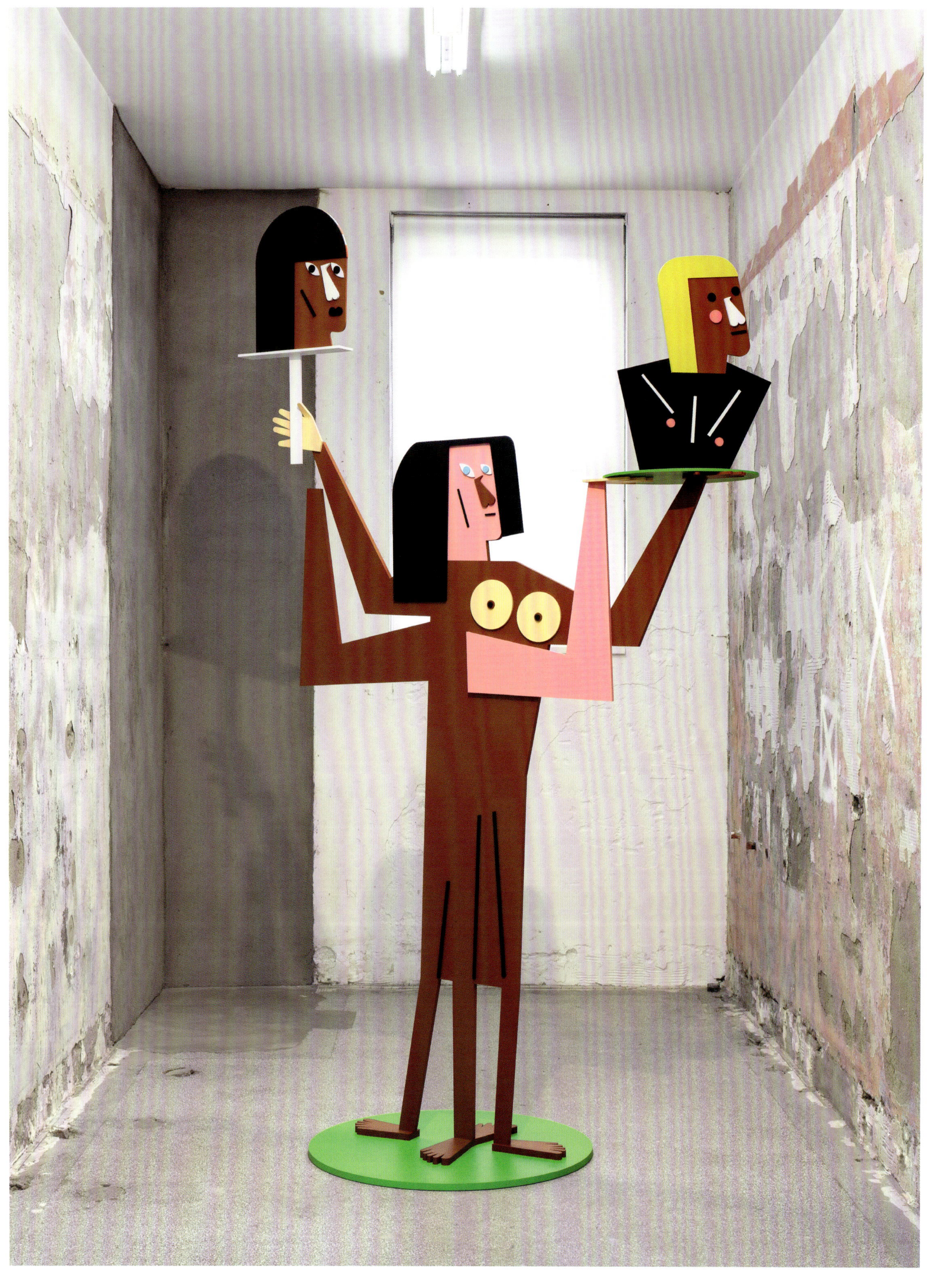

[ABOVE & OPPOSITE] TOK, 2024 (multiple views)

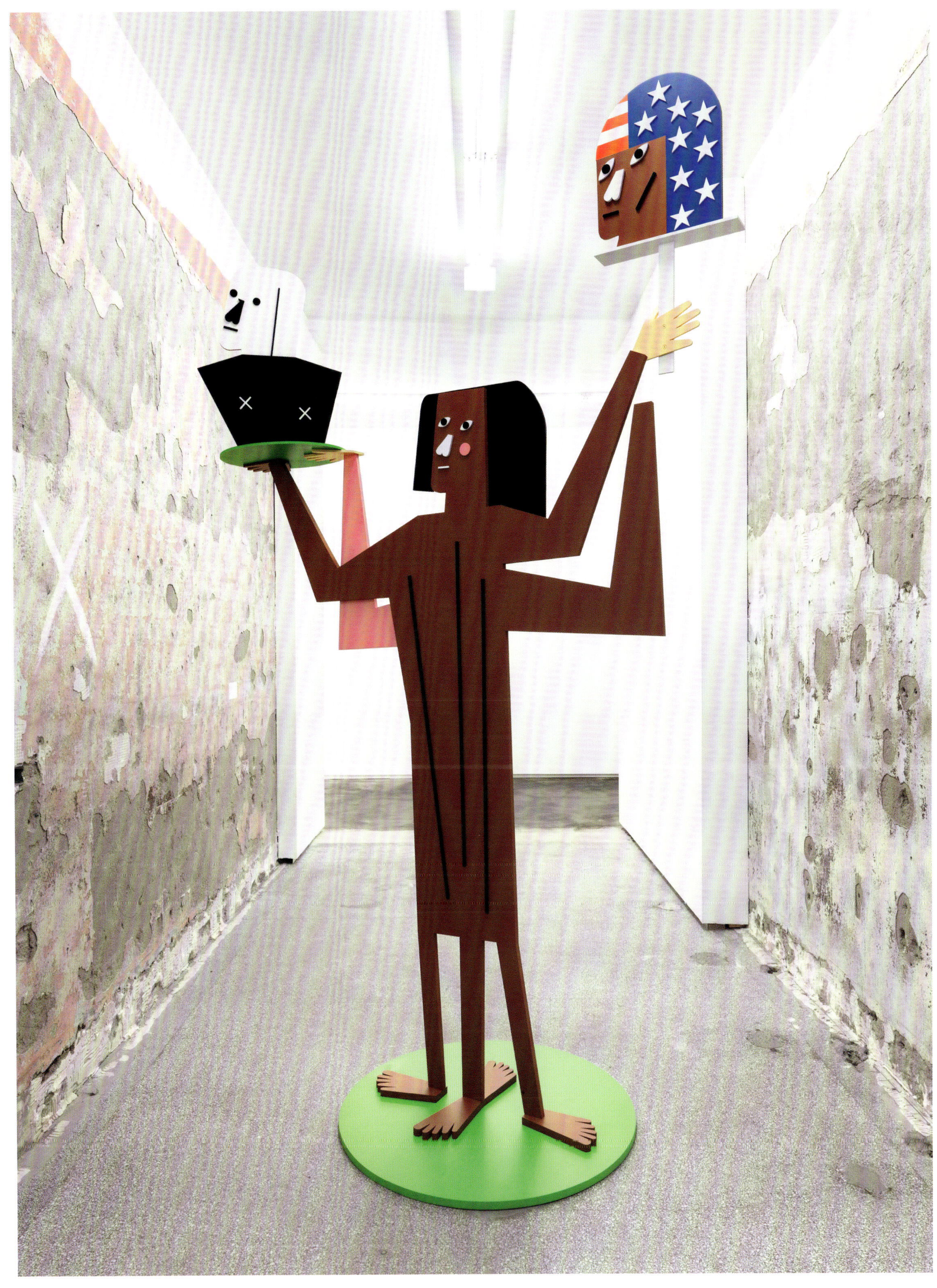

[OVERLEAF] Installation view, Soup Kitchen, 2024

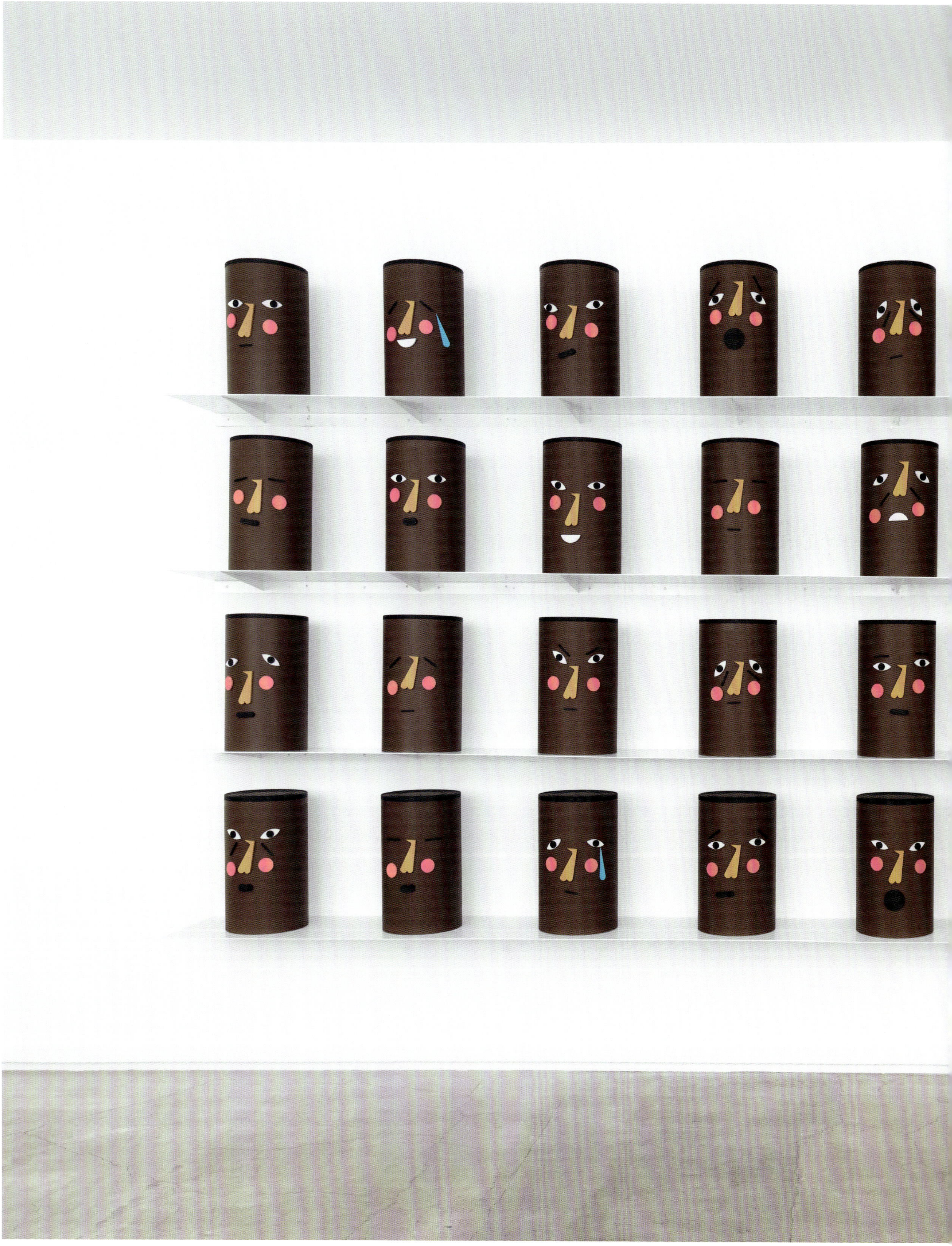

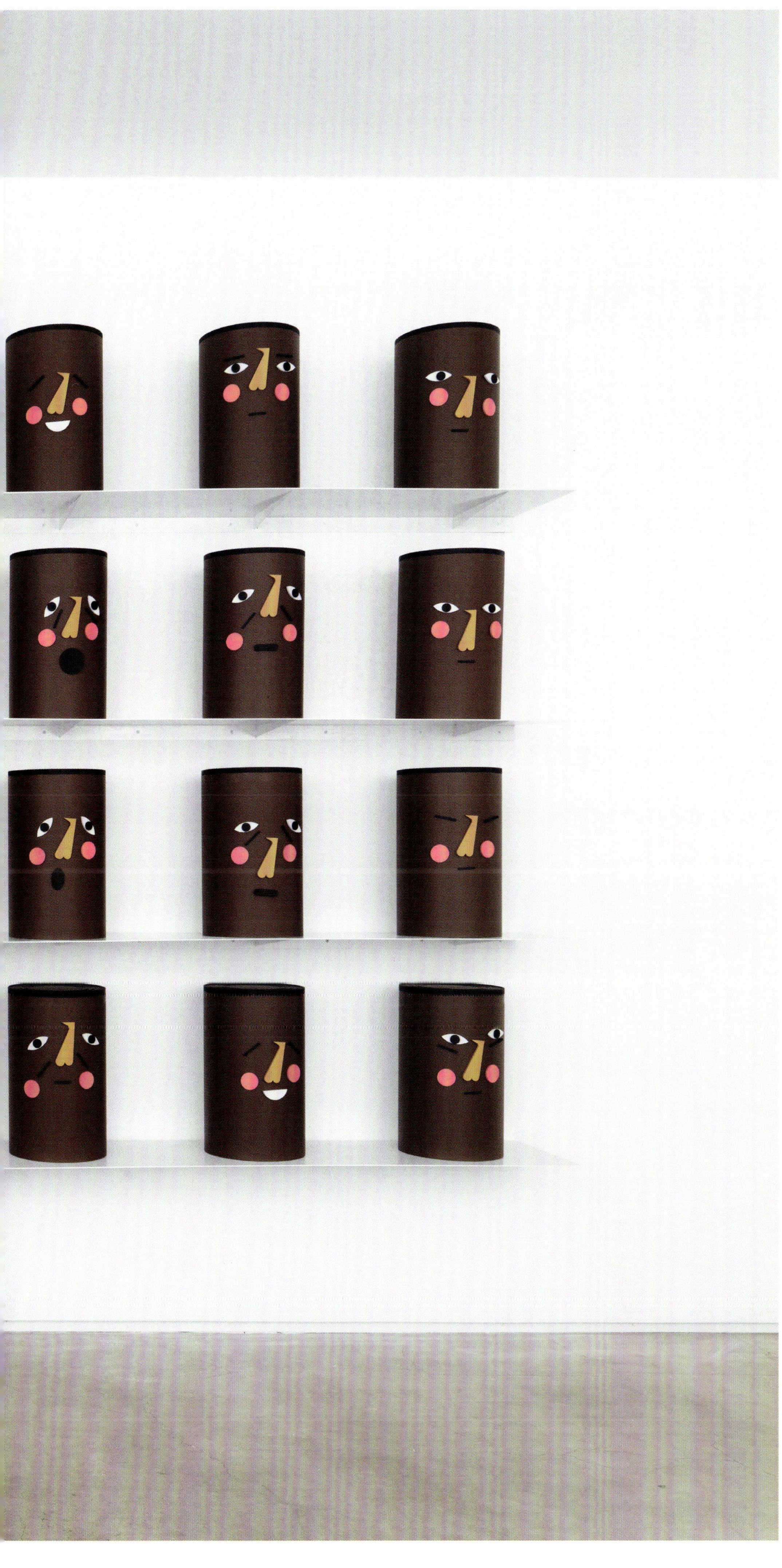

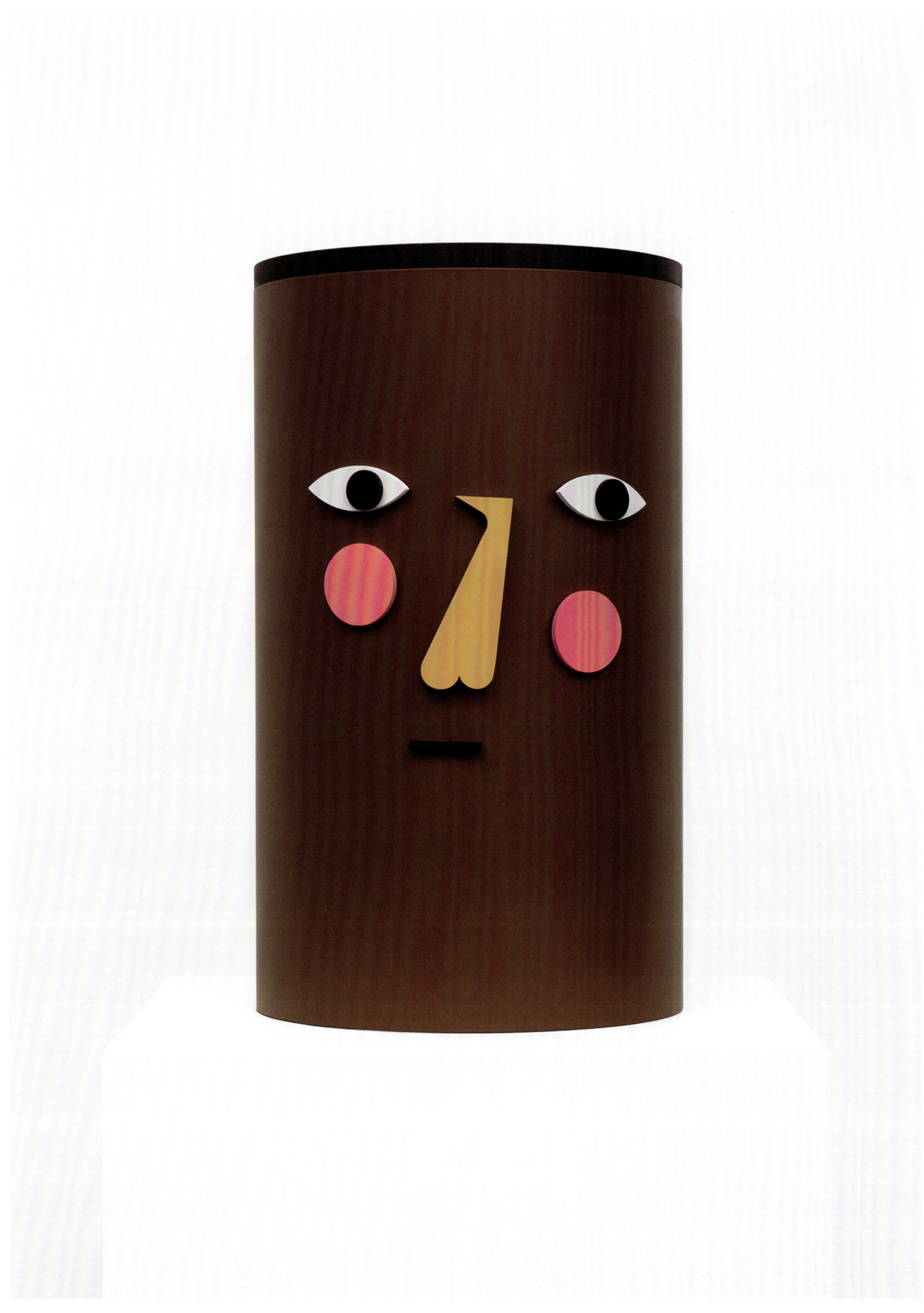

Soup Kitchen 1, 2024

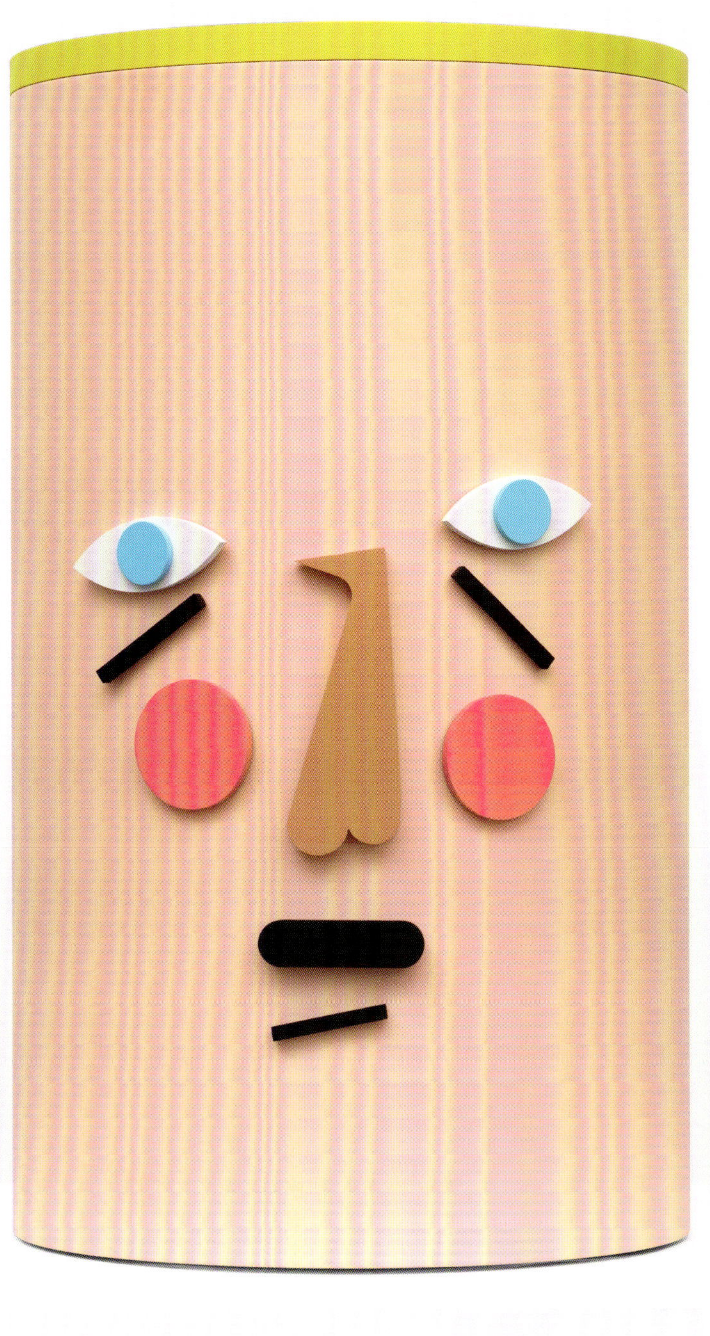

Soup Kitchen 34, 2024

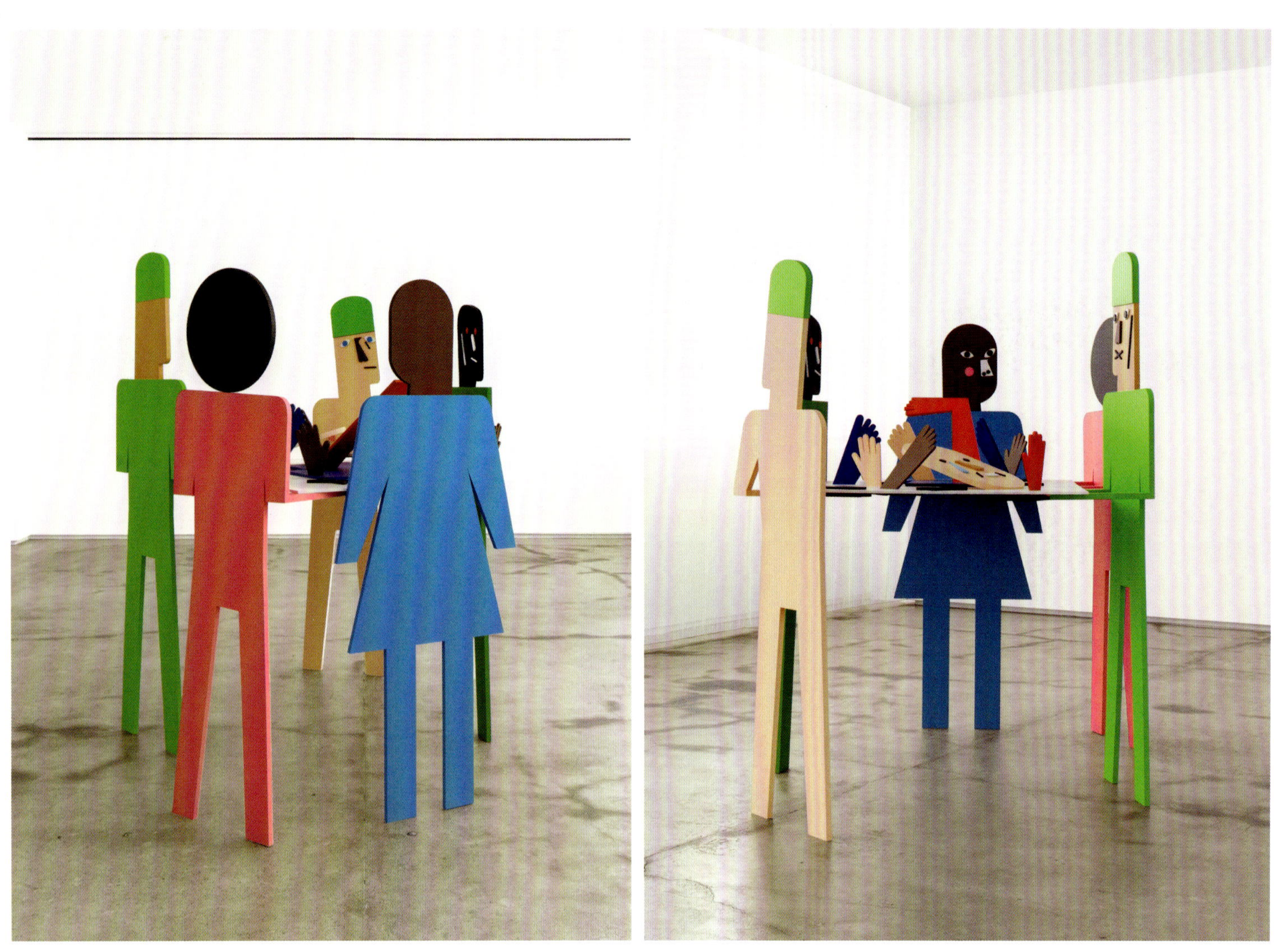

[ABOVE] Four and a Possible, 2024 (multiple views)
[OPPOSITE] Pursuit of Happiness, 2025

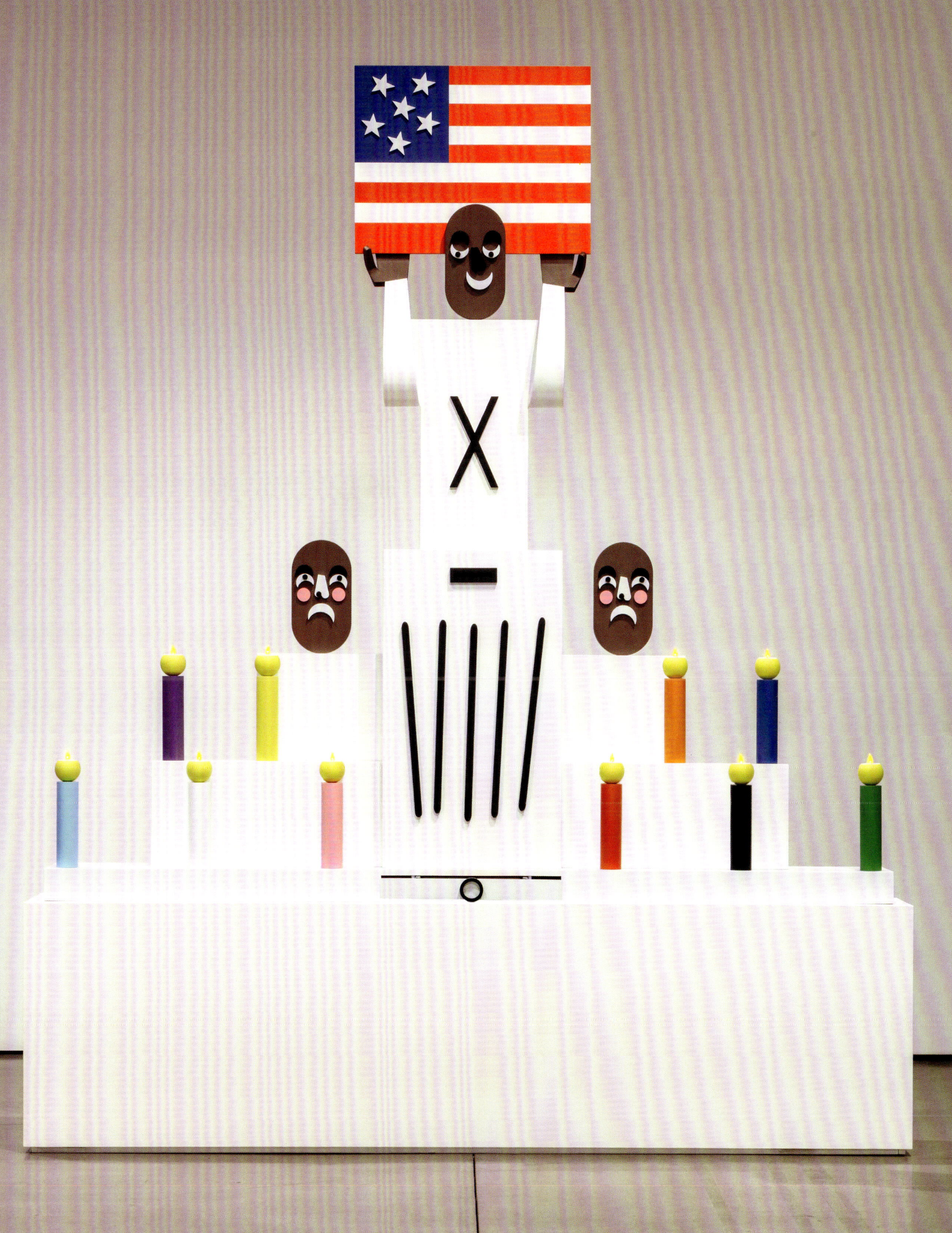

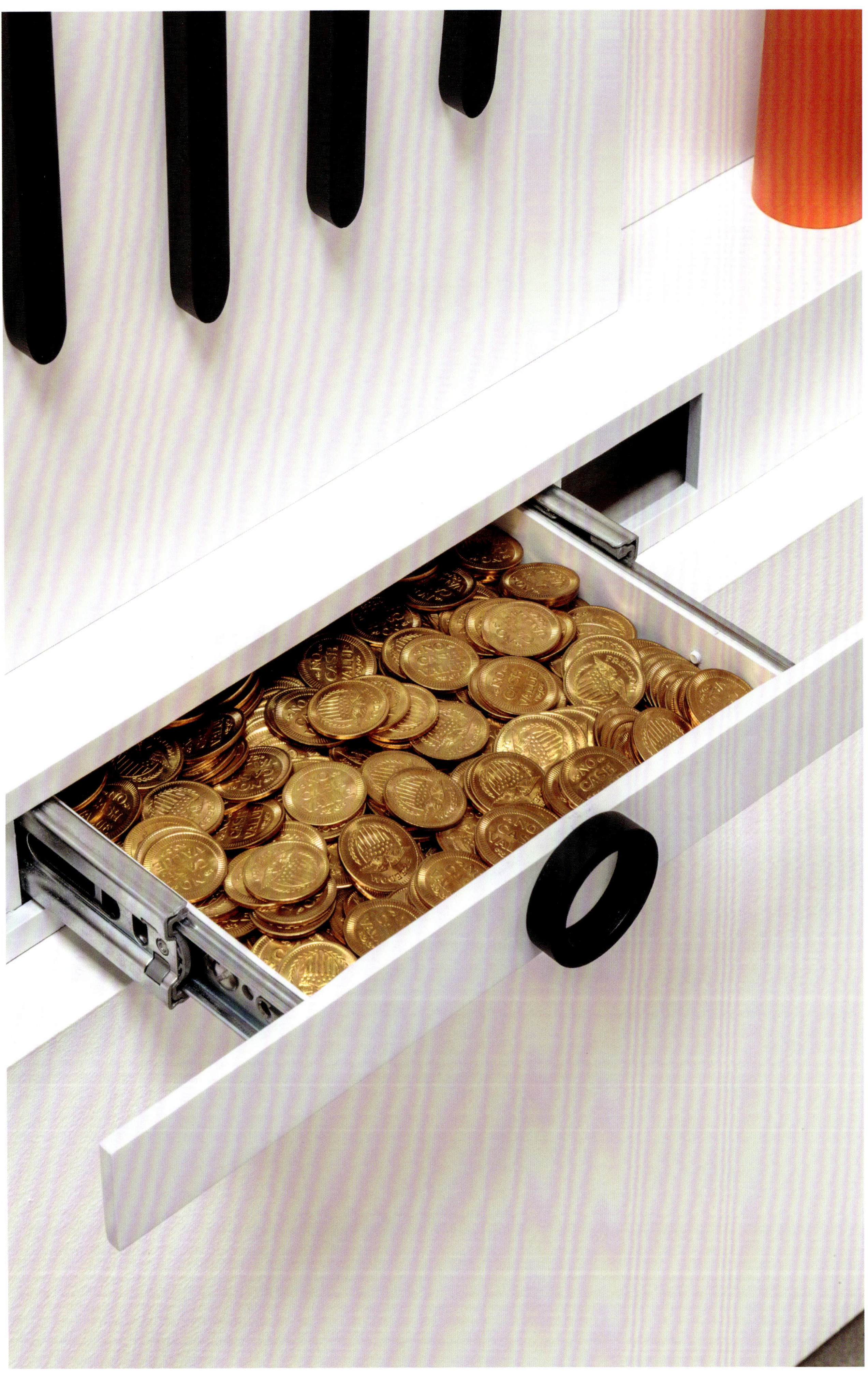

Detail, Pursuit of Happiness, 2025

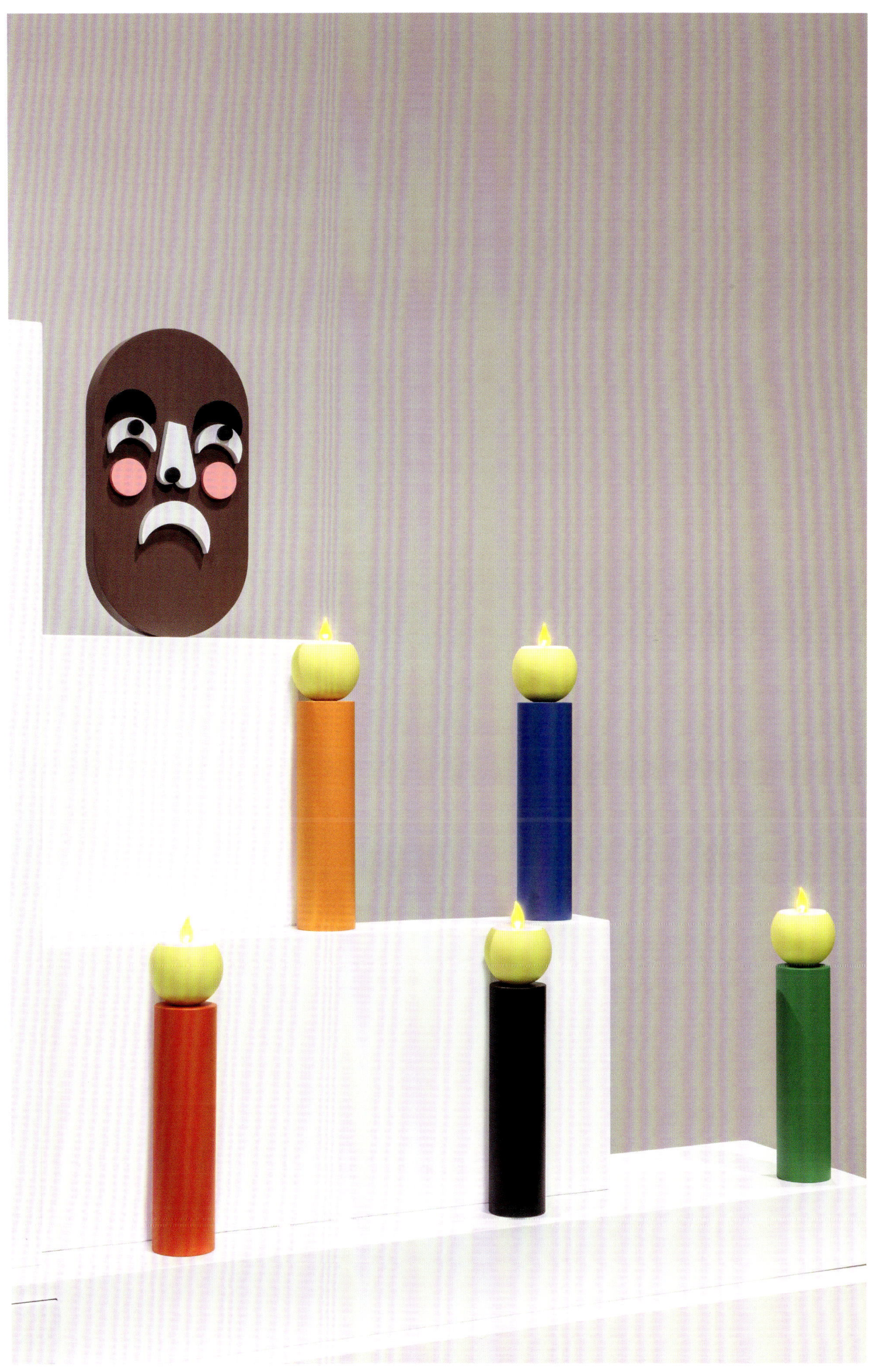

Detail, Pursuit of Happiness, 2025

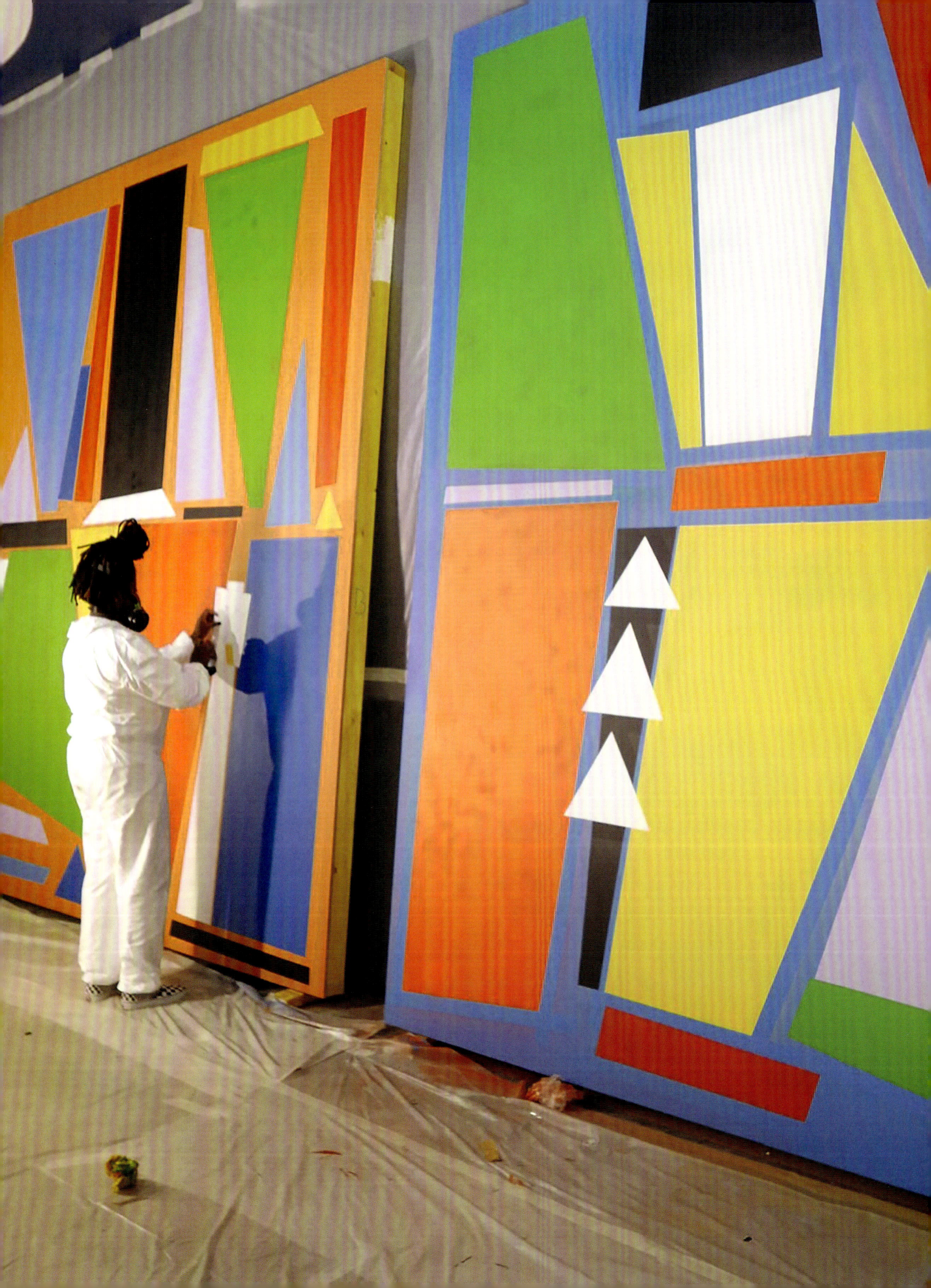

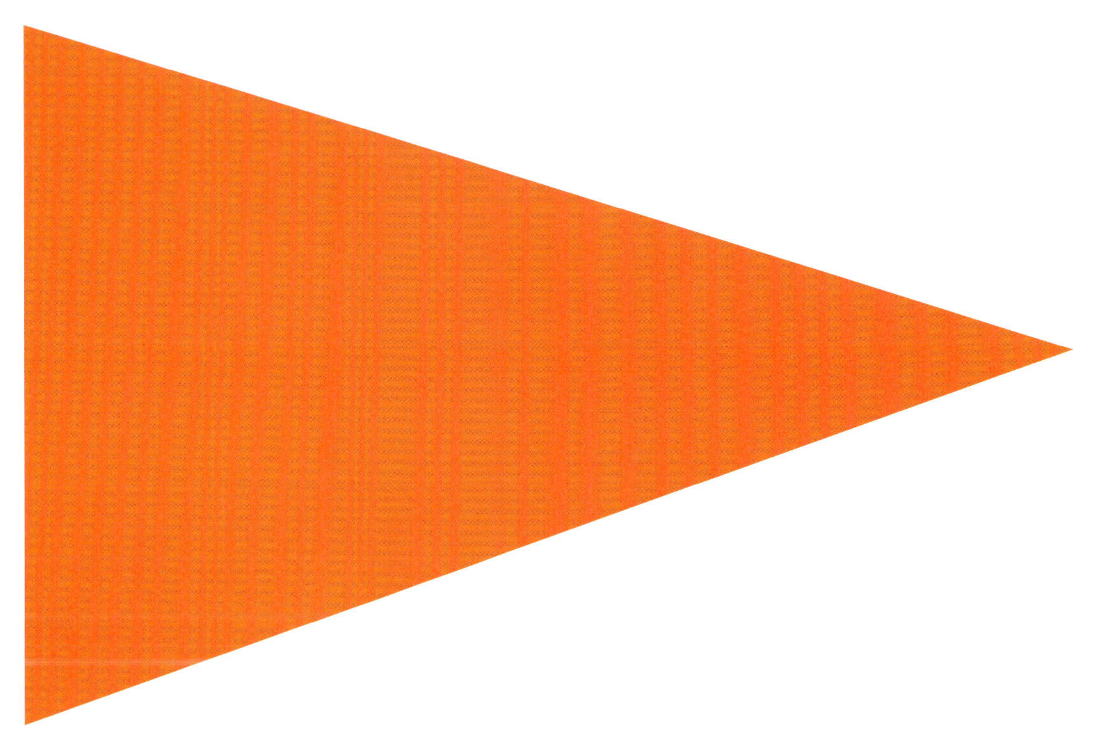

INSTALLATIONS

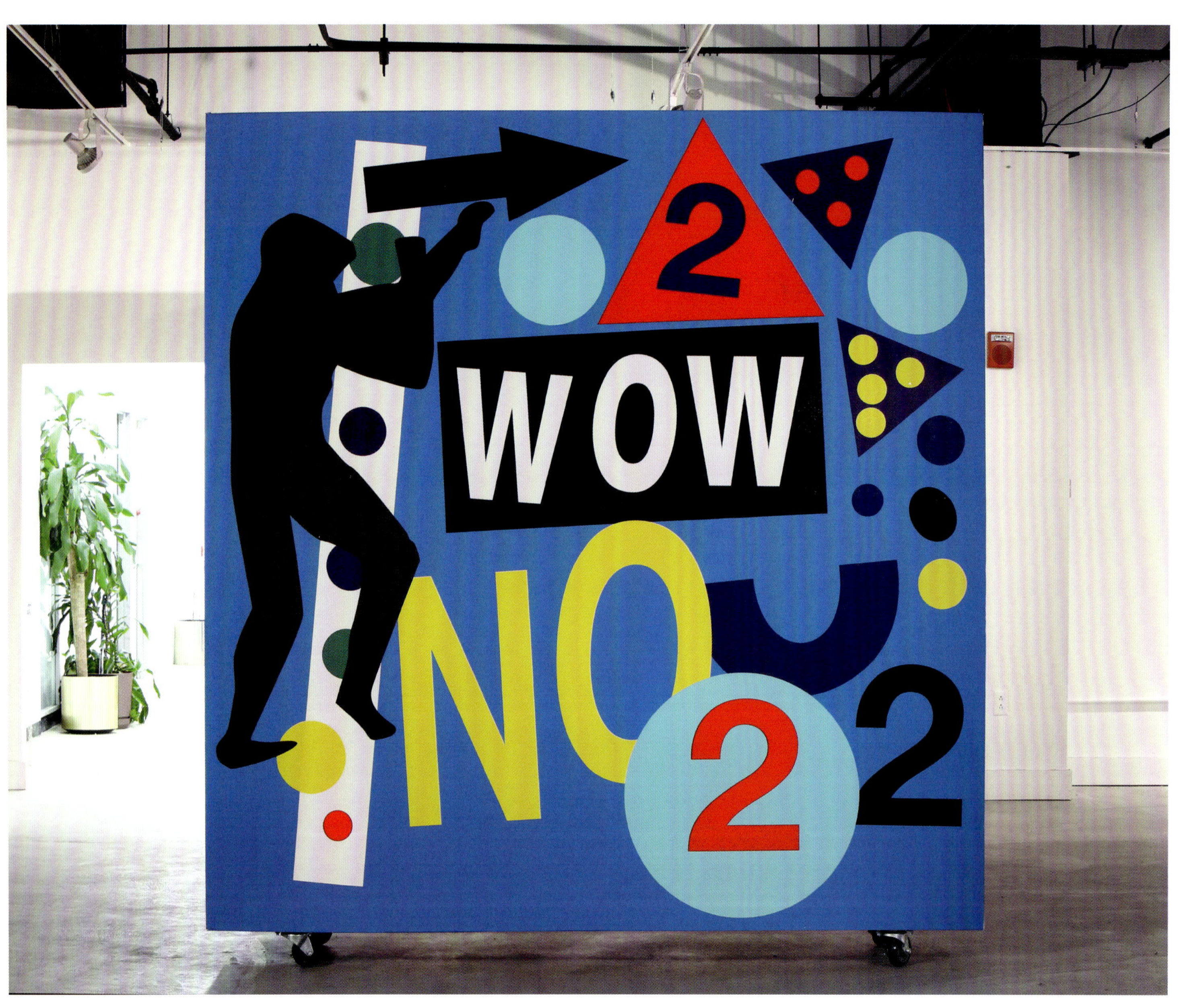

Untitled, 2016

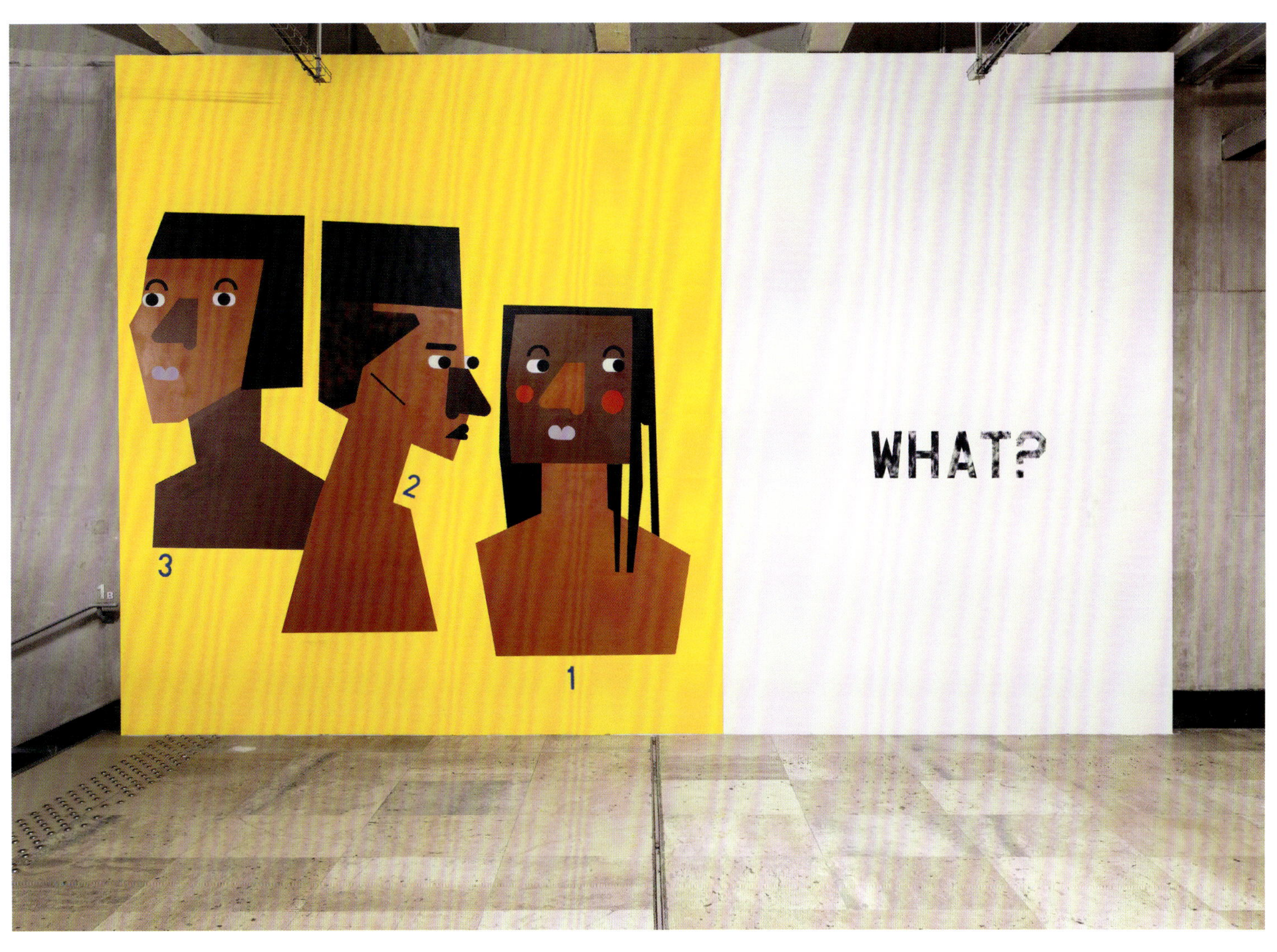

Installation view, Hot to Trot. Not., 2018

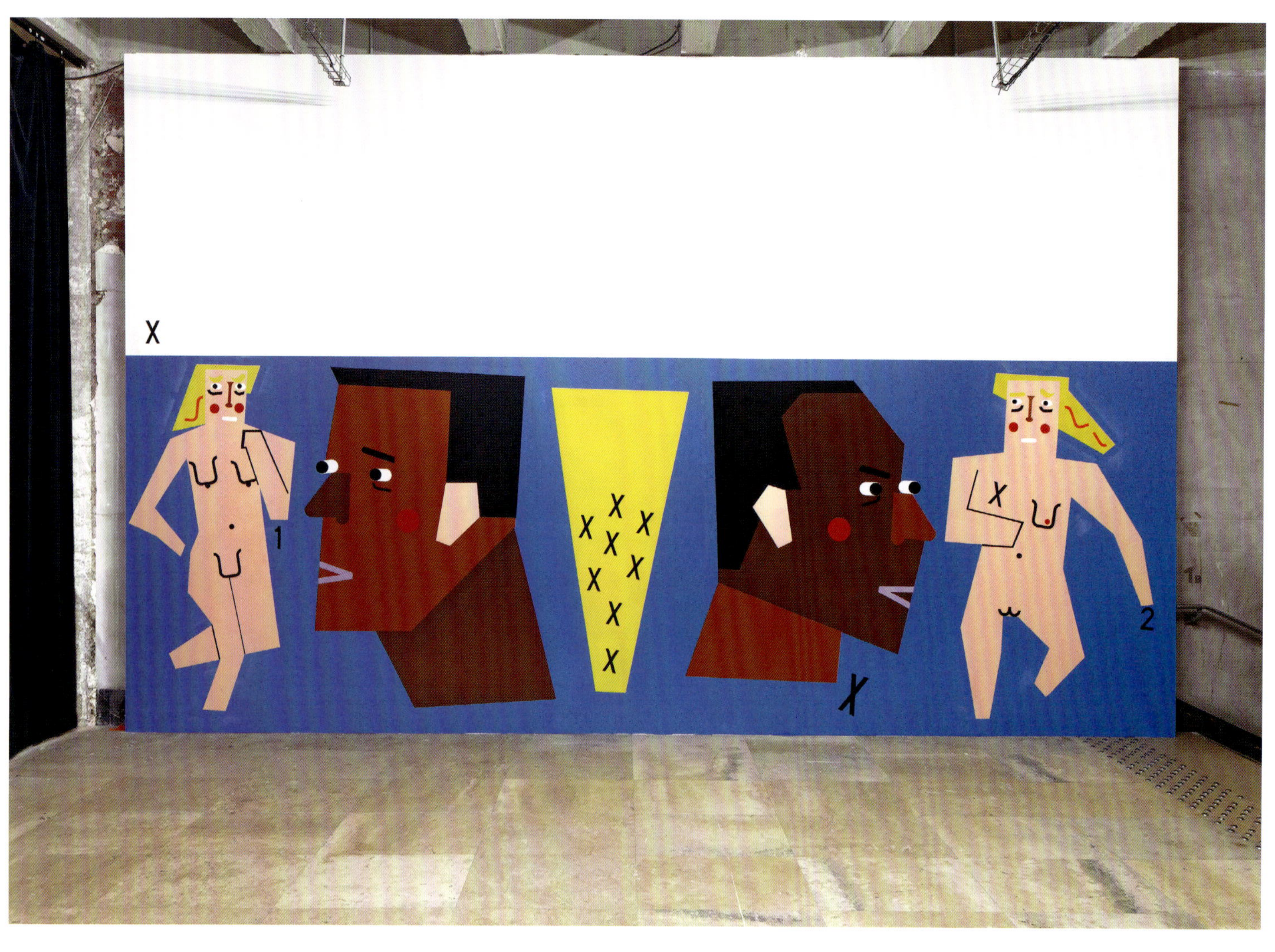

[ABOVE] Installation view, Hot to Trot. Not. , 2018
[OPPOSITE] Installation view, Hot to Trot. Not. , 2018
[OVERLEAF] Installation view, Art Wall, the Institute of Contemporary Art / Boston, 2019

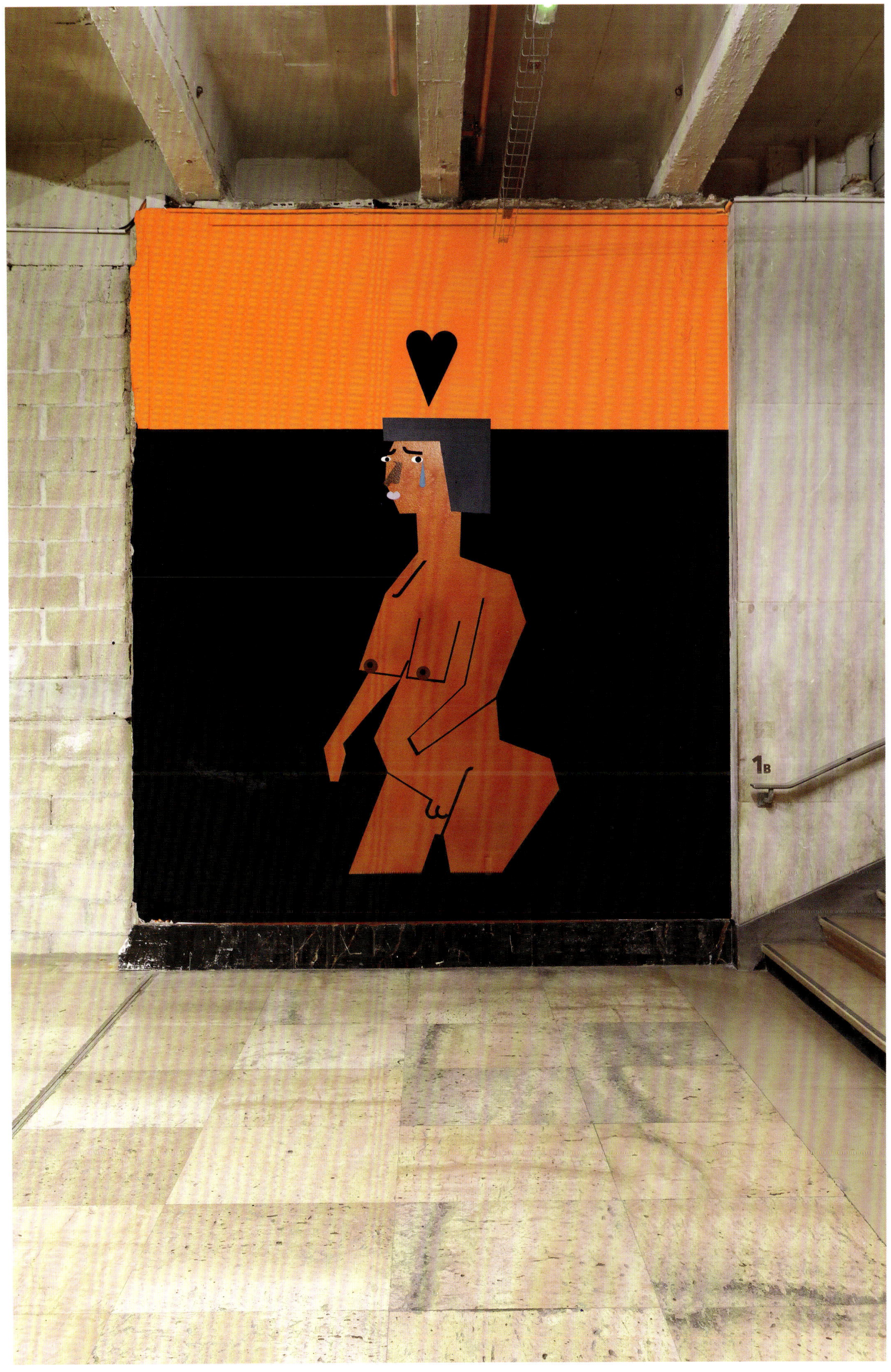
1B

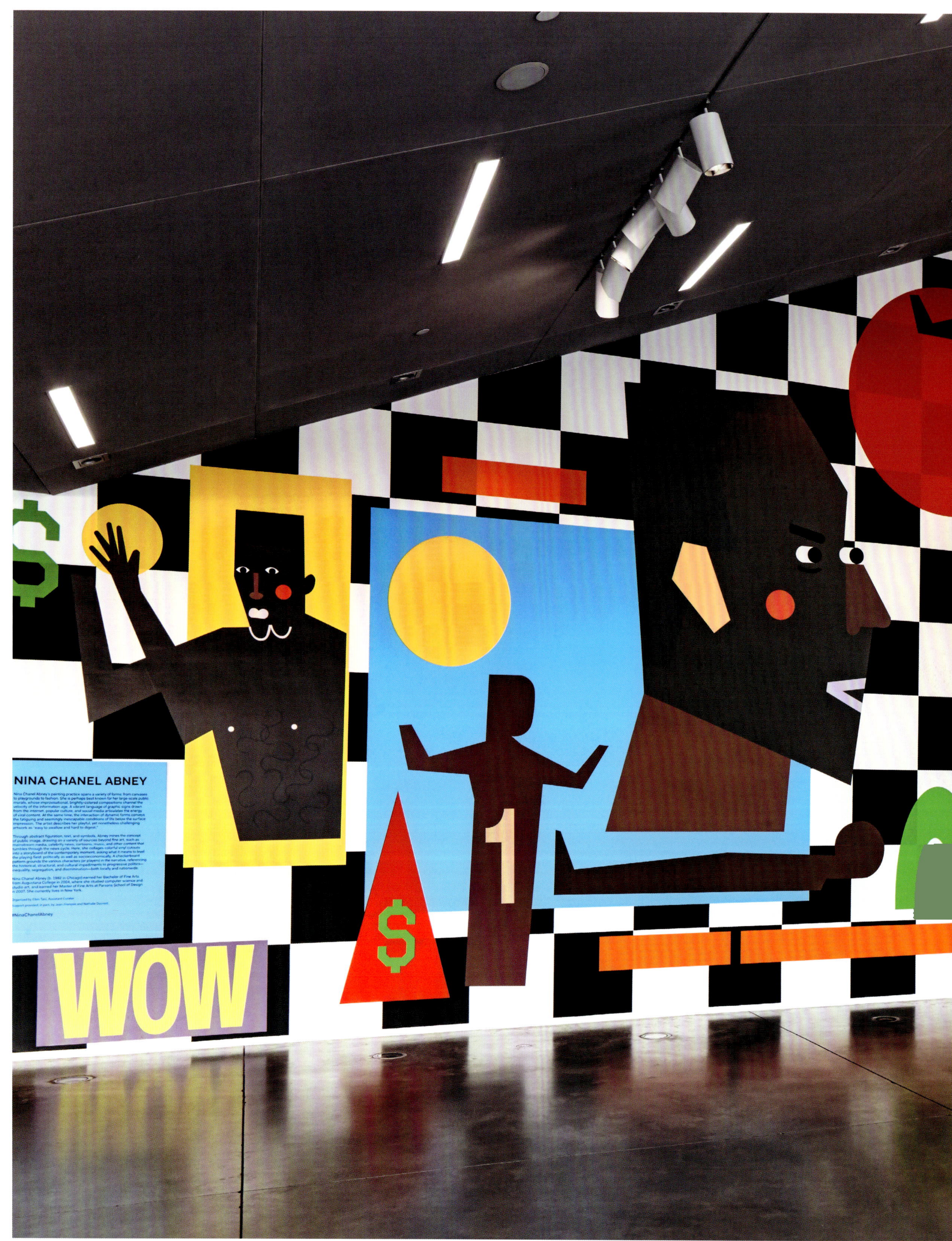
$
NINA CHANEL ABNEY
#NinaChanelAbney
1
$
WOW

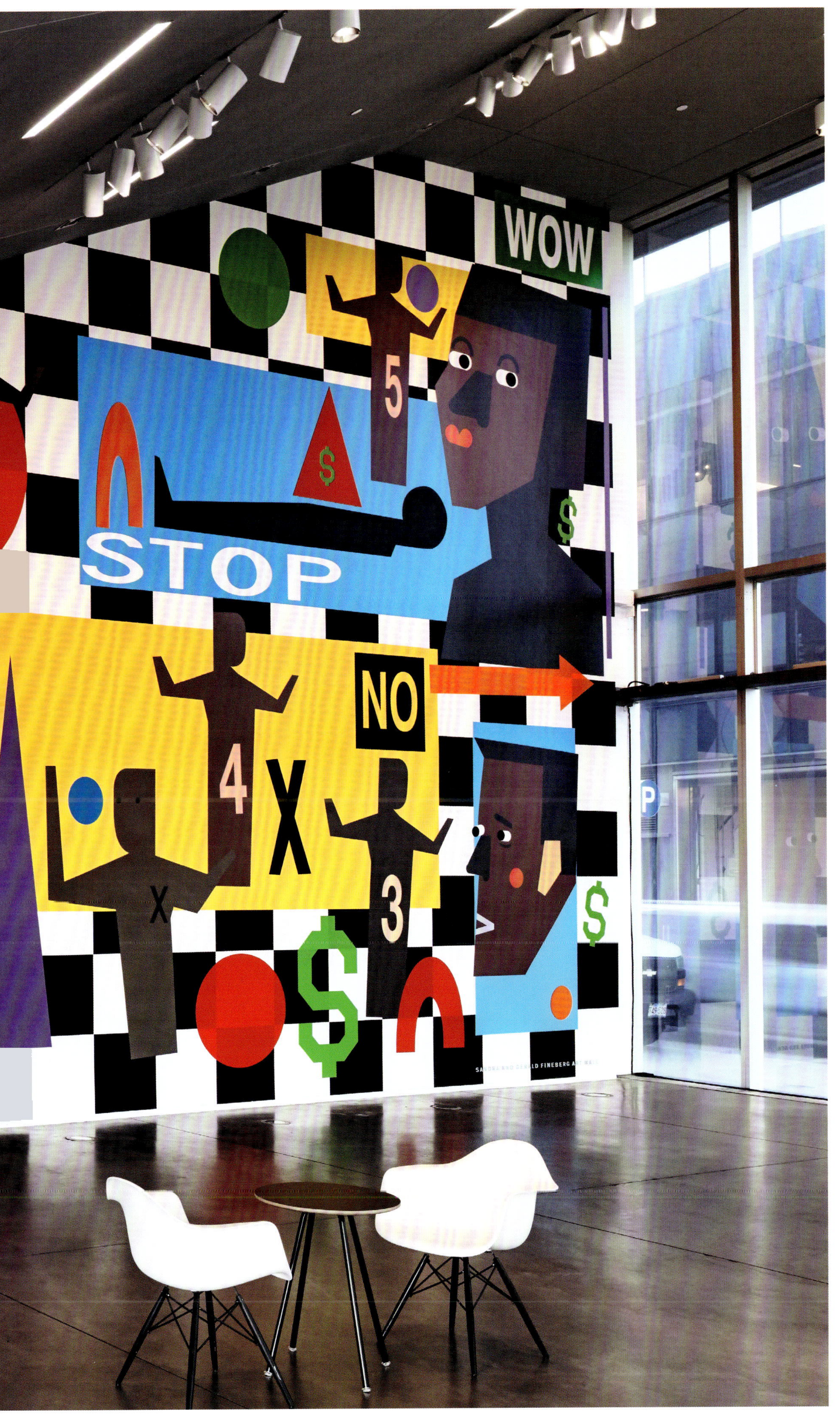
WOW
5
STOP
NO
4
X
3

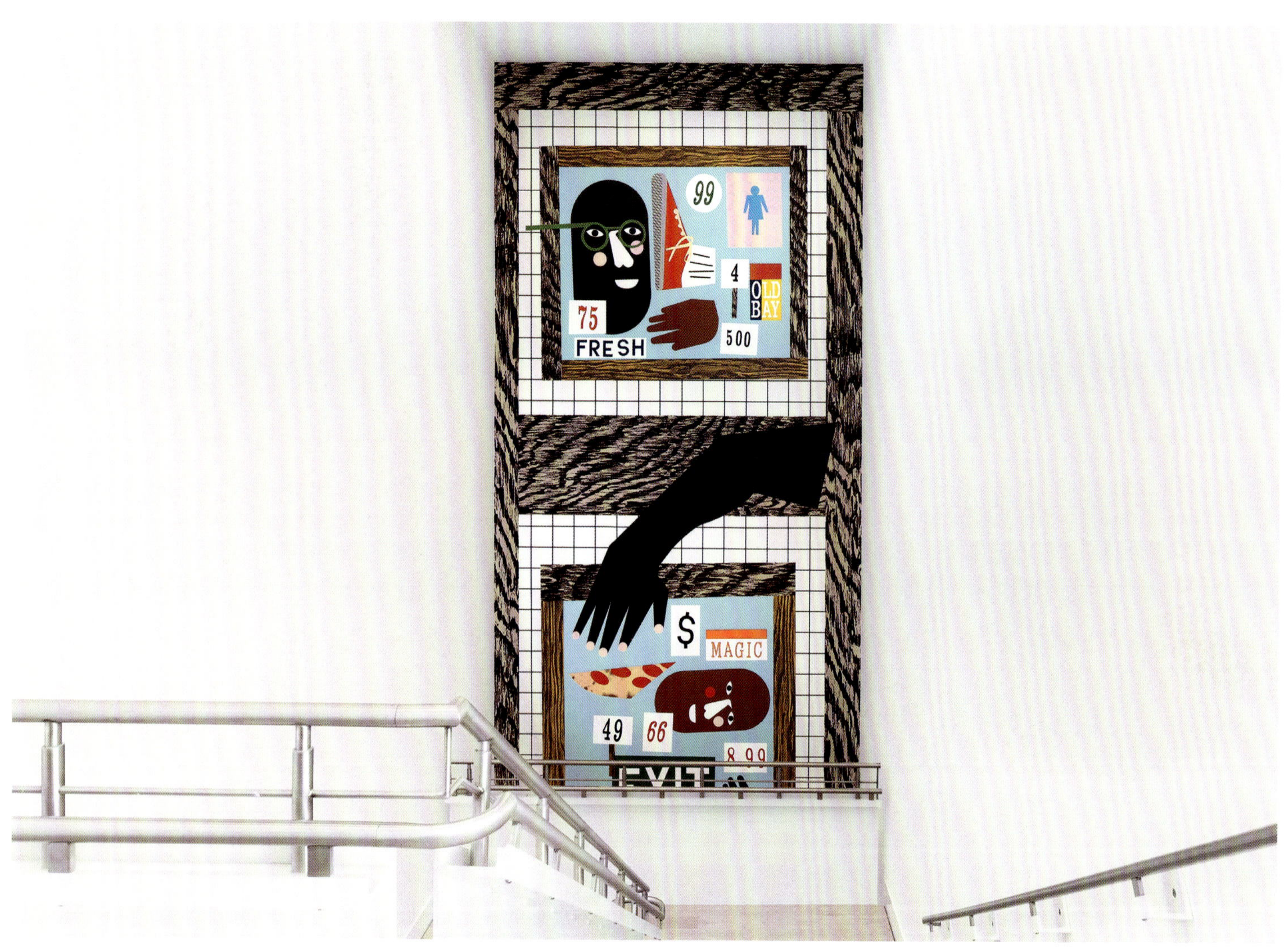

Cafeteria, 2022

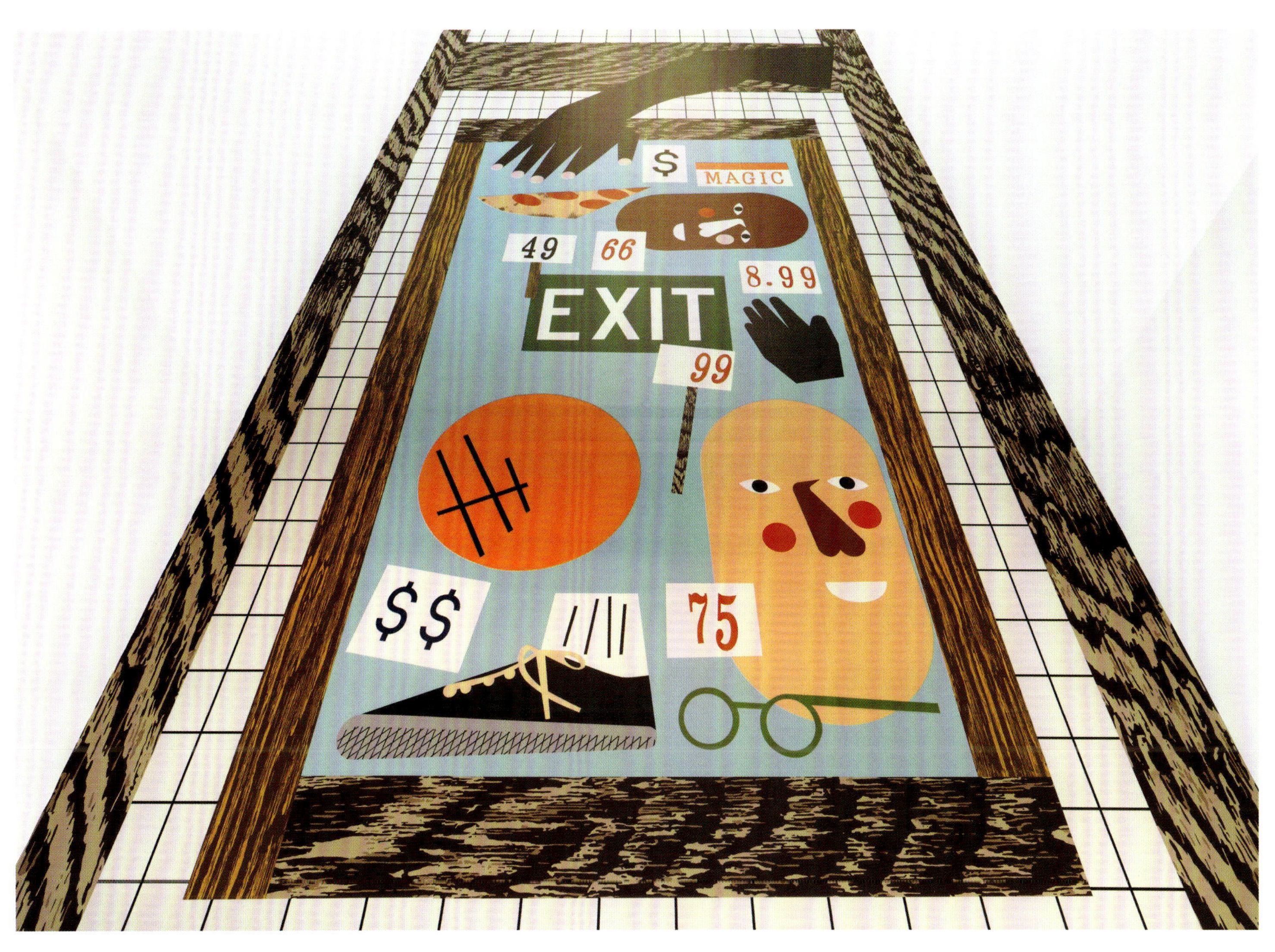

Cafeteria, 2022

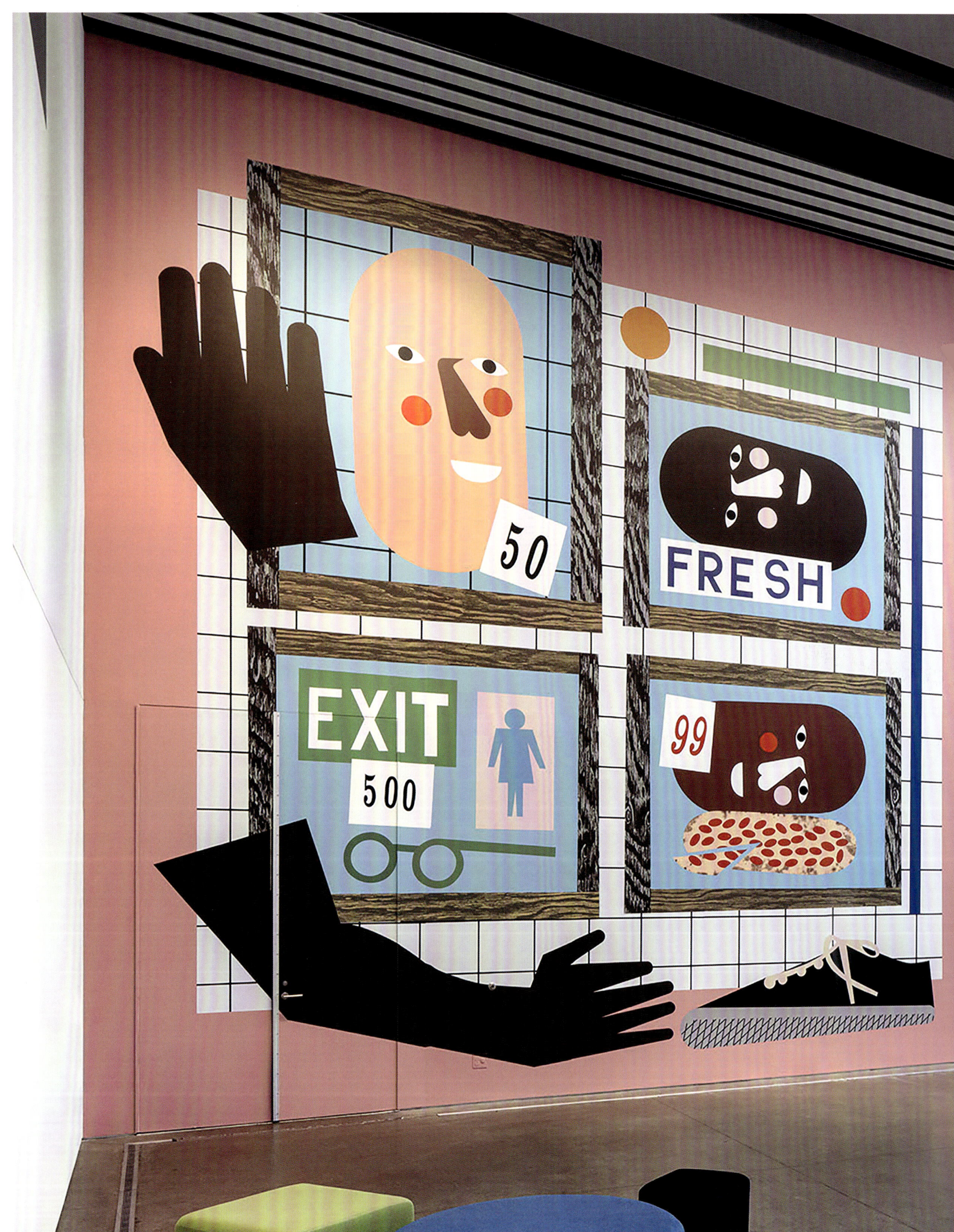
50
FRESH
EXIT
500
99

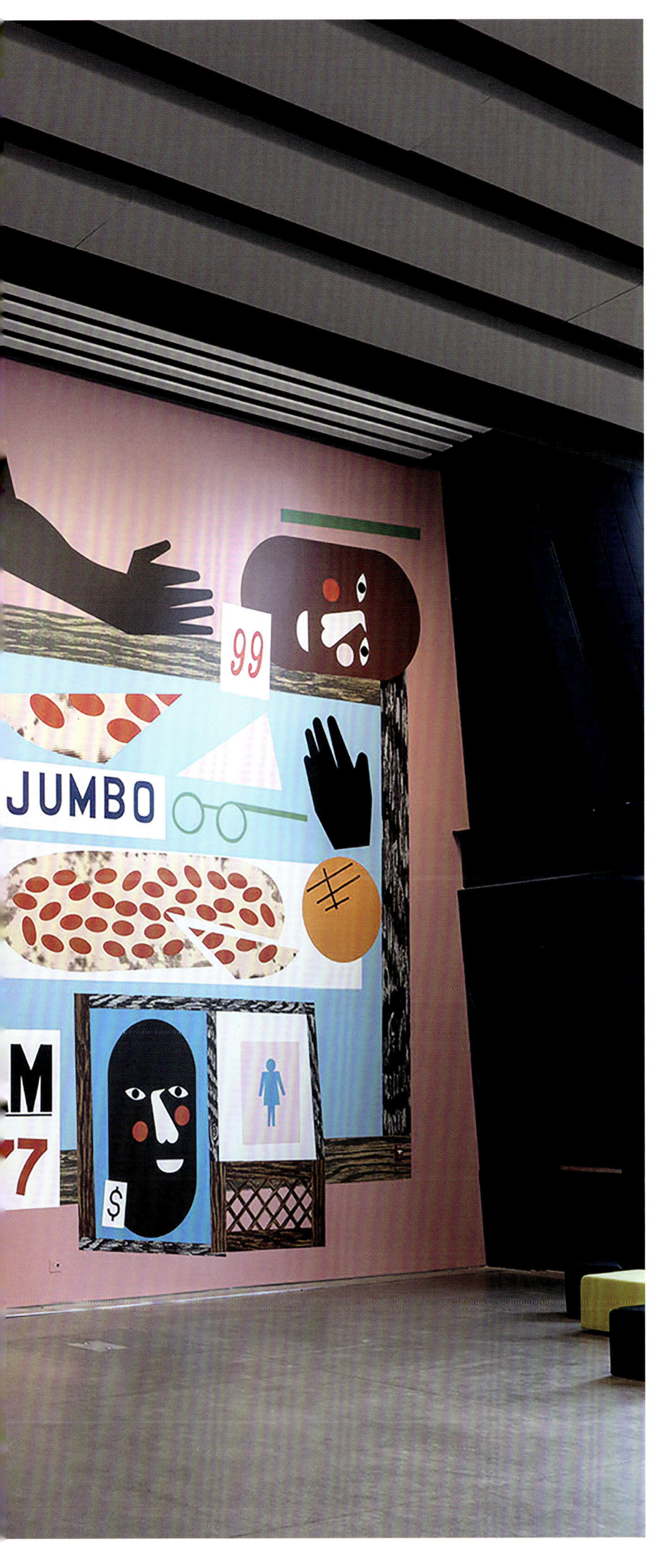

[LEFT] Cafeteria 2, 2023
[OVERLEAF] Heaven's Hotline, 2025

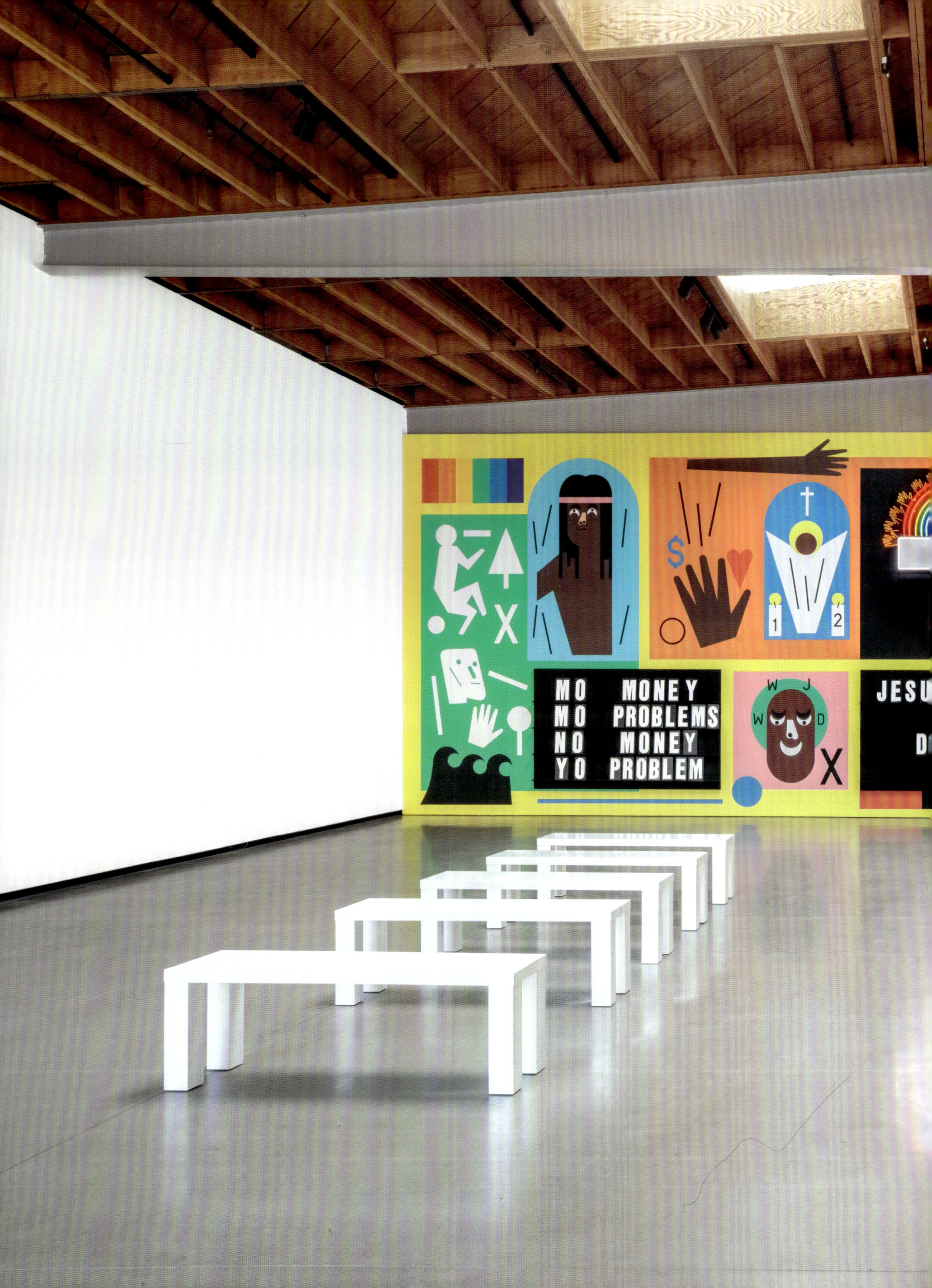
MO MONEY
MO PROBLEMS
NO MONEY
YO PROBLEM

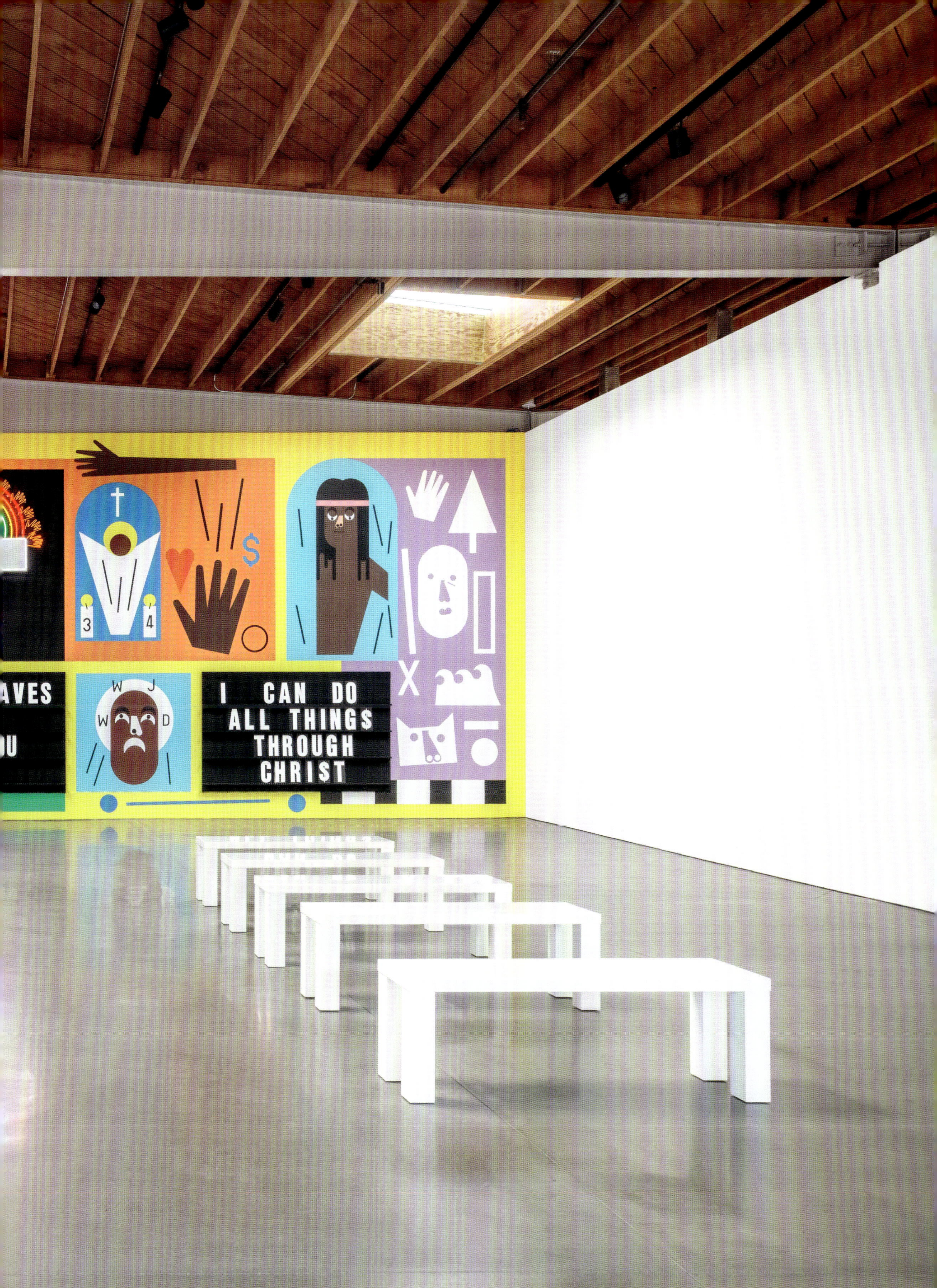
I CAN DO
ALL THING$
THROUGH
CHRI$T

CONTRIBUTORS

Nina Chanel Abney (b. 1982, Harvey, Illinois) is a contemporary artist who lives and works in New York. She received her BFA from Augustana College, Rock Island, Illinois, in 2004 and her MFA from Parsons School of Design, New York, NY, in 2007.

Abney presented her work in 2024 solo exhibition at The School | Jack Shainman Gallery, Kinderhook, NY, and a 2025 exhibition at Jeffrey Deitch, Los Angeles. She previously was honored with solo exhibitions at the Savannah College of Art and Design, Georgia (2023); the Museum of Contemporary Art, Cleveland (2023); the Institute of Contemporary Art, Miami (2022); the Gordon Parks Foundation, Pleasantville, New York (2022; traveled to Henry Art Gallery, Seattle); the Institute of Contemporary Art, Boston (2019–21); Palais de Tokyo, Paris (2018); and the Contemporary Dayton, Ohio (2021). Additionally, her solo exhibition at the Nasher Museum of Art, Duke University, Durham, North Carolina (2017), traveled to the Chicago Cultural Center; Institute of Contemporary Art, Los Angeles, and the California African American Museum, Los Angeles; and the Neuberger Museum of Art, Purchase College, State University of New York. Abney was recently commissioned to transform Lincoln Center's new David Geffen Hall facade in New York, drawing from the cultural heritage of the neighborhood previously known as San Juan Hill that comprised African American, Afro-Caribbean, and Puerto Rican families. Abney's recent public mural at the Miami World Center was similarly inspired by Overtown, a historically Black neighborhood in Miami. Abney's work is held in the collections of the Whitney Museum of American Art, New York; the Museum of Modern Art, New York; the Brooklyn Museum, New York; the Bronx Museum, New York; the Dallas Museum of Art, Texas; the Rubell Family Collection, Miami, Florida; the Nasher Museum of Art, North Carolina; and the Pennsylvania Academy of the Fine Arts; among others.

Jeffrey Deitch is an art dealer and curator. His first exhibition in New York titled *Lives* (1975) featured works by Vito Acconci, Joseph Beuys, Adrian Piper, Andy Warhol, and Hannah Wilke, positioning Deitch at the heart of the art world, where he has continued to receive recognition as an art advisor, dealer, writer, artist, and curator. Deitch now operates contemporary galleries in New York and Los Angeles and continues to advise private art collectors and institutions.

Thelma Golden is the Director and Chief Curator of the Studio Museum in Harlem, the world's leading institution devoted to visual arts by artists of African descent. Under Golden's leadership, the museum has gained increased renown as a global leader in the exhibition of contemporary art, a center for innovative education, and a cultural anchor in the Harlem community. Born and raised in New York City, Golden holds a BA from Smith College. She has received honorary doctorates from the New School (2022), Columbia University (2018), Barnard College (2010), the City College of New York (2009), San Francisco Art Institute (2008), and Smith College (2004). In 2024, Golden was listed in *Time* magazine's TIME100 list of the hundred most influential people in the world. Golden is a recognized authority on Black art and an active lecturer and panelist who speaks about contemporary art and culture at national and international institutions.

Jazmine Hughes is a writer, editor, and professor based in Brooklyn, New York, and Oaxaca, Mexico. She is a former staff writer for the *New York Times Magazine*. She has won two National Magazine Awards for profile writing as well as an award from the National Association of LGBTQ+ Journalists. She has served as a part-time lecturer in journalism at Cornell University and the New School.

Richard J. Powell is the John Spencer Bassett Professor of Art and Art History at Duke University, is a recognized authority on African American art and culture, and a frequent lecturer and media commentator on this topic both in the United States and abroad.

Along with teaching courses in American art, the arts of the African Diaspora, and contemporary visual studies, he has written extensively on topics ranging from primitivism to postmodernism, including the book *Going There: Black Visual Satire* (2020). From 2007 until 2010, Powell was Editor-in-Chief of the *Art Bulletin*, the world's leading English language journal in art history. Among the major museums where his curated exhibitions have been presented are the Phillips Academy's Addison Gallery of American Art, the Art Institute of Chicago, the Fine Arts Museums of San Francisco, the Los Angeles County Museum of Art, the New Orleans Museum of Art, the Whitney Museum of American Art, and London's Whitechapel Art Gallery.

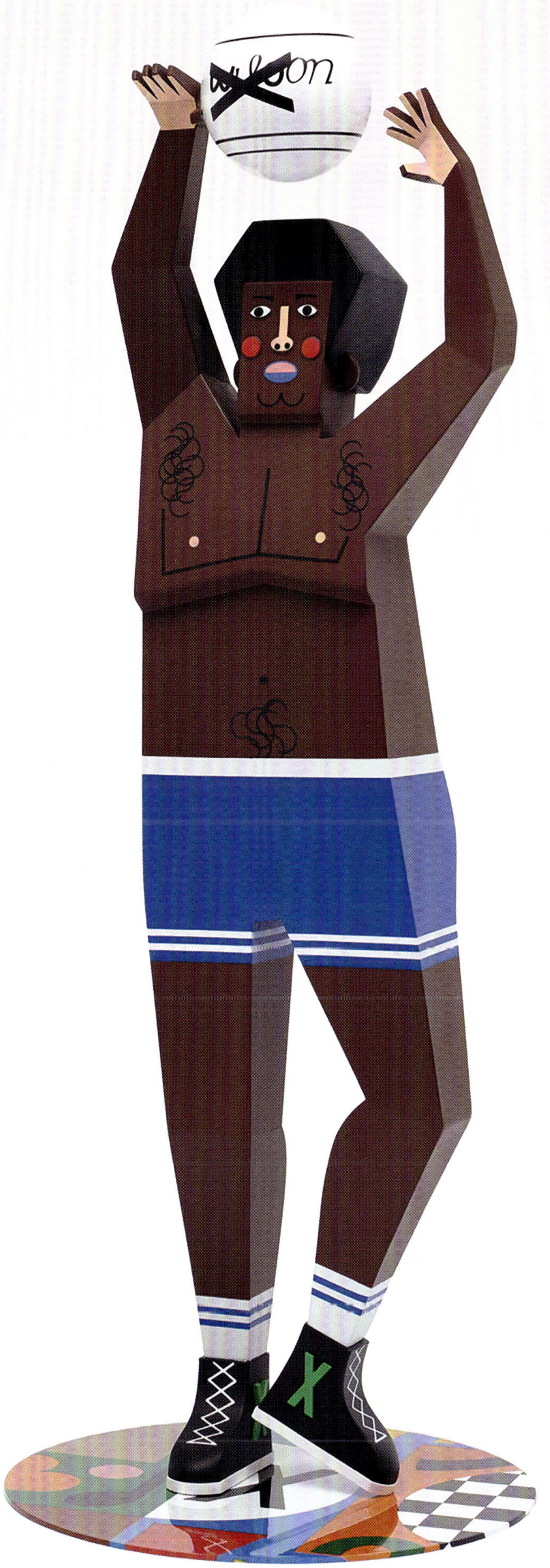

Boobie, 2019

LIST OF WORKS

Class of 2007, 2007
Acrylic on canvas
114 in. × 15½ ft.
(289.6 cm × 4.7 m)
Rubell Museum, Miami and Washington, DC
pp. 26–27

Untitled (Black Soap), 2007
Acrylic on canvas
64 × 229 ft.
(19.5 × 69.8 m), overall
pp. 28–29

Rainblow, 2008
Acrylic on canvas
89¾ × 92 in.
(233.7 × 233.7 cm)
p. 30

The Ugly, 2008
Acrylic on canvas
90½ × 52 in.
(229.9 × 132.1 cm)
p. 31

The Good, The Bad, 2008
Acrylic on canvas
90½ × 52 in.
(229.9 × 132.1 cm)
p. 32

Randaleeza, 2008
Acrylic on canvas
90 × 94 in.m
(228.6 × 238.8 cm)
p. 33

The Takeover, 2008
Acrylic on canvas
67 in. × 12 ft. 9⁄10 in.
(170.2 cm × 3.9 m)
p. 34

Close, But No Cigar, 2008
Acrylic on canvas
diptych, 84 in. × 12 ft. ⅕ in.
(213.4 cm × 3.7 m), overall
p. 35

The Paris Portrait, 2008
Acrylic on canvas
22 × 24 in. (55.9 × 60.9 cm)
p. 36

Another Midnight Run, 2009
Acrylic on canvas
48½ × 36½ in.
(123.2 × 92.7 cm)
p. 37

Forbidden Fruit, 2009
Acrylic on canvas
77½ × 67 in.
(196.8 × 170.2 cm)
Brooklyn Museum
p. 38

Make it Reign, 2009
Acrylic on canvas
36 × 48 in. (91.4 × 121.9 cm)
p. 39

Who, What, When, 2009
Acrylic on canvas
72½ × 77½ in.
(184.2 × 196.9 cm)
p. 40

Your Gig Is Up, 2009
Acrylic on canvas
first panel: 69½ × 55 in.
(176.5 × 139.7 cm);
second panel: 71½ × 77½ in.
(181.6 × 196.8 cm)
pp. 42–43

King of Sorrow, 2011
Acrylic on canvas,
diptych, 73 × 36 in.
(185.4 × 91.4 cm), overall
pp. 11, 41

Untitled, 2012
Acrylic on canvas
48 × 36 in. (121.9 × 91.4 cm)
Studio Museum in Harlem; bequest of Peggy Cooper Cafritz (1947–2018), Washington, DC, collector, educator, and activist, 2018.40.1.
p. 22

Superstar Ken, 2012
Acrylic on canvas
15 × 42 in. (38.1 × 106.7 cm)
pp. 44–45

Untitled, 2012
Acrylic on canvas
diptych, 3 × 3 ft.
(0.9 × 0.9 m), each
pp. 46–47

Mad 51st, 2012
Acrylic on canvas
40 × 30 in. (101.6 × 76.2 cm)
p. 48

I Dread to Think (1 of 3), 2012
Acrylic on canvas
one of three panels,
76 in. × 21 ft.
(193 cm × 6.4 m), overall
pp. 50–51

I Dread to Think (2 of 3), 2012
Acrylic on canvas
one of three panels,
76 in. × 21 ft.
(193 cm × 6.4 m), overall
pp. 8, 52–53

I Dread to Think (3 of 3), 2012
Acrylic on canvas
one of three panels,
76 in. × 21 ft.
(193 cm × 6.4 m), overall
pp. 54–55

Let's Go Hoop, 2013
Acrylic on canvas
48 × 36 in. (121.9 × 91.4 cm)
p. 49

Untitled (Mannequins), 2013
Acrylic on canvas
60 × 60 in.
(152.4 × 152.4 cm)
p. 56

Incite (COM), 2015
Unique UltraChrome pigmented print, spray paint, and acrylic on canvas
47⅗ × 35⅘ in.
(121 × 90.9 cm)
p. 57

*Untitled (FUCK T*E *OP)*, 2014
Acrylic and spray paint on canvas
72 × 108 in.
(182.9 × 274 cm)
pp. 11, 58–59

Who, 2015
Unique UltraChrome pigmented print, acrylic, and spray paint on canvas
96 × 112 in.
(243.8 × 284.6 cm)
p. 60

What, 2015
Unique UltraChrome pigmented print, acrylic, and spray paint on canvas
96 × 112 in.
(243.8 × 284.5 cm)
p. 61

Why, 2015
Unique UltraChrome pigmented print, acrylic, and spray paint on canvas
96 in. × 16 ft. 2 in.
(243.8 cm × 4.9 m)
pp. 62–63

Where, 2015
Unique UltraChrome pigmented print, spray paint, and acrylic on canvas
96 × 96 in.
(243.8 × 243.8 cm)
p. 64

Untitled, 2015
Acrylic and cut paper collage on wood panel diptych, 20 × 30 in.
(50.8 × 76.2 cm), each
p. 65

Untitled, 2015
Unique UltraChrome pigmented print, acrylic, and spray paint on canvas
96 × 96 in.
(243.8 × 243.8 cm)
p. 66

Brazil -3, 2015
Acrylic, spray paint, cut paper collage on paper
38 × 27 in. (96.5 × 68.6 cm)
p. 68

Sorry We're Closed, 2015
Spray paint on canvas
48 × 36 in. (121.9 × 91.4 cm)
p. 69

Potato, Potata, 2015
UltraChrome pigmented print, acrylic, and spray paint on canvas
18 ft. 4in. × 23 ft. 8 in.
(5.6 × 7.2 m)
Pennsylvania Academy of the Fine Arts
pp. 70–71

Untitled, 2016
McCarter Highway, Newark, NJ
p. 5

Untitled, 2016
Coney Island Art Wall, Brooklyn, NY
p. 5

Brazil -4, 2016
Acrylic, spray paint, cut paper collage on paper
38 × 27 in. (96.5 × 68.6 cm)
p. 67

Hothouse, 2016
Acrylic and spray paint on canvas
8 ft. 6 in. × 17 ft. 2 in.
(2.6 × 5.2 m)
Whitney Museum of American Art
pp. 14, 72–73

Untitled, 2016
Wall paint and vinyl
8 × 8 ft. (2.4 × 2.4 m)
p. 250

Catch Me If You Can, Catch 22, 2017
Acrylic and spray paint on canvas
96⅛ × 60¹⁵⁄₁₆ in.
(244.2 × 154.8 cm)
pp. 74–75

Pooh-Pooh, 2017
Unique UltraChrome pigmented print, acrylic, and spray paint on canvas
96 × 72 in. (243.8 × 182.8 cm)
p. 76

Non Action Satisfaction, 2017
Unique UltraChrome pigmented print, acrylic, and spray paint on canvas
96 × 72 in. (243.8 × 182.8 cm)
p. 77

Guns and Butter, 2017
Unique UltraChrome pigmented print, acrylic, and spray paint on canvas
96 × 72 in. (243.8 × 182.8 cm)
p. 78

In the Land Without Feelings, 2017
Unique UltraChrome pigmented print, acrylic, and spray paint on canvas
96 × 72 in. (243.8 × 182.8 cm)
Marciano Art Foundation
p. 79

Fruit of the Womb, 2017
Unique UltraChrome pigmented print, acrylic, and spray paint on canvas
96 × 96 in. (243.8 × 243.8 cm)
p. 82

People at Peoples Beach, 2017
Unique UltraChrome pigmented print, acrylic, and spray paint on canvas
96 × 96 in. (243.8 × 243.8 cm)
p. 83

All These Flavors and You Choose to be Salty, 2017
Unique UltraChrome pigmented print, acrylic, and spray paint on canvas
96 × 96 in.
(243.8 × 243.8 cm)
p. 84

Si, Mister, 2017
Unique UltraChrome pigmented print, acrylic, and spray paint on canvas
96 × 48 in. (243.8 × 121.9 cm)
p. 85

Black and Blues, 2017
Acrylic and spray paint on canvas
84 × 120 in.
(213.4 × 304.8 cm)
p. 86

Penny Dreadful, 2017
Acrylic and spray paint on canvas
84 × 120 in.
(213.4 × 304.8 cm)
p. 87

White River Fish Kill, 2017
Acrylic and spray paint on canvas
84 × 120 in.
(213.4 × 304.8 cm)
Whitney Museum of American Art
p. 88

Whet, 2017
Acrylic and spray paint on canvas
60 × 60 in.
(152.4 × 152.4 cm)
p. 89

Always Ready, Always There, 2018
Acrylic and spray paint on canvas
84 × 120 in.
(213.4 × 304.8 cm)
p. 90

Anytime, Anyplace, 2018
Acrylic and spray paint on canvas
72 × 72 in.
(182.8 × 182.8 cm)
p. 91

#33, 2018
Acrylic and spray paint on canvas
72 × 48 in.
(182.9 × 121.9 cm)
p. 92

#5, 2018
Acrylic and spray paint on canvas
72 × 48 in.
(182.9 × 121.9 cm)
p. 93

#13, 2018
Spray paint on canvas
40 × 30 in.
(101.6 × 76.2 cm)
p. 94

#21, 2018
Acrylic and spray paint on canvas
40 × 29 in.
(101.6 × 73.7 cm)
pp. 12, 95

Untitled, 2018
Acrylic and spray paint on panel
7 ft. 6 in. × 24 ft. 6 in.
(2.3 × 7.5 m)
pp. 96–97

Ooh La, La, 2018
Five-panel monoprint
5 ft. 6 in. × 16 ft. 6 in.
(1.7 × 5 m), overall
pp. 146–47

Third Time's the Charm, 2018
Four-panel monoprint
66¼ × 139⅝ in.
(168.3 × 354.6 cm), overall
pp. 148–49

Let's Work, Let's Play, Let's Live Together, 2018
Diptych monoprint
68½ × 84 in.
(174 × 213.4 cm), overall
pp. 150–51

What Beats What, 2018
Triptych monoprint
65⅞ × 118⅞ in.
(167.3 × 302 cm), overall
pp. 152–53

Snoops, 2018
Four-panel monoprint
80¾ × 80¾ in.
(205.1 × 205.1 cm), overall
p. 154

Snoops' Friend, 2018
Four-panel monoprint
80 ¾ × 80 ¾ in.
(205.1 × 205.1 cm), overall
p. 155

Fast Draw, 2018
Triptych monoprint
59⅝ × 108½ in.
(151.4 × 275.6 cm), overall
pp. 160–61

Installation view,
Hot to Trot. Not., 2018
Fresco in-situ
Palais de Tokyo, Paris FR
pp. 251–53

Junk Mail Scribble, 2019
Acrylic and spray paint
on canvas
84 × 120 in.
(213.4 × 304.8 cm)
pp. 15, 98–99

Junk Mail Scribble #2,
2019
Acrylic and spray paint on
canvas
84 × 120 in.
(213.4 × 304.8 cm)
pp. 100-01

555 Wow, 2019
Acrylic and spray paint
on canvas
60 × 60 in.
(152.4 × 152.4 cm)
p. 102

Wow Money, 2019
Acrylic and spray paint on
canvas
60 × 60 in.
(152.4 × 152.4 cm)
p. 103

A Vanilla Position, 2019
Acrylic and spray paint on
canvas
five panels, 40 × 30 in.
(101.6 × 76.2 cm), each
pp. 104–05

Bizarre Blazaar, 2019
Acrylic and spray paint
on canvas
96 × 96 in.
(243.8 × 243.8 cm)
p. 106

Issa Saturday (Study), 2019
Acrylic and spray paint
on canvas
60 × 60 × 11¼ in.
(152.4 × 152.4 × 28.6 cm)
p. 107

Explicit Bias, 2019
Acrylic and spray paint on
canvas
96 × 96 in.
(243.8 × 243.8 cm)
p. 108

Peep, 2019
Acrylic and spray paint
on canvas
five panels, 84 × 60 in.
(213.6 × 152.4 cm), each
pp. 13, 116–19

Temporary Friends, 2019
Relief prints
39¼ × 29½ in.
(99.7 × 74.9 cm)
pp. 156–59

Untitled, 2019
Monoprints
65⅞ × 118⅞ in.
(167.3 × 301.9 cm)
pp. 162–63

Untitled, 2019
Monoprints
65⅞ × 118⅞ in.
(167.3 × 301.9 cm)
pp. 164–65

Installation view, Art Wall,
the Institute of Contem-
porary Art / Boston, 2019
pp. 254–55

Boobie, 2019
Alloy and mixed media
4½ × 16¾ × 84 in.
(11.5 cm × 42.5 × 8.4 cm)
Edition of 40,
10 AP editions
p. 263

Taking My Flowers, 2020
Acrylic and spray paint
on canvas
24 × 24 in. (61 × 61 cm)
p. 109

Femme Games, 2020
Acrylic and spray paint
on canvas
96 × 96 in.
(243.8 × 243.8 cm)
pp. 12, 110

Bird Talk, 2020
Acrylic and spray paint
on canvas
48 × 48 × 1¾ in.
(121.9 × 121.9 × 4.4 cm)
p. 111

Off, 2020
Acrylic and spray paint
on canvas
48 × 48 in. (121.9 × 121.9 cm)
p. 112

*Being Mixie with My
Fixie*, 2020
Acrylic and spray paint
on canvas
84 × 84 × 1⅝ in.
(213.4 × 213.4 × 4.1 cm)
p. 113

Where's the Remote, 2020
Spray paint on canvas
48 × 72 × 2¼ in.
(121.9 × 182.9 × 5.7 cm)
pp. 114–15

Thirsty, 2020
Acrylic and spray paint
on canvas
36 × 48 in. (91.4 × 121.9 cm)
p. 120

Cut Em' Off, 2020
Acrylic and spray paint
on canvas
36 × 48 in. (91.4 × 121.9 cm)
p. 121

Plenty of Fish, 2020
Acrylic and spray paint
on canvas
48 × 48 × 1¾ in.
(121.9 × 121.9 × 4.4 cm)
p. 122

Bring Me A Cutie, 2020
Spray paint on canvas
24 × 24 in.
(61 × 61 cm)
p. 123

*Storytime – Learn How
to Read*, 2020
Acrylic on canvas
96 × 96 in.
(243.8 × 243.8 cm)
p. 124

He's Catty, 2020
Acrylic and spray paint
on canvas
48 × 48 in.
(121.9 × 121.9 cm)
p. 125

House of Reps, 2020
Triptych collage on panel
85½ × 73½ × 1⅜ in.
(217.2 × 186.7 × 3.5 cm)
each, framed
pp. 166–67

WA and Up for Whatever,
2020
Collage on panel
85½ × 85½ × 1⅜ in.
(217.2 × 217.2 × 3.5 cm),
framed
p. 168

*She Was a Real Trouper –
Acts of Service*, 2020
Collage on panel
85½ × 73½ × 1⅜ in.
(217.2 × 186.7 × 3.5 cm),
framed
Museum of Modern Art
p. 169

Outer Space, Inner Circle,
2020
Collage on panel
85½ × 85½ × 1⅜ in.
(217.2 × 217.2 × 3.5 cm),
framed
p. 170

2 Step, 2021
Acrylic and spray paint on canvas
five panels, 7 × 25 ft. (2.1 × 7.6 m), overall
pp. 126–27

Untitled, 2021
Collage on panel
58 × 59 in.
(147.3 × 149.9 cm)
p. 171

White, 2021
Collage on panel
$60\frac{11}{16}$ → 60 × $60\frac{11}{16}$ × 1⅜ in.
(152.4 × 154.1 × 3.5 cm), framed
p. 172

Green, 2021
Collage on panel
$60\frac{7}{16}$ × $60\frac{15}{16}$ × 1⅜ in.
(153.5 × 154.8 × 3.5 cm), framed
p. 173

CREW, 2021
Set of seven collage works on panels
Dimensions variable
pp. 174–75, 178–79

Kiyanna, 2021
Collage on panel
$84\frac{7}{16}$ × 50⅝ × 1⅜ in.
(214.5 × 128 × 3.5 cm), framed
p. 180

Me, 2021
Collage on panel
75¼ × 34 × 1⅜ in.
(191.1 × 86.4 × 3.5 cm), framed
p. 181

Mary, 2022
Spray paint on canvas
72 × 54½ in.
(182.9 × 138.4 cm)
p. 128

Courtney, 2022
Spray paint on canvas
72 × 54½ in.
(182.9 × 138.4 cm)
p. 129

Jordan, 2022
Spray paint on canvas
72 × 54½ in.
(182.9 × 138.4 cm)
p. 129

Jackie, 2022
Spray paint on canvas
72 × 54½ in.
(182.9 × 138.4 cm)
p. 130

Keisha, 2022
Spray paint on canvas
72 × 54½ in.
(182.9 × 138.4 cm)
p. 131

Captain F.M., 2022
Collage on panel
61¼ × 61¼ × 1⅜ in.
(155.6 × 155.6 × 3.5 cm), framed
p. 182

#BRUTHAS WHO #FISH, 2022
Collage on panel
68⅜ × 79½ × 1⅜ in.
(173.7 × 201.9 × 3.5 cm), framed
p. 183

Fish Tales, 2022
Collage on panel
48 × $36\frac{11}{16}$ × 1⅜ in.
(121.9 × 93.2 × 3.5 cm), framed
p. 184

Anthony, 2022
Collage on panel
47⅞ × $36\frac{11}{16}$ × 1⅜ in.
(121.6 × 93.2 × 3.5 cm)
p. 185

Sea & Seize, 2022
Collage on panel
63⅜ × 72¾ × 1⅜ in.
(161 × 184.8 × 3.5 cm), framed
p. 186

My Old Bae, 2022
Collage on panel
57¾ × 37½ × 1⅜ in.
(146.7 × 95.2 × 3.5 cm), framed
p. 187

Johnny X, 2022
Collage on panel
79¼ × 68 × 1⅜ in.
(201.3 × 173.4 × 3.5 cm), framed
p. 188

Fish Head, 2022
Collage on panel
$36\frac{7}{16}$ × $48\frac{7}{16}$ × 1⅜ in.
(92.5 × 123 × 3.5 cm), framed
p. 189

Black People (BP), 2022
Triptych collage on panel
73¼ × 85¼ × 1⅜ in.
(186 × 216.5 × 3.5 cm) each, framed
pp. 190–91; Insert B, p. 9

Homiesexuals 1, 2022
Collage on panel
73¼ × 97¼ × 1⅜ in.
(186.1 × 247 × 3.5 cm), framed
p. 192

Homiesexuals 2, 2022
Collage on panel
73¼ × 97¼ × 1⅜ in.
(186.1 × 247 × 3.5 cm), framed
p. 193

I Am- Somebody, 2022
Diptych collage on panel
85¾ × 61½ × 1⅜ in.
(217.8 × 156.2 × 3.5 cm), each, framed
pp. 194–95

The Light Skinned Comeback, 2022
Diptych collage on panel
85¾ × 62 × 1⅜ in.
(217.8 × 157.5 × 3.5 cm) each, framed
p. 196

Mama Gotta Have A Life Too, 2022
Diptych collage on panel
85¾ × 61½ × 1⅜ in.
(217.8 × 156.2 × 3.5 cm) each, framed
p. 197

You Spot It, You Got It, 2022
Collage on five panels
97½ × 73½ × 1⅜ in.
(247.6 × 186.7 × 3.5 cm) each, framed
pp. 198–99

What I Wanted vs. What I Got, 2022
Tryptich collage on pigmented Pace Paper handmade cotton, mounted on panel
80⅛ × 60¾ × 1⅜ in.
(203.5 × 154.3 × 3.5 cm), each, framed
pp. 200–01

Day Party, Gay Party, 2022
Triptych collage on panel
96 × 72 in.
(243.8 × 182.9 cm), each
pp. 202–03

Dance 2, 2022
Collage on panel
57 × 39 in.
(144.8 × 99.1 cm)
p. 204

Light-Footed, 2022
Collage on panel
71 × 78 in.
(180.3 × 198.1 cm)
National Museum of African American History and Culture
p. 205

Pump, 2022
Diptych collage on panel
96 × 72 in.
(243.8 × 182.9 cm), each
pp. 206–07

Cafeteria, 2022
Site-specific vinyl mural
139 in. × 535 ft. $\frac{1}{16}$ in.
(353 cm × 163.1 m)
pp. 256–57

Cafeteria 2, 2023
Site-specific vinyl mural
26 ft. 1 in. × 44 ft. 7 in.
(8 × 14 m)
pp. 258–59

Throwing Light, Catching Shade, #4, 2024
Collage on panel
90 15/16 × 30 9/16 in.
(229.4 × 77.6 cm)
p. 6

Marabou, 2024
Acrylic on canvas
diptych, 84 × 84 in.
(213.4 × 213.4 cm)
pp. 16, 132–33

Miss Opportunity, 2024
Acrylic on canvas
four panels, 108 × 84 in.
(274.3 × 213.4 cm), each
pp. 134–35; Insert B, p. 7

Flint Fuel, 2024
Acrylic on canvas
four panels, 84 × 60 in.
(213.4 × 152.4 cm), each
pp. 136–37; Insert B, p. 7

Picnic at Butler, 2024
Acrylic on canvas
60 × 60 in.
(152.4 × 152.4 cm)
p. 138

All Fun and Games Until, 2024
Acrylic on canvas
diptych, 108 × 48 in.
(274.3 × 121.9 cm), each
p. 139

Stock 2, 2024
Acrylic on canvas
120 × 48 in.
(304.8 × 121.9 cm)
p. 140

Stock 1, 2024
Acrylic on canvas
120 × 48 in.
(304.8 × 121.9 cm)
p. 141

Humble Gifts #12, 2024
Cast paper frames
with collage
28 × 24½ in.
(71.1 × 62.2 cm)
p. 208

Humble Gifts #7, 2024
Cast paper frames
with collage
28 × 24⅝ in.
(71.1 × 62.5 cm)
p. 209

Humble Gifts #9, 2024
Cast paper frames
with collage
22¾ × 18⅝ in.
(57.8 × 47.3 cm)
p. 210

Humble Gifts #11, 2024
Cast paper frames
with collage
22⅝ × 18¾ in.
(57.5 × 47.6 cm)
p. 211

Breaking Bread, 2024
Collage on four panels
87⅞ × 67 11/16 in.
(223 × 171.9 cm), overall
pp. 212–15

Loads of Grace, 2024
Collage on four panels
87⅞ × 67 11/16 in.
(223 × 171.9 cm), overall
pp. 216-17

Installation view,
Patchwork, 2024
Twenty-four hand-painted gouache flags
on paper
p. 220

Let the Dollar Circulate #1, 2024
Unique gouache on paper
diptych
22 × 30 in.
(55.9 × 76.2 cm), each
p. 221

Wrath, 2024
Painted aluminum
19½ × 15 13/16 × 2⅞ in.
(49.5 × 40.1 × 7.4 cm)
Edition of 3 + 1 AP
p. 224

Limbo, 2024
Painted aluminum
11⅞ × 18 11/16 × 16⅞ in.
(30.2 × 47.5 × 42.9 cm)
Edition of 3 + 1 AP
p. 225

Greed, 2024
Painted aluminum
13½ × 15 13/16 × 5 5/16 in.
(33.5 × 40.1 × 13.5 cm)
Edition of 3 + 1 AP
p. 225

Heresy, 2024
Painted aluminum
19⅝ × 8 13/16 × 5 in.
(49.8 × 22.3 × 12.7 cm)
Edition of 3 + 1 AP
p. 226

Gluttony, 2024
Painted aluminum
19⅝ × 8 13/16 × 5 in.
(49.8 × 22.3 × 12.7 cm)
Edition of 3 + 1 AP
p. 226

Fraud, 2024
Painted aluminum
16⅝ × 12½ × 8⅛ in.
(42.2 × 31 × 20.6 cm)
Edition of 3 + 1 AP
p. 226

Treachery, 2024
Painted aluminum
19 11/16 × 16½ × 4⅝ in.
(50 × 41.9 × 11.7 cm)
Edition of 3 + 1 AP
p. 226

Lust, 2024
Painted aluminum
21⅞ × 15 13/16 × 4⅞ in.
(55.6 × 40.1 × 12.4 cm)
Edition of 3 + 1 AP
p. 227

Pig Out 1, 2024
Painted aluminum
48¼ × 47 × 45¼ in.
(122.6 × 119.4 × 114.9 cm)
Edition of 3 + 1 AP
p. 228

Pig Out 2, 2024
Painted aluminum
48¼ × 47 × 45¼ in.
(122.6 × 119.4 × 114.9 cm)
Edition of 3 + 1 AP
p. 229

Pig Out 3, 2024
Painted aluminum
48¼ × 47 × 45¼ in.
(122.6 × 119.4 × 114.9 cm)
Edition of 3 + 1 AP
p. 230

Pig Out 4, 2024
Painted aluminum
48¼ × 47 × 45¼ in.
(122.6 × 119.4 × 114.9 cm)
Edition of 3 + 1 AP
p. 231

Gated Community, 2024
Painted and patinated
brass
58⅞ × 131⅞ × 13/16 in.
(149.6 × 335 × 2 cm)
Edition of 3 + 1 AP
pp. 234–35

The Qing, 2024
Painted aluminum
69 11/16 × 44⅛ × 11 13/16 in.
(177 × 112 × 30 cm)
Edition of 3 + 1 AP
pp. 236–37

TOK, 2024
Painted aluminum
116⅝ × 71 11/16 × 36⅛ in.
(296.2 × 182.1 × 91.7 cm)
Edition of 3 + 1 AP
pp. 17, 238–39

Installation view,
Soup Kitchen, 2024
pp. 240–41

Soup Kitchen 1, 2024
Painted stainless steel
and aluminum
19 11/16 × 11 13/16 × 12 in.
(19.7 × 30 × 30.5 cm)
Edition of 2 + 1 AP
p. 242

Soup Kitchen 34, 2024
Painted stainless steel and aluminum
$19\frac{11}{16} \times 11\frac{13}{16} \times 12$ in.
(19.7 × 30 × 30.5 cm)
Edition of 2 + 1 AP
p. 243

Four and a Possible, 2024
Painted aluminum
$74\frac{13}{16} \times 58\frac{5}{16} \times 75\frac{11}{16}$
(190 × 148.1 × 192.3 cm)
Edition of 3 + 1 AP
p. 244

IYKYK #1, 2025
Acrylic on canvas
72 × 72 in.
(182.9 × 182.9 cm)
p. 142

IYKYK #2, 2025
Acrylic on canvas
72 × 72 in.
(182.9 × 182.9 cm)
p. 143

Installation view, *Winging It*, 2025
pp. 218–19

Pursuit of Happiness, 2025
Painted aluminum, tea light candles, and metal coins
$61\frac{1}{2} \times 64\frac{13}{16} \times 7$ in.
(156.3 × 164.6 × 18.5 cm)
Edition of 3 + 1 AP
pp. 245–47

Heaven's Hotline, 2025
Vinyl mural, neon, and wooden letterboards
Dimensions variable
pp. 260–61

Public Works (Insert A)

Mural for the Morrison Residence Hall basketball court, 2018
Duke/UNC Nannerl O. Keohane Distinguished Visiting Professor
University of North Carolina at Chapel Hill
Insert A, pp. 2–3

Untitled, 2018
Imagined Borders: Gwangju Biennale
Gwangju, South Korea
Insert A, pp. 4–5

Mull it Over, 2021
Mural for OZ Art NWA
Bentonville, AR
Insert A, p. 16

R&R, 2022
Miami Worldcenter
Miami, FL
Insert A, p. 1

San Juan Heal, 2022
Latex ink and vinyl mounted on glass
68 × 150 ft.
(20.7 × 45.7 m)
Facade of David Geffen Hall, Lincoln Center
New York, NY
pp. 20; Insert A, pp. 6–7

NYC LOVE, 2022
High Line Art
The High Line
New York, NY
Insert A, p. 8–9

Schoolyard basketball court, Juan Morel Campos Secondary School, 2022
Brooklyn, NY
Part of Trust for Public Land's New York City Playgrounds Program
Insert A, pp. 10–11

FUN #1, 2022
NYC Health + Hospitals/Elmhurst
Elmhurst, NY
In collaboration with RxART
Insert A, pp. 12–13

Mural for the launch of FIFA 22, 2022
In collaboration with EA Sports
Site-specific installation at the Ground,
New York, NY
Insert A,pp. 14–15

Commercial Works (Insert C)

HUF × STORY × PEANUTS × SKATE DECK, 2018
Offset lithograph in colors on skate deck (maple wood)
$31\frac{1}{2} \times 7\frac{9}{10}$ in.
(80 × 20 cm)
Insert C, p. 5

Baby, 2020
Painted cast vinyl
$10\frac{1}{4} \times 3$ in. (26 × 7.6 cm)
Insert C, pp. 1, 16

Peanuts (Triptych), 2020
Three skateboards, 7-ply grade A Canadian maple wood
33 × 9 in.
(85 × 23 cm), overall
The Peanuts Global Artist Collective
Produced by The Skateroom
Insert C, p. 4

UNO® Artiste: Nina Chanel Abney, 2020
Paper
10 × 6 × 4 in.
(25.4 × 15.2 × 10.2 cm)
Edition of 1,000
In collaboration with Pharrell's Black Ambition
Insert C, p. 6

Air Jordan 2 × Nina Chanel Abney, 2022
Insert C, pp. 2–3

Air Jordan 2 × Nina Chanel Abney, 2022
Insert C, p. 3 (top right)

Air Jordan 2 Low × Nina Chanel Abney, 2022
Insert C, p. 3 (bottom left)

MoMA Exclusive: Nina Chanel Abney Jigsaw Puzzle, 2022
95% recycled greyboard printed with non-toxic ink
20 × 30 in. (51 × 76.3 cm)
Insert C, p. 7

Super Cool World × Ledger Nano X, 2022
Insert C, p. 12

Timberland® × Nina Chanel Abney Future73 Collection, 2023
Insert C, pp. 10–11

Air Jordan 3 Retro × Nina Chanel Abney, 2024
Insert C, pp. 8–9

Avante Art, Super Cool World Prints, 2024
Digital NFT
Insert C, p. 13

Super Punk World Logo, 2024
Insert C, p. 14

Super Punk World #10, 2024
Digital NFT
Insert C, p. 14

Super Punk World #70, 2024
Digital NFT
Insert C, p. 14

Super Punk World #276, 2024
Digital NFT
Insert C, p. 14

Super Punk World Astronaut #1, AP, 2024
Digital NFT
Insert C, p. 15

Super Punk World Astronaut #2, AP, 2024
Digital NFT
Insert C, p. 15

Super Punk World Cop #1, AP, 2024
Digital NFT
Insert C, p. 15

Super Punk World Cop #2, AP, 2024
Digital NFT
Insert C, p. 15

ACKNOWLEDGMENTS

So much love to my mom, Aunt Jackie, Lindsey, and fam for always cheering me on and seeing the vision before it was real.

Endless love to Jet—for riding every high, low, and chaotic detour with me—and somehow still liking me after all of it.

◁○▷○◁○▷

Putting this book together has been a real labor of love, and I'm so grateful to everyone who helped bring it to life.

Huge thanks to the galleries who continue to champion and support my work—Jeffrey Deitch, Pace Prints, Perrotin, and Jack Shainman Gallery. I'm lucky to work with people who not only believe in the vision but help expand it in ways I couldn't have imagined.

Thank you to Caroline Newman and Ali Scotland for making the behind-the-scenes magic (and miracles) happen.

To Sean Newcott—thank you for being such a steady hand through this process. Your eye, your edits, and your calm energy made this feel less like a deadline and more like a collaboration I actually looked forward to.

I'm especially thankful to Jeffrey Deitch, Thelma Golden, Jazmine Hughes, and Rick Powell for lending your voices and insights to this book. Your perspectives added so much depth, and I'm honored to have your words alongside the work.

And to everyone who's been following the journey—collectors, fans, friends, and folks who just stumbled on the work and stuck around—thank you. Whether you've been there since day one or just picked up this book out of curiosity, your support means the world. I see you and appreciate you.

Nina Chanel Abney

CREDITS

Every reasonable effort has been made to supply complete and correct credits; errors or omissions will be corrected in subsequent editions.

Interior

2, 24: Todd Midler; **5 (top):** Charles David – elevatewelcomereimagine.com; **5 (bottom), 98–101, 142, 218–19, 245–47, 260–61:** Courtesy Jeffrey Deitch, Los Angeles, CA and New York, NY; **6, 144, 146–71, 172–75, 178–89, 192–217, 263:** Courtesy Pace Prints; **8, 11 (top & bottom), 30–32, 34, 36–71:** Courtesy Kravets Wehby Gallery, New York, NY; **12 (top & bottom), 15, 16, 17, 74–75, 84–89, 90–95, 102–103, 109–115, 120–127, 128–141, 143, 190–91, 224–31, 236–44:** Courtesy Jack Shainman Gallery, New York, New York; **13:** Courtesy Norton Museum of Art, West Palm Beach, Florida; **14, 72–73:** Courtesy Whitney Museum of American Art; **20:** Nicholas Knight Studio; **22:** John Berens–Brooklyn, NY; **26–27:** Rubell Museum, Miami and Washington, DC; **28-29:** Courtesy William Bunch Auctions & Appraisals; **33, 35:** Courtesy the Nasher Museum of Art at Duke University. Photo by Peter Paul Geoffrion; **76–79, 82–83:** Courtesy Mary Boone Gallery; **96–97:** Kevin Todora, courtesy the Modern Art Museum of Fort Worth; **104–08**: © Jacek Garcarz; **117–18:** Courtesy Norton Museum of Art, West Palm Beach, Florida. © Jacek Garcarz; **220–21:** Courtesy Anthony Gallery, Chicago, IL; **234–35:** Courtesy Kunstgiesserei St.Gallen; **250:** Courtesy Project for Empty Space; **251–3:** Courtesy the Palais de Tokyo, as part of the LASCO PROJECT. Photo: Aurélien Mole; **254–55:** Charles Mayer Photography; **256–57:** Zachary Balber; **258–59:** Jacob Koestler, Museum of Contemporary Art, Cleveland

Insert A

1: Oriol Tarridas; **2–3:** Nathan Klima; **6–7, 12–13:** Nicholas Knight Studio; **8–9:** Timothy Schenck; **16:** Raymesh Cintron for Justkids.art

Insert B

1: Courtesy AllRightsReserved; **2, 3 (top left & bottom right), 8, 9 (bottom left):** Shaniqwa Jarvis; **4–5:** The Skateroom; **6:** ©Mattel. UNO™ and related trademarks are owned by Mattel; **7:** Courtesy MoMA Design Store; **9 (top left, top right & bottom left):** Tyler Mansour; **10–11:** Joe Perri; **12:** Charlie Tronchot

Insert C

1: Marisa Langley; **3, 5, 12:** Todd Midler; **11:** Tiffany & Co.

Phaidon Press Limited
2 Cooperage Yard
London E15 2QR

Monacelli
A Phaidon Company
111 Broadway
New York, NY 10006

Phaidon SARL
55, rue Traversière
75012 Paris

phaidon.com/monacelli

First published 2025

Cover art: Detail, Nina Chanel Abney, *Blue*, 2021
Collage on panel, 60¼ × 60⅞ × 1⅜ in.
(153 × 154.6 × 3.5 cm), framed

ISBN 978-1-58093-700-9
ISBN 978-1-58093-723-8 (signed copies)

Library of Library of Congress Control Number:
2025931303

Editor: Sean Newcott
Production: Michael Vagnetti
Design: Marwan Kaabour

Printed in China